ADULT DEVELOPMENT & AGING

BIOPSYCHOSOCIAL PERSPECTIVES

ADULT DEVELOPMENT & AGING

BIOPSYCHOSOCIAL PERSPECTIVES

Seventh Edition

Susan Krauss Whitbourne, Ph.D.
University of Massachusetts Boston

Stacey B. Whitbourne, Ph.D.
VA Boston Healthcare System

VP AND EDITORIAL DIRECTOR	Veronica Visentin
EXECUTIVE EDITOR	Glenn Wilson
EDITORIAL ASSISTANT	Jannil Perez
EDITORIAL MANAGER	Judy Howarth
CONTENT MANAGEMENT DIRECTOR	Lisa Wojcik
CONTENT MANAGER	Nichole Urban
SENIOR CONTENT SPECIALIST	Nicole Repasky
PRODUCTION EDITOR	Vinolia Benedict Fernando
COVER PHOTO CREDIT	Courtesy of Susan K. Whitbourne & Stacey B. Whitbourne

This book was set in 9.5/11.5 BerkeleyStd-Book by SPi Global.

Founded in 1807, John Wiley & Sons, Inc. has been a valued source of knowledge and understanding for more than 200 years, helping people around the world meet their needs and fulfill their aspirations. Our company is built on a foundation of principles that include responsibility to the communities we serve and where we live and work. In 2008, we launched a Corporate Citizenship Initiative, a global effort to address the environmental, social, economic, and ethical challenges we face in our business. Among the issues we are addressing are carbon impact, paper specifications and procurement, ethical conduct within our business and among our vendors, and community and charitable support. For more information, please visit our website: www.wiley.com/go/citizenship.

ISBN: 978-1-119-60787-8 (PBK)
ISBN: 978-1-119-60939-1 (EVALC)

Library of Congress Cataloging-in-Publication Data

Names: Whitbourne, Susan Krauss, author. | Whitbourne, Stacey B., author.
Title: Adult development and aging : biopsychosocial perspectives / Susan
    Krauss Whitbourne, e, Ph.D., University of Massachusetts Boston, Stacey
    B. Whitbourne, Ph.D., VA Boston Healthcare System.
Other titles: Adult development & aging
Description: Seventh Edition. | Hoboken : Wiley, 2020. | Revised edition of
    the authors' Adult development & aging, [2017] | Includes
    bibliographical references and index.
Identifiers: LCCN 2020004059 (print) | LCCN 2020004060 (ebook) | ISBN
    9781119607878 (paperback) | ISBN 9781119609438 (adobe pdf) | ISBN
    9781119609377 (epub)
Subjects: LCSH: Gerontology. | Older people—Psychology. | Older
    people—Health and hygiene. | Older people—Social conditions.
Classification: LCC HQ1061 .W48 2020 (print) | LCC HQ1061 (ebook) | DDC
    305.26—dc23
LC record available at https://lccn.loc.gov/2020004059
LC ebook record available at https://lccn.loc.gov/2020004060

The inside back cover will contain printing identification and country of origin if omitted from this page. In addition, if the ISBN on the back cover differs from the ISBN on this page, the one on the back cover is correct.

SKY10033669_030722

PREFACE

Everyone ages. This very fact should be enough to draw you into the subject matter of this course, whether you are the student or the instructor. Yet, for many people, it is difficult to imagine the future in 50, 40, or even 10 years from now. The goal of our book is to help you imagine your future and the future of your family, your friends, and your society. We have brought together the latest scientific findings about aging with a more personal approach to encourage you to take this imaginative journey into your future.

The seventh edition of *Adult Development and Aging: Biopsychosocial Perspectives* incorporates material that we believe is vital to your understanding of this rapidly developing and fascinating field of study. Much of what you will read comes directly from Susan's classroom teaching of the psychology of aging course at the University of Massachusetts Boston. She continues to incorporate her day-to-day teaching of the course into the text, which keeps the material current, fresh, and engaging. At the same time, her active involvement in research on the psychology of adult development and aging gives her the ability to sift through the available findings and pull out those that are central to an understanding of individuals as they change from the years of early adulthood through late life.

Stacey was inspired to pursue the field of aging after taking her mother's course at the University of Massachusetts Amherst. She continued her graduate work in social and developmental psychology, focusing on cognitive functioning in later adulthood. Stacey is the program director for a major national initiative that is building a health and genomic database for future studies of military veterans. Having also taught adult development and aging at Brandeis University and the University of Massachusetts Boston, she is also attuned to student needs and interests.

We are proud to say that Stacey is the third generation of her family to be involved in the field of gerontology. Theodore C. Krauss, M.D., Susan's father, was an innovator in geriatric medicine. Susan became interested in the scholarly field of aging as an undergraduate when she decided to write a paper on personality and adaptation in a developmental psychology course. At the same time, her father's professional activities had a profound influence and made the choice of gerontology (the scientific study of aging) a natural one.

It is our hope and belief that you will find yourself as engrossed in the psychology of adult development and aging as we are. Not only is everyone around you aging but also the issues that researchers in field examine range all the way from the philosophical to the practical. Why do living things age? Is there a way to slow down the aging process? How will society deal with the aging of the Baby Boomers? How will job markets be affected by an aging society? Will the young adults of today age differently than did their parents and grandparents? Bringing it to a personal level, as you take the course, you'll start to ask questions about your own life. What challenges await you as you begin your career? What will it be like to start a family? How will you manage the transition into your early adulthood as you leave college behind to pursue your own life? All of these, and more, are questions that you will find yourself asking as you explore the many complexities of the process that causes people to change and grow throughout life. You will learn not only how people grow older but also how to grow older in a way that is healthy and satisfying.

THEMES OF THE BOOK

The biopsychosocial model emphasized in our text is intended to encourage you to think about the multiple interactions among the domains of biology, psychology, and sociology. According to this model, changes in one area of life have effects on changes in other areas. The centerpiece of this model is identity, your self-definition. You interpret the experiences you have through the framework provided by your identity. In turn, your experiences stimulate you to change your self-definition.

This is an exciting time to be studying adult development and aging. The topic is gaining increasing media attention and tremendous momentum as an academic discipline within life span development. The biopsychosocial model fits within the framework of contemporary approaches taking hold in the sciences in general that emphasize the impact of social context on individuals throughout all periods of life. Entirely new concepts, sets of data, and practical applications of these models are resulting in a realization of the dreams of many of the classic developmental psychologists whose work shaped the field in the early 20th century.

Adult development and aging are areas that have no national boundaries. Aging is now being recognized as a priority for researchers and policy makers around the world, not only in the United States and Canada. We can all benefit from this international perspective both for our own countries and for those of citizens around the world.

ORGANIZATION

If you read the chapters of this book in order from start to finish, you will progress from the basics in the first three chapters to more complex issues, starting in Chapter 4, that place relatively more emphasis on the "bio," the "psycho," and the "social." However, not all instructors choose to proceed in this fashion, and we have designed the book with this flexibility as an option. We emphasize the biopsychosocial model throughout, in that many of the topics, regardless of where they appear in the book, span areas as diverse, for example, as driving and diabetes.

We do recommend, though, that the last chapter you read is not the one on death and dying, as is often the case in other books in the field. Our last chapter covers successful aging. Many students and instructors have shared with us their appreciation of our ending on a "high note." Even though death is obviously the final period of life, we each have the potential to live on after our own ending through the works we create, the legacies we leave behind, and the people whose lives we have touched. These are the themes that we would like you to take with you from this book in the years and decades ahead.

FEATURES

Up-to-Date Research   The topics and features in this text are intended to involve you in the field of aging from a scholarly and personal perspective. You will find that the most current research is presented throughout the text, with careful and detailed explanations of the studies that highlight the most important scholarly advances. We have given particular attention to new topics and approaches, including neuroscience and genetics, as well as continuing to bring to students the latest advances in cognition, personality, relationships, and vocational development as well as highlighting sociocultural influences on development, including race, ethnicity, and social class.

AgeFeed   The chapters begin with our very own "Age-Feed" openers to give you an introduction to the topic. These are in the form of fact versus myth challenges, self-tests, or lists relevant to each chapter that take one of several formats. For AgeFeed openers that involve a challenge or self-test, the answers are provided for you so that you can score yourself. Your instructor may decide to assign these to tests, so be sure to read them over carefully. We hope you like them!

Engaging Figures and Tables   All of the figures and photographs in this seventh edition were redesigned from the previous editions with updated information and formats. These will help you learn and remember the key information presented in the text. Our selection of these materials connects to the PowerPoint slides that instructors can download from the Wiley website.

Contemporary Approach   With coauthors literally one generation apart, it's been our goal to find the balance between the "professor" and the "student" perspectives. As a result, you will find many current examples relevant to people in your age group, whether you're a returning student or a student of traditional college age. Instructors, too, will find material that they can relate to their own experiences, whether they are relative newcomers or more seasoned academics.

STUDENT LEARNING AIDS

Glossary Terms   We have made a concerted effort in this edition to provide a large number of glossary terms, indicated in bold in each chapter, and listed at the end of the book. Although it may seem like you will have a great many terms to memorize, the fact of the matter is that you will need to learn them anyway, and by having them provided in your glossary, you'll find it easier to spot them when it comes time to review for your exams. Susan finds that her students like to study from flashcards that they make up, and if you find this a useful study tool, the glossary terms will make that process much more straightforward. The majority of these terms relate specifically to adult development and aging, but where we felt it was helpful for you to review a term that you may not have encountered for a while, we also included several terms of a more general nature.

Numbered Summaries   You will find a numbered summary for each chapter that will supplement your studying and help you narrow down your reviewing to the chapter's main points. Together with the glossary terms, these will give you a comprehensive overview, though they will help you the most if you actually read the chapters themselves.

CHANGES IN THE SEVENTH EDITION

The first edition of *Adult Development and Aging: Biopsychosocial Perspectives* was intended to provide a fresh and engaging approach to the field of the psychology of adult development and aging by focusing on three themes: a multidisciplinary approach, positive images of aging, and the newest and most relevant research. We continue this tradition in the seventh edition because we want you, our readers, to feel as connected to the material as possible. Our thinking is that students will be more motivated to complete their reading if they like the text and feel that they can relate to it. At the same time, instructors will find their job that much easier because students sitting in their classrooms will come to class ready to discuss what they've read.

Instructors who have developed their course based on earlier editions will not need to change the basic structure of their lectures and assignments. However, to reflect this ever-changing field, we shifted material within the chapters, in some cases deleting topics that by now are no longer considered relevant in order to make room to cover the newer approaches that have come into prominence within the past 3 years.

Although many of the classics remain, we have included over 500 references from the past 3 years, up through mid-2019. In virtually all cases where we reference population data, we rely on sources from 2018 and 2019. We also give expanded coverage to global population and health data in keeping with our stated goal of providing an international perspective.

In the sixth edition, we revamped much of the topical organization to be consistent with new developments in theory and research. In the present edition, we have trimmed some areas that had become outdated even further in order to be able to cover the emerging literature. Additionally, to make the new material consistent with the illustrations, we have provided narratives that will allow readers to understand the main points of each of the revamped figures. These changes came about, in part, as a result of feedback from students in Susan's undergraduate course in gerontology.

Several trends in the literature that are reflected in the seventh edition include greater appreciation of the role of social context as an influence on development such as income inequity, variations according to such areas of diversity as race, ethnicity, and sexual orientation. We also expand our treatment of international variations and include considerable material from the World Health Organization's focus on "Active and Healthy Ageing." All references prior to 2015 have been checked to determine whether newer information is available. Where sections of the text covered topics that have diminished in importance in the field, these have been condensed or eliminated. As a result, although the text's structure remains consistent, there are new areas of emphasis reflecting the growth of the field.

Our goal is to provide the latest findings while preserving information of relevance to the "classic" studies in the field. Students will therefore have the best of all worlds, with the opportunity to learn about cherished traditions in adult development and aging but also to learn where this exciting field is headed in the coming decades.

Supplements   Wiley is pleased to offer an online resource containing a wealth of teaching and learning materials at http://www.wiley.com/college/whitbourne.

Website Links   References in this edition show the websites that students and instructors can consult to gather updated information on changes in the field.

INSTRUCTOR RESOURCES

Instructor's Manual   The content in the Instructor's Manual reflects the 45 years of experience that Susan has in teaching this course. You will find chapter outlines, key terms, learning objectives, and lecture suggestions. We have updated our suggestions for videos, taking advantage of the new resources available through YouTube, and also provide instructors with resources for films, music, and literature.

PowerPoint Slides   Prepared for use in lectures, we provide you with a complete set of PowerPoint slides tested in Susan's class and designed specifically for this book. Instructors can easily adapt them for their own specific needs.

Test Bank   Instructors have access to a complete downloadable test bank that includes 50 questions in each chapter that follow the order in which concepts are presented in the text. Each multiple-choice question is labeled according to the concept it tests, along with its difficulty level (based on class testing). We include short answer and essay questions that correspond with each section of the chapter. Because they are in convenient Microsoft Word format, instructors can adapt them to their own particular needs.

ACKNOWLEDGMENTS

Our first set of acknowledgments goes to our families. Husbands Richard O'Brien and Erik Gleason have graciously provided important support that allowed us to spend the many hours we needed over the period of a year to revise the book. Jennifer O'Brien, daughter and sister, is a wonderful sounding board for our ideas; as she continues her career in clinical psychology, we look forward to continued "collaboration" with her. We would also like to thank the newest members of our family—namely Theodore James Gleason, age 8 at the time of this writing, and Scarlett Beth Gleason, who has just turned 6. Susan is thrilled to be a grandmother, experiencing the joys of this special status on a first-hand basis.

Throughout the writing of this book, students in the Mental Health and Aging class at the University of Massachusetts Boston have provided valuable insights and observations. As we were revising the book and preparing the lectures, students continued to provide us with fresh perspectives. Their good humor, patience, and willingness to experiment with some new ideas have made it possible to add the all-important student viewpoint to the finished product. We also appreciate the contributions of Susan's graduate teaching assistants, who serve as sounding boards in her preparation and review of lecture content.

Our final thanks go to the reviewers over the years who provided helpful comments. Their insightful observations and thoughtful proposals for changes helped us tighten and focus the manuscript and enhance the discussion of several key areas of interest in the field. Thank you to Alex Bishop (Oklahoma State University), Sue Burdett-Robinson (Hardin-Simmons University), Alvin House (Illinois State University), Gary Montgomery (The University of Texas-Pan American), and Nancy Partika (Triton College). We have also benefited from informal reviews provided by our colleagues who use the book in their teaching. We greatly appreciate their helpful suggestions.

In conclusion, we hope that we have given you something to look forward to as you venture into the fascinating field of adult development and aging and that the subsequent pages of this book will fulfill these expectations. We aim to present a comprehensive but clear picture of the area and hope that you will be able to apply this knowledge to improve your own life and the lives of the older adults with whom you may be preparing to work. We hope you will come away from the course with a positive feeling about what you can do to "age better" and with a positive feeling about the potentialities of later life. And maybe, just maybe, as has happened on many past occasions with people who read this book and take our courses, you will decide to pursue this field and we can welcome you as colleagues in the coming years.

Finally, we would like to comment on the process of working together as a mother–daughter team. The first author was pregnant with the second author when she embarked on her first textbook in the field, the precursor to the present volume. Little did she know that the child she was about to have would become a psychologist, much less a specialist in aging. Indeed, because Susan recently relocated to Boston, where Stacey and her family live, we have had more opportunities to talk about this revision in depth, including some lively debates about several of the topics. The AgeFeeds reflect Stacey's desire to engage readers with the type of material that students encounter in their own informal Web searches and daily online news updates. We greatly enjoy writing this book and are proud and happy to be able to share our perspectives with you, the reader.

Susan Krauss Whitbourne, Ph.D.
Stacey B. Whitbourne, Ph.D.
January 2020

ABOUT THE AUTHORS

Susan Krauss Whitbourne, Ph.D., is a Professor Emerita of Psychological and Brain Sciences at the University of Massachusetts Amherst and Adjunct Professor and Faculty Fellow in Gerontology at the University of Massachusetts Boston. She received her Ph.D. in developmental psychology from Columbia University in 1974 and completed a postdoctoral training program in clinical psychology at the University of Massachusetts at Amherst, having joined the faculty there in 1984. Her previous positions were as associate professor of education and psychology at the University of Rochester (1975–1984) and assistant professor of psychology at SUNY College at Geneseo. Formerly the Psychology Departmental honors coordinator at the University of Massachusetts Amherst, she was also director of the Office of National Scholarship Advisement where she advised students who apply for the Rhodes, Marshall, Fulbright, Truman, and Goldwater Scholarships, among others. In addition, she was faculty advisor to the University of Massachusetts Chapter of Psi Chi, a position for which she was recognized as the Eastern Regional Outstanding Advisor for the year 2001 and as the Florence Denmark National Faculty Advisor in 2002. She served as eastern region vice president of Psi Chi in 2006–07 and as chair of the program committee for the National Leadership Conference in 2009. Her teaching has been recognized with the College Outstanding Teacher Award in 1995 and the University Distinguished Teaching Award in 2001. Her work as an advisor was recognized with the Outstanding Academic Advisor Award in 2006. In 2003, she received the American Psychological Association (APA) Division 20 (Adult Development and Aging) Master Mentor Award and the Gerontological Society of America (GSA) Behavioral and Social Sciences Distinguished Mentorship Award.

Over the past 20 years, Dr. Whitbourne has held a variety of elected and appointed positions in APA Division 20 including president (1995–96), treasurer (1986–89), secretary (1981–84), program chair (1997–98), education committee chair (1979–80), Student Awards Committee chair (1993–94), Continuing Education Committee chair (1981–82), and Elections Committee chair (1992–93). She has chaired the Fellowship Committee and serves as the Division 20 representative to the APA Council (2000–06 and 2009–14, and 2017–present). She is a fellow of Divisions 1 (General Psychology), 2 (Teaching of Psychology), 9 (Society for the Study of Social Issues), 12 (Clinical Psychology), 20, and 35 (Society for the Psychology of Women). She served on the APA Committee on Structure and Function of Council, chaired the Policy and Planning Board in 2007, served on the APA Membership Board, served on the Board of Educational Affairs, chaired Women's Caucus and Coalition of Scientists and Applied Researchers in Psychology, and is now on the Board of Educational Affairs. In 2011, her contributions were recognized with an APA Presidential Citation.

Dr. Whitbourne is also a fellow of the American Psychological Society and was President of the Eastern Psychological Association (2017–18). She is the Chair of the Behavioral and Social Sciences Section of the Gerontological Society of America. She is past president of the Council of Professional Geropsychology Training Programs. Having received her Diplomate in Geropsychology in 2015, she currently serves as the Treasurer for the ABGERO board of the American Board of Professional Psychology. A founding member of the Society for the Study of Human Development, she was its president from 2005 to 2007. She is also a founding member of the Society for the Study of Emerging Adulthood. She also served on the Board of Directors of the National Association of Fellowship Advisors. In her home of Amherst, Massachusetts, she served on the Council on Aging (2004–07) and was the president of the Friends of the Amherst Senior Center (2007–09).

Her publications include 19 published books, many in multiple editions, and more than 175 journal articles and chapters, including articles in *Psychology and Aging, Psychotherapy, Developmental Psychology, Journal of Gerontology, Journal of Personality and Social Psychology*, and *Teaching of Psychology*, and chapters in the *Handbook of the Psychology of Aging, Clinical Geropsychology, Comprehensive Clinical Psychology (Geropsychology)*, the *Encyclopedia of Psychology*, and the *International Encyclopedia of the Social and Behavioral Sciences*. She has been a consulting editor for *Psychology and Aging*, serves on the editorial board of the *Journal of Gerontology*, and was a consulting editor for *Developmental Psychology*. She is editor-in-chief of the Wiley-Blackwell *Encyclopedia of Aging*. Her presentations at professional conferences number over 250 and include several invited addresses, among them the APA G. Stanley Hall Lecture in 1995, the EPA Psi Chi Distinguished Lecture in 2001, and the SEPA Invited Lecture in 2002. In addition to her professional writing, she writes a blog for *Psychology Today* called "Fulfillment at Any Age" and has consulted for publications of the National Geographic Society in psychology and serves on the Prevention.com health review board.

Stacey B. Whitbourne, Ph.D., received her Ph.D. in social and developmental psychology from Brandeis University in 2005 where she was funded by a National Institute on Aging training fellowship. She completed her postdoctoral fellowship at the Boston University School of Public Health, Department of Epidemiology, funded by a National Institute on Aging Grant and a Department of Veterans Affairs Rehabilitation Research and Development Service Grant. Currently, she is a research health scientist at the Massachusetts Veterans Epidemiology and Research Information Center (MAVERIC), a research center housed within the VA Boston Healthcare System. She serves as the Program Director of Recruitment and Enrollment for the Million Veteran Program, a longitudinal health and genomic cohort funded by the Department of Veteran's Affairs Office of Research and Development. In addition, she is an instructor of medicine at Harvard Medical School and an associate epidemiologist at the Division of Aging at Brigham and Women's Hospital. The author of several published articles, she is also a coauthor on a chapter for the Sage Series on Aging in America. She is a member of the American Psychological Association Division 20 and the Gerontological Society of America. A member of the

Membership Committee of Division 20, she has also given more than 30 presentations at national conferences. As an undergraduate, she received the Psi Chi National Student Research Award. In graduate school, she was awarded the Verna Regan Teaching Award and an APA Student Travel Award. She has received numerous commendations and awards for her work with the Million Veteran Program from the Department of Veterans Affairs. She has taught courses on adult development and aging at Brandeis University and the University of Massachusetts Boston.

CONTENTS

CHAPTER 6

CHAPTER 7

CHAPTER 8

CHAPTER 9

CHAPTER 10

Work, Retirement, and Leisure Patterns   201

CHAPTER 11

Mental Health Issues and Treatment   225

CHAPTER 12

Long-Term Care   243

1

Themes and Issues in Adult Development and Aging

At the beginning of each chapter, we invite you to check out "Age Feed" to see top 10 lists, take quizzes, or learn fun facts about the chapter ahead.

To get started, as you will learn in Chapter 1, there are many myths about aging. See if you're able to separate fact from fiction in these statements and check your answers on the next page.

AGEFEED

1. All older adults are alike.

2. Most older adults live in nursing homes.

3. Loss of interest in sex and intimacy is a normal part of aging.

4. Most older adults stay socially active.

5. Alzheimer's disease is an inevitable part of aging.

6. Older adults are unable to learn new skills.

7. Memory loss is a normal as people grow older.

8. People become more pessimistic in later life.

9. Creativity peaks early in adulthood and declines after that.

10. As people get older, they need more assistance in daily life.

AGEFEED

...the facts

1. All older adults are alike.
   Myth! The range of ages among older adults spans 5 decades; they differ more than any other age group.

2. Most older adults live in nursing homes.
   Myth! Only about 5% of older adults in the United States are in nursing homes although this rises to 13% for those 85+.

3. Loss of interest in sex and intimacy is a normal part of aging.
   Myth! Although the frequency of sexual activity may decrease, most older adults continue to enjoy a fulfilling sex life.

4. Most older adults stay socially active.
   Fact! Many older adults continue working, volunteer, and are part of a family social network.

5. Alzheimer's disease is an inevitable part of aging.
   Myth! Alzheimer's disease and other forms of cognitive loss occur in a minority of older adults.

6. Older adults are unable to learn new skills.
   Myth! Learning new skills may take longer, but the ability to learn continues throughout later life.

7. Memory loss is a normal as people grow older.
   Fact and myth! Short-term memory may be less efficient, but long-term memory is maintained in later life.

8. People become more pessimistic in later life.
   Myth! Older adults are more likely to feel satisfied with their lives and to be optimistic about getting older.

9. Creativity peaks early in adulthood and declines after that.
   Myth! There are many examples of famous creative older adults but even ordinary individuals can be creative throughout their lives.

10. As people get older, they need more assistance in daily life.
    Fact! The need for assistance increases in later adulthood, but only reaches as high as 53% for women aged 85 and older.

Aging affects everyone. Your aging process began the moment you were born. If you are of traditional college age, you're undergoing a time of transition that lasts from adolescence to adulthood. The concept of being an adult may be new to you, and the idea of being an older adult may seem far off. Our purpose in writing this book is to help you think about your own aging as well as the aging process more generally. You may have decided to take this course to help you understand your aging family members or trends in society and before long, we hope that you also think about what will happen to you as you yourself get older.

Let's start by asking you what comes to mind when you think of your current age. Is it an important part of who you are or do you not think about your actual age? Next, ask yourself whether you consider yourself to be an adult. What does the word *adult* mean to you? Is it a term you would use to describe others who are older than you are now? Finally, what are your thoughts about the aging process? When you think of older adults, do you immediately regard them as unable to care for themselves? What is the "typical" older adult like, in your eyes?

Just by thinking about these questions, you've already started to focus on what age means in terms of your overall sense of self. These are the types of questions that we'll explore throughout the book. Even as we discuss in-depth the effects of the aging process throughout adulthood, we will often come back and question how much we really know about a person based on age alone. We'll also show you that some age distinctions are almost arbitrary. Someone decided that a certain age means you're in a certain stage of life; from that point forward, people attribute a great deal of meaning to that particular number. In reality, however, the aging process isn't completely linked to the passage of time alone.

Our goal is to encourage you to take personal explorations as you gain factual information about the aging process. Not only will the material help you in your career regardless of what field you go into, but it will also help you understand yourself and how you change over time. You'll also learn, perhaps surprisingly, that you don't have to sit back and let the aging process passively affect you. There are active steps you can be taking now to make sure that you keep functioning as well as possible for as long as possible throughout your entire life. With a few simple precautions, you can avoid the illnesses that limit people's ability to enjoy themselves into their later decades.

If you're a traditional college-age student heading into your 20s, we hope to help you appreciate that it is never too early to start incorporating these changes into your lifestyle. And for our readers of nontraditional college age, we hope to help you see that it's never too late to initiate behaviors that can maintain, if not enhance, your everyday functioning. A key goal we have in writing this book is to involve you in the progression of your aging process and show you ways to be an active part of your own development.

THE BIOPSYCHOSOCIAL PERSPECTIVE

We organize the book around the biopsychosocial perspective, a view of development as a complex interaction of biological, psychological, and social processes. Aging is not a simple, straightforward progression through time. Your body undergoes biological changes largely influenced by your genetics or physiology. At the same time, you change psychologically in ways that reflect what's happening to your body that, in turn, affect your body's changes. All of this takes place in a social context. Holding biology and psychology constant, people age differently depending on where and when they live, whom they interact with, and what resources they have available to them.

Figure 1.1 captures this complex biopsychosocial interaction. Biological processes refer to how the body's functions and structures change throughout the aging process. We cover these changes in the chapters on normal aging and health. Psychological processes include the individual's thoughts, feelings, and behaviors related to growing older. We examine these changes in the chapters on

FIGURE 1.1

The Biopsychosocial Model

According to the biopsychosocial perspective, adult development and aging are understood as involving biological, psychological, and sociocultural influences.

cognition, personality, and emotions. The social processes of aging reflect the cultural, historical, and interpersonal influences on the individual. We cover these in chapters about relationships, family, work, and institutionalization. In Chapter 2, we will explore how life-span development theories grapple with explaining how these complex processes all interrelate. You'll find that there's a great deal more to aging than you probably imagined when you first started reading this chapter.

As you can see from the biopsychosocial model, we intend to go beyond "psychology" in teaching you about the processes involved in adult development and aging. In fact, gerontology, the scientific study of the aging process, is an interdisciplinary field. People who devote their professional lives to the study of gerontology come from many different academic and applied areas—biology, medicine, nursing, sociology, history, and even the arts and literature. It's almost impossible to be a gerontologist without applying this integrative view to your work. Knowledge, theories, and perspectives from all disciplines contribute importantly to the study of the individual over time. Gerontology is distinct from geriatrics, which is the medical specialty in aging.

To help put it all together for you as you develop throughout adulthood, we will pay special attention to the concept of identity. Identity is defined as a composite of how people view themselves in the biological, psychological, and social domains of life. The interaction of these domains forms an overall view of the "self."

FOUR PRINCIPLES OF ADULT DEVELOPMENT AND AGING

We begin our study of adult development and aging by sharing a set of four principles that form the foundation of our biopsychosocial approach (see Figure 1.2). As you read the book, you'll find that we return frequently to these principles, which we highlight when they appear in the chapter. If you begin to understand them now, you will find the course material much easier to master.

Principle 1: Changes Are Continuous Over the Life Span

First and foremost, changes over the life span happen in a continuous fashion. According to the continuity principle, the changes that people experience in later adulthood build on the experiences they had in their earlier years. This means we can never isolate the later years of life without considering the years preceding them. Since time moves

FIGURE 1.2

The Four Principles of Adult Development and Aging

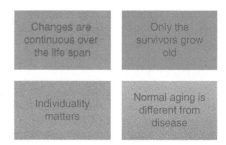

in a forward direction, the changes throughout life build upon themselves in a cumulative fashion. If you were hard on your body as a young adult, chances are the changes you'll undergo when you're older will be more negative than if you took good care of yourself.

The continuity principle also applies to the way that people think about their own identities. You know that you're the same person you always were, despite getting older. Birthdays don't transform you into a different person. You don't look the same to others, but you feel essentially the "same" on the inside.

When others look at you, however, they don't necessarily share this perspective. People don't meet you for the first time and think about what you were like when you were younger—they see you as you are now. Unless they are close relatives or friends, they have no way of knowing what you were like when you were in your childhood or teenage years. Anyone meeting you now judges you on the basis of your current appearance because he or she has no other data from which to draw.

Similarly, when you look at a middle-aged or older adult, it's unlikely that you judge that person on the basis of how he or she may have been in the past. You see an older woman, perhaps walking with a little difficulty, and don't stop to think that she might have been a marathon runner in her youth. However, that very same older woman knows that she is the "same" person she's always been. True, she can no longer compete for a marathon, but this accomplishment is part of her identity. She knows her physical abilities have changed, but to herself she's still the Jane, Barbara, or Mary she has been her entire life.

There's an important implication of the continuity principle for anyone working with older adults. You need to remember that they would prefer to be treated as the people they always were, rather than as "old people." As we'll see later, older adults are often stereotyped as weak and infirm, when in reality, they want to be viewed as individuals who possess strengths they have built up over

The principle of continuity is illustrated here, showing that an individual may feel the same inside even though their outer appearance changes.

Gerd Altmann/Pixabay

their entire lives. They don't want to be stereotyped on the basis of the way they look to the world right now. Some nursing home administrators, eager to remind their employees of this fact, display pictures of the residents from their younger years on the nameplates outside their doors. The residents and their visitors think of them in this way, and it's helpful if those who work with them are reminded of this fact as well.

Principle 2: Only the Survivors Grow Old

The survivor principle states that the people who live to old age are the ones who managed to outlive the many threats that could have caused their deaths at earlier ages. Perhaps this is obvious because clearly, to grow old, you have to not die. However, the survivor principle is a bit more complex than that. Contrary to the Billy Joel song "Only the Good Die Young," it's not the good who die young, but the ones who fall victim to the forces that cause people to lose their lives. Some of these are random, to be sure, such as being killed by someone else in an accident, by an act of war, or in a natural disaster. However, many other factors that lead some to survive into old age are nonrandom. Survivors not only manage to avoid random causes of their own fatalities but also are more likely to take care of their health, not engage in risky behaviors (such as driving too fast or getting involved in crime), or using drugs and alcohol excessively.

The survivor principle exemplifies the biopsychosocial perspective. The very fact that survivors avoid death until late in life suggests that they may have inherited good genes or at least managed to maintain their physical abilities (biological factors), are cognitively and emotionally healthy (psychological factors), and have surrounded themselves with a good support system (social factors). Furthermore, these factors build on each other. People with stronger

cognitive skills are more likely to attend college which, in turn, provides them with greater economic resources that can sustain their health and well-being. A combination of mental and physical health and adequate resources, plus a dose of good luck, allow them to be with us today.

Figure 1.3 illustrates the survivor principle. Across the years of adulthood, the population of people born around the same time thins out so that, by the later years, only the hardiest are still alive. Gerontologists must take the survivor principle into account when interpreting the results of their research because it is quite likely that survivors are not like the people born at the same time as they were. They may have been born with greater resilience, but they also likely took care to maintain their health and preserve their longevity. There are so many ways to lose one's life as you get older, from such causes as terminal illness or accidents, that to become an older adult, you have to possess some incredibly special characteristics.

The survivor principle also impacts the way we understand research on aging. Clearly, all older adults who participate in research are survivors of the conditions that others did not endure. As time goes by, more and more of the older population will die. When they reach age 90 or 100, they most likely represent a different population than their now-deceased age mates. The older they get, the more select they become in such key characteristics as physical functioning, health, intelligence, and even personality (Baird et al., 2010).

Consequently, when we examine differences between younger and older people, we must keep in mind that older people alive today were a special group when they were young. The younger adults have not yet been subjected to the same conditions that could threaten their lives. Some of them will die before they reach old age. Knowing who will be the survivors is almost impossible to predict, of course, meaning we may be comparing highly select older adults with a wider range of younger adults. Therefore, we cannot conclude that age "caused" the older adults to have the characteristics they have now because they might always have been a special subset of their own age group.

To help illustrate this principle, consider data on the psychological characteristic of cautiousness. One of the tried and true findings in the psychology of adult development and aging contends that older people are less likely to take risks than are younger people. Similarly, older adults are less likely to engage in criminal behavior. It's possible that as people age they are better able to avoid behaving in ways that could bring them harm or get them arrested. Alternatively, it's possible that they did not change at all and are the only ones left standing from their generation. The people more likely to make risky decisions early on

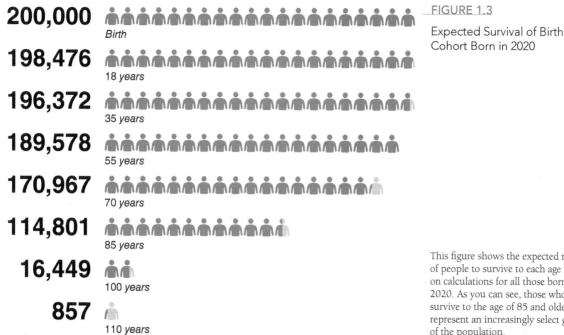

200,000 *Birth*

198,476 *18 years*

196,372 *35 years*

189,578 *55 years*

170,967 *70 years*

114,801 *85 years*

16,449 *100 years*

857 *110 years*

FIGURE 1.3

Expected Survival of Birth Cohort Born in 2020

This figure shows the expected number of people to survive to each age based on calculations for all those born in 2020. As you can see, those who survive to the age of 85 and older represent an increasingly select group of the population.

in life died at younger ages or were imprisoned. Certainly, those who made poor health decisions would be less likely to have survived into old age.

As a result of the survivor principle, you need to remind yourself continually throughout this book that the older adults we study may have become less risky, more honest, or better able to take care of their health. On the other hand, they may not have changed at all—only survived long enough for us to study them.

Principle 3: Individuality Matters

A long-held myth regarding development is that as people age, they all become alike. This view is refuted by the principle of individuality, which asserts that as people age, they become more different from each other. This divergence occurs in people's physical functioning, psychological performance, relationships, interest in work, economic security, and personality.

In one often-cited study, still considered relevant, researchers examined a large number of studies of aging to compare the divergence among older versus younger adults on measures of the same characteristics (Nelson & Dannefer, 1992). Research continues to underscore the notion that individuals continue to become less alike from each other with age. Such findings suggest that diversity becomes an increasingly prominent theme during the adult

years, a point we will continue to focus on throughout this book.

The idea of increasing divergence among older adult populations does not mean that everyone starts out at exactly the same point when they're young. There are always going to be differences within any sample of people in almost any characteristic you can name. The issue is that as people get older, these differences become magnified. The top-performing person in a sample of young adults may be 10 points higher than the next highest performer. By the time, this person reaches his or her 70s or 80s, these differences may grow by a factor of two, three, or more. In part, this is a statistical fluke. As you'll learn in Chapter 3, it's difficult to find a sample of older adults who are as close in age as are the young adults researchers tend to study (who are often within 2 or 3 years of each other). If age is related to performance, then the odds are that the older group will differ simply because they differ more in age.

However, the increasing variation among older adults isn't just a statistical artifact. Even if you had a sample of older adults who were exactly the same age, it's likely that they would differ more among themselves than they would have when they were younger because they've lived through more experiences affecting everything from their health to their psychological well-being. Those experiences have cumulative effects, causing them to change at different rates and to differing degrees.

FIGURE 1.4

Inter- and Intraindividual Differences in Development

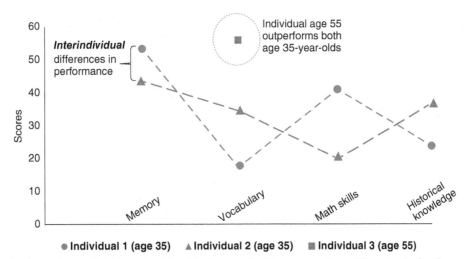

These illustrative data from a theoretical study on cognition show how people of the same age show different levels of performance on different tasks (intraindividual variability) but also that on particular tasks, such as vocabulary, older individuals can perform better than younger individuals (interindividual variability).

Consider what's happened to you and the people you grew up with by this point in your life. You have made the decision to go to college, while others in your age group may have enlisted in military service. You may meet your future spouse in college, while your best friend remains on the dating scene for years. Upon graduation, some may choose to pursue graduate studies as others enter the workforce. You may or may not choose to start a family, or perhaps have already begun the process. With the passage of time, your differing experiences build upon each other to help mold the person you become. The many possibilities that can stem from the choices you make help illustrate that the permutations of events in people's lives are virtually endless. Personal histories move in increasingly idiosyncratic directions with each passing day, year, and decade of life.

There are actually two types of differences that come into play when we talk about individuality. Interindividual differences are differences *between* people. Intraindividual differences refer to the variations in performance within the same individual. In other words, not all systems develop at the same rate within the person. Some functions may increase over time, others decrease, and others stay the same. Even within a construct such as intelligence, an individual may show gains in one area, losses in another, and stability in yet another domain. Intraindividual differences illustrate the fact that development can proceed in multiple directions within the

same person (Baltes & Graf, 1996), a concept known as multidirectionality.

Figure 1.4 illustrates interindividual and intraindividual differences by showing scores of two 35-year-old individuals and one 55-year-old individual on four psychological tests. These illustrative data from a theoretical study on cognition show how people of the same age show different levels of performance on different tasks (intraindividual variability) but also that on particular tasks, such as vocabulary, older individuals can perform better than younger individuals (interindividual variability).

Principle 4: "Normal" Aging Is Different From Disease

The principle that normal aging is different from disease means that growing older doesn't necessarily mean growing sicker. It is important for both practical and scientific reasons to distinguish between normal aging and disease. Health care specialists who work with middle-age and older adults need to recognize and treat the onset of a disease rather than dismiss it simply as "getting older." For example, an 80-year-old man exhibiting symptoms of depression can be successfully treated, assuming that the clinician does not write his symptoms off as a feature of normal aging. Personality development in adulthood does not inevitably lead to the depressive symptoms of lowered self-esteem, excessive guilt, changes in appetite, or lack of interest in activities. Older adults may experience some moderation in personality qualities such as becoming a bit less judgmental in relation to others. However, the development of psychological disorders for the first time in later life is not typical. Clinicians who mistakenly think that these symptoms are part of the normal aging process won't take the proper course of treatment that could alleviate the depressed person's suffering.

Gerontologists translate the principle that normal aging is different from disease into terms that distinguish these processes. Primary aging (or normal aging) refers to the normal changes over time that occur due to universal, intrinsic, and progressive alterations in the body's systems. Changes over time leading to impairment due to disease rather than normal aging are referred to as secondary or impaired aging. These changes are not due to universal, intrinsic processes but are a function of an abnormal set of changes afflicting a segment rather than the entirety of the older population (Aldwin & Gilmer, 1999). Skin wrinkling and discoloration represent primary aging but skin cancer represents secondary aging.

The third type of aging process sets in toward the very end of life, when individuals experience a rapid loss of functions across multiple areas of functioning. This precipitous decline is called tertiary aging (Gerstorf et al., 2013). Representing the impact of disease on perhaps already compromised areas of functioning, tertiary aging deserves mention in its own right as distinct from primary or even secondary aging.

Primary, secondary, and tertiary aging refer to processes that, over time, accumulate, and in the absence of accident or injury, cause the individual's death. Gerontologists believe that despite changes in the body that lead to loss, aging can also involve gains. The term **optimal aging** refers to age-related changes that improve the individual's functioning. Changes due to optimal aging may reflect the preventative or compensatory measures that adults take to counter the toll that aging would normally take on their physical and psychological functioning. However, some individuals do not even make special efforts to alter their own aging, but for reasons not always entirely clear, seem to age at a slower rate than their peers. They may be the ones who never seem to get sick right until the very end of their lives, when a sudden illness leads to their death.

Throughout life, age-related losses due to primary, secondary, and tertiary aging occur contemporaneously, as we show in Figure 1.5. Thus, even while optimal aging can slow the deleterious changes of primary and secondary aging, eventually tertiary aging takes over and the individual's life comes to an end. Remember that, according to the principles of intraindividual and interindividual variability, the rates of each type of aging vary within individuals and from person to person.

THE MEANING OF AGE

The study of aging implies that age is the major variable of interest. However, the scientific study of aging faces a challenge in that age carries with it a number of problems as that major variable of interest. To be sure, there is value in categorizing individuals in later life based on their age. At the same time, attaching a numerical value to people on the basis of their date of birth carries with it a certain arbitrariness. Chronological age is a number based on measures of the Earth's movement around the

JEGAT MAXIME/MaxPPP/Newscom

An example of optimal aging is Charles Eugster, shown here on the far left. Beginning his fitness program when he was 85 years old, he broke world records for masters athletes, winning more than 100 fitness awards prior to his death at age 97.

Losses

Primary aging
Normal age-related changes

Secondary aging
Disease-related impairments

Tertiary aging
Rapid decline shortly before death

Gains

Optimal aging
Changes that improve the individual's functioning

FIGURE 1.5

Age-Related Losses and Gains

Normal aging is also referred to as primary aging, which is different from secondary aging related to disease and tertiary aging, which includes the rapid loss of function before death. There are also gains associated with aging referred to as "optimal aging" in which people become better with age in certain functions.

sun; however, we don't know how much the changes in the physical universe relate to what goes on inside the body in any kind of precise fashion.

Consider what happens when people's ages change at a major birthday such as reaching the age of 40. The crossing from an age that ends in 9 to an age that ends in 0 may lead people to engage in self-scrutiny just because we've all been socialized to believe that 40 means something important. This belief is reinforced by birthday cards that invoke the "over the hill" metaphor. In truth, your body does not change in discrete fits and starts when you pass a particular birthday.

The body does keep time in a cycle that approximates a 24-hour period, but there is no evidence at the moment to suggest that this time pacemaker is related to aging. To say that chronological age (or time) "means" anything with regard to the status of the body's functioning is, based on current evidence, questionable. The popularity of such phrases as "30 being the new 20" and "60 the new 50" capture the difficulty of defining people's aging processes based solely on a number. Chronological age does have some value in describing a person, but like other descriptive features of a person, such as gender or eye color, it is the social meaning attached to chronological age that often outweighs any intrinsic usefulness. As we have already discussed, people of the same age can vary substantially from one another, and people of different ages can be more similar to each other than their differing age might lead you to expect.

Using Age to Define "Adult"

Now that we have you thinking about the meaning of age, we will move on to the next challenge—the meaning of the word "adult." Earlier, we asked you to decide whether you consider yourself an adult. When you think of that word,

perhaps the synonym of "mature" comes to mind. This, in turn, may conjure up images of a person reaching a certain level of accomplishment or growth. Consider, for example, the term "mature" in reference to an apple. A mature apple is one that is ready to be eaten, and you can judge that by examining the apple's color, size, and texture. An apple's maturity level is relatively easy to measure compared to judging the maturity of humans. The complexity of the biopsychosocial processes that occur within us are far more difficult to quantify.

You might think that the most logical definition of maturity should be based on physical development. Yet, you also know that girls and boys who have passed through puberty in their teenage years would, in contemporary Western society, be regarded as anything but an adult. Although their physical attributes define them as adults, the psychological and social standards would not.

Perhaps a standard based on ability is a better option. Consider 16 years, the age when most people can legally drive. Or, alternatively, consider age 18, when U.S. society ordains the person with the right to vote. Using the age of 21 presents another possible point of entry into adulthood. Because it is the age when American adults can legally drink alcohol, for many, the turning of 21 represents a defining mark of the beginning of adulthood. However, the United States is in a small minority of nations that set the drinking age at 21. Some Canadian provinces set the drinking age at 19 (though it is 18 in most); countries such as Germany, Barbados, and Portugal set it at 16. These conflicting age demarcations for even such a seemingly concrete behavior as drinking alcohol show that deciding when a person is an adult on this basis has very limited utility.

Parenthetically, the variations in the legal drinking age shown from country to country (and even within a country) illustrate the interaction of biological and socio-cultural factors in setting age-based parameters around human behavior. People in Canada who are 18 years old are, on average, not all that physiologically distinct from 18-year-olds who live in the U.S. For that matter, they are probably not even psychologically different. It's the culture that distinguishes whether they're able to drink alcohol without getting arrested.

If you're like many students, the age of 25 may hold special importance for you. This is the age where, in the United States, you can rent a car without having to pay a tremendous surcharge. This age has no inherent meaning, but it is used by car rental companies because the chances of having an auto accident are lower after the age of 25. It's possible that a switch is flicked on a person's 25th birthday so that the unsafe driver now has become a model of good behavior on the road. However, the odds are statistically higher that people under age 25 are more likely to engage in the risky combination of drinking and driving, which is what leads to the higher insurance premiums.

Another set of criteria related to the age of adulthood pertains to when people can marry without the consent of their parents. There again, we find huge variation. Within the United States alone, the age of consent varies from state to state from 16 to 18 years of age, though the age at which individuals can legally consent to sex may be younger. In South Carolina, for example, 14-year-old girls are considered old enough to consent to having sex with partners who are 18 or older. Moreover, the age when people actually marry reflects factors such as the health of the economy; in bad economic times, the median age of marriage goes well above the age of consent. During these times, people in their 20s (or older) may find they're forced to move back in with their parents because they aren't earning sufficient income to rent or buy their own place. Does that mean that people become less "adult" when the economy lags?

Given these contradictory definitions of "adult," it might be wise to recommend that we set the threshold into adulthood based on the individual's having reached the chronological age associated with the expectations and privileges of a given society or subculture. For example, in the United States, individuals may be considered to have reached adulthood at the age when they are eligible to vote, drink, drive, and get married. For the majority of U.S. states, the age of 21 is therefore considered the threshold to adulthood. In other countries, these criteria may be reached at the age of 18. Regardless of the varying definitions, up to as many as the first 10 or 11 years of adulthood represent the period of emerging adulthood, or the transition prior to assuming the full responsibilities associated with adulthood, normally the years 18 to 29 (Arnett, 2000). Here again, however, there is a debate about whether age can provide a useful definition even of this relatively narrow period of life (Côté, 2014).

Divisions by Age of the Over-65 Population

Traditionally, 65 years of age has been viewed as the entry point for "old age." The origins of this age of retirement can be traced to Germany when, in 1889, the German Chancellor Otto von Bismarck proposed an old-age social insurance program. Although the original age in Germany was 70 years, it became changed in 1916 to age 65, and now this is the age traditionally associated with "old age."

Gerontologists recognized long ago that not only was 65 an arbitrary number for defining old age, but that it also resulted in people being placed into too broad of a category when defined as older adults. All other things being equal, a 65-year-old faces very different issues than someone who is 85 or 90. There are certainly 65-year-olds in very poor health and 95-year-olds who have no serious ailments. But because, on average, 65-year-olds are so different than those who are 20 or more years older, we use a convention to break the 65-and-older category into subgroups.

The subgroups most frequently used in gerontology are young-old (ages 65 to 74); old-old (ages 75 to 84); and oldest-old (ages 85 and older). We shouldn't place too much credence on numbers, as we've already said, but these are good approximations for roughly categorizing the 65-and-older population. Bernice Neugarten, one of the early pioneers in psychological gerontology, proposed these distinctions in the mid-1970s, and they have remained in use to this day even though 85 may be the "new" 65 with the oldest-old being in better health than they were 50 years ago (Neugarten, 1974).

With more and more people living to the oldest-old category as defined in this manner, gerontologists are reexamining the divisions of the 65+ age group. Specifically, people over the age of 100, known as centenarians, are becoming more and more commonly represented in the population, as we will show later in the chapter. It will not be long before the very highest age category becomes more prominent—the supercentenarians, who are 110 and older. Typically, the oldest person in the world at any given time is between the ages of 114 and 116. Jeanne Louise Calment, the oldest documented living human, was 122 at the time of her death. Supercentenarian will probably retain its definition as 110 and over, though, at least for the foreseeable future.

Functional Age

Discontented with the entire concept of chronological age, a number of gerontologists are devising a new classification system that is based not on what the calendar says but on functional age, which is how people actually perform

FIGURE 1.6

Measures of Functional Age

Functional age measures use scores on given indicators to represent age rather than chronological age.

(see Figure 1.6). With functional instead of chronological age as the basis for a system of studying aging, we could gain a better grasp of a person's true characteristics and abilities. When we talk about research methods in Chapter 3, we'll see further advantages to using measures other than chronological age to study the aging process.

Biological age is the age of an individual's bodily systems. Using biological age instead of chronological age would tell us exactly how well people are able to perform such vital functions as the heart's pumping blood through the arteries and getting oxygen to the lungs. With biological age, you could also help people learn how best to improve their muscle and bone strength.

In order to be able to use biological age as an index, we would need a large repository of data showing what's to be expected for each major biological function at each age. For example, we'd need to know the population values for blood pressure readings in people with different chronological ages. Then, we would assign people a "blood pressure age" according to which chronological age of healthy people their numbers most closely match. A 50-year-old whose blood pressure was in the range of normal 25- to 30-year-olds would then have a biological age that was 20 or 25 years younger than his or her chronological age.

Popular culture has certainly caught on to the notion of biological rather than chronological age. There are a multitude of online calculators in which you answer various questions to estimate how long you will live. In addition, there are slightly more sophisticated "biological age tests" that let you calculate your "lung age," for example.

Another, far more sophisticated approach, involves measuring cellular aging. When exposed to harmful environmental conditions, the body's cells undergo important changes affecting their ability to function normally. By indexing these changes, researchers can develop a scale that assesses biological functioning at this very basic level (Hannum et al., 2013).

Psychological age refers to the performance an individual achieves on measures of such qualities as reaction time, memory, learning ability, and intelligence (all of which are known to change with age). Like biological age, a person's performance on these tasks would be compared with those of other adults and then scaled accordingly.

Social age is calculated by evaluating where people are compared to the "typical" ages expected for people to be when they occupy certain positions in life. These positions tend to center on family and work roles. For example, a grandparent would have an older social age than would a parent, although the grandparent might easily be chronologically younger than the parent.

Social age can have some interesting twists. For example, people can be grandparents in their late 20s (with a social age of 60 or older). Conversely, women can become mothers in their late 60s. Perhaps you have a friend whose grandmother is 93 and another whose grandmother is 57. We see the same issue with regard to work roles. A 70-year-old who is still working has a younger social age than a 66-year-old who has retired. Athletes and politicians present a similar contrast. A gymnast may be forced to give up her sport at 18 years of age and thus have an older social age than a still-employed legislator who continues to win elections into her 70s or beyond.

As we stated earlier, an advantage of using functional indices of aging is that they can be more accurate than chronological age. However, it's much easier to use chronological age than these sophisticated calculations. Adding to the problem is the fact that, functional ages must be constantly calibrated and recalibrated to ensure that they continue to be accurate. For example, a biological index based in part on blood pressure may require adjustments as health practitioners change the definition of what is considered "normal." Changes in both medical knowledge and population norms for particular age groups may mean that the definition of normal blood pressure for an average 60-year-old shifts to be more typical of a person in the 70s. Psychological age and social age indices are also likely to change over time.

Despite its faults, chronological age may be the most expedient index for many areas of functioning. Just keep in mind that it does not tell the whole story.

Personal Versus Social Aging

The aging process occurs within the individual, but as you have learned already, it is shaped by events occurring in the individual's social context. When developmental psychologists study the aging process, it is difficult to disentangle those internal changes from those that reflect a changing world, though we try to do so by applying the appropriate controls in our research.

Personal aging refers to changes that occur within the individual and reflect the influence of time's passage on the body's structures and functions. This is how people ordinarily think of the aging process and, indeed, it is what is implied in primary, secondary, and tertiary aging.

Social aging refers to the effects of a person's exposure to a changing environment. Over time, the changes we see within the individual represent the unique blend of personal and social aging as these play out in that individual's life.

Within the category of social aging, the changes that take place in an individual's life are seen as reflecting a multitude of interacting factors. At any one time, the individual's life reflects one or more of three basic categories of three social influences. These influences, identified by psychologist Paul Baltes (1979) and still seen as relevant today, include normative age-graded influences, normative history-graded influences, and nonnormative influences. We'll look at each of these in turn.

Normative age-graded influences lead people to choose experiences that their culture and historical period attach to certain ages or points in the life span. The term "normative" stems from the term "norm," which is a social expectation for behavior. In Western society, age norms traditionally dictate that individuals graduate from college in their early 20s, get married and begin a family in their 20s or 30s, retire in their 60s, and become grandparents in their middle to later years, usually in the decades of the 50s, 60s, and beyond. These are influences on behavior to the extent that people believe that they should structure their lives according to these age demarcations.

Events that occur in response to normative age-graded influences occur in part because a given society has developed expectations about what is assumed appropriate for people of certain ages. The decision to retire at the age of 65 years can be seen as a response to the norm more true perhaps in the past than today, that 65 is the correct age to leave the labor market. Graduation from high school generally occurs at the age of 18 years for most because in most industrialized societies, children start school at the age of 5 or 6 and the educational system is based on 12 or 13 grades.

Normative age-graded influences exert their impact beyond what the norms themselves imply because people are socialized into believing that they *should* structure their lives so that they conform to these influences. When people don't adhere to these norms, for whatever reasons, they feel that there is something wrong with them. For example, a 40-year-old office worker may consider retiring but feel reluctant to do so because it is not what is expected for a person of that age in that field of employment. Similarly, a 35-year-old may prefer not to marry or to have children, but feel pressured into doing so by other family members, friends, or the society at large by virtue of having reached their mid-30s.

The normative age-graded influences are partly linked to the biological aging process. Parenthood traditionally occurs between the ages of 20 and 40, at the peak of a woman's reproductive cycle. This age range sets the normative age period for biologically becoming a parent. Once this age is set, then a lower limit is set on the age at which the adult can become a grandparent. If the child also follows a normative age-graded influence, the parent will likely become a grandparent for the first time between the ages of 55 and 65 years. Similarly, manual laborers or athletes may be at peak physical capacity up to their 40s, when they may experience loss of strength and speed.

Now let's turn to the second set of influences on development, those that relate to the impact of events in the outside world on the individual. **Normative history-graded influences** are events that occur to everyone within a certain culture or geopolitical unit (regardless of age) and include large-scale occurrences, such as world wars, economic trends, or sociocultural changes in attitudes and values. One such example is a natural disaster that impacts thousands of people living in a particular location or area of the world. The California wildfires (shown in the photo) of 2019 affected large parts of the state, causing many to lose their homes and places of work. The impact of these events on people's lives may be felt immediately. They can continue to have a lasting impact for many years on the subsequent patterns of work, family, and quality of life of the people affected by those events.

An individual does not have to experience a historical event directly to be affected by a normative history-graded influence. For example, a terrorist attack or a mass shooting not only creates victims but also has wider influences on a society's sense of security as well as potential governmental actions that are the result of the incident. In 2019, a partial shutdown of the U.S. government not only caused nearly 800,000 federal workers to lose their paychecks but also affected the effectiveness of the agencies for whom they worked as well as the larger economy.

If the life course was influenced only by normative age- and history-graded influences, predicting the course of development of people of the same age living in the same culture would not be easy, but it would be a manageable problem. Plug in a person's age and the year of the person's birth, and you'd be able to figure out which combination of age-graded and history-graded influences set the course of that person's life. However, people's lives are also affected by nonnormative influences, which are the random idiosyncratic events that occur throughout life. They are "nonnormative" because they occur with no regular predictability.

There are almost an infinite number of examples of nonnormative influences. Some are due to good luck, such as winning the lottery or making a smart investment. Nonnormative influences can also be negative, such as a car accident, fire, or the untimely death of a relative. One moment your life is routine and predictable, and in the next, a single event irrevocably alters it. Other nonnormative influences may unfold over a gradual period, such as being fired from a job (due to personal, not large-scale economic reasons), developing a chronic illness not related to aging, or going through a divorce. In everyday language, you talk about someone benefiting from the "right place, right time" effect or—conversely—suffering a negative fate from the opposite set of coincidences.

As you have read about the various types of influences on life, it may have crossed your mind that the way in which they interact with each other is also important. Consider the example of divorce. Although society's norms have changed considerably regarding this life event, many would still consider this a nonnormative occurrence because the norm (and certainly the hope) of married couples is to remain married. And although a divorce is a personal occurrence, it may be seen in part as a response to larger social forces. For example, a couple who is exposed to financial hardship because one or both partners lost a job due to living in harsh economic times (normative historical influence) is now faced with severe emotional stress. If they are in their middle years, when couples are expected to have reached a degree of financial comfort (age-graded normative influence), their problems may be exacerbated. Yet, some couples may feel closer to each other when exposed to such adversity, and this is where the idiosyncratic nonnormative factors come into play.

This example illustrates the dilemmas faced by researchers in human development who attempt to separate out not only personal from social aging but also the impact of particular influences that fall into the category of social aging. Though challenging, the very complexity of the equation fascinates those of us who try to understand what makes humans "tick" and what causes that ticking to change over the decades of the human life span.

U.S. Marine Corps photo by Cpl. Dylan Chagnon

An example of a normative history-graded influence is a natural disaster such as the wildfires that affected the lives of many thousands of Californians in the late 2010s.

KEY SOCIAL FACTORS IN ADULT DEVELOPMENT AND AGING

As we've just seen, social factors play an important role in shaping the course of our lives. Here we make explicit exactly how we define and use the key social factors that we will refer to in this book.

Sex and Gender

In discussing the aging process, there are important male–female differences related to the socialization experiences of men and women. We will use the term gender to refer to the individual's identification as male, female, or nonbinary. Gender is distinct from biological sex, which refers to the individual's inherited predisposition to develop the physiological characteristics typically associated with maleness or femaleness. Both sex and gender are important in the study of adult development and aging. Physiological factors relevant to sex influence the timing and nature of physical aging processes, primarily through the operation of sex hormones. For example, the sex hormone estrogen is thought to play at least some role in affecting a woman's risks of heart disease, bone loss, and possibly cognitive changes.

Social and cultural factors relevant to gender are important to the extent that the individual assumes a certain role in society based on being viewed as a male or female. Opportunities in education and employment are two main areas in which gender influences the course of adult development and becomes a limiting factor for women. Although progress has certainly occurred in both domains over the past several decades, women continue to face a more restricted range of choices and the prospects of lower earnings than do men. Furthermore, these differences are important to consider when studying the current generation of older adults, as they were raised in an era with more traditional gender expectations.

The phenomenon of transgendered individuals (i.e., those who adopt the sex other than what they were born with) is too recent to have produced enough information relevant to aging. We might expect that this will become an area studied by gerontologists, particularly because it also highlights the role of social influences on development. Prior to the decade of the 2010s, there was relatively little social awareness of the experience of transgendered individuals and aging but this is rapidly changing (Kimmel et al., 2015).

Race

A person's race is defined in biological terms as the classification within the species based on physical and structural characteristics. However, the concept of race in common usage is broader than these biological features. Race is used in a more widespread fashion to refer to the cultural background associated with being born within a particular biologically defined segment of the population. The "race" that people use to identify themselves is more likely to be socially than biologically determined. In addition, because few people are solely of one race in the biological sense, social and cultural background factors assume even greater prominence.

The U.S. census, a count of those living in the United States conducted every 10 years, attempts to provide an accurate depiction of the size and makeup of the country. The 2020 U.S. census defined race on the basis of a person's self-identification. The most frequently used racial categories in data reported from the census are White, Black or African American, American Indian or Alaska Native, Asian, and Native Hawaiian or Other Pacific Islander. In addition to these racial categories, the census also included categories based on national origin and allowed individuals to select more than one racial category.

To the extent that race is biologically determined, racial differences in functioning in adulthood and aging may reflect differences in genetic inheritance. People who have inherited a risk factor that has been found to be higher within a certain race are more likely to be at risk for developing that illness during their adult years.

Racial variations in risk factors may also interact with different cultural backgrounds associated with a particular race. For example, people at risk for a disease with a metabolic basis (such as inability to metabolize fats) will be more likely to develop that disease if cooking foods high in fat content are a part of their culture.

Social and cultural aspects of race may also alter an individual's development in adulthood through the structure of a society and whether there are systematic biases against people who identify with that race. As we will demonstrate throughout this book, many illnesses have a higher prevalence among the African American population than among the White population in the United States, and this has led to significant disparities in the health of the two groups. Part of the differences in health may be attributed to lack of opportunities for education and well-paying jobs, but systematic discrimination is also believed to take a toll on health by increasing the levels of stress experienced by African Americans (Green & Darity, 2010).

Ethnicity

The concept of ethnicity captures the cultural background of an individual, reflecting the predominant values, attitudes, and expectations in which the individual has been raised. Along with race, ethnicity is often studied in adult development and aging as an influence on a person's familial attitudes and experiences. For example, people of certain ethnic backgrounds are thought to show greater respect for older adults and feel a stronger sense of obligation to care for their aging parents. Ethnicity also may play a role in influencing the aging of various physiological functions, in part through genetic inheritance, and in part through exposure to cultural habits and traditions. Finally, discrimination against people of certain ethnic backgrounds may serve the same function as race in limiting the opportunities for educational and occupational achievements.

The term *ethnicity* is gradually replacing the term *race* as a categorical variable in social research. We will follow that tradition in this book unless there is a clear-cut reason to refer specifically to race (i.e., if we are describing research that also uses this term). However, there are occasional points of confusion in that the U.S. census occasionally combines race (White or Black) and ethnicity (Hispanic or non-Hispanic). Many census statistics break down the distributions they report into White non-Hispanic, White Hispanic, Black non-Hispanic, and Black Hispanic.

Socioeconomic Status

Socioeconomic status (SES), or "social class," reflects people's position in the educational and occupational ranks of a society. Technically, SES is calculated through a weighted formula that takes into account a person's highest level of education and the prestige level of his or her occupation. There is no one set way to calculate SES, however. Various researchers have developed scales of SES that give differing weights to these values in coming up with a total score. People with higher levels of education tend to have occupations that are higher in prestige, and so some researchers use level of education alone as the index of SES.

Income levels are not necessarily associated with SES. High-prestige jobs (such as teachers) are often associated with mid- or even low-level salaries. However, as a proxy for or in addition to SES, some researchers use income as the basis for analyzing social class differences in health and opportunities. Income inequity can be expressed in statistical terms. Figure 1.7 illustrates the Gini coefficient, an index of income inequality in a given economy. If income is equally distributed, 100% of the population earns 100% of the accumulated wealth. Income equality is reflected when a smaller percent of the population earns a higher proportion of the wealth, such as when 10% of the population earns 90% of the wealth. In the United States, the Gini coefficient has risen steadily since 1990, indicating the consolidation of wealth in the upper income brackets.

SES is an exceptionally important, but often unrecognized, influence on the aging process. In our book,

FIGURE 1.7

Gini Coefficient

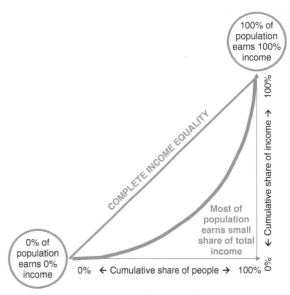

The Gini coefficient makes it possible to classify an economy according to the distribution of its wealth. The green line of complete income equality occurs when income is distributed equally across the population. The red curve shows an economy characterized by inequity in which a small percentage of the population earns the largest share of income as when the wealthiest 10% of the population earns 90% of the income generated in that economy.

we will highlight studies that connect aging with SES. One in particular stands out because of its size, length of time of follow-up, and complexity. This is the landmark investigation known as Whitehall II, a survey of a large sample of British adults focusing on the relationships among health, social class, and occupation. Whitehall I (the original study) was established in 1967 and involved 18,000 men working in civil service occupations in the United Kingdom. This study showed that the men in the lowest employment brackets had poorer health than their health habits would predict.

Whitehall II was initiated by Sir Michael Marmot in 1985 to investigate specifically social and occupational influences on health and illness including psychological work load, control over work pacing and content, opportunity for using one's skills, and social support at work. Sir Marmot currently chairs the Commission on Equity and Health Inequalities in America and was Chair of the World Health Organization's Commission on Social Determinants of Health. Whitehall II continues to produce important findings that we will share throughout the text.

Religion

Religion, or an individual's identification with an organized belief system, is surprisingly one of the least well-understood but presumably important influences on aging. Organized religions form a set of social structures that transcend nationality and which, additionally, are partly connected with race and ethnicity. More important, religion provides many people with a source of coping strategies, social support in times of crisis, and a systematic basis for interpreting life experiences (Klemmack et al., 2007).

Religion is distinct from spirituality, or the set of beliefs than an individual holds about such areas as the afterlife, a sense of meaning in life, and feelings of connections to others. Spirituality and its relationship to psychological well-being in later life is becoming an increasing focus of researchers in the field and will undoubtedly grow in importance over the coming years (Tomás et al., 2015).

THE BABY BOOMERS GROW UP: CHANGES IN THE MIDDLE-AGED AND OLDER POPULATIONS IN THE UNITED STATES AND THE WORLD

A quick snapshot of the U.S. population according to age and sex appears in Figure 1.8. The age–sex structure provides a useful way of looking at the population. A "young" population is shaped like a pyramid, an "old" population is depicted by an upside-down pyramid, and a population considered stable is shaped like a rectangle.

You can clearly see in this figure the prominence of the Baby Boom generation, the term used to describe people born in the post-World War II years of 1946 to 1964. This period really did represent a "boom" in that more babies were born in 1946 than ever before (3.4 million); more than 4 million were born every year from 1954 to 1964. By then, the Baby Boom generation made up nearly 40% of the entire U.S. population.

We now have several other terms for generations of Americans born in other decades, including the "Silent Generation" (those in their teens in the 1950s), the "Greatest Generation" (those who fought in World War II), "Gen X" (the children of the Baby Boomers), and the Millennials, also called "Gen Y," born in the 1990s, at the tail end of the Gen Xers. The assumption with this terminology is that you are defined in important ways by the year of your birth, clearly an overgeneralization. Nevertheless, the terms persist and at least for the Baby Boomers, they will most likely never go away. These generational terms provide convenient categories and therefore remain popular.

What's important about the Baby Boom generation, apart from whatever it might mean in terms of defining any one individual, is the preponderance of individuals of similar ages moving through the population together. Not only do these groups share certain historical events, but

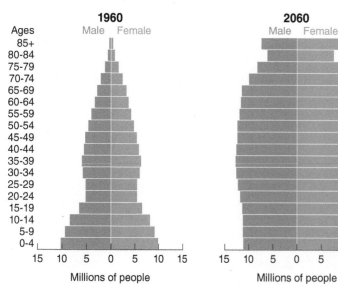

From Pyramid to Pillar: A Century of Change
Population of the United States

FIGURE 1.8

Age and Sex Structure of the Population of the United States, 1960–2060

This is the age–sex structure of the U.S. population, showing the millions of people in each 5-year age bracket divided by sex. The 2060 structure reflects projections that there will be more people alive than was the case in 1960 in the upper age brackets of the population.

Source: U.S. Bureau of the Census (2018a). Public Domain.

they also create their own set of dilemmas (Whitbourne & Willis, 2006). We will learn later in the book about the implications for the economy, for example, of having so many people reach their 60s at similar times.

United States

In 1900, the number of Americans over the age of 65 years was 3.1 million people, making up about 4% of the population. By 2017, the number of people 65 and older in the United States was estimated to be 50.9 million, or 5.6% of the total population (U.S. Bureau of the Census, 2018a). There were 6.5 million Americans 85 and older in 2017 (U.S. Bureau of the Census, 2018b). Figure 1.9 shows the growth of the total 65 and older population from 1960 to 2060 (Vespa et al., 2018).

By 2060, the U.S. Bureau of the Census estimates that there will be 94.7 million adults 65 and older, representing 23% of the total population; and older adults alone will number 19 million, or triple the number in 2017 (Vespa et al., 2018). Perhaps most impressive is the estimate in the growth in the number of centenarians. In 1990, an estimated 37,306 people over the age of 100 lived in the United States. By 2015, this number had increased to 72,000; by 2060, it will increase eight times to 604,000 (U.S. Bureau of the Census, 2017a).

FIGURE 1.9

Projections of the Older Adult Population: 2020–2060

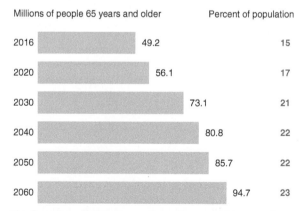

Millions of people 65 years and older / Percent of population

Year	Millions	Percent
2016	49.2	15
2020	56.1	17
2030	73.1	21
2040	80.8	22
2050	85.7	22
2060	94.7	23

This figure from the U.S. Census shows the expected increases from 2016 to 2060 in the number and percent of the population who will be 65 and older.

Source: From Jonathan Vespa, David M. Armstrong, and Lauren Medina. Current Population Reports. Issued March 2018. U.S. Census Bureau. Public Domain.

The major explanation for these large increases in the 65 and older population can be accounted for by the movement of the Baby Boomers through the years of middle and later adulthood. It is important to consider not just that these individuals were born during a period of high birth rates but that they are expected to live into their 80s, 90s, and 100s. This will increase the number of very-old individuals that society will experience throughout the century.

Increases in the aging population reflect the vast advances that have taken place in the average length of life. Life expectancy is the average number of years of life remaining to the people born within a similar period of time. To calculate life expectancy, statisticians take into account death rates for a particular group within the population and use these figures to project how long it will take for that entire group to die out completely. Life expectancy is not the same as life span, which is the maximum age for a given species. The life span of humans has not changed, but more people are living to older ages, leading to the life expectancy increase we are currently witnessing.

Life expectancy from birth rose overall from 62.9 years in 1940 to 78.8 years in 2015. Many factors have contributed to increases in life expectancy, including reduced death rates for children and young adults. People are also living longer once they reach the age of 65, at which point the life expectancy becomes 84.4 years of age (i.e., people turning 65 in 2013 could expect to live an additional 19.4 years) (Murphy et al., 2017).

A related concept is health expectancy, which is the number of years a person could expect to live in good health and with relatively little disability if current mortality and morbidity rates persist. The ideal situation in a given society is that individuals have both long health and life expectancy, meaning that they are able to be productive and free of chronic illness until close to the time that they die. This is also called compression of morbidity, meaning that the illness burden to a society can be reduced if people become disabled closer to the time of their death (Vita et al. 1998).

Geographic Variations Within the United States. As you can see from Figure 1.10, the over-65 population of the United States population is very unevenly distributed geographically. As of 2016, slightly over one half of persons 65 and over lived in 10 states. With 5.3 million people 65 and older, California has the largest number of older adults, but because the state's population is so large, this age group constitutes a relatively small proportion (13.6%) of the population. As you may have guessed, Florida has the highest percentage of people 65 and older (19.9%). The greatest increases in percentage of aging population

FIGURE 1.10

Percent 65 and Over by State as a Percentage of Total Population, 2016

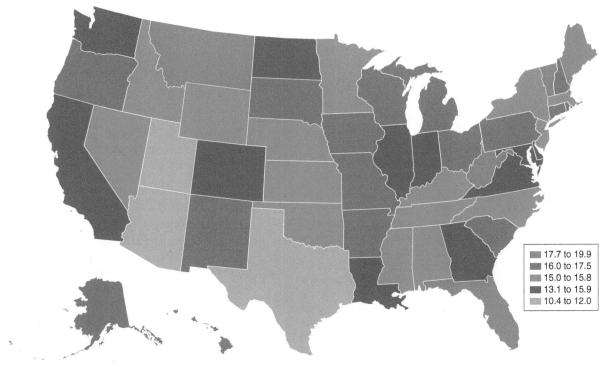

17.7 to 19.9
16.0 to 17.5
15.0 to 15.8
13.1 to 15.9
10.4 to 12.0

This map of the United States shows the states with the highest percentage of individuals ages 65 and older.

Source: From Administration on Aging (2018). Public Domain.

between the years 2006 to 2016 occurred in the states of Alaska (65.6%), Nevada (57.3%), and Colorado (55%) (Administration on Aging, 2018).

Gender and Racial Variations in the Over-65 Population. Women over the age of 65 currently outnumber men, amounting to approximately 56% of the total over-65 population. This gender disparity is expected to diminish somewhat by the year 2050 as the last of the Baby Boomers reach later adulthood. At that time, 54% of the 65 and older population in the United States will be female (U.S. Bureau of the Census, 2017a).

Changes are also evident in the distribution of White and minority segments of the population (see Figure 1.11). In 2016, 23% of all persons in the United States 65 and older were members of racial or ethnic minority populations; persons of Hispanic origin represented 8% (Administration on Aging, 2018). Between 2014 and 2060, there will be dramatic shifts in the racial/ethnic distribution of the 65 and older population of the United States. As shown in Figure 1.11, the percentage of those 65 and older

who are non-minority (shown as "White") will decrease from 78% to 55%; correspondingly, all other racial and ethnic groups will increase. People of Hispanic origin will show the largest overall increase across this period, from 8% to 22% (Federal Interagency Forum on Aging-Related Statistics, 2016). These demographic shifts will occur in part due to increasing migration into the United States. In 2030, net international migration will outpace natural population growth, with a growth of 1 million due to number of births minus number of deaths compared to 1.1 million through net international migration (Vespa et al., 2018).

Aging Around the World

Data from around the world confirm the picture of an increasingly older population throughout the 21st century. In 2015, there were 617 million people worldwide over the age of 65. Predictions suggest that this number will triple to 1.57 billion by the year 2050. China had the largest number of older adults in 2015 (136.9 million), but Japan

FIGURE 1.11

Population Age 65 and Over, by Race and Hispanic Origin, 2016 and Projected 2030 and 2060

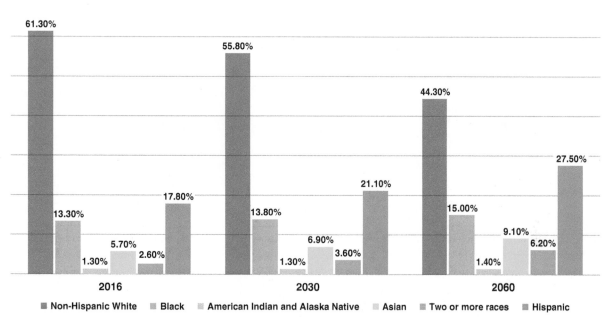

Within the United States, between the years 2016 and 2060, there will be a relative decrease in the percent of those 65 and older who are non-Hispanic white, and relative increases in all other racial/ethnic groups, reflecting overall shifts in the United States to a "majority–minority" country.

Source: From Jonathan Vespa, David M. Armstrong, and Lauren Medina. Current Population Reports. Issued March 2018. U.S. Census Bureau. Public Domain.

had the highest percentage of people 65 and older (26.6%) (He et al., 2016).

The population worldwide is aging at disproportionate rates from region to region. Figure 1.12 shows the distribution of percentage increases according to world region (He et al., 2016). The greatest increases will occur in Asia and Africa, and there will be corresponding decreases in percentage of the 65 and older population in Europe, North America, Oceania (Pacific Ocean countries), and Latin America. The oldest countries in the world (with the highest percentages 65 and older) were Japan, Germany, Italy, Greece, and Finland. Japan will remain the oldest country in 2050, but the next oldest will become South Korea, Hong Kong, Taiwan, and Slovenia. Canada is the sixth oldest now, but will disappear from the top 25 by 2050.

The aging of the world's population will disproportionately occur in the 80-and-older population. Worldwide, those 80 years and older will increase from 126 million in 2015 to 447 million by 2050, with Asia showing particularly rapid growth in this segment of the population. Between 2015 and 2050, 23 countries in Asia

will experience a quadrupling of the 80-and-older population and older compared to only one European country, Bosnia and Herzegovina. The larger proportion of the aging population in the world will place a strain on the economies and health care systems of all nations but particularly those that lack the resources to support the rise in the older adult population, particularly those in low-income countries (He et al., 2016).

What are the implications of these figures for your future as you enter into and move through your adult years? First, you will likely have more friends and associates than the current older population does, simply because there will be more peers of your age group to socialize with. If you are male, the news is encouraging; you will be more likely to live into old age compared to the current cohorts of older adults. For those of you who are younger than the Baby Boomers, the statistics are also encouraging if you are considering a career related to the field of aging, given the higher number of older clientele. Changes in various aspects of lifestyle can also be expected in the next decades, as adjustments to the aging population in the entertainment world and media are made. Just as society

FIGURE 1.12

Percentage Distribution of Population Aged 65 and Over by Region: 2015 and 2050

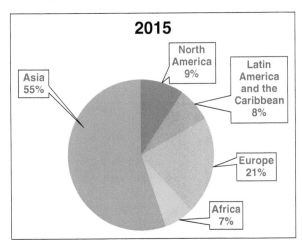
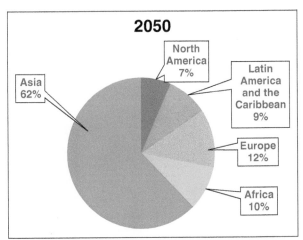

These graphs show the relative increases in the world's older adult population between 2015 and 2050 with Asian countries becoming an increasingly large share of the world's older population by 2050.

Source: From Kowal, P., Goodkind, D. and He, W. (2016) An Aging World 2015, International Population Reports. U.S. Government Printing Office, Washington DC. Public Domain.

is getting used to the idea of an aging Paul McCartney, many others will follow in his footsteps to change views about prominent celebrities in Western society and, indeed, around the world.

SUMMARY

1. This book uses the biopsychosocial perspective, which regards development as a complex interaction of biological, psychological, and social processes. The four principles of adult development and aging include the assumptions that changes are continuous over the life span; only the survivors grow old; individual differences are important to recognize; and "normal" aging is different from disease. Distinctions must be drawn between primary aging (changes that are intrinsic to the aging process) and secondary aging (changes due to disease).

2. It is difficult to define the term "adult" given the range of possible criteria. For purposes of this book, we will consider the ages of 18 to 22 to serve as a rough guideline. The over-65 population is generally divided into the subcategories of young-old (65 to 74), old-old (75 to 84), and oldest-old (85 and over). Centenarians include individuals 100 and older, and supercentenarians are those 110 and older. These divisions have important

policy implications as well as highlight the need to make distinctions among individuals over 65.

3. The idea of functional age bases age on performance rather than chronological age. Additionally, biological, psychological, and social age all provide alternative perspectives to describe an individual. Whereas personal aging refers to changes within the individual over time, social aging refers to the effects of exposure to a changing environment and includes normative age-graded influences, normative history-graded influences, and nonnormative influences.

4. Social factors important to the study of adult development and aging include gender, race, ethnicity, SES, and religion. The Gini coefficient quantifies the extent to which a country experiences income inequity.

5. Society will experience a great impact as the Baby Boom generation begins to enter later adulthood. 50.9 million Americans are over the age of 65, constituting 15.6% of the total U.S. population; these numbers are expected to rise dramatically in the coming years as a result of the Baby Boomers. Gender and racial variations are also expected to change. Countries around the world will show increases in the over-65 population as well, particularly among Asia and Africa. These changes will impact the way in which you view your own later adulthood, as well as prepare for what will happen in your later years.

2

Models of Development: Nature and Nurture in Adulthood

We're sure you are familiar with plenty of stereotypes about aging. Some positive, some negative, and many of them contradictory. From driving to intelligence, here are some common ones. Which do you agree with? Check your answers on the next page.

AGEFEED

? test yourself

1. Older adults are bad drivers.
2. In later life, people lose all interest in sex.
3. Older adults are cute.
4. Grumpiness is common in older adults.
5. Older adults are warm and kind.
6. All older adults are senile.
7. The older you get, the wiser you become.
8. Older adults are wrinkly and saggy.
9. Nothing excites older adults more than the early bird special.
10. Older adults are helpless with technology.

AGEFEED ⓘ
...the scores

All of the statements were stereotypes, representing different forms of ageism. Here's what your scores might suggest about your own attitudes toward aging:

1–3: You hold some negative views about older adults, but for the most part you have managed to avoid too many stereotypes. Even if you agreed with "positive" statements, these still represent overgeneralizations.

4–5: Your views about older adults reflect some of the typical stereotypes but you are still hold some nonstereotyped views.

6–8: Almost all of your views about older adults represent common stereotypes. Keep an open mind to what you'll learn in this text to counteract those views!

9–10: You definitely have room for improvement in your understanding of older adults. We hope this text will educate you otherwise!

The study of adult development and aging has evolved from the field of developmental psychology to incorporate the years beyond childhood and adolescence into a unified view of the life span. For many years, the field of developmental psychology was synonymous with the field of child development. Starting in the 1960s, several influential theorists determined that the emphasis in the field should extend through the entire life span. They argued that designating a point when people stopped developing did not make sense because people do not stop growing and changing once they reach full maturity. Although there are still theorists and researchers in developmental psychology who retain an emphasis on the early years, the emphasis in the field is increasingly coming to embrace the middle and later years of life.

Reflecting the expanded view of developmental psychology beyond the early years of life, the term developmental science emerged in the 1960s to promote a more integrative, life-span view of individual growth and change (Magnusson, 1996). The use of the term "science" rather than "psychology" additionally conveys a shift from focusing solely on what happens to the individual over time to understanding the systematic effects of multiple influences that all play a role in the developmental process.

Developmental scientists look, then, at the multiple intersecting factors that impact change. According to this approach, to understand development, we have to go beyond the unit of the individual and look at social context. Contextual influences on development include sex, race, ethnicity, social class, income, religion, and culture.

Another key feature of developmental science is that it goes beyond psychological domains such as cognition and personality and instead examines areas of functioning traditionally used in other disciplines relevant to behavior such as biology, health, and sociology. The inclusion of social context implies that it is not sufficient to look only within the individual's immediate environment in order to understand change over time (Ford & Lerner, 1992). Particularly important to the field of developmental science is a desire to understand the dynamic interactions among and within each level of analysis of change, from the biological to the social (Lerner, 1996).

With the refocus toward developmental science, researchers now attempt to explain the underlying processes of development rather than simply use a descriptive approach to catalog the changes over time that occur as people get older. The descriptive approach to development was practiced for many decades as scholars attempted to establish the ages at which particular events occur within the individual. Developmental scientists are now attempting to discover orderly principles underlying growth through life: the "whys," not just the "whats."

Developmental science is also increasingly relying on advances in the field of neuroscience, or the study of brain-behavior relationships. Researchers in developmental neuroscience use brain scanning methods to correlate changes in the structures of the nervous system with changes in behavior from birth through later life. They also draw from research on species other than humans in which experimental methods can be used to manipulate both genes and the environment in ways that are not possible with humans.

In summary, the emerging field of developmental science suggests that individuals continue to grow and change over the entire course of their lives. Additionally, developmental scientists believe that it is important to consider multiple influences, particularly the way in which social context influences change over time.

MODELS OF INDIVIDUAL–ENVIRONMENT INTERACTIONS

What causes people to change over time? We know that nature and nurture influence the individual's growth, but how much can we attribute to nature and how much to nurture? When you think about your own development, do you tend to say you must have your mother's this or your father's that? Or do you connect your current behaviors with the city or town you grew up in, what your friends were like, and where you went to school? Questions such as these fall into the category of individual–environment interactions in development. Just as you think about the causes of your own behavior, so do developmental scientists.

Early in the 20th century, developmental psychologists took a largely "nature" approach. They regarded growth in childhood as a clocklike process that reflected the unfolding of the individual's genetic makeup. This was the assumption of early 20th-century writers such as Arnold Gesell (1880–1961), who took on the task of chronicling a child's changes from birth to adolescence. According to these early developmental theorists, such changes reflected the influence of ontogenesis, or maturational processes, as they unfolded within the child. Early scholars such as Gesell gave minimal emphasis to the environment. They believed that parents needed to provide the right growing conditions, much as you would provide water and light to a plant seedling. Other than that, the child's genes would dictate the pace and outcome of development.

Challenging the nature position was the founder of American behaviorism, John B. Watson (1878–1958). Writing some 20 years after Gesell, Watson took the extreme "nurture" position that a child's development was

The young soccer players shown here have found their "niche" in athletics, in which they continue to develop their interests and abilities.

entirely dependent on the environment the parents provided. Similarly, the behaviorist B.F. Skinner (1904–1990) believed that development consisted of the acquisition of a series of increasingly complex habits reflecting the child's exposure to new experiences.

The nature–nurture debate stimulated many of the classic studies in child development. Researchers from the opposing viewpoints attempted to prove their positions by contrasting, for example, differences between identical twins reared together and those reared in separate homes. The theory behind these studies was that since identical twins shared 100% of their genetic material, any differences between those reared apart would be due to the environment in which they grew up.

Perhaps the most hotly debated of these discussions was the issue of whether intelligence is inherited or acquired. The debates took on a different tone as researchers understood more and more that neither influence alone could account for individual differences in performance on intelligence tests—in children or adults. One contribution that changed the tone of the nature–nurture debate occurred when developmental psychologist Sandra Scarr introduced the concept of niche-picking (Scarr & McCartney, 1983), the proposal that genetic and environmental factors work together to influence the direction of a child's life. According to this concept, children quite literally pick out their "niche," or area in which they develop their talents and abilities. Once they start down that particular pathway, they experience further changes that influence the later development of those particular abilities.

Consider the example of a child whose genetic potential predisposes her to be a talented dancer. She has a great deal of flexibility, poise, and a good sense of rhythm—all characteristics that reflect strong "dance" genes. At the age

of 4, her parents take her to a ballet performance. She sits glued to her seat, fascinated by the pirouetting and leaping of the performers who she sees on stage. This event triggers pleas to her parents to enroll her in ballet lessons, and soon they do. The child has chosen dancing as her "niche," having been exposed to the ballet performance, and once allowed to pursue her talent, she continues to thrive. Thus, her "dance genes" lead her to develop an interest in exactly the activity that will allow her talents to flourish. Similarly, had she possessed strong athletic abilities, she would have pursued a game such as soccer or field hockey that, in turn, would have given her the niche in which to develop those strengths.

There are three prominent models in developmental science; not, each gives differing emphasis to genetics, the environment, and the interaction of the two (Lerner, 1995). Figure 2.1 illustrates these models.

According to the organismic model (taken from the term "organism"), heredity drives the course of development throughout life. Changes over time occur because the individual is programmed to exhibit certain behaviors at certain ages in a stage- or step-wise fashion. Thus, development reflects primarily the influence of maturational forces arising within the individual due to genetic programming.

In contrast, the mechanistic model of development (taken from the word "machine") proposes that people's behavior changes gradually over time, shaped by the outside forces that cause them to adapt to their environments. Developmental scientists working from the mechanistic model propose that growth throughout life occurs by exposure to experiences that present new learning opportunities. Because this exposure is gradual, the model assumes that there are no clear-cut or identifiable stages. Instead, development is a smooth, continuous set of gradations as the individual acquires new experiences.

The interactionist model takes the view that not only do genetics and environment interact in complex ways to produce their effects on the individual but that individuals actively shape their own development. This model is most similar to niche-picking because it proposes that you can be shaped by and, in turn, shape your own environments.

With increasing evidence from studies showing that genetics and environmental influences on development in fact interact with one another, the interactionist model perhaps has the most empirical support. The nature–nurture controversy ultimately appears to boil down to "nature and nurture," and further, that each influences the other in a continuous fashion throughout life.

A related concept is also becoming increasingly accepted: that individuals can alter not only the nature of their interactions with the environment but also the rate and direction of the changes associated with the

FIGURE 2.1

Models of Development

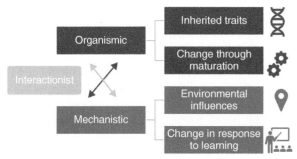

Organismic models regard development as reflecting inherited traits that change through maturation. Mechanistic models propose that environment and learning are the main forces in development. Interactionist models view development as reflecting interactive processes between the two.

aging process. According to the principle of **plasticity in development**, the course of development may be altered (is "plastic"), depending on the nature of the individual's specific interactions in the environment. The type of interactions most likely to foster plasticity involve active interventions such as mental and physical exercise. Other ways to promote plasticity include taking steps to prevent causing harm to the body and mind by avoiding, as much as possible, engaging in risky behaviors. The biopsychosocial perspective falls within the interactionist model of development because it considers multiple influences on development and views the individual as an active contributor to change throughout life.

We have already discussed the need to examine the aging process from a multidimensional point of view and along with this notion is the idea that development can proceed in multiple dimensions across life. The concept of plasticity fits very well with the notion of compensation and modifiability of the aging process through actions taken by the individual, a concept that we will continue to explore throughout this book. From our point of view, the interactionist model provides an excellent backdrop for the biopsychosocial perspective and a basis for viewing the processes of development in later life on a continuum with developmental processes in the early years.

Reciprocity in Development

You can see that an important assumption of the interactionist model is that individuals are shaped in part by their experiences. Additionally, this model implies that individuals also shape their own experiences, both through

active interpretation of the events that happen to them and through the actions they take. We would like to explore this idea now because it is so fundamental to the principles we articulate throughout the text.

The concept of **reciprocity in development** states that people both influence and are influenced by the events in their lives (Bronfenbrenner & Ceci, 1994). This model, then, explicitly proposes that not only are you shaped by your experiences but that you in turn shape many of the experiences that affect you.

Consider the reciprocal process as it has affected your own life. Earlier events in your life influenced you to choose a particular course that has brought you to where you are right now. Perhaps you and your best friend from high school decided to apply to the same college, and as a result you are at this college and not another one. Perhaps you chose this college because you knew you wanted to major in psychology and you were impressed by the reputation of the faculty in your department. Or perhaps your choice seemed to be made randomly, and you are unsure of what exactly led to your being in this place at this time even though there must have been something that led you to where you are now. In any case, you are where you are, having been influenced one way or another by your prior life events. That is one piece of the reciprocal process.

The second piece of the reciprocity puzzle relates to the effect you have on your environment; this, in turn, will affect subsequent events in your life. For example, by virtue of your existence, you affect the people who know you, your "life footprint," as it were. It is not only very possible but very likely that their lives may have already been altered by their relationship with you.

Indeed, your impact as a student at your college may have a lasting effect on both you and your institution. Everyone knows of great student athletes, scholars, or musicians who bring renown to their institutions. Even if you don't become a famous alum, your contributions to the school may alter it nevertheless. Have you ever asked a question in class that may have taken your professor by surprise? Perhaps, as a result, you may have permanently altered the way that professor approaches the problem in the future. It is not improbable to imagine that your question stimulates your professor to investigate a new research question. The investigation may ultimately produce new knowledge in the field, changing it permanently by virtue of your own, perhaps unwitting, contribution.

Though you may not become the source of ground-breaking research by one of your professors, you may nevertheless influence the people around you in much smaller ways that lead to important changes. Some of these influences may be good ones, as when you express kindness to a stranger who in turn has reason to smile, and for that instant, feels a bit better about the world. Others may prove disastrous, as when a single wrong turn while you are behind the wheel has the unfortunate effect of causing an accident that injures your passengers or those in other vehicles. In a split second, any person can influence others for better or worse, forever changing the course of someone's life.

To sum up, the reciprocal process takes as a basic assumption the idea that people are not passive recipients of environmental effects nor of their own heredity. Instead, choices and behaviors that each and every one of us makes leave a mark on the world. Subsequently, the changes in that environment may further alter people in significant ways, which leads to further impacts on society. Reciprocal views of development regard these continuing processes as both ongoing and, to some extent, unpredictable.

SOCIOCULTURAL MODELS OF DEVELOPMENT

The models of development we have just examined set the stage for looking in greater depth at particular theoretical approaches to adult development and aging. We begin by focusing on those approaches that give relatively more emphasis to the environment as an influence on development.

Ecological Perspective

The **ecological perspective**, proposed by pioneering developmental scientist Urie Bronfenbrenner (1994), identifies multiple levels of the environment as they affect the individual over time. As shown in Figure 2.2, the ecological perspective defines five levels of the environment or "systems," all of which interact in their influence on the individual. You are aware of some of these influences, but the further you go out from the center, the less likely you are to have direct experiences with those systems (Swick & Williams, 2006).

Rather than see these as static circles, imagine them as having the ability to interact fluidly and in multiple directions. The individual is shown here at the center. In keeping with the reciprocity principle, though, keep in mind that you are affected by the outer rings but can also have influence on each of them, to varying degrees. Closest to the individual is the **microsystem**, the setting in which people have their daily interactions and which therefore have the most direct impact on their lives. The **mesosystem**

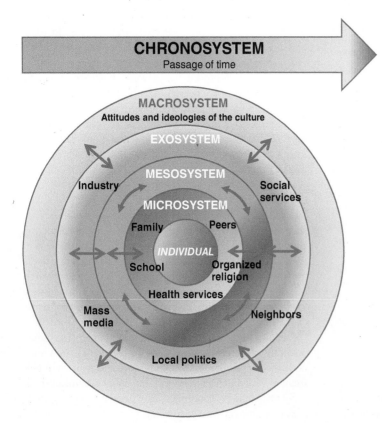

FIGURE 2.2

Bronfenbrenner's Ecological Perspective

The ecological model of development proposes that development occurs over time (the "chronosystem") within the individual, who is at the center of the systems reflecting environmental influences.

is the realm of the environment in which interactions take place among two or more microsystems. For example, you may be having difficulties at home that you carry over into your relationships with co-workers. The exosystem includes the environments that people do not closely experience on a regular basis but that impact them nevertheless. These environments include such institutions as the workplace and community centers as well as extended family, whom you may not see very often. The macrosystem includes the larger social institutions ranging from a country's economy to its laws and social norms. The macrosystem influences the individual indirectly through the exosystem.

All of these systems interact over time. The chronosystem refers to the changes that take place over time. The interacting systems within the ecological model are affected by historical changes. These can include events within the family, for example, as well as events in the larger society that indirectly affect the individual by affecting the macrosystem.

Now that you have seen the different levels of the ecological model, you can experiment in your mind with ways that they interact. Consider a situation perhaps close to your own right now. Many college students in the United States, at least as of 2020, are forced to take out student loans. They graduate with significant debt, affecting their well-being for years to come. If the government either provided more funding for higher education, or at least debt service relief, students would not be burdened with so much debt.

You could, alternatively, influence the outer ring of the ecological system by speaking out against student debt. You could organize a movement on your campus to lobby for student loan forgiveness. Perhaps you are able to bend the ear of a legislator who, in turn, proposes new laws that lead to student debt relief. Individuals who bring about broad social changes exemplify how reciprocity can work at all levels. On a smaller scale, however, as we showed before, you can also influence those around you in more direct and immediate ways.

The ecological model can also apply to such areas as health. Although you may typically think of your overall health as functioning within your inner biological level, researchers working within the Whitehall II study have demonstrated the significance of relations with others on health. In one study, participants who reported negative characteristics of close relationships had a higher likelihood of being overweight (Kuovonen et al., 2011). Social support from a relationship identified as the closest related to physical activity, even after controlling for factors such as physical functioning and self-rated health.

Other studies from Whitehall II show that, even more surprisingly, the location in which people live can shorten their life expectancy. In one study, researchers mapped life expectancy in the city of London, England, according to the underground (Tube) station nearest to their home. Even across only a 13 km distance, life expectancy varies dramatically, ranging from as high as 97 years or older near the affluent areas of central London to 75 years in the poorer sections of the city. The estimates are that a year of life expectancy is lost for each station moving eastbound to the lower-income areas of the London Tube (Cheshire, 2012).

Figure 2.3 depicts these disparities in the comparison between the wealthier Kensington and Chelsea districts and the regions of Barking and Dagenham, which represent the poorer neighborhoods in East London (Cheshire, 2012).

The Life Course Perspective

The ecological model's emphasis on social context provides an excellent background for understanding a concept central to social gerontology. According to the life course perspective, norms, roles, and attitudes about age have an impact on the shape of each person's life (Settersten, 2006). It's important to recognize, right at the start, that the term life "course" is not the same as life span. The life "course" refers, literally, to the course or progression of a person's life events. This course is theorized to be heavily shaped by society's views of what is appropriate and expected to occur in connection with particular ages.

Within the life course perspective, specific theories attempt to link society's structures to the adaptation, satisfaction, and well-being of the people who live in that society. Social gerontology focuses on age as the primary structure that influences an individual's quality of adaptation. Social class, family roles, and work are additional areas of study by gerontologists studying the life course.

For many people, the social clock can create stress as they measure their progress toward achieving goals associated with age norms.

FIGURE 2.3

Life Expectancy at Birth in London

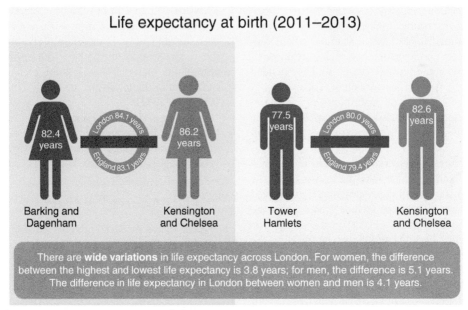

Reinforcing Bronfenbrenner's ecological model, a study of life expectancy according to wealth within London, England, shows how men and women living in the wealthy areas of Kensington and Chelsea outlive those living in the poorer districts along the London Underground of Barking/Dagenham and Tower Hamlets.

Related to the concept of the life course is the social clock, the expectations for the ages at which a society associates with major life events (Hagestad & Neugarten, 1985). These expectations set the pace for how people think they should progress through their family and work timelines. People evaluate themselves according to these expectations, deciding whether they are "on-time" or "off-time" with regard to the social clock. Those who see themselves as off-time may feel that they've failed, especially when they are criticized by others who expect people to follow the normative prescriptions for their age group. In this sense, the "nonevents" of life, those that don't happen but are believed to be normative, may have as much of an influence on an individual's life as actual events.

Increasingly, however, individuals are setting their own unique social clocks with one of the most famous being former astronaut and Ohio senator John Glenn (1921–2016). At the age of 77, Glenn joined the space shuttle *Discovery* crew on a 9-day orbital mission in 1998. His ability to meet the arduous physical requirements of the voyage was aptly captured in his statement: "Too many people, when they get old, think that they have to live by the calendar." More recently, actress Betty White (born in 1922), challenged the views that older women need to be staid and serious with her performances in comedic roles on television and in the movies.

Not only is age linked to the social clock, but also to people's social roles, the resources available to them, and the way they are treated by those with whom they interact. One of the guiding frameworks regarding age and role satisfaction is activity theory, the view that older adults are most satisfied if they are able to remain involved in their social roles (Cavan et al., 1949). If forced to give up their roles, according to this view they will lose a major source of identity as well as their social connections. According to activity theory, older adults should be given as many opportunities as possible to be engaged in their work, families, and community.

A contrasting perspective to activity theory is disengagement theory (Cumming & Henry, 1961), which proposed that the normal and natural evolution of life causes older adults to loosen purposefully their social ties. This natural detachment, according to disengagement theory, is not only inevitable but also desirable. Aging, furthermore, is accompanied by a mutual withdrawal process of the individual and society that is sought after, and favorable to, the older person. It follows from disengagement theory that retirement and isolation from family members

Budimir Jevtic/Shutterstock.com

Treating older adults as if they lack technological skills is one example of ageism, as shown by this young woman who is placing pressure on this older adult.

are sought out by older adults and result in higher levels of well-being.

When first proposed in the early 1960s, gerontologists were highly skeptical if not outraged by the propositions of disengagement theory. The idea that older adults wanted to be put "on the shelf" and could even benefit from social isolation only reinforced negative treatment of older adults by society. Rather than describing a desirable end product of a mutual withdrawal process, critics of disengagement theory regarded it as disrespectful of older adults and as a justification for what is already harsh treatment by society of its older adult members, as you will learn more about in the next section.

Yet, it makes sense that not all older adults wish to be as active and involved in their work, family, and community as they were when they were younger. **Continuity theory** (Atchley, 1989) proposes that whether disengagement or activity is beneficial to the older adult depends on the individual's personality. Some older adults prefer to withdraw from active involvement with their families and communities; others are miserable unless they are in the thick of the action. Either forced retirement or forced activity will cause poorer adjustment and self-esteem in middle-aged and older adults than finding the amount of involvement that is "just right."

Ageism as a Social Factor in the Aging Process

The social context in which aging occurs is, unfortunately, one that is not necessarily favorable to the overall well-being of older adults. Many are affected by ageism, a set of

beliefs, attitudes, social institutions, and acts that denigrate individuals or groups based on their chronological age. Similar to other "isms" such as racism and sexism, ageism occurs when an individual is assumed to possess a set of stereotyped traits.

Ageism can apply to anyone, regardless of age. Teenagers are often stereotyped as lazy, impulsive, rebellious, and self-centered. However, for all practical purposes, ageism is used to refer to stereotyped views of the *older adult* population. Disengagement theory was thought of by its critics as a justification for ageism, as a way to move older people conveniently, and with justification, to the backdrop of society. Moreover, by implying that all older adults have the same drive to withdraw, the theory perpetuates the stereotype that all older adults have similar personalities.

The primarily negative feature of ageism is that, like other stereotypes, it is founded on overgeneralizations about individuals based on a set of characteristics that have negative social meaning. Ageism applies to any view of older adults as having a set of characteristics, good or bad, that are the same for everyone. Even though ageism may have a positive spin (Kite & Wagner, 2002), its overall thrust is negative. Calling an older adult "cute" or "with it" is as much an expression of ageism as is referring to that person as "cranky" or "senile."

One effect of ageism is to cause younger people to avoid close proximity to an older person. In fact, ageism may also take the form of not being openly hostile but of making older adults "invisible": that is, not worthy of any attention at all. Ageism is often experienced in the workplace, and although prohibited by law (a topic explored in Chapter 10), older workers are penalized for making mistakes that would not incur the same consequence if made by younger workers (Rupp et al., 2006).

Ironically, aging is the one stereotype that, if you are fortunate enough to survive to old age, you will most likely experience. Unlike the other "isms," people who hold aging stereotypes will eventually become the target of their own negative beliefs as they grow old. What are your stereotypes about aging? Research on college students shows that the ones most likely to harbor ageist attitudes are those who identify most strongly with their own age group (Packer & Chasteen, 2006). In other words, the more likely you are to think of yourself as a teen or twenty-something, the more likely you'll hold biased views of older adults. As a result of taking this course, however, we hope you will gain knowledge that will cause you to challenge your own stereotypes about aging and older adults.

Ageism takes many forms, and its effects can be significant, both on older adults and on society at large. Figure 2.4 summarizes the facts that counter the most common misconceptions about aging and presents the policy implications were each fact to be heeded by world leaders and policy makers (World Health Organization, 2018). For example, the fact that availability of resources influences diversity in older adults, as shown in the London Tube study, suggests that policies should be aimed at reducing inequity, allowing more older adults to experience healthy aging.

Why does ageism exist? Of the many possible causes, perhaps at the root is that older adults remind us of the inevitability of our own mortality (Greenberg et al., 2017). According to terror management theory, people regard with panic and dread the thought that their lives will someday come to an end (Darrell & Pyszczynski, 2016). They engage in defensive mechanisms to protect themselves from the anxiety and threats to self-esteem that this awareness produces. Younger people therefore unconsciously wish to distance themselves as much as possible from older adults. Having acquired ageist attitudes when younger, older adults themselves may start to view themselves and their own opportunities for the future in a more limited manner (Barber & Tan, 2018).

An alternative perspective, advanced by sociologists, is that older adults are seen negatively because they have lost their utility to society. According to the modernization hypothesis, the increasing urbanization and industrialization of Western society is what causes older adults to be devalued (Cowgill & Holmes, 1972). They can no longer produce, so they become irrelevant and even a drain on the younger population.

Current views of modernization as an explanation of ageism criticize the theory as being overly simplistic. Instead of considering the extent to which a country has become modernized as the only factor affecting the status of older adults, it is necessary to take employment status into account. When older adults are employed at higher rates, their social status even in modernized countries is viewed more favorably (Vauclair et al., 2015).

Whatever its cause, older adults must nevertheless cope with ageist attitudes. Many too must cope with other "isms" that affect the way they are regarded in society. According to the notion of intersectionality, multiple "isms" such as ageism, sexism, and racism do not just add up but interact with one another to influence the discriminatory ways in which people reflecting more than one group are treated. The multiple jeopardy hypothesis (Ferraro & Farmer, 1996) states that older individuals who fit more than one discriminated-against category are affected by biases against each of these categorizations. Women are subject to ageism and sexism, and minority-status women are subject to racism, ageism, and sexism. Regardless of minority status, women may also experience "lookism," in which older women (but not men) are judged as less attractive on the basis of looking older. They may also be treated differently as consumers based on their age and sex. One study of retail sales employees revealed that 95% of female and 54% of male attendants gave preferential treatment to well-dressed, young female customers (Palmeira, 2014). Thus, classism (biases against people of working class backgrounds) further adds to multiple jeopardy. These systematic biases interact with age to produce greater risk for discrimination in attitudes and the provision of services to specific subgroups of older adults.

It's possible, however, that older adults are somehow protected from multiple jeopardy. The age-as-leveler view proposes that as people become older, age overrides all other "isms." Older adults, whatever their prior status in life was, all become victims of the same stereotypes. Regardless of minority status, gender, or other social characteristics, all older adults are viewed with the same harshly negative views. Consider the case of a wealthy older adult white male and an older lower-income minority woman. Though the man almost certainly would have enjoyed many advantages over the woman when he was younger, the age-as-leveler view proposes they are now seen as having an equally low social ranking because they are old. Therefore, there's only a single jeopardy of ageism facing older adults rather than multiple jeopardy resulting from a combination of "isms".

Older adults potentially facing multiple jeopardy may also be protected from its effects and even perhaps fare better than those with higher social standing. According to the inoculation hypothesis, older minorities and women have managed to become immune to the effects of ageism through years of exposure to discrimination and stereotyping. These years of maltreatment help them to develop a tolerance, so that they are better able to withstand the negative attitudes applied to older adults than are their counterparts. The upper-income white male may actually find it more difficult to accept the stereotypes of ageism than does the low-income minority woman, who is used to being treated as a less desirable member of society after years of discrimination. Even so, his privileged status may have granted him more economic resources from which to draw, which in turn could buffer him from this newly acquired lower status by virtue of his age.

These perspectives of ageism become important in examining the health and well-being of older adults. Interestingly, neither ageism nor multiple jeopardy appears to have deleterious effects on feelings of happiness and well-being, a topic we explore in Chapter 14. However, the effects of less access to health care and exposure to negative views of aging on those who are subjected to the "isms" may take their toll on physical health and are therefore a matter of vital concern.

PSYCHOLOGICAL MODELS OF DEVELOPMENT IN ADULTHOOD

In the broadest sense, psychological models attempt to explain the development of the "person" in the person–environment equation from the standpoint of how adaptive abilities unfold over the course of life. Psychologists approach aging by focusing on the changes that occur over time in the individual's self-understanding, ability to adjust to life's challenges, and perspective on the world.

Erikson's Psychosocial Theory

According to developmental psychologist Erik Erikson (1963), people pass through a series of eight stages as they progress from birth through death. A psychoanalyst by training, Erikson attempted to understand how people navigate the major psychological issues that they face when they encounter each of life's new challenges.

Erikson's psychosocial theory of development proposes that at certain points in life, biological, psychological, and social changes come together to influence the individual's personality. He defined each stage of development as a "crisis" or turning point that reflects the combination of these three sets of influences. The "crisis" is not truly a crisis in the sense of being a catastrophe or disaster. Instead, each psychosocial stage is a time during which the individual may move closer to either a positive or negative resolution of a particular psychosocial issue.

The easiest way to understand Erikson's theory is by examining an 8 × 8 matrix with the individual's approximate age along one dimension and the major psychosocial issue along the other. As shown in Figure 2.4, this creates eight points of intersection at which the individual's age meets a main issue. The typical course of development,

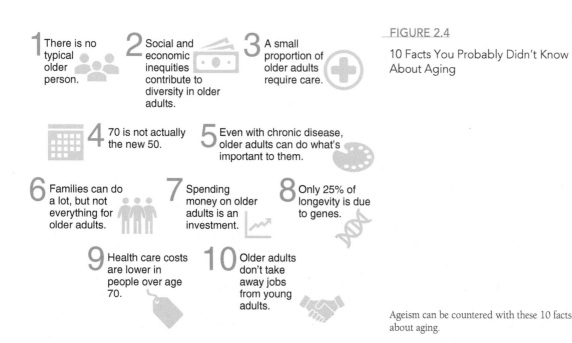

FIGURE 2.4

10 Facts You Probably Didn't Know About Aging

Ageism can be countered with these 10 facts about aging.

1 There is no typical older person.

2 Social and economic inequities contribute to diversity in older adults.

3 A small proportion of older adults require care.

4 70 is not actually the new 50.

5 Even with chronic disease, older adults can do what's important to them.

6 Families can do a lot, but not everything for older adults.

7 Spending money on older adults is an investment.

8 Only 25% of longevity is due to genes.

9 Health care costs are lower in people over age 70.

10 Older adults don't take away jobs from young adults.

according to Erikson, is to proceed along this upward diagonal. However, there can be exceptions, as we will note shortly.

Erikson proposed the epigenetic principle to apply to the course of development, meaning that each stage along the diagonal unfolds from the previous stage in a predestined order. Biological processes of development account for the individual's maturation from infancy to later adulthood, and thus, the stages Erikson proposed, are built into the hard-wiring of the human being.

Turning now to the stages themselves, which are summarized in Figure 2.5, each represents the ratio of favorable to unfavorable resolution achieved by the individual at that particular point in life. The earliest four stages are central to the adult's ability to build a solid sense of self and engagement with others. Basic trust versus basic mistrust involves the infant's establishing a sense of being able to rely on care from the environment (and caregivers). In autonomy versus shame and doubt, young children

learn ways to act independently from their parents without feeling afraid that they will venture too far off on their own. In the initiative versus guilt stage, the child becomes able to engage in creative self-expression without fear of making a mistake. The last stage associated with childhood, industry versus inferiority, involves the individual's identifying with the world of work and developing a work ethic.

The first of the eight stages directly relevant to adulthood is identity achievement versus identity diffusion (shown in Figure 2.5 as "identity vs. identity diffusion"), which is when individuals must decide "who" they are and what they wish to get out of life. This stage emerges in adolescence, yet continues to hold importance throughout adulthood, forming a cornerstone of subsequent adult psychosocial crises (Erikson et al., 1986; Whitbourne & Connolly, 1999). An individual who achieves a clear identity has a coherent sense of purpose regarding the future and a sense of continuity with the past. By contrast, identity

FIGURE 2.5

Stages in Erikson's Psychosocial Theory

Ages (approx.)	Reliance on others	Independence	Self-expression	Work ethic	Sense of self	Close relationships	Care for younger generation	Mortality and acceptance
65 and older								Ego integrity vs. Despair
30 to 65							Generativity vs. Stagnation	
21 to 30						Intimacy vs. Isolation		
12 to 21					Identity vs. Identity diffusion			
6 to 12				Industry vs. Inferiority				
3 to 6			Initiative vs. Guilt					
1-1/2 to 3		Autonomy vs. Shame and doubt						
0 to 1-1/2	Trust vs. Mistrust							

Erikson's theory proposes that there are eight psychosocial issues (shown in the diagonal) that people confront over the life span. The top row of the chart shows these eight issues and the vertical axis illustrates the typical age at which each becomes prominent.

diffusion involves a lack of direction, vagueness about life's purposes, and an unclear sense of self.

In the intimacy versus isolation stage, individuals are faced with making commitments to close relationships. Attaining intimacy involves establishing a mutually satisfying close relationship with another person to whom a lifelong commitment is made. We can think of the perfect intimate relationship as the intersection of two identities, not a total overlap because each partner preserves a sense of separateness. The state of isolation represents the other end of the spectrum, in which a person never achieves true mutuality with a life partner. Theoretically, isolation is more likely to develop in individuals who lack a strong identity because in a close relationship, each partner has to "give up" a piece of his or her identity.

The motive for caring for the next generation emerges from the resolution of the intimacy psychosocial crisis. During the stage of generativity versus stagnation, middle-aged adults focus on the psychosocial issues of procreation, productivity, and creativity. The most common pathway to generativity is through parenthood, an endeavor that involves direct care of the next generation. However, individuals who do not have children can nevertheless develop generativity through such activities as teaching, mentoring, or supervising younger people. A career that involves producing something of value that future generations can enjoy is another form of generativity. Conversely, not all parents demonstrate a strong sense of generativity with regard to their own children. They may focus instead on other young people or prefer to invest their emotional resources on their friends or romantic partners.

The main feature of generativity is that the individual feels and shows concern over what happens to the younger generation, along with a desire to make the world a better place for them. Stagnation, by contrast, occurs when the individual turns concern and energy inward or solely to others of one's own age group rather than to the next generation. A person who is high on the quality of stagnation lacks interest or may even go so far as to reject the younger generation. The next time you hear someone complaining about "Millennials" being unwilling to work hard and completely obsessed with themselves, you might consider this to be an example of that individual's own sense of stagnation.

Toward the end of adulthood, individuals face psychosocial issues related to aging and facing their mortality, the key issues in the stage of ego integrity versus despair. Older individuals who establish a strong sense of ego integrity can look back at their experiences with acceptance. Ego integrity also involves an ability to look at and accept the positive and negative attributes of one's life and self, even if it may be painful for people to acknowledge their past mistakes or personal flaws. This sense of acceptance of the past and present self allows the

Eleanor Addison/Pixabay

Mentoring is one example of generativity in which a senior business executive provides a model for her younger employees.

individual also to view mortality with the acceptance that life inevitably must end.

It may be difficult for a young person to imagine how a person who is happy with life could also be happy with, or at least not devastated by, the thought of death. According to Erikson, acceptance of the past and present helps people attain acceptance about being at the end of their lives. In contrast, despair is the outcome of the individual's realization that death is coming too soon to help him or her achieve major life goals or rectify mistakes. The individual in a state of despair feels discontent with life and is melancholic, perhaps to the point of despondency, at the thought of death.

Erikson presented an organized, cohesive view of the life span that is both elegant and deceptively simple. At first glance, it might appear that he viewed development as proceeding in a series of steps moving steadily from childhood to old age. The diagonal in the matrix of ages and psychosocial issues shows how each age period is associated with a crisis. However, the intersection of ages and psychosocial issues along the diagonal is not the only possibility for development. People may experience a psychosocial issue at an age other than the one shown where it crosses the diagonal. Thus, the issues characterizing each stage (such as trust versus mistrust for infancy) may coexist as relevant concerns throughout adulthood. Any stage may reach ascendancy in response to events that stimulate its reappearance.

Let's look at an example to show how these "off-diagonal" situations might occur. An 80-year-old woman walking on a city sidewalk is suddenly attacked, robbed of her purse, and left alive but physically injured and emotionally shaken. This incident may traumatize her for some time and in the process, she becomes fearful of leaving her home. In Eriksonian terms, she is reliving the issues of "trust" experienced in infancy and must regain the feeling of safety in her environment. The woman may also be left feeling vulnerable that with her increasing years, she appears to be an easy target for a person with criminal intent.

Another implication of the epigenetic matrix is that a crisis may be experienced before its "time." A 35-year-old woman diagnosed with breast cancer may be faced with issues relevant to mortality, precipitating her to contemplate the psychosocial issues that normally confront much older people. The crisis stages can be considered "critical periods" during which certain issues are most likely to be prominent, but they are not meant to be discrete steps that proceed from youth to old age.

Erikson's views about development were a radical departure from the personality theories prevalent in the mid-1900s, when childhood was given sole emphasis as a time of important change. By reenvisioning the life span, Erikson provided a new but enduring perspective that recognized development as a lifelong set of processes that help to mold and shape and reshape the individual.

Piaget's Cognitive-Developmental Theory

Just as Erikson crafted a new model of personality development throughout the life span, a Swiss psychologist by the name of Jean Piaget brought an entirely new perspective to bear on the process of cognitive development. Rather than being content simply with describing children's development, as his predecessors had done, Piaget tried to explain the processes underlying their growth of cognitive abilities. Stimulated in part by watching his own young children explore their environment while at play, Piaget hypothesized the existence of a set of underlying processes that allowed them eventually to achieve understanding and mastery of the physical world.

Piaget believed that development involves continuing growth of the individual's knowledge about the world through a set of opposing, complementary processes. These processes target what Piaget called schemas, the

mental structures we use to understand the world. Children's schemas change and mature as they explore their environment—a process that, ideally, helps them to bring their schemas increasingly in tune with reality.

Through the process that Piaget called assimilation, people use their existing schemas as a way to understand the world around them. In this context, the term assimilation does not have its usual meaning, as when you say that a person has become assimilated to a new culture. Rather, in Piaget's model, assimilation has the opposite meaning: it refers to the situation in which individuals change their interpretation of reality to fit the schemas they already hold. Instead of changing themselves to fit the culture, they change their perception of the culture to fit their own way of understanding it.

When you change your schemas in response to new information about the world you are, in Piaget's terms, using the process of accommodation. This process is actually more like the way we commonly speak about cultural "assimilation." In Piaget's terms, when you change yourself in order to fit the larger culture that you're now a part of, you are engaging in accommodation: You are the one who is changing. Throughout development, people's schemas change and mature as a result of interactions with other people, objects in the environment, and, of course, education. Ideally, as schemas mature, they become closer and closer, where possible, to "reality," but even these views may shift as new "realities" emerge.

As an example of the continuous changes that people make in their schemas, consider what happens when you change your mind about your musical preferences. Perhaps you have always found classical music to be intensely boring. A friend invites you to a concert in the park, and, much to your surprise, you actually enjoyed the violinist's performance of a Mozart concerto. Your schema about music now becomes revised and you find yourself downloading other selections to add to your workout playlist. This process, summarized in Figure 2.6, shows how people change their ideas, knowledge, and preferences over time.

It's unfortunate that Piaget's terms mean the opposite of their use in common speech, especially the concept of

FIGURE 2.6

Piaget's Theory

Piaget's theory proposes that people change their schemas in response to new experiences. In this figure, the original schema of not liking classical music is changed when the individual enjoys a classical music concert, leading to a revised schema as shown in a new workout playlist.

assimilation. However, it might be easier to understand assimilation and accommodation in the Piagetian sense if you remember that Piaget was describing the process of schema development. You impose your schemas onto the world, making the world fit you, in assimilation. You change your schemas about the world, changing in response to knowledge from experiences, in accommodation. (If all else fails, think of the "s" in assimilation standing for "same," and the "c" in accommodation for "change.")

The processes of assimilation and accommodation occur continuously throughout development. Children are constantly exploring their worlds, changing their schemas as they accommodate them to fit the reality of their experiences. At certain points in childhood, according to Piaget, there are major shifts in children's understanding of their experiences. These correspond to the stages associated with early infancy (sensorimotor stage), preschool (preoperational period), middle childhood (concrete operations stage), and adolescence through adulthood (formal operations stage). Each stage represents a time of equilibrium, when assimilation and accommodation are perfectly balanced. The equilibrium achieved in formal operations is the most stable because it is when the individual is able to use the highest level of thought to understand and learn from experience. However, throughout life, people rely on all forms of thought, ranging from sensorimotor (nonverbal) to concrete (the here and now).

Identity Process Theory

According to Erikson's theory, identity is a central issue in adulthood. How identity changes is a question that we will explore throughout this book. We will rely heavily on the framework of identity process theory (Whitbourne et al., 2002), which proposes that identity continues to change in adulthood in a dynamic manner.

In identity process theory, identity is defined as a set of schemas that the person holds about the self. Your identity is your own answer to the question "Who am I?" For most people, this includes their views about their physical self, their cognitive abilities, their personality characteristics, and their social roles. Identity also includes the individual's sense of connection to his or her cultural heritage, a process of particular importance to adolescents and emerging adults from immigrant and minority groups (Rodriguez et al., 2010; Schwartz et al., 2012).

Identity Assimilation, Identity Accommodation, and Identity Balance.   Refer to Figure 2.7, which depicts two pathways through which individuals change their self-schemas, or identities. Age-related changes occur continuously throughout adulthood, but trigger identity processes only when they are regarded as important by the individual. Such age-related changes can be interpreted through identity assimilation, or a tendency to interpret new experiences in terms of existing identity. This process will minimize the impact of the age-related change on the individual's sense of self, putting off any identity change.

Alternatively, the age-related change may trigger identity accommodation in which people make changes in their identities in response to experiences that challenge their current view of themselves. Initially, this response to change may potentially create the feeling of being "over the hill," as shown in Path 2.

Eventually, the individual either finds denial no longer possible (Path 1) or is able to gradually reestablish a more stable sense of self (Path 2) and eventually achieves identity balance, the dynamic equilibrium that occurs when people tend to view themselves consistently but can make changes when called for by their experiences.

To illustrate the process of identity change proposed by identity process theory, consider an example from your own life as a student. You may have a positive identity of yourself as a student, seeing yourself as achieving your educational goals. This view of yourself colors your academic experiences. If you are, in fact, a good student, you'll have plenty of instances that bolster this view. You receive good grades, your professors seem to like you, and other people come to you for help. Occasionally, however, you may have experiences that contradict this self-image. You do poorly on an exam, an assignment is returned with many critical comments, or you're stumped in class when you're called upon to answer a question. How do you reconcile these experiences with your positive identity as a student? If you're using identity assimilation, you won't change your identity at all. Instead, you'll still see yourself as a good student, but one who ran into some rough material, an unfair test, or an inordinately harsh professor.

When people use identity assimilation, they tend to resist changing their identities in the face of criticism or disconfirming experiences. In fact, most people prefer to see themselves in the positive light of being physically and mentally competent, well liked, honest, and concerned about the welfare of others. The advantage of identity assimilation is that it allows people to feel reasonably happy and effective, despite being less than perfect. The downside of identity assimilation is that it can lead you to distort your interpretation of experiences when change would truly be warranted. Returning to our example of seeing yourself as a good student, by blaming the material or the professor for your bad grade, you may not realize how your own academic weaknesses contributed to the trouble you're in now.

We can see, then, that although identity assimilation has the advantage of allowing you to preserve a positive view of who you are, there may be negative consequences of refusing to incorporate these experiences into your identity. If you continue to blame the professor or the test for your poor grades, you will never find that you need to change. Eventually, these limitations need to be confronted. Whether this signifies that you are in the wrong major, are not studying hard enough, or may not be as smart as you once thought, learning to accept your imperfections is vital to your own growth.

Thus, ideally, people eventually use identity accommodation, in which they make changes in their identities in response to experiences that challenge their current view of themselves. Identity change may be difficult, particularly at first, because you must come to grips with your weaknesses. However, the result will ultimately produce a self-image that is more in sync with reality.

It's possible, also, for an individual to use identity assimilation to bolster a negative rather than a positive view of the self. As we will learn later in the book, people who suffer from chronic depression often take an unduly pessimistic view of their identities, focusing on their weaknesses to the exclusion of seeing their strengths. In that case, identity accommodation can help them develop a more realistically positive set of schemas about their personal characteristics and strengths.

Identity process theory proposes that both identity assimilation and identity accommodation are most beneficial when they operate in tandem. If you had that tendency to avoid letting your academic disappointments permeate your identity through identity assimilation, it would benefit you to use identity accommodation to acknowledge your areas of weakness, such as not being well-suited to your college major, perhaps. Although you wouldn't want to go overboard and conclude that you should give up school altogether, by using some identity accommodation, you could first admit to your problems and then set up a plan to improve your study habits.

As with identity assimilation, however, relying too heavily on identity accommodation can have destructive consequences. Individuals who define themselves entirely on the basis of their experiences, such as being viewed negatively by others, may be devastated by an event when they feel rejected. Imagine if every criticism ever leveled at you throughout your life caused you to question your personal qualities and think that you are a deeply flawed person. You would become extremely insecure, and your identity would fail to include the central compass that would ultimately allow you to have confidence in your abilities. In this case, you would benefit by ignoring those experiences that unrealistically caused you to question yourself.

For some individuals, age-related changes in appearance can serve to stimulate identity accommodation.

Piaget proposed that the natural tendency is to use assimilation when confronted with a new situation. People use what has worked in the past to help understand what is happening in the present. However, when the situation warrants changes, you should be able to make those adjustments. Though it would hardly be ideal to change your self-view completely when someone criticizes you, if the criticism is consistent enough and comes from enough different quarters, you may be well advised to look honestly at yourself and see whether you should change something.

When identity balance is operating successfully, the individual feels that he or she has a strong sense of self-efficacy, a term used in the social psychological literature to refer to a person's feelings of competence at a particular task (Bandura, 1977). As we will see throughout the book, older adults high in particular types of self-efficacy recognize that they have experienced age-related changes but nevertheless feel in control of their ability to succeed.

The Multiple Threshold Model. Figure 2.7 depicts the process of identity change in response to age-related changes in functioning. These changes can be thought of as occurring through a sequence of phases over time (Whitbourne & Collins, 1998). The multiple threshold model of change in adulthood proposes that individuals realize that they are getting older through a stepwise process as aging-related changes occur. Each age-related change (such as wrinkling of the skin or increased reaction time) brings with it the potential for another threshold to be crossed. People are likely to monitor the areas of the greatest significance to their identities with great care or

FIGURE 2.7

Identity Process Theory

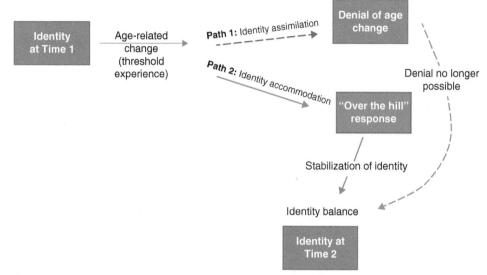

Identity process theory proposes that age-related changes become threshold experiences. Paths 1 and 2 illustrate alternate pathways in responding to these experiences in terms of identity.

vigilance, while paying less attention to the thresholds that don't mean as much to them. You may be preoccupied with the fact that your hair is thinning or turning gray but less focused on the changes in your muscles. Someone else may feel oppositely, and disregard gray hair but fixate on the loss of muscle strength.

Whatever the area of greatest relevance, at the point of crossing a threshold, people are prompted to recognize the reality of the aging process in that particular area of functioning. It is during the process of moving from identity assimilation to identity accommodation through the occurrence of these thresholds that a new state of balance is reached. Ultimately, people will only be able to adapt to age-related changes once they have examined the meaning of the change and incorporated it into their existing view of the self.

In Western society, because of ageism, this youthful image is one that many people would like to preserve and therefore they resist making changes to this image. You perhaps feel this way now. It's true that you're no longer an adolescent, but you almost certainly still regard yourself as being young. You may feel this way for years, if not decades, identifying yourself with the younger generation.

It won't be too long, however, until you encounter experiences that lead you to your first "threshold." Perhaps you feel a little stiff when you get up from a chair or find out that your blood pressure is higher than it used to be.

Many people say that the first time they felt old was when someone called them "sir" or "ma'am." At that point, you may start to challenge the view you had of yourself as a young person. Your options now are to disregard the whole experience and not change your identity (identity assimilation). Or you might become completely thrown by the experience and conclude that you are heading more swiftly than you hoped to middle age (identity accommodation). It's also possible that you might note the experience, admit that you're not a teenager any more, and feel perfectly fine with the fact that people are treating you with a bit more dignity (identity balance).

Identity assimilation can be healthy or unhealthy. The unhealthy type of identity assimilation occurs when people ignore warning signs that the changes their body is going through require attention. If your blood pressure really is too high, you should explore ways to lower it, no matter what your age. It would not be healthy to deny the condition. On the other hand, a healthy denial occurs when people avoid becoming overly preoccupied with age-related changes that are truly inconsequential to their overall health and well-being, especially if there is nothing they can do to ameliorate the process. Healthy deniers continue or begin engaging in preventive behaviors without overthinking their actions and reflecting at length about their own mortality (Path 1 in Figure 2.7). However, at some point, everyone needs to confront these changes, to some extent. You can't completely ignore the fact that you are getting older no matter what your age. Ultimately, this need to deal with the reality of aging leads the individual to incorporate these changes into identity.

Let's look next at identity accommodation in which people change their identities in response to experiences. Theoretically, identity accommodation helps to keep identity assimilation in check. However, people who conclude that one small age change means they are "over-the-hill" may be just as likely to avoid taking preventative actions as those who engage in unhealthy denial. They incorrectly conclude that there's nothing they can do to slow down the aging process, so why try? Similarly, people who are told they must watch their blood pressure may go overboard and do nothing but worry about what this means for their health. They "become" their illness, which they allow to take over their identity.

Eventually, if the pendulum swings from identity accommodation back to identity assimilation, the individual can reestablish a middle ground between becoming overly preoccupied with change versus pretending that changes are not occurring (Path 2 in Figure 2.7). People who use identity balance accept that they are aging without adopting a defeatist attitude. They take steps to ensure that they will remain healthy but do not become demoralized about conditions or limitations they may already have developed. Additionally, they are not deluded into thinking that they will be young forever.

The advantages of identity balance (and to an extent healthy denial) are that the older adult adopts an active "use-it-or-lose-it" approach to the aging process. By remaining active, people can delay or prevent many if not most age-related negative changes. On the other hand, there are many "bad habits," or ways in which a person's behavior can accelerate the aging process. Some of the most common negative behaviors, include overexposure to the sun and smoking. Ideally, people adapt to the aging process by taking advantage of the use-it-or-lose-it approach and avoiding the bad habits. Less of a strain will be placed on both identity assimilation and accommodation if people can take advantage of the many strategies receiving increasing publicity designed to promote good health for as long as possible.

The Selective Compensation with Optimization Model

We see, then, that people adapt mentally to the age-related changes they experience by shifting their priorities. Although it does not refer specifically to identity, a related model focuses on how people balance gains and losses as they age. According to the selective optimization with compensation model (SOC), adults attempt to

FIGURE 2.8

Selective Optimization with Compensation Model

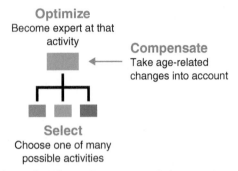

According to the Selective Optimization with Compensation model, aging involves selecting which activities are of greatest importance, compensating for age-related changes, and then optimizing performance of that activity.

preserve and maximize the abilities that are of central importance and put less effort into maintaining those that are not (Baltes & Baltes, 1990) (see Figure 2.8). Older people make conscious decisions regarding how to spend their time and effort in the face of losses in physical and cognitive resources.

The SOC model implies that at some point in adulthood, people deliberately begin to reduce efforts in one area in order to focus more on achieving success in another. It is likely that the areas people choose to focus on are those that are of greater importance and for which the chances of success are higher. However, they may also switch within the same general area to make it possible to retain as much of the original activity as possible. Older adults with mobility issues substitute walking for running, for example. Similar processes may operate in the area of intellectual functioning. The older individual may exert more effort toward solving word games and puzzles and spend less time on pastimes that involve spatial and speed skills, such as fast-moving computer games. If reading becomes too much of a chore due to fading eyesight, the individual may compensate by switching to audio books.

Concepts from the multiple threshold model would seem to fit well with the SOC model. People may make choices to optimize those areas of functioning that are central to their identities. Those who value the mind will compensate for whatever changes in their ability to solve mental puzzles by finding other intellectually demanding activities that they can still perform. People who enjoyed crafts that required very fine motor movements that they can no longer perform may switch to projects that they complete on a somewhat larger scale and still feel satisfied. It may be difficult at first, but people who are able to make accommodations to age-related changes without becoming overwhelmed or preoccupied will be able to reestablish their sense of purpose and well-being.

Although the SOC model may seem to present a negative view of aging, in that it emphasizes the way that people adapt to loss, it can also be seen as offering a realistic perspective on the fact that there are losses in adulthood that can often outweigh the gains (Heckhausen, 1997). However, people adapt to these changes by readjusting their goals and, in the process, can maintain their sense of well-being (Frazier et al., 2012).

BIOLOGICAL APPROACHES TO AGING IN ADULTHOOD

Biological approaches to aging tackle the fundamental question of why the body changes over the course of life. As stated by Stanford University's Walter Bortz (2010, p. 383): "What are the generic properties of life, which establish its essence? What is aging? Whatever the answer, it must transcend biology as everything in the universe ages, galaxies, canyons, Chevrolets, redwoods, and turtles." For reasons we don't now understand, the body's biological clock continues to record the years with the passage of time. Ultimately, the aging of the body sets the limit on life's length, but most gerontologists agree that people can compensate through behavioral measures for many of the changes associated with the aging process to alter the timing of these events.

Acknowledging the role of biology begs the question: Why do living organisms grow old and die? If you are a fan of science fiction, you have surely read stories of a world in which aging does not occur or occurs so slowly that people live for hundreds of years. While these fictional accounts may be engrossing and even tempting to imagine, there are some obvious problems associated with such a world. Outcomes such as overpopulation, a lack of adequate resources, and intergenerational strife are just some of the possibilities. Presumably, to keep the population in check, birthrates would be reduced to a virtual standstill.

Some scientists believe that organisms are programmed to survive until they reach sexual maturity. Having guaranteed the survival of their species, living creatures are programmed to deteriorate or diminish once the genes programmed to keep them alive past that point are no longer of use to the species. Biologically speaking, according to this view, reproduction is the primary purpose of life, and once this criterion has been met, there are no specific guidelines to determine what happens next. Although it's not possible to know "why" aging occurs, the fact is that it does. Researchers who study aging continue to explore whether aging is in fact the result of a correctable defect in living organisms. We may not be able to guarantee that the aging process can be ground to a halt, even with the most advanced scientific methods; however, researchers who study aging believe that their efforts will result in concrete improvements to people's lives.

Genes and DNA

To understand the biological approaches to aging, we need to explain several basic concepts about genetics. Our focus will be on those aspects of genetics most relevant to theories of aging to give you some of the background needed to understand this material.

To begin, inherited characteristics are found in the genome, the complete set of instructions for "building" all the cells that make up an organism. The human genome is found in each nucleus of a person's many trillions of cells. The genome is contained in deoxyribonucleic acid (DNA), a molecule capable of replicating itself that encodes information needed to produce proteins. There are many kinds of proteins, each with different functions. Some proteins provide structure to the cells of the body, whereas other proteins called enzymes assist biochemical reactions that take place within the cells. Antibodies are proteins that function in the immune system to identify foreign invaders that need to be removed from the body.

A gene is a functional unit of a DNA molecule carrying a particular set of instructions for producing one of those proteins. Some of the proteins that the genes encode provide basic housekeeping duties in the cell. These genes constantly stay active in many types of cells; more typically, a cell activates just the genes needed at the moment to carry out a task and suppresses the rest. Through this process of selective activation of genes, a cell becomes a skin cell, for example, rather than a bone cell.

Human genes vary greatly in length, but only about 10% of the genome actually contains sequences of genes used to code proteins. The rest of the genome contains sequences of bases that have no apparent function.

The genome is organized into chromosomes, which are distinct, physically separate units of coiled threads of DNA and associated protein molecules. In humans, there are two sets of 23 chromosomes, one set contributed by each parent. Each set has 23 single chromosomes: 22 are called "autosomes" and contain non-sex-linked information, and the 23rd is the X or Y sex chromosome. The presence of the Y chromosome determines maleness, so that a normal female has a pair of X chromosomes and a male has one X and one Y in the 23rd chromosome pair. There is no rhyme or reason to the distribution of genes on chromosomes. A gene that produces a protein that influences eye color may be next to a gene that is involved in cellular energy production.

FIGURE 2.9

DNA Structure

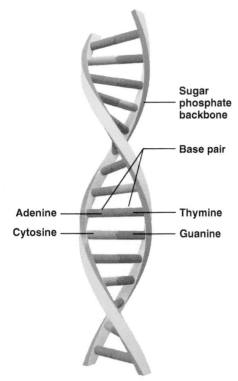

The structure of DNA is shown here, illustrating the four nucleotides as arranged in the double helix along a backbone of sugar phosphate.

All the genes in DNA are formed by the pattern of four nucleotides: adenine (A), guanine (G), thymine (T), and cytosine (C) as shown in Figure 2.9. One DNA segment, for example, might be composed of a sequence such as AATCGCGTAC. A single-nucleotide polymorphism (SNP) is a small genetic variation that can occur in a person's DNA sequence in which one nucleotide is substituted for another (see Figure 2.10). To qualify as a SNP, the variation must occur in at least 1% of the population.

When DNA reproduces itself, the process often occurs without a problem, and the DNA copy is the same as the original molecule. However, for various reasons, genes may undergo the alterations known as mutations. Genetic mutations are either inherited from a parent or acquired over the course of one's life. Inherited mutations originate from the DNA of the cells involved in reproduction (sperm and egg). When a gene contains a mutation, the protein encoded by that gene will most likely be abnormal. Sometimes, the protein can function despite the damage, but in other cases, it becomes completely disabled. If a protein vital to survival becomes severely damaged, the results of the mutation can be serious.

When reproductive cells containing mutations are combined in one's offspring, the mutation is in all the bodily cells of that offspring. Inherited mutations are responsible for diseases such as cystic fibrosis and sickle cell anemia. They also may predispose an individual to developing cancer, major psychiatric illnesses, and other complex diseases.

Acquired mutations are changes in DNA that develop throughout a person's lifetime. Remarkably, cells possess the ability to repair many of these mutations. If these repair mechanisms fail, however, the mutation can be passed along to future copies of the altered cell. Mutations can also occur in the mitochondrial DNA, which is the DNA found in the tiny structures within the cell called mitochondria. These structures are crucial to the functioning of the cell because they are involved in producing cellular energy. Unlike DNA found elsewhere in the cell, mitochondrial DNA is inherited solely from the mother.

Geneticists have provided many fascinating and important perspectives on the aging process. The completion of the Human Genome Project in 2003 and progress by the International HapMap project (Frazer et al., 2007; Green et al., 2015) paved the way for researchers to identify successful analytic techniques to map complete sets of DNA. A genome-wide association study is a method used in behavior genetics in which researchers search for genetic variations related to complex diseases by scanning the entire genome. Another method in behavior genetics is a genome-wide linkage study, in which researchers study the families of people with specific psychological traits or disorders. These methods offer a promising avenue for research on the genetics of aging. Hundreds of studies have successfully identified novel genes involved in aging-related diseases such as heart failure (Velagaleti & O'Donnell, 2010), Alzheimer's disease (Harold et al., 2009), and osteoarthritis (Richards et al., 2009). Genetic sequencing studies are also becoming the basis for understanding the mechanisms of action of therapeutic drugs (Choi et al., 2018).

As genomic research continues to make advances in understanding the complexity of disease and genes, more and more individuals will be offered the opportunity to have their genome scanned to determine their risk for developing a disease. The availability of online genetic testing through commercial websites also makes it possible for anyone to explore their own genetic risks, as well as family ancestry. These approaches will bring genomics increasingly into people's everyday lives and could ultimately help

FIGURE 2.10

Example of a SNP

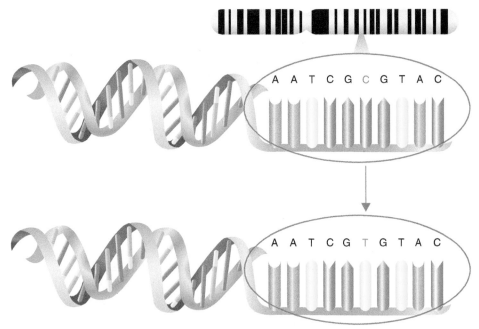

As shown in this figure, which represents a genetic sequence, a single nucleotide differentiates one genetic variation from another (i.e., single-nucleotide polymorphism).

individuals make lifestyle and medical decisions in a more informed manner than has ever been possible.

Programmed Aging Theories

Genetics are involved in all biological theories of aging, but to differing degrees (Hayflick, 1994). Programmed aging theories propose that aging and death are built into the hard-wiring of all organisms and therefore are part of the genetic code. Every living organism has, then, "aging genes" that count off the years past maturity, just as "development genes" lead to the point of maturity in youth.

One argument long used to support programmed aging theories is based on the fact that species have different life spans (see Figure 2.11). For example, butterflies have life spans of 12 weeks, and giant tortoises have life spans of 180 years. Humans have the longest life span of any mammals at 120 years. The fact that life spans vary so systematically across species supports the role of genetics in the aging process, according to many biologists.

Variations among species in life spans are clearly illustrated when age is plotted against death rates. The Gompertz function plots the relationship between age and death rates for a given species. The originator of this

idea, Benjamin Gompertz, was an 18th-century British mathematician who worked as an actuary, a profession where the financial impact of risk is calculated. In 1825, he applied calculus to mortality data and showed that the mortality rate increases in a geometric progression with age (Gompertz, 1825). In other words, the longer an individual lives, the higher the chances that the individual will die, a fact that Gompertz represented mathematically. Gompertz's work is still considered relevant today, 350 years after his groundbreaking paper (Kirkwood, 2015).

Within humans, researchers estimate that longevity is at least 25% inherited. However, the estimate of longevity's genetic influence increases for life spans that go beyond the age of 60 years. Perhaps as much as 33% of the life span in women and 48% of that in men living to 100 can be attributed to genetics (Sabastiani & Perls, 2012).

Findings in support of genetic theories of aging are particularly intriguing in view of the considerable progress being made in the field of genetics in general. The ability to identify and then control the "aging" gene or genes would go a long way toward changing the very nature of aging. The idea that there is one single gene or small combination of multiple genes that control the aging process from birth to death is very appealing, but the approach has its limits.

FIGURE 2.11

Life Spans of Different Species

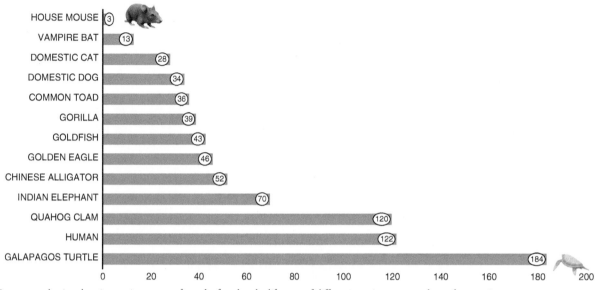

Programmed aging theories receive support from the fact that the life span of different species appear to be set by genetics.

We cannot say for sure that evolution has selected for the aging process so that old generations die in order to make room for new ones. Historically, few species survive long enough to provide data relevant to the evolutionary selection process.

A more defensible alterative to genetic theory is that evolution has selected for species that are vigorous through the period of optimal sexual reproduction and then less important once that period has passed. According to the "good genes gone bad" theory (Hayflick, 1994), also known as the quasi-programmed aging theory (Blagosklonny, 2013), aging genes take over in the postreproductive years and lead to the ultimate destruction of the organism. Researchers continue to investigate the notion that the very genes that have a positive effect on development during early life lower the susceptibility to a variety of diseases in later life (Caruso et al., 2000). For example, senescent cells may act as a protective device against the continued growth of cancerous cells. The senescent cells, in turn, are eliminated by the immune system. However, the immune system does not destroy all of the senescent cells, and so they continue to remain present in the body's tissues (Hornsby, 2009).

The first important set of theories that attempt to explain aging through genetics are based on the principle of replicative senescence, or the loss of the ability of cells to reproduce. Scientists have long known that there are a finite number of times (about 50) that normal human cells can proliferate in culture before they become terminally incapable of further division (Hayflick, 1994). Until relatively recently, scientists did not know why cells had a limited number of divisions. It was only when the technology needed to look closely at the chromosome developed that researchers uncovered some of the mystery behind this process.

As we saw in Figure 2.9, the chromosome is made up largely of DNA. However, at either end of the chromosomes are telomeres, repetitive DNA sequences at the ends of chromosomes (see Figure 2.12). The primary function of the telomeres is to protect the chromosomes from the damage to them that accumulates over repeated cell replications. With each cell division, the telomeres shorten, eventually leading to damage of the genome. Once telomeres shorten to the point of no longer being able to protect the chromosome, adjacent chromosomes fuse, the cell cycle is halted, and ultimately the cell dies. Evidence linking telomere length to mortality in humans suggests that the telomeres may ultimately hold the key to understanding the aging process (Shay, 2018).

However, biology does not completely explain the loss of telomeres over the course of life. Supporting the idea of biopsychosocial interactions in development, researchers have linked telomere length to social factors. Initial findings indicated that socioeconomic status and lifestyle (i.e., exercise) seemed to be related to telomere length in women (Cherkas et al., 2006, 2008). However, a large-scale

FIGURE 2.12

Telomere Theory of Aging

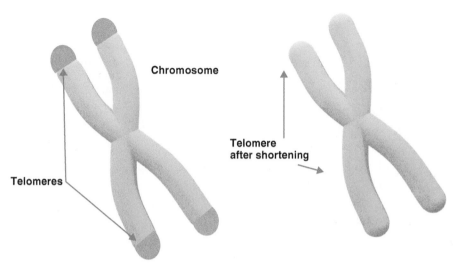

The telomere theory of aging proposes that with each cellular replication telomeres shorten until they are no longer present to protect the ends of chromosomes.

analysis of 29 different study populations including men and women pointed to education, but not current social status, as having a weak link to biological aging as measured by telomere length (Robertson et al., 2013).

On the other hand, at least for older men, participation in high levels of exercise over a prolonged period could serve to have a protective role in preserving telomere length. Indeed, the longer and higher intensity of the activity, the more beneficial the effects on telomere length (Arsenis et al., 2017).

Although many cells in the body are thought to be affected by the shortening of the telomeres, not all experience this effect of the aging process. For example, when tumor cells are added to normal cells, they replicate indefinitely. Because of the danger posed by these multiplying tumor cells, senescence may be thought of as a form of protection against cancer. The key to extending the life span based on the telomere theory would be for scientists to find a way to keep cells replicating longer without increasing the risk of cancer cell proliferation (Ohtani et al., 2009).

Another compelling candidate for a genetic cause of aging involves the **FOXO genes**, a group of genes that influence crucial cellular processes regulating stress resistance, metabolism, the cell cycle, and the death of cells. FOXO is actually shorthand for "forkhead box O," with the forkhead referring to its winged helix (butterfly-like) structure (Stefanetti et al., 2018). The FOXO3 variant includes approximately 40 SNPs associated with longevity in humans and is also associated with healthier skeletal

muscle and the functioning of cells that maintain healthy functioning in the brain. The exact mechanisms through which FOXO3 operates remain yet to be determined, but research on how it exerts its longevity effects will undoubtedly produce important results in the coming years (Stefanetti et al., 2018).

Random Error Theories

Random error theories are based on the assumption that aging reflects unplanned changes in an organism over time. The **wear and tear theory** of aging is one that many people implicitly refer to when they say they feel that they are "falling apart" as they get older. According to this view, the body, like a car, acquires more and more damage as it is exposed to daily wear and tear from weather, use, accidents, and mechanical insults. Programmed aging theories, in contrast, would suggest that the car was not "built to last" but rather meant to deteriorate over time in a systematic fashion.

Cross-linking theory proposes that aging causes deleterious changes in cells of the body that make up much of the body's connective tissue, including the skin, tendons, muscle, and cartilage. The cross links develop in collagen, the fibrous protein that makes up about one-quarter of all bodily proteins (see Figure 2.13). Collagen provides elasticity and strength to tissues that are involved in mechanical function, including skin, cartilage, tendons, and bones. The collagen molecule is composed of three chains of amino

FIGURE 2.13

Aging of the Collagen Molecule

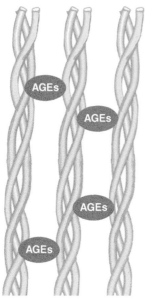

According to the cross-linking theory of aging, advanced glycation end products ("AGEs") form between collagen molecules, causing them to lose elasticity.

acids wound together in a tight helix. Strands of collagen molecules are attached through horizontal strands of proteins, similar to rungs on a ladder.

Increasingly with age, the rungs of one ladder start to connect to the rungs of another ladder, causing the molecules to become increasingly rigid and shrink in size. The process of cross linking occurs because exposure to certain types of sugars leads to a process known as glycation, which in turn leads to the formation of what are called advanced glycation end products (appropriately

named "AGE"). The AGEs induce cross-linking of collagen, which in turn can contribute to increased stiffness in skeletal muscle and cartilage (Semba et al., 2010) as well as tendons (Snedeker & Gauteri, 2014).

An issue yet to be determined is whether the cross-linking theory adequately explains the cause of aging or whether it describes a process that occurs due to the passage of time and cumulative damage caused by a lifetime of exposure to sugar in the diet. Another theory focuses on free radicals, unstable oxygen molecules produced when cells create energy (see Figure 2.14). The primary goal of a free radical is to seek out and bind to other molecules. When this occurs, the molecule attacked by the free radical loses functioning. According to free radical theory (Sohal & Orr, 2012), the cause of aging is the increased activity of these unstable oxygen molecules that bond to other molecules and compromise the cell's functioning.

Although oxidation caused by free radicals is in fact a process associated with increasing age, researchers have questioned the utility of free radical theory to explain the aging process in general (Gladyshev, 2014). Antioxidants, chemicals that prevent the formation of free radicals, are advertised widely as an antidote to aging. The active ingredient in antioxidants is the enzyme superoxide dismutase (SOD). No doubt you have seen advertisements that promote the intake of foods high in vitamins E and C, including grapes, blueberries, strawberries, and walnuts. There is scientific evidence supporting the role of antioxidants in cognitive aging, especially when combined with physical activity (Freitas et al., 2017).

Although free radical theory itself does not seem to be able to explain the aging process, there are variants of the theory that focus on antioxidants as contributors to rate of aging. One of these is caloric restriction, the view that the key to prolonging life is to restrict the total number of calories that individuals consume (Walford et al., 2002). Caloric restriction is thought to have a

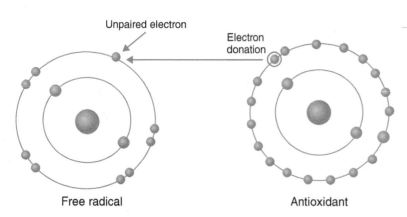

FIGURE 2.14

Free Radical Theory of Aging

The free radical theory of aging proposes that free radicals (unpaired electrons) cause cellular damage. Antioxidants protect the cell by contributing electrons to stabilize the free radicals.

beneficial impact in part because it reduces the formation of free radicals. After many years of experimental research involving nonhuman species, including primates, evidence is beginning to emerge to support the value of caloric restriction in humans, with or without exercise (Colman et al., 2014).

Another offshoot of free radical theory suggests that resveratrol, a natural compound found in grapes and consequently wine, could be a highly potent antioxidant (Pearson et al., 2008). However, for humans, the amount of wine needed to approximate the beneficial effects of resveratrol on mice would be so high that no one person could drink enough in a day to be able to see life-extending effects. There is still considerable interest in resveratrol, though, and researchers believe that its effects could be comparable to those achieved by caloric restriction (Li et al., 2017).

The autoimmune theory of aging is not a major theory of aging, yet deserves mention as another approach to understanding the causes of aging. The autoimmune theory proposes that aging is due to faulty immune system functioning in which the immune system attacks the body's own cells. Although not a major theory of aging in its own right, it deserves mention because autoimmunity is at the heart of certain diseases prevalent in older adults, such as some forms of arthritis, systemic lupus erythematosus, and cancer (Watad et al., 2017). Additionally, as you will learn in Chapter 4, there are significant effects of aging on the immune system. Despite the importance of the immune system to health, as a theory of biological aging, the autoimmune theory does not seem to provide a broad enough explanation to account for the aging process in general.

Error theories of aging propose that mutations acquired over the organism's lifetime lead to malfunctioning of the body's cells. According to the error catastrophe theory, the errors that accumulate with aging are ones that are vital to life itself. The source of the errors, furthermore, may be associated with the mutations in the mitochondrial DNA, the so-called "powerhouse" of the cell, passed down from the mother (Sun et al., 2016). This process is shown in Figure 2.15. For example, mice with mutations in the mitochondrial DNA show accelerated signs of aging, including graying, hair loss, and loss of muscle mass and spine strength. (Kukat & Trifunovic, 2009). Researchers continue to investigate the role of mitochondrial DNA as they seek to translate findings from mouse models to human aging (Ma et al., 2018; Payne & Chinnery, 2015).

At present, we can conclude that biologists have made significant advancements in trying to solve the puzzle of why humans and our counterparts across the animal kingdom experience the changes associated with aging that eventually lead to death. However, no one theory has

FIGURE 2.15

Error Catastrophe Theory

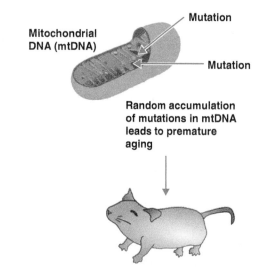

When mitochondrial DNA is damaged by mutations, as shown here, specially bred mice show signs of premature aging.

emerged as more compelling than any other. At the present time, genetic theories are considered more likely to hold the ultimate answer, but other approaches cannot yet be ruled out. Though it is likely that aging ultimately will be accounted for by a combination of these theories, it is also likely that some theories provide better ways to understand age-related changes in the body than others. Rather than exploring one overarching theory, many researchers take the approach of applying specific theories to specific alterations with age in particular organ systems or tissues, such as using cross-linking theory to explain changes in the body's connective tissues. Other researchers may propose, in contrast, that defects in the mitochondrial DNA are the most important biological changes to understand in regard to aging.

Although not yet elevated to the status of a theory, the impact of environmental stress on DNA is one of the newest areas of investigation in the biology of aging. In a process known as DNA methylation, the sequences of amino acids in a gene are altered by exposure to harmful conditions. These can have pronounced effects during fetal development, such as when the mother experiences stress during pregnancy but can also alter genetic expression throughout life influencing the individual's susceptibility to diseases that become more prevalent in later life (Johnson et al., 2012). In this way, environmental factors interact with genetic predisposition to influence the individual's rate of aging.

Finally, in looking at perspectives on the aging process that derive from the social sciences, it is important to keep in mind the central role of biological factors. These factors form the "nature" component to the complex "nature–nurture" interactions assumed to characterize development in the adult years. Clearly, all three models must be brought to bear in attempting to understand the complexities of nature and nurture.

SUMMARY

1. The life-span perspective views development as continuous from childhood to old age and incorporates the effects of sex, race, ethnicity, social class, religion, and culture. The term "developmental science" is emerging to reflect the need to take a broad, interdisciplinary approach to the study of change over time, including the fields of biology, health, and sociology.

2. The three prominent models of developmental science offer differing emphasis on genetics, the environment, and the interaction of the two. The organismic model proposes that heredity drives the course of development throughout life and that changes occur in a series of stages over time because individuals are programmed to exhibit behaviors at certain ages. The mechanistic model proposes that people's behavior changes gradually over time, shaped by the outside forces that cause them to adapt to their environments. Rather than clear-cut stages, development is viewed as a smooth, continuous set of gradations as the individual acquires new experiences. The interactionist model of development emphasizes processes such as niche-picking, in which there is a reciprocal interaction between the individual and the environment. The concepts of multi-dimensionality and multidirectionality are central, and plasticity is considered an important element of development. The biopsychosocial perspective fits within the interactionist model.

3. Sociocultural models of development emphasize the effects of the environment on individuals, focusing on variables such as age and sex structures within the population, income, and social class. Ecological perspectives examine multiple levels of organization within the environment, such as the proximal social relational level and the sociocultural level. The life course perspective highlights age-related norms, roles, and attitudes as influences on individuals. Age norms in adulthood are tied to the social clock, the expectations for the ages at which a society associates with major life events. Theories that relate the well-being of the older individual to the level of social involvement include disengagement theory, activity theory, and continuity theory. These propose different relationships between individuals and society.

4. Ageism is a set of stereotyped views about older adults, reflected in negative as well as positive images. Some historians believe that older adults were more highly regarded in preindustrial societies, a view known as the modernization hypothesis. However, it appears that mixed views of aging have existed throughout history and across cultures. According to the multiple jeopardy hypothesis of aging, older adults who are of minority status and are female face more discrimination than White male individuals. In contrast, the age-as-leveler view proposes that as people become older, age overrides all other "isms." Older adults potentially facing multiple jeopardy may also be protected from its effects and even perhaps fare better than those with higher social standing. According to the inoculation hypothesis, older minorities and women have actually become immune to the effects of ageism through years of exposure to discrimination and stereotyping.

5. Erikson's psychosocial development theory is an important psychological model of development in adulthood. It proposes a series of eight psychosocial crisis stages that correspond roughly to age periods in life in the growth of psychological functions. The eight stages follow the epigenetic principle, which means that each stage builds on the ones that come before it. However, later stages can appear at earlier ages, and early stages can reappear later in life. According to Piaget's theory of development, individuals gain in the ability to adapt to the environment through the processes of assimilation and accommodation. The ideal state of development is one of equilibration or balance. According to the identity process theory, identity assimilation and identity accommodation operate throughout development in adulthood as the individual interacts with experiences. The multiple threshold model was proposed as an explanation of how identity processes influence the interpretation of age-related events such as changes in physical or cognitive functioning.

6. According to the selective optimization with compensation (SOC) model, adults attempt to preserve and maximize the abilities of central importance and put less effort into maintaining those that are not. Older people make conscious decisions regarding how to spend their time and effort in the face of losses in physical and cognitive resources.

7. There are two major categories of biological theories, all of which regard aging as the result of changes in the biological makeup of the organism. Programmed aging theories are based on the observation that species differ in life spans (represented by the Gompertz equation) and propose that aging is genetically determined. The telomere theory, which emerged in part from observations of replicative senescence, proposes that cells are limited in the number of times they can reproduce by the fact that each replication involves a loss of the protective ends of chromosomes known as telomeres. Random error theories view aging as an accident resulting from cellular processes that have gone awry, including the cross-linking, free radical, autoimmune, and error theories. As yet, there is no one biological theory that has gained widespread acceptance, and it is likely that aging will ultimately be understood as due to some combination of biological, psychological, and sociocultural processes.

3

The Study of Adult Development and Aging: Research Methods

We know how exciting adult development and aging research methodology can be. Here are some fun facts about aging based on the latest research methods in the field.

AGEFEED

#trending

1. The Terman Study of the Gifted and Talented was started almost **100** years ago and is still up and running.

2. Aging is one of top 20 research areas supported by the National Institute of Aging (NIA), with **$2.5** billion spent each year.

3. Did you love playing with worms as a kid? The nematode worm is giving us new insights into how to slow down aging and prevent disease.

4. The Los Angeles Gerontology Research Group tracks the number of living supercentenarians. The current number is **36**, and counting!

5. The home of research on aging in the American Psychological Association is the Division of Adult Development and Aging. It was formed **75** years ago.

6. Gerontology education is on the rise. As of 2016, there were about **98** higher education institutions offering degrees in gerontology. In that same year, about **1,450** gerontology degrees were awarded.

7. Did you know sharks don't get cancer? Research at the Save Our Seas Foundation Shark Research Centre in Florida suggests that they are protected by DNA mutations. These findings may help with treating age-related diseases in humans.

8. "Artificial intelligence (AI)" isn't just for robots. AI is helping medical researchers to sort through medication data to help treat human disease.

9. Looking at life under water helps understand ways to treat and prevent diseases, with reports of this type of research dating all the way back to China in **2953** B.C.E.!

10. There are nearly **500,000** research articles on aging in the U.S. Library of Medicine.

Researchers in the field of adult development and aging may not agree on the cause of aging, but it is clear that aging is inherently linked with the passage of time. In this chapter, we will examine the innovative research strategies developed to tackle the unique challenges in research on aging, as well as the procedures in collecting information that form the knowledge base of the field.

VARIABLES IN DEVELOPMENTAL RESEARCH

Understanding why people vary as a function of their age is at the heart of the study of development. A characteristic that "varies" from individual to individual is known as a variable. In scientific research in general, the dependent variable is the outcome that researchers observe. The independent variable is the factor that the researcher manipulates. The researcher can set the value of the independent variable according to the study's conditions. Researchers choose these variables to test a particular hypothesis. The hypothesis, in turn, is based on the question the researcher wishes to investigate. Typically, these questions arise from a theoretical interest of the researcher. Age is indeed a variable, and the trick in developmental research is to show both how and why people with different ages differ on particular measures, whether of physical, psychological, or sociocultural factors.

In an experimental design, researchers study a question of interest by deciding on conditions that will allow them to manipulate a particular independent variable. Participants receive assignment to groups that either receive the treatment (the "treatment" or "experimental" group) or do not receive the treatment ("control" group). The key to the experimental method is the random assignment of participants to these groups. There can be no systematic basis for the researcher to determine that some people receive the treatment and others do not.

This condition of random assignment of participants to groups makes it difficult to conduct experimental research on aging. An experimenter cannot randomly assign people to a particular age group by making some people young and some people old. This means that you can never state with certainty that aging "causes" people to receive certain scores on a dependent variable of interest. Studies on aging therefore suffer from the problem that age is not a true "independent" variable because its value cannot be set by the experimenter.

Researchers cannot assign ages to their participants, but they can devise experiments that make it possible to study how different experimental conditions affect people of different ages. For example, consider an experiment in which the experimenter wishes to test the hypothesis that the memory performance of older adults is particularly sensitive to instructions that help them to feel more confident going into the experiment. To test this hypothesis, the researcher compares older and younger adults in two conditions. In the experimental condition, the researcher gives the confidence-boosting instructions to both age groups prior to the memory test. In the control condition, the researcher provides standard instructions to both age groups prior to the test. The independent variable is the instructions and the dependent variable is memory performance. The experimenter then compares memory scores in the two age groups and the two conditions. If people in both age groups get higher scores in the experimental group, but the older adults improve more, the researcher would have evidence to support the hypothesis that the memory performance of older adults is influenced by the wording of instructions and that this might be a function of age. Further steps would be needed to ensure this possibility, as we will discuss later, but at least one aspect of the nonrandom assignment to groups would have been addressed.

Because age cannot be experimentally manipulated, we say that studies of aging have a quasi-experimental design in which researchers compare groups on predetermined characteristics. You can think of this situation as similar to studies of such other preassigned qualities that people have such as sex/gender, ethnicity, social class, nationality, and religion. You cannot conclude that the predetermined characteristic caused the variations in the dependent variable, but you can use the results to describe the differences between groups. Whitehall II is an example of a study using social class as a quasi-experimental variable. The researchers can describe the relationship between social class and health but cannot conclude that social class "caused" different groups of workers to have different levels of health or even different types of health conditions. Researchers can, however, try to rule out as many competing explanations as possible, using methods we will describe later in the chapter.

DESCRIPTIVE (SINGLE-FACTOR) RESEARCH DESIGNS

Because studies of aging are, by definition, quasi-experimental, researchers cannot draw cause-and-effect conclusions from the findings. Studies on aging suffer additionally because effects that appear to be due to age may also represent effects of historical time. The problem of disentangling personal from social aging is more than theoretical; it also impacts the conclusions that researchers can draw from their own studies. To be able to make legitimate claims about "age" and not the social or historical period, researchers must be able to build controls into their data, designs, and analyses that can rule out these factors. Fortunately, there are such tricks up the developmental researcher's sleeve. Therefore, even though age is an imperfect variable, many researchers have figured out ways around the thorniest problems it creates.

However, the great majority of studies on aging actually do not build these controls into their designs. Instead of attempting to rule out factors other than age that could influence the pattern of findings, they only categorize the scores of participants on the basis of their age. We use the term descriptive (single-factor) designs to refer to studies that catalog information about how people perform based on their age but do not attempt to rule out social or historical factors.

Age, Cohort, and Time of Measurement

The main problem with descriptive research designs is that, because they only use age to categorize the responses from participants, they cannot rule out competing factors related to historical time. These two factors relate to the period in which the individual was born and the period in which the results are being obtained. To help you understand this problem, we need to explain the concepts of age, cohort, and time of measurement.

Age is an objectively determined measure of how many years (and/or months or days) a person has lived up to the present moment. Cohort is the term we use to describe the year (or period) of a person's birth. Time of measurement tells us the year or period in which a person is tested. Single-factor designs intended to study age cannot separate the effects of age from these two factors of cohort and time of measurement.

Consider the historical circumstances that affect the performance of people now in their later adult years. People in their 80s now were born at a time (approximately the 1940s) in which many people experienced economic hardship. People born in the "Baby Boomer" generation and who are now entering later adulthood grew up during the 1960s and 1970s, a very different historical era than that encountered by their parents.

You may not be particularly familiar with the term "cohort," but you almost certainly know about "generational" effects. A generation is simply a period that spans about a 20- to 30-year time frame. Cohort can be any length of time, which is why researchers use it rather than generation.

Cohort effects refer to the social, historical, and cultural influences that affect people during a particular period

of time. In many cases, cohort effects are taken to mean the influences present during the early years of development that cause individuals to behave in a certain way at the current time. For example, the Baby Boomers were thought to have become rebellious because their parents were permissive in raising them, a fact that could be traced to the popularity of a particular parenting advice book. When the Baby Boomers reached their adolescent years, this "anything goes" attitude combined with the natural tendency of teenagers to forge their own paths to produce an authority-flaunting generation. Another way to think about cohort effects, going back to our terminology in Chapter 1, is that they are normative history-graded influences present at or around the time of a person's birth.

Social, historical, and cultural influences that are presently affecting people participating in developmental research are called time of measurement effects. As used in developmental research designs, time of measurement effects are similar to cohort effects in that they are also normative history-graded influences that affect many people who are alive at the same time. In the 2010s, such time of measurement effects could include the rapid growth of personal technology, a slowing of the world's economy, and the impact of political and social change in the Middle East on global relations. As in Bronfenbrenner's ecological model, time of measurement effects may be far removed from the individual but still impact people indirectly by affecting the conditions that actively impinge on their lives. For example, rising energy costs can limit a family's finances, which, in turn, has an effect on the health of individual family members.

Age will always equal time of measurement minus time of birth (cohort). Similarly, time of measurement is a sum of age plus time of birth (cohort). Time of birth must be the difference between time of measurement and age. Because knowing two factors completely explains the third, a simple descriptive design does not allow researchers to conduct appropriate statistical tests. Ordinarily, experimental data do not have this inherent dependency, and it is this dependency that compromises research on aging from a methodological point of view. Descriptive research designs are thus unable to offer any solutions to the inevitable confound between age and context.

Longitudinal Designs

In a study using a longitudinal design, people are followed repeatedly from one test occasion to another. By observing and studying people as they age, researchers aim to determine whether participants have changed over time as a result of the aging process. Figure 3.1 shows the data from a typical longitudinal study, in which people are followed

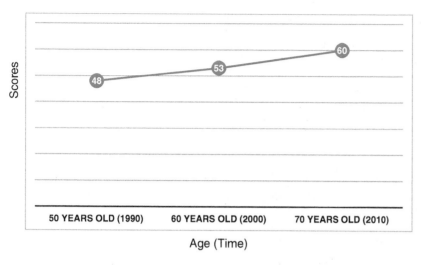

FIGURE 3.1

Sample Longitudinal Study

In an experimental study, the independent variable is randomly assigned; in quasi-experimental studies, the independent variable (such as age) is not randomly assigned.

over several decades, and their scores compared at each time of testing.

A variant of the longitudinal design is the **prospective study**, in which researchers draw from a population of interest before the sample develops a particular type of illness or experiences a particular type of life event. For example, researchers who wish to study widowhood may recruit participants from a population of married individuals while they are still married. Over the ensuing period of the study, the researchers can expect that a certain percentage of these individuals will suffer the death of their spouses. After that point, the now-widows can be compared to the way they were prior to the loss.

The typical longitudinal studies that psychologists carry out in their labs are very similar to those that you experience in your own life as you watch the people around you change over time. Consider your own experience from the start of kindergarten to high school graduation. Perhaps you attended school with the same set of students throughout high school, watching your friends and peers grow and develop along with you. Perhaps you marveled at how some friends remained the same over the years while others were not at all like they were when they were younger. Now that you are in college, your relationships with your childhood friends will change even more with the passage of time. You may attend their weddings or even find romance with past loves.

Fast forward to your 10-year reunion (or if you have already attended yours, reflect back), when you are reminded of the person you were during your adolescent development. Many of your former classmates will look and act the same, and you may remark that the years have done little to change these people. However, other classmates may be difficult or impossible to recognize. Of course, you are also changing along with them. Maybe you

were too harsh to judge the cheerleader or nerd and it is only now that you can see them as the complex and multifaceted people they were all along.

Just as psychologists develop hypotheses about why the participants in their studies change over time, you also develop your own hypotheses regarding reasons for the changes in the people you know. Did the cheerleader who joined the Peace Corps change her personality because of the influence of volunteering in an impoverished nation, or did she choose to volunteer for the Peace Corps because she had a hidden side that none of her friends saw in high school? How about the math whiz? Did he blossom because his business acumen gave him access to a broader social network? Or was he really more social than you realized and simply waiting until he had more financial resources before letting his true personality shine through?

As with these two examples, researchers also face the challenge of determining whether changes observed over time in longitudinal studies result from the person's own aging or the result of the changing environment in which the person functions. The individual cannot be removed from the environment to see what would happen if he or she had lived in a different time or place. It is simply not possible to know if people are inherently changing or whether they alter due to the circumstances in which they are aging. This is the key limitation to longitudinal studies: the inability to differentiate between aging within the individual from changes in the social and historical context.

In addition to this thorny theoretical problem, practical problems also plague longitudinal research. The most significant is perhaps the most obvious. It takes years, if not decades, to see the study come to fruition, making it both expensive and technologically challenging—in other words, it takes money and a great deal of clerical effort to keep the project going. On top of this, the results are not

Roanoke college

A longitudinal study in action as shown in the 50-year reunion of Roanoke College graduates held in 2012.

available for many years, meaning that researchers cannot focus their entire professional energy on this one study. In many cases, the original investigator may not even live long enough to see the results come to fruition.

Further complicating the longitudinal study is the problem of losing participants to death, relocation, or lack of sustained interest. As the number of participants diminishes, researchers find it increasingly difficult to make sense of the data because there are too few participants left to allow for statistical analyses across the multiple time points of the study.

The problem of losing participants is compounded by selective attrition, the fact that the people who drop out of a longitudinal study are not necessarily representative of the sample that was originally tested. This nonrandom loss of participants can occur for a variety of reasons, from illness or death to having become unable to continue in the study in a way related to the study's purpose. If the participants who dropped out were systematically different when the study began from those who remained in it, this creates particularly thorny problems.

Thus, one direct consequence of selective attrition is that the data from the study become increasingly skewed as the study wears on. In a process called terminal decline, individuals gradually lose their cognitive abilities as they draw closer to death (Hūlūr et al., 2015). After that point, they quite obviously cannot be tested; however, while they were in the sample in their declining years, they may have pulled down the group's average. The researcher may erroneously conclude that participants in the sample "improved" when, in reality, it's just that the sicker and perhaps less motivated are simply gone from the sample, leaving the higher performers alone to contribute scores.

You can compare this to a marathon run. As the race nears its conclusion, only the hardiest remain on their feet to make it to the finish line. If you measured the finishers at the beginning of the race, they would have scored higher than the dropouts on such critical factors as endurance and speed.

Figure 3.2 illustrates the problem of selective attrition with a hypothetical longitudinal study conducted over four time points. The bottom line shows the data from Times 1 through 3 of the subgroup who had died by the Time 4 data were collected. As you can see, their scores steadily declined prior to that point. The top line shows the people who remained in the study across all four times of testing. Their scores did not change at all. However, look now at the average score reflecting the means of scores of people who survived and those who died between Times 3 and 4. This average line heads downward after Time 1 and then spikes up between Times 3 and 4. On average, scores showed a remarkable increase between Times 3 and 4, but the only reason is that the ones who were in terminal decline (i.e., died after Time 3) are gone. Overall, instead of showing relative stability (as was evident in the top line), the average shows what appear to be distinct patterns of change.

Selective attrition is a special case of nonrandom sampling, as the successive samples in a longitudinal study become increasingly unlike the populations they were intended to represent and thus were "nonrandomly" sampled.

To address the problem, longitudinal researchers typically conduct analyses to determine whether the pattern of participant dropout was random, or whether it reflected a systematic bias that kept the healthier and more motivated participants in the sample.

FIGURE 3.2

Effect of Selective Attrition in a Longitudinal Study

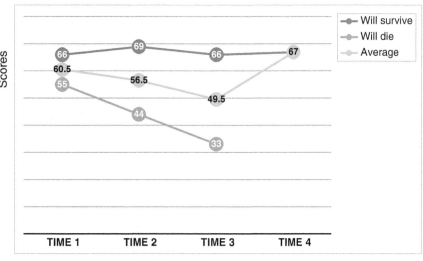

Time of testing

Longitudinal studies suffer from the problem of selective survival. Participants who will die before Time 4 had a steeper decline between Times 2 and 3 than those who will survive. The average seems to have increased between Times 3 and 4 because those who died were no longer in the sample; however, those who will survive show no actual change in scores.

Various statistical techniques are available to determine whether nonrandom sampling has occurred, and if so, whether relationships between the variables of interest are affected. Without such procedures, the study's results become difficult to interpret. Beyond a certain point, however, there is little that the researcher can do. The healthiest individuals will always be the last ones standing at the end of a study and therefore may never have been representative of their age group (Hofer & Sliwinski, 2006). In fact, we know that the super centenarians studied in the New England Centenarian Study not only lived longer than their age peers who did not survive but also were remarkably healthy for their age (Sabastiani & Perls, 2012).

Practice effects are another theoretically thorny issue that complicate longitudinal studies (Hoffman, Hofer, & Sliwinski, 2011). Because they repeatedly take the same tests, participants may improve simply because they become better able to answer the questions. If the test measures intelligence, as hard as this might seem to believe, the highly motivated participants may purposely learn the answers in between testing occasions. Similarly, in studies examining personality, a participant may suspect or find out the meaning of a response that implies something personally unfavorable. On the next test occasion, the respondent may be less likely to respond honestly so as to avoid appearing to have unfavorable qualities.

The investigator faces a far more serious dilemma with regard to the nature of the tests themselves which, over time, may become outdated. The cutting-edge theory developed in the 1980s may have since been refuted, but the researcher is still left with measures based on that theory. One way to address this problem is to reanalyze or rescale the test scores to correspond to the newer theory, if possible. This was the strategy used in studies of personality development by researchers at the Institute for Human Development in Berkeley, who began a study of child development in the late 1920s, a project that continued far longer than initially planned. By the time participants were in their adult years, the original measures were no longer theoretically relevant. The researchers rescored the data using newer theoretical and empirical frameworks.

A variety of methods can also address the practical problems that researchers encounter when they conduct longitudinal studies. Most importantly, investigators need to monitor and maintain their databases of contact information. Administrative personnel whose job it is to retain study participants can maintain the "care and feeding" of the sample in between testing occasions. Research staff may send out greeting cards for holidays and birthdays or update participants on study progress via newsletters and emails. Many longitudinal studies use websites to allow participants to engage interactively. Creating a personal touch encourages respondents to continue their involvement and also enables investigators to keep better track of moves, deaths, or email updates.

The problem of having to wait years, if not decades, for results can also be partly overcome. Investigators often publish multiple studies from the same investigation, some of which may be spinoffs addressing slightly different research questions. They can also look at analyses based on measures taken at the same testing point that are not dependent on the longitudinal analyses.

Despite their flaws, longitudinal studies have the potential to add invaluable data on psychological changes in adulthood and old age. Furthermore, as data accumulate from multiple investigations concerning related variables, a body of evidence builds up that helps to inform the larger research questions. Even though one study may have its problems, convergence across several investigations allows researchers to feel greater confidence when findings are similar from one study to the next.

Cross-Sectional Designs

In a study using a cross-sectional design, researchers compare groups of people with different ages at one point in time. Figure 3.3 illustrates a cross-sectional design of three cohorts carried out in the year 2010. The cross-sectional design is by far the more frequently used research method in the field of developmental science in general but particularly in research on aging.

Because research on aging is focused on age *changes*, the cross-sectional design, which looks at *age differences*, would seem to hold limited value. However, given the expense, technical, and practical problems that plague longitudinal studies, many researchers have little choice other than to turn to the cross-sectional method. It is then up to the researchers to come up with creative ways to control for those cohort effects, to make sure that they are actually studying the effects of age rather than simply documenting differences between cohorts.

The key to controlling for cohort differences is for researchers to select younger samples comparable in important ways to the older sample. For instance, in a study of aging and verbal memory, it would be important for researchers to ensure that the age groups being compared have similar vocabulary or verbal comprehension skills if not actually similar educational backgrounds.

The cross-sectional design reflects not only differences between cohorts but also the effects of current social and cultural influences. In other words, everyone participating in the study at about the same time is affected by normative history-graded influences. For example, you and everyone else living now are going through the same events affecting

FIGURE 3.3

Sample Cross-Sectional Study

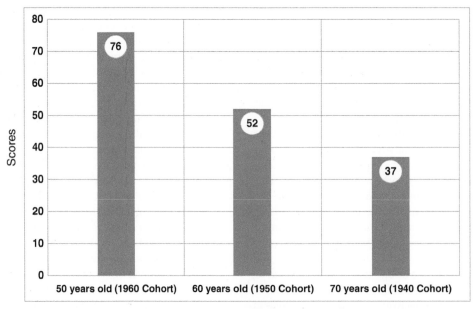

The design of a cross-sectional study showing the scores of three different age groups, who also represent different cohorts tested in 2010.

your country, if not the world. What would make this even more problematic from the standpoint of studies on aging is if younger and older adults experienced these events differently.

Researchers conducting cross-sectional studies must also control for cohort differences in factors related to the variable of interest on which the cohorts are being compared. Consider the data shown in Figure 3.3, displaying lower scores among the oldest cohort. If these scores were, for example, based on a test of health status, the researchers would need to ensure that the participants from the three age groups were drawn from similar social class groups. Based on Whitehall II, the study showing links between health and social class, such controls would be important to ensure that results attributed to age are not due to sociocultural factors.

Selective survival, the bane of longitudinal investigators, also serves to challenge the work of researchers whose primary work involves the cross-sectional design. Study participants, by definition, are survivors of their respective age groups. Thus, they may represent a healthier or luckier group of people than those in their cohort who did not live as long. Perhaps they are the ones who are more cautious, smarter, and genetically hardier and so were able to avoid the many diseases that could have caused their death prior to old age. As a result, older adults in a cross-sectional study may look different from the younger ones because the two groups are drawn from two different populations—those who will die young (but are still represented in the young adult group) and those who survive to be old. Similarly, samples of young adults drawn exclusively from a college population, a common technique in psychological research, may not be representative of the younger cohort either.

Unlike a longitudinal study, however, cross-sectional studies do not lend themselves to examinations of terminal decline. Because the participants are not followed over time, deteriorations in performance as they become ill or impaired cannot be observed. It is possible that on any given occasion, a participant who will be dying in the next few months or years is in the sample of a cross-sectional study. However, this person's scores will not be tracked over time and so will not appear in the data.

Beyond these considerations, researchers conducting cross-sectional studies must make numerous decisions as they plan their sample. For example, if researchers wish to compare "young adults" with older adults, they have to decide whether to restrict themselves to the sort of typical 18- to 22-year range or instead allow the age range to expand to the mid- or even late-20s. As it turns out, the age range of older adult samples is rarely defined as narrowly as is the range of those in college. Often, researchers have to settle for an age range for the older group that is larger than is desirable. In some studies, the range is as large

as 20 to 30 years (or more). Some researchers define the "older" sample as all respondents over the age of 50 or 60 and, having done so, fail to look for any possible age differences within the older sample. By the time all is said and done, age differences in the older sample may be as great, if not greater than, differences between the older and younger samples.

A problem related to the researcher's need to set acceptable age ranges is the question of how to divide samples when sampling the adult years. Is it better to divide samples of people in cross-sectional studies into decades and then examine age differences continuously across the adult years? Or is it better to compare people at the two extremes of the adult span? Researchers increasingly include middle-aged samples along with the younger and older adults rather than compare only those at the two extremes of the age distribution. The inclusion of three age groups creates a more justifiable basis for "connecting the dots" between their scores on measures of psychological functioning across the adult years.

Another area of concern to researchers conducting cross-sectional studies is the need to take into account the problem of task equivalence for the older and younger samples. Different age groups may very well react differently to the test materials, causing performance differences to be an artifact of the design. In studies of memory, for example, there is a risk that the older adults will find some of the measures challenging and perhaps intimidating because they are not used to having their abilities evaluated in a formal setting such as the psychology lab. Young adults are far more comfortable with test situations either because they are currently or have recently been in school, where testing is part of the fabric of everyday life. To an older adult, particularly one who is sensitive to memory loss, anxiety about the situation rather than actual performance can result in decreased scores, a topic we address further below.

Steve Buissinne/Pixabay

Research involving smartphone technology may make participation more difficult for some older adults, exaggerating any cohort differences.

Task equivalence also applies to the way different cohorts react to measures of personality and social attitudes. For example, a measure of depression may have been tested on a young adult sample but not on an older sample. Items on such a scale concerning physical changes, such as alterations in sleep patterns (a symptom of depression), may in fact reflect normal age-related differences and not differences in depression. Older adults will therefore receive a higher score on the depression scale by virtue of changing their sleep patterns alone, not because they are actually suffering from depression.

These problems aside, cross-sectional studies are relatively quick and inexpensive compared to longitudinal studies. Another advantage of cross-sectional studies is that the latest and most up-to-date technology can be brought to bear on the problem. If a new tool or technique comes out 1 year, it can be tested through a cross-sectional method the next year. Researchers are not tied to obsolete methods that were in use some 30 or 40 years ago.

The best cross-sectional studies, though never able to permit causal inferences about aging, employ a variety of controls to ensure that differences other than age are kept to a minimum and that the ages selected for study span across the adult years. Most researchers regard their cross-sectional findings as tentative descriptions of the effects of aging on the function of interest. They are aware of the importance of having their findings replicated and verified through studies employing a longitudinal element.

Throughout this book, we endeavor to sift through and find the best available evidence to report to you about the aging process. We will emphasize the studies that do the best job of controlling for factors extraneous to age, whether they are longitudinal or cross sectional. The next section covers methods that are superior to descriptive designs; however, unfortunately these methods are still only rarely used. In areas where there is relatively little research, we may find that we have to turn to studies that didn't necessarily control that well for confounds other than age. However, we will aim to point these problems out to you so that you are still getting the best information possible. Even if you do not pursue a research career, you will learn to be an educated consumer of research on a topic that is so vital to many areas of your life.

SEQUENTIAL RESEARCH DESIGNS

We have probably convinced you by now that the perfect study on aging is virtually impossible to conduct. Age can never be a true independent variable because it cannot be manipulated. Furthermore, age is inherently linked with time, and so personal aging can never be separated from social aging. However, considerable progress in some areas of research has been made through the application of **sequential designs**. These are data collection strategies that consist of different combinations of the variables age, cohort, and time of measurement.

Simply put, a sequential design involves a "sequence" of studies, such as a cross-sectional study carried out twice (two sequences) over a span of 10 years. The sequential nature of these designs is what makes them superior to the truly descriptive designs conducted on one sample, followed over time (longitudinal design) or on different-aged samples, tested on one occasion (cross-sectional design). Not only do sequential studies automatically provide an element of replication, but when they are carried out as intended, statistical analyses can permit remarkably strong inferences to be drawn about the effect of age as distinct from cohort or time of measurement.

The Most Efficient Design

One of the most influential articles to be published in the field of adult development and aging was the landmark work by psychologist K. Warner Schaie (1965), in which he outlined what would later be called the **Most Efficient Design**, a set of three designs manipulating the variables of age, cohort, and time of measurement. It is "most efficient" because it enables the most amount of information to be condensed into the most inclusive data framework.

The three designs that make up the Most Efficient Design and the respective factors they include are the **time-sequential design**, in which the data are organized by age and time of measurement, the **cohort-sequential design**, in which cohorts are compared at different ages, and the **cross-sequential design**, in which cohorts are examined at different times of measurement (the only design that does not specifically include age as a factor). Figure 3.4 illustrates the combination of factors included in each of the sequential designs.

FIGURE 3.4

Factors Examined in Each of the Sequential Designs

	Age	Time	Cohort
Time-sequential	✓	✓	
Cohort-sequential	✓		✓
Cross-sequential		✓	✓

Each type of study in the "Most Efficient Design" involves different combinations of the factors of age, cohort, and time of measurement.

As you can see, then, each sequential design involves arranging the data obtained from more than one cohort at more than one age and across more than one time period. Figure 3.5 shows the cohort-sequential design, in which each of three cohorts is investigated over three time points. The figure shows three differing patterns of change. If only one cohort were tested, as would be true in a longitudinal study, it would appear that either the scores went up with age, they were flat, and then increased, or were almost completely unchanged. Notice, also, that the design ignores the fact that the three time points come from different years of testing (e.g., for age 30, the data came from 1970, 1980, and 1990).

In the time-sequential design, shown in Figure 3.6, researchers examine the two factors of age and time of measurement. The bars reflect the scores of 30-year-olds tested in 1970, 1980, and 1990; 40-year-olds tested in 1980, 1990, and 2000; and 50-year-olds tested in 1990, 2000, and 2010. At each time of testing, there were age differences, but because those age groups had different times of birth, the findings could reflect cohort rather than age effects.

The cross-sequential design, illustrated in Figure 3.7, shows the findings displayed according to cohort and time of measurement and does not take age into account at all. The lines connect data points for each cohort across the three times of measurement. For the first two cohorts, there is a continuous rise in scores between 1980 and 1990, but the 1950 cohort increases between 1990 and 2000, while the 1960 cohort shows no change at all and has consistently lower scores.

The cross-sequential design suggests, then, that historical time does interact with age as an influence on patterns of scores. The time-sequential makes it possible to examine the effects of time of testing in contrast to age, and the cohort-sequential to examine the effects of cohort. The interpretation the researchers make of these patterns of findings will be informed by the availability of evidence to tie scores on the scales of interest with those sociocultural, environmental, and historical factors. Keep these in mind as you read subsequent chapters, particularly where sequential data are available on the variables of interest.

CORRELATIONAL DESIGNS

The above developmental designs are all quasi-experimental, in that even in the sophisticated sequential approach, researchers are not able to manipulate the age of participants. An alternative approach to describing group differences using the quasi-experimental design is the correlational design, in which relationships are observed among variables as they exist in the world. The researcher makes no attempt to divide participants into groups or to manipulate variables.

FIGURE 3.5

Sample Findings from a Cohort-Sequential Design

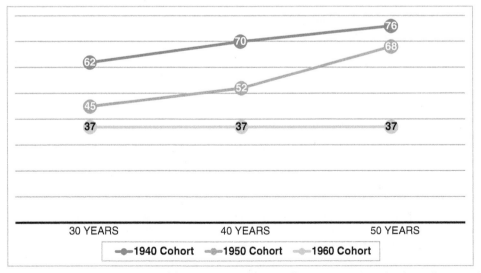

In a cohort sequential design, two or more cohorts are followed across at least two different age periods. In this figure, the 1950 cohort is the only one to show increases from ages 40 to 50, and the 1940 and 1960 cohorts have different mean scores at each age.

FIGURE 3.6

Sample Findings from a Time-Sequential Design

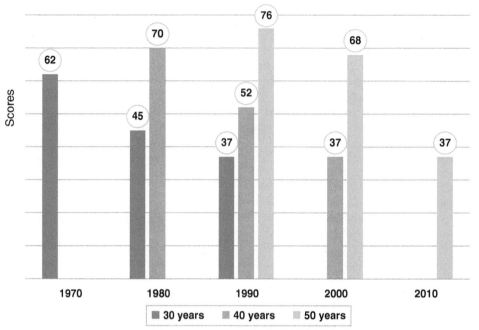

In a time sequential design, scores are compared at different times of testing for groups that differ in age. In this figure, 50-year-olds had higher scores than the younger groups in 1990 and 2000. The 40-year-olds had higher scores in both 1980 and 1990.

FIGURE 3.7

Sample Findings from a Cross-Sequential Design

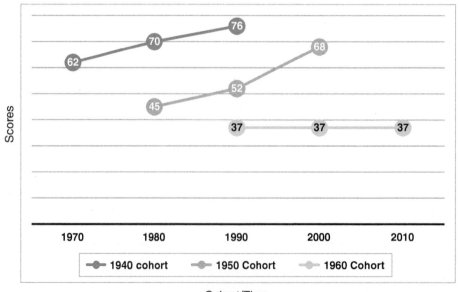

In a cross-sequential design, different cohorts are compared at different times of testing. In this figure, the 1960 cohort did not change over the three times of testing. The 1950 cohort showed increases, and the 1940 cohort was higher throughout from 1970 to 1990.

Simple Correlational Designs

Comparisons of age groups or groups based on divisions such as year of birth or time of measurement are useful for many research questions in the field of gerontology. However, often this approach is neither the most efficient nor the most informative. By grouping people into categories, researchers lose a great deal of information that could be preserved if they used actual age in years. Age is a continuous variable, meaning that it does not have natural cutoff points, as does a categorical variable such as gender. There may be a difference between people of 42 and people of 49 years of age, but when they are all grouped in the "40-year-old" category, this distinction is obscured.

In the correlational design, age can be treated as a continuous variable and it is therefore unnecessary or even desirable to put people into arbitrarily defined groups. The relationship between age and another variable is expressed through the statistic known as the correlation (represented by the letter r), whose value can range from $+1.0$ to -1.0. A significant positive correlation indicates that the two variables are positively related so that when the value of one variable increases, the other one does as well. A significant negative correlation indicates that the two variables are negatively related so that when one increases in value, the other one decreases. A correlation of zero indicates no relationship between the variables.

In a correlational study, the researcher makes no assumptions about what caused what—there are no "independent" or "dependent" variables. A correlation between two variables means simply that the two variables are related, but like the proverbial chicken and egg, the researcher cannot say which came first.

Consider the example shown in Figure 3.8 depicting the relationship between age and memory (a negative correlation). Each dot represents the score of one person in the study, and as you can see, people in the higher age range have lower memory scores than people in the lower age range. Although it would seem clear that higher age would "cause" poorer memory, rather than that poorer memory would "cause" aging, the age-memory relationship could reflect unmeasured variables such as health status, education, or even confidence in one's memory, all factors that we will examine in subsequent chapters. A simple correlational design does not make it possible to rule out these competing explanations.

When examining data from a typical correlational study, then, it is important to keep in mind that causation cannot be inferred from correlation and to be on the lookout for competing hypotheses related to unmeasured variables. Because arguments that increasing age "causes" changes in other variables are so compelling, it is difficult

FIGURE 3.8

Sample Results from a Correlational Study of Age and Memory

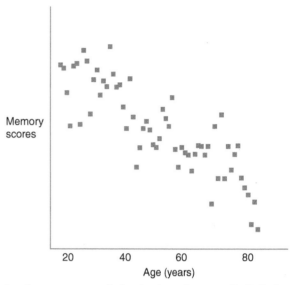

Data from a memory study showing the performance of individuals ranging from 20 to 80 years of age, with each person's scores represented by a point on the graph.

to remember that there can be other causes lurking in the background.

Correlational studies contain a wealth of information despite their inability to determine cause and effect. The value of the correlation itself provides a useful basis for calculating the strength of the relationship. Furthermore, it is possible to manipulate a larger number of variables at one time than is generally true in studies involving group comparisons. Advanced correlational methods have become increasingly available in the past 20 years that allow researchers to navigate the difficulties involved in causality with traditional correlational methods, and we will turn to those next.

Multivariate Correlational Designs

In contrast to simple correlational designs, which involve determining the statistical relationship between two variables (called a bivariate relationship), a multivariate correlational design involves the analysis of relationships among more than two variables. Researchers using a multivariate design can simultaneously evaluate the effects of many potentially important factors rather than being restricted to the study of two variables, which can lead to overlooking an important third (or fourth) variable.

Multivariate correlational methods also enable researchers to test models in which a set of variables is used to "predict" scores on another variable. In multiple regression analysis, one set of variables are designated as predictors of performance on another variable designated as the outcome.

A variant of multiple regression is logistic regression, in which researchers test the likelihood of an individual receiving a score on a discrete yes–no variable. For example, a group of investigators may want to test the probability that a person will receive a diagnosis of cardiovascular disease or not, depending on whether the person has one of several risk factors. Logistic regression is often used to determine whether nonrandom sampling has occurred, as discussed earlier with subject attrition in longitudinal studies. Using the yes–no variables of "survivor" and "dropout," researchers can attest to whether differences between survivors and dropouts are due to chance or to other factors.

Multivariate correlational designs have the potential to test complex models that reflect multiple influences, including age, on the outcome variables of interest to the researcher. For example, the researcher may believe that education positively affects life satisfaction in older adults because of a third variable, such as health status. The researcher can conduct a statistical test of mediation, in which the correlation between two variables is compared with and without their joint correlation to a third variable. If the correlation between education and life satisfaction is smaller when health status is included than when it is not, then the researcher can assume that health serves in this mediational role. Researchers can also test for moderation, when two variables are believed to have a joint influence on a third. For example, both age and education may separately relate to life satisfaction.

Researchers can test for multiple types of mediation and moderation by conducting a single analysis that includes different types of proposed relationships. In path analysis, researchers test all possible correlations among a set of variables to see if they can be explained by a single model. In our example of education, health, age, and life satisfaction, a path analysis would allow the researcher to test whether education and age both affect life satisfaction (moderation) through their joint effect on health (mediation), which in turn affects life satisfaction.

Depending on the data available to a researcher, there may be several measures that all tap a similar construct. In this case, they can use a latent variable, which is a statistical composite of several variables that were actually measured. In the example we are using, the researchers may have three measures of life satisfaction rather than just one. They can construct a latent variable that then serves to capture all three measures. In structural equation modeling (SEM), researchers test models involving relationships that include latent variables. As in path analysis, researchers propose a set of relationships among variables; however, some are directly measured and others are constructed as latent variables.

Figure 3.9 shows an example of the results of a sample study using structural equation modeling to examine the predictors of life satisfaction from health, age, social class, and exercise frequency. Health is shown as a circle because it is a latent variable made up of the components of blood pressure, weight, and mobility limitations. Age, social class, and exercise frequency serve as additional predictors of the

FIGURE 3.9

Structural Equation Modeling of Relationship between Health and Life Satisfaction

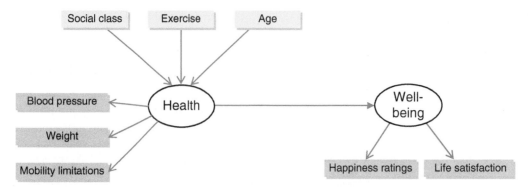

Data from a study using structural equation modeling to represent the relationship between health and well-being. Health represents a combination of blood pressure, weight, and mobility limitations. Well-being represents a combination of happiness ratings and life satisfaction. Social class, exercise, and age are all factors that can affect health.

latent variable of health. In the model, health is compared to these three additional variables in predicting the outcome of well-being.

SEM is typically used to assess the relationships among variables collected at one point in time. To take advantage of data obtained in longitudinal studies, researchers turn to a multivariate method that takes into account the patterns of people's scores over time. In hierarchical linear modeling (HLM) (Raudenbush & Bryk, 2002), individual patterns of change are examined over time rather than simply comparing mean scores of people at different ages. Such a technique is particularly important in longitudinal research because not every participant exhibits the same patterns of change over time. While some individuals may increase, others may decrease, and some may not change at all. Solely looking at overall mean scores fails to capture this individual variation. In HLM, individual patterns can be explored statistically in addition to examining whether particular variables affect some individuals more than others.

TYPES OF RESEARCH METHODS

Data on adult development and aging can be captured using a variety of data collection strategies or research methods. Each method has advantages and disadvantages that are important to consider according to the particular field of study, the nature of the sample, available resources, and desired applications.

Laboratory Studies

The majority of information about physical and cognitive changes associated with the aging process comes from laboratory studies, in which participants are tested in a systematic fashion using standardized procedures. The laboratory method is considered the most objective way of collecting data because each participant is exposed to the same treatment, using the same equipment and the same data recording procedures. For example, in a study of memory, participants may be asked to recall a set of items presented on a computer. At a later point, they may be asked to recall as many of those items as possible using some type of automated response system.

There are obvious advantages to the laboratory study. The objective and systematic ways in which data are recorded provide the investigator assurance that the results are due to the variables being studied rather than to extraneous factors. For instance, in the memory study, all participants would be presented with the recall items systematically, in a way that does not depend on the voice inflections of the researcher, the quality of the visual stimuli, or the amount of time used to present the items.

A limitation of the laboratory study is the inability to apply the stimuli presented to real-life experiences of most adults. It is possible that the older person feels uncomfortable when tested in an impersonal and possibly intimidating manner using unfamiliar equipment. Consequently, the findings may underestimate the individual's abilities in everyday life and may not generalize to real-world scenarios.

Qualitative Studies

There are often instances in which researchers wish to explore a phenomenon of interest in an open-ended fashion. The investigation of social influences on adult development such as, for example, personal relationships, may demand the researcher use a method that captures potentially relevant factors within a broad spectrum of possible influences (Allen & Walker, 2000). The qualitative method allows for the exploration of such complex relationships outside the narrow restrictions and assumptions of quantitative methods. In other cases, researchers may be working in an area in which conventional methods are neither practical nor appropriate for the problem under investigation. Qualitative methods are also used in the analysis of life history information, which is likely to be highly varied from person to person and not easily translated into numbers. The main advantage of using qualitative methods is that they provide researchers with alternative ways to test their hypotheses. The qualitative method can be adapted in a flexible manner to the nature of the problem at hand.

Archival Research

In archival research, investigators use existing resources that contain data relevant to a question about aging. The archives might consist of a governmental data bank, or the records kept by an institution, school, or employer. Another source of archival data is newspaper or magazine reports.

An advantage of archival research is that the information is readily accessible, especially given the growth of Web-based data sets including those of the U.S census. Data files can be downloaded directly from the Internet, or publications can be accessed using portable document files (PDFs) that are easily read and searched. Disadvantages are that the researcher does not necessarily have control over the form of the data. For instance, a governmental agency may keep records of employment by age that do not include information on specific occupations of interest to the researcher. Another disadvantage is that the material may not be systematically collected or recorded. Newspaper or school records, for example, may have information that is biased or incomplete.

Surveys

Researchers rely on the survey method to gain information about a sample that can then be generalized to a larger population. Surveys are typically short and easily administered with simple rating scales to use for answers. For instance, poll voters are surveyed on for whom they will cast their ballots in upcoming elections. Occasionally, more intensive surveys may be given to gain in-depth knowledge about aging and its relationship to health behaviors, health risks, and symptoms. The U.S. Census is collected through survey methodology. However, it is considered archival in that it has extensive historical records going back to the year 1750 when the first U.S. Census was conducted.

The American Community Survey (ACS) is a nationwide sample survey of approximately 3 million households collected every month on about 250,000 households. Many of the statistics we present in this book about families, work, and other key social indicators come from the ACS. The ACS website has many downloadable tables, making up-to-date statistics more accessible than has ever been the case in prior years.

Surveys have the advantage of providing data that allow the researcher to gain insight into the behavior of more people than could be studied in the laboratory or other testing site. They can be administered over the telephone or, increasingly, via the Web. Interview-based surveys given by trained administrators provide knowledge that is easily coded and analyzed while still providing comprehensive information about the behavior in question. On the other hand, many surveys tend to be short, with questions that are subject to bias by respondents who may attempt to provide a favorable impression to the researcher (e.g. "How happy are you?"). Consequently, although the data may be generalizable to a large population, the quality of the data itself may be limited.

Several surveys carried out by collaborations of researchers have provided particularly important data for the study of adult development and aging. The Midlife in the United States Survey (MIDUS) was conducted in 1995 on over 7,100 adults aged 45 and older (MIDUS I). The investigators then received further funding to conduct follow-ups and were able to reach over 4,900 of the original participants in 2004 (MIDUS II). The interdisciplinary nature of MIDUS, the fact that it had a longitudinal component, and its inclusion of the midlife years have made it an important data source for studies spanning such wide-ranging areas as genetics, personality, mental and physical health, and sociodemographic factors.

Epidemiological Studies

Governments, funding agencies, or interested researchers often need to gather data on the frequency of a particular disease in the population. Epidemiology is the study of the distribution and determinants of health-related states or events (including disease), and the application of this study to the control of diseases and other health problems.

An epidemiological study may use a survey methodology in which questionnaires asking about a particular disease or set of diseases are sent to a representative sample of the population. Epidemiologists may also collect data through interviews and, increasingly, by obtaining biological samples for genetic and genomic analysis.

The results of epidemiological studies can provide researchers with two types of population estimates as shown in Figure 3.10. Prevalence statistics provide estimates of the percentage of people who have *ever* had symptoms in a particular period. Incidence statistics provide estimates of the percentage of people who *first* develop symptoms in a given period. For example, the lifetime prevalence of a disorder signifies what percentage of the population had the disease at any time since they were born. A 1-year incidence estimate would tell you what percentage of the population develops symptoms of the disease within a 1-year period.

Case Reports

When researchers want to provide an in-depth analysis of particular individuals, they use the case report, which summarizes the findings from multiple sources for

FIGURE 3.10

Types of Data Used in Epidemiological Studies

Prevalence:
Estimate of percentage who *ever* had symptoms in given period

1-month... 6-month, 1-year- ...lifetime

Incidence:
Estimate of percentage who *first* develop symptoms in given period

Past month   Past 6 months   Past year

Epidemiological studies are based either on prevalence or incidence data.

Pixabay/Pexels

In research based on surveys, participants complete measures such as ratings of personality or attitudes.

those individuals. Data may be integrated from interviews, psychological tests, observations, archival records, or even journal and diary entries. The focus of the case report is on the characteristics of the individual and what has influenced his or her development and life experiences. Personal narratives may also be obtained with this method, in which individuals describe their lives as they have experienced them along with their ideas about why their lives have evolved in a given manner.

Although the case report has the benefit of providing insights into the lives of individuals as they change over time, it relies heavily on clinical judgments by the researcher. Therefore, for a case report to provide valuable information, a high level of expertise is required so that the findings are presented in a manner that balances the objective facts with the subjective analysis of the researcher.

Focus Groups

A less formal research method is a focus group, which is a meeting of respondents asked to provide feedback about a particular topic of interest. In a focus group, an investigator attempts to identify important themes in the discussion and keep the conversation oriented to these themes. The goal is to develop concrete research questions to pursue in subsequent studies. For example, attitudes toward mental health providers by older adults may be assessed by a focus group in which participants 65 and older share their concerns and experiences with counselors and therapists.

An advantage of the focus group is that issues can be identified prior to conducting a more systematic investigation. This approach, often considered a pilot study, is particularly useful when little preexisting research on the topic is available. An obvious disadvantage is that the method is not particularly systematic, and the data cannot readily be analyzed or systematically interpreted.

Daily Diaries

Researchers who wish to examine the day-to-day variations in a measure of interest use the daily diary method in which participants enter data on a daily basis. The data may consist of ratings on such variables as happiness, perceived stress, or interactions with friends, family, or coworkers. The participants may be asked to record their ratings at the same time every day, or they may be sent messages on a mobile device reminding them to enter their data. Typically, these studies are carried out over a period of weeks or months.

By obtaining data on a frequent basis over a period of time, researchers can track small variations in conditions that they believe may influence people's day-to-day functioning. Moreover, the statistical analyses made possible by these numerous data points provide researchers with more extensive information than they could obtain by single-point investigations.

Observational Methods

In the observational method, researchers draw conclusions about behavior through careful and systematic examination in particular settings. Recordings may be made using videotapes or behavioral records. In one type of observational method known as participant observation, the researcher participates in the activities of the respondents. For example, a researcher may wish to find out about the behavior of staff in a nursing home. The researcher may spend several days living with people in the nursing home. The researcher's subjective experiences would become part of the "data."

There are elaborate procedures available for creating behavioral records in which the researcher precisely defines the behavior to be observed (the number of particular acts) and specifies the times during which records will be made. Figure 3.11 shows a sample behavioral observation record.

This procedure may be used to determine whether an intervention is having its intended effects. If an investigator is testing a method to reduce aggressive behavior in people with Alzheimer's disease, behavioral records could be made before and after the intervention is introduced. After observing the effects of the intervention, the method's effectiveness could be determined by a return to baseline condition to assess whether the aggressive behavior increases without the intervention.

Meta-Analysis

In comparing the findings across investigations that examined similar phenomena, researchers can take advantage

FIGURE 3.11

Behavioral Observation Record

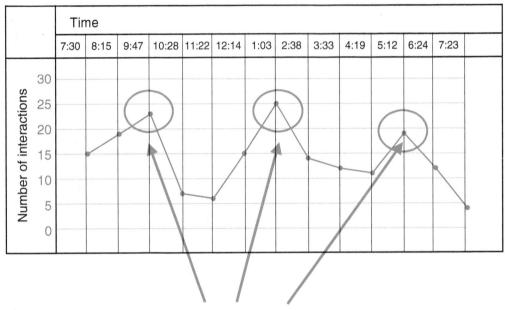

In behavioral observations, researchers count the number of behaviors shown at given intervals.

of meta-analysis, a statistical procedure that allows them to combine findings from independently conducted studies. For example, it is common for multiple researchers to test the effect of a particular psychological treatment, such as psychotherapy. The investigator who conducts the meta-analysis sets criteria for including particular studies such as the type of therapy, use of similar outcome measures, and gender distribution of the sample. Then the investigator calculates a statistic that reflects the extent of the therapy's effect, known as the "effect size." This statistic can then be used to estimate, across studies, the statistical significance of the outcomes observed in the studies included in the analysis.

Studies on aging also benefit from meta-analysis. In these cases, investigations that include estimates of age differences or age changes can then be compared using a single statistic. That statistic then provides an estimate that incorporates all the studies that the researcher includes.

Meta-analysis is far superior to the approaches previously used in which researchers used subjective judgment or simple counting to combine the information from a group of related studies. Although somewhat rare at this point in the field, with the accumulation of more research investigating similar problems, meta-analyses may become more common and therefore provide a more accurate picture of how a given variable or set of variables change over the adult years.

MEASUREMENT ISSUES IN ADULT DEVELOPMENT AND AGING

Research designs, no matter how cleverly engineered, are unable to yield worthwhile results if the methods used to collect the data are flawed. Researchers in adult development and aging, like all other scientists, must concern themselves with the quality of the instruments they use to capture data. The task is made more difficult because the instruments must be usable with people who are likely to vary in ability, educational background, and sophistication with research instruments. Earlier we pointed out the problems involved in comparing older and younger adults on measures used in cross-sectional studies. Here we will look specifically at some of the ways developmental researchers can ensure that their measures are equivalent across age groups.

The first measurement issue to consider is that of reliability. A measure is reliable if it yields consistent results every time it is used. The importance of reliability is highlighted by considering the analogy of measurements used in cooking. If your tablespoon were unreliable (say, it was made of floppy plastic), the amount of ingredients added would vary with every use. Your cookies may be hard and crunchy one time and soft and gooey the next. A psychological test must also provide similar scores upon repeated administration. Reliability can be assessed by test–retest reliability, which is determined by giving the test on two occasions to assess whether respondents receive similar scores across both administrations. Another form of reliability relates to internal consistency, which indicates whether respondents answer similarly on comparable items.

The second criterion used to evaluate a test is validity, meaning that the test measures what it is supposed to measure. A test of intelligence should measure intelligence, not how good your vision is. Returning to the example in the kitchen, if a tablespoon were marked "teaspoon," it would not be measuring what it is supposed to measure, and your baked products would be ruined. Tablespoons are fairly easy to assess for validity; however, psychological tests unfortunately present a far greater challenge. For this reason, validity is a much more difficult quality to capture than reliability.

The concept of validity varies depending on the intended use of the measure. Content validity provides an indication of whether a test designed to assess factual material accurately measures that material. Your next exam may very well include questions testing how well you have understood the topics covered in this chapter. Criterion validity indicates whether a test score accurately predicts performance on an indicator measure, as would be used in a test of vocational ability that claims to predict success on the job. Finally, construct validity is used to assess the extent to which a measure intended to assess a psychological construct is able to do so.

Construct validity is difficult to establish and requires two types of evidence: convergent and discriminant validity. Convergent validity is needed to determine that the measure relates to other measures that are of theoretical similarity. A test of intelligence should have a positive relationship to another test of intelligence that has been well validated. Discriminant validity demonstrates that the measure does not relate to other measures that have no theoretical relationship to it. A test of intelligence should not be correlated with a test of personality, unless the personality test assesses some aspect of intelligence.

Although psychologists are generally aware of the need to establish the reliability and validity of measures used in both research and practical settings, less attention is focused on psychometric properties when used in gerontological research. Measures whose reliability and validity were established on young adult samples are often used inappropriately without testing their applicability to samples of adults of varying ages. The process can become quite complicated. If Form A of a measure is found to be psychometrically sound with college students but only Form B has adequate reliability and validity for older adults, the researcher is faced with the prospect of having to use different forms of a test within the same study.

Nevertheless, sensitivity to measurement issues is crucial if conclusions drawn from the research are to have value.

ETHICAL ISSUES IN RESEARCH

All scientists who engage in research with humans or other animals must take precautions to protect the rights of their participants. In extreme cases, such as in medical research, the life of an individual may be at stake if he or she is subjected to risky procedures. Research in which respondents are tested or put through stressful experimental manipulations also requires that standard protocols are followed. Recognizing the importance of these considerations, the American Psychological Association developed a comprehensive set of guidelines for psychologists that includes the appropriate treatment of human participants in research (American Psychological Association, 2018). The main features of these guidelines appear in Figure 3.12.

Researchers must present a potential respondent as full a disclosure as possible of the risks and benefits of

FIGURE 3.12

Summary of Key Components of APA Ethical Guidelines

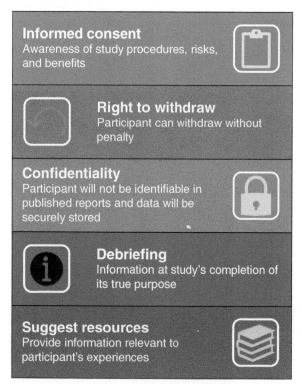

This graphic shows the four key areas of research ethics.

becoming involved in any research project. When the individual is a minor child or an adult who is not able to make independent decisions, the researcher is obligated to inform the individual's legal guardian about the nature of the study. Having provided information about the study, the researcher must then obtain a legal signature indicating that the participant understands the risks and benefits involved in the study. At this point, the researcher is able to obtain the full informed consent of the respondent or the respondent's legal representative. When the individual is an animal, the researcher is similarly bound to ensure that the animal is not mishandled or subjected to unnecessary harm, although different protective procedures are followed.

Research participants are also entitled to know what the study was about after they completed it, a process called debriefing. If you have ever participated in research, you may have been curious during the course of the study to know what was being tested. In some cases, you might have been surprised to find out about the "real" purpose of the study. Perhaps you were told that you were going to be asked to fill out a series of questionnaires in a quiet laboratory room. In the middle of the questionnaire, you hear a loud noise in the hallway, followed by a man screaming. Although you may think the point of the study is to gather information about you through the questionnaires, the actual goal of the research was to find out whether you would offer help to the man in the hallway. After the experiment is over, the researcher is obligated to tell you the truth about the purpose of the study. You may be embarrassed if in fact you did not get up to help, but you at least had a right to know that you were being tested on this attribute. The debriefing might make you feel better if the experimenter explains that your behavior was not all that atypical and, in fact, could be considered normal under such conditions.

Even though the study's purpose was explained to you, it's still possible that you regret your failure to offer help to the man in distress. In fact, ethical guidelines for research in psychology dictate that the researcher not only provide feedback but also must be ready to suggest support or counseling for people who become distressed while involved in the experiment. Respondents are also entitled to withdraw from a study without risk of penalty should they choose to do so. The experimenter should not coerce them into completing the study, and even if they decide to discontinue participation, they should still receive whatever reimbursement was initially promised. If they are students in a class or clients receiving services (such as hospital patients), they should not fear having their grades lowered or services withheld from them.

Finally, research participants are entitled to know what will happen to their data. In all cases, the data must be kept confidential, meaning that only the research team will have access to the information provided by the participants. The other condition usually attached to the data is that of anonymity. Participants are guaranteed that their names will not be associated with their responses. The condition of anonymity obviously cannot be kept if the study is a longitudinal one because the researchers must maintain access to names for follow-up purposes. In this case, the condition of confidentiality applies, and the researchers are obligated to ensure that all records are kept private and secure.

These ethical standards are enforced in all institutions receiving federal or local funding for research through Institutional Review Boards (IRBs), which review all proposed studies to be carried out at that institution or by anyone employed by that institution. These reviews ensure that the rights of research participants are adequately protected according to the criteria discussed.

In addition, the American Psychological Association's ethical guidelines ensure that studies conducted specifically in the field of psychology meet predetermined criteria for protection of human and animal subjects. An important development in the area of protection of human participants was the implementation in April 2003 of national standards within the United States to protect the privacy of personal health information. The Health Insurance Portability and Accountability Act, referred to as HIPAA, is the first-ever federal privacy standards to protect patients' medical records and other health information provided to health plans, doctors, hospitals, and other health care providers. HIPAA protects research participants by ensuring that a researcher must meet standards to maintain the privacy of health-related information. With these guidelines in place, there is assurance that respondents in research will be appropriately treated and their rights protected.

SUMMARY

1. The study of aging is intimately linked with the passage of time, making research on aging difficult to design and implement. A variable is a characteristic that "varies" from individual to individual. The dependent variable is the outcome that researchers observe, while the independent variable is the factor that the researcher manipulates. In experimental study designs, researchers decide on conditions that will allow them to manipulate a particular independent variable based on the question of interest using random assignment. Because aging can never be randomly assigned, studies on aging are considered quasi-experimental.

2. Descriptive (single-factor) research designs include longitudinal and cross sectional. Both of these designs are quasi-experimental because they do not involve the manipulation of age as an independent variable.

Each has advantages and disadvantages, but the main problem is that they do not allow for generalizations to be made beyond a single cohort or period of history.

3. The variables in developmental research are age, cohort, and time of measurement. Age represents processes going on within the individual, and cohort and time of measurement are regarded as measures of social aging. These three variables are interdependent because as soon as two are known, the third is determined. Cohort effects refer to the social, historical, and culture influences that affect people during a particular period of time.

4. Longitudinal research designs involve people being followed repeatedly from one test occasion to another in an attempt to determine whether participants have changed over time as a result of the aging process. A variant of longitudinal research is the prospective study, in which researchers sample from a population of interest before they develop a particular type of illness or experience a particular type of life event. Longitudinal designs have several limitations, including selective attrition, terminal decline, practice effects, outdated tests, and length of time to follow the results. A variety of methods can be employed to account for these limitations.

5. A cross-sectional design compares groups of people of different ages at one point in time and is the more frequently used method in research on aging. The challenge of cross-sectional designs is to ensure that the effects of age are studied rather than differences between cohorts. Researchers design cross-sectional studies to control for cohort effects as best as possible. Limitations of cross-sectional research include concerns about survival effects, unrepresentative populations, age range definitions, test material reaction, and task equivalence. Despite these drawbacks, researchers employ a variety of controls to ensure that differences other than age are kept to a minimum.

6. Sequential designs consist of different combinations of the variables of age, cohort, and time of measurement, and attempt to control for the effects of social aging by allowing the researchers to make estimates of the influence of factors other than age on performance. The Most Efficient Design was developed by Schaie to provide a framework for three types of sequential studies and involves a set of three designs manipulating the variables of age, cohort, and time of measurement.

7. Correlational designs involve studying the relationship between age (or another variable) and other measures of interest. A simple correlational design involves two variables, and a multivariate correlational design involves analyzing relationships among multiple variables. Structural equation modeling is a form of multivariate correlational analysis in which complex models involving age can be statistically evaluated. In hierarchical linear modeling, patterns of change over time are analyzed, taking into account individual differences in change.

8. There are several methods of research available to investigators who study aging. In the laboratory study, conditions are controlled and data are collected in an objective manner. Qualitative studies allow for exploration using an open-ended method. Archival research uses existing records, such as census data or newspaper records. Surveys involve asking people to provide answers to structured questions, with the intention of generalizing to larger populations. Epidemiologic studies gather data on the frequency of a particular disease in the population. Case reports are used to provide in-depth analyses of an individual or small group of individuals. Focus groups gather information about people's views on particular topics. Observational methods provide objective data on people in specific settings and under specific conditions. Meta-analysis allows for a statistical procedure that allows researchers to combine findings from independently conducted studies.

9. Researchers in adult development and aging must concern themselves with finding the most appropriate measurement tools available. The science of studying measurement instruments is known as psychometrics. Of particular concern is the need to establish the appropriateness of the same measurement instrument for adults of different ages. Reliability refers to the consistency of a measurement instrument, and validity assesses whether the instrument measures what it is intended to measure.

10. Ethical issues in research address the proper treatment of participants by researchers. Informed consent is the requirement that respondents be given adequate knowledge about a study's procedures before they participate. Debriefing refers to notification of participants about the study's real purpose. Respondents also have the right to withdraw at any time without penalty. Finally, respondents must be told what will happen to their data, but at all times, the data must be kept confidential. All research institutions in the United States are required by federal law to guarantee the rights of human and animal subjects.

4

Physical Changes

Plastic surgery is big business for U.S. adults 55 and older. Check out these 2018 facts!

AGEFEED

#top10facts

1. Total number of cosmetic procedure: **4.2 million**
2. Number of invasive cosmetic surgeries: **400,000**
3. Number of facelifts or eyelifts: **180,000**
4. Number of Botox® treatments: **1.7 million;** average cost: **$397**
5. Number of filler injections: **927,000;** average cost: **$669**
6. Percent of all procedures by 55+ adults: **23%**
7. Average cost of facelifts: **$7655**
8. Increase in yearly number of procedures: **50,000**
9. Reasons for plastic surgery: **Reentering the dating scene**
10. Newest trend in plastic surgery: **The "Daddy-do-over":** designed to get rid of the "dad bod" by reshaping the midsection.

In this chapter, we examine changes in the body, brain, and sensory systems throughout middle and later adulthood, all of which can interact with an individual's identity. People's feelings about themselves strongly reflect perceptions of their physical appearance and ability to do what they want to with their bodies. Furthermore, reflecting the interactionist model of development, physical changes affect a person's behavior, which, in turn, can modify the actions the individual takes to slow or modify those changes. As people experience mobility changes, for example, they may exercise less often, only making it more difficult to engage in the exercise that can benefit their overall physical functioning.

In accordance with the interactionist model, you will find that there are behaviors people can engage in to prevent many age-related changes, or at least substantially slow them down. If you adopt these changes now, you can grow older more successfully, regardless of your current age. Physical activity isn't always the remedy for age-related changes, but it certainly goes a long way toward minimizing their effects. Both of us follow our own advice and work out at the local gym at least four times a week, or more if possible. This choice is one that research continues to support. If you're not doing so already, we hope this book will inspire you to consider incorporating exercise into your own daily routine.

In keeping with the biopsychosocial perspective, physical changes reflect the influence of social factors, including social class, race, gender, and income. These social factors, in turn, affect how people interpret changes in their physical functioning. For example, women in Western culture are socialized to care more about their appearance than are men. This means that women are more likely to feel negatively about themselves as they lose their so-called youthful "beauty." However, women may also be more likely to take measures to maintain their appearance, such as wearing face makeup with sunscreen, which has the added benefit of preventing harmful exposure to the environment.

Physical changes also interact with identity in important ways throughout adulthood. This adds the "psych" to the biopsychosocial model as applied to aging of the body. The way that people interpret age-related changes in their physical functioning can have significant influences on their sense of self.

APPEARANCE

When you think about which physical features are the most telling about the aging process, wrinkles and gray hair are probably the first changes to come to mind. Because people so commonly judge others by their appearance, even if

not consciously, many adults regard these as the most important aspects of the changes that occur as they get older. Although there may not be a clear-cut relationship between observable and unobservable changes in the body, some researchers believe that the appearance you project to others could contain clues to the actual state of your health (Christoffersen & Tybjaerg-Hansen, 2016).

Skin

Skin, the largest organ in the body, is most vulnerable to a series of age-related changes that become visible as early as the 20s and continue throughout adulthood. Figure 4.1 summarizes the major age-related changes in the structures of the skin.

The first signs of aging generally appear in the 30s, and by the 50s, the skin shows distinctive marks of the passage of time. These changes are most apparent in the exposed areas of the skin, which include the face, hands, and upper arms.

The age changes that appear on the skin's surface reflect the changes that occur underneath. The outermost layer of the skin, known as the epidermis, consists of a thin covering of cells that protects the underlying tissue. Over time, and not visible to the naked eye, the epidermal skin cells lose their regular patterning.

The dermis is the middle layer of the skin, made up of connective tissue, among which reside nerve cells, glands, and the hair follicles. Over time, the connective tissue in the dermis undergoes a set of changes due to changes in the two types of protein molecules of which it is composed. Collagen undergoes cross-linking, as we described in Chapter 2, leading the skin to become more rigidified and less flexible. Elastin, a molecule that is supposed to provide flexibility, becomes less able to return to its original shape after it is stretched during a person's movements. With the changes in collagen and elastin, the skin eventually can no longer return to its original state of tension and begins to sag. At the same time, the sebaceous glands, which normally provide oils that lubricate the skin, become less active. Consequently, the skin surface becomes drier and more vulnerable to damage from being rubbed or chafed.

The subcutaneous fat layer is the bottommost layer of skin, giving the skin its opacity and smoothing the curves of the arms, legs, and face. Starting in middle adulthood, this layer starts to thin, providing less support for the layers above it, which then exacerbates the wrinkling and sagging caused by changes in the dermis. The blood vessels beneath the skin therefore become more visible.

The skin's coloring also changes over the course of adulthood, most visibly in fair-skinned people. People develop discolored areas referred to in colloquial terms

FIGURE 4.1

Age-Related Changes in the Skin

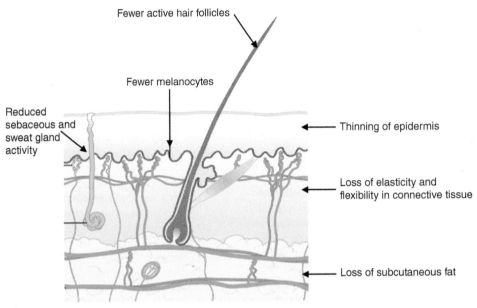

This diagram shows the major age-related changes in the structure of the skin.

as "age spots" (officially called *lentigo senilis*). These areas of brown pigmentation that show up on the skin of fair-skinned people are more likely to occur in the sun-exposed areas of the face, hands, and arms. Also developing on the skin are pigmented outgrowths (moles) and elevations of small blood vessels on the skin surface (angiomas).

Nails are a part of the skin and are also subject to age-related changes. Toenails, in particular, grow more slowly and may become yellowed, thicker, and ridged. In addition to normal age-related changes in the nails, many older adults develop fungal infections in their toenails, causing the nails to thicken and separate from the nail bed. Older adults with limited joint movement and flexibility experience more difficulty caring for their own feet and lower extremities (Mitty, 2009). Medications that older adults may be taking can also affect the hair, skin, and nails, further exacerbating changes due to the aging process.

The general changes that occur in the skin contribute to the aging of the face; however, the face's underlying structure also changes as a result of bone loss in the skull, particularly in the jaw. Changes in the cartilage of the nose and ears cause them to become longer, further altering the face's shape. The muscles of the face also lose their ability in an older adults to contract, leading to a reduction in smiling width, particularly for males (Chetan et al., 2013).

Loss of enamel surface leads the teeth to become yellow: stains accumulate from a lifetime intake of coffee and tea, certain types of food, and—for smokers—tobacco. With increasing age, many people lose their teeth, a process that affects not only their appearance but aspects of their health in general. In the United States, about 19% of all adults 65 and older have lost all their natural teeth, with the highest rates (29%) in non-Hispanic black older adults. By age 75, 26% of all older adults have experienced complete tooth loss (Dye et al., 2015). The rates are double for people in lower income brackets and those without private medical insurance. Middle-aged adults may suffer less from problems related to tooth loss than previous generations; this is due to improvements in dental hygiene in the past several decades, particularly increased rates of flossing. Nevertheless, some changes in the teeth are bound to occur, along with a rise in the associated prevalence of gum disease (Persson, 2018).

Changes in the skin also affect the appearance of the eyes, which develop bags, small lines at the creases (crows feet), areas of dark pigmentation, and puffiness. The need for eyeglasses, which increases in middle adulthood as we discuss later in this chapter, means further changes.

Genetic background plays an important role in the rate of skin aging. Fair-skinned people tend to display more rapid effects of aging than those with darker skin. Above and beyond genetic inheritance, lifestyle habits are perhaps the next greatest influence on the aging of the skin. The most significant lifestyle habit is exposure to the sun.

FIGURE 4.2

Photoaging

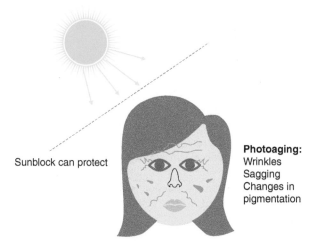

Sunblock can protect

Photoaging:
Wrinkles
Sagging
Changes in
pigmentation

Photoaging causes changes in the collagen and elastin molecules that contribute to wrinkling and sagging of the skin, as well as areas of discoloration due to changes in pigmentation.

As shown in Figure 4.2, age-related changes in the skin due to radiation from the sun are called photoaging (Maddodi et al., 2012). The sun's ultraviolet rays accelerate the process of cross-linking, causing mutations that alter protein synthesis by the cells and increasing the production of free radicals. Other harmful habits can interact with exposure to the sun, most notably cigarette smoke (Hodges & Walker, 2017).

This list of changes in the skin is daunting, indeed. Many of these changes are intrinsic to the aging process, but even these vary depending on the individual's lifestyle habits. One of the most significant habits is the use of sunscreen to protect the skin from photoaging. Because it is not possible to avoid the sun's rays completely, people who want to protect themselves from photoaging should use sunscreen with a sun protection factor (SPF) of at least 15. The sunscreen should also block both UVA and UVB light. Though most health-conscious people are aware of the importance of sunscreen, they may not realize the importance of avoiding sunburn (Centers for Disease Control and Protection, 2012).

Additional ways to prevent skin aging involve the use of products that take advantage of improved micro delivery systems for ingredients such as collagen and tretinoin, the active ingredient in retinol (Ghate et al., 2016). Even so, not all antiaging products are able to live up to their advertised promise, so it is best for consumers to do their research before buying expensive creams with no proven clinical effectiveness. The best type of moisturizer combines such active ingredients with SPF-15 and UVA/UVB protection. If used on a daily basis, a good moisturizer can help to counteract the fragility, sensitivity, and dryness of the exposed areas of skin. The addition of alpha-hydroxy acid agents to a basic moisturizer can help stimulate cell growth and renewal to offset sun damage (Tran et al., 2015).

Other antiaging treatments for the face can only be provided by a plastic surgeon or dermatologist. The most popular is the injection of botulinum toxin (Botox®). In a Botox treatment, a syringe containing a small amount of a nerve poison is injected into the area of concern, such as around the eyes or in the middle of the forehead muscle. This procedure paralyzes the muscle, relaxing the skin around it and causing a temporary reduction in the appearance of the wrinkle. Although cosmetics companies have invested heavily in finding over-the-counter alternatives, at present there are no substitutes for this procedure.

Dermatologists and plastic surgeons perform a host of other antiaging interventions: injections of artificial fillers, laser resurfacing treatments, and microdermabrasion. Increasingly, products that simulate these procedures are being introduced into the market; in the coming years, people who seek to reverse or alter the facial aging process will have a wider variety of affordable, effective, and convenient options.

Hair

You are most likely familiar with the fact that one of the most obvious changes to occur as the body ages is the graying of the hair. But what you might not realize is the fact that the hair does not, literally, turn gray. Instead, the number of pigmented (colored) hairs diminishes over time while the number of hairs that are no longer pigmented increases. Hair loses its pigment when the production of melanin, which gives hair its color, slows and eventually ceases. It is very likely that by the time a person reaches the age of 75 or 80, there are virtually no naturally colored hairs left on the scalp or other hair-covered areas of the body. There are variations in the rate at which this change takes place. You may have an older relative or friend whose hair is only slightly gray or, conversely, know people in their 20s who have a significant amount of gray hair already.

The thinning of the hair, though more visible in men, actually occurs in both sexes. In general, hair loss results from the destruction of the germination centers that produce the hair in the hair follicles. The most common form of hair loss with increased age is androgenetic alopecia, in which hair loss occurs according to a pattern, and is classified differently for men and women. This is a condition that affects 95% of adult men and 20% of adult women, to some degree. Androgenetic alopecia causes the hair follicles

Friedhelm Brandenburg/Pixabay

Graying and thinning of the hair are a common feature of physical aging in middle and later adulthood.

to stop producing the long, thick, pigmented hair known as terminal hair and instead produce short, fine, unpigmented, and largely invisible hair known as vellus hair. Eventually, even the vellus hair is not visible, because it no longer protrudes from the follicle, which itself has shrunk. Although hair stops growing on the top of the head where it is desired, it may appear in larger amounts in places where it is not welcome, such as the chin on women, the ears, and in thicker clumps around the eyebrows in men.

Pharmaceutical companies are actively working to find a solution for baldness. The multitude of products designed to stop or mask the balding process range from chemicals applied directly to the scalp, most notably topical minoxidil (Rogaine), to herbal remedies and surgically implanted hair plugs. Available by prescription only, oral finasteride (Propecia) is another alternative considered to be effective against hair loss, although it has side effects that can interfere with a man's sexual functioning (Chiriaco et al., 2016).

Although there is no "cure" for gray hair or baldness, improvements in products that stimulate hair growth and the production of melanin are probably not far off in the future.

BODY BUILD

The concept of being "grown up" implies that you are done growing and your body has reached its final, mature form. However, throughout adulthood, the body is a dynamic entity, continuously changing in size and shape. By the time people reach their 50s and 60s, their bodies may have only a passing resemblance to what they looked like when they first reached physical maturity.

The first set of changes in body build involves height. Cross-sectional and longitudinal studies convincingly show that people get shorter as they get older, a process

that is more pronounced for women. You may think of yourself as remaining for the rest of your life at the height, for example, of 5 feet 9 inches. However, the chances are good that you will lose as much as an inch of height over the coming decades. This decrease in height is due to the loss of bone material in the vertebrae. With the weakening of the vertebrae, the spine collapses and shortens in length (Kaiser et al., 2018). In one intriguing longitudinal study, however, decreases in disk height were compensated by increases in adjacent vertebra heights (Videman et al., 2014).

The body's shape also changes significantly for most people in the adult years. The body's lean tissue, or fat-free mass (FFM), decreases. Changes in body composition over adulthood are reflected in the body mass index (BMI), an index used to estimate body fat. The BMI is calculated by dividing weight (in kilograms) by height (in meters squared). According to the Centers for Disease Control and Prevention (2017), the ideal BMI is between 18.5 and 24.9. Figure 4.3 shows the chart used to illustrate BMI in relation to your weight and height. Calculate your BMI by converting your weight to kilograms (2.2 kg = 1 pound) and height into centimeters (1 cm = .40 inch).

The overall pattern of body weight in adulthood shows an upside-down U-shaped trend by age. Most people experience an increase in their weight from their 20s until their mid-50s, after which they tend to lose those added pounds. The weight gain during middle adulthood is mainly due to an increase in BMI representing the accumulation of body fat around the waist and hips (commonly referred to as the "middle-aged spread"). Unfortunately for most people, when they lose body weight in their 60s and beyond, it's not due to a loss of fat but to a loss of muscle. Furthermore, the individual's BMI when entering later life predicts loss of physical functioning and lean mass, with obese individuals showing the greatest patterns of decline (Reinders et al., 2015). Obese men had the highest risk of decline in physical function despite similar weight loss between trajectories, whereas overweight and obese women who lost the most weight had the greatest risk of lean mass loss.

At the other end of the spectrum, some older adults continue to gain weight to the point of developing a BMI that places them in the overweight or obese categories. The World Health Organization (2019) has estimated that BMIs of adult men and women increased significantly from 1975 to 2016. Even the average BMI in one of the lowest-BMI countries, Ethiopia, has increased from 17 to 21. The average BMI of Canadians increased over this period from under 25 to 27, with Americans showing a slightly larger increase from 25 to 29 (World Health Organization, 2019a).

Much of the impact of aging on body build and composition can be offset by exercise. One 12-week study

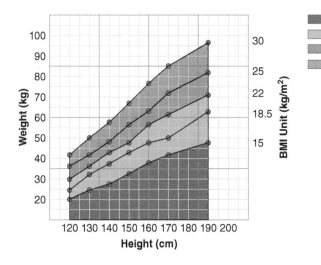

Underweight
Normal weight
Overweight
Obese

FIGURE 4.3

BMI Calculator

This chart can be used to obtain a rough calculation of BMI. Smartphone apps and online calculators are readily available to provide more precise estimates.

involving resistance training showed improvements in percent of body fat, lean mass, and quadriceps strength, although the improvements in obese older adults were less favorable than normal-weight and overweight individuals (Geirsdottir et al., 2019).

On the basis of extensive research on both short- and long-term exercise benefits, the American College of Sports Medicine and the American Heart Association (ACSM/AHA) (Garber et al., 2011) recommend specific amounts and forms of exercise for older adults, as shown in Figure 4.4.

These guidelines are meant to be adjusted for the older adult's individual needs. The ACSM/AHA states that the

intensity and duration of physical activity should be low at the outset for older adults who are functionally limited or have chronic conditions that affect their ability to perform physical tasks. It recommends that the progression of activities should be tailored to the individual and that strength and/or balance training may need to precede aerobic training until the individual has gained some strength. Even if the individual is unable to engage in the minimum amount of activity, he or she should perform some type of physical activities to avoid being sedentary. For example, older adults who have impaired balance and mobility can be given chair aerobics to perform, such as raising and lowering their arms. Individuals who have mobility problems or are frequent fallers can be given balance training that includes progressively difficult postures, dynamic movements—such as turning in circles, heel stands, toe stands—and standing with their eyes closed.

Exercise, even in small doses, can have beneficial effects not only on physiological status but also on feelings of psychological well-being. Recall our discussion at the beginning of the chapter on the interactions of aging and identity. One intriguing study provides dramatic support for this relationship. Researchers tested older adults on a measure of "social physique anxiety," the extent to which one is afraid of what other people think of one's body. Over the course of a 6-month exercise training study, older adults decreased their social physique anxiety and felt more fit. They also gained on a measure of self-efficacy, or the feeling of confidence in being able to complete physically demanding tasks (McAuley et al., 2002). In a subsequent study, both social physique anxiety and confidence about one's appearance while exercising among sedentary, moderately obese women predicted their level of involvement in physical activity (Pearson et al., 2013).

FIGURE 4.4

Recommendations for Exercise from the ACSM and AHA

Aerobic
• 150 minutes of moderate activity per week
• No less than 10 minutes for each session

Resistance
• Each major muscle group 2–3 days per week
• 2–4 sets of each exercise
• Previously sedentary should start with light intensity

This is a summary of the recommendations for type and amount of exercise from the American Heart Association and American College of Sports Medicine.

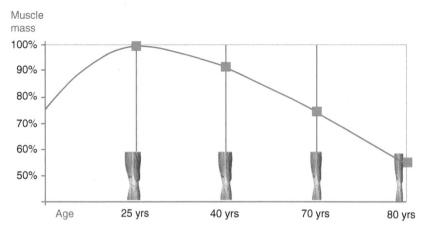

FIGURE 4.5

Sarcopenia in Relation to Age

Changes with age in muscle mass, or sarcopenia, occur gradually throughout adulthood.

MOBILITY

You are able to move around in your environment due to the actions of the structures that support this movement, including your bones, muscles, tendons, and ligaments. In the average person, all these structures undergo age-related changes that compromise the ability to function effectively.

Beginning in the 40s (or earlier in the case of injury), each component of mobility undergoes significant age-related losses. The changes in gait that occur in later adulthood include slowing, impaired balance and stability, lower extremity strength, and a fear of falling (Cruz-Jimenez, 2017). Foot problems alone affect 71% to 87% of the older adult population, leading to pain and limitations in the ability to carry out everyday activities (Rodriguez-Sanz et al., 2018). Consequently, people walk more slowly as they get older (Shumway-Cook et al., 2007), although they can make up for their slower gait by taking longer steps more frequently (Jerome et al., 2015). Barring this adaptation, older adults may find it hard to adapt to their slower walking speed, leading them to be more likely than the young to make mistakes when predicting how long it will take them to cross the street (Dommes et al., 2012). Thus, there are practical implications of these changes in mobility that can have far-reaching consequences on the older adult's life and health.

Muscles

The adult years are characterized by a progressive age-related loss of muscle mass with a consequent loss of strength, a process known as sarcopenia. The number and size of muscle fibers decrease, especially the fast-twitch muscle fibers that you use in speed and strength. As indicated by research from cross-sectional studies, muscle strength as measured by maximum force peaks in the 20s and 30s, remains at a plateau until the 40s to 50s, and then declines at a faster rate of 12% to 15% per decade (Kostka, 2005), with more pronounced decreases for men (see Figure 4.5).

In contrast to the declines in speed and strength, people retain their muscular endurance, as measured by isometric strength (Lavender & Nosaka, 2007). There are also relatively minor effects of age on eccentric strength, the action involved in activities such as lowering arm weights (such as the downward motion of a bicep curl) or going down the stairs. Eccentric strength is preserved through the 70s and 80s in men and women (Roig et al., 2010).

Changes in muscle mass strongly predict age-related reductions in strength in adulthood (Walston, 2012). The second contributor to loss of muscle strength comes from disrupted signals that the nervous system sends to the muscles telling them to contract (Clark & Fielding, 2012). Third, the tendons become stiffer, which makes it more difficult to move the joint and thus exert muscular strength (Carroll et al., 2008).

The loss of muscle mass brings with it a set of negative consequences, including increased risk of falling, limitations in mobility, and reduced quality of everyday life. Unfortunately, sarcopenia can become part of a vicious cycle: the greater the loss of muscle mass, the greater the difficulty the person experiences in undertaking exercise, leading to more muscle loss weakening (Lang et al., 2009). If sarcopenia occurs in the presence of gains in fat, a condition known as sarcopenic obesity may develop, in which the individual both loses muscle and gains body fat (Tyrovolas et al., 2016).

Strength training with free weights or resistance machines is the top preventative measure that can counteract the process of sarcopenia in adulthood (Nascimento et al., 2019). Although older adults do not achieve as high a degree of improvement as do younger adults, even a program as short as 16 weeks of resistance training can build fast-twitch muscle fiber numbers to the size of those found in the young (Negaresh et al., 2019). There seems to be no age limit on who can benefit, as adults in their 90s also show improvements in muscle strength after training (Kryger & Andersen, 2007).

Effective muscle strength training typically involves 8 to 12 weeks, three to four times per week, at 70% to 90% of the one-repetition maximum. In order for these benefits to be maintained, the individual has to keep exercising. It's not enough to exercise for a year or two and then stop. Resistance training also has added benefits for cardiovascular functioning by improving the ability of peripheral arteries to circulate blood (Parmenter, 2019).

One of the major benefits of muscle training is that the stronger the muscles become, the more pull they exert on the bones. As we will see next, loss of bone strength is an equally significant limitation on the health and well-being of older adults as is loss of muscle mass.

Bones

Bone is living tissue. It constantly reconstructs itself through a process of **bone remodeling**, in which old cells are destroyed and replaced by new cells. The general pattern of bone development in adulthood involves an increase in the rate of bone destruction compared to renewal and greater porosity of the calcium matrix, leading to loss of bone mineral content. The remodeling process that leads to these changes is controlled in part by a set of protein-like substances that act on the bone cells (Cao et al., 2005). These substances are, in turn, under the influence of the sex hormones estrogen for women

(Messier et al., 2011) and testosterone for men (Travison et al., 2009). Therefore, as people experience decreases in sex hormones, they also lose bone mineral content (Sigurdsson et al., 2006).

Estimates of the decrease in bone mineral content over adulthood are about 0.5% per year for men and 1% per year for women (Emaus et al., 2006), although the rates become higher for women in their 50s (3% to 5% per year; Ferrucci et al., 2014) (see Figure 4.6). Among women, White postmenopausal individuals show bone loss at higher rates than do their Black counterparts (Conradie et al., 2015); the reverse is true for men (Sheu et al., 2009). Further weakening occurs due to microcracks that develop in response to stress placed on the bones (Diab et al., 2006). Part of the older bone's increased susceptibility to fracture can be accounted for by a loss of collagen, which reduces the bone's flexibility in response to pressure (Saito & Marumo, 2009). The problem is particularly severe for the upper part of the thigh bone right below the hip, which does not receive much mechanical pressure during walking and therefore tends to thin disproportionately (Mayhew et al., 2005).

In addition to genetic influences on bone loss (Ralston, 2007) are the effects of lifestyle factors including mobility and weight with obese sedentary individuals showing higher rates of bone loss (Shapses & Sukumar, 2012).

As shown above, lifestyle factors influence the rate of bone loss; conversely, taking advantage of lifestyle and dietary influences on bone health can at least partially offset age-related changes in bone strength. The keys to minimizing bone loss are engaging in exercise (both aerobic and resistance), not smoking, eating sufficient

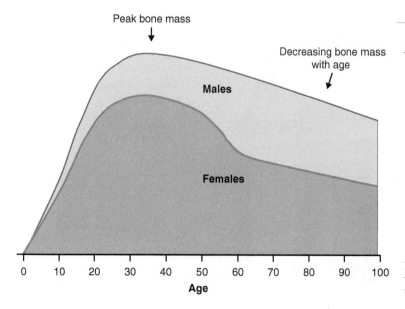

FIGURE 4.6

Bone Mineral Content in Relation to Age

Bone mass peaks in early adulthood for men and women, declining more abruptly for women due to changes associated with the menopause.

amounts of dietary protein, and ensuring adequate intake of calcium and vitamin D. Additional foods to include in the diet are sources of magnesium such as bananas, certain types of nuts, and potatoes, as well as carotenoids found in carrots, squash, and apricots (Devine et al., 2005; Dawson-Hughes & Bischoff-Ferrari, 2007; Ryder et al., 2005; Sahni et al., 2009). The key lifestyle factors are to exercise, not smoke, and maintain a BMI of approximately 25 (Wilsgaard et al., 2009). Resistance training with weights in particular can help slow the rate of bone loss (Tolomio et al., 2008). Eating high amounts of dietary protein can further stave off bone loss (Devine et al., 2005) as can increasing calcium intake prior to menopause and taking vitamin D (Dawson-Hughes & Bischoff-Ferrari, 2007). Beginning a program of resistance training prior to menopause is another important intervention that women can use to minimize bone loss after menopause (Ferrucci et al., 2016).

Environmental factors also play a role in maintaining bone health. People who live in climates with sharp demarcations between the seasons appear to be more likely to suffer from earlier onset of bone loss; for example, people living in Norway have among the highest rates of bone fracture of anyone in the world (Forsmo et al., 2005).

Not only can taking advantage of methods to reduce bone loss improve physical functioning and mobility, but there is also evidence that people with stronger bones live longer. This mortality advantage remains even after controlling for other relevant health measures, including grip strength (Hauger et al., 2018).

Joints

Although most people do not feel that they are getting "creaky" until their 40s, your joints are already undergoing significant changes even before you reach the age of skeletal maturity in late adolescence. By the 20s and 30s, the articular cartilage that protects the joints has already begun to degenerate, and as it does so, the bones start to suffer as well. The fibers in the joint capsule become less pliable, reducing flexibility even further. Within the knees, at least, these changes have a greater impact on women beginning in their 40s (Ding et al., 2007).

Unlike muscles, joints do not benefit from constant use. On the contrary, stress and repeated use cause the joints to wear out more rapidly. As they become less flexible and more painful, people find it increasingly hard to move the affected limbs, hands, and feet. As you will learn in Chapter 5, extreme joint pain and loss of mobility are associated with diseases that affect the musculoskeletal system, which become increasingly prevalent in later life.

Because joint pain is associated with overuse, individuals who wish to exercise to benefit other bodily systems must use caution (Nielson et al., 2019). To protect the

FIGURE 4.7

Safe Workstation Guidelines from the U.S. Occupational Safety and Health Administration

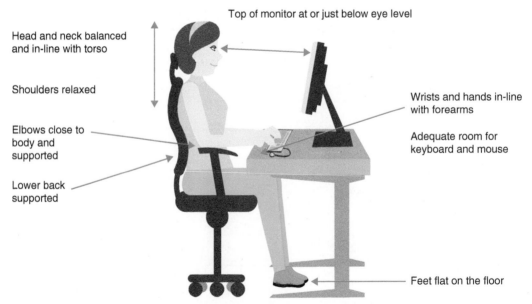

Proper workstation equipment can help offset age-related changes in the joints to preserve mobility.

joints and take advantage of benefits of exercise on other bodily systems, it is best to work on strengthening the muscles that support the joints and increasing the flexibility of the tendons and ligaments that allow the joints to move more comfortably (Reeves et al., 2006). Because the increased weight associated with obesity contributes to joint pain and stiffness and loss of cartilage volume (Teichtahl et al., 2009), an exercise program should also focus on lowering body fat.

Individuals can begin to take precautions in young adulthood that will reduce the risk of developing joint pain later in life. As shown in Figure 4.7, consider repositioning your work desk so that you minimize the pressure you place on your upper limbs, back, and feet. Protecting your lower extremities, furthermore, can also allow you to experience better joint health as you age. This means wearing appropriate shoes in high-impact sports or exercise as well as, for women, opting for shoes that support your feet rather than high, spiky heels (Dufour et al., 2009).

VITAL BODILY FUNCTIONS

The major organs of the body that keep us alive are in the cardiovascular, respiratory, urinary, and digestive systems.

Each of these systems undergoes age-related changes on their own. However, it is difficult to separate the systems completely due to interactions in their structures and functions that change across the adult years. At the same time, changes due to aging in each separate system can be modified by exercise, diet, lifestyle, and psychosocial factors.

Cardiovascular System

The cardiovascular system includes the heart, the arteries that circulate blood throughout the body away from the heart, and the veins that bring the blood back to the heart. The most significant changes in the cardiovascular system involve the heart muscle itself and the arteries, leaving the veins relatively spared (see Figure 4.8).

The left ventricle is the chamber in the heart that pumps the oxygenated blood out to the arteries; therefore, its performance is key to the efficiency of the entire cardiovascular system. However, due to a combination of aging of the muscle and changes in the arteries themselves, the walls of the left ventricle lose their ability to contract enough so that they can accomplish an efficient distribution of blood through the arteries (Nikitin et al., 2006). The arteries accommodate less blood flow that, in turn, further stresses the left ventricle (Otsuki et al., 2006).

FIGURE 4.8

Age Changes in the Heart

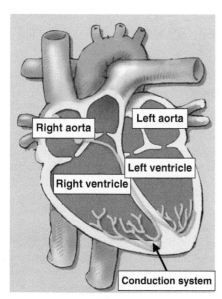
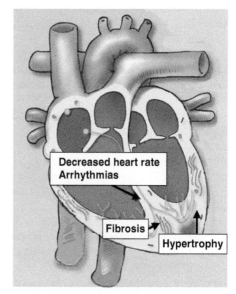

Young adult   Older adult

The structure of the heart, showing major age-related changes that affect its function across adulthood.

The reason the arteries accommodate less blood flow is that fats circulating throughout the blood eventually form hard deposits inside the arterials walls known as plaque, consisting of cholesterol, cellular waste products, calcium, and fibrin (a clotting material in the blood).

Cardiovascular efficiency is indexed by aerobic capacity, the maximum amount of oxygen that can be delivered through the blood, and cardiac output, the amount of blood that the heart pumps per minute. When viewed as an average between 20 and 70 years of age, the decline in aerobic capacity is 5% to 10% per decade. However, the overall decline is not a linear one. In the 30s and 40s, the decline amounts on average of 3% to 6% per decade, but by age 70, the rate rises to over 20% per decade. Fortunately, although the rate of decline cannot be slowed significantly, people can improve their chances of staying fit into later adulthood through high levels of physical activity earlier in life (Ades & Toth, 2005).

Middle-aged and older adults who continue to exercise at a high level of intensity do experience declines in aerobic capacity, but at a lower rate than individuals who do not exercise (Tanaka & Seals, 2003). Another health benefit shown by masters athletes is that, despite consuming more food energy than sedentary adults, they maintain lower body weight (Rosenbloom & Bahns, 2006). Indeed, masters athletes, or those who continue to engage in team and individual sports designed for older adults, maintain high physical functioning throughout their later years (Geard et al., 2017). However, it is important to be cautious in interpreting data showing the well-maintained physical functioning of masters athletes, given that only highly functioning middle-aged and older adults can continue to participate at such intense levels (Fien et al., 2017).

Short-term training studies on middle-aged and older adults show that even previously sedentary individuals can benefit from exercise training (Falck et al., 2019). Added benefits to physical functioning include improved cognitive functioning, a topic we will return to in Chapter 6 (Chodzko-Zajko et al., 2009). To be maximally effective, exercise must stimulate the heart rate to rise to 60% to 75% of maximum capacity, and this training must take place three to four times a week. People benefit from many forms of aerobic activities, including walking, hiking, jogging, bicycling, swimming, and jumping rope. However, even moderate- or low-intensity exercise can have positive effects on previously sedentary older people.

Lipid metabolism also plays an important role in regulating the functioning of the arteries. High-density lipoproteins (HDLs), or "good" cholesterol, transport lipids out of the body. Low-density lipoproteins (LDLs), or "bad" cholesterol, transport cholesterol to the arteries. Measures of an individual's cholesterol levels reflect the

For older adults with mobility limitations, exercises performed while seating can provide a healthy alternative.

ratio of HDLs and LDLs. Blood levels of triglycerides reflect the amount of fat stored in the body's cells.

Cholesterol metabolism, then, is an important component of overall cardiovascular fitness. Moderate levels of exercise can have beneficial effects on cholesterol metabolism (Walker et al., 2009). However, the greatest benefit appears in long-term endurance athletes who have maintained active lifestyle (Campbell et al., 2019). Conversely, individuals with a lifetime history of cigarette smoking are more likely to experience poor cardiovascular health as reflected by higher levels of inflammatory markers in their blood (Yilmaz & Kayancicek, 2018).

Developments in wearable technology are making it increasingly feasible for individuals to track the intensity of their workouts as well as the number of steps they take on a daily basis. As wearable technology increases in ease of use and popularity, we might hope that adults of all ages will be more motivated to engage in healthy habits, particularly exercise. In one study on focus groups of older adults regarding the use of wearable technology, participants expressed favorable attitudes although to commit to long-term use also required internal motivation and social support (Kononova et al., 2019). If you are a fan of wearable technology, you probably know from your own experience that sharing your activity records with family members or friends can boost your motivation as well.

In summary, although there are a number of deleterious cardiovascular changes associated with aging, they are by no means uniformly negative. More importantly, there are many ways that you can both prevent and compensate for these changes. With regard to aerobic functioning, exercise is one of the best ways you can slow down the rate of your body's aging process.

Respiratory System

The function of the respiratory system is to bring oxygen into the body and move carbon dioxide out. The respiratory system accomplishes these goals through the mechanical process of breathing, a process that involves several structures, including the diaphragm and the muscles of the chest wall. The exchange of gases takes place within the innermost reaches of airways in the lungs, in the tiny air sacs known as the alveoli.

Aging affects all components of the respiratory system. The respiratory muscles lose the ability to expand and contract the chest wall, and the lung tissue itself is less able to expand and contract during inspiration (Adachi et al., 2015). Consequently, starting at about age 40, all measures of lung functioning in adulthood tend to show age-related losses. These losses are more severe in women (Harms & Rosenkranz, 2008). Unfortunately, changes in the respiratory system can lead to breathing difficulties under duress, potentially limiting older adults' ability to maintain an exercise regimen (Roman & Rossiter, 2016).

Overall, the normal age-related changes contribute to the measure of lung age, which is a mathematical function showing how old your lung is based on a combination of your age and a measure obtained from a spirometer called forced expiratory volume. By calculating lung age, individuals can determine how much they are placing themselves at risk by engaging in behaviors such as smoking that are known to compromise respiratory function.

People who want to minimize the effects of aging on the lungs have two main strategies they can follow. The first may be the most obvious—to stay away from or quit smoking cigarettes. People who smoke lose more forced expiratory volume in later adulthood than those who do not (Yohannes & Tampubolon, 2014). Although it is better to quit smoking than continue smoking, there are unfortunately deleterious changes in the body's cells that remain for at least several decades after a person has quit smoking (Masayesva et al., 2006).

Exercise is the second strategy to minimize the effect of aging on the respiratory system. By strengthening the muscles of the chest wall, individuals can improve the ability of the lungs to expand and contract while breathing (Abrahin et al., 2014).

Urinary System

The function of the urinary system is to excrete waste from the body through the urine. The urinary system is made up of the kidneys, bladder, ureters, and urethra. The kidneys are composed of nephrons, cells that serve as millions of tiny filters that cleanse the blood of metabolic waste (see Figure 4.9). These waste products combine in the bladder

FIGURE 4.9

Aging of the Kidneys

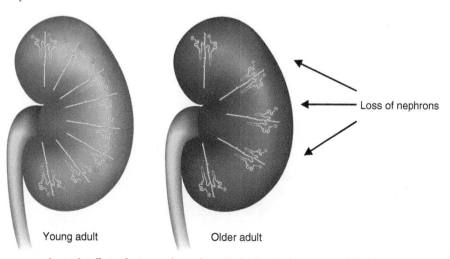

Young adult   Older adult

Loss of nephrons

Changes in the kidneys occur due to the effects of aging on the nephron, the basic unit of structure and function.

with excess water from the blood and are eliminated as urine through the urethra.

Various structures in the kidney undergo age-related changes in adulthood, leading to a lowering in the rate at which wastes are filtered through the nephrons (Bitzer & Wiggins, 2016), a change in blood flow through the kidneys, and a decrease in the ability to raise and lower the urine's concentration (Karam & Tuazon, 2013). The functional reserve of the kidney can become compromised, even in healthy older adults, leading to less effective responses to stress placed on the kidneys through illness, exertion, or extreme heat (Esposito et al., 2007). Health care professionals working with older adults must take care to factor normal age-related changes in the kidney when calculating prescription dosages, particularly for antianxiety medications, anticoagulants, and antibiotics (Guerville et al., 2019).

Changes with aging may also occur in the elastic tissue of the bladder, making it no longer capable of efficiently retaining or expelling urine. Even though the bladder does not become smaller with age, older adults also experience slight changes in the perception that they need to urinate (Pfisterer et al., 2006). Adding to intrinsic changes in the bladder that lower the rate of urinary flow in men is the fact that many men experience hypertrophy (enlargement) of the prostate, a gland located on top of the bladder. This puts pressure on the bladder and can lead men to feel frequent urges to urinate.

Approximately 30% of all adults 65 and older suffer from urge incontinence, a form of urinary incontinence in which the individual experiences a sudden need to urinate and may even leak urine. In stress incontinence, the individual is unable to retain urine while engaging in some form of physical exertion. According to one estimate (Anger et al., 2006), the prevalence of daily incontinence ranges from 12% in women 60 to 64 years old to 21% in women 85 years old or older. Of all women reporting incontinence, 14% experience it on a daily basis and 10% on a weekly basis. The experience of incontinence in women is linked to poorer health, decreased mobility, current use of hormone replacement therapy, being overweight, history of falls, and heart disease (Bresee et al., 2014). A condition related to urge incontinence is overactive bladder; in addition to incontinence, symptoms include a need to urinate more frequently than normal. Epidemiologists estimate that overactive bladder affects nearly 30 million adults aged 40 and older in the United States (Coyne et al., 2011).

It is important to remember that, despite the distressing nature of urinary incontinence and related conditions, the large majority of older adults are symptom free. Those who do have overactive bladder and incontinence, however, are likely to experience a number of associated psychological problems, including symptoms of depression, difficulty sleeping, and various forms of sexual dysfunction. These individuals are also likely to experience embarrassment, shame, and concern over having an accident. Misunderstanding the causes of the bladder dysfunction, some may blame themselves for their difficulties (Kinsey et al., 2016).

A variety of treatments are available to counteract incontinence; however, because people often mistakenly assume that bladder dysfunction is a normal part of aging, they are less likely to seek active treatment. In one study of more than 7.2 million patients diagnosed with overactive bladder, 76% went untreated (Helfand et al., 2009).

Yolya Ilyasova/Shutterstock.com

Kegel exercises, or pelvic floor muscle training, can help compensate for or even prevent urinary incontinence.

Treatment of overactive bladder and incontinence typically involves a combination of medication, exercise, and behavioral control. The first-line treatment involves behavioral controls, such as monitoring fluid intake, maintaining regular schedules for emptying the bladder, and pelvic floor ("Kegel") exercises in which the individual strengthens the urinary sphincters by contracting and relaxing them several times per day (Felicissimo et al., 2010). Behavioral treatment in which individuals learn to use these schedules and perform Kegel exercises can be administered individually or in group format (Diokno et al., 2018). Additionally, physicians may prescribe medications that reduce bladder contractions via the nervous system, preferably in conjunction with behavioral treatment (Jayarajan & Radomski, 2013).

Digestive System

The digestive system is responsible for extracting nutrients out of food and eliminating as solid waste the undigested products. Digestion begins with the secretion of saliva by the salivary glands in the mouth. Aging is associated with decrease in saliva production (Elliason et al., 2006), which can result in less efficient processing of food as it prepares for the next phases of digestion. Furthermore, loss in the ability of the lower jaw to move while chewing can lead to difficulties in eating food that is hard in texture (Wada et al., 2019). Changes in the esophagus include lowering of its effectiveness in contracting and expanding as it moves food down into the stomach (Cock & Omari, 2018). Within the stomach, fewer gastric juices are secreted, and its digestive products leave more slowly than in younger adults (O'Donovan et al., 2005). The consequence of these changes in the gastrointestinal tract can have the combined effect of leading older adults to become malnourished (Remond et al., 2015).

Fecal incontinence affects only 4% of the over-65 population (Alameel et al., 2010). Though relatively rare, then, it is troubling when it occurs, described as "trying to control the daily life that is out of control" (Olsson & Berterö, 2014, p. 141). As is true with urinary incontinence, training in behavioral controls can help to manage the condition (Byrne et al., 2007). Increasing the amount of fiber in the diet can, however, help older adults maintain bowel regularity and prevent incontinence (Markland et al., 2009).

Physiology is not the only determinant that regulates how well a person's digestive system functions in later life. Many lifestyle factors that change in middle and later adulthood contribute to overall digestive health. For example, families typically become smaller as children move out of the home, financial resources may decrease when people retire, and age-related mobility and cognitive problems can make cooking a more difficult task for the older adult to manage. As a result, the older adult may be less motivated to eat, or to eat a healthy diet. To offset these effects, older adults can maintain their digestive health by eating a diet that includes a balance among foods containing protein, complex carbohydrates, and fats.

BODILY CONTROL SYSTEMS

Each of the organ systems we have discussed so far plays a crucial role in a person's daily physical and mental well-being; however, for these systems to work properly, their functioning must be coordinated. This is the job of the endocrine and immune systems. Together, these systems have important roles in a variety of areas related to health and quality of life.

Endocrine System

The endocrine system is a large and diverse set of glands that regulate the actions of the body's organ systems (referred to as "target" organs). Hormones are the chemical messengers produced by the endocrine systems (see Figure 4.10). The hormones ultimately reach the target organs where they regulate their activity.

Changes with age in the endocrine system can occur at many levels. Because there are so many complex regulatory pathways, changes in one can have numerous effects on others. For example, the endocrine glands themselves may release more or less of a particular hormone. The target organs may also respond differently to stimulation from the hormones. Complicating matters is the fact that the endocrine system is highly sensitive to levels of stress and physical illness. These outside factors can further disturb whatever intrinsic changes would normally occur due to aging.

The hypothalamus and anterior (front) section of the pituitary gland, located deep within the base of the brain, are the main control centers of the endocrine system. Hypothalamus-releasing factors (HRFs), hormones produced by the hypothalamus, regulate the secretion of hormones in turn produced by the anterior pituitary gland. HRFs are not the only source of stimulation for pituitary hormones, however. The pituitary hormones also respond to signals from target organs carried through the blood, indicating that more pituitary hormones are needed. The HRFs then stimulate greater hormone production by these endocrine glands. Because the hypothalamus is also a part of the nervous system and thus a neuroendocrine structure, it also may release HRFs in response to information sent from other parts of the nervous system.

FIGURE 4.10

Overview of the Endocrine System

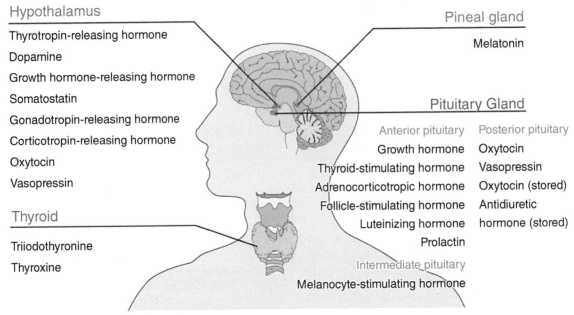

The endocrine system includes a complex set of structures that produce hormones via feedback loops involving the body's organs.

Six hormones are produced by the anterior pituitary: growth hormone (GH, also called somatotropin), thyroid-stimulating hormone (TSH), adrenocorticotropic hormone (ACTH), follicle-stimulating hormone (FSH), luteinizing hormone (LH), and prolactin. Each of these hormones acts on specific target cells within the body and some (such as TSH) stimulate the production of other hormones. Next we focus on the GH and TSH as they relate to the aging process.

Growth Hormone (GH). In youth, GH stimulates the growth of bones and muscles and regulates the growth of most internal organs. Throughout life, GH affects the metabolism of proteins, lipids, and carbohydrates. A related hormone produced by the liver, IGF-I (insulin-like growth factor-1), stimulates muscle cells to increase in size and number.

Together, GH and IGF-1 are called the somatotrophic axis (GH and IGF-1). A decline in their activity, called **somatopause of aging**, is thought to account for a number of age-related changes in body composition across adulthood, including loss of bone mineral content, increases in fat, and decreases in muscle mass as well as losses in strength, exercise tolerance, and quality of life in general (Lombardi et al., 2005). There are also age differences in the activity of GH. In young people, GH production

shows regularly timed peaks during nighttime sleep; in older adults, this peak is smaller, a pattern that may contribute to changes in sleep (Espiritu, 2008), a topic we will discuss shortly. GH also rises during exercise, but in adults aged 60 and older this response is attenuated (Weltman et al., 2006).

Given the importance of GH to so many basic processes affected by aging, GH replacement therapy (also called hGH replacement therapy) has been increasingly viewed by some as an antidote to reverse or at least slow the effects of the aging process. Although GH treatment increases lean and reduces fatty mass, there is no evidence that it has positive effects on muscle strength and performance or overall quality of life (Sattler, 2013). Ironically, despite the fact that GH replacement therapy has no proven impact on athletic performance (Hermansen et al., 2017), some professional athletes put their careers at risk to give them what they believe will be a competitive edge.

In addition to its lack of proven effects, many questions remain about the practicality of GH alone or GH in combination with testosterone as a way to counter the effects of aging. In addition to being extremely expensive (US $12,000 to $60,000 per year), there is insufficient evidence on long-term use to justify its continued administration to older adults (Samaras et al., 2014). These side effects include joint pain, enlargement of the heart, enlargement of the bones, diabetes, high blood pressure, and heart failure. Alternative treatments are currently being explored that do not carry GH's risks and expense. There is some evidence that supplements containing soy isoflavone could have the potential to remediate the symptoms of somatopause (Ajdzanovic et al., 2018).

Cortisol. We turn next to cortisol, the hormone produced by the adrenal gland. Cortisol serves the function of energizing the body, making it ready to react to a stressful encounter. Given that cortisol provides energy to the muscles to prepare them for action, researchers regard it as the "stress hormone."

The idea that aging causes dangerous increases in cortisol levels is known as the glucocorticoid cascade hypothesis (Angelucci, 2000). According to this view, increased cortisol levels accelerate neuronal loss in the hippocampus. Repeated (cascading) increases in cortisol over the lifetime lead to further degeneration. Unfortunately the increase in cortisol negatively affects memory and other forms of cognitive functioning in older adults (Comijs et al., 2010). These findings are called into question by a fascinating study in which older and younger adults were compared in the relationship between hippocampal volume and cortisol levels under differing conditions of environmental stress. It was only when the testing conditions were made to be stressful based on the individual's age group that the relationship appeared (Sindi et al., 2014).

Thyroid Hormones. Hormones produced by the thyroid gland control the rate of metabolism also known as the basal metabolic rate or BMR. Beginning in midlife, the BMR begins to slow, increasing the chances of weight gain even when an individual's caloric intake remains the same. Changes in BMR are at least in part related to age-related decreases in thyroid hormones over adulthood (Meunier

et al., 2005). Subclinical hypothyroidism can affect as many as 15% to 18% of adults over the age of 60 (Diez & Iglesias, 2004) and can progress to clinical levels in approximately half of those affected (Diez & Iglesias, 2009).

Melatonin. Sleep–wake cycles are controlled in part by melatonin, the hormone manufactured by the pineal gland, located deep within the brainstem. Circadian rhythm, the daily variations in various bodily functions, is therefore affected by this hormone (see Figure 4.11). Significant changes in circadian rhythm that occur throughout middle and later adulthood appear to correspond to the timing of peak melatonin production throughout the day (Scholtens et al., 2016).

A segment of the research community believes that melatonin supplements can reduce the effects of aging and age-associated diseases, especially in the brain and immune system. Melatonin supplements can help to offset the natural alterations in this hormone and may even have beneficial effects on other bodily systems, including cardiovascular diseases (Favero et al., 2017). However, melatonin use can produce significant side effects, including confusion, drowsiness, headaches, and constriction of blood vessels, posing a danger to people with high blood pressure. Furthermore, melatonin supplements can interfere with sleep cycles if taken at the wrong time of day. If older adults nevertheless wish to take melatonin supplements, they are advised to take amounts as small as possible to mimic normal physiological circadian rhythms (Vural et al., 2014).

DHEA. The most abundant steroid in the human body, dehydroepiandrosterone (DHEA), is a weak male steroid (androgen) produced by the adrenal glands. DHEA is a precursor to the male and female sex hormones and is believed to have a variety of functions, such as increasing the production of other sex steroids and the availability

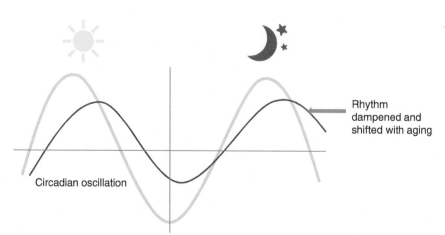

Circadian oscillation

Rhythm dampened and shifted with aging

FIGURE 4.11

Shifts in Circadian Rhythms with Age

Changes in circadian rhythms occur due to alterations in the hormone melatonin, released by the pineal gland.

of IGF-1 as well as positively influencing some central nervous system functions.

DHEA, which is higher in males than females, shows a pronounced decrease over the adult years, decreasing by 60% between the ages of 20 and 80 (Feldman et al., 2002). This phenomenon, termed adrenopause, is greater in men, although men continue to have higher levels than women throughout later life because they start at a higher baseline.

Although there are no definitive answers about DHEA's role in aging, DHEA replacement therapy rivals GH and melatonin in the antiaging industry. However, like GH therapy, DHEA use presents notable health risks, mainly liver problems and an increase in risk of prostate cancer (Arnold et al., 2007). A natural substitute for some of the positive effects of DHEA replacement therapy is exercise, which can help to compensate for its loss in the later adult years, at least in men (Al-Turk & Al-Dujaili, 2016).

Female Hormonal Changes. Technically speaking, menopause is the point in a woman's life when menstruation stops permanently. As used in common speech, however, menopause has come to mean a phase in middle adulthood covering the years in which a woman's reproductive capacity diminishes. The more precise term for this gradual winding down of reproductive ability is climacteric, a term that applies to men as well. For women, the climacteric occurs over a 3- to 5-year span called perimenopause, which ends in menopause when the woman has not had her menstrual period for 1 year. The average age of menopause is 50 years, but the timing varies among individuals. Menopause occurs earlier in women who are thin or malnourished or who smoke.

Throughout perimenopause, there is a diminution in the production by the ovarian follicles of estrogen, the primary female sex hormone. Because the other female hormone, progesterone, is produced in response to ovulation, progesterone levels also decline during this time. The process of estrogen decline begins about 10 to 15 years before menopause, at some point in the mid-30s. By the mid-40s, the ovaries have begun to function less effectively and produce fewer hormones. Eventually, menstrual cycles by the early to middle 50s have ended altogether. There is still some production of estrogen, however, as the ovaries continue to produce small amounts and the adrenal glands stimulate the production of estrogen in fat tissue. FSH and LH levels rise dramatically during the perimenopausal period, as the anterior pituitary sends out signals to produce more ovarian hormones. In turn, the hypothalamus produces less gonadotropin-releasing factor (GnRH).

Although women vary considerably in their progression through the menopause (as they also do during puberty), there are certain characteristic symptoms, many of which you have probably heard discussed by middle-aged and older women. One of the most prominent symptoms is the occurrence of "hot flashes," which are sudden sensations of intense heat and sweating that can last from a few moments to half an hour. These are the result of decreases in estrogen levels, which cause the endocrine system to release higher amounts of other hormones that affect the temperature control centers in the brain. Fatigue, headaches, night sweats, and insomnia are other physiological symptoms that result from fluctuating estrogen levels. Menopausal women also report that they experience psychological symptoms such as irritability, mood swings, depression, memory loss, and difficulty concentrating; however, the evidence regarding the connection between these symptoms and the physiological changes involved in menopause is far from conclusive.

Along with hormonal changes, menopause is associated with alterations in the reproductive tract. Because of lower estrogen levels, there is a reduction in the supply of blood to the vagina and surrounding nerves and glands. The tissues become thinner, drier, and less able to produce secretions to lubricate before and during intercourse. The result is the possibility of discomfort during intercourse (da Silva Lara et al., 2009). Sexual functioning can also be affected by negative societal attitudes toward menopause (Heidari et al., 2019).

The impact of decreasing estrogen levels also includes effects on other bodily systems. Weaker bones, high blood pressure, and cardiovascular disease become more prevalent among postmenopausal women. Estrogen appears to provide protection against these diseases, but is lost at menopause. There are also deleterious changes in cholesterol levels in the blood associated with menopause, causing postmenopausal women to be at higher risk of atherosclerosis and associated conditions.

Estrogen replacement therapy (ERT) was introduced in the 1940s to counteract the negative effects of estrogen loss on postmenopausal women. Later, estrogen was combined with the hormone progestin to reduce cancer risk. Administration of both hormones is referred to as hormone replacement therapy (HRT).

Initial studies on HRT's effects on the body provided enthusiastic support, citing positive impact on skin tone and appearance, bone mineral density, immune functioning, thickness of the hair, sleep quality, prevention of accidental falls, and improvements in memory and mood. However, starting in 2002, the pros and cons of HRT were hotly debated by researchers such as whether HRT increases the risk of mortality, due to its possible relationships to breast cancer and deep vein thrombosis (blood clots). In 2015, the United Kingdom's National Health Service published a nearly 300-page report extensively documenting the risks and benefits of HRT for a variety of physical and psychological symptoms associated with menopause (National Collaborating Centre for Women's and Children's Health, 2015). As is usual, women trying to decide whether to embark on HRT should consult a health professional (Stuenkel et al., 2015). In addition to determining the timing of any such intervention, it is important to consider the form of HRT, as there are differing risks for transdermal (skin) applications compared to those associated with oral ingestion.

For women not willing to experiment with HRT given the conflicting data, alternatives are available. Locally administered vaginal creams containing estrogen can help offset dryness and pain associated with intercourse (Tyagi et al., 2019). Other recommended approaches to counteract the effect of hormonal changes include exercise, quitting smoking, lowering the cholesterol in the diet, and perhaps, more enjoyably, having one alcoholic drink a day.

Male Hormonal Changes.   Although men do not experience a loss of sexual function comparable to menopause (despite what you might hear about "male menopause"), men undergo andropause, which refers to age-related declines in the male sex hormone testosterone. The decline in testosterone is equal to about 1% per year after the age of 40, a decrease in longitudinal studies conducted across cohorts (Liu et al., 2007). The term "late-onset hypogonadism" or "age-associated hypogonadism" has begun to replace the term andropause, although all three terms are currently in use.

Abnormally low levels of testosterone levels are found in 6% to 10% of men between the ages of 40 and 70, but these rates are far higher (15% to 30%) in men who are diabetic or obese (Tostain & Blanc, 2008). Testosterone supplements for aging men were long considered an unnecessary and potentially dangerous proposition. However, with greater empirical support and acceptance in the medical community, testosterone supplements are in greater use, with the stipulation that treatment is accompanied by regular medical screening (Theodoraki & Bouloux, 2009). However, evidence is still lacking on the safety of long-term testosterone supplementation (Jakiel et al., 2015), including effects on bone strength (Piot et al., 2019).

Erectile dysfunction (ED), a condition in which a man is unable to achieve an erection sustainable for intercourse, is estimated to increase with age in adulthood, from a rate of 31% among men aged 57 to 65 to 44% of those 65 and older. Compared to younger men, however, premature climax is less common in the 65 and older population (Waite et al., 2009). However, ED is related to health problems in older men, including metabolic syndrome (Lee et al., 2012).

You are no doubt familiar with the "cure" for ED, the little blue pill known as Viagra. Phosphodiesterase type 5 inhibitors, including Viagra (the technical term is sildenafil), can be effective in treating ED, as demonstrated in a randomized control trial (Schneider et al., 2011). For men with testosterone deficiency, sildenafil may be combined with testosterone supplements (Corona & Maggi, 2010). However, these treatments must be conducted under careful medical supervision. Other treatments for ED include mechanical prostheses and implants that allow the man to experience an erection.

Based on the relationship between ED and metabolic syndrome as well as hypertension, diabetes, and obesity (Chitaley et al., 2009), however, a safer alternative, at least as an initial approach, would be to adopt a healthier diet (Esposito et al., 2010) and to exercise more frequently to reduce these conditions (Lamina et al., 2009).

Immune System

Regulating the body's ability to fight off stress, infection, and other threats to well-being and health is the immune system. In addition to protecting the body, the immune system is closely linked to the nervous system and, consequently, to behaviors, thoughts, and emotions (Lupien et al., 2009).

The two primary types of immune cells found in the blood are "T cells" and "B cells," both of which are involved in destroying bodily invaders known as antigens. Researchers believe that there are widespread age-related declines in immune system functioning, a process known as immune senescence. As a result of immune senescence, these cells lose their ability to perform effectively, causing older adults to be less resistant to infections (Grubeck-Loebenstein, 2010). Thus, although children are more likely to develop an influenza infection during flu season, mortality from such a disease occurs almost entirely among older adults unless the flu viruses were ones to which they were exposed as children or young adults. Conversely, other cells in the immune system show deleterious changes, including those that reflect the presence of some age-related chronic diseases (Valiathan et al., 2016).

Age-related changes in the immune system may also be affected by such factors as diet, exercise, and exposure to stress. Zinc is an important nutrient related to the functioning of the immune system, and decreases in zinc intake can therefore exacerbate immune senescence (Maywald & Rink, 2015). Similarly, deficient protein intake can lower immune functioning in older adults (Aoi, 2009). Obesity in later life can negatively alter immune functioning to accelerate deleterious changes (Garg et al., 2014), but lifetime patterns of high-intensity exercise can offset age-related declines in immune system functioning in later adulthood (Turner & Brum, 2017). Chronic stress has deleterious effects on the immune system and can therefore accelerate its rate of aging, whether experienced later in life (Gouin et al., 2008) or during early development (Dich et al., 2015). Furthermore, older adults who are clinically depressed may be more likely to experience more pronounced rates of immune senescence (Vogelzangs et al., 2014).

Previous research examining the effects of aging on the immune system may have failed to control (statistically) for the host of variables that can influence its functioning. Perhaps for this reason, studies produce differing results on how aging affects the immune system (Dorshkind et al., 2009). There may also be some protective mechanisms not completely understood at present that help maintain the immune functioning of certain healthy agers. A study of so-called "semisupercentenarians" (ages 105 to 109) suggests that resistance to immunosenescence could be an important contributor to longevity (Sizzano et al., 2018).

The many conflicting studies on aging and the immune system support the principle of interindividual variability in the aging process. This variability may reflect as much the different samples who were studied as the fact that health, diet, and exercise, not to mention biological differences, all play a role in affecting the rates at which any one individual experiences immune system changes.

NERVOUS SYSTEM

It is no exaggeration to say that the nervous system controls all behavior. The central nervous system makes it possible to monitor and then prepare responses to events in the environment, conceive and enact thoughts, and maintain connections with other bodily systems. The autonomic nervous system controls involuntary behaviors, the body's response to stress, and the actions of other organ systems that sustain life.

Central Nervous System

Early research on nervous system functioning in adulthood was based on the hypothesis that individuals progressively lose brain tissue over the life span because neurons do not have the ability to replace themselves when they die. This view is referred to as the neuronal fallout model.

The data to support the neuronal fallout model came primarily from autopsy studies in which neuroanatomists counted the number of neurons in the brains of people of different ages. These studies tended not to take into account the cause of death, the fact that brain tissue may be destroyed after death by the methods used to study it, and the possible diseases that the subjects suffered from while alive. All of these factors may have biased the results and caused an exaggerated picture of the extent to which nerve cell populations change later in life.

Neurons in the brain communicate with each other through complex networks of synapses.

Newer findings are presenting a more optimistic view of the effect of aging on the nervous system. It now seems clear that in the absence of disease, the aging brain maintains much of its structure and function. Moreover, it is possible that neurons may actually gain in both structure and function even until late in life (see Figure 4.12). The plasticity model proposes that neurons which remain alive are able to take over the function of those that die (Goh & Park, 2009). The myelination of neurons, an indication of the speed with which neurons can communicate with each other, shows decreases in some brain regions, but not in others from childhood through late life (Grydeland et al., 2019). Diet and physical exercise are important ways to maintain brain function (Murphy et al., 2014) and, consequently, cognitive functioning. Aerobic exercise in particular appears to be most beneficial in preserving and maximizing the functioning of the brain (Matta Mello Portugal et al., 2013), particularly in areas involved in attentional control and verbal memory (Bherer, 2015) (see Figure 4.12).

Researchers also propose that older adults can show neural plasticity by compensating for declines in certain brain regions by activating other areas that remain intact. According to the Hemispheric Asymmetry Reduction in OLDer adults (HAROLD) model, the brains of older adults become activated in the opposite hemisphere when the original area suffers deficits (Manenti et al., 2011). Similarly, the Posterior–Anterior Shift with Aging (PASA) model proposes that the front (anterior) of the brain in older adults becomes more responsive to make up for the lower responsiveness found in the rear (posterior) of the brain (Ansado et al., 2012).

The Compensation-Related Utilization of Neural Circuits Hypothesis (CRUNCH) model (Schneider-Garces et al., 2010) incorporates both of these models, proposing that the demands of cognitively challenging

FIGURE 4.12

Plasticity in the Aging Brain

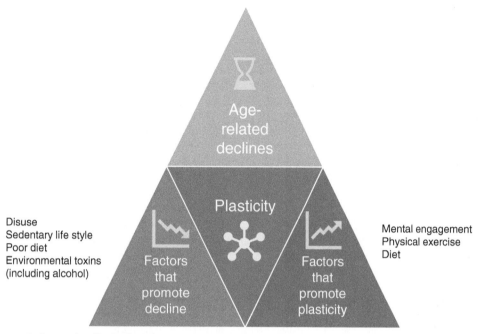

Disuse
Sedentary life style
Poor diet
Environmental toxins
(including alcohol)

Mental engagement
Physical exercise
Diet

Factors that promote decline can be offset by those that can promote plasticity across the adult years.

tasks cause an overall excitation of brain activity in older adults leading to overall patterns of compensation not limited to one particular area (Berlingeri et al., 2013).

Related to the idea of plasticity is that of brain reserve, or untapped resources primarily in the cerebral cortex (Cabeza et al., 2018). Educational, occupational, and health-promoting activities can help recruit the brain's own capacity to draw upon its additional resources to combat aging's impact (Whalley et al., 2016).

The findings to support these models are made possible by the increasing availability of brain scanning methods now being used in many laboratories that in the past were either not yet developed or, even after they were, only accessible in hospitals or major research centers. There are several types of scanning methods that can produce pictures of brain structures or activity, depending on the goal of the research.

The **electroencephalogram (EEG)** is a brain scanning method that measures electrical activity in the brain. EEG activity reflects the individual's state of consciousness and the state of the brain's arousal while the individual is asleep. The EEG pattern also shows particular patterns of brain waves when an individual engages in particular mental tasks. Clinicians use EEGs to evaluate clients for conditions such as epilepsy, sleep disorders, and brain tumors.

Computed axial tomography (CAT or CT scan) is an imaging method that clinicians and researchers use to provide an image of a cross-sectional slice of the brain from any angle or level. CT scans provide an image of the fluid-filled areas of the brain, the ventricles. The method is useful when clinicians are looking for structural damage to the brain.

Magnetic resonance imaging (MRI) is a brain imaging method that uses radio waves to construct a picture of the living brain based on the water content of various tissues. The person is placed inside a device that contains a powerful electromagnet. This causes the nuclei in hydrogen atoms to transmit electromagnetic energy (hence the term *magnetic resonance*), and the activity from thousands of angles is sent to a computer, which produces a high-resolution picture of the scanned area. The picture from the MRI differentiates areas of white matter (nerve fibers) from gray matter (nerve cells) and is useful for diagnosing diseases that affect the nerve fibers that make up the white matter.

Neither the CT scan nor the MRI can show changes in the brain when the individual is involved in a task because they both provide static images. In contrast, **functional magnetic resonance imaging (fMRI)** is a type of scan that can be used to show changes in the brain over the course of a mental activity. Researchers are increasingly using fMRIs to understand the brain areas involved in the processing of information, giving an "inside look" at age differences in cognition.

Diffuse tensor imaging is a brain scanning method that reveals the structure and integrity of white matter. It therefore is used to show the quality of connections among brain regions. Two other scans show brain activity but require injections of radioactively labeled compounds into the blood. Positron emission tomography (PET) scan and single-photon emission computed tomography (SPECT) detect these radioactive compounds as they pass through the brain. The images they provide show blood flow, oxygen or glucose metabolism, and concentrations of brain chemicals. Vibrant colors at the red end of the spectrum represent higher levels of activity, and colors at the blue-green-violet end of the spectrum represent lower levels of brain activity.

Using these scanning techniques, researchers have accumulated a rapidly growing body of evidence about how aging affects the normal brain. The areas most affected include the prefrontal cortex, the area of the brain most involved in planning and the encoding of information into long-term memory, and the temporal cortex, which is involved in auditory processing (Fjell et al., 2009). The hippocampus, the structure in the brain responsible for consolidating memories, becomes smaller across adulthood (Fraser et al., 2015).

Aging is also associated with changes in the frontal lobe in the form of abnormalities known as white matter hyperintensities (WMHs). These abnormalities, which appear at first as abnormalities on DTIs (Pelletier et al., 2015), are thought to be made up of parts of deteriorating neurons. Their presence appears to be related to the extent of brain atrophy and some measures of cognitive functioning (Habes et al., 2016), but their exact roles in normal aging and disease are as yet unclear.

Sleep

The literature on sleep in adulthood clearly refutes a common myth about aging, namely, that as people grow older they need less sleep. Regardless of age, everyone requires 7 to 9 hours of sleep a night (Ancoli-Israel & Cooke, 2009). There is evidence that, for women, longer sleep durations are correlated with increased risk of stroke (Wassertheil-Smoller et al., 2014). Middle-aged and older adults who experience changes in sleep-related behavior and sleep problems can suffer adverse effects on their mental and physical well-being (Hausler et al., 2019). Unfortunately, sleep problems seem to affect up to half of all older adults (Neikrug & Ancoli-Israel, 2009). Changes in circadian rhythms seem to be important in creating these

changed sleep patterns, as shown in Figure 4.11, which compares melatonin release and core body temperature in older adults, both of which are involved in regulation of sleep cycles.

Sleep problems in middle and later life relate in part to lifestyle as well as physiology. You almost certainly know from your own experience that your sleep is more disrupted when you are experiencing periods of stress. For instance, middle-aged adults who live with high degrees of job-related stress suffer sleep disturbances. Other lifestyle factors also play an important role, including obesity, physical inactivity, and alcohol use (Janson et al., 2001).

Whatever the cause, we know that older adults spend more time in bed relative to time spent asleep. They take longer to fall asleep, awaken more often during the night, lie in bed longer before rising, and have sleep that is shallower, more fragmented, and less efficient (Fetveit, 2009). Their sleep patterns on an EEG show some corresponding age alterations, including a rise in Stage 1 sleep and a large decrease in both Stage 4 and REM (rapid-eye movement) sleep (Kamel & Gammack, 2006). These changes occur even for people who are in excellent health.

At some point during middle to late adulthood, people also shift from a preference to working in the later hours of the day and night to a preference for the morning. Adults over 65 tend to classify themselves as "morning" people, while the large majority of younger adults classify themselves as "evening" people (Hasher et al., 2005). The biological basis for this shift in preferences presumably occurs gradually throughout adulthood, along with changes in hormonal contributors to sleep and arousal patterns. As can be seen from Figure 4.11, the circadian rhythms of older adults are shifted so that they are slightly earlier than are those of young adults relative to clock time. In general, older adults have higher rates of sleep–wake disorders than do younger adults and they are less able to adjust their sleep patterns to such conditions as jet lag and shift work (Duffy et al., 2015).

One intriguing implication of the changes in circadian rhythm with age is the possible confound that time of day presents in studies of aging and cognitive functioning. Older adults tested at their nonoptimal hours (such as late afternoon) are more disproportionately affected than are young adults (Rowe et al., 2009). This can result in a systematic bias that exaggerates the extent of age differences in performance. However, the effect of time of day on memory performance is less pronounced among older adults who engage in regular patterns of physical activity compared with their sedentary peers (Bugg et al., 2006).

There are concrete steps older adults can take to offset age-related changes in sleep patterns. The first is to make changes in sleep-related behaviors and adopt healthy sleep habits (Schroeck et al., 2016). Exercising (early in the day) can help both to promote healthy sleep and offset other effects of a sedentary lifestyle on physical functioning. Another behavior that can interfere with sleep is napping during the day. Older adults who have difficulty sleeping at night therefore need to cut down on daytime naps until they can reestablish regular nighttime schedules.

Older individuals should also avoid reading late at night on their mobile devices or e-readers as bright light can interfere with circadian rhythms (Chinoy et al., 2018). Because psychological disorders can interfere with sleep in middle-aged and older adults, psychological interventions that promote mental health can have additional benefits on sleep (Kim et al., 2009).

A number of changes in other systems can interfere with the sleep of older adults. These include normal age-related changes in the bladder that lead to a more frequent urge to urinate during the night. As a result of these changes, the individual is likely to experience sleep disruptions. It is also possible that age-related changes in circadian rhythms create a vicious cycle in that urine production may itself undergo alterations in timing throughout the night (Duffy et al., 2016). Menopausal symptoms can also lead to frequent awakenings during the night (Chedraui et al., 2010). Periodic leg movements during sleep (also called nocturnal myoclonus) are another source of nighttime awakenings (Ferri et al., 2009).

The sleep of older adults can also be interfered with by sleep apnea, a disorder in which the individual becomes temporarily unable to breathe while asleep. People who suffer from this condition typically let out a loud snore followed by silence due to the closing of the airway. The respiratory control centers in the brain respond to the lack of oxygen, and the sleeper awakens. The periods of snoring and choking may occur as many as 100 times a night. To make up for the lack of oxygen that occurs during each episode, the person's heart is forced to pump harder to circulate more blood. As a result, the person experiences large spikes in blood pressure during the night and elevated blood pressure during the day. Over time, the person's risk of heart attack and stroke is increased.

Sleep apnea is more common in older adults with chronic diseases such as chronic respiratory diseases, heart disease, and diabetes (Okuro & Morimotu, 2014). The condition can be treated with a continuous positive airway pressure (CPAP) device, which keeps airways open during sleep; however, users often complain that the burdensome equipment inhibits sleep patterns.

Although changes in sleep occur as a normal feature of the aging process, severe sleep disturbances do not. Exercise can help in improving disturbed circadian rhythms (Benloucif et al., 2004). Sleep specialists can offer innovative approaches such as light therapy, which "resets" an out-of-phase circadian rhythm, and encouragement of improvements in sleep habits (Klerman et al., 2001). Additionally, with the greater availability and accuracy of fitness monitors, adults of all ages can benefit from tracking and improving their sleep patterns.

Temperature Control

Every summer or winter, when regions of the country suffer extreme weather, older adults are among those reported to be at greatest risk of dying from hyper- or hypothermia, conditions known together as dysthermia. Between 2015 and 2017, deaths due to hypothermia increased for all age groups, in both rural and urban settings in the United States. The greatest increase was reported for those 85 and older living in rural areas (7.3 per 100,000 in 2017), which was greater than the rates for the same age group in urban areas (3.8 per 100,000) (Centers for Disease Control and Prevention, 2019a). Heat-related deaths are lower, even in the oldest age groups (1.3 per 100,000). Perhaps reflecting the lack of resources to cope with extreme temperatures, such as air-conditioning, weather-related death rates are higher in counties with lower median incomes than in wealthier counties (Berko et al., 2014).

Physiologically, the cause of the higher death rates under conditions of hypothermia may be an impaired control of the sympathetic nervous system to constrict the blood vessels in the skin in response to cold environmental temperatures (Greaney et al., 2015).

In less extreme conditions, older adults are less able to adjust their internal bodily temperature. This is because their sweat output is reduced, causing their core temperatures to rise (Dufour & Candas, 2007). Adding to this is the fact that the dermal layer of the skin becomes thinner, making it more difficult to cool the skin (Petrofsky et al., 2009).

SENSATION AND PERCEPTION

A variety of changes occur in adulthood throughout the parts of the nervous system that affect sensation and perception.

Vision

You may associate growing older with the need to wear reading glasses, and in fact, this is what occurs. Most people require some form of corrective lenses by the time they reach their 50s or 60s.

Presbyopia is the loss of ability of the lens to focus on objects that are close to the viewer and therefore is the primary culprit for the need for reading glasses. Presbyopia is caused by changes in the proteins within the lens leading to the thickening and hardening of the lens, which is the focusing mechanism of the eye (Lampi et al., 2014). By the age of 50, presbyopia affects the entire population.

There is no cure for presbyopia. Bifocals had been the only correction available since the time of Benjamin Franklin (who invented them). Although several alternatives to bifocals are available, none at present provide an ideal solution (Wolffsohn et al., 2019).

Though you cannot cure presbyopia, you may be able to alter its onset; lifestyle habits seem to affect the rate at which the presbyopic aging process occurs. For example, smoking accelerates the aging of the lens (Kessel et al., 2006). Additionally, blue-blocking lenses can help promote eye health, including offsetting changes due to presbyopia (Downes, 2016).

Older adults are also likely to experience the loss of visual acuity, or the ability to see details at a distance. The level of acuity in an 85-year-old individual is approximately 80% less than that of a person in his or her 40s. Turning up the lights is one effective strategy to compensate for loss of acuity, but at the same time, older adults are more sensitive to glare. For example, older drivers are more vulnerable to the glare caused by the lights of oncoming traffic on a dark road at night or the light of the setting sun shining directly on the windshield. As a result, making lights brighter may actually impair rather than improve an older person's visual acuity.

In addition to experiencing normal age-related changes in vision, older people become increasingly vulnerable to visual disorders. In fact, about 50 percent of adults over the age of 65 years report that they have experienced some form of visual impairment. The most common impairment and the main form of eye disease is a cataract, a clouding or opacity in the lens. This results in blurred or distorted vision because the retina cannot clearly focus the images. The term "cataract" reflects a previous view of this condition as a "waterfall" behind the eye that obscured vision.

Cataracts affect about 17% of the over-40 population (Congdon et al., 2004). There are variations by race in cataract prevalence with highest rates in Whites (18.10%) and lowest in Hispanics (11.8%) (see Figure 4.13).

Cataracts start as a gradual cloudiness that progressively grows more opaque and bothersome. Although they are most often white, cataracts may also appear to be yellow or brownish in color. If the cataracts have a yellow or brown tone, colors will take on a yellow tinge similar to the effect of wearing colored sunglasses. Cataracts appear to develop as a normal part of the aging process, but other than the changes that occur in the lens fibers, their cause is not known. A variety of health conditions can

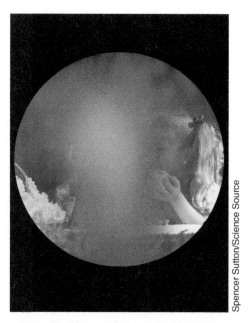

Spencer Sutton/Science Source

How the world may appear to an individual with cataracts.

affect the development of cataracts, including obesity, high blood pressure, high glucose levels, and excess blood lipids (Poh et al., 2016). On the protective side, blue-blocking lenses can further help protect against cataracts as can beta-carotene and vitamin C (Sideri et al., 2019).

As the cataract develops, the person's vision becomes increasingly impaired both under conditions of low light, as acuity is reduced, and under conditions of bright light, due to increased susceptibility to glare. Bright lights may seem to have a halo around them. These are significant limitations and can alter many aspects of the person's everyday life. It is more difficult to read, walk, watch television, recognize faces, and perform work, hobbies, and leisure activities. Consequently, people with cataracts may become more dependent on others because they cannot drive or go out at night on their own.

Fortunately, cataracts can be successfully treated with little inconvenience or pain. Enormous strides have been made in the treatment of cataracts due to advances in surgical procedures. Currently, people who undergo cataract surgery are through in an hour or less, under local anesthesia and with no hospital stay. They recover their vision within 1 to 7 days, and many people's vision is so improved that they rely only minimally on corrective lenses.

A second significant form of blindness that becomes more prevalent in later adulthood is age-related macular degeneration (ARMD), a condition caused by damage to the photoreceptors located in the central region of the retina known as the macula. This area of the retina is normally

FIGURE 4.13

Prevalence of Cataracts by Race (2010)

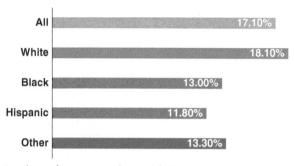

Prevalence of cataracts vary by race/ethnicity.

Source: From Cataract Data and Statistics, National Eye Institute. U.S. Department of Health & Human Service. Public domain. https://nei.nih.gov/eyedata/cataract

used in reading, driving, and other visually demanding activities so that the selective damage to the receptors in the macula that occurs is particularly incapacitating because central vision is impaired. ARMD is prevalent among increasingly older age groups of adults, affecting about 8% of adults aged 40 to 85 years; it is the fourth most common form of blindness worldwide (Jonas et al., 2017).

There are two forms of ARMD. In the "dry" form, individuals develop drusen in the macula, which are yellow deposits under the retina. In the "wet" form, blood vessels in the retina leak blood or fluid. The wet form is most likely to progress rapidly, causing a sudden loss of central vision. The majority of people with ARMD have the dry form.

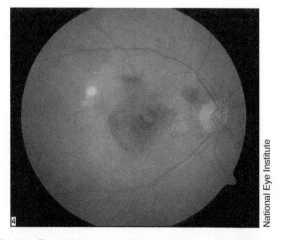

An eye affected by age-related macular degeneration, filled with abnormal blood vessels and yellow deposits called drusen. The white spot at the right is where the optic nerve leaves the eye.

Although there is no known treatment for ARMD, the measures individuals can take to prevent its development are similar to those to maintain good eye health in general, particularly including beta-carotene in the diet and wearing glasses that protect from blue and UV light.

Glaucoma is the term used for a group of conditions that lead to blindness due to destruction of the neurons leading from the retina to the optic nerve by increased pressure inside the eyeball. The most common type of glaucoma develops gradually and painlessly without symptoms. Therefore, it may not be detected until the disease reaches advanced stages. Glaucoma causes a loss of peripheral vision and, over time, may cause the remaining vision to diminish altogether. More rarely, the symptoms appear suddenly: they include blurred vision, loss of side vision, perception of colored rings around lights, and experience of pain or redness in the eyes. The causes of some form of glaucoma can be controlled but not cured, and others can be treated successfully through surgery.

The third leading cause of blindness around the world, glaucoma affects approximately 64 million adults and is expected to rise to nearly 112 million by 2040. Glaucoma is more common in men (Flaxman et al., 2017), and its prevalence is highest in Blacks and people living in urban areas (Tham et al., 2014). Glaucoma affects more than 70 million people around the world, about 10% of whom are blind in both eyes (Quigley et al., 2006). In the United States, glaucoma affects about 3 million individuals with new cases diagnosed at a rate of nearly 100,000 per year. In addition to variations by race and sex, glaucoma is higher in people who are nearsighted, have diabetes, or have a family history of glaucoma. Arthritis (Perruccio et al., 2007) and obesity (Imai et al., 2010) are additional risk factors.

Visual disturbances in older adults, whatever their cause, require the attention of health care professionals. Not only might they be treatable, but even if not, their presence can relate to psychological symptoms, including depression and isolation. Moreover, visual problems can create difficulties in other areas of functioning, such as increasing the likelihood of a person's falling or making medication errors that can have serious consequences in their own right (Pelletier et al., 2009).

Hearing

Age-related hearing loss occurs progressively through later adulthood. The most common form of age-related hearing loss is presbycusis, in which degenerative changes occur in the cochlea or auditory nerve leading from the cochlea to the brain. Presbycusis is most often associated with loss of high-pitched sounds, because the receptor cells that are triggered by high-frequency stimuli are located toward the front of the cochlea (the sensory structure responsible for hearing), the area that receives the most stimulation by noise waves in general.

Hearing loss clearly has an effect on the older adult's ability to engage in conversation (Murphy et al., 2006). In turn, older adults may be more likely to avoid potentially noisy situations, such as eating at a restaurant.

Presbycusis can result from metabolic changes that affect the tissue in the wall of the cochlea, leading to less amplification of sound. Sensory presbycusis is the result of chronic noise exposure. Increasing age in middle to later adulthood is associated with increases in the metabolic form of presbycusis (Vaden et al., 2017).

The single best way to minimize the risk of developing significant hearing loss due to presbycusis is to reduce your exposure to noise. The next time you turn up the music playing in your headphones or go to a loud concert, think about the long-term effects on your hearing, particularly if you wake up the following morning with your ears still ringing.

Another hearing disturbance that is relatively common in older people is tinnitus, a symptom in which the individual perceives sounds in the head or ear (such as a ringing noise) when there is no external source. The condition can be temporarily associated with the use of aspirin, antibiotics, and anti-inflammatory agents. Changes in the bones of the skull due to trauma and the buildup of wax in the ears may also contribute to tinnitus. Although treatments are available for tinnitus (generally dependent on the cause of the symptom), there is no cure.

Using hearing aids can help adults with hearing loss overcome many hearing-related problems. With increasing improvements in the quality of hearing aids as well as reductions in their size, people no longer need to rely on devices that are visible to others. These miniature devices considerably reduce the social stigma many associate with the need to wear a hearing aid. They are also more effective, and particularly so because people are more likely to use them given that they are so small and easily hidden.

Even without a hearing aid, however, it's possible for older adults to improve their ability to understand speech if they take advantage of various communication strategies. The first is to look directly at the person speaking to them and to make sure that there is enough light so that they can clearly see the person's face. Older adults should also turn down background noise that could interfere with the audio stream they are trying to follow, whether it's a person, a television, or the radio. At restaurants and social gatherings, they should find a place to talk that is as far as possible from crowded or noisy areas. They can also ask the people speaking to them not to chew food or gum while talking and not to speak too quickly (Janse, 2009).

Many people talking to an older adult (with or without hearing loss) tend to overcompensate and raise their voices unnecessarily high. This has the unfortunate effect of interfering with the speech signal. It is also important for the speaker to enunciate carefully, speak in a low tone (to offset presbycusis) and look straight at the older adult. Most importantly, if you're the speaker, you should avoid talking to the person as if he or she were a child. This also includes referring to the individual in the third person or leaving the person out of the conversation altogether (based on the assumption that he or she can't hear).

Providing context is also useful because this provides additional cues to the listener about your topic of conversation. You can also gauge whether you are being understood

Listening to loud music through headphones can place individuals at risk for noise-induced presbycusis.

by paying careful attention to how the other person is responding to you, both verbally and nonverbally. Finally, rather than becoming frustrated or upset with the listener, maintaining a positive and patient attitude will encourage the listener to remain more engaged in the conversation.

Balance

As important as the maintenance of visual and auditory functioning are with increasing age, the sense of balance can mean the difference between life and death. Loss of balance is one of the main factors responsible for falls in older adults (Dickin et al., 2006). In 2016, there were 29,688 deaths of individuals 65 and older who died due to injuries related to falls (Xu et al., 2018). Each year, more than 300,000 older adults are hospitalized for hip fractures, and more than 95% of hip fractures are caused by falling, usually by falling sideways. Falls are also the most common cause of traumatic brain injury (Centers for Disease Control and Prevention, 2019b).

In addition to experiencing changes in balance, people who are more likely to fall have a history of previous falls, are weaker, have an impaired gait, and are more likely to be on medications (Tinetti & Kumar, 2010). Older individuals who have more difficulty detecting body position are more

Uneven pavements can increase the risk of falls in older adults.

Chuti/Shutterstock.com

likely to lose their balance or fail to see a step or an obstacle in their path on a level surface.

It is natural that people who have had a painful and perhaps frightening experience of a fall become anxious in a subsequent situation where they feel insecure; they then become even more unsteady in their gait (Reelick et al., 2009). The fear of falling can create a vicious cycle in which older individuals increasingly restrict their movement. In this regard, fear of falling becomes an unhealthy form of identity accommodation, in which individuals lose all confidence in the ability to avoid a fall. This, in turn, increases their perceived instability, making them perhaps more physiologically unstable as well (Horslen et al., 2015).

The two symptoms most frequently associated with age-related vestibular dysfunction are dizziness and vertigo. Dizziness is an uncomfortable sensation of feeling light-headed and even floating. Vertigo refers to the sensation of spinning when the body is at rest.

Because the vestibular system is so intimately connected to other parts of the nervous system, people may experience symptoms of vestibular disturbance in the form of problems such as headache, muscular aches in the neck and back, and increased sensitivity to noise and bright lights. Other signs of vestibular disturbance include fatigue, inability to concentrate, unsteadiness while walking, and difficulty with speech. Increased sensitivity to motion sickness is another common symptom. Some of these changes may come about with diseases that are not part of normal aging; others may occur as the result of normative alterations in the vestibular receptors.

Exercise can help older adults learn to compensate for factors that increase their chance of falling. The most beneficial forms of exercise include functional training in control of the core bodily muscles involved in posture and balance. These are exercises that can be practiced on a daily basis in the individual's own home (Olij et al., 2019). Tai Chi is another form of exercise that helps to promote balance and flexibility. Together, such interventions are estimated to result in a significant reduction of fall risk as high as 34% (Sherrington et al., 2019).

Falls can also be prevented if a person wears proper eyeglasses, uses a prosthetic aid in walking, outfits the home with balance aids such as handrails, and develops greater sensitivity to the need to take care while walking. Having an accurate eyeglass prescription is crucial, given that vision provides important cues to navigating the environment. Accordingly, older adults with uncorrected visual problems are more vulnerable to falls (Vitale et al., 2006).

Although a person may resist using a walking stick, this is an adaptation to changes in balance that can lead to significant improvements in mobility. At home, people can also make relatively simple adaptations that prevent falls, such as getting a shower chair or bath bench in the tub and installing a handheld shower head. Learning to sit while performing ordinary grooming tasks, such as shaving, further reduces a person's risk of falling. People can also outfit their kitchens to minimize the fall risk, such as bringing in a tall (but stable) chair or stool that they use while they cook. Having multiple telephones in the home is another useful strategy so that the need to hurry to reach the phone (and possibly fall) is avoided. Even better, keeping a cell phone close by or using smart watch technology reduces this risk. The person at risk of falling can also derive feelings of security, and a lower risk of falling, by having the cell phone nearby in case he or she actually does fall and needs help.

In addition to practical strategies, older individuals can learn to develop greater sensitivity to the floors that they navigate, such as when they step onto a tile floor from a carpet. They can also be trained to recognize situations that realistically should be avoided, such as bumpy sidewalks or wet floors. As they do, they gain a greater sense of personal control over the likelihood of falling, lowering their fear of it and increasing their ability to navigate around their environments within safe limits.

Smell and Taste

Smell and taste belong to the sensory system referred to as chemosensation. The sensory receptors in these systems are triggered when molecules released by certain substances stimulate special cells in the nose, mouth, or throat. Despite the fact that the olfactory receptors (responsible for smell) constantly replace themselves, the area of the olfactory epithelium shrinks with age, and ultimately the total number of receptors becomes reduced throughout the adult years. At birth, the olfactory epithelium covers a wide area of the upper nasal cavities, but by the 20s and 30s, its area has started to shrink noticeably.

The rates of olfactory impairment are higher in older than in middle-aged adults, with 13% of 60 to 69 year olds and 39% of those 80 and older showing some form of dysfunction. The environmentally important odors of smoke and natural gas show impairments among those 70 and older, with 20% misidentifying smoke and 31% natural gas (Hoffman et al., 2016). Perhaps for this reason, mortality rates are higher in older adults with olfactory deficits, but these individuals also are in poorer health (Liu et al., 2019).

There are also other potential contributors to poorer olfaction in older adults, including a history of smoking, sinus problems, certain medications, and chronic disease (Rawson, 2006). Tobacco smoke is a major source of interference with taste and smell. Although people who quit smoking eventually experience an improvement in

their sense of smell, this can take many years (equal to the number of years spent smoking). Dentures are another cause of loss of taste sensitivity: they may block the receptor cells of the taste buds. Add to this the fact that certain medications also interfere with taste disorders (Schiffman, 2009), and it is difficult to determine whether aging brings with it inherent changes in taste or not.

Cognitive changes are also believed to be associated with a loss of smell sensitivity. Older adults who have experienced the greatest impairment in cognitive functioning may be the most vulnerable to loss of odor identification abilities. In one longitudinal study, researchers followed older adults over a 3-year period and observed that people with the most rapid decline in cognitive processes had the greatest rate of decline in the ability to label various odors (Wilson et al., 2006).

Taste disorders in older adults appear to affect all five forms of taste (salty, sweet, bitter, sour, and umami), with the most pronounced increase in detection ability involving sour and bitter tastes. There are dietary implications of these changes, with reports that older adults have higher consumption rates of sweet and salty foods (Sergi et al., 2017). Rather than being due to intrinsic processes involved in aging, however, it appears that taste disorders have other causes including drug use, zinc deficiency, and both oral and chronic diseases (Imoscopi et al., 2012).

Although nothing can be done to reverse age-related losses of smell and taste once they occur, people who suffer from severe losses may benefit from medical evaluations and treatments for underlying conditions. Apart from such interventions, older people can also take advantage of strategies to enhance the enjoyment of food, such as expanding their food choices, planning meals in pleasant environments, and finding good dining companions.

Somatosensory System

You are able to move around in the environment through the operation of the somatosensory system, which translates information about touch, temperature, and position to your nervous system. Awareness of bodily position is made possible by proprioception, which provides information about where your limbs are placed when you are standing still. Kinesthesis applies to the knowledge that receptors in your limbs provide when your body is moving. Through proprioception, you would know that you are poised at the top of a staircase, ready to take your first step downward; through kinesthesis, you would know that you are actually moving down those stairs.

Touch. A well-established body of evidence links the loss of the ability to discriminate touch with the aging process throughout adulthood as a result of changes in the receptors underneath the skin (Garcia-Piqueras et al., 2019). In the hands, loss of touch sensitivity seems to be greater for men than for women across adulthood. Changes in touch sensitivity in the feet can contribute to difficulties with balance contributing to other changes in the vestibular system to increase older adults' risk of falling (Hafstrom et al., 2018).

Pain. The question of whether older adults are more or less sensitive to pain is a topic of considerable concern for health practitioners. Changes in pain perception with age could make life either much harder or much easier for individuals with illnesses (such as arthritis) that cause chronic pain.

There is no evidence that older adults become somehow immune or at least protected from pain by virtue of age changes in this sensory system. Lower back pain for at least 30 days in the past year was reported among 12% of a large-scale sample of Danish elders (Leboeuf-Yde et al., 2009). Chronic back pain is exacerbated by osteoarthritis in the hip; together restrictions in hip mobility and back pain can increase older adults' quality of life, particularly in the areas of social functioning, mental health, and limitations in the ability to carry out everyday activities (Hicks et al., 2018). Limitations in the range of motion in the knee create further difficulties for some older adults (Jung et al., 2018).

The experience of pain can also interfere with cognitive performance, in addition to being a limitation in an individual's everyday life. In one sample of more than 300 older adults, poorer performance on tests of memory and spatial abilities was observed among individuals who suffered from chronic lower back pain (Weiner et al., 2006). In a study of more than 11,000 elders in the United Kingdom, researchers found that regardless of the presence of other complicating conditions such as depression and anxiety, the experience of chronic pain had a direct relationship to cognitive symptoms (Westoby et al., 2009). You should keep this finding in mind when you evaluate studies of cognitive performance in older adults, because it is possible that many reports of age differences reflect the fact that they are distracted by pain.

People can reduce the risk of pain in later adulthood by controlling for the factors related to greater pain prevalence. Obesity is highly associated with chronic pain even after controlling for education and related conditions such as diabetes, hypertension, arthritis, and depression (Ray et al., 2011). Thus, controlling for weight would seem to be an important and effective intervention. At the same time, rather than relying on pain medications, all of which carry the risk of abuse or at least interactions with treatments for other conditions, it is also advisable for older adults to learn to manage their pain through holistic methods (Bruckenthal et al., 2016).

Depression, stress, and lack of sleep can contribute to the experience of pain in older adults, outweighing even the benefits that can be provided by social support (Musich et al., 2019).

In summary, changes in physical functioning have important interactions with psychological and sociocultural factors, and can influence the individual's identity in the middle and later years of adulthood. Fortunately, there are many preventative and compensating steps that people can take to slow the rate of physical aging.

SUMMARY

1. Appearance is an important part of a person's identity, and throughout adulthood, the components of appearance all undergo change. Following the interactionist model of development, physical changes affect a person's behavior, which can modify the actions the individual takes to slow or modify those changes. Many age changes in the skin are the result of photoaging. The hair thins and becomes gray, and in men in particular, baldness can develop. There are significant changes in body build, including loss of height, increase of body weight into the 50s followed by a decrease, and changes in fat distribution. However, adults of all ages can benefit from exercise, which can maintain muscle and lower body fat.

2. Mobility reflects the quality of the muscles, bones, and joints. Age-related losses in mobility typically start in the 40s. The process of sarcopenia involves loss of muscle mass, and there is a corresponding decrease in muscle strength although muscular endurance is maintained. Strength training is the key to maintaining maximum muscle functioning in adulthood. Bones lose mineral content throughout adulthood, particularly among women, in large part based on genetic factors. Diet and exercise are important areas of prevention. The joints encounter many deleterious changes, and although exercise cannot prevent these, middle-aged and older adults can benefit from strength training, which builds muscles that support the joints, and flexibility training, which maintains range of motion even in damaged joints.

3. The cardiovascular system undergoes changes due to alterations in the heart muscle and arteries that lower aerobic capacity, cardiac output, and maximum heart rate. It is crucial for adults to avoid harmful fats in the diet and to engage in a regular pattern of aerobic exercise

to minimize changes in the cardiovascular system. The respiratory system loses functioning due to stiffening of lung tissue starting at about age 40. Important preventive actions include avoiding (or quitting) cigarette smoking and maintaining a low BMI. Although age changes in the kidney are likely due to nephron loss, other environmental factors, such as smoking, illness, or extreme exertion appear to play a role. Changes in the urinary system make the kidney more vulnerable to stress and less able to metabolize toxins, including medications. The bladder of older adults becomes less able to retain and expel urine, but the majority of people do not become incontinent. Behavioral methods and/or medication can correct normal age-related changes in urinary control. The digestive system becomes somewhat less efficient in older adults, but there is not a significant loss of functioning. In addition to the physiological changes, lifestyle factors impact overall digestive health. Improved dietary habits can also affect the digestive health of older adults.

4. The endocrine system is the site of many changes in the amount and functioning of the body's hormones as people age. The hormones affected by age include growth hormones, cortisol, thyroid hormones, melatonin, and DHEA. The climacteric is the period of gradual loss of reproductive abilities. After menopause, which typically occurs at the age of 50, women experience a reduction in estrogen. Decreases in testosterone levels in older men, referred to as andropause, are not consistently observed. Erectile dysfunction is observed in 44% of men age 65 and older. Changes in the immune system, referred to as immune senescence, are observed primarily in a decline in T cell and B cell functioning. Diet and exercise can counteract the loss of immune responsiveness in older adults while chronic stress can accelerate the immune system's aging.

5. Normal age-related changes in the nervous system were once thought of as neuronal fallout, but it is now recognized that there is much plasticity in the aging brain. The increasing availability of brain scanning methods for research purposes has revealed considerable variation in age-related alterations in brain structure. Changes in circadian rhythms lead older adults to awaken earlier and prefer the morning for working. Poor sleep habits and the coexistence of psychological or physical disorders (such as sleep apnea) can interfere further with the sleep patterns of middle-aged and older adults. In many cases, dysthermia (including hyper- or hypothermia) is related to the presence of disease.

6. Visual acuity decreases across adulthood, and presbyopia leads to a loss of the ability to focus the eye on near objects. Cataracts, age-related macular degeneration, and glaucoma are medical conditions that can lead to reduced vision or blindness. Presbycusis, the most common form of age-related hearing loss, can interfere with the ability to communicate. Hearing aids can help older adults overcome many hearing-related problems. Older adults are more vulnerable to a loss of balance, particularly when they suffer from dizziness and vertigo. Balance training can compensate for these changes and help reduce the fear of falling. There is loss of the perception of the position of the feet and legs, adding to other age-related changes in balance. Smell and taste show some losses with age, but both senses are extremely vulnerable to negative effects from disease and environmental damage, in particular from tobacco smoke. A loss of the ability to discriminate touch is observed in aging, particularly in the hands and feet. Findings on changes in pain perception with aging suggest important connections to everyday functioning as well as cognitive performance.

5

Health and Prevention

Think you know what it takes to stay healthy into adulthood? Check out some of the top 10 ways. It's never too late to get a head start!

1. **Stay connected to friends and family.** Loneliness can be harmful to your health.

2. **Eat a healthy diet.** High-fiber fruits, veggies, and whole grains help keep the digestive system functioning. Avoid sugar, salt, prepackaged foods, butter, and fatty meats.

3. **Watch your weight to avoid arthritis.** Excess weight puts pressure on the weight-bearing joints eventually leading to irreversible damage.

4. **Stay physically active.** Strength training and balance exercises can help reduce falls as you age.

5. **Practice sleep healthy habits.** Turn off technology before bed and stick to a consistent schedule.

6. **Stop smoking or using any tobacco products.** Now!

7. **Take good care of your teeth.** Brushing, flossing, and seeing the dentist can help prevent later-life oral problems including gum recession, staining, decay, and tooth loss.

8. **Learn to manage stress.** Coping with stress can promote physical and mental health.

9. **Stay on top of your health.** Get regular checkups and follow your medical professional's advice.

10. **Take dance classes.** You'll get your exercise while benefiting from the mental stimulation involved in learning new moves and remembering choreography.

Chronic illnesses can significantly interfere with the quality of a person's daily life, adding to normal age-related changes in physical functioning to affect the individual's psychological well-being and identity. Psychologists providing services to older adults with chronic illnesses may find that these chronic illnesses make it more difficult to diagnose and treat psychological disorders. Although it is important to distinguish illness from normal aging, there are significant chronic diseases to which people become increasingly susceptible with age.

KEY CONCEPTS IN HEALTH AND PREVENTION

Health is more than the absence of illness or disability. According to the World Health Organization (1948), health is a state of complete physical, mental, and social well-being. This multidimensional definition fits well with the biopsychosocial model, as it emphasizes all realms of the individual's functioning. In addition, as we shall see throughout this chapter, people who are healthy are not just not ill but are able to maintain a sense of well-being.

It is important to keep in mind, then, that health is not simply the absence of disability. However, disability can limit the individual's ability to adapt to the requirements of everyday life. Many health researchers and practitioners find it useful to assess an older adult's ability to perform activities of daily living (ADL), which are the tasks of

bathing, dressing, transferring, using the toilet, and eating. An expanded measure evaluates the instrumental activities of daily living (IADL), which include the ability to use the telephone, go shopping, prepare meals, complete housekeeping tasks, do the laundry, use private or public transportation, take medications, and handle finances (Lawton & Brody, 1969). These measures provide a functional assessment of health status by indicating the degree of independence the individual can maintain whether living at home or in an institution.

The behavioral risk factors for chronic disease include a sedentary lifestyle, smoking, alcohol use, and unhealthy diets (see Figure 5.1). According to the World Health Organization (2018), noncommunicable (i.e., chronic) diseases account annually for the deaths of 41 million people worldwide. Over 85% of those deaths occur in low- and middle-income countries where they are more likely to target people less than 70 years old. To the extent that individuals are able to reduce their risk factors for chronic disease, they therefore improve not only their quality of life but also the economic health of society.

DISEASES OF THE CARDIOVASCULAR SYSTEM

We begin with cardiovascular disease, a term that refers to a set of abnormal conditions that develop in the heart and arteries. The number one cause of death worldwide,

FIGURE 5.1

Behavioral Risk Factors for Chronic Diseases in Adulthood

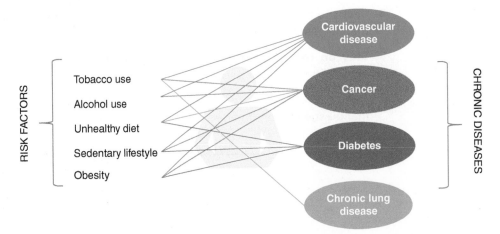

This model shows the relationship between unhealthy behaviors and the development of chronic disease in adulthood.

cardiovascular disease can also cause chronic disability. Because the distribution of blood throughout the body is essential for the normal functioning of all other organ systems, cardiovascular disease can have a widespread range of effects on the individual's health and everyday life.

Cardiac and Cerebrovascular Conditions

Chronic diseases that fall into the category of cardiac and cerebrovascular conditions are linked by the fact that they involve disturbances of the cardiovascular system.

As we described in Chapter 4, fat and other substances accumulate in the walls of the arteries throughout the body as part of the normal aging process. One of the most pervasive chronic diseases is atherosclerosis, a term that derives from the Greek words *athero* (meaning paste) and *sclerosis* (meaning hardness). In atherosclerosis, fatty deposits collect at an abnormally high rate, substantially reducing the width of the arteries and limiting the circulation of the blood (see Figure 5.2). Arteriosclerosis is a general term for the thickening and hardening of arteries. Everyone experiences some degree of arteriosclerosis as part of normal aging.

It is possible to live with atherosclerosis and not encounter significant health problems. However, atherosclerosis can eventually lead to a buildup in plaque

FIGURE 5.2

Process of Atherosclerosis

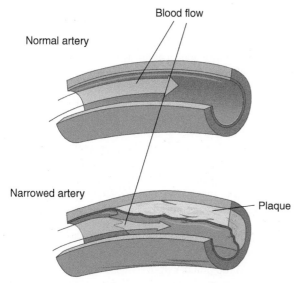

Development of atherosclerosis through the buildup of plaque in the arteries.

in a particular artery causing the blood flow to that part of the body to be blocked. The organs or tissues that are fed by that artery then suffer serious damage due to the lack of blood supply. When this process affects arteries that feed the heart muscle, the individual is said to have coronary (or ischemic) heart disease. The term myocardial infarction refers to the acute condition in which the blood supply to part of the heart muscle (the myocardium) is severely reduced or blocked.

An individual with hypertension suffers from chronic abnormally elevated blood pressure. The technical definition of hypertension is based on the two measures of blood pressure. Systolic is the pressure exerted by the blood as it is pushed out of the heart during contraction, and diastolic is the pressure when the blood is relaxed between beats. Blood pressure is measured in units of "mm Hg," or millimeters of mercury, referring to the display on a blood pressure scale. A person is diagnosed with hypertension when his or her blood pressure is greater than or equal to 140 mm Hg systolic pressure or 90 mm Hg diastolic pressure.

Atherosclerosis contributes to hypertension in the following way. The accumulation of plaque forces the blood to be pushed through narrower and narrower arteries. As a result, the pressure on the blood as it is being pumped out of the heart becomes greater and greater, and the person now is at risk for hypertension.

Hypertension itself creates dangerous changes in the arteries. The more pressure that the blood exerts in its passage through the arteries, the greater the strain on the arteries' delicate walls. Over time, these walls become weakened and inflamed. As they do, they accumulate even more plaque, which tends to settle into those cracks and weak areas. Consequently, the individual's hypertension becomes even more pronounced. This problem is more severe in the larger arteries, particularly the ones leading from the heart, which take the full force of the heart's pumping action.

In addition to damaging the arteries, hypertension increases the workload of the heart. Because the arteries have narrowed, the heart must pump harder and harder to push out the blood. The heart muscle in the left ventricle (the part that pumps out the blood) becomes thickened and overgrown. This hypertrophy of the left ventricle further compromises the health of the cardiovascular system. Referring back to Figure 4.8, you can see normal changes in the left ventricle's wall; these changes are accentuated in the case of cardiovascular disease.

Congestive heart failure (or heart failure) is a condition in which the heart is unable to pump enough blood to meet the needs of the body's other organs. Blood flows out of the heart at an increasingly slower rate, causing the blood returning to the heart through the veins to back up. Eventually, the tissues become congested with fluid. This condition can result from a variety of diseases, including coronary heart disease, scar tissue from a past myocardial infarction, hypertension, disease of the heart valves, disease of the heart muscle, infection of the heart, or heart defects present at birth. People with congestive heart failure are unable to exert themselves without becoming exhausted and short of breath. Their legs may swell due to edema, a condition in which fluid builds up in their bodies. They may also experience fluid buildup in their lungs along with kidney problems.

The term "cerebrovascular disease" refers to disorders of circulation to the brain. This condition may lead to the onset of a cerebrovascular accident, also known as a "stroke" or "brain attack," an acute condition in which an artery leading to the brain bursts or is clogged by a blood clot or other particle. The larger the area of the brain deprived of blood, the more severe the deterioration of the physical and mental functions controlled by that area. Another condition caused by the development of clots in the cerebral arteries is a transient ischemic attack (TIA), also called a ministroke. The cause of a TIA is the same as that of a stroke, but in a TIA, the blockage of the artery is temporary. The tissues that were deprived of blood soon recover, but chances are that another TIA will follow. People who have had a TIA are also at higher risk of subsequently suffering from a stroke.

Incidence

Heart disease is the number one killer in the United States, resulting in 23% of all deaths in the year 2016. Together, heart and cerebrovascular disease accounted for 31% of all deaths in the United States of people 65 and older (Xu et al., 2018), a figure that is comparable to the rate observed in Canada (Statistics Canada, 2019). Thus, deaths from heart disease and strokes are proportionately highest among the oldest segment of the population. In addition, heart disease is the leading diagnosis for health care expenditures in the United States, accounting for $213.8 billion combined across heart disease, hypertension, other circulatory conditions, and stroke (Benjamin et al., 2019).

As mentioned, cardiovascular disease is the leading cause of death worldwide, causing 17.9 million deaths in 2015, or 31% of all deaths (World Health Organization, 2017). Eastern Europe has the highest prevalence of deaths from heart disease (adjusted for age) followed by Central Asia and Central Europe. The lowest rates of heart disease are in Central Sub-Saharan Africa, with similar low rates in southern Latin America and the high-income countries in the Asia-Pacific region (Roth et al., 2017).

Behavioral Risk Factors

Lifestyle factors contribute significantly to all forms of heart disease. Even people who have a strong genetic predisposition to cardiovascular disease can reduce (or raise) their risks through the choices they make on a daily basis. Referring back to Figure 5.1, we will now consider each of the four risk factors in terms of cardiovascular disease.

Looking first at tobacco smoking, 14% of American adults are current smokers. The rates of current smokers decrease across age groups of adults from 16% among adults 25 to 44 to a low of 8.2% among those age 65 and older (Centers for Disease Control and Prevention, 2019c). It is very possible that the smoking rates decrease not only because older adults are less likely to smoke but also because the nonsmokers are more likely to survive.

Although it is not known exactly why smoking increases the risk of heart disease, most researchers believe that the smoke itself damages the arteries, making them more vulnerable to plaque formation and ultimately leading to the deleterious changes we outlined earlier. Research on factors predicting longevity shows that smoking has a more significant impact on the aging process than other behaviors, speeding up the process of DNA methylation (Fiorito et al., 2019).

A sedentary lifestyle is the next major risk factor for heart disease. There is a well-established relationship between exercise and heart disease (Campbell et al., 2019). Combining aerobic exercise and resistance training produces even more beneficial effects on blood pressure and other measures of cardiovascular health and may also produce longer-term adherence (Ruangthai & Phoemsapthawee, 2019).

Unfortunately, the majority of adults at highest risk for heart disease (i.e., those 75 and older) are the least likely to exercise. Rates of physical inactivity increase from 25% in ages 50 to 64, 27% in 65 to 74, and 35% in 75 and older. However, the rates of physical inactivity are greatly reduced (14%) in college graduates (Watson et al., 2014).

An unhealthy diet places the individual at risk of developing a BMI in the overweight or obese range. An analysis of 239 prospective studies conducted in four continents showed a causal relationship between a high BMI and mortality due to vascular disease (Global BMI Mortality Collaboration, 2016). According to the CDC, dramatic increases in the number of overweight and obese individuals have occurred among United States adults over the past 20 years. Currently, 39% of the U.S. population is considered obese by government standards (Hales et al., 2017). This is far higher than the worldwide rate of adult obesity, which is 13% (World Health Organization, 2018a).

Finally, high intake of alcohol to the point of being harmful is the fourth major risk factor for cardiovascular disease. This is in part because alcohol is high in calories, but also because excessive alcohol use can damage the cardiovascular system and the brain.

Illustrating how dangerous the combination of these risk factors can become, the so-called "stroke belt" includes the 8 to 12 states in the southeastern United States that represent the population most likely to experience all four (see Figure 5.3). Within the stroke belt, North Carolina, South Carolina, and Georgia have the highest rates and are referred to as the "stroke buckle." The high rates of stroke are attributed in part to diets in this region that are based on high consumption of sodium, monounsaturated fatty acids, polyunsaturated fatty acids and cholesterol, and the low consumption of dietary fiber.

Although stroke rates are in general elevated for the stroke belt, they are particularly high for Blacks. In a study of more than 23,000 men and women 45 years and older, researchers found higher scores for Blacks than Whites living in the stroke belt on measures related to stroke risk, including hypertension, systolic blood pressure, diabetes, smoking, and hypertrophy of the left ventricle of the heart (Cushman et al., 2008). The stroke belt's higher risk also reflects the fact that the region has lower levels of education and less access to health care than is true for other areas within the United States. Geographic factors aside, Black women between the ages of 50 and 60 have higher risk of stroke even after adjusting for behavioral and lifestyle factors (Jimenez et al., 2019).

FIGURE 5.3

Stroke Death Rates by County U.S. 2014–2016

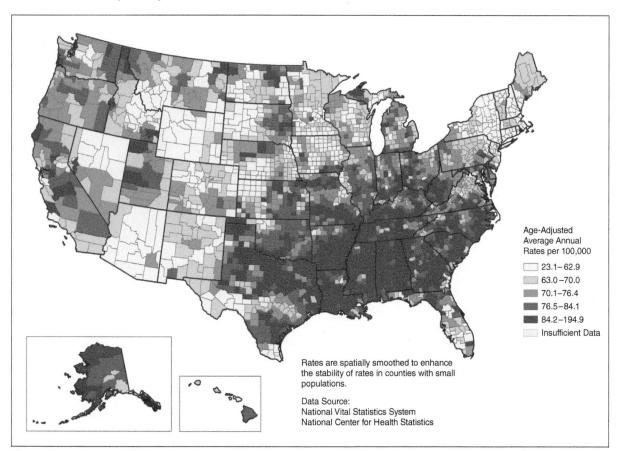

Within the United States, stroke deaths are more likely to occur in the "stroke belt," or Southeast area of the country.

FIGURE 5.4

Metabolic Syndrome

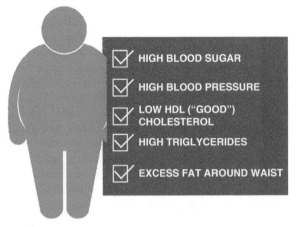

Metabolic syndrome is a term used to characterize people who show three of the five risk factors illustrated here.

As shown in Figure 5.4, metabolic syndrome is a term applied to people who have a cluster of symptoms associated with high risk factors for cardiovascular and related diseases.

The criteria for metabolic syndrome include abdominal obesity, high levels of trigylcerides, low levels of HDL ("good" cholesterol), high levels of LDL ("bad" cholesterol), hypertension, and high levels of glucose. According to the American Heart Association and the National Heart, Blood, and Lung Institute, three of these criteria must be present for the person to be considered to have metabolic syndrome (Grundy et al., 2006).

Prevention of Heart Disease and Stroke

Advances in the understanding of the cause of heart disease and stroke have resulted in safer and more effective medical and dietary supplements, contributing to substantial improvements of mortality rates due to cardiovascular disease. Much of this improvement is due to the widespread use of medications known as statins, which work by lowering the levels of harmful cholesterol (LDL) in the blood. However, in addition to or instead of medication, anyone can benefit from control of diet and participation in exercise as preventive strategies; the earlier you begin to follow these strategies, the better.

Healthy heart diets are high in fruit and vegetable intake (Crowe et al., 2011). The so-called Mediterranean diet is a regimen that includes fruits and vegetables as well as nuts, seeds, whole grains, and olive oil along with minimal intake of red meat and dairy foods and moderate intake

of red wine during meals. People who follow this diet have reduced risk of developing metabolic syndrome, particularly when combined with high levels of physical activity (Malakou et al., 2018). Additionally, treatments that incorporate relaxation training can help address psychosocial contributors to cardiovascular disease (Tang et al., 2011). Novel approaches to treatment also may incorporate music to aid in relaxation (do Amaral et al., 2016).

As we noted earlier, there are significant national differences in rates of cardiovascular disease. These are almost certainly related to diet. An analysis of the dietary habits and food intake of almost 27,000 people living in the countries of Central and Eastern Europe suggested that poor dietary habits contribute significantly to the high rates of morbidity and mortality in these countries (Boylan et al., 2009). Additionally, psychosocial and socioeconomic factors may contribute further to the high risk for cardiovascular disease in these countries, further exacerbating problems related to unhealthy diets (Tillmann et al., 2017).

It is important to remember in our discussion of available preventive treatments that people are reluctant to change their lifestyle habits, particularly when they must make these changes after decades of unhealthy habits. Health care professionals must therefore not only educate high-risk individuals but also give them encouragement that change is possible (Resnick et al., 2009).

CANCER

Cancer is a generic term that includes a group of more than 100 diseases. Each type of cancer has its own symptoms, characteristics, treatment options, and overall effect on a person's life and health.

In the United States, over 1.7 million new cases of cancer were diagnosed in 2018, and 609,640 individuals in the United States died from the disease. The most common forms of cancer are breast (in women), lung and bronchus, prostate (in men), colon and rectal, and melanoma of the skin. As of 2016, there were 15.5 million cancer survivors in the United States (National Cancer Institute, 2019). The breakdown of cancer cases and deaths by sex and race is summarized in Figure 5.5.

Worldwide, there were 9.6 million deaths from cancer in 2018, with 70% of them occurring in low- and middle-income countries. Approximately one-third of cancer deaths around the world are due to the risk factors of high BMI, low intake of fruits and vegetables, sedentary lifestyle, and use of tobacco and alcohol. The most common cancers are lung, breast, colorectal, prostate, skin, and stomach, with the most number of deaths due to lung cancer (World Health Organization, 2018b).

FIGURE 5.5

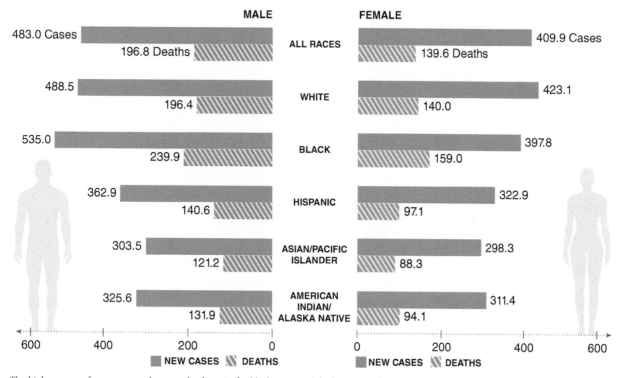

Number of New Cases and Deaths from Cancer Each Year
Per 100,000 Persons by Race/Ethnicity and Sex: All Cancers

The highest rates of new cases and cancer deaths exist for black men, and the lowest are for Asian/Pacific islander women.

Risk Factors and Prevention

All cancer is genetically caused in the sense that it reflects damage to the genes that control cell replication. Some damage is associated with genetic mutations that people inherit. These inherited risks are particularly important for breast and colon cancer. About 5% of women with breast cancer have a hereditary form of this disease. Similarly, close relatives of a person with colorectal cancer are themselves at greater risk, particularly if many people within their extended family have had the disease. However, most cancer is not of the inherited variety. Instead, cancer develops when random mutations occur that cause the body's cells to malfunction. The mutations develop either as a mistake in cell division or in response to injuries from environmental agents such as radiation or chemicals. Thus, cancer is due to an interaction between a person's genetic inheritance and exposure to the harmful risk factors of physical carcinogens (e.g., radiation), chemical carcinogens (e.g., asbestos), or biological carcinogens.

Most cancers become more prevalent with increasing age in adulthood because age is associated with greater cumulative exposure to harmful toxins (carcinogens) in the environment. Skin cancer is directly linked to exposure to ultraviolet (UV) radiation from the sun. In the United States, for example, melanoma is most common in Utah, a state with a high proportion of the population who have fair skin and who live in elevated areas where sunlight is reflected onto the body by ice, snow, and water. There is concern that as ozone levels in the air are depleted due to global warming, the risk of skin cancer will continue to rise (World Health Organization, 2019a).

Even as awareness of the need for sunblock as a prevention against skin cancer increases, tanning beds that expose users to artificial sources of UV radiation continue to be in use. Researchers estimate that women in developed countries who use tanning beds before the age of 30 increase their risk of developing skin cancer by 75%; despite knowing the risks, women use tanning beds anyway (Farley et al., 2015).

Cigarette smoking is in many ways more dangerous than UV exposure because the forms of cancer related to cigarettes are much more lethal than skin cancer. Most lung cancer is caused by cigarette smoking. People who smoke also place themselves at risk for developing cancers of the mouth, throat, esophagus, larynx, bladder, kidney, cervix, pancreas, and stomach. The risk of lung cancer begins to diminish as soon as a person quits smoking. People who had lung cancer and stopped smoking are less likely to get a second lung cancer than are people who continue to smoke. Being exposed to cigarette smoke ("secondhand smoke") can present just as great a risk, if not greater, for lung cancer (Chung et al., 2015).

Though you are probably aware of the risks of cigarette smoke in developed countries such as the United States, Canada, and Europe, you may not realize that carcinogens are present in substances such as betel quid, which includes the toxic substance areca nut. Over 90% of esophageal cancers in the world occur in countries in the "esophageal cancer belt," located in the region from the Caspian Sea to Central Asia to the West Pacific (Chung et al., 2015).

Being overweight is linked to a variety of cancers of the gastrointestinal system (see Figure 5.6). A nationwide study of over 900,000 adults in the United States who were studied prospectively from 1982 to 1998 played an important role in identifying the cancer risks associated

FIGURE 5.6

Cancers Associated with Overweight and Obesity

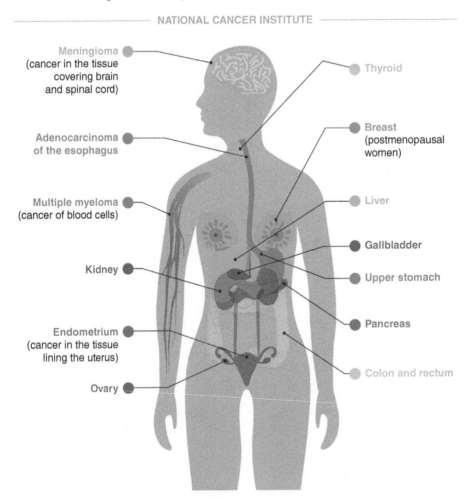

Overweight and obesity present risk factors for cancer among women.

with a high BMI. During this period of time, there were more than 57,000 deaths within the sample from cancer. The people with the highest BMIs had death rates from cancer that were 52% higher for men and 62% higher for women compared with men and women of normal BMI. The types of cancer associated with higher BMIs included cancer of the esophagus, colon and rectum, liver, gallbladder, pancreas, and kidney. Significant trends of increasing risk with higher BMIs were observed for death from cancers of the stomach and prostate in men and for death from cancers of the breast, uterus, cervix, and ovary in women (Calle et al., 2003). In addition to the other health benefits of a low BMI, then, it appears that maintaining normal weight is an important way to prevent the development of cancer.

In addition to BMI, eating specific foods seems to play a role in cancer risk. Stomach cancer is more common in parts of the world—such as Japan, Korea, parts of Eastern Europe, and Latin America—in which people eat foods that are preserved by drying, smoking, salting, or pickling. By contrast, fresh foods, especially fresh fruits and vegetables, may help protect against stomach cancer. Similarly, the risk of developing colon cancer is thought to be higher in people whose diet is high in fat, low in fruits and vegetables, and low in high-fiber foods such as whole-grain breads and cereals. A prospective study in the United Kingdom showed increases of 20% in colorectal cancer among individuals with higher intake of red meat (Bradbury et al., 2019).

There are several additional specific types of environmental toxins in the air, food, and water that make certain people more vulnerable to cancer. Such compounds include asbestos, arsenic, beryllium, cadmium, chromium, and nickel. Exposure to these compounds significantly increases a person's risk of cancer in various sites in the respiratory system, including the lung and nasal cavity. People exposed to arsenic are at risk for bladder cancer, and those to asbestos more likely to develop ovarian cancer. In addition, people exposed to leather, silica, and wood dust are more likely to develop respiratory cancers (Straif et al., 2009). People in certain occupations are more at risk for exposure to these carcinogenic substances, including those who work in iron and steel founding or manufacture isopropyl alcohol, paint, and rubber (Baan et al., 2009).

People make many other lifestyle choices that can further contribute to their risk of developing cancer. In the intensive efforts to find the causes of breast cancer, a variety of lifestyle factors have been suggested, such as amount of alcohol consumed and having an abortion or a miscarriage. The evidence is somewhat stronger for the effect of personal history in the case of cervical cancer, which has a higher risk among women who began having sexual intercourse

before age 18 and/or have had many sexual partners. For men, efforts are under way to determine whether having had a vasectomy increases their risk for prostate cancer.

In addition to a person's lifestyle and history of disease, people's race and ethnicity may contribute to certain types of cancers. Skin cancer is more likely to develop in people with fair skin that freckles easily; Black people are less likely to develop any form of skin cancer. Uterine cancer is more prevalent among Whites, and prostate cancer is more prevalent among Blacks. Stomach cancer is twice as prevalent in men and is more common in Black people, as is colon cancer. Rectal cancer is more prevalent among Whites.

Finally, certain hormones may increase the risk of cancer, interacting in complex ways with other factors that we have already mentioned. Although the cause of prostate cancer is not known, the growth of cancer cells in the prostate, like that of normal cells, is stimulated by male hormones, especially testosterone. Estrogen taken as part of HRT in postmenopausal women is thought to increase their likelihood of developing uterine cancer. However, other sources of estrogen, such as the endocrine-disrupting chemicals in certain consumer products (in the form of bisphenol A [BPA]) can also increase a woman's risk of developing cancer (Rutkowska et al., 2016).

Treatments

The best way to avoid cancer is to prevent it by staying away from known carcinogens. People at risk based on their age, sex, and lifestyle should also undergo screenings as recommended by health care professionals. Organizations in the United States such as the American Cancer Society and the Canadian Cancer Society publicize the need for tests, such as breast self-examination and mammograms for women, prostate examinations for men, and colon cancer screenings for both men and women.

As important as detection is, however, public health officials often revise their recommendations for the frequency and nature of cancer screening. For example, in November 2009, the U.S. Preventive Services Task Force (USPSTF) released a controversial update to the 2002 recommendation statement for breast cancer screening. The 2002 recommendation advocated breast mammography every 1 to 2 years for women over 40. The 2009 statement, citing insufficient evidence to assess the benefits and harms of screening, recommends against routine mammography screening in women between the ages of 40 and 49. Biennial screening mammography is recommended for women between the ages of 50 and 74. For women over the age of 75, the USPSTF determined insufficient evidence to assess the additional benefits and harms of mammography. Uncertainties pertaining to the harm of screening (including misdiagnosis) were cited as a basis for the recommendations. When the report was made public, countless groups and organizations were quick to harshly criticize the recommendations, sparking debate in the medical field and media outlets (Woolf, 2010).

In order to determine the impact of the USPSTF recommendations, researchers examined self-reported mammography rates between 2006 and 2010. Although mammography rates declined slightly across all age groups over 40 (adjusted for a variety of demographic factors including race/ethnicity) in 2010, the differences were not statistically significant (Howard & Adams, 2012). A national telephone survey conducted a year after the revised recommendations suggested that less than half of women surveyed were aware of the changes in screening guidelines and that those who were younger and had higher rates of education and income were more aware of the changes (Kiviniemi & Hay, 2012).

The debate on mammograms continues, however, and was once again in the headlines in 2015 when the American Cancer Society revised its previous guidelines. An important and controversial element of this revision was the advice that women not perform breast self-examinations or have these examinations be part of their ordinary physicals with their primary health care provider. The risk now is that the pendulum has swung too far in the direction of insufficient screening, leading to new concerns about failing to detect treatable cancers (Schattner, 2019). Similar concerns as those involving breast cancer occur in guidelines for colon and prostate cancer screening. In each case, physicians and their patients must weigh the risks incurred by undergoing screening (and possibly receiving a false positive) against the failure to detect a treatable cancer.

Depending on the stage of cancer progression at diagnosis, various treatment options are available (see Figure 5.7). Radiation therapy involves the use of high-energy X-rays to damage cancer cells and stop their growth. Surgery is the most common treatment for most types of cancer when it is probable that all of the tumor can be removed. Chemotherapy uses drugs to kill cancer cells. Patients are most likely to receive chemotherapy when the cancer has metastasized to other parts of the body. Targeted drug therapies aim at cancer's specific genes, proteins, or the tissue environment that contributes to cancer growth and survival.

As more information is gathered through the rapidly evolving program of research on cancer and its causes, new methods of treatment and prevention can be expected to emerge over the next few decades. Furthermore, as efforts grow to target populations at risk for the development of preventable cancers (such as lung cancer), we can expect that cancer deaths will be reduced even further in the decades ahead.

DISORDERS OF THE MUSCULOSKELETAL SYSTEM

Musculoskeletal diseases include a range of conditions that develop in the bones and joints. Not fatal in and of themselves, these diseases can be crippling and may lead to injury or bodily harm that can eventually lead to the death of the afflicted individual.

Osteoarthritis

Arthritis is a general term for conditions affecting the joints and surrounding tissues that can cause pain, stiffness, and swelling in joints and other connective tissues. Osteoarthritis, the most common form of arthritis in older adults, affects joints in the hips, knees, neck, lower back, and small joints of the hands. These are joints vulnerable to injury that people sustain due to repeated overuse in the performance of a particular job or a favorite sport. The diagram in Figure 5.8 illustrates arthritic changes in

FIGURE 5.7

Forms of Cancer Treatment

Radiation   **Surgery**   **Chemotherapy**   **Targeted drug therapies**

Cancer treatments currently include these four methods, with targeted drug therapies becoming better refined through research.

FIGURE 5.8

A Joint with Severe Osteoarthritis

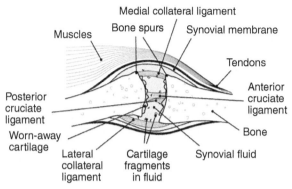

As shown in this diagram of the knee, osteoarthritis creates pain and stiffness due to wearing away of the cartilage and accumulation of bone spurs.

the knee. The impact from injury and repeated use of the joints contributes to osteoarthritis by thinning or wearing away the cartilage that cushions the ends of the bones in the joint as they rub together. The synovial fluid that fills the joint loses its shock-absorbing properties as well, further contributing to the development of osteoarthritis. Bony spurs and joint swelling also develop as the disease progresses. These changes in the joint structures and tissues cause the individual to experience pain and loss of movement. People who are overweight or obese are at further risk for osteoarthritis, particularly in the lower joints which must support their extra weight.

Because osteoarthritis has no cure, people who develop this disease require pain management. Medications used to help alleviate the pain of osteoarthritis include aspirin, acetaminophen, ibuprofen, and nonsteroidal anti-inflammatory drugs (NSAIDs). Although these can help alleviate the individual's pain, NSAIDs can create their own set of problems. People who take NSAIDs on a chronic basis are at risk for kidney disease as well as ulcers. Another strategy is to inject corticosteroids directly into joints to reduce swelling and inflammation. These drugs are used sparingly, however, because they can themselves destroy bones and cartilage.

Even the best pain medications only alleviate symptoms; they do not provide a cure for the disease. More active forms of treatment for osteoarthritis are increasingly becoming available. One approach is to receive an injection of a synthetic material into an arthritic joint to replace the loss of synovial fluid. A second option is to be injected with sodium hyaluronate directly into the joint. This is a

version of a chemical normally present in high amounts in joints and fluids.

When these pain or injectable treatments no longer produce relief, the individual with osteoarthritis may undergo the total replacement of the affected joint. Although hip or knee replacement surgery may seem like a drastic measure, it is one that typically proves highly satisfactory. Following the surgery, many individuals are able to lead not only pain-free lives but are also able to resume some of their former activities.

Exercise can also help to reduce the pain of osteoarthritis, but it must be geared to the individual's ability, perhaps requiring less extensive bouts throughout the course of the day than one intense exercise session (Kraus et al., 2019). The best exercise for osteoarthritis helps the individual strengthen the muscles around the joint (Verweij et al., 2009) and stretch the tendons. Swimming is another form of exercise that can help offset the pain and limitations of osteoarthritis (Alkatan et al., 2016). People whose osteoarthritis is made worse by their obesity can also benefit from a program of exercise that focuses on weight loss. Another benefit of exercise is that it can offset the effects on mood of the chronic pain associated with osteoarthritis.

Osteoporosis

As we saw in Chapter 4, people steadily lose bone mineral content throughout the decades of adulthood. This loss of bone mineral content occurs due to an imbalance between the rates of bone resorption versus bone growth. Osteoporosis (literally, "porous bone") is said to occur when the bone mineral density reaches the point that is more than 2.5 standard deviations below the mean of young, White, non-Hispanic women.

As many as 8 million women and 2 million men in the United States suffer from osteoporosis. The percent of older adults with osteoporosis is 6% at the femur neck, 8% at the lumbar spine, and 11% at either site (Looker et al., 2017). Women (particularly postmenopausal women) are at higher risk than men because they have lower bone mass in general. However, osteoporosis is a significant health problem in men. Women vary by race and ethnicity in their risk of developing osteoporosis; White women are twice as likely (15.8%) as Black women (7.7%) to have osteoporosis; Mexican American women have the highest rates of all subgroups (20.4%). About half of all women 50 and older in the United States have low bone mass, and 35% of all men (Wright et al., 2014). In addition, women who have small bone structures and are underweight have a higher risk for osteoporosis than heavier women.

Excessive use of alcohol and a history of cigarette smoking increase an individual's risk of developing osteoporosis. Conversely, people can reduce their risk by taking in adequate amounts of calcium present in dairy products, dark-green leafy vegetables, tofu, salmon, and foods fortified with calcium such as orange juice, bread, and cereal (a regimen similar to that recommended to prevent heart disease). Other dietary measures include eating foods high in protein and nutrients such as magnesium, potassium, vitamin K, several B vitamins, and carotenoids. Vitamin D, obtained through exposure to sunlight (while wearing sunblock, of course!), or as a dietary supplement, is another important preventative agent. Exercise and physical activity are also significant factors in reducing a person's risk of osteoporosis, particularly when that exercise involves resistance training with weights (Rizzoli et al., 2014).

Once an individual develops osteoporosis, there are a variety of medications currently available to slow or stop bone loss, increase bone density, and reduce fracture risk. The bisphosphonate known as alendronate is a medication used to increase bone density. Unfortunately, it can have serious side effects, particularly bone loss in the jaw. In severe cases, individuals may have no choice other than to take these medications. To minimize the side effects of the medications, such individuals can benefit from a "drug holiday," as the medications have long-lasting effects (Villa et al., 2016). The naturally occurring hormone calcitonin was once proposed as a treatment to regulate calcium and bone metabolism, but its use is no longer recommended (Khan et al., 2017). Conversely, there is some evidence that intake of dietary silicon can help promote bone regeneration (Rodella et al., 2014).

In summary, osteoporosis is a potentially disabling condition that limits an older individual's ability to carry out daily tasks without pain or restriction. However, new methods of prevention and treatment are making it possible to reverse or at least stave off the disease.

DIABETES

Diabetes is a chronic disease in which people are unable to metabolize glucose, a simple sugar that is a major source of energy for the body's cells. Adult-onset diabetes, also known as type 2 diabetes, develops over time, gradually reducing the individual's ability to convert dietary glucose to a form that can be used by the body's cells.

Characteristics of Diabetes

Normally, the digestive process breaks food down into components that can be transported through the blood to the cells of the body. The presence of glucose in the blood stimulates the beta cells of the pancreas to release insulin, a hormone that acts as a key at the cell receptors within the body to "open the cell doors" to let in the glucose. Excess glucose is stored in the liver or throughout the body in muscle and fat, at which point its level in the blood returns to normal.

In type 2 diabetes, the pancreas produces some insulin, but the body's tissues fail to respond to the insulin signal, a condition known as insulin resistance. Because the insulin cannot bind to the cell's insulin receptors, the glucose cannot be transported into the body's cells to be used. As a result, large amounts of glucose remain in the blood.

The symptoms of diabetes include fatigue, frequent urination (especially at night), unusual thirst, weight loss, blurred vision, frequent infections, and slow healing of sores. If blood sugar levels dip too low (a condition known as hypoglycemia), the individual can become nervous, jittery, faint, and confused. The only way to correct for this condition is for the individual to eat or drink a sugary substance as quickly as possible. Alternatively, in hyperglycemia, when blood glucose levels become too high, the person can also become seriously ill. Type 2 diabetes is associated with long-term complications that affect almost every organ system, contributing to blindness, heart disease, strokes, kidney failure, the necessity for limb amputations, and damage to the nervous system.

Incidence and Risk Factors

A large fraction of the over-65 population suffers from type 2 diabetes. Diabetes is estimated to afflict 12 million people 65 years of age and older, which is approximately 25.2% of adults in this age category. As shown in Figure 5.9, among all adults 20 years and older, American Indian/Alaska Native have the highest age-adjusted prevalence; Black non-Hispanic adults have the next highest age-adjusted prevalence. The lowest prevalence rates are for White, non-Hispanic; Asian individuals have slightly higher rates. Sex differences vary by race/ethnicity (Centers for Disease Control and Prevention, 2017).

More children are developing type 2 diabetes consistent with the rise in childhood obesity (Centers for Disease Control and Prevention, 2017). Such findings will have important health implications for future generations of older adults.

According to the World Health Organization, the global prevalence of diabetes is estimated to be 8.5%, having risen from 4.7% in 1980. Approximately 1.6 million deaths in 2016 were estimated to be due to diabetes (World Health Organization, 2018c). Countries in the eastern Mediterranean region showed the most precipitous rise

FIGURE 5.9

Estimated Age-Adjusted Prevalence of Diagnosed Diabetes by Race/Ethnicity and Sex among Adults Aged 18 or Older, U.S. 2013–2015

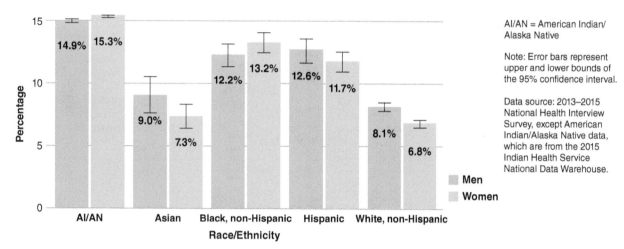

AI/AN = American Indian/Alaska Native

Note: Error bars represent upper and lower bounds of the 95% confidence interval.

Data source: 2013–2015 National Health Interview Survey, except American Indian/Alaska Native data, which are from the 2015 Indian Health Service National Data Warehouse.

in diabetes prevalence between 1980 and 2014, but all regions of the world showed at least a doubling rate as well (World Health Organization, 2016).

Diabetes can be understood in terms of the biopsychosocial perspective in that it involves physical, behavioral, and sociocultural risk factors noted earlier in the chapter as risk factors for heart disease. Researchers in this area warn that older adults are becoming increasingly likely to experience metabolic syndrome, insulin resistance, high lipid levels, and hypertension, leading to greater risk of cardiovascular and kidney disease (Grundy, 2016).

Prevention and Treatment

Given the clear relationship between obesity and diabetes, the most important means of preventing type 2 diabetes include the control of glucose intake, blood pressure, and blood lipids along with exercise and weight control.

People with diabetes require frequent testing, usually accomplished by measuring blood levels. Depending on the severity, once an individual has type 2 diabetes, diet and exercise may be sufficient to control its symptoms. If not, then the individual requires insulin injections or oral forms of diabetes medications. Additionally, people with diabetes need to be aware of the potential interaction of their treatment with any over-the-counter medications they use for other conditions, including herbal remedies, NSAIDs, and cough and cold medicines (Taylor, 2017).

RESPIRATORY DISEASES

The main form of respiratory disease affecting adults in middle and late life is chronic obstructive pulmonary disease (COPD), a group of diseases that involve obstruction of the airflow into the respiratory system. Two related diseases—chronic bronchitis and chronic emphysema—often occur together in this disease (see Figure 5.10). People with COPD experience coughing, excess sputum, and difficulty breathing even when they carry out relatively easy tasks, such as putting on their clothes or walking on level ground.

Chronic bronchitis is a long-standing inflammation of the bronchi, the airways that lead into the lungs. The inflammation of the bronchi causes an increase in mucus and other changes, which in turn leads to coughing and expectoration of sputum. People with chronic emphysema are more likely to develop frequent and severe respiratory infections, narrowing and plugging of the bronchi, difficulty breathing, and disability.

Chronic emphysema is a lung disease that causes permanent destruction of the alveoli. Elastin within the terminal bronchioles is destroyed, causing the airways to lose their ability to become enlarged during inspiration and to empty completely during expiration. The result is that the exchange of carbon dioxide and oxygen becomes compromised. People with COPD experience this situation as shortness of breath, making it difficult for them to complete the tasks of daily life (Johansson, 2019).

FIGURE 5.10

Chronic Obstructive Pulmonary Disease

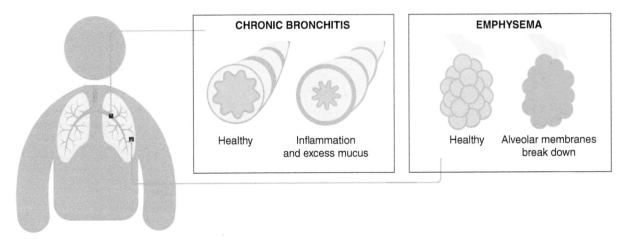

COPD is a chronic respiratory disease that is composed of chronic bronchitis and emphysema.

Although the cause of COPD is not known, most who study the disease generally agree that its main cause is cigarette smoking. Exposure to environmental toxins such as air pollution and harmful substances in the occupational setting also may serve as contributing causes.

The specific mechanism involved in the link between smoking and emphysema is thought to involve the release of an enzyme known as elastase, which breaks down the elastin found in lung tissue. Cigarette smoke stimulates the release of this enzyme and results in other changes that make the cells of the lung less resistant to elastase. Normally there is an inhibitant of elastase found in the lung, known as alpha-1 antitrypsin (AAT). However, cigarette smoke inactivates AAT and allows the elastase to destroy more lung tissue. Of course, not all smokers develop COPD, and not all people with COPD are or have been smokers. Heredity may also play a role. There is a rare genetic defect in the production of AAT in about 2% to 3% of the population that is responsible for about 5% of all cases of COPD.

Apart from quitting smoking, a necessary first step in prevention and treatment, individuals with COPD can benefit from medications and treatments. These include inhalers that open the airways to bring more oxygen into the lungs or reduce inflammation, machines that provide oxygen, or, in extreme cases, lung surgery to remove damaged tissue. As suggested by preliminary studies, individuals with COPD may also benefit from using a handheld device known as a SpiroTiger® that provides stimulation to the respiratory muscles (Wlodarczyk & Barinow-Wojewodzki, 2015). Such an approach would be of obvious benefit in building respiratory fitness.

NEUROCOGNITIVE DISORDERS

People receive the diagnosis of neurocognitive disorder when they experience a loss of cognitive function severe enough to interfere with normal daily activities and social relationships. You may be familiar with the term dementia, which is also used in common speech to refer to a loss of cognitive abilities. Clinicians distinguish major neurocognitive disorder from mild neurocognitive disorder, which, like the term mild cognitive impairment (MCI), refers to a form of neurocognitive disorder that signifies that the individual may be at risk for developing Alzheimer's disease.

People who suffer from amnesia have as their main symptom profound memory loss. Their amnesia may involve an inability to learn or remember information encountered after the damage (anterograde—into the future) or the inability to recall information learned prior to the damage (retrograde—going back into the past). Amnesia can be caused by chronic substance use, medications, exposure to environmental toxins, head trauma, loss of oxygen supply to the brain, or the sexually transmitted disease of herpes simplex.

Alzheimer's Disease

Alzheimer's disease is a form of neurocognitive disorder in which the individual suffers progressive and irreversible neuronal death. Over the years, Alzheimer's disease has been called by a variety of names, including senile dementia, presenile dementia, senile dementia of the Alzheimer's type, and organic brain disorder.

Identified as a disease in 1906, Alzheimer's disease is named after Aloysius Alzheimer (1864–1915), the German neurologist who was the first to link changes in brain tissue with observable symptoms. Alzheimer treated Auguste Deter, a woman in her 50s who suffered from progressive mental deterioration marked by increasing confusion and memory loss. Taking advantage of what was then a new staining technique, he noticed an odd disorganization of the nerve cells in her cerebral cortex. In a medical journal article published in 1907, Alzheimer speculated that these microscopic changes were responsible for Auguste Deter's dementia. The discovery of brain slides from this patient confirmed that these changes were similar to those seen in the disease (Enserink, 1998). In 1910, as a resulting number of autopsies from severely demented individuals showed the same abnormalities, a foremost psychiatrist of the era, Emil Kraepelin (1856–1926), gave the name described by his friend Alzheimer to the disease.

Prevalence.   The World Health Organization estimates a prevalence of all forms of neurocognitive disease (dementia) at 5% to 8%, with 60% to 70% being due to Alzheimer's disease. Slightly over half of these (58%) live in low- to middle-income countries (World Health Organization, 2019b).

In contrast to the World Health Organization's estimates, the Alzheimer's Association in the United States has typically cited a far higher prevalence rate amounting to 5.8 million Americans, which equals, in their estimates, 10% of the population ages 65 and older (Alzheimer's Association, 2019). The lower prevalence rate used for worldwide statistics conforms to the latest approach to estimate Alzheimer's disease prevalence in which researchers use a multistage modeling formula that separates the steps in the disease's progression. By applying this method, the most recent estimate places the number in the United States with the disease as of 2018 at 3.65 million (Brookmeyer et al., 2018). Furthermore, more refined approaches to measuring prevalence rule out other causes of neurocognitive disorders, which can account for roughly 25% of Alzheimer's dementia cases (Boyle et al., 2018).

Prospective studies that follow individuals over time support the interpretation that U.S. prevalence statistics are biased by the inclusion of non-Alzheimer's patients. In one such study, the autopsied brains of 553 individuals diagnosed in life as having Alzheimer's disease were found, upon autopsy, to have another neurocognitive disorder (Shim et al., 2013). Similarly, research based on the long-term Framingham (MA) Heart Study (Satizabal et al., 2016) carefully distinguished among causes of dementia across four successive groups of older adults studied between 1977 and 2008. Reporting on incidence (new cases), the Satizabal et al. study showed that vascular dementia and Alzheimer's disease both decreased over the three-decade period. At the same time the overall cardiovascular health of participants improved, the cohorts studied were successively better educated. Earlier studies on Alzheimer's disease prevalence in the United States might not only have failed to differentiate forms of neurocognitive disorder but also failed to account for educational influences on prevalence estimates.

The distinction between Alzheimer's disease and other forms of neurocognitive disorder is an important one. Other forms of neurocognitive disorder are different in their cause, prognosis, and treatment. They may even be preventable, as you will soon learn.

From a sociocultural point of view, what the public hears about the prevalence of Alzheimer's disease is also important because this information shapes people's attitudes about their own cognitive functioning. People who see these statistics may inaccurately conclude that they are doomed to develop the disorder and that there is nothing they can do to prevent it. In fact, not all neurocognitive disorders have the same inexorable progression as does Alzheimer's disease, and some can be prevented.

Psychological Symptoms.   The psychological symptoms of Alzheimer's disease evolve gradually over time. The earliest signs are occasional loss of memory for recent events or familiar tasks. Changes in personality and behavior eventually become evident as the disease progresses. By the time the disease has entered the most advanced stage, the individual has lost the ability to perform even the simplest and most basic of everyday functions.

The rate of progression in Alzheimer's disease varies from person to person, but there is a fairly regular pattern of loss over the stages of the disease. The survival time following the diagnosis is 4.2 years for men and 5.7 for women on average, but is shorter for individuals with more severe cognitive impairment at the time of diagnosis (Larson et al., 2004).

Biological Changes.   One of the most pervasive set of changes to occur in the brain of a person with Alzheimer's disease is the formation of abnormal deposits of protein fragments known as **amyloid plaques**. Amyloid is a generic name for protein fragments that collect together in a specific way to form insoluble deposits (meaning that they do not dissolve). The form of amyloid most closely linked with Alzheimer's disease consists of a string of 42 amino acids and is therefore referred to as **beta-amyloid-42**.

Beta amyloid is formed from **amyloid precursor protein (APP)**, a protein found naturally in the brain. As APP is manufactured, it embeds itself in the neuron's membrane. A small piece of APP is lodged inside the neuron, and a larger part of it remains outside. In healthy aging, the part of APP remaining outside the neuron is trimmed by enzymes called secretases so that it is flush with the neuron's outer membrane. In Alzheimer's disease, something goes wrong with this process so that the APP is snipped at the wrong place, causing beta-amyloid-42 to form. The cutoff fragments eventually clump together into beta-amyloid plaques, the abnormal deposits that the body cannot dispose of or recycle (see Figure 5.11).

The second major change to occur in the brain is a profusion of abnormally twisted fibers within the neurons themselves, known as neurofibrillary tangles (literally, tangled nerve fibers). It is now known that the neurofibrillary tangles are made up of a protein called tau (see Figure 5.12), which seems to play a role in maintaining the stability of the microtubules that form the internal support structure of the axons. The microtubules are like train tracks that guide nutrients from the cell body down to the ends of the axon. The tau proteins are like the railroad ties or crosspieces of the microtubule train tracks. In Alzheimer's disease, the tau is changed chemically and loses its ability to separate and support the microtubules. With their support gone, the tubules begin to wind around each other and they can no longer perform their function.

This collapse of the transport system within the neuron may first result in malfunctions in communication between neurons and may eventually lead to the death of the neuron.

Proposed Causes.   The theory guiding most researchers is that genetic abnormalities are somehow responsible for the neuronal death that is the hallmark of Alzheimer's. The genetic theory began to emerge as an explanation after the discovery that certain families seemed more prone to develop a form of the disease that struck at the relatively young age of 40 to 50 years. These cases are now referred to as early-onset familial Alzheimer's disease. Although the situation is tragic for the afflicted individuals, geneticists have learned a tremendous amount from studying their DNA.

Since the discovery of the early-onset form of the disease, genetic analyses have also provided evidence of a large number of genes potentially numbering as many as 21 that can individually or in combination increase the likelihood of developing the form of Alzheimer's disease that starts at a more conventional age of 60 or 65 years. This form of the disease is called late-onset Alzheimer's disease.

One of the prime genes thought to be involved in the late-onset form of the disease is the apolipoprotein E (ApoE) gene, located on chromosome 19. ApoE is

FIGURE 5.11

Plaque Formation in Alzheimer's Disease

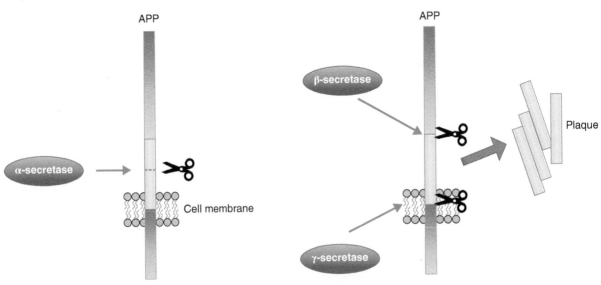

Normal cleavage of APP occurs when it is snipped by α-secretase, releasing a neuroprotective fragment along with the snipped APP. In the formation of a plaque, the snipping by β-secretase and γ-secretase results in abnormal cleavage and the production of plaques.

FIGURE 5.12

Neurofibrillary Tangle Formation in Alzheimer's Disease

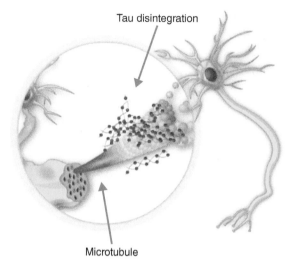

Tau disintegration

Microtubule

Neurofibrillary tangles are formed when tau disintegrates leading microtubules to become twisted and tangled.

Source: From Mark C. Surles. Used with permission of ScienceMedia, Inc.

a protein that carries cholesterol throughout the body, but it also binds to beta-amyloid, possibly playing a role in plaque formation. A host of other genes have been proposed, perhaps as many as 21, which can individually or in combination be involved in the disease. The newer approaches to understanding the genetics of Alzheimer's disease use genome-wide association study to look for genetic associations that may not be predicted by existing theory (Jansen et al., 2019).

Even as inherited contributions to Alzheimer's disease were being identified with the advent of new genetic methods of testing, researchers were also becoming intrigued with the role of environmental contributions. In a unique longitudinal study of aging among the Sisters of Notre Dame, nuns who agreed to donate their brains upon their death were studied while alive and their cognitive performance related to the studies of their brain upon autopsy. One of the original findings of the study was that despite the appearance of plaques and tangles in autopsy, many of the sisters did not show symptomatic deficits in cognitive performance. More recently, researchers found that higher mental activity in early adulthood seemed to protect the sisters from showing signs of cognitive decline in later life despite the presence of these changes in the brain (Iacono et al., 2015).

Evidence for other protective factors continues to accumulate showing that even people who might be otherwise at risk for Alzheimer's disease never show symptoms during their lifetimes. Exercise is one of these protective factors. In one large study conducted in Japan, a group of highly active older individuals who exercised at least once a week had a lower rate of Alzheimer's disease than did the nonactive participants (Kishimoto et al., 2016).

Predicting who will develop Alzheimer's disease, even in genetically at-risk individuals, is a challenging proposition given the many as yet unknown processes that lead to its development. The good news is that there are protective factors and as we learn more about what they are and how they operate, even those with a genetic predisposition may be able to take advantage of "nurture" in reducing their chances of developing Alzheimer's disease. Indeed, the improved health of the population may be playing a role in reducing the chances of even genetically susceptible individuals to developing Alzheimer's disease.

Diagnosis.   The diagnosis of neurocognitive disorder is in general made when there is significant and progressive cognitive decline in one or more areas including social cognition, memory, aphasia (loss of language ability), apraxia (loss of ability to carry out coordinated movement), agnosia (loss of ability to recognize familiar objects), and disturbance in executive functioning (loss of the ability to plan and organize) (American Psychiatric Association, 2013).

The diagnosis of Alzheimer's disease through clinical methods is traditionally carried out using the process of exclusion, where other possible diagnoses are systematically ruled out. This is because no one specific test or clinical indicator can definitively identify the disorder. Though methods of diagnosis are improving considerably, it is still the case that only an autopsy will reveal the presence of neurofibrillary tangles and beta-amyloid plaques that are the sure signs of the presence of Alzheimer's disease rather than another form of neurocognitive disorder.

The NINCDS-ADRDA criteria (McKhann et al., 1984) are considered currently to be a gold standard for diagnosing Alzheimer's disease. The acronym stands for National Institute of Neurological and Communicative Disorders and Stroke and Alzheimer's Disease and Related Diseases Association. The criteria are based on medical and neuropsychological screening tests, behavioral ratings, and mental status measures. The NINCDS-ADRDA criteria are said to be 85% to 90% accurate in the disease's later stages.

Through the continued improvement of brain scanning, the ability to provide a reliable diagnosis in the early to moderate stages of the disorder is becoming ever more likely (Panegyres et al., 2016). Ultimately, as treatments improve, early diagnosis would make it possible for clinicians to intervene and either slow or stop the degeneration of the patient's brain.

Medical Treatments. As researchers continue to make advances in identifying the cause or causes of Alzheimer's disease, the hope is that medications will be found that can reverse its course.

One category of Alzheimer's medications targets acetylcholinesterase (also called cholinesterase), the enzyme that normally destroys acetylcholine after its release into the synaptic cleft. The actions of this enzyme seem to reduce the amount of acetylcholine available to the hippocampal neurons, thus leading to memory loss. Anticholinesterase treatments inhibit this enzyme. The anticholinesterase treatments approved by the U.S. Food and Drug Administration (FDA) are tetrahydroaminoacridine (THA), also called tacrine and given the brand name Cognex; donepezil hydrochloride, called Aricept; galantamine, called Razadyne; and rivastigmine, with the brand name of Exelon. By inhibiting the action of acetylcholinesterase, these drugs slow the breakdown of acetylcholine, maintaining it at normal levels in the brain.

Memantine (Namenda) is the fourth type of medication for Alzheimer's disease. It acts by targeting the excitatory neurotransmitter, glutamate. The theory is that glutamate overstimulates excitatory synapses, damaging the neurons involved. By targeting glutamate, memantine is thought to exert a protective effect against this damage (Lipton, 2006).

Neither of the major types of medications, either alone or in combination, have shown conclusive scientific evidence for their efficacy. At best, they could only treat symptoms, and only for a limited time as they do not stop disease progression (Stella et al., 2015). There are a number of possible explanations for the failure to demonstrate significant effects of these medications (Schott, 2019), not the least of which may be that pharmaceutical companies are beginning to invest fewer dollars into finding a cure. Additionally, no one disease mechanism has been isolated, and, unlike other medical conditions, the diagnostic criteria are not clearly established.

The side effects of medications used to treat neurocognitive disorders, including Alzheimer's disease, are considerable and can range as high as 37% of all patients (Kanagaratnam et al., 2016). These side effects include gastrointestinal effects; dizziness; drowsiness; fainting; frequent or painful urination; headache; joint pain, stiffness, or swelling; depression; unusual bleeding or bruising; weight loss; clumsiness or unsteadiness; confusion; changes in blood pressure; loss of bladder or bowel control; aggression; agitation; delusions; irritability; nervousness; restlessness; tremors; and respiratory difficulties.

Other than medications, a diet rich in antioxidants has long been touted as a way to prevent Alzheimer's.

Antioxidants such as ginkgo biloba, melatonin, polyphenols, and vitamins E and C have been proposed to help improve memory and thinking in people with Alzheimer's although researchers have yet to validate these claims.

Psychosocial Treatments. Given that the pathway to medical treatments is not clearly established, people with this disease and their families must nevertheless find ways to deal on a daily basis with the incapacitating cognitive and sometimes physical symptoms that accompany the deterioration of brain tissue. Clearly, until a cure can be found, mental health workers will be needed to provide assistance in this difficult process, so that the individual's functioning can be preserved for as long as possible.

A critical step in providing conscientious symptom management is for health care professionals to recognize that Alzheimer's disease involves families as much as it does the patients. Family members are most likely to be the ones providing care for the patient, particularly when the patient is no longer able to function independently. This responsibility most likely falls to spouses and their children.

Caregivers are those individuals, usually family, who provide support to people with chronic diseases. They have been the focus of considerable research efforts over the past 30 years. We now know that caregivers are very likely to suffer adverse effects from the constant demands placed on them. The term caregiver burden is used to describe the stress that caregivers experience in the daily management of their afflicted relative. As the disease progresses, caregivers must provide physical assistance in basic life functions, such as eating, dressing, and toileting. As time goes by, the caregiver may experience health problems that make it harder and harder to provide the kind of care needed to keep the Alzheimer's patient at home.

Given the strain placed on caregivers, it should come as no surprise that health problems and rates of depression, stress, and isolation are higher among these individuals than among the population at large. Fortunately, support for caregivers of people with Alzheimer's disease is widely available. Local chapters of national organizations in the United States such as the Alzheimer's Association provide a variety of community support services for families in general and caregivers in particular. Caregivers can be taught ways to promote independence and reduce distressing behaviors in the patient as well as to learn ways to handle the emotional stress associated with their role (Piersol et al., 2017).

An important goal in managing the symptoms of Alzheimer's disease is to teach caregivers behavioral methods that will help to maximize the patient's ability to remain independent for as long as possible (see Figure 5.13). The idea behind this approach is that, by maintaining the patient's independence, the caregiver's burden is somewhat reduced. For example, the patient can be given prompts, cues, and guidance in the steps involved in getting dressed and then be positively rewarded with praise and attention for having completed those steps.

Second, caregivers can also use behavioral strategies to reduce or eliminate the frequency of actions such as wandering or being aggressive. In some cases, this strategy may require ignoring problematic behaviors, with the idea that by eliminating the reinforcement for those behaviors in the form of attention, the patient will be less likely to engage in them. However, it is more likely that a more active approach will be needed, especially for a behavior such as wandering. In this case the patient can be provided with positive reinforcement for not wandering.

Third, caregivers should, as much as possible, operate according to a strict daily schedule. The structure provided by a regular routine of everyday activities can give the patient additional cues to use as guides for which behaviors to carry out at which times of day.

Fourth, the caregiver should identify situations in which the patient becomes particularly disruptive, such as during bathing or riding in the car. In these cases, the caregiver can learn how to target those aspects of the situation that cause the patient to become particularly upset and then modify them accordingly. For example, if the problem occurs while bathing, it may be that a simple alteration such as providing a terry cloth robe rather than a towel helps reduce the patient's feeling of alarm at being undressed in front of others.

It is also important for caregivers to understand what to expect as the disease progresses. In a study of more than 300 nursing home patients with advanced neurocognitive disorder, fewer interventions considered burdensome, such as tube feeding, were used when those responsible for the patient's treatment were aware of the prognosis and typical course of the disease (Mitchell et al., 2009).

Other Forms of Neurocognitive Disorder

The condition known as neurocognitive disorder is frequently caused by Alzheimer's disease in later life; however, many other conditions can affect the status of the brain and cause the individual to experience loss of memory, language, and motor functions.

People with vascular neurocognitive disorder progressively lose cognitive functioning due to damage to the arteries supplying the brain. The most common form of vascular neurocognitive disorder is multi-infarct dementia (MID), caused by transient ischemic attacks. In this case, a number of minor strokes (infarcts) occur in which a clogged or burst artery interrupts blood flow to the brain. Each infarct is too small to be noticed, but over time, the progressive damage caused by the infarcts leads the individual to lose cognitive abilities.

There are important differences between MID and Alzheimer's disease. The development of MID tends to be more rapid than Alzheimer's disease. The higher the number of infarcts, the greater the decline in cognitive functioning (Dhamoon et al., 2018).

Vascular neurocognitive disorder seems to be related to risk factors that are similar to those for cardiovascular disease. Diabetes mellitus is associated with a higher risk of vascular dementia, or neurocognitive disorder, particularly in individuals who are older and have a history of stroke and/or hypertension (Sherzai et al., 2016). Metabolic syndrome also is associated with a higher risk of vascular neurocognitive disorder (Ng et al., 2016). Excess fat (adiposity) in the midsection further increases the risk of neurocognitive disorder in late life (Arnoldussen et al., 2018).

Neurocognitive disorder that specifically involves the frontal lobes of the brain is known as frontotemporal neurocognitive disorder (FTD). The individual with FTD experiences personality changes such as apathy, lack of inhibition, obsessiveness, addictive behaviors, and loss of judgment. Eventually the individual becomes neglectful of personal habits and loses the ability to communicate.

People who develop Parkinson's disease show a variety of motor disturbances, including tremors (shaking at rest), speech impediments, slowing of movement, muscular rigidity, shuffling gait, and postural instability or the inability to maintain balance. Neurocognitive disorder can develop during the later stages of the disease, and some people with Alzheimer's disease develop symptoms of Parkinson's disease. Patients typically survive 10 to 15 years after symptoms appear.

FIGURE 5.13

Psychosocial Treatments

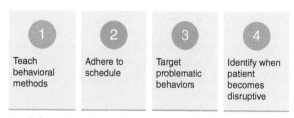

Four behavioral methods to help caregivers of patients with Alzheimer's disease.

There is no cure for Parkinson's disease, but medications are available that can treat its symptoms. The primary drug used is Levodopa (L-dopa); however, over the years, this medication loses its effect and may even be toxic. Another, more radical, approach involves applying high-frequency deep brain stimulation of subcortical movement areas of the brain that in the past were excised surgically (Sharma et al., 2016). Research examining the activation of brain cells with flashes of light offers promising treatment for Parkinson's disease. This quickly emerging field of optogenetics presents exciting avenues to better understand the mechanisms involved in Parkinson's disease to advance and improve treatment (Delbeke et al., 2017).

Lewy bodies are tiny spherical structures consisting of deposits of protein found in dying nerve cells in damaged regions deep within the brains of people with Parkinson's disease. Neurocognitive disorder with Lewy bodies, first identified in 1961, is similar to Alzheimer's disease in that it causes progressive loss of memory, language, calculation, and reasoning as well as other higher mental functions. Neurocognitive disorder with Lewy bodies can fluctuate in severity, at least early in the disease. The disease also includes episodes of confusion and hallucinations, which are not typically found in Alzheimer's disease. Fortunately, progress in diagnostic methods are making it possible to recognize the symptoms of the disorder, but its cause is still not yet well understood (McKeith et al., 2017).

A relatively rare cause of neurocognitive disorder is Pick's disease, which involves severe atrophy of the frontal and temporal lobes. This disease is distinct from frontotemporal neurocognitive disorder because, in addition to deterioration of these areas, the individual's brain accumulates unusual protein deposits (called Pick bodies). The symptoms of Pick's disease include disorientation and memory loss in the early stages, but the disorder eventually progresses to include pronounced personality changes and loss of social constraints, similar to frontotemporal neurocognitive disorder. Eventually the individual becomes mute, immobile, and incontinent.

Reversible neurocognitive disorders are due to the presence of a medical condition that affects but does not destroy brain tissue. If the medical condition is left untreated, permanent damage may be done to the central nervous system, and the opportunity for intervention will be lost. Furthermore, if the condition is misdiagnosed as Alzheimer's disease, the patient will be regarded as untreatable and not be given the appropriate care at the appropriate time.

A neurological disorder known as normal-pressure hydrocephalus, though rare, can cause cognitive impairment, dementia, urinary incontinence, and difficulty in walking. The disorder involves an obstruction in the flow of cerebrospinal fluid, which causes the fluid to accumulate in the brain. Early treatment can divert the fluid away from the brain before significant damage has occurred.

Head injury can cause a subdural hematoma, which is a blood clot that creates pressure on brain tissue. Again, surgical intervention can relieve the symptoms and prevent further brain damage. The presence of a brain tumor can also cause cognitive deficits, which can be prevented from developing into a more severe condition through appropriate diagnosis and intervention.

Delirium is an acute cognitive disorder that is characterized by temporary confusion. It can be caused by diseases of the heart and lung, infection, or malnutrition. Unlike neurocognitive disorder, however, delirium has a sudden onset. Because this condition reflects a serious disturbance elsewhere in the body, such as infection, it requires immediate medical attention.

Delirium has many causes, including substance use, intake of medications, head injury, high fever, and vitamin deficiency. Most cases of delirium subside within days, but the condition may persist for as long as a month. Although relatively frequent in acute care medical settings, occurring in up to nearly 40% of hospitalized older adults (Boustani et al., 2010), the condition is uncommon within community-residing populations. Within institutionalized settings, the onset of delirium appears to be associated with the presence of pain and use of antipsychotic medications (Cheung et al., 2018). Unfortunately, the individual with delirium may be misdiagnosed with dementia, and an opportunity for intervention will have been lost or at least made more complicated. Furthermore, older adults whose inability to care for themselves renders them as frail (e.g., low on functional independence) may be discharged from the hospital with their delirium untreated or mismanaged (Verloo et al., 2016).

Prescribed medications given in too strong a dose or in harmful combinations are included as other potentially toxic substances that can cause neurocognitive disorder-like symptoms. A condition called polypharmacy, in which the individual takes multiple drugs sometimes without the knowledge of the physician, can be particularly lethal. Recall that the excretion of medications is slower in older adults because of changes in the kidneys, so that older adults are more vulnerable to such toxic effects of medications.

Wernicke's disease is an acute condition caused by chronic alcohol abuse involving delirium, eye movement disturbances, difficulties maintaining balance and movement, and deterioration of the nerves to the hands and feet. Providing the individual with vitamin B1 (thiamine) can reverse this condition. Unfortunately, if it is not treated, Wernicke's disease progresses to the chronic form of alcohol-induced neurocognitive disorder known as Korsakoff syndrome.

Older adults who suffer from clinical depression may show cognitive changes that mimic those involved in Alzheimer's disease. The symptoms of depression in older adults may include confusion, distraction, and irritable outbursts, symptoms that may be mistaken for Alzheimer's disease. When these cognitive symptoms appear, causing impairment similar to neurocognitive disorder, the individual is said to have pseudodementia. Depression may also occur in conjunction with dementia, particularly in older adults who are in the early stages of a dementing disorder. In either case, the depression is treatable, and when appropriate interventions are made, the individual's cognitive functioning can show considerable improvement. We will discuss these issues further in Chapter 11.

The many possible causes of neurocognitive disorder, and the difficulty in distinguishing neurocognitive disorder due to Alzheimer's disease from other forms of cognitive decline, supports the notion that the prevalence of Alzheimer's disease may be overestimated, particularly with the rise in obesity in the United States, which presents a significant risk factor for certain forms of neurocognitive disorder.

Clearly, Alzheimer's disease and the variety of neurocognitive disorders described here are major potential limitations on the lives of older adults. Contrary to the impression given by the media, they afflict a minority of older people. Nevertheless, breakthroughs in their treatment, along with contributions to understanding other major diseases, will be among the most significant achievements of science in the 21st century.

SUMMARY

1. Diseases in middle and later adulthood can significantly interfere with quality of life. Risk factors for chronic disease include a sedentary lifestyle, smoking, alcohol use, and unhealthy diets. Cardiovascular diseases, in which there are pathological changes in the arteries in the form of arteriosclerosis and atherosclerosis, are the number one cause of death worldwide. Heart disease also includes coronary artery disease, myocardial infarction, hypertension, and congestive heart failure. Cerebrovascular accidents involve a cutting off of blood to the brain and may be acute or transient. Cardiovascular diseases are the leading cause of death in the over-75 population, with men having a higher risk, particularly Black men. Behavioral risk factors include a sedentary lifestyle, smoking, high BMI, and excessive alcohol intake. Metabolic syndrome refers to the cluster of symptoms including abdominal obesity, high blood fats, abnormal levels of blood cholesterol, hypertension, and high glucose associated with high-risk factors for cardiovascular diseases. Preventive medication, diet, and exercise are advised to reduce or prevent the prevalence of heart disease.

2. Cancer is a group of diseases in which there is abnormal cell growth. There are many behavioral risk factors for cancer, including smoking, sun exposure, and lack of control over diet. Environmental toxins can increase cancer risk. Cancer treatment includes surgery, radiation therapy, chemotherapy, and targeted drug therapy.

3. Several musculoskeletal disorders are more common in older adults than in the younger population. Osteoarthritis is a degenerative joint disease in which the cartilage deteriorates. Osteoporosis is an extreme loss of bone mineral content that primarily affects women. Preventative steps include calcium intake, vitamin D, exercise, dietary control, and estrogen-replacement therapy.

4. Type 2 diabetes is an increasingly common chronic disease in older adults caused by a defect in metabolizing glucose; estimates suggest that a substantial proportion of the over-60 population are afflicted. Prevention and treatment involve weight control, exercise, and medication.

5. Respiratory diseases, including chronic obstructive pulmonary disease, chronic emphysema, and chronic bronchitis, are thought to be caused primarily by cigarette smoking. They have no cure at present.

6. Neurocognitive disorder is a clinical condition involving loss of memory and other cognitive functions. Alzheimer's disease is thought to have genetic causes but may also reflect lifestyle factors and may co-occur with other forms of neurocognitive disorders. Other neurocognitive disorders include vascular, frontotemporal, Parkinson's, Lewy Body, and Pick's Disease. There are also reversible neurocognitive disorders which, if treated, and can lead to a return of normal cognitive functioning.

6

Basic Cognitive Functions: Information Processing, Attention, and Memory

Although declines in memory and attention occur with age, there are ways to slow this process. Take a look at some of the strategies used by older adults to help improve their cognitive functioning. Chances are, you already use some of these strategies!

1. **Train your brain.** Look for new challenges every day, from crossword puzzles to videogames to taking different routes to get to the same place.

2. **Limit distractions.** Easier said than done in this age of multitasking, but focusing on one task at a time boosts your memory (hint: stay off social media during class!).

3. **Keep organized.** Make lists, reduce clutter, and keep common items in the same location.

4. **Practice mindfulness.** Focus on your current inner state while you remain aware of your surroundings.

5. **Stay healthy.** Good physical health promotes mental agility.

6. **Use mnemonics.** Memory tricks can help you remember everything from gardening advice ("leaflets of three, let it be" to avoid poison ivy) to people's names ("Joy has a baby boy").

7. **Stay hydrated.** Drinking plenty of water can help you avoid sluggishness and memory loss.

8. **Use visualization.** Ever go into another room to get something and forget what it was? Imagine that you're picking the item up as soon as you decide to go get it.

9. **Write things down.** Like, with a pen or pencil. Handwriting outweighs typing on a computer or phone, in part because your brain is better activated when creating each letter's shape rather than hitting keys that all have the same shape and feel.

10. **Make new brainpaths.** Use your fingertips to trace the outlines of objects. Each repetition will help you build new synapses.

Cognition refers to the way the mind works, specifically, the processes of attention, memory, intelligence, problem-solving, and the use of language. We know that aging affects each of these areas of functioning, leading to important changes in many of people's ability to carry out their everyday activities.

PROCESSING SPEED AND ATTENTION

One of the most widely studied areas in cognition and aging, processing speed is the amount of time it takes for an individual to analyze incoming information from the senses, formulate decisions, and then prepare a response on the basis of that analysis. One of the fundamental units of study in cognitive and aging, researchers have used processing speed as an indicator of the integrity of the central nervous system.

Reaction Time

The basic measure of processing speed is reaction time. To measure reaction time, researchers ask their participants to complete an action such as pushing a computer key when the screen flashes a particular stimulus, known as a target. Stimuli that do not fit the criteria for the target are called distractors.

In simple reaction time tasks, participants are instructed to make a response such as pushing the key as soon as they see the target, such as a red circle appearing on the screen in front of them. In choice reaction time tasks, participants must make one response for one stimulus and another response for a different stimulus. For example, they would push the "F" button for a red circle and the "J" button for a blue circle.

In some studies, participants see a cue prior to the target's presentation. This cue directs them to look in a particular area of the computer screen. The cue may or may not direct them to the exact spot on the screen where the actual target will appear. In some studies, researchers use misleading or irrelevant cues to determine how distracting information alters the individual's responses and compare performance in response to these cues to performance in response to relevant cues.

Researchers know with certainty that the reaction time of a young adult will be lower (i.e., the person will be quicker) than when that individual gets older. The question is, by how much and under what circumstances will it increase? The documented changes in reaction time with age in adulthood are typically a matter of several hundreds of milliseconds, not enough to be particularly noticeable in everyday life, but enough to be significant under the scrutiny of the laboratory researcher.

People vary greatly in the rate at which they experience a slowing in reaction time and seem to do so more among older groups than younger groups of adults. Despite this increasing variability in reaction times with age, overall, reflecting, in part, variations in health and fitness (Dreary & Ritchie, 2016).

Why do reaction times slow as people age? According to the general slowing hypothesis, the increase in reaction time reflects a general decline of information processing speed within the nervous system of the aging individual (Salthouse, 1996). The age-complexity hypothesis proposes, furthermore, that through a slowing of central processes in the nervous system, older adults perform progressively more poorly as the tasks become more complex and their processing resources are stretched more and more to their limit (Cerella et al., 1980).

The age-complexity hypothesis is reflected in the Brinley plot, in which the reaction times of older groups of adults are plotted against the times of younger adults (see Figure 6.1). If you look closely at this graph, you can see that in the 500 ms range (half a second), older and younger adults have similar performance. These are the tasks that are relatively easy; this is why they are performed so quickly. However, on tasks that take longer for young adults to complete (1,000 ms or 1 s), older adults take proportionately longer (1,500 to 2,000 ms) than they do

FIGURE 6.1

Relationship between Reaction Times of Younger and Older Adults

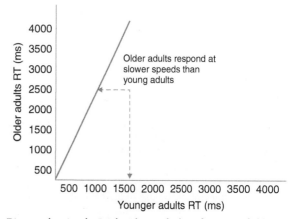

Diagram showing the Brinley plot in which performance of older adults is plotted against performance by younger adults, revealing that as the task becomes more difficult (requires more time), older adults are disproportionately slower.

on the 500 ms tasks. The hardest tasks take young adults about 2,500 ms to complete, but take older adults as long as 4,000 ms.

The general slowing hypothesis is consistent with a large body of data on reaction time performance in adulthood. This hypothesis does not identify any particular stage or component of information processing as the culprit for causing age differences in reaction time, though there is the assumption that the slowing reflects a lack of efficiency in the central rather than peripheral nervous system. As we will see later, the general slowing hypothesis is also used to explain age differences in memory. A loss of speed leads to memory impairments, as a backlog develops in cognitive processes calling for multiple operations to be completed simultaneously or within a limited time.

Attention

Attention involves the ability to focus or concentrate on a portion of experience while ignoring other features of that experience, to be able to shift that focus as demanded by the situation, and to be able to coordinate information from multiple sources. Once your attention is focused on a piece of information, you are then able to perform further cognitive operations, such as those needed for memory or problem-solving.

If you have difficulty concentrating or focusing your attention for long periods of time, you are certainly aware of how frustrating it can be to miss important information or details when you divert your mental resources away from the task. Persistent and serious attentional problems characterize people with attention deficit disorder who, as a result, may have difficulty learning new information or performing more than one task at a time. The attentional deficits associated with the normal aging process can lead to difficulties of a similar nature, particularly when individuals have to make complex decisions within a short period of time.

Types of Attentional Tasks. Studies of attention are important for understanding the cognitive functions of adults of varying ages and their abilities to function in various real-life situations in which cognitive resources must be focused on some target or goal. Researchers approach these issues by breaking down the attentional tasks involved in everyday life into components to examine in the laboratory. For the most part, these studies suggest that people become less efficient in the use of attentional processes as they get older.

Two methods used in studies on attention and aging involve visual search tasks which require that the observer locate a specific target among a set of distractors. In simple visual search, the target differs from the other stimuli by only one feature, such as shape, color, or size. Your task would be to respond by pushing a computer key every time you saw a specific target appear on the screen in front of you. The target might be an "X" appearing among a set of distractors, such as "+" signs of the same size and color.

Participants completing tests of simple visual search can generally reach high levels of performance very quickly across the trials of an experiment. When this occurs, the target is said to "pop out" among the distractors. At that point, the search is automatic. Because the target is so easy to detect, reaction time tends not to increase as the number of items in the stimulus array gets larger. There could be 10 or 50 "Xs" in the array but, as long as the participant can see all the stimuli, participants will find it easy to see if that "+" is there or not.

In conjunction visual search, the target differs from the distractors in more than one way. If the target is a red X, the distractors could be blue +'s, red +'s, and blue X's. To register a correct response, the respondent must indicate that the target is present only when the field contains the red X.

Researchers propose that simple visual search relies on parallel processing, meaning that you can scan the whole array at once, just looking for the one feature that matches that of the target. It's as if you were at a home basketball game and wanted to spot your friend, a fan of the visiting team, in the large crowd. If all the home fans were wearing the school colors (e.g., maroon), your friend's light blue shirt would easily jump out at you. Older and younger adults perform at similarly high levels in simple visual search tasks, finding the targets quickly and accurately (Whiting et al., 2005).

Conjunction search relies on the more time-consuming task of serial processing because each stimulus must be examined in sequence to determine whether it has all the qualities of the target. You first have to detect color (or shape) and then detect the second attribute. The larger the number of stimuli to scan, the longer the participant will take to decide whether the target is present or not. In the case of your friend at the basketball game, should the visiting team's shirts also be maroon, it would take you much longer to find your friend's face among the fans, especially in a large arena.

Comparisons of older and younger adults on conjunction search show that both age groups perform less efficiently than they do on simple search tasks. However, the cost to performance is higher for older adults, in part because they require more eye movements while processing the stimuli (Porter et al., 2010).

On the other hand, older adults have greater experience in making decisions in real-life settings, which can benefit them when they scan actual environments. When compared to younger adults on a search task that included context to guide their attention, older adults were more likely than younger adults to benefit from background cues (Neider & Kramer, 2011). Furthermore, older adults can benefit from training that gives them practice and guidance in performing even very difficult conjunction searches (Neider et al., 2010).

One particularly important area of attentional performance that you undoubtedly know about is called "multitasking," in which people have to attend to more than one input source at a time. While multitasking, most people pay a price in terms of the quality of their performance. This includes lower academic performance by college students who go on social media or who text while in class (Junco, 2012). It is not only college students, though, who perform more poorly when multitasking. The disadvantages of multitasking that people experience increase progressively in older age groups (Kramer & Madden, 2008).

A number of investigators who study attention and aging are interested in the way that older adults mentally juggle the information they must manage when it comes in from different sources. In particular, researchers try to determine whether older adults have difficulty turning off one response while performing another in what is called inhibitory control. One of the best known inhibitory attention tasks is the Stroop test, in which you are told to name the color of ink in which a word is printed. In the critical trials on the Stroop test, your response time and accuracy are compared when the color and the word match (e.g., the word "red" printed in red) with your performance when the color and the word do not match ("red" is printed in green). People with good inhibitory control can quickly state the color name without being distracted by the color of the printed letters.

In a sustained attention task, participants must respond when they see a particular target appear out of a continuous stream of stimuli. This is the type of attention that many video games require when players monitor a constantly changing visual array. Laboratory tasks of sustained attention are similar in principle, though not as elaborate. For example, in a typical experimental task, participants watch a computer screen with a series of stimuli; they're told to respond only when the target stimulus appears (such as the letter "X" moving onto a screen containing all "Y"s). In some conditions, the experimenter provides cues that give participants notice about whether and where to look for the target just before it appears. Older adults typically have more difficulty on sustained attention tasks than do younger adults in part because they take longer to shift their focus from trial to trial (Golub & Mock, 2019).

There are key ways in which attention may be preserved in older adults. For example, although older adults are typically slower when processing information from visual displays, they can remember the location of an item presented in a visual display and may be even be more efficient at this task than are younger adults (Kramer et al., 2006). Additionally, healthy older adults, with practice, can activate different areas of the brain than can younger adults to raise their performance on the Stroop task to comparable levels (Schulte et al., 2009). Such results support models proposing that aging involves a degree of neural plasticity, a topic we will return to shortly.

Theories of Attention and Aging. Researchers appear to divide into two camps in accounting for age differences in attention (Figure 6.2). The attentional resources theory regards attention as a process reflecting the allocation of cognitive resources. When you focus on a particular object, you must dedicate a certain proportion of your mental operations to that object. According to this theory, older adults have greater difficulty on attentional tasks because they have less energy available for cognitive operations than do their younger counterparts (Kilb & Naveh-Benjamin, 2015).

The second theory of attention and aging, the inhibitory deficit hypothesis, suggests that aging reduces the individual's ability to inhibit or tune out irrelevant information (Butler & Zacks, 2006). As we discussed earlier, one important feature of attention is the ability to focus on one element of a stimulus array while ignoring others. If older adults cannot ignore irrelevant information, their attentional performance will suffer.

General slowing

Loss of attentional resources leads to longer times to respond

Inhibitory deficit

Inability to tune out irrelevant information

FIGURE 6.2

Theories of Aging and Attention

The two primary approaches to aging and attention/speed contrast the general slowing hypothesis with the inhibitory deficit model.

The inhibitory deficit hypothesis implies that middle-aged and older adults perform best when they have few distractions. One source of such distraction may be their own concern over how they are performing, which therefore may cause them to perform even more poorly than they otherwise would. Imagine that you are a computer programmer anxious about the possibility of being laid off or reassigned because you are not as quick as you once were in your job of inspecting arrays of new data. The more you worry about how you are performing, the less able you are to concentrate on your task. Your performance deficits might ultimately lead you to lose your job or be reassigned to other duties. Thus, people who are worried about the aging of their cognitive abilities may be more likely to engage in identity accommodation (the "over-the-hill" mentality), a process that will ultimately contribute to poorer performance.

The inhibitory deficit hypothesis initially received widespread support from studies in which electrical activity of the brain was used to indicate the ability to block out distracting stimuli on visual tasks (West & Schwarb, 2006). However, more recent evidence suggests that older adults are not entirely disadvantaged in inhibitory attentional tasks. As we noted earlier, they can benefit from practice with the Stroop test in ways similar to younger adults (Davidson et al., 2003), suggesting that performance on certain types of attention can be improved regardless of age. Additionally, older adults may even perform better than young adults on inhibitory tasks by activating their frontal lobes in a compensatory manner (Staub et al., 2014). Furthermore, if stimuli are presented in two modalities, such as auditory and visual, older adults are capable of showing levels of inhibition comparable to those of young adults (Guerreiro et al., 2015).

Drawing upon the idea that older adults can overcompensate for attentional deficits, they can also take advantage of their greater experience when confronted with situations that tap into that experience can compensate for age-related changes in sustained attention. In a simulated air-traffic control experiment, older adults who showed deficits on laboratory attentional tasks were able to perform well on the complex tasks required in the situations they encountered on the job on a daily basis (Nunes & Kramer, 2009). Education and verbal experience may also protect against increases in distraction while reading (McGinnis, 2012). Thus, although aging may affect attentional performance, the roles of experience and training may mitigate some of these effects to preserve important areas of functioning.

Coming to the problem from an entirely different perspective, Ramscar et al. (2014) argue that the deficits shown by older adults in cognitive tasks can be explained by their lifetime's accumulation of knowledge. Because they have more experience, older adults also have more information to sort through when they must make a decision. In a laboratory task, where every millisecond counts, they may therefore appear "slower." In everyday life, though, such delayed responding would be unlikely to have a measurable impact.

Video Games and Attention

With the increasing popularity of video games, many of which demand quick decisions and response speed, researchers have taken to the lab to investigate whether older adults can be trained in playing these games to improve their attentional control in real-life situations. In action video games, such as first-person shooter games (*Call of Duty, Halo,* and *Battlefield*) or third-person shooter games (*Grand Theft Auto, Gears of War*), the player must have excellent hand–eye coordination, play at a fast pace, and track multiple inputs. The aggressive content of these games aside, their cognitive benefits are becoming well established.

Young adults who play action video games have improved attentional capacity (Green & Bavelier, 2003). Experienced players have more efficient eye movements (West et al., 2013) and scan a display more quickly, automatically appraising such features as the number of

FIGURE 6.3

Example of a Useful Field of View (UFOV) Task

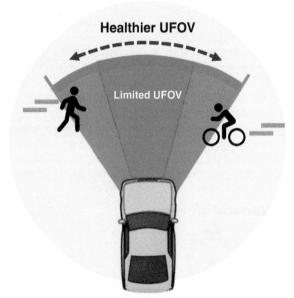

The Useful Field of View is the amount of visual information a person can take in with a glance without eye or head movements.

items in a display without having to count (Riesenhuber, 2004). Players of these games also have more attentional resources that they can devote to rapidly changing inputs, meaning that they will make finer-grained distinctions and, therefore, better decisions. They are also better able to focus their attention and ignore distracting or irrelevant information. However, it is important to keep in mind that there may be a self-selection bias operating so that people with better attentional resources also gravitate toward playing these games (Boot et al., 2008).

Experimental studies using action video games as a training tool show that they can enhance a variety of skills, including peripheral attention (seeing a target at the outer edges of a display), ability to process a rapidly changing stream of information, and keeping track of multiple targets (Bavelier et al., 2012). Video game training may also improve probabilistic learning, in which the individual becomes more adept at predicting the outcomes of particular actions (Schenk et al., 2017). Training also seems to improve the driving-relevant task called Useful Field of View (UFOV), which tests people's ability to respond to stimuli appearing in the periphery of their vision (see Figure 6.3) (Green & Bavelier, 2006).

If video games can have these beneficial effects on young adults, it would make sense that they could also improve the attentional abilities of older adults

(Dye et al., 2009). Studies going back to the early 1990s show that among older adults, training in video games can improve speeded performance (Dustman et al., 1992; Goldstein et al., 1997).

With the continued development of personal computer-based video games, researchers are able to investigate the effects on attention and speeded performance in a wider variety of formats. Older adults do not prefer to play first-person shooter games (McKay & Maki, 2010) but are instead drawn to casual video games played on a personal computer (Whitbourne et al., 2013). These ordinary computer games, as well as those specifically intended to improve cognition in older adults ("brain training"), appear to have beneficial effects on focused and sustained attention (Peretz et al., 2011).

On a cautionary note, however, consumers should be aware of the possibility that companies which sell brain training games provide misleading promotional materials about the benefits of their products. In 2016, the U.S. Federal Trade Commission charged that Lumosity, the producer of one of these games, was doing just that, and the company was given a warning to desist along with a $2 million fine. A randomized control trial study concluded that these games can have some positive effects on everyday functioning but inconsistent effects on cognition (Motter et al., 2016).

FIGURE 6.4

MV Crashes and Age

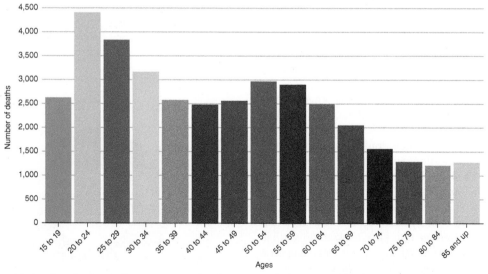

As shown here, with data from the Centers for Disease Control and Prevention, the highest number of motor vehicle deaths occurs in the 20- to 24-year-old age group.

Source: Data from Centers for Disease Control and Prevention. U.S. Department of Health and Human Services. Public domain.

DRIVING AND AGING

The ability to drive is undoubtedly one of the most important functional areas of an adult's life, particularly for people who live in areas that are not well served by public transportation. Changes in basic cognitive functions threaten to impair the older adult's ability to perform this vital task. Furthermore, as we saw in Chapter 4, there are also a number of changes in the visual system that can impair the performance of older drivers, including loss of visual acuity, increased sensitivity to glare, and difficulty seeing in the dark. Physical changes may also limit the older driver's ability to get in and out of a car, fasten a seat belt, change the seat position, turn the steering wheel, or cope with a breakdown (Arbesman & Pellerito, 2008). Finally, many medications used to treat chronic conditions in older adults can impair their driving ability due to side effects such as drowsiness, confusion, and dizziness (Sargent-Cox et al., 2011). Driving with pets, especially in the front seat, is another potential source of motor vehicle accidents for older adult drivers (Huisingh et al., 2016).

It is also important to consider the "low mileage bias" in statistics on crash rates involving older drivers. As you can see in Figure 6.4, older adult drivers have fewer crashes that are fatal than do younger drivers. However, because they drive fewer miles, older adults are reported as having higher crash rates and rates of fatality. Nevertheless, some form of vision screening seems warranted even though current methods to do so are not necessarily accurate (Desipriva et al., 2014).

Although previous research identified left-hand turns (in countries with right-side driving) and lane merging as particular risks for older adults, a more careful analysis of physiological responses during difficult maneuvers, as well as performance, yielded no evidence of differences from younger drivers (Koppel et al., 2015). In fact, for younger drivers, distracted driving due to cell phone use and manipulation of complex dashboard information panels pose just as significant a risk as vision changes in older adults (Klauer et al., 2015). The other major source of fatal accidents for younger drivers is drinking and driving with 27% of all fatal crashes due to elevated blood alcohol levels compared to 5% of those 75 and older (National Center for Statistics and Analysis, 2017).

As you can see from Figure 6.4, drivers under the age of 25 are also far more likely than older drivers to drink and drive. Younger drivers are also more likely to drive while distracted, particularly by talking or text messaging on a cell phone. Research suggests that even hands-free devices do not negate the effect of distracted driving (Kunar et al., 2018). In other words, any type of talking on the phone while driving is unsafe.

Counteracting the effects of age on rapid, complex, decision-making is the fact that older adults avoid many of the causes of motor vehicle accidents that injure, or take the lives of, younger adults. Many older drivers are able to self-regulate their behaviors to compensate for the changes they experience in their visual and cognitive abilities. They avoid driving at night, on interstate highways, and during rush hour (Desipriya et al., 2014). They also self-limit their driving if they become aware of limitations in their cognitive functioning (Pyun et al., 2018) in which they must make risky left-hand turns (Okonkwo et al., 2008). Older adults, perhaps rightly so, are concerned about unsafe drivers on the road, a concern that translates into their increased use of seat belts (Allen et al., 2019).

Another factor to consider is that older drivers have decades of experience behind the wheel that can compensate for their slower reaction times, particularly if they don't need to make a response within a fraction of a second. Under icy conditions, for example, experienced older drivers know how to control the car to avoid a spinout. They may also be better able to predict what other drivers will do in certain situations, such as whether someone will pull out of a parking spot without signaling.

Driving provides a perfect example of the importance of adopting a biopsychosocial perspective to understand the aging process (see Figure 6.5). Biology (changes in vision and reaction time) and psychology (internal distractions causing anxiety) each play important roles. The sociocultural component of the equation provides further insight into this comprehensive model. Driving is necessary in order to live independently in many regions of the United States and in other countries that lack comprehensive public transportation. Older adults who live in suburban or rural areas with limited or no public transportation lose

FIGURE 6.5

Biopsychosocial Model of Driving

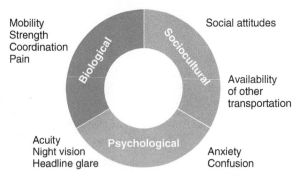

Driving and aging can be thought of in terms of the biopsychosocial model.

an important connection to the outside world and risk becoming housebound and socially isolated, particularly if they restrict their own driving due to loss of confidence in their abilities (Wong et al., 2016).

In terms of identity, older adults may also incorporate social attitudes about aging and driving that serve to impair their performance beyond what would occur due to the normal aging process. Older adults who doubt themselves more frequently will hesitate before making a response due to worries about their abilities or may suffer internal distractions because they are so preoccupied with their own concerns. Prejudice against them by younger people can exacerbate whatever fears and concerns older drivers already have about their changing abilities. They may hear derogatory phrases such as "driving while old" or "gray head" and become even more concerned and hence distracted.

As the number of older drivers continues to grow—due to the increased longevity of the Baby Boomer generation—appropriate safeguards are being considered for them by public officials, such as driving tests and safety classes. Highway safety experts are also exploring alternatives to the traditional intersection, such as substituting well-designed roundabouts for the type of complex junction that can cause so many accidents while turning. Older drivers can also benefit from easy fixes to their automobiles, such as adjusting the head restraints, steering wheel tilt, and mirror. In one survey of aging drivers, researchers found that over half needed to have their head restraints readjusted to provide proper support. Furthermore, through new technologies, such as collision avoidance systems, automobiles will eventually become better adapted to the needs of older drivers (Arbesman & Pellerito, 2008).

Nevertheless, there is value to maintaining precautions that protect all drivers from accidents caused by distracted driving, visual losses, or slowing of response speed. Current licensing policies and procedures are not well equipped to handle the influx of older drivers. Recommendations to address this growing public safety concern include identifying older drivers who may be medically at-risk and impaired rather than restricting all older drivers (Dobbs, 2008).

It's also worthwhile to consider that speed is not everything when it comes to navigating your way around the highways and byways of your community. Allowing more time for older drivers to get where they are going might not be such a bad idea and could even make the roads safer for everyone. It is also important to remember that prevention efforts should focus on the avoidable fatalities involving younger drivers who are under the influence of alcohol or other substances. The real "number one killer"—in the United States, at least—is not heart disease but fatal accidents involving drivers who are under the influence: people die at much younger ages than biology would dictate.

Interestingly, the data on aging and driving correspond closely to research about aging and crash prevalence among older airline pilots, who have fewer fatal and nonfatal accidents than younger pilots (Broach et al., 2003). Although older airline pilots may have better records, however, they do seem to be more vulnerable to fatigue from disrupted sleep schedules, taking longer to recover from

Jaroslaw Igras/Pixabay

Although the many roundabouts in this intersection appear potentially confusing, the British government is now investing in redesigns of roadways to ease traffic patterns.

jet lag, particularly if they were physically inactive, low in self-rated health, and moderate consumers of alcohol (van Drongelen et al., 2017).

MEMORY

One of the changes people fear the most about getting older is that they will lose their memory. It is perhaps for this reason that nutritional supplements supposedly targeting memory and those "brain games" have become so commercially popular. The data on the effects of aging on memory suggest that the aging process indeed has negative effects on many aspects of memory. However, as was true for attention, not all aspects of memory are affected in the same way by aging, nor is everyone affected the same way by aging, so that the process of memory loss is by no means completely inevitable.

Working Memory

After you attend to information, the next step is to register that information into consciousness. This process is known as working memory, which keeps information temporarily available and active in consciousness. You use your working memory when you are trying to learn new information or bring to mind information you learned previously that you are trying to recall. Working memory and attention are closely linked, as controlled attention is required to juggle multiple thought processes.

Researchers assess working memory by assigning a task to participants that prevents them from consciously rehearsing the information they are supposed to remember. The "n-back" task, a commonly used working memory test, requires you to repeat the "nth" item back in a list of items presented to you in serial order. For example, you might see a series of visual stimuli, such as a yellow triangle, a red square, a green circle, and a blue diamond. In each instance, you are asked whether the stimulus is new or one previously seen. In the "1-back" task, you are shown the yellow triangle followed by the red square followed by the yellow triangle and asked to remember the stimulus shown prior to the red square (the yellow triangle). The further back in the series (for example, in the "3-back"), the harder the task because more demands are placed on working memory.

You can see an example of an n-back working memory task in Figure 6.6. The letters would be presented starting with H and then move through the series. The H would be a 2-back task and the C would be a 3-back task. One advantage of this task is that it can be easily applied to neuroimaging studies because the stimuli can be presented

FIGURE 6.6

Example of a Working Memory Task

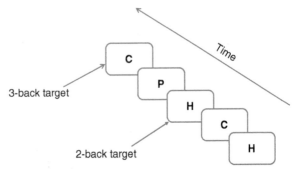

Schematic of n-back working memory task. Participants see the letters in the order shown on the screen, from "H" to "C."

on a screen that the subject views in a brain scanner such as an fMRI.

Through neuroimaging studies that connect how individuals perform on memory tasks to patterns of their brain's activity, researchers are beginning to understand the structural basis for the effects of aging on working memory. These studies look not just at what individual brain regions do during cognitive tasks but also at how these brain regions communicate with each other through networks. These studies are also able to test neuroplasticity models we discussed in Chapter 4 by documenting which regions of the brain are more activated in older adults than younger adults during a working memory task. Although this field is still relatively young, there are signs of promise that the proposed models of neuroplasticity can be traced to patterns of brain activation during working memory tasks (Froudist-Walsh et al., 2018).

Also relevant to working memory performance is the default network, a circuit in the brain that is active when the brain is at rest while processing internal stimuli (see Figure 6.7). The default network includes the hippocampus, parts of the prefrontal cortex, the parietal lobe, the temporal lobe, and part of the cingulate cortex involved in visualization. During tasks such as those involved in working memory, other areas become activated and the default network becomes deactivated. The default network may itself be subdivided into those regions involved in thinking about your own experiences and those that process your knowledge about events and facts that did not happen to you (Kim, 2012). In both cases, the network needs to turn itself off when you're trying to remember new information.

Age-related changes in the ability to deactivate the default network may contribute in part to poorer working memory performance in older adults (Hafkemeijer et al.,

FIGURE 6.7

Default Network

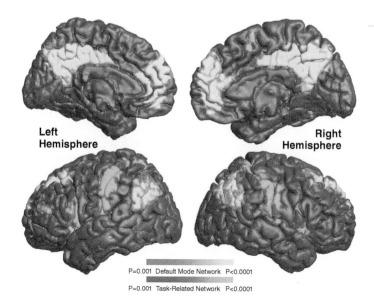

Left
Hemisphere

Right
Hemisphere

P=0.001 Default Mode Network P<0.0001

P=0.001 Task-Related Network P<0.0001

Default mode and task-related maps for healthy participants. On a green background, the default mode network is highlighted in warm colors (red and yellow) and the task-related network is highlighted in cold colors (blue and green).

2012). Instead of focusing on the information they need to be remembering, they use their cognitive resources on inwardly oriented stimuli.

On the other hand, by drawing on their inner resources, older adults may be able to use previous knowledge of stored information, which would represent an adaptive shift in the allocation of cognitive resources (Spreng et al., 2014).

Effects of Aging on Long-Term Memory in Adulthood

We turn next to long-term memory, the repository of information that is held for a period of time ranging from several minutes to a lifetime. Long-term memory contains information that includes the recent past, such as remembering where you put your cell phone half an hour ago, to information from many years ago, such as what happened at your fourth birthday party. The processes of long-term memory include encoding, storage, and retrieval. You encode information when you first learn it, keep it in long-term storage, and retrieve it when you need to use it on a subsequent occasion.

Episodic memory is long-term memory for events (episodes). Research suggests that older adults experience impairments in episodic memory, both in encoding and retrieving information (Shing et al., 2010). Episodic memory also depends on the integrity of connections among the frontal cortex, temporal and parietal lobes, and areas of the subcortex, including the thalamus. Age-related damage to the white matter, which shows up as white matter

hyperintensities, may be associated with memory changes in these regions (Lockhart et al., 2012).

However, in normal aging, these structural changes in areas of the brain involved in working memory may be compensated by heightened activation of the prefrontal cortex. According to scaffolding theory, older adults are able to recruit alternate neural circuits as needed by task demands to make up for losses suffered elsewhere in the brain (see Figure 6.8). Thus, working memory may decline in later adulthood, but individuals can circumvent these declines by bringing compensatory mechanisms into play. Additionally, life course factors may come into play, such as education, stress, exposure to toxins, health and physical activity, and personality changes over time (Reuter-Lorenz & Park, 2014).

Remote memory involves the recall of information from the distant past. In general, information stored and not accessed from remote memory becomes increasingly difficult to retrieve with passing years. A popular myth is that older people can remember information from many years in the past better than they can remember more recent information. However, this myth is not supported by data on remote memory (Aizpurua et al., 2015). In one study, Boston Red Sox fans were asked to recall details of the 2003 and 2004 league championship games between the Red Sox and the New York Yankees. Nearly 10 years later, older participants consistently showed poorer recall than younger participants (Breslin & Safer, 2013).

The exception to this research on remote memory occurs in the area of autobiographical memory, or the recall of information from your own past. Many people

FIGURE 6.8

Scaffolding Theory

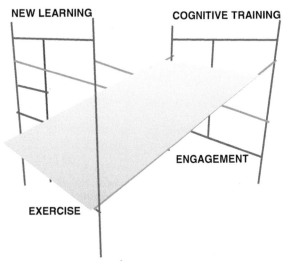

According to the scaffolding theory, older adults can recruit alternate neural circuits as needed by task demands as shown by these potential routes.

seem to experience a reminiscence bump of very clear memories for the ages of from about 10 to 30 years (Rubin et al., 1998), an effect that is particularly strong for happy memories (Gluck & Bluck, 2007). Researchers believe that these memories are preserved in part because they are central to identity (McLean, 2008). Remote memories that are not as personally relevant fade with the passage of time.

Flashbulb memory is the recall of important and distinctive events that stand out from other memories of past events. For example, you may remember where you were and what you were doing on February 14, 2018, when you heard the news that a gunman opened fire with a semi-automatic rifle at Marjory Stoneman Douglas High School in Parkland, Florida, killing 17 students and staff members and injuring 17 others. When older adults form such memories, the emotional meaning that makes them distinct can prove to enhance their ability to recall the event. For example, in the case of the 2000 U.S. Presidential election, even older individuals with slight cognitive impairments were able to remember factual details of the event (Waring et al., 2014).

In contrast to episodic memory, there are no declines in normal older adults in semantic memory, or the ability to recall word meanings and the factual information. Additionally, older adults seem to have well-preserved abilities to remember the names of famous people from viewing their faces, although their associations to those name-face

combinations may differ from those formed by younger adults (Pistono et al., 2019).

Long-term memory also includes your ability to remember actions. Procedural memory is recall of the actions involved in particular tasks, such as sewing on a button, playing the piano, and riding a bike. Like semantic memory, procedural memory holds up well with age. In one particularly impressive study, a sample of approximately 500 adults ranging from 18 to 95 years were tested on their ability to learn a fine motor task in which they had to use their fingers to slide a small metal nut off a rod as quickly as possible. Not only did older adults show significant improvement in performance over a series of five learning trials, but they retained their memory for the task for as long as 2 years later with no drop-off in performance (Smith et al., 2005). Similarly, in a two-handed motor learning task, older adults performed as well as, if not better than, their younger counterparts (Bhakuni & Mutha, 2015).

A well-maintained procedural memory contributes to the ability of older adults to compensate for some of their loss of speed and working memory in diverse areas including bridge playing, chess, reading, cooking, gardening, and typing (Mireles & Charness, 2002). The experienced bridge player, for example, is able to examine a round of cards without giving each individual card a great deal of thought or study. Through years of playing, many of the choices about which card to play follow established conventions and rules, so that the older bridge player does not have to remember as much about each of the hand of 13 cards they are dealt for each round of play.

Implicit memory is long-term memory for information that people acquire without intending to do so. It is another long-term memory process that does not appear to be affected by the aging process (Ward, 2018). In testing implicit memory, researchers present participants with a task that involves manipulating but not necessarily remembering information. For example, you might be presented with a list of words and asked to place them into categories but not to recall them. Later, you would be asked to remember the words you had previously only been told to categorize.

Remembering where you heard or saw something is sometimes as important as remembering the information itself. Source memory is the recall of where or how an individual acquires information. In everyday life, you use source memory when you are trying to remember which of your friends said she would give you tickets to an upcoming concert or which professor hinted at an impending pop quiz.

Older adults seem to have greater difficulty on source memory tasks when they must judge where they saw an item on a previous occasion (Kuhlmann & Boywitt, 2016). They also are more susceptible to false or illusory memories in which they say they remember something that never happened. The age differences in source memory may be due, in part, to the tendency for older adults to form more global memories ("the gist") which then leaves them open to false memories about some of the details that experimenters plant by inserting new information that was not part of the original stimuli (Webb et al., 2016).

However, older adults may be helped to improve their ability to overcome the susceptibility to false memory. In one intriguing study, participants were prompted to remember stops they had actually taken while on a museum tour but also shown prompts of stops they had not made. The prompts served to strengthen the memories for the stops in older adults, and in the process, reduced their susceptibility to a false memory effect (St. Jacques et al., 2015).

Another category of memory tasks involves remembering to do something that has not yet happened. Prospective memory encompasses the recall of events to be performed in the future. In prospective memory, you must remember your intention to perform an action, such as calling that friend who promised the tickets to decide where to meet.

Older adults commonly complain (and you may too) that they cannot remember what they were supposed to get when they went into a room. Although a nuisance, this type of forgetting is not as detrimental as the type of forgetting involved in not taking a medication at a certain time. Older people do indeed appear to have more prospective memory slips than do younger adults. Because prospective memory is so important in many real-life situations, difficulties in prospective memory seem to affect the older individual's everyday quality of life (Woods et al., 2015).

The tip-of-the-tongue phenomenon, more formally known as retrieval-induced forgetting, is another source of frequent memory complaints. This is what happens to you when you are unable to remember information that you knew at one time. For example, you might forget the name of a movie one of your favorite stars was in even though you knew it very well at the time. Eventually, it might come back to you, but for several minutes, you're just drawing a blank.

Whether in the lab or in everyday life, older adults seem more susceptible than younger adults to retrieval-induced forgetting. Young adults occasionally experience this effect when they are trying to retrieve an abstract word, but older people are more likely to forget a person's name (Shafto et al., 2007), particularly when the person has a name that sounds similar to someone else's (O'Hanlon et al., 2005). Evidence from imaging studies suggests that the area of the brain used for phonological production is subject to

age-related neural declines, a fact that might explain this form of retrieval failure in older adults (Shafto et al., 2009).

One important influence on retrieval failure is the frequency with which the information is typically drawn upon for everyday use. If you rarely see or talk about a person, it is more likely that you will have trouble coming up with that person's name should you happen to meet accidentally. Thus, when older adults must search among their larger repository of names, it requires more time and effort and they are unable to produce the correct response within the constraints of either ordinary conversation or a laboratory task. Additionally, making matters more difficult for older adults is that current common names are far more varied than they were when older adults were younger (Ramscar et al., 2014). For example, "Apple" or "Sky" have not been used as female names until recently. This means that there are even more names, many of them unfamiliar, that older adults must consider when they bump into that acquaintance on the street.

Finally, education may also play a role as an influence on retrieval failure in older adults. In one study comparing higher and lower educated older adults, there was greater interference in face-naming than word naming the less well-educated older adults. This finding suggests that education may help buffer against at least some of the face-naming deficits associated with aging (Paolieri et al., 2018).

Summing up the effects of aging on long-term memory, the "long-term memory scorecard" in Figure 6.9 illustrates

FIGURE 6.9

Long-Term Memory Scorecard

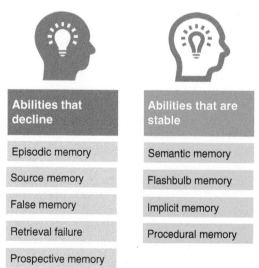

The long-term memory and aging scorecard contrasting abilities that decline with those that are stable.

those memory abilities that do and those that do not show age-related declines.

Psychosocial Influences on Memory

The empirical evidence we have just covered supports in part the commonly held belief that at least some forms of memory suffer as people get older—what varies is perhaps how much, exactly which type, and when. However, there is also evidence to suggest that how you think about your memory may play just as important a role as your actual age or state of the brain.

The identity process model predicts that undue concern about memory loss can translate into an "over-the-hill" attitude of identity accommodation that turns into a self-fulfilling prophecy. Believing that their memory is failing, and experiencing such embarrassing situations as forgetting someone's name, older adults can come to believe that their minds are on a hopeless downhill course. Evidence suggests that middle-aged adults are highly sensitive to age-related changes in memory (Whitbourne & Collins, 1998), but how does this sensitivity affect their actual performance?

Memory self-efficacy is a form of self-efficacy that refers to the confidence you have in your memory; specifically, the degree to which you feel that you can successfully complete a memory task. This should, in turn, affect how well you actually perform. Unfortunately, people feel less and less confident about their memory and consequently their self-efficacy suffers (West et al., 2003). Adding to this is the fact that people with objectively poorer cognitive function also feel less confident in their memory abilities (Payne et al., 2017), further placing them at risk for suffering continued memory losses. These negative beliefs can further affect their memory self-efficacy and feelings of depression (Cherry et al., 2019).

An impressive display of the power of memory self-efficacy comes from a 6-year longitudinal study conducted in the Netherlands of a healthy community sample of more than 1,800 individuals aged 55 and older (Valentijn et al., 2006). Individuals with a lower sense of memory self-efficacy, particularly with regard to the belief that their memory had declined, showed poorer memory performance over the course of the study. Whether their lower self-efficacy caused their poorer performance or whether it reflected actual negative changes was impossible to determine. Similarly, although not specifically focused on memory self-efficacy, in a large representative U.S. sample of adults 55 and older, Zahodne et al. (2015) observed positive relationships between overall self-efficacy

and working memory, even among older adults with lower hippocampal volumes (Zahodne et al., 2019).

An older **individual's identity** and self-efficacy may also be influenced by social attitudes toward aging. This makes the older adult more likely to experience stereotype threat, a concept drawn from research on the standardized test performance of African Americans suggesting that people perform in ways consistent with negative stereotypes of the group to which they see themselves as belonging (Steele et al., 2002). Research on stereotype threat and aging suggests that the older person's self-identification as "old" contributes to lower memory test scores. Because older adults are stereotyped as having poorer memories, this belief causes poorer performance. Although older adults can overcome stereotype threat through identity assimilation (Whitbourne & Sneed, 2002), it is difficult to resist the "essentialist" views of aging as involving inevitable memory decline (Weiss, 2018).

Researchers in the area of stereotype threat and aging propose that identification with negative images of aging interferes with memory performance in older adults by lowering their feelings of self-efficacy. Ultimately, they become less able to take advantage of mnemonic strategies, systematic procedures designed to enhance memory such as ROY G. BIV to remember the colors in the rainbow (Hess et al., 2003). The effect, furthermore, seems particularly pronounced when stereotype threat is invoked prior to the retrieval phase of memory rather than prior to encoding (Krendl et al., 2015). However, in keeping with the premise of identity process theory, people vary in the way they respond to stereotype threat; sometimes, the oldest participants are the least rather than the most affected by stereotype threat. Supporting this view, one study of aging and stereotype threat showed that the oldest participants (those in their 80s) were least affected by these negative unconscious attitudes (Hess & Hinson, 2006). Although identity processes were not investigated in this particular study, the investigators proposed that individual differences in response to threat may mediate the way that older individuals react to negative information about aging and memory.

Some may go so far as to say that there is no way of knowing just how much stereotype threat could account for many of the findings on aging and memory. The slightest hint of a memory test can be enough to activate stereotype threat, ultimately leading to poorer performance by older adults. In a study comparing traditional and nontraditional instructional conditions in relation to memory for trivia, age differences were observed in the traditional, but not nontraditional, instructional condition (Rahhal et al., 2001). Conversely, when older adults are encouraged to view aging from a positive perspective, their memory performance is enhanced, even in those who feel negatively about getting older (Fernandez-Ballesteros et al., 2015).

Memory controllability refers to beliefs about the effects of the aging process on memory, such as the extent to which the individual believes that memory decline is inevitable with age (Lachman, 2006). Older people who rely heavily on identity accommodation are more likely to hold negative beliefs about their ability to control their memory as they age (Jones et al., 2009). If people believe that they can control their memory, however, then they are more likely to take advantage of the strategies to ensure they actually do achieve higher performance (Lachman & Andreoletti, 2006).

The importance of identity also became highlighted indirectly as part of the Australian Longitudinal Study of Aging (ALSA) carried out from 1992 to 2004 (Luszcz et al., 2015). The older adult participants in this study (65 to 100 years at first test) completed several measures of subjective memory beliefs and complaints about their memory as well as a recall task and measures of functional health. Contrary to prediction, changes in memory complaints did not correlate overall with changes in memory. Instead, it seemed that participants "attribute to themselves and take responsibility for their memory decline" (p. 248). This appears to be very much like the process of identity accommodation in which older individuals, especially the ones who are vigilant about their memory, become overly pessimistic as they evaluate their own cognitive performance.

Memory and Health-Related Behaviors

Given the relationship of various health-related behaviors to the functioning of the central nervous system, as we discussed in Chapter 4, it should be no surprise that memory in later adulthood is also related to health-related behaviors (see Figure 6.10). For example, cigarette smoking

FIGURE 6.10

Health Behaviors and Memory

Memory in older adults can be modified through these four health-related lifestyle factors.

is known to cause deleterious changes in the brain over the long term, although short-term effects may include a temporary boost in cognition (Campos et al., 2016). One longitudinal study conducted in Scotland provided impressive data showing that people tested as children who eventually became smokers had significantly lower memory and information processing scores when followed up at ages 64 and 66 years, controlling for early life intelligence (Starr et al., 2007).

A second health-related behavior relevant to memory involves diet and specifically the consumption of fish. You have probably heard the saying that fish is "brain food," and evidence suggests that it can be, particularly fish, high in omega-3 fatty acids (such as salmon or tuna). Participants in the large-scale Chicago Health and Aging Study (with over 3,700 participants) were followed over a 6-year period during which they were asked to report their food consumption. Approximately 20% of the sample ate two or more meals containing fish per week. Controlling for a host of relevant factors, the rate of cognitive decline in individuals who consumed one or more fish meals a week was reduced by 10% to 13% per year (Morris et al., 2005). A subsequent study of nearly 900 older adults from England and Wales showed that socioeconomic status may also play a role in affecting the relationship between cognitive performance and fish consumption, in that people with higher social status are more likely to include fish in their regular diets (Dangour et al., 2009).

Investigators continue to search for sources of natural dietary supplements, vitamins, minerals, and flavonoids in enhancing cognitive functioning for individuals experiencing normal aging and who therefore do not have neurocognitive disorders or mild cognitive impairment. One comprehensive review of 28 studies involving more than 83,000 individuals evaluated vitamin B12, folic acid, vitamin B6, beta-carotene, vitamin C, vitamin E, selenium, vitamin D3, calcium supplements, zinc, copper, and antioxidant vitamins. There were no demonstrated effects of any of these supplements on cognitive function, with the possible exception of antioxidant vitamins (Rutjes, 2018). In part, this failure to demonstrate positive effects of most supplements may be due to the short-term nature of the studies.

Although not a supplement, one popular natural memory "cure," however, is known to show no effects at all. It continues to be marketed as such, and that is ginkgo biloba (Snitz et al., 2009). Similarly, the protein found in jellyfish (apoaequorin), the chief ingredient of the widely advertised supplement "Prevagen," has no effects on cognitive functioning (Morrill, 2017) despite the claims it makes in its commercials.

In Chapter 4, we saw that aerobic exercise can contribute to increases in brain areas involved in cognition. Research on exercise and cognition repeatedly illustrates that attention, memory, accuracy, and information processing all improve with each heart-pumping activity session (Erickson et al., 2009; Marks et al., 2009). Moderate- to high-intensity strength training contributes to more efficient information processing (Chang & Etnier, 2009) and the ability to make decisions (Liu-Ambrose et al., 2010). To be most effective, older adults benefit from exercise that focuses on functional training with, for example, resistance bands, rather than exercise that is more focused on recreation (Ponce-Bravo et al., 2015).

Exercise may have indirect effects on memory by helping older adults feel stronger and more competent. Research on exercise self-efficacy and control beliefs among a group of older adults engaged in a strength training intervention demonstrated that higher exercise beliefs during the intervention were related to higher levels of resistance and maintenance of exercise after the intervention (Neupert et al., 2009).

Health may also play a role in cognition through the route of metabolic factors. As we saw in Chapter 5, people with metabolic syndrome are at increased risk for Alzheimer's disease. Impaired glucose tolerance, a component of metabolic syndrome, shows a clear relationship to cognitive functioning in normal aging individuals (Di Bonito et al., 2007). Older adults with type 2 diabetes are more likely to experience slowing of psychomotor speed as well as declines in executive functioning (Yeung et al., 2009).

One possible route through which metabolic factors can affect psychomotor slowing and memory involves the hormone insulin growth factor-1 (IGF-1). Among 1,320 cognitively unimpaired participants ages 50 and older in the Mayo Clinic Study of Aging, higher levels of IGF were associated with improved attention and overall cognition, including visuospatial abilities, but only in women. These relationships were independent of walking speed, a measure of functional health (Wennberg et al., 2018).

As we also discussed in Chapter 5, health-related behaviors include those that are involved in the management of stress. Given that stress takes its toll on health and emotions, it makes sense that it would also affect cognitive functioning. You undoubtedly have had the experience of forgetting something important when you were preoccupied with other concerns such as financial strains, increased demands at school or work, or problems in your close relationships. Researchers investigating this issue have provided support for the notion that stress can interfere with memory performance among older adults. In one intriguing investigation, a sample of more than 300 older adults in the Veterans Affairs Normative Aging Study were asked to keep a daily diary of their interpersonal stressors and their memory failures. By tracking the relationship of stressful experiences to memory on a daily basis, researchers were able to establish the lagged effect showing that stressors on one day predicted memory failures on the next (Neupert et al., 2006).

Interference of emotions, such as feelings of depression, may also contribute to poorer performance in older adults by depleting valuable cognitive resources (Meijer et al., 2009). A prospective longitudinal study of widows (begun before the widows lost their husbands) confirmed this idea among older women. Independent of the effect of losing a spouse on depressive symptoms, women in the Longitudinal Aging Study Amsterdam were found to have lower memory performance at the end of a 6-year period. Although the women who eventually lost their husbands started out with lower memory scores, even after controlling for this difference, the widows showed greater memory loss than did the nonwidows over the course of the study (Aartsen et al., 2005).

Looking directly at memory performance and its relationship to stress, another group of investigators provided impressive evidence to support the idea that the deficit shown by older adults on working memory tasks can be accounted for in part by the experience of daily stressors (Stawski et al., 2006). In this study, a group of more than 100 older community-living adults with intact mental status were compared to young adults on the n-back working memory task. The amount of daily stress in their lives was determined through an interview in which participants were asked questions such as, "Did you have an argument or disagreement with anyone?" and "Did anything happen to a close friend or relative that turned out to be stressful for you?" Testing occurred over six occasions, allowing the investigators to examine within-person variations in the relationship between stress and memory as well as between-person age group differences.

Interestingly, the young adults in the sample were more likely to say "yes" to these and the other four questions assessing interpersonal stress. For instance, young adults said they had an argument on 26% of the days on which a given stressor occurred compared to 5% for older adults. The study's main finding was that on days in which people experienced stress, the performance of people in both age groups was significantly poorer. Emotional strains can interfere with memory in anyone regardless of age.

Why does stress have this impact on memory? Stawski and his colleagues (2006) maintain that preoccupation with stress occupies attentional resources that could otherwise be devoted to the memory task. There is evidence that older adults are perhaps more anxious than younger adults about their memory performance and therefore their memories are more vulnerable to this emotional interference (Andreoletti et al., 2006).

A final factor to consider in understanding the relationship between memory and health is that of sleep. In young adults, long-term memory is strongly linked to slow-wave sleep. Experimental participants allowed to sleep in between learning and testing consistently achieve better memory performance than participants who spend an equivalent period of time awake (Diekelmann et al., 2012). Indeed, as shown in the Canadian Longitudinal Study on Aging, there is a link between chronic insomnia and memory performance, even after controlling for other health-related factors (Cross et al., 2019).

Memory Training Studies

One mission of aging and memory research is to find ways to help older adults offset deleterious changes in memory. Many researchers in this field are true "gerontological optimists" who believe that their work can help improve cognitive functioning in older adults. They have established, for example, the fact that even simple practice can produce significant improvements in memory task performance, offsetting the negative effects of mental inactivity. Interventions aimed at improving episodic memory can be beneficial even for individuals suffering from the clinical condition known as mild cognitive impairment (MCI).

Although the simple task of practice can result in enhanced memory performance, there are advantages to encouraging strategy use among older adults. Providing training intended to improve the memories of older adults also has the benefit of increasing feelings of the individual's self-efficacy (West et al., 2008). When this training is provided in a group setting, it can be particularly effective in boosting not only self-efficacy but also memory performance (Hastings & West, 2009).

Older adults can also benefit from interventions that provide them with additional support during the encoding stage, while they are inputting information into long-term memory (Craik & Rose, 2012). This support can take the form of additional cues such as having them see pictures as well as words when learning a word list. Older adults would benefit, according to this approach, by using "deep" processing, in which they think about the meaning of the information they are trying to remember rather than simply repeating information by rote.

One of the most ambitious cognitive training interventions is a multisite study known as Advanced Cognitive Training for Independent and Vital Elderly (ACTIVE) that was carried out over a 2-year period on more than 2,800 adults 65 to 94 years of age (Ball et al., 2002). Training

consisted of 10 one-hour sessions over a 5- to 6-week period. The participants were trained in one of three types of cognitive skills—memory, reasoning, or speed of processing—while a control group received no training. These cognitive functions were selected because they show the most improvement in laboratory work and are related to everyday living tasks (e.g., telephone use, shopping, food preparation, housekeeping, laundry, transportation, medication use, and management of personal finances). For instance, those who received memory training were taught ways to remember word lists and sequences of items, text, and the main ideas and details of stories. Training in the area of reasoning involved learning how to solve problems that follow patterns, such as reading a bus schedule or filling out an order sheet. Training in the speed of processing involved learning how to identify and locate visual information quickly for use in tasks such as looking up a phone number, finding information on medicine bottles, and responding to traffic signs.

Testing conducted at the end of the training period demonstrated that the majority of participants in the speed (87%) and reasoning (74%) groups showed improvement; about one-quarter (26%) in the memory group showed improvement. Two years later, the gains were still evidenced, although these were larger for participants who participated in booster sessions.

These gains continued over the decade following the conclusion of training. In the 10-year ACTIVE follow-up

FIGURE 6.11

Method of Loci

Imagine a place you know well.

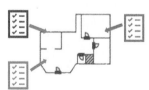

Mentally walk through each room, associating items you want to remember with that room.

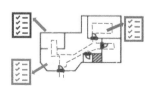

To recall those items, retrace your steps.

The use of method of loci as a way to improve long-term memory.

(Rebok et al., 2014), improvements in memory persisted to at least 5 years for memory training and up to the full 10 years for reasoning and speed-of-processing training. Furthermore, a large proportion (60% and over) reported having less difficulty performing IADLs, and 60% to 70% felt they were as well off as, or better, than before they were at the beginning of the training.

Memory training can not only improve an individual's performance but can even alter the brain. In a study carried out in Norway, middle-aged and older adults learned to use the "method of loci" (associating words with rooms in your home) (see Figure 6.11). They were given intensive training, involving 25-minute sessions, 5 days a week, for 8 weeks. Compared to a control group, the training group showed increased white matter density, a change that would help them process new information more quickly and efficiently (Engvig et al., 2012). In the ACTIVE study, training in method of loci helped older adults become more consistent in their use of this strategy, producing both immediate and long-term memory improvement (Gross et al., 2014).

In conclusion, attentional and memory processes in adulthood play vital roles in life. Older adults appear to suffer deleterious changes, but these changes are neither universal nor irreversibly negative. Identity and other memory-related beliefs play an important role in determining whether individuals are able to take advantage of compensatory strategies. Future research will help uncover more of these personality–memory linkages as well as to identify which strategies can be most effective in maximizing cognitive performance throughout middle and later adulthood.

SUMMARY

1. Cognition refers to the way the mind works, including the processes of attention, memory, intelligence, problem-solving, and the use of language. Aging affects each of these areas, leading to changes in many of people's ability to carry out everyday activities. Processing speed, measured by reaction time, is an important variable in research on cognitive aging. There is a consistent increase in reaction time throughout adulthood. The general slowing hypothesis explains this increase as a decline of information processing speed, and the related age-complexity hypothesis proposes that the loss is greater for more difficult tasks.

2. Attention involves the ability to focus while ignoring other features, to shift that focus, and to coordinate information from multiple sources. Laboratory studies suggest that people become less efficient in the use of attentional processes with age. Multitasking involves the ability to monitor multiple input sources, with older adults experiencing greater disadvantages. Inhibitory control refers to the process of turning off one response while performing another and is often measured using the Stroop test. Studies on aging and attentional performance suggest that not all abilities decline. Two approaches to understanding age differences in attentional tasks include the attentional resources theory and the inhibitory deficit hypothesis. Experience can compensate for age-related changes in sustained attention. Based on research suggesting the attentional benefits video games offer to younger adults, researchers are beginning to explore the use of video games in interventional studies as training tools to enhance attentional skills among older adults. Older adults prefer computer games rather than first-person shooter video games, which may benefit focused and sustained attention.

3. Challenges facing older adult drivers include age-related increases in reaction time and changes in visual functioning. However, accidents are higher among younger drivers, perhaps due in part to increased rates of drinking and driving and engaging in distracting behaviors. Older adults compensate for changes in driving ability by modifying behaviors and relying on experience.

4. One of the greatest fears about aging is the loss of memory, and, indeed, data suggests that the aging process has negative effects on many, but not all, aspects of memory. Working memory, which keeps information temporarily available and active, is significantly poorer in older adults. However, individuals can compensate for these declines by activating different neural circuits.

5. Long-term memory refers to information that is held from several minutes to a lifetime and includes various types; these are impacted by age differently. Episodic, remote, and autobiographical memory are sensitive to age effects, with the exception of a phenomenon known as the reminisce bump, the period of time between the ages of 10 and 30. Flashbulb memory and semantic memory are not affected by the normal aging process. Procedural memory is also retained in older adults, as is implicit memory. However, older adults have more difficulty with tasks involving source memory and prospective memory.

6. Researchers are investigating the interaction of memory changes with changes in self-efficacy, control beliefs, and identity. The concept of stereotype threat implies that older adults may perform more poorly on memory tasks that activate negative stereotypes about aging and memory.

7. Memory in later adulthood is related to a variety of health-related behaviors that promote cardiovascular and metabolic health. Aerobic exercise can contribute to increases in brain areas involved in cognition. Health may also play a role through the route of metabolic factors. Impaired glucose tolerance, a component of metabolic syndrome, shows a clear relationship to cognitive functioning in normal aging individuals. Stress can also interfere with memory performance.

8. Interventions aimed at improving episodic memory can be beneficial, particularly those that teach strategy use among older adults. One of the most ambitious cognitive training interventions was a multisite study known as Advanced Cognitive Training for Independent and Vital Elderly (ACTIVE), which found that training in memory and reasoning improved the performance of older adults on daily living tasks, gains that were maintained over a 10-year period.

7

Higher-Order Cognitive Functions

Think you're good at solving problems? Answer True or False to each of these 10 statements and check your answers on the next page:

 **AGEFEED**

? **test yourself**

1. You don't always need to be right.
2. Asking for help is how you learn from others and see different perspectives.
3. You visualize the worst-case scenario and ways to get out of that scenario.
4. Problems are challenges that you use as learning opportunities.
5. You tend to be a positive thinker and surround yourself with like-minded people.
6. You look for more than one solution to a problem and have backup plans for as many scenarios as possible.
7. You don't have a lot of drama or stressful interactions in your life.
8. You make decisions based on fact rather than intuition.
9. When it comes to solving problems, you take your time to think through all possible solutions.
10. You look for feedback from others when solving a problem.

AGEFEED ⓘ
...the scores

All of these are excellent problem-solving approaches. Here's what your score means:

Mostly Trues—You are an expert problem solver who can adapt to different situations and don't seek confrontation!

Mix of Trues and Falses—You may not be an expert problem solver, but chances are you will get better with age and experience!

Mostly Falses—Problem-solving may not be your strong suit, but that's okay, many people become better at solving certain kinds of problems with age!

Information processing and memory are basic cognitive operations that make it possible for you to perform a variety of critical adaptive functions in your everyday life. They also form the basis for your ability to analyze, reason, and communicate with others.

Researchers are interested in understanding higher-level cognitive functions in adulthood and later life for a number of reasons. First, these functions play a major role in areas such as educational success, health, occupational performance, and even relationships. Second, information on the way that individuals think and learn in later adulthood can provide a greater understanding of the potential everyone has for benefiting from educational opportunities throughout life. With many adults retooling in order to find new positions in the rapidly changing labor market, educators and employers must find ways to help people past traditional school age prepare for incorporating technological and other advances into their work. Finally, there are practical applications of this knowledge in the area of diagnosis and treatment for the neurocognitive disorders that may develop in middle and later adulthood.

EXECUTIVE FUNCTIONING AND ITS MEASUREMENT

The higher-order cognitive skills needed to make decisions, plan, and allocate mental resources to a task are called executive functioning. Specifically, an individual's executive functioning draws upon several abilities, including working memory, selective attention, mental flexibility, and the ability to plan and inhibit distracting information (Miyake et al., 2000).

Clinicians and researchers are particularly interested in learning how aging affects executive functioning because it is central to so many activities that older adults need to use in order to be able to care for themselves. For example, driving depends heavily on speed but, just as importantly, on executive functioning due to the need to be able to plan and make decisions while you are behind the wheel (Adrian et al., 2019). You need to use your executive functions to determine the route to take to your destination, alternate between input from the road and that of your vehicle's dials and instruments, and make any changes in your route to account for traffic, construction, or obstacles in the road. Studies on aging and executive functioning and aging are also increasingly focusing on interventions that can protect and maximize these important skills.

Intelligence Tests

The higher-order cognitive functions that make up executive functioning contribute, at least in part, to an individual's overall intelligence. An intelligence test provides an assessment of an individual's overall cognitive status along a set of standardized dimensions. The scores on an intelligence test may be used in a research context, particularly when investigators are seeking to understand the effects of aging. They are also used by clinicians as part of a larger neuropsychological evaluation to establish a diagnosis of a neurological or psychiatric disorder. Psychologists working in human resource departments may also use intelligence testing as part of a larger process of personnel selection or evaluation.

Through intelligence testing, psychologists obtain a set of standardized scores that allow them to evaluate the cognitive strengths and weaknesses of their research subjects, clients, or personnel. The most commonly used intelligence tests in clinical settings are given on a one-to-one basis, providing a comprehensive view of the client's abilities to perform a range of perceptual, memory, reasoning, and speeded tasks.

The Wechsler Adult Intelligence Scale (WAIS) is one of the most well-known individually administered intelligence tests. Originally developed in 1939 by David Wechsler as the Wechsler–Bellevue test, the WAIS, first published in 1955, is now in its fourth edition (WAIS-IV) (Wechsler, 2008). Intended as a tool to be used for assessing psychiatric patients, the WAIS first contained scales that measured "verbal" abilities and a second set that measured "performance." The scores on these scales have the abbreviation "IQ," for "intelligence quotient," although technically they were not quotients. The WAIS IQ scores were actually calculated by comparing a person's raw scores with the norms for that person's age group, with the IQ score constituting deviation from those age-adjusted norms. As the terms imply, Verbal IQ tests knowledge of areas such as vocabulary and general information. Performance IQ tests measure nonverbal abilities such as spatial relationships and reasoning.

In the versions prior to the WAIS-IV, people received Verbal and Performance IQ scores along with an overall IQ. The test developers of the WAIS-IV decided to revise the entire scoring system to reflect developments in the fields of neuropsychology and cognitive psychology. Furthermore, some of the items and stimuli had become outdated and needed to be replaced. The WAIS-IV includes new test items, several new tests, and a completely different scoring system.

The four indexes that the WAIS-IV produces, as you can see from Figure 7.1, are Verbal Comprehension, Perceptual Reasoning, Working Memory, and Processing Speed. There are 10 standard tests and five optional tests, which the examiner may give depending on the specific purpose of the assessment. The Full-Scale IQ reflects general

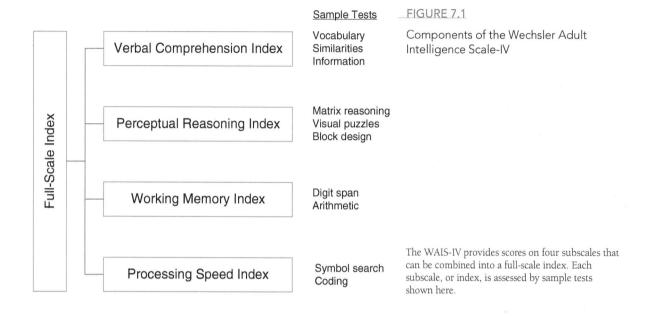

Components of the Wechsler Adult Intelligence Scale-IV

The WAIS-IV provides scores on four subscales that can be combined into a full-scale index. Each subscale, or index, is assessed by sample tests shown here.

cognitive functioning but is perhaps less informative than the four index scores, each of which captures a different facet of the individual's strengths and weaknesses.

One scale of Perceptual Organization is the Matrix Reasoning test, shown in Figure 7.2. Each row shows a progression as the dark-shaded quadrant occupies positions starting from the top left to the bottom right. The test taker would decide which of several choices would fit into that empty square.

In addition to scoring the individual's responses, the examiner would also record any relevant behaviors or concerns that could affect the test taker's scores. These could include fluency in the language of administration, problems with vision or hearing, and difficulties with attention and concentration. Such observations could be helpful in further interpreting the individual's numerical scores.

Although not currently in use by clinicians, another intelligence test worth noting is extensively used in research on aging. The Primary Mental Abilities Test (PMAT) assesses the seven abilities of Verbal Meaning, Word Fluency (the ability to generate words following a certain lexical rule), Number (arithmetic), Spatial Relations, Memory, Perceptual Speed, and General Reasoning. Unlike the WAIS-IV, psychologists administer the PMAT in a group format rather than an individualized manner, which also makes it more practical for research purposes. The PMAT's scales roughly parallel at least some of those included in the WAIS-IV, such as Memory and Working Memory, and Perceptual Speed and Processing Speed.

Neuropsychological Assessment

There are a variety of specialized tests that can evaluate an individual's cognitive status, including the quality of executive functioning. The process of neuropsychological assessment involves gathering information about a client's brain functioning from a series of standardized cognitive tests. In cases involving older adults with cognitive deficits, in particular, neuropsychologists may adapt their assessment to try to target the specific area in the brain that they believe has suffered damage or decline. They conduct this assessment individually rather than in group format.

Tests of executive functioning are typically part of the total process of neuropsychological assessment. However, most neuropsychological assessments of older adults also include other measures of cognitive functioning and may incorporate some we have already discussed as part of intelligence testing. There are enough available neuropsychological tests within each category so that if a clinician wishes to investigate one area in depth for a particular client, then he or she will be able to probe into the individual's possible disorder by administering more tests from that category.

You might be surprised to learn that there is no one set procedure for conducting a neuropsychological assessment. In fact, particular neuropsychologists may have preferences for certain tests, especially if they tend to see the same type of client in their practice or their area of research expertise. In clinical settings, though, neuropsychologists are expected to have training in enough types of

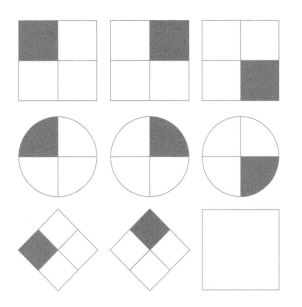

FIGURE 7.2

Sample Perceptual Item from the WAIS-IV

A sample item from the Raven Progressive Matrices where the task is to choose the next pattern that would go in the series, as shown here.

tests to be able to adapt the assessment to the individual's symptoms. In working with older adults, neuropsychologists are also expected to be familiar with the tests that are appropriate for people in this age group rather than those used in diagnosing a child or adolescent.

Several neuropsychological tests are either derived from or the same as tests from the WAIS-IV, such as Digit Span (used to assess verbal recall and auditory attention) and Similarities (used to assess verbal abstraction abilities). Other tests, such as the Trail Making Tests, also called "Trails," were developed specifically to assess the individual's so-called "frontal lobe functioning," which includes attention, visual scanning ability, and numerical sequencing (see Figure 7.3). The examiner shows the test taker a pattern of numbered circles, with the instructions to draw lines to connect the circles in order. Another variant of the Trail Making Test displays a pattern of numbered circles and letters, and the test taker's job is to connect them in order, from 1 to A to 2 to B, and so on.

The Wisconsin Card Sorting Test (WCST) measures the individual's ability to form mental sets in categorizing cards with related features, such as number of items, color, or shape. The WCST is now administered on a computer rather than with physical cards, reflecting a growing trend in neuropsychology to use computerized test batteries. A sample item from the WCST is shown in Figure 7.4. The three yellow diamonds could be an example of the color yellow (which would fit with card 2), the number 3 (fitting with card 4), or triangles (care 1). By your series of choices, you should eventually learn which concept should be used for classifying the cards (such as yellow). Once you have that concept, a new concept would be introduced

and you would have to learn that concept next (such as the number 3).

In addition to the convenience factor, computerized testing allows the psychologist to administer an adaptive test, in which the client's responses to earlier questions determine which questions will be subsequently asked. For example, the Cambridge Neuropsychological Testing Automated Battery (CANTAB) consists of 22 subtests that assess visual memory, working memory, executive function and planning, attention, verbal memory, decision-making, and response control. Having these tests on a laptop or tablet device has clear advantages to handling the equipment needed for 22 (or more) physical tests. However, there

FIGURE 7.3

Example of Trail Making Test

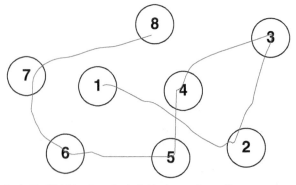

In the Trail Making Test, the individual must draw a line connecting the circled numbers in sequence.

FIGURE 7.4

Wisconsin Card Sorting Test

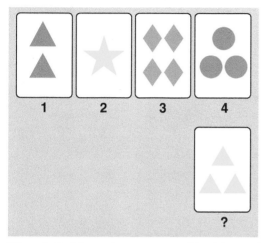

The Wisconsin Card Sorting Test is a measure of the ability to adapt to changing rules of organization. The test-taker is shown screens with a set of four stimuli and must guess whether the stimulus shown below matches or not.

may be drawbacks to the use of computerized assessment for current cohorts of older adults who may have limited experience taking tests in this format. The psychologist must take this into account when evaluating the results.

Aging and Executive Functioning

Researchers conducting laboratory studies that examine the relationship between age and executive functioning may draw from the intelligence and neuropsychological tests we have just discussed. Additionally, they may employ specific measures designed to pinpoint a particular type of executive functioning. One measure that taps cognitive flexibility is the task-switching method, in which participants respond to one type of stimulus in one set of trials (judging if a number is odd) and the opposite in the next set of trials (judging if a number is even). Thus, the first set of trials leads participants to adopt a particular decision rule, which they must then change in responding to the second set of trials.

Another experimental task measures verbal fluency, a form of executive functioning that depends on the individual's ability to generate multiple items meeting a single criterion. Tests of verbal fluency ask participants to produce as many items as possible in response to one stimulus, such as listing as many possible words that begin with the letter "K" in a set amount of time. However, because it is dependent on language, verbal fluency tests may not be pure measures of executive function (Whiteside et al., 2016).

Scores on measures of executive functioning appear to show steady declines in later adulthood, though most of the research is cross sectional, and therefore cannot detect age changes. In one 4-year longitudinal study of older adults, there were no changes in overall measures of executive functioning; additionally, language scores improved (Castellano et al., 2019). These declines are important because they are related to negative changes in a number of everyday cognitive functions that individuals need in their daily lives (Overdorp et al., 2016). Interestingly enough, older adults themselves may not perceive themselves to be affected by these changes in their own self-reports of their ability to manage daily tasks (Tucker-Drob, 2011). It is possible that this self-perception reflects the process of identity assimilation due to older adults' desire to see themselves as cognitively in control of their lives.

Performance on the WCST appears to be maintained through midlife (Garden et al., 2001). Age-related effects start to become apparent by later adulthood, however (Head et al., 2009). These changes may be related to changes in regions of the brain that support the ability to plan, make decisions, and adapt flexibly to changing situations (Burzynska et al., 2012).

Furthermore, differences among older adults in background factors such as education can also play a role in influencing performance on measures of executive functioning. One study of verbal fluency showed that older adults were more likely to perseverate, meaning that they continue to produce the same words, such as "king," "keel," "kept," "king," and "kite," where "king" counts as a perseveration. However, the tendency to perseverate is less evident in people with higher levels of verbal abilities (Methqal et al., 2019).

Fortunately, there are ways that older adults can perhaps compensate for these changes in executive functioning. Following similar models as studies on brain plasticity, researchers are showing that physical exercise can benefit executive functioning in older adults. Not only do people who exercise have better executive functioning, but also experimental studies show that aerobic exercise training improves performance on tests of mental flexibility, attention, and inhibitory control (Erickson et al., 2019). Lifetime habits of greater physical activity also help to preserve executive functioning in older adults. In one long-term investigation following individuals from adolescence through later life, positive effects of physical activity among older adults were associated with better cognitive functioning, effects even stronger in those who had lifetime habits of physical exercise (Reas et al., 2019).

Videogames would also seem to have positive effects on executive functioning, given that even casual games readily available on the market often require players to switch targets and the games themselves require multiple strategies for winning as players move through a game's levels. However, one comprehensive investigation of a novel videogame package intended to promote cognitive flexibility through a 12-week training program showed no effects other than improvements in game-playing itself (Buitenweg et al., 2017). As discussed in Chapter 6, although these games might be enjoyable to players, it is still premature to regard videogame interventions as having measurable real-life effects.

Another approach combines physical exercise and videogame playing. Known as "exergaming," in this approach players ride an exercise cycle while playing videogames on a screen in front of them. One initial study investigated exergaming's impact on trail making performance after a 3-month intervention. The older adults who exercised more often, more rigorously, and did more complex tasks showed improvements (Barcelos et al., 2015). However, the question of just how different exergaming is from physical activity in general has yet to be determined (Stojan & Voelcker-Rehage, 2019).

As research on video game training and executive functioning continues, it is likely that as the training tasks become better understood, more robust transfer to everyday abilities will be demonstrated.

LANGUAGE

The use of language involves a wide range of cognitive functions, including comprehension, memory, and decision-making. As we discussed in Chapter 6, many of these functions are negatively affected by the aging process. However, the majority of researchers believe that the average healthy older adult does not suffer significant losses in the ability to use language effectively under normal speaking conditions (Shafto & Tyler, 2014). The basic abilities to carry on a conversation, read, and write remain intact throughout later life. The "Language and Aging Scorecard" in Figure 7.5 summarizes this research.

Cognitive Aspects of Language

Although many cognitive functions relevant for language are preserved in older adults, the scorecard shows that there are changes that can have a detrimental effect on the older adult's ability to use and maximize language most effectively. One of the most significant is a slower processing speed while reading (Malyutina et al., 2018). While reading, older adults may have greater difficulty forming visual images to accompany concrete words, a process that can benefit the memory of younger adults for written material (Huang et al., 2012). While reading, older adults

FIGURE 7.5

Aging and Language Scorecard

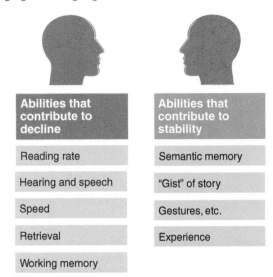

Abilities that contribute to decline	Abilities that contribute to stability
Reading rate	Semantic memory
Hearing and speech	"Gist" of story
Speed	Gestures, etc.
Retrieval	Experience
Working memory	

The language and aging scorecard shows which abilities contribute to decline in language skills with aging and which contribute to stability.

appear to preserve the ability to process and remember general features of a story but are less likely to remember specific details. Consistent with the CRUNCH model of neuroplasticity, however, it seems that older adults appear to compensate for changes in comprehension ability by activating more neural circuits than do younger adults (Martin et al., 2018).

As we saw in Chapter 4, changes in hearing and speech perception have the potential to influence the ability to comprehend spoken language. For example, older adults may find it more difficult to hear all the words spoken in a conversation; they then must work harder to make sense out of what other people are saying (Janse, 2009). More generally, hearing deficits create additional strain on an older adult's processing resources, so that semantic judgments that would otherwise be automatic now require more effort. These changes negatively impact working memory and hence the individual's ability to correctly identify spoken words (Peele & Wingfield, 2016).

In using written language, retrieval errors could make it more difficult for them to correct misspellings. In one study of proofreading, older adults were found to be able to detect errors but not to be able to correct those errors (Shafto, 2015)

Adults' slower cognitive processes may also have an effect on the complexity of grammatical structures that they use. As you form sentences, you must keep one clause in mind while you compose the next one, a process that places demands on your working memory. As we saw in Chapter 6, working memory undergoes significant changes with age. Consequently, compared with young adults, older adults speak in simpler sentences (Kemper et al., 2001). Their writing also becomes simpler, in both the expression of ideas and the use of grammatical complexity (Kemper, Greiner, et al., 2001). Thus, although older adults retain their knowledge of grammatical rules (a form of semantic memory), declines in working memory can cause older adults to lose track of what they mean to say while they are saying it, especially when the language they are producing requires thought and preparation (Harley et al., 2011).

Interestingly, the speeches and interviews given by political figures allow for unique insights to be gained in the nature of language production by older adults. An analysis of President Donald Trump's interviews showed an increase in filler words prior to his election in 2016 although there were no comparable measures of cognitive ability against which these changes could be compared (Coutanche & Paulus, 2018). As you learned already, semantic memory is not impaired by aging, meaning that older adults should have no difficulty understanding word meanings.

On the positive side, experience is an important way that older adults compensate for changes in memory and speed. This is particularly true for highly educated older adults, whose extensive vocabularies allow them to take advantage of the context in language, particularly when the task is cognitively challenging (Zekveld et al., 2011). In general, though, older adults also have a rich backlog of experiences from which to draw when they listen or read, even without a rich vocabulary (Benichov et al., 2012). They can also take advantage of interpreting the paralinguistic aspects of speech, including gestures and facial expressions. You have likely encountered this experience of filling in missing information in speech that is directed toward you. Someone approaches you at a loud party, and it is probably safe to assume, even if you are unable to hear, that he or she is saying "Hello" or "What's up?" You are pretty safe in returning the greeting.

Also, on the positive side, health status may play a role in affecting language abilities of older adults. Two measures of language known to be affected negatively by aging, word finding (lexical retrieval) and sentence processing, were found by one set of researchers to be less efficient in older adults who met the criteria for metabolic syndrome (Cahana-Amitay et al., 2015). Thus, by controlling the factors that contribute to metabolic syndrome, older adults may be able to preserve key features of language processing.

In summary, older adults have well-developed structures of information that allow them to anticipate and organize information that may typically overwhelm a novice. Even in situations that do not involve expert knowledge of a skill, previous experience can make up for slower processing of new linguistic information. For example, an avid soap opera watcher can anticipate what the characters will say (and often do) rather than needing to hear every single spoken word in a particular interchange between characters. When reading magazines or newspapers, a knowledgeable older reader is able to make up for changes in working memory by relying on more effective structures for retrieving related information from written text (Payne et al., 2012).

Social Aspects of Language

Corresponding to changes in language use and comprehension throughout adulthood are changes in the way that older adults use language socially. Perhaps most striking is the tendency of older adults to reminisce with others about experiences from the past. As they do so, they often polish and refine their storytelling so that by the time their reminiscences have been practiced and rehearsed, the stories have considerable impact on the listener. In your own family you may have heard an older relative tell the same story over and over again so often that you can repeat it by heart. Watching the reaction of your friends when they first hear the same story may cause you to realize that it is a pretty good story after all. This is perhaps one reason why comedians in their 60s, 70s, and beyond have become such masters of the punch line.

Reminiscences about the past may also serve a function for older adults in solidifying relationships and building shared identities with others from their generation. As they do so, they can enhance and strengthen their relationships with their long-time friends and family members.

Younger adults may become annoyed with the older adults they know well and feel that the older people's speech is too repetitive or focused on the past (Bieman-Copland & Ryan, 2001). At times, older adults may also speak more off-topic, particularly when they are giving instructions about how to perform an action. Younger adults seem to be better able to focus their speech in such situations (Trunk & Abrams, 2009). In a related vein, older adults may experience "mental clutter" due to an inability to inhibit irrelevant information. This tendency causes their speech to become somewhat rambling. However, these slight changes seem more related to altered executive functioning than to age, per se, because we know that inhibition is a key component of frontal lobe control over behavior.

The problem of intergenerational communication is made worse if the older person tends to focus on his or her current disabilities or health limitations. Talking extensively about a topic in which the listener has no interest or that makes the listener uncomfortable can have an effect opposite to that intended and possibly isolate the older individual. Such examples highlight the downside to changes in these conversational patterns when they have the unintended effect of turning off the listener.

Intergenerational communication can take a decidedly nasty turn. **Elderspeak** is a speech pattern directed at older adults similar to the way people talk to babies. If you have ever heard an older adult referred to as "cute," or being called "honey," or "sweetie," you have heard one form of elderspeak. More generally, elderspeak involves simplifying your speech much as you would talk to a child by leaving out complex words or talking in a patronizing or condescending tone of voice. Younger people who speak in this manner do so because, either consciously or unconsciously, they equate the older and perhaps frailer adult as being equal in status to a child. Offering unnecessary help, making personal comments about clothing or appearance, or talking in short, simple sentences are just some examples of this type of speech pattern.

Researchers investigating elderspeak have proposed that its use fits into the **communication predicament model** of aging. The predicament is that older adults are thought of as mentally incapacitated, leading younger people to speak to them in a simplified manner; over time, this can reduce the older adult's actual ability to use language (see Figure 7.6). In addition, failure to encourage independent behaviors in the older person, a part of the communication predicament, leads to a further spiraling downward of the older person's abilities (Ryan et al., 1995).

The communication predicament model is part of a larger phenomenon known as infantilization, in which the older person loses the incentive to attempt to regain self-sufficiency in the basic activities of daily life (Whitbourne et al., 1995). Moreover, when older adults in a residential facility are treated by younger staff in an infantilizing manner, they lose the desire to socialize with each other, potentially leading to social isolation (Salari & Rich, 2001). The self-fulfilling nature of infantilization can also increase the older person's awareness of age stereotypes, causing a self-fulfilling prophecy to spread across a wide domain of areas of functioning. If you think you are unable to carry out a task because you are too old, infirm, or feeble, then the chances are you will eventually lose the ability to carry out that task. According to one analysis, infantilization may even produce symptoms of neurocognitive disorder, particularly in institutional settings where residents may feel they have no escape from the control of their caregivers (Marson & Powell, 2014).

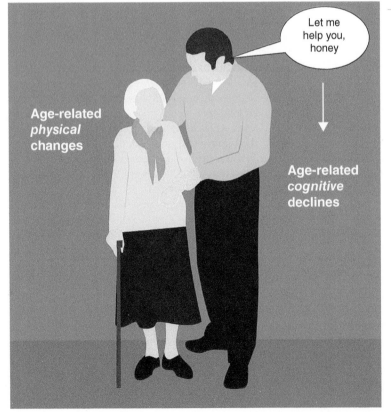

FIGURE 7.6

Example of Communication Predicament Model

In the Communication Predicament Model, when older adults who experience age-related physical changes are treated in infantilizing ways, they can experience age-related cognitive declines.

Because infantilization results in a loss of independence, researchers believe that it is important to sensitize those who work with older adults so that they avoid falling into this pattern. These programs have started, at least within assisted living facilities (Williams & Warren, 2009), but clearly more work in this area would have wide-ranging benefits.

Bilingualism and Aging

In contrast to common belief, being able to speak and think in two languages appears to benefit the individual. This advantage begins in infancy and continues through old age (Bialystok et al., 2009). Even if the speaker no longer relies on one of the languages, that second language remains active. This means that the bilingual speaker must add the step of deciding which language to use in a given situation depending on its context. As a result, bilingual individuals continually practice and therefore build their executive functions. This constant strengthening of their executive functioning may result in protection against the effects of Alzheimer's disease (Bialystok, 2011).

It is interesting to think that the use of two languages benefits executive function tasks, such as task-switching, that do not depend on verbal skills. Imaging studies suggest that the advantage conferred to bilinguals reflects better connectivity among networks in the brain (Luk et al., 2011) as well as helping to preserve cortical thickness (Li et al., 2017).

The advantage of bilingualism does not extend to all cognitive tasks. In working memory tasks, bilingual older adults seem to have greater difficulty with verbal than spatial stimuli, even after controlling for vocabulary (Luo et al., 2012). In a comparison of bilinguals to monolinguals on the Stroop interference task, which may be considered at least in part a measure of executive functioning, older bilinguals did not show a performance advantage (Kousaie & Phillips, 2012). Part of the reason for inconsistent results across studies of bilinguals may be that a large number of factors are at play. In a review paper evaluating the evidence on possible benefits and mechanisms of bilingualism's impact on executive functioning, it appears that "a many-many-many-many relation holds among executive function, tasks, experiences, and mechanisms" (Valian, 2014, p. 4).

EVERYDAY PROBLEM-SOLVING

From figuring out why your computer is freezing up the night before a paper is due to managing your dwindling bank account, you must constantly deal with problems requiring solutions in your daily life. Researchers have increasingly moved these daily challenges into the laboratory to evaluate the ability of older adults to manage such everyday tasks as handling their personal finances, maintaining their medication schedules, and monitoring their diets. Everyday problem-solving refers to the ability to solve problems that typically occur in people's daily lives, that can be solved in more than one way, and that require the problem solver to decide which strategy will lead to the desired result. The processes involved in

FIGURE 7.7

Problem-Solving Steps as Illustrated by the Rubik's Cube

The Rubik's cube provides a well-defined problem in which the solver must transform the randomly arranged cube into six sides that all have the same color.

Photo Credit: Popartic/Shutterstock.com; christianchan/123RF; Pedro Campos/123RF

everyday problem-solving involve key cognitive abilities as well as the contributions of education, other demographic variables, and health (Burton et al., 2006).

Characteristics of Problem-Solving

Psychologists approach the topic of problem-solving by identifying types of problems and the stages involved in successfully approaching and resolving them. Essentially, problem-solving involves the steps of assessing a current situation, deciding on a desired end-state, and finding ways of transforming the current into the desired state. At the end of this process, the final stage involves evaluating how well the desired state was achieved. The Rubik's cube shown in Figure 7.7 provides an example of these stages of problem-solving. You begin by looking at the random configuration of the cube (shown on the left), and then switch the layers around until each side of the cube has the same color. At that point, you will know you have successfully solved the problem.

Problems vary tremendously in their structure and complexity. The Rubik's cube is an example of a well-defined problem because it has only one correct solution. Figure 7.8 shows a less well-defined problem whose correct solution may not be so clear. When you're about to give

FIGURE 7.8

Example of Problem without Clear Solution

Some everyday problems do not have a clear end state, as shown here when the person offering the flowers must decide on the right moment to propose marriage.

flowers to your romantic partner, you won't necessarily know the "right" words you should use to communicate your feelings until your partner responds. Because this problem has no clear solution, it will require more of your cognitive (and perhaps emotional) resources as you sift through the many possible ways to express yourself.

Advances in technology are providing new areas in which to practice your problem-solving skills. However, these problems often involve heavy cognitive burdens because the correct solutions are not always so clearly laid out for you. You have most likely become quite skilled in figuring out how to add applications to your smartphone or laptop computer without having to rely on any written instructions. However, at some point the problem becomes too complex and you have to turn to website resources after having done an online search. For people accustomed to learning how to use technology by reading instruction manuals rarely provided now, you can see what a challenge this can become.

Making matters worse, instructions for new products assume a level of expertise with either the hardware itself or the software you need to install to make it work. Furthermore, you need the hardware itself (i.e., a computer you can connect to the Internet) in order to use that very same hardware.

Complexity and vagueness in instructions are not limited to high-tech areas, though. Cooking recipes often are based on the assumption that you know whether to grease a pan before adding dough, what "simmer" means, and whether a piece of meat is truly "brown" or onions are "wilted." Prescription bottles have warning labels that instruct the patient to take the medication with "plenty of water" but also may indicate not to eat or drink before or after taking the medication. The only saving grace in all of this is the more widespread availability of "how-to" videos, but even these require that the user can separate good advice from ads or testimonials who do not actually have the expertise they claim. All of these complications make everyday problem-solving a particular challenge for people not familiar with technology.

Problem-Solving in Adulthood

As we have just noted, everyday problems are multidimensional, and the steps in solving them are not always clear. As people get older, they gain in some problem-solving skills at the expense of others. They may become slower and have more memory lapses; however, if they are very familiar with a problem or a type of problem, they can get to a solution more quickly and effectively than can a novice. If you have stood by in awe as your grandmother produced a perfectly formed piecrust in less than 2 minutes while your own dough sticks limply to the rolling pin, then you can relate to this observation. Indeed, researchers have found that the more extensive experience of older adults can enhance not only their problem-solving performance (Crawford & Channon, 2002) but also their feelings of self-efficacy (Artistico et al., 2003).

Because middle-aged and older adults have acquired expertise through their years of exposure to certain kinds of problems associated with their jobs, hobbies, or daily routines, they have many advantages in everyday problem-solving. They develop the ability to scan quickly for the important factors in a problem and avoid those that are irrelevant. As a result, expert problem solvers avoid information overload by honing in on specific areas that experience has taught them are important particularly in areas relevant to their current life concerns (Artistico et al., 2010). Figure 7.9 summarizes the balance exhibited by older problem solvers between analytics, or taking a problem apart bit by bit, and heuristics, in which older adults use their experience to guide their steps through a problem.

Older adults may also make choices that are better founded and less subject to extraneous factors. One study on decision-making found that, in general, older adults avoid what is known as the "attraction effect." In tests of the attraction effect, participants must choose from either two (A vs. B) or three (A vs. B vs. C) alternative options. For example, option A may represent a product of medium quality costing $30, while option B is a product of somewhat higher quality costing $40. These two options are about equal in their desirability. Researchers then present a different group of participants with three choices. A and B remain the same, but C is the least desirable of all three ($100 for a product of only slightly higher quality than B). The addition of choice C should have no effect on

people's decision to choose either A or B, but it does. Even though no one would choose C, its presence drives them to be more likely to pick the alternative between A and B that seemed the closest to C (choice B in this example).

A comparison of older and younger adults in the case of shopping for groceries showed a greater susceptibility of younger adults to demonstrate the attraction effect, meaning that their choices were less rational than those of older adults (Tentori et al., 2001). In a follow-up study (Kim & Hasher, 2005), researchers tested the possibility that older adults were less vulnerable to the attraction effect because they had more experience with grocery shopping. The actions of younger and older adults were compared on an additional task that would be more typical for college students, namely, a choice between options for extra experimental credit. Younger adults showed the attraction effect once again in the grocery shopping case, but not in the experimental credit case. Older adults, though less familiar with the ins and outs of experimental credits, nevertheless did not show the attraction effect in either situation.

These studies are particularly interesting because they relate to behavioral economics, an emerging field that investigates the illogical choices that consumers make in everyday situations. According to the results of the attraction effect study, then, older adults should be wiser consumers, particularly when those decisions have real economic consequences (Lichters et al., 2015).

Increased experience enhances problem-solving in the later years by allowing older adults to sift quickly through information, honing in on what is relevant and arriving at a solution. As we have just seen, this ability to mobilize a familiar strategy can have advantages but can create difficulties in some situations, particularly when it is important to look at possible alternative approaches. For example, an automobile mechanic who goes directly to the distributor as the source of a stalled engine may not notice a more serious wiring flaw elsewhere. Older problem solvers may think that they are doing a better job at solving the problem but, by objective criteria, they may not be considering alternative solutions as effectively as do younger adults and therefore can make an erroneous decision. In a comparison of young, middle-aged, and older adults on ill-defined problems, older adults were found to generate the fewest possible solutions, even when the problems were ones for which their greater experience should have proved helpful (Thornton et al., 2013).

Memory problems can also contribute to difficulties in problem-solving. If you are unable to remember the steps you've taken to try to solve a problem, you'll be more likely to repeat ineffective solutions. This was the pattern of results observed in a study of Japanese monkeys (Kubo et al., 2006). Their task was to find which of nine small

FIGURE 7.9

Heuristics versus Analytics

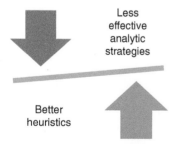

Less
effective
analytic
strategies

Better
heuristics

Problem-solving in later life involves a balance between the less effective analytic strategies an older adult may use, perhaps, balanced against the better heuristics obtained through previous problem-solving experience.

openings in a panel contained food. In the experimental condition, the food was hidden behind white plastic circles, so the monkeys had to move the plate to see what was behind it. In the control condition, the food was visible through clear plastic plates. The older monkeys in the experimental condition were hampered in their problem-solving abilities because they went back and checked behind plates they had already moved.

Making up for losses in their strategic planning ability, older problem solvers have the advantage of more experience and more access to information that could help them in a larger variety of situations. As we have already pointed out, people with experience have well-organized storehouses of knowledge that they can easily access and put to use. You may have an older relative who likes to travel abroad and can quickly tell you the pros and cons of a trip you are planning to a foreign country that you have never visited. After years of traveling internationally, this sage advisor can give you knowledge about the country's hotels, places of interest, weather patterns, and the best travel deals. Sports trivia buffs have a similar mastery of large amounts of content matter because they have that knowledge organized into systematic units, such as which 16 teams are in the U.S. American Football Conference versus the 16 in the National Football Conference. These are good people to know if you are looking for information but not good people to challenge in a trivia contest: you will undoubtedly lose.

Research on the speed at which adults make decisions confirms that older people are able to reach answers more quickly than younger people who either lack the knowledge or the ability to categorize that knowledge. However, older persons are also more apt to make quicker decisions in areas in which they may not have expertise. Furthermore, they are less likely to seek additional information once their decision has been made. It is possible that the rapid problem-solving shown by older adults reflects the fact that their experience gives them an advantage in the many areas of decision-making. Therefore, they are not as dependent on incoming information as younger adults. The other possibility is that older adults are less able to organize multiple sources of information, leading their decisions to be based on prior experience rather than on new data related to the problem (Marsiske & Margrett, 2006).

The finding that older adults are faster at solving problems conflicts with the majority of research on adult development and cognition. The types of measures and outcomes used in studies of problem-solving do not always capture timed responses, as is true for studies of psychomotor speed. Rather, studies of problem-solving involve measures based on the amount of information that the participant gathers prior to making a decision, and these measures are not as sensitive to small changes in reaction time.

The most extensive measure of problem-solving ability in daily life is the Everyday Problems Test (EPT), which presents test takers with problems they may encounter in a variety of real-world contexts. You can see an example of the type of item used in the EPT in Figure 7.10. You would answer the questions shown about cereal

	Cereal A	Cereal B	Cereal C	Cereal D
Calories	210	190	100	140
Sodium (mg)	250	0	180	0
Dietary fiber (g)	5	6	5	4
Sugars (g)	12	11	5	3
Total fat (%)	2.0	1.0	0.5	6.0
Price per serving ($)	0.58	0.39	0.26	1.14

FIGURE 7.10

Everyday Problems Test

EPT-type questions:
1. If you wanted to cut calories, which cereal should you buy?
2. If you need to stick to a budget, which cereal is most affordable?
3. Which cereal would you eat if your physician told you to eat a low-sodium diet?
4. If you wanted to cut down on fats, which cereal would be the unhealthiest?

In the Everyday Problem-Solving Test, the individual is presented with information that needs to be used to answer a series of practical questions.

choices with the information presented in the comparison chart. Performance on the EPT is related to reaction time (Burton et al., 2006), education (Burton et al., 2009), and, among African Americans, health status (Whitfield et al., 2004).

When it comes to making practical decisions in situations with which they are familiar, then, middle-aged and older adults may have an advantage. This possibility was tested in a study on decision-making comparing younger and older adults in a task where a prior choice was either relevant or not to the opportunity to receive future rewards (Worthy et al., 2011). Younger adults earned more points when the best strategy was to select which of two cards per trial would pay off with the higher reward and when there was no carryover from trial to trial. Older adults, in contrast, earned more points when the value of the reward on each trial depended on the sequence of choices made on prior trials. These and later findings (Worthy & Maddox, 2012) support the idea that older adults are more likely to base their decisions on the knowledge they develop from prior experience.

As a result of their greater experience and expertise in terms of content and process, older adults may be better able than their younger peers to enact the stages of problem-solving in which they appraise the problem, come up with a strategy, and then carry out that strategy. However, when a familiar dilemma appears with a new twist, or when a premature decision leads to avoiding important information, older adults are relatively disadvantaged. Young problem solvers may suffer from their lack of familiarity with many situations, but because they can process larger amounts of information in a shorter time, they may avoid some of the traps of failing to see alternatives that befall their elders.

Adult Learners

The literature on problem-solving in adulthood emphasizes the ability to come to a resolution when dealing with a dilemma. However, the ability to "find" problems seems to be an equally compelling aspect of adult cognition. Research and theory on this aspect of adult cognition were stimulated, in part, by Swiss psychologist Jean Piaget's concept of formal operations, the ability of adolescents and adults to use logic and abstract symbols in arriving at solutions to complex problems. Adult developmental researchers have proposed that there is a stage of postformal operations, referring to the way that adults structure their thinking over and beyond that of adolescents (Commons et al., 1984; Sinnott, 1989).

Thinking at the postformal operational level incorporates the tendency of the mature individual to use logical processes specifically geared to the complex nature of adult life. The postformal thinker is also able to judge when to use formal logic and when, alternatively, to rely on other and simpler modes of representing problems. For example, you do not need to use the rules of formal logic to unplug a stopped drain. Hands-on methods are generally suitable for dealing with practical situations like this one involving actions in the physical world.

Related to the postformal stage of cognitive development is dialectical thinking, which is an interest in and appreciation for debate, arguments, and counterarguments (Basseches, 1984). Dialectical thinking involves the recognition that often the truth is not "necessarily a given" but that common understandings among people are a negotiated process of give and take. People may not be able to find the ideal solution for many of life's problems, but through the process of sharing their alternative views with

FIGURE 7.11

The Trolley Problem as an Example of Postformal Logic

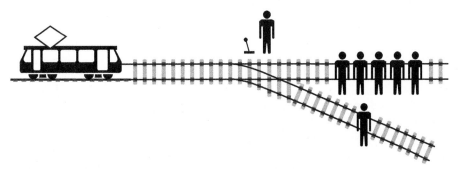

The Trolley Problem can be seen as a test of postformal logic because there is no "right" answer in deciding whether to pull the switch to save the five and kill the one or do nothing and the five will be hit by the trolley.

each other, most reasonable adults can at least come to some satisfactory compromises. Although you may not agree with some of your friends who have vastly different political opinions than your own, you have learned to respect their viewpoints, no matter how difficult it may be for you to do so and remain on speaking terms.

On a daily basis, average adults face many ambiguities and uncertainties in dilemmas ranging from how to resolve conflicts with their friends to how to make the best choices for their children's education. Many people actively seek out the opportunity to engage others in dialogue and intellectual engagement. The ability to integrate diverging viewpoints as well as see the advantages to different points of view may be the key to understanding the way that adults think (Kallio, 2011).

Moral dilemmas present one particularly important implication of these concepts related to postformal logic and dialectical thinking. In what's known as the "Trolley Problem" (see Figure 7.11), you are presented with the very unpleasant choice of a trolley proceeding toward a track junction. If you do nothing, the trolley will run over the five people standing in its way. The only way to save them is to pull the switch lever, which will now result in the death of one person standing on that track. The question is, then, whether you kill the one to save the five or let the five die by taking no action at all. Rather than using logical probabilities as presented to them in this dilemma, it appears that most people instead rely on their own intuition in deciding whether to pull the lever or not (Ryazanov et al., 2018). Logic, then, may only go so far in the actual decisions made by adult problem solvers.

These ideas about adult cognition present interesting implications about adults as thinkers, problem solvers, and, particularly, learners. Adult learners are increasingly becoming part of the concerns of those who teach at the college level. In 2016, 17% of the undergraduate population was age of 35 or older (National Center for Education Statistics, 2019). As you can see from Figure 7.12, 44% of all U.S. adults aged 17 and older were involved in some form of adult education, with 21% of all adult education students aged 70 and older. Many of these students were in courses related to work (27%), but almost as many (21%) were taking courses out of personal interest (National Center for Education Statistics, 2013).

Increasingly, within the United States, adults are enrolling in classes for English as a second language (ESL). As of 2012, 40% of the 1.7 million taking some form of state-administered adult education were enrolled in ESL programs. Over one-quarter of these students lived in the state of California (National Center for Education Statistics, 2013).

In the classroom, adult learners may attempt to master the material through using strategies such as taking more copious notes and relying on them more heavily as

FIGURE 7.12

Facts About Adult Learners

Adults 17 and older engaged in some form of adult education

Taking courses relevant to work

Ages 70 years or older

Taking some form of ESL

The distribution of adult learners showing that as many as one-fifth of adult learners are ages 70 or older. Of those taking adult education, about one-quarter are taking courses relevant to work, and 40% are involved in English as a Second Language.

they are trying to acquire new information (Delgoulet & Marquie, 2002). The adult learner is also more likely to challenge the instructor to go beyond the information and explore alternative dimensions. Such tendencies, though fascinating in the classroom, can lead to problems when it comes to evaluation. For a person who can see all the alternate angles to a standard multiple-choice exam question, it can be very difficult to arrive at the correct answer because more than one has virtues that merit attention. The adult thinker and learner may find it equally fascinating to ponder ambiguities rather than settle on one choice even though only one choice is graded as correct.

The preference that many adult learners have for applying their real-world experiences to what they gain from the classroom suggests that instructors should incorporate problem-centered teaching as much as possible (Papa & Papa, 2011). Flexible models of instruction that allow learners to apply what they are learning to their own lives through active decision-making can also fit well with the learning style of nontraditional adult students (Cornelius et al., 2011). Online courses with opportunities for personalization seem particularly well suited to the style preferred by the adult learner (Ausburn, 2004).

Educators must also adapt their methods of instruction to accommodate the learning styles and preferences of adult students at different levels of ability and literacy. For example, in the case of second language learning, students with low literacy skills and less prior education in their home countries behave differently in the classroom than students who already have more classroom experience. They are less likely to ask for help and participate in classroom interactions. To reach these students, instructors may adopt methods such as asking the students with more education and classroom experience to mentor them, starting with oral exercises before moving to written exercises, and encouraging them to use language in new ways (Ramírez-Esparza et al., 2012). Furthermore, the needs of these adult learners may involve broader issues relating to socialization, ideology, and pedagogical preferences (Mori, 2014).

INTELLIGENCE

If you were asked to define the term "intelligence," you would probably guess that it represents the quality of a person's ability to think. In the most general sense, psychology defines intelligence as an individual's mental ability. We know that "some people are cleverer than others" (Deary, 2012, p. 454); the question is why, and how this cleverness changes over adulthood.

The existence of age effects on intelligence in adulthood has many practical and theoretical ramifications. For practical reasons, it is important to find out the relative strengths and weaknesses of younger versus older workers. As we noted earlier in our discussion of problem-solving, there appear to be fairly distinct differences in the styles that adults of different ages use when making decisions. Employers in the public and private sectors can put to practical use the data that psychologists produce from studies using standard intelligence test scores. From a theoretical standpoint, research on intelligence in adulthood has provided new perspectives on the components of thought. This research has also provided insight into the perennial question of how mental processes are affected by "nature versus nurture," as researchers have continued to exploit and explore the application of complex research designs to data on intelligence test scores in adulthood.

Just as physical abilities partially define a person's identity, intelligence serves as an attribute of the person that forms part of the sense of self. People have a good idea of whether they are "smart" or "not as bright," a self-attribution that they can carry for years (Leonardelli et al., 2003). Your theory about your own intelligence can even affect how much you study, although just as important, an influence on your study habits may be how much you think you can control your school performance (Bodill & Roberts, 2013). In either case, as you get older your views about your intelligence may change as you come

to adopt some of society's negative stereotypes about aging and mental abilities. Fortunately, the results of research on intelligence provide considerable encouragement about how you can maintain those skills.

The earliest findings on adult intelligence proposed that age differences across adulthood followed the classic aging pattern of an inverted U-shape, with a peak in early adulthood followed by steady decline (Botwinick, 1977). Results from the Wechsler scales, which supported the view that intelligence generally erodes over successive decades in adulthood, contrasted a smaller but uniform body of evidence from longitudinal studies. When samples of adults were followed through repeated testings using the Wechsler scales or other standardized tests, the finding was either no decline or a decline that did not become apparent until very late in life.

Theories of intelligence differ in the number and nature of abilities proposed to exist. However, many adult development and aging researchers believe that there are two main categories of mental abilities corresponding roughly to verbal and nonverbal intelligence.

Theoretical Perspectives on Adult Intelligence

The earliest theory of intelligence, that proposed by British psychologist and statistician Charles Spearman (1904, 1927), proposed the existence of g or general factor, defined as the ability to infer and apply relationships on the basis of experience. According to Spearman, g could not be directly observed but could be estimated through tests that tap into specific mental abilities. Psychologists now find it more useful to divide intelligence into a set of multiple components. Raymond B. Cattell and John L. Horn proposed fluid-crystallized theory (Gf-Gc), the view that intelligence should be divided into two distinct factors (Cattell, 1963; Horn & Cattell, 1966). Fluid reasoning (Gf) is the individual's innate ability to carry out higher-level cognitive operations (Cattell, 1971). Originally called crystallized intelligence, comprehension knowledge (Gc) represents the acquisition of specific skills and information that people gain as a result of their exposure to the language, knowledge, and conventions of their culture. These broad abilities each reflect distinct abilities that are measured by specific tests.

In addition to these two factors, the "extended" Gf-Gc theory proposes that there are eight other broad factors that incorporate cognitive skills such as memory, speed, sensory processing, reading, writing, and mathematical knowledge. Each of these broad factors is measured by a specific test or tests that tap narrower, related, abilities. In the extended Gf-Gc model, each broad ability has its own predictive power rather than each reflecting different aspects of g.

Although Cattell and Horn regarded Gf and Gc as being distinct factors, his own analysis of the available studies at the time led educational psychologist John B. Carroll to propose that intelligence is organized into a three-level structure (Carroll, 1993). Combining these theories, the Cattell–Horn–Carroll (CHC) model of intelligence proposes that there is a three-tier structure to intelligence. Figure 7.13 illustrates the CHC model. As shown in this figure, there are five broad areas of intelligence (motor, perception, controlled attention, knowledge, and speed). Within each area, the specific abilities are represented by "Gs," whose definitions appear in the accompanying labels (e.g., "Gh" represents tactile intelligence, a component of perception).

In keeping with the CHC's proposed specific abilities, researchers testing the model use tests that measure those abilities such as WAIS-IV scales. The "Knowledge" domain, for example, can be tested with WAIS-IV verbal abilities scales. The advantage of using existing tests for assessing CHC intelligence is that the findings from previous studies can be fit into that larger model. In support of the CHC model, Benson and colleagues (2010) showed the existence of considerable overlap between the WAIS-IV and the CHC model among a sample of participants ages 16 to 90.

Research on Adult Intelligence

What happens to intelligence as you get older? This seemingly simple question is hotly debated in the literature on adult development and aging. Some researchers claim that intelligence starts to dip as early as the 20s; others are convinced by their data that the changes only become noticeable after the decade of the 60s.

The most comprehensive study of adult intelligence was conducted by K. Warner Schaie. Begun in the 1950s, what is now known as the Seattle Longitudinal Study (SLS) has produced extensive information about what happens to people's intellectual skills as they age. In addition to providing a picture of how age alters intelligence, the SLS also has provided important evidence about how cohort and time of measurement influence patterns of performance on basic intellectual abilities. Additionally, more recent offshoots of the SLS have explored the relationship of intelligence to personality, lifestyle, and the activity of various brain structures as well as patterns of intellectual development across generations.

When he began the SLS, Schaie's intention was to conduct a one-time cross-sectional study in which he would compare 500 people divided into 10 five-year age intervals or cohorts in their performance on the PMAT.

FIGURE 7.13

Cattell–Horn–Carroll (CHC) Model of Intelligence

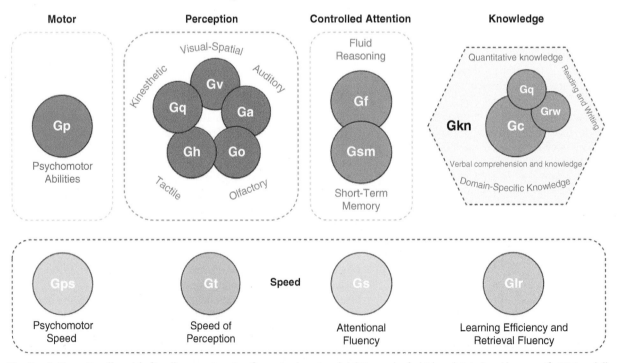

The Cattell–Horn–Carroll model of intelligence categorizes five major domains of abilities, each of which each is indexed by a specific "G," or skill.

His participants were drawn from the insured members of a prepaid medical plan. Schaie decided to expand on the study several years later, when he instituted a series of follow-ups that he then went on to conduct every seven years. As a result of adopting this method, Schaie was able to analyze the data in a series of sequential studies. This made it possible for him to test the effects of age as distinct from time of measurement and cohort. Schaie's foresight in planning a study that would allow analyses using the sophisticated developmental research designs described in Chapter 3 has provided a wealth of information on intelligence in adulthood and the factors that affect its fluctuations.

The first set of findings the SLS produced was based on the cross-sectional analyses comparing all 10 cohorts on the PMAT at one point in time. Replicating the classic aging pattern, the scores of the older adults were lower than those of the younger adults. It was not until 7 years later that Schaie was able to show that the classic aging pattern reflected not the effect of age changes, but the combined effects of age, cohort, and time of measurement. For most abilities, even the oldest age group increased or showed no change between the first and second testings. The stage was set for what has now become a 40-year-plus exploration for the factors accounting for why people change, or not, across the adult years.

The findings that Schaie and his collaborators published in a comprehensive review (2006) showed distinct patterns of age changes across the primary abilities. Vocabulary, a measure of Gc, showed the least amount of change, holding up fairly steadily until the age of 74. The largest drop in scores occurred on Numeric Ability, which in the CHC model represents Gq (quantitative knowledge). Supporting these findings are analyses from the University of Manchester Longitudinal Study, conducted over a 20-year period on over 6,000 middle-aged and older adults (Ghisletta et al., 2012). In this study, tests measuring Gf declined at a faster rate than did those of Gc. However, confirming findings from the SLS, there were large individual differences, particularly during the midlife years.

Even in the face of the compelling nature of the SLS findings, Salthouse (2009) concluded from his own analysis of cross-sectional data that the "decline" occurs in intelligence starting at age 20. Schaie (2009), arguing that cross-sectional data cannot prove or disprove the existence of age changes, regards this assertion as unfounded. Moreover, challenging Salthouse's treatment of intelligence as a unitary quality, Schaie along with others maintains that not only do people vary from each other in the rate and extent of change (interindividual change) but also within themselves and their own abilities (intraindividual change) (Nilsson et al., 2009). Indeed, in an unusual "retrodiction" paradigm using a Scottish sample followed from ages 11 to 77, reading ability measured as correct word pronunciations were found to predict, retrospectively, intelligence scores the individuals had received at age 11 (Deary & Brett, 2015). Thus, even as intelligence may change over the course of adulthood, it does so in a way that reflects individual differences far earlier in life.

In an analysis specifically investigating differences between earlier- and later-born cohorts in the SLS data, a team headed by Gerstorf (2011) showed that some abilities seem particularly sensitive to cohort effects. The later-born cohort had higher scores throughout the entire age range on all abilities except number. Moreover, the earlier cohort also had lower rates of decline.

Why would there be such powerful cohort influences on the rates of cognitive change in later adulthood? Gerstorf et al. (2011) controlled for such possible contributors as years of education and disease (cardiovascular and cancer). The remaining effects may be due to differences in the quality of education (i.e., discovery vs. rote learning), exposure to technology, the increasing complexity of work environments, and changes in gender roles associated with greater labor force participation among women. The authors concluded, essentially, that their findings support the common belief now that "60 is the new 40," or at least "the new 50."

A host of other health and lifestyle factors can affect intelligence test scores across adulthood (see Figure 7.14). As we saw in Chapter 3, retrospective studies show that people close to death show diminished intellectual functioning. Findings from the SLS suggest that health status is indeed related to intelligence test performance. Arthritis, cancer, and osteoporosis are health conditions associated

FIGURE 7.14

Factors Affecting Aging of Intelligence

Greater decline among smokers	Among men, obesity predicts lower intelligence scores	People with more active engagement show less decline

These three health-related factors can affect the rate of aging of intelligence in adulthood.

with intelligence test scores (Schaie, 1996), as is metabolic syndrome (Akbaraly et al., 2009). These effects are not limited to Western countries; similar findings were reported among a study of more than 3,200 Chinese age 60 and older, even after controlling for age, smoking, hypertension, and diabetes (Liu et al., 2009).

Taking advantage of the types of healthy behaviors we discussed in Chapter 5 also seems to help preserve "executive function," or the ability to allocate cognitive resources. The Whitehall II study showed greater declines in this type of intellectual ability among those in the sample who smoked, abstained entirely from alcohol, did not participate in exercise, and consumed low amounts of fruits and vegetables (Sabia et al., 2009). Not surprisingly, these were also the individuals who showed the largest increase in BMI over adulthood.

Lifestyle choices also play a role in helping to preserve intellectual functioning in later life. A 4-year follow-up study of nearly 32,000 European older adults showed a protective role of social network involvement on tests of memory and semantic fluency, two indicators of intelligence. Additionally, cognitive functioning in these individuals was positively affected by engagement in diversified leisure activities (Miceli et al., 2019).

Having a stimulating job may also benefit an individual's intellectual performance in later life. A study in the Netherlands comparing teachers with nonteachers showed that teachers were technically "younger" on measures of verbal fluency and working memory (Van der Elst et al., 2012). Carrying this notion forward, as shown in the SLS, being exposed to a stimulating environment after retirement can also help individuals maintain their intellectual abilities (Schaie et al., 2001). Exercise training can also benefit intelligence by promoting brain plasticity (Eggermont et al., 2009).

Expertise may also play a role in preserving an individual's intellectual abilities. An intriguing study of players of the Chinese game "Go" revealed that among those with high levels of expertise, the expected decline in memory-based measures of fluid intelligence was not observed (Masunaga & Horn, 2001).

There is increasing evidence showing that these factors affect intelligence test scores through their impact on brain health. Activation of the prefrontal cortex seems to play a role in fluid intelligence among both older and younger adults even when memory performance is controlled (Waiter et al., 2010). Aging individuals showing greater variation in reaction time have lower scores on episodic memory and crystallized intelligence, as well as steeper declines over time (Grand et al., 2016).

This finding supports earlier work showing that older adults with lower fluid intelligence show greater fluctuations in their scores over time (Ram et al., 2005). Perhaps these older individuals are more vulnerable to the physiological changes that can exacerbate the aging of the abilities that underlie fluid intelligence. In fact, researchers in the Canadian Study of Health and Aging have observed a predictive effect of low fluid intelligence test scores in a higher rate of mortality in older adults (Hall et al., 2009).

In addition to whatever lifestyle and health factors can affect intelligence across adulthood, personality also plays a role in the maintenance of intellectual abilities. People who score high on measures of anxiety exhibit poorer performance on a variety of fluid and crystallized tests (Wetherell et al., 2002). Conversely, being flexible and open-minded is related to better intellectual performance over time, as revealed in the SLS (Schaie et al., 2004).

The predictive power of personality openness may start to exert its influence very early in life. In a longitudinal study begun on the Aberdeen Scotland Birth Cohort of 1936 when the participants were children, those high in the personality trait of openness to experience had higher scores on measures of reading ability in their mid-60s (Hogan et al., 2012). Similarly, an Australian study on adults ages 74 to 90 found that participants who scored high on a measure of enjoyment of fantasy had higher Gf, Gc, and scores on a measure of everyday functioning (Gregory et al., 2010). However, in both of these studies, personality alone did not serve to predict intellectual functioning. In the Aberdeen study, childhood intelligence was a stronger predictor of cognitive ability in later adulthood than was personality. The Australian study showed that fluid intelligence interacted with personality openness in influencing cognitive abilities. It is possible that people with higher intelligence are higher in personality openness, which in turn affects their cognitive performance in later life.

This latter study raises the problem of cause and effect when examining research on lifestyle and intelligence. Do the intellectually more able seek out more stimulating environments, or does involvement in a rich environment lead to greater preservation of mental abilities? Perhaps older people with high levels of intelligence purposefully search for ways to maximize their abilities. They may also seek out certain complex problems and situations because these fit with their abilities. Research suggests that crystallized intelligence exhibits a stronger relationship to lifestyle than fluid intelligence among older adults who engage in cognitively demanding activities (Dellenbach & Zimprich, 2008). Another possibility is that people with higher intellectual abilities and better problem-solving abilities are better able to take advantage of health maintenance and treatment strategies.

The personality–intelligence conundrum was specifically addressed in another large-scale study of intelligence, the Berlin Aging Study, comparing the two directions of this relationship (Ziegler et al., 2015). According to the "environmental enrichment hypothesis," higher levels of personality openness would lead older adults to better preservation of intelligence. The "environmental success hypothesis," the one you're probably more familiar with, states that people high in intelligence are able to succeed in many arenas in life, allowing them to remain high on openness to experience. Over its 14 years, the Berlin study appeared to support the environmental enrichment hypothesis in that individuals higher in personality openness showed less of a decline in fluid intelligence than their less open counterparts. Crystallized intelligence can also facilitate learning among older individuals. This research lends support to the Openness-Fluid-Crystallized-Intelligence (OFCI), which regards personality openness as a protective factor against cognitive decline in later adulthood (Ziegler et al., 2018).

Further support for the role of the environment as an influence on intelligence comes from studies of aging twins. In the Swedish Twin Study, which followed twin pairs from 41 to 91 years of aging, there was evidence of hereditary influences on individual differences in intelligence. However, environmental factors exerted effects on the rates of change over time (Reynolds et al., 2002).

Similar findings were obtained in a study of Danish twins, who were measured using a cohort-sequential design and retested every 2 years for up to four testings. As with the Swedish study, overall intellectual ability appeared to be a function of genetics, but the rate of change over time was a function of environmental influences (McGue & Christensen, 2002).

Training Studies

Researchers have for decades tried to develop effective intervention strategies to examine ways to counteract the effects of age on intelligence. There is a long tradition within the developmental perspective advocated by Schaie, Baltes, and Willis of seeking ways to help preserve people's functioning as robustly and as for long as possible (Willis & Schaie, 2009).

The underlying theoretical and philosophical perspective for this approach evolved from some of the earliest work in this area by Baltes and Schaie (1976): "Our central argument is one for plasticity of intelligence in adulthood and old age as evidenced by large interindividual differences, multidirectionality, multidimensionality, the joint significance of ontogenetic and historical change components, and emerging evidence on modifiability via intervention research" (p. 724). To put it more simply, Baltes and Schaie argued for the need to see intelligence as "plastic" or modifiable rather than simply an attribute that declines with age. Much like the debate between the neuronal fallout and plasticity models of aging of the central nervous system, the view of intelligence as "plastic" assumes that declines are not inevitable even though some resources may be sensitive to the effects of aging. The basic assumption that adult intelligence is responsive to interventions was a driving force behind later research, particularly for training studies carried out within the SLS (Willis et al., 2009).

Underlying the plasticity model is the idea that older adults possess reserve capacity, abilities that are there to be used but are currently untapped (Staudinger et al., 1995). You can think of reserve capacity as your ability to perform to your highest level when you are positively motivated by a teacher, coach, competitor, or friend. You may not have even imagined that such a strong performance was possible until you completed it successfully. Training studies operate according to the same principle. Tapping into an individual's reserve capacity involves testing the limits, the process of continuing to train people until they show no further improvements (Baltes & Kliegl, 1992).

The earliest studies to demonstrate plasticity were conducted in the early 1970s at Penn State University by Baltes, Willis, and their colleagues. These studies demonstrated that, given practice and training in test-taking strategies, older adults could improve their scores on tests of fluid intelligence (Hofland et al., 1980; Plemons et al., 1978; Willis et al., 1981). Keeping in mind that fluid intelligence is theoretically intended to be a "pure" measure of ability, educational experiences should not have had an impact on the scores of older adults. Applying these methods to individuals in the SLS sample, the Penn State group was able to show that training in fluid intelligence tasks such as inductive reasoning could produce gains that lasted for at least seven years (Schaie, 1994).

The most impressive findings on reserve capacity and the possibility for training to improve an older adult's everyday life comes from ACTIVE, the large multisite intervention study we described in Chapter 6. Over the course of the 10-year follow-up, the training groups maintained their superiority over the controls in IADLs. It is most impressive that even a relatively brief intervention could have such a long-term effect, not only in cognitive abilities but also in areas relevant to everyday functioning. Such findings, along with other studies on cognitive plasticity via other intervention methods (Hertzog et al., 2008), provide hope that cognitive training can enable older adults to live independent lives and prevent functional disability.

THE PSYCHOLOGY OF WISDOM

Some might argue that the most advanced form of cognition is the capacity for wisdom. Unlike the ability to score well on a traditional intelligence test, wisdom reflects a far less quantifiable phenomenon. If you were asked to define wisdom, you might come up with a meaning that incorporates the individual's knowledge of the ways of the world and understanding of how other people feel, think, and behave. However, you may feel that even this general definition doesn't capture the true meaning of the word as you use it in your own life.

Psychologists who take on the task of defining wisdom actually start by asking lay people what they think it means and, further, to nominate people they think are wise. Baltes and his team of researchers decided to explore this topic after they realized that traditional views of intelligence were focusing only on the mechanics of intelligence, which involve cognitive operations such as speed, working memory, and fluid intelligence. He believed that adults become increasingly capable of dealing with higher-level conceptual issues and that conventional tests, by measuring the mechanics of intelligence, fail to capture these abilities. The central element of the Baltes wisdom model proposes that wise people are experts in the pragmatics of intelligence, meaning that they can apply their abilities to the solution of real-life problems. According to Baltes, cognitive development in adulthood involves growth in this ability to provide insight into life's many dilemmas, particularly those that are psychosocial or interpersonal.

According to the Berlin Wisdom Paradigm, wisdom is a form of expert knowledge in the pragmatics of life (Baltes & Smith, 2008) (see Figure 7.15). For many people, wisdom evolves in the later years of life as they become aware of the role of culture in shaping their lives and personalities (called "life span contextualism"). Wise people become less likely to judge others and have a greater appreciation for individual differences in values, life experiences, and beliefs (value relativism). People who are wise also have a rich base of factual or declarative knowledge and an extensive background of procedural knowledge, meaning that they know how things work (Baltes et al., 1995). Wise people also have the ability to take other people's perspectives into account (Kunzmann et al., 2018) as

FIGURE 7.15

Berlin Wisdom Paradigm

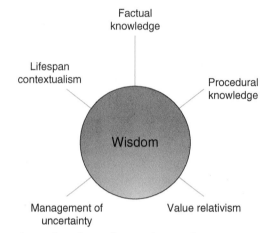

According to the Berlin Wisdom Paradigm, wisdom incorporates a set of complex cognitive abilities.

well as the ability to recognize and manage uncertainty as a fact of life (Ardelt, 2004).

These conclusions about wisdom initially developed through studies identifying the characteristics of people nominated by others to be wise who were then asked to comment about another person's personal difficulties. Continued work on the Berlin Wisdom Paradigm has focused on defining wisdom, measuring it, understanding its development, investigating its plasticity, and applying knowledge about wisdom in practical contexts (Staudinger & Glück, 2011).

In a related attempt to study wisdom, Grossman and colleagues (2010) developed a simulated task in which respondents describe how they would resolve social problems presented to them in the form of stories requiring complex judgments, such as resolving conflicts between different ethnic groups. The researchers then rated their responses along six dimensions, including being able to see multiple points of view, recognizing that knowledge of any situation is limited, making multiple predictions of how the situation may unfold, and trying to resolve the conflict through compromise. A group of professional counselors and wisdom researchers validated these rating scales. The findings supported the view that, relative to middle-aged and younger adults, older adults are better able to take multiple perspectives, try to forge compromises, and recognize the limitations of knowledge. The same individuals who received higher scores on the wisdom ratings had also received lower scores on a measure of fluid intelligence, supporting the Baltes distinction between pragmatics and mechanics.

Cultural influences also play a role in the development of wisdom over the adult years. Using the same wisdom scenarios, a subsequent study showed that young and middle-aged Japanese adults had responses that were wiser than those of their American counterparts. For the older adults in the sample, however, the Japanese–American differences were weaker. In fact, older Americans gave responses that were considered wiser than their Japanese counterparts for conflicts involving groups rather than individuals (Grossmann et al., 2012).

Wisdom may also play a role in facilitating the individual's own adjustment to life. Older adults who scored higher on the wisdom ratings using the scenario measure had higher life satisfaction, lower negative affect, less of a tendency to have depressive thoughts, and better social relationships. Five years after participating in the study, the wisest participants also were most likely to still be alive, even after controlling for other factors such as gender, social class, income, perceived health, and verbal abilities (Grossmann et al., 2012). The role of emotions in wisdom is also supported by more recent studies showing how "emodiversity" (a rich and balanced emotional life) can be an important contributor to wiser reasoning (Grossman et al., 2019).

Adding further to the idea that noncognitive factors can play a role in promoting wisdom is Gardner's theory of multiple intelligences (see Figure 7.16). According to this theory, intelligence includes several traditional abilities (logical/mathematical, verbal, visual/spatial) as well as others not usually tapped in intelligence tests (naturalistic, interpersonal, intrapersonal, musical, bodily "kinesthetic," or athleticism). This approach would seem to be an ideal way to capture the complexity of intelligence required for adaptation to daily life. In this sense, wisdom might be seen as most relevant to the domains of interpersonal (knowledge of others) and intrapersonal (knowledge of self), paralleling the distinction between mechanics and pragmatics of intelligence. We might hope that future researchers will explore these alternate and important forms of ability that clearly impact many areas of functioning throughout the adult years.

FIGURE 7.16

Gardner's Theory of Multiple Intelligences

Gardner's theory of multiple intelligences proposes that intelligence is made up of more than abilities tested in standard intelligence tests.

SUMMARY

1. The higher cognitive functions include language, problem-solving ability, and intelligence. Changes in memory contribute in part to age-related losses in language, such as the ability to derive meaning from spoken or written passages, spell, and find words. As a result, older adults use simpler and less specific language. However, many language abilities are maintained, and older adults are able to use nonlanguage cues to help them derive meanings from language. The way that younger persons speak to older adults can also be problematic if this involves elderspeak, which is patronizing and infantilizing speech directed at an older person. The communication predicament describes the negative effects on cognition and language when older people are communicated to in this manner.

2. Throughout the adult years, there is a trade-off in the factors affecting everyday problem-solving between alterations in speed of processing and working memory and gains in experience as individuals encounter a wider variety of problems as well as more depth in their own fields of expertise. However, because experienced problem solvers tend to seek answers to familiar problems by seeking familiar solutions, they may miss something important that is unique to a particular problem. In addition to focusing on one solution rather than considering others, older adults may also tend to stick with one pattern of responding when the situation calls for being able to call on a range of ideas.

3. There are a number of theories of intelligence, but the majority of research on adult intelligence is based on the fluid-crystallized theory. Studies on the primary mental abilities support the theory's proposal that fluid (unlearned, nonverbal) abilities decrease gradually

throughout adulthood. By contrast, the crystallized abilities that are acquired through education and training steadily increase through the 60s and show a decrease only after that point. The CHC theory combines existing theories into one that involves three levels of abilities.

4. The most extensive study of adult intelligence is the SLS, in which sequential methods have been applied to the PMAT. In addition to providing data on age patterns in intelligence test scores, this study has highlighted relationships with intelligence among health, personality, lifestyle, and sociocultural factors.

5. Intervention studies in which older adults are given training in the abilities tapped by intelligence test scores have yielded support for the notion of plasticity. Even 5 hours of training can result in improved scores across tests for as long as a 10-year period. Following from these training studies, researchers have proposed establishing the reserve capacity of older adults not demonstrated in ordinary life by using a method known as testing the limits.

6. Many older adults turn to the pragmatics of intelligence, or the practical use of knowledge, and away from the mechanics of intelligence, or the skills typically measured on tests of ability. The quality of wisdom in later life develops as individuals become more interested in developing their abilities in the pragmatics of life.

8

Personality

How well can you separate myth from reality about what happens to personality with age? Check your answers on the next page.

AGEFEED

FACT? MYTH?

1. Personality is set in stone and does not change with age.
2. Aging brings fewer social responsibilities, allowing people to do more of what they want.
3. People become nicer as they get older.
4. Personality change is constant throughout life.
5. Younger adults are better than older adults at controlling their negative emotions.
6. Almost everyone experiences a midlife crisis.
7. Personality traits can predict health in older adults.
8. Pessimists report a higher quality of life.
9. Being in love can reduce neuroticism.
10. Certain personality traits help people live longer.

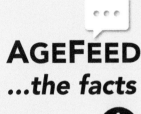

AGEFEED
...the facts

1. Personality is set in stone and does not change with age.
   Myth! People's personalities change over time, typically for the better.

2. Aging brings fewer social responsibilities, allowing people to do more of what they want.
   Fact! Without the demands of work and raising a family, older adults are often able to pursue their passions and not worry about conforming to social norms.

3. People become nicer as they get older.
   Fact! Adults tend to become nicer and more forgiving with age; however, this is likely because the not so nice adults die at younger ages.

4. Personality change is constant throughout life.
   Fact and Myth! Personality changes most early in adulthood, but people still continue to change after that.

5. Younger adults are better than older adults at controlling their negative emotions.
   Myth! Older adults tend to manage stress by understanding the situation rather than younger adults, who are more apt to take out frustrations on others.

6. Almost everyone experiences a midlife crisis.
   Myth! Believe it or not, there is very little empirical evidence supporting that midlife crises are a certainty.

7. Personality traits can predict health in older adults.
   Fact! For example, extraversion is related to lower blood pressure and neuroticism to higher blood pressure.

8. Pessimists report a higher quality of life because they're less likely to be disappointed.
   Myth! Optimists are less likely to believe in aging stereotypes, which can help maintain a higher quality of life.

9. Being in love can reduce neuroticism.
   Fact! Love may help stabilize personality, which can reduce some of the traits associated with being neurotic such as anxiety and dissatisfaction with life.

10. Certain personality traits help people live longer.
    Fact! Resiliency and adaptability to change are traits found in people who live into their 90s and beyond.

In everyday language, people use the term "personality" to describe a person's characteristic way of feeling or behaving. For example, you might say that someone does you a favor because that person has a "nice," "generous," or "friendly" personality. Although psychologists use a variety of ways to define personality, there is no one consistent meaning that all psychologists use. Instead, psychologists who study personality approach its definition from the vantage point of their particular theoretical preference.

PSYCHODYNAMIC PERSPECTIVE

We begin with the first recognized theory of personality, that of Sigmund Freud. Credited with having "discovered" the unconscious in psychology, his work indeed placed special importance on hidden motives and feelings within the mind. His approach, called the psychodynamic perspective, emphasizes the ways in which unconscious motives and impulses express themselves in people's personalities and behavior.

Current theories of adult development and personality based on the psychodynamic perspective continue to emphasize such Freudian ideas such as the importance of early development and the ways in which people cope with such emotions as fear, anxiety, and love. However, the methods used to study these phenomena are far different than the clinical approach of the traditional Freudians.

Although he left a rich body of work that later theorists would subsequently revise and reshape, many believe that Freud's legacy in the area of adult development and aging was to make the unfounded claim that personality does not change after early childhood. According to Freud, the major tasks of personality development are completed by the time the child turns 5 years old. Some changes continue to occur through adolescence, but by early adulthood, the individual's psychological development is essentially over. As a result, according to this traditional Freudian view, therapy is of little value to individuals over the age of 50, who he believed had personalities so rigidly set that they could not be radically altered.

Contemporary followers of traditional Freudian thinking share his emphasis on early development but do not share the pessimistic view that adults are incapable of change. Freudian theory today as applied to adult development is divided into three main branches, as shown in Figure 8.1. This framework will help you keep the differences among these three branches straight while also seeing their common basis in the psychodynamic perspective.

FIGURE 8.1

Overview of Psychodynamic Theory

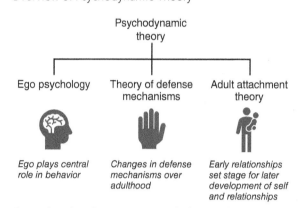

The tree branches of contemporary psychodynamic theory.

Ego Psychology

According to Freud's theory, the mind is made up of three structures that he named id, ego, and superego. As you might recall from your introductory psychology course, the id refers to the individual's biological instincts, which include the needs for food, sex, and water. Id instincts can also include the need to hurt, kill, and exert power over others. The superego attempts to control the id's irrational instincts in part through imparting society's moral standards (the conscience) and in part by providing the individual with an image of goodness to which the individual can aspire (the ideal self).

In Freudian theory, the ego is the part of the mind that controls rational thought. Its job is to negotiate a way for people to meet their biological needs without putting themselves at risk of violating society's expectations or falling short of their ideals. Although Freud regarded the ego as acting in the service of the id, other theorists propose that the ego is the central part of the mind and carries out the important functions of helping people find a balance between expressing their inner selves while finding ways to adapt to the world's demands. Psychologists in the area of ego psychology believe that the ego plays a central role in actively directing behavior.

Erikson's theory of psychosocial development proposes that it is the ego that matures throughout life as the individual faces particular biological, psychological, and social forces. He defined each point in the ego's development in terms of a push and pull that leads the individual toward a favorable outcome (such as attaining a sense of identity) or an unfavorable outcome (such as not attaining a sense of identity). As each stage is navigated, the individual moves on to the next set of issues following the epigenetic principle, as each stage unfolds in a predetermined order.

Although the theory proposes that particular issues are most likely to arise at particular ages, earlier issues may arise at a later point in life, and the later stages may move to the forefront in earlier periods if conditions develop that stimulate the individual to confront those issues. Research based on Erikson's theory includes studies that cover a single stage and those that incorporate all or most of the stages. Of all eight stages, identity and generativity receive the greatest attention, particularly among researchers whose work covers adolescence, emerging adulthood, and midlife.

Identity.   Erikson's conception of the stage of identity achievement versus identity (or role) diffusion portrays adolescents as struggling to define themselves in the face of physical changes associated with puberty, cognitive changes, and particularly role changes where they are expected to find a place for themselves in society.

Starting with this conceptual view, James Marcia (1966) developed the identity status interview, which examines the degree of commitment held by the individual to identity issues and the degree of exploration the individual used to arrive at this commitment. Figure 8.2 shows the model used in grouping people into identity statuses. The two dimensions are commitment—no commitment and exploration—no exploration. People who have strong identity commitments and have gone through a period of exploration fall into the identity achieved quadrant. Those with strong identity commitments without exploration are considered foreclosed. Turning now to the two statuses low in commitment, those who are identity diffuse have had no period of exploration moratorium and are still in a period of actively exploring alternative identity commitments.

FIGURE 8.2

The Four Identity Status in Marcia's Theory

In the identity status model, there are four combinations of identity statuses based on the two dimensions of commitment—lack of commitment and exploration—no exploration.

The traditional areas within the identity status framework of occupation, religion, and politics have expanded to the areas of racial and gender identity (Graham-Bailey et al., 2018) and acculturation status (Schwartz et al., 2013).

The identity status interview expanded on Erikson's theory by showing that people could have strong identities without going through traditional periods of "crisis" or exploration. For example, they may have taken on the views of their parents in religion, politics, or even of career. Those in moratorium are chronically in crisis, another possibility not considered by Erikson in his twofold distinction.

Marcia's work on the identity statuses has yielded a wealth of research that elaborated on his initial framework, including hundreds of studies that detail the personalities and behavioral profiles of emerging adults in each of the identity statuses (Kroger & Marcia, 2011). For example, people in the identity achievement status tend to be balanced in their thinking, mature in their relationships to others, and thoughtful about their life options. People in the moratorium status tend to be open and curious, on the positive side, and also anxious, depressed, and low in self-esteem. Individuals who are in the foreclosed status appear to be higher in self-esteem but closed-minded and rigid. Those who are identity diffuse are more likely to engage in delinquent and drug-related behaviors as well as having low self-esteem. Within the identity diffuse statuses, however, there are further distinctions that can be made between the "carefree" diffuse, who do not care about identity issues, and the undifferentiated, who are trying unsuccessfully to arrive at a set of commitments (Schwartz et al., 2011). College-age individuals involved in identity exploration may, at least temporarily, engage in high-risk behaviors involving sex, unsafe driving (Ritchie et al., 2013; Bersamin et al., 2014), and drinking games (Zamboanga et al., 2015).

As is clear from the large body of research based on the identity status model, this approach is a useful one for helping to understand the identity formation process during adolescence and emerging adulthood. However, it is less clear how it can be applied to adults in midlife and beyond. Technically, using the identity status framework, you could be considered "identity achieved" if you went through a period of exploration during your college years or even your early teens. Some 30 years later, would it still be appropriate for you to retain that same set of commitments despite the many opportunities for change that would have ensued since then? Technically, you would be identity achieved, but for all intents and purposes, if you never questioned your identity since adolescence, you would be different from someone who occasionally revisits these important commitments.

The identity process model, by looking at adult development in terms of identity accommodation, identity

FIGURE 8.3

Four Ways of Expressing Generativity in Adulthood

Redemption   Parenting   Mentoring   Grandparenting

assimilation, and balance, makes it possible to describe the adult's position on issues relevant to the sense of self at any point in life. People who retain their adolescent commitments without questioning or challenging them, in this framework, are not identity achieved but instead considered high on identity assimilation (Sneed & Whitbourne, 2003).

Generativity. Midlife adults must also come to terms with issues relating to generativity, according to Erikson's theory. Figure 8.3 shows the four components of generativity as studied in midlife adults. Because Erikson defined generativity as showing care and concern for guiding the next generation, it would follow that parents would be higher in generativity than nonparents. However, not just having children but also successfully parenting them seems to be more consistent with Erikson's views. Peterson et al. (2006) found that, indeed, parents higher in generativity not only felt closer to their college-age children but also had children who were happier, more likely to be able to plan for the future, higher in prosocial personality attributes, and higher in social interest as indicated by their interest in politics, a feature of generative midlife adults as well (Hart et al., 2001). The desire to secure a legacy is another component of generativity, involving a desire to contribute not just to one's family, but to the common good (Newton et al., 2019). Grandparenting is another way to express generativity, not only by the fact of having grandchildren but also being involved in mentoring, spending time with them, and strengthening the bonds of mutual family ties (Hebblethwaite & Norris, 2011).

Generativity is not completely selfless, however. According to McAdams (2008), generative behaviors also expand and enrich one's own ego in a process he calls the "redemptive self." By being generative, in other words, you are benefiting your own development as well as the people you are helping. In truly generative behavior, though, the balance shifts more toward concern about others rather than concern about your own personal accomplishments. Along the same lines, Bauer (2008) talks about the "noisy ego" versus the "quiet ego." Bauer proposes that people high on generativity have moved past the phase when their "noisy" ego causes them to focus on their own self-interest and can instead have a "quiet" enough ego to allow them

to hear what others need and help without thought or concern of how these actions will benefit them.

Although people high in generativity may be better parents, at least according to some criteria, the idea of the redemptive self suggests that generativity goes beyond even good parenting to extend to concern with larger society. If this is true, then it seems that people high in generativity should also show greater interest in and concern for helping others beyond their own families, such as participating in volunteer work in their communities; in this regard, generativity shares certain features with altruism (Agostinho & Paço, 2012). In research testing whether people who are committed to environmental causes (which may also be seen as reflecting care toward future generations), Matsuba et al. (2012) found that both college students and midlife adults high in generativity were also more likely to be concerned with environmental issues. Similarly, people scoring high on generativity are more likely to believe in, and engage in, environmentally responsible behavior (Urien & Kilbourne, 2011), a process that may be related to the idea of leaving behind a positive legacy (Zaval et al., 2015).

Overall Psychosocial Development. Researchers also approach studying Erikson's theory by measuring development along all eight stages simultaneously. In contrast to studies that focus on specific stages, the broad-spectrum approach examines individual differences both in levels of psychosocial development and in the relationships among the stages. According to Erikson, anyone can confront any psychosocial issue at any point in life. Measuring individual differences on all stages at once allows researchers to test this notion.

One of the earliest measures used to investigate psychosocial development across a range of stages was the Inventory of Psychosocial Development (IPD) (Constantinople, 1969), the questionnaire used in the Rochester Adult Longitudinal Study (RALS). The original sample of more than 300 students in the classes of 1965–1968 was followed up in 1977, when they were in their early 30s. At the same time, a new sample of 300 undergraduates entered the study, making it possible to conduct sequential analyses (Whitbourne & Waterman, 1979). Both of these samples participated again in 1988–1989, when the third undergraduate sample was added. At this point, the sample contained three cohorts of college students and two cohorts of adults in their early 30s (Van Manen & Whitbourne, 1997; Whitbourne et al., 1992). The most recent follow-up took place in 2000–2002 (Whitbourne et al., 2009), when the two oldest cohorts were in their 40s and 50s (Sneed et al., 2012).

The latest published follow-up of the RALS used hierarchical linear modeling (HLM), making it possible to look at how individuals changed over time relative to themselves and to others in the sample. Previous follow-ups relied on comparing the entire sample's means, obscuring those individual change curves. By using HLM, it was possible not only to see how much change occurred but also who was most and who was least likely to change.

One question was whether people who were in a committed relationship right after college would show more or less growth of intimacy in the ensuing decades. As it turned out, those who became involved in marriage or a cohabiting relationship after the age of 31 started out with lower intimacy scores in college. However, over the subsequent two decades, these late-bloomers showed a steeper growth curve than did the individuals who married or cohabited within a few years of college graduation.

Moreover, the individuals in the 1946 Cohort (who were in college in the 1960s) showed a different pattern than those in the 1957 Cohort (in college in the 1970s). Within the 1946 cohort, those in a relationship by age 31 started out with higher intimacy scores in college than did those not in a relationship. However, those not in relationships by age 31 showed a steeper growth curve and therefore had reached the same intimacy level as their peers by the time they reached their 40s and 50s. These trends also occurred for the younger cohort but to an even greater degree.

Similar patterns of "catching up" occurred for people who got a later start in their careers. During college, they had low scores on the Eriksonian quality of industry (identifying with a work ethic); however, in the subsequent 20 years, they showed a steeper increase and eventually caught up with their higher-achieving counterparts. Current work on the 2012–2014 testing of the RALS samples continues to reinforce the conclusion that psychosocial development continues along multiple dimensions across the adult years.

These findings from the RALS show that continued personality development is not only possible but predictable. Even the psychosocial stages associated with childhood showed continued gains for many of the RALS members during adulthood. The RALS data did not, unfortunately, include the kind of rich personal narratives that investigators can obtain when they test their participants in face-to-face interviews. However, the questions that participants answered about their work and family histories provided descriptive life history information that supplemented the questionnaire scores. By studying the patterns of life changes, the first author extracted enough narrative material to identify five patterns of "life pathways" (Whitbourne, 2010).

The five pathways are shown in Figure 8.4, and, as you can see, they represent divergent ways of navigating the course of adult life. Those in the Authentic Road pathway had made a series of changes in their lives, but with each change, sought greater identity clarity and opportunities for growth. The Triumphant Trail pathway included people who did not seek change specifically, but instead were handed significant challenges that they were able to overcome such as death of children, spouses, and partners. It appeared that early childhood, during which these individuals developed favorable resolutions of the first psychosocial issues in life, helped prepare them for those difficult periods in their later years.

In contrast to the two more positive pathways, the remaining three pathways each reflected a differing pathway marked by less favorable identity resolutions. In the Straight and Narrow pathway were individuals who made virtually no self-initiated life changes but instead maintained highly consistent patterns for decades. In the Meandering Way were people who made a series of very different life commitments, but never seemed to settle on one direction to follow. Finally, the people in the Downward Slope pattern made a series of decisions throughout their lives, which set the stage for unfulfilling outcomes such as leaving public service and entering a profitable, but unsatisfying, profession.

There are connections between the pathways and the identity processes of assimilation, accommodation, and balance. In identity assimilation, individuals attempt to maintain a consistent view of themselves over time. Like those on the Straight and Narrow pathway, people who use identity assimilation also fear change and prefer to think of themselves as stable even when situations might require that they change. Identity accommodation is the predominant identity process of those in the Meandering Way because this identity process involves excessively changing in response to experiences when it would be preferable to maintain some consistency. Identity balance is very much like the Authentic Road; people who use identity balance are able to change flexibly in response to experiences but still maintain consistency of their sense of self over time.

A second longitudinal study of college students, this one focusing on women, began in the 1950s to 1960s by Ravenna Helson and her colleagues at Mills College, a private school in California. Although not originally

FIGURE 8.4

Pathways Model from the Rochester Adult Longitudinal Study

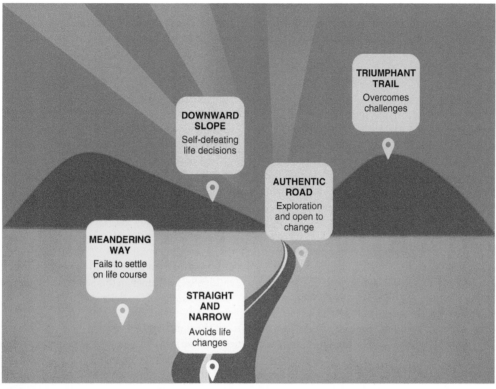

According to the pathways model, there are five differing routes that individuals take through adulthood.

intended as a study of Eriksonian development, a number of the findings were interpreted in terms of his theory. The study's founders originally intended to study leadership and creativity among college women (Helson, 1967) but, like the RALS, the study's scope continued to expand to include the years of later adulthood.

The initial findings reported by Helson and her team in the early years presented evidence for considerable personality stability. However, there were several notable exceptions. The Mills women increased in the qualities of assurance, independence, and self-control and decreased on a scale measuring their perceived femininity. There was also evidence of substantial individual differences in personality change patterns, which the investigators linked to variations in level of ego development and identity. For example, women higher in identity at age 43 were more likely to have achieved higher levels of generativity at age 48 (Vandewater et al., 1997). Similar findings were obtained in a later analysis in which the identity of a woman at age 43 served to predict her well-being at age 60 (Helson & Srivastava, 2001). Social roles also influenced the development of women in this sample through late midlife of such qualities as dominance, masculinity/femininity, flexibility, and achievement (Helson & Soto, 2005). The Mills study findings also support the notion of patterns or pathways throughout adulthood, which suggest consistent variations in well-being are related to a sense of purpose in life (Mitchell & Helson, 2016).

These studies of psychosocial development support the view that personality continues to evolve throughout adulthood but not in a single, universal direction. This conclusion provides an important contrast to studies, which we will examine later, that attempt to relate personality change to age alone rather than to individual variations in life events and personal developmental patterns.

Vaillant's Theory of Defense Mechanisms

The second psychodynamic approach is based on the work of Vaillant (2000), who emphasizes the development of defense mechanisms in adulthood. As we mentioned earlier, intended to help protect the conscious mind from knowing about unconscious desires, defense mechanisms are strategies that people use almost automatically as protection against morally unacceptable urges and desires.

The question, from Vaillant's point of view, is how defense mechanisms change over time, as individuals find themselves presented with new circumstances to which they must adapt ranging from stress at work to problems in their close relationships. This is a very different position from that of Freud, who proposed that there was no personality change of any substance after people reached the age of 50, if not before.

For Vaillant, the major shift that adults experience in their adaptation to life involves using fewer of the so-called "immature" and more of the "intermediate," and eventually "mature" defense mechanisms. You can see these three categories of defense mechanisms in Figure 8.5. Over time, Vaillant proposed, people use increasingly mature and adaptive defenses and fewer immature and maladaptive ways of minimizing anxiety. Immature defense mechanisms include acting out and denial.

The immature defense mechanisms involve reacting to a stressful situation in a way that fails to contain your emotions or help you feel better. In denial, you refuse to acknowledge a bad situation, in projection you blame others, in acting out you release your feelings impulsively, and in passive aggression you try to get back at others by finding a way to harm them without being obvious about it.

The intermediate defense mechanisms allow you to turn your anxiety or other negative feelings into slightly more productive outlets. In displacement, you transfer perhaps your angry feelings from their true target to someone who is less threatening, you forget an unpleasant experience in repression, and in reaction formation, you act in a way opposite to your true feelings.

Finally, the mature defense mechanisms allow you to feel better by channeling your anxiety into a constructive activity (such as cooking or gardening), stifle your feelings through suppression, and in anticipation, try to plan ahead so the problem will not seem quite so bad, The other two mature defense mechanisms involve acting to benefit other people in order to feel better (altruism) or using humor to see the funny side of even the worst situations.

In the Vaillant Study of Adult Development (1993), Vaillant and his research team investigated the use of defense mechanisms in three diverse samples of individuals. The first consisted of men in what was known as the Harvard Grant Study. Begun in 1938, this study was intended to characterize the physical and psychological functioning of Harvard undergraduates on a wide variety of measures. Over the course of the subsequent decades, it continued to follow the men as they made their way through the early and middle years of life. Men in the second group, called the Core City sample, were a socioeconomically and racially diverse group chosen as a comparison to the Harvard men. In order to extend the findings beyond men, Vaillant eventually recruited a sample of women from a study originally focused on gifted children. The women in this sample were interviewed again for the purpose of the defense mechanism study when they were in their late 70s.

The initial set of findings provided evidence within each of the three samples for a positive relationship between maturity of defenses and various outcome measures. For instance, Core City men who used immature defenses (such as acting out) were more likely to experience alcohol problems, unstable marriages, and antisocial behavior (Soldz & Vaillant, 1998). However, the use of mature defense mechanisms increased over the course of later life up through the oldest age tested of 75 years. Supporting the notion of patterns of development through adulthood, however, there were differing patterns of changes based on the extent to which participants reported having been raised in warm childhood environments (Martin-Joy et al., 2017).

FIGURE 8.5

Defense Mechanisms in Vaillant's Theory

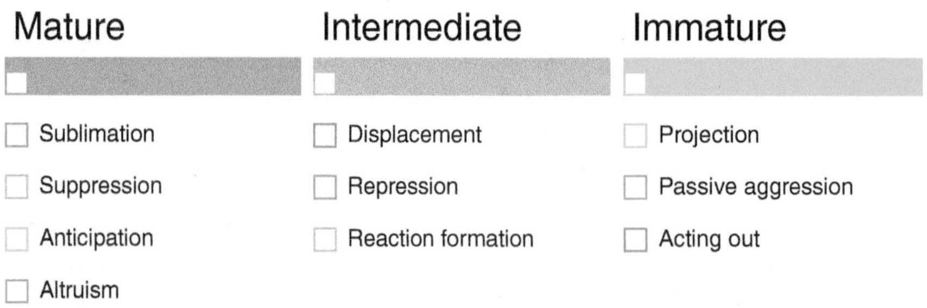

Mature	Intermediate	Immature
☐ Sublimation	☐ Displacement	☐ Projection
☐ Suppression	☐ Repression	☐ Passive aggression
☐ Anticipation	☐ Reaction formation	☐ Acting out
☐ Altruism		

Vaillant's theory of defense mechanisms proposes three categories based on maturity of the defense mechanism used for adapting to stress.

Other longitudinal investigations support the general direction of defense mechanism changes from less to more mature. Cramer (2003) conducted a 24-year longitudinal study in which she followed more than 150 men and women from early to middle adulthood. As in the Vaillant studies, age was associated with the use of more mature defenses. In the subsequent 20 years from middle to later adulthood, Cramer and her colleagues found that the maladaptive defense mechanisms used by people with a narcissistic personality (whose gratification depends on the admiration of others) became less psychologically healthy (Cramer & Jones, 2008). Consistently, these studies show that older adults are able to manage their emotions through the use of mature defense mechanisms that involve the control of negative emotions or trying to put the situation into perspective.

The general pattern that emerges is that older adults cope with anxiety, stress, or frustration by reacting in less self-destructive or emotional ways than they would have when they were younger. Rather than getting frustrated and giving up on a solution, older adults are more apt to try and understand the situation and figure out a way around it. They can suppress their negative feelings or channel them into productive activities. By contrast, younger people (including adolescents and young adults) are more likely to react to psychologically demanding situations by acting out against others, projecting their anger onto others, or regressing to more primitive forms of behavior.

These findings from studies of the use of defense mechanisms in adulthood further support the notion that change is possible throughout life. However, they also suggest that people do not change in reliably consistent ways on the basis of age alone. The role of early life predictors, furthermore, is shown in research based on adult attachment theory, to which we turn next.

Adult Attachment Theory

Adult attachment theory proposes that the early bond between the infant and caregiver set the stage for all of the individual's later significant relationships. Through interactions with their caregivers (usually the mother), infants develop attachment styles that are mental representations or frameworks about what to expect in a relationship. These mental representations form models not only of relationships but also of the self, and so they are important for understanding both an individual's personality and close relationships.

According to adult attachment theory, if people feel safe and cared for, they will carry forward into their adult relationships a secure attachment style in which they feel confident about themselves and confident that others will treat them well. People who were either abandoned as infants or felt that they would be, develop an anxious attachment style in which they imagine that their adult partners will also abandon them. Being neglected in infancy may also produce adults who show the avoidant attachment style with a fear of abandonment so intense that they stay away from close relationships altogether.

There is very little research specifically on aging and adult attachment style in samples, in part because it is seen as a theory about how people choose and relate to romantic partners relatively earlier in adulthood. In fact, we will explore the implications of attachment style for long-term relationship satisfaction in Chapter 9.

Nevertheless, there is reason to examine attachment style as a quality of an individual's personality independently of relationship status. As shown earlier, several investigations of adult personality identify differing trajectories of development in later life as a function, in part, of early influences. Attachment style would clearly fit into this framework as well, relating to a favorable resolution of the Eriksonian stage of trust versus mistrust, and to the quality of a warm childhood environment discussed by Vaillant. For example, older adults recalling their childhood in terms of a secure attachment style report being happier on a daily basis than those who report an insecure attachment style (Consedine & Magai, 2003).

Older adults with insecure attachment styles, by contrast, may be more likely to experience social isolation than their securely attached counterparts (Spence et al., 2018). Another risk presented to older adults with insecure attachment style involves health. A subsample of over 3,200 Whitehall II participants ages 50 to 73 provided saliva samples over the course of a day that were analyzed for cortisol levels, an index of stress (Kidd et al., 2013). Additionally, they rated their subjective stress levels. Individuals who fit the criteria of one type of anxious attachment had higher levels of cortisol and perceived stress shortly after awakening, remaining higher than the other attachment groups throughout the day. The group highest in both physiological and psychological stress seemed to spend the day on the watch for signs of rejection by the people closest to them. Understandably, such an approach to one's daily interactions can have cumulatively deleterious effects that take their toll on health.

Older adults, whatever their early attachment styles, may face challenges as they outlive their prior attachment figures (i.e., spouses/partners, siblings, other relatives). Instead, they may turn to a variety of other potential attachment figures or "safe havens" who provide them with emotional security during times of stress (Cicirelli, 2010; see Figure 8.6). Pets provide one such safe haven, because they are with the individual on a daily basis. Others in older adults' life may serve similar purposes, including clergy, health care professionals, and more distant relatives.

FIGURE 8.6

Safe Haven Attachment Figures

Pets and other attachment figures can provide "safe havens" for older adults

In attachment theory as applied to later life, a variety of attachment figures can provide "safe havens."

As you can see from this discussion of the psycho-dynamic approach, there are a number of concepts that can be useful in understanding personality development throughout the adult years. The next approach takes a very different view of adult personality but similarly provides useful perspectives from which adult personality can be examined.

TRAIT APPROACHES

This next approach in personality is based on the concept of traits, or stable enduring dispositions that persist over time. When you think about how to describe the personality of a friend, relative, or coworker, you most likely begin by listing a set of a characteristics or qualities that seem to fit the person's observable behavior. These characteristics typically take the form of adjectives such as "generous," or "outgoing," or perhaps, "quiet" and "unfriendly." Trait theories of personality propose that adjectives such as these capture the essence of the individual's psychological makeup based on the concept of the trait, which is a stable, enduring disposition that persists over time.

The trait perspective in personality is based on the assumption that the organization of the personal dispositions known as traits guide the individual's behavior. Trait theorists view adult development in large part from the perspective of early psychologist William James (1842–1910)

who claimed that personality is "set in plaster" by the age of 30, a position not unlike that of Freud's. More recently, however, even these views about personality stability are coming under scrutiny, as you will see shortly. The most generally accepted trait theory in the field of personality and aging is based on Costa and McCrae's proposal that there are five major dimensions to personality (Figure 8.7). The Five-Factor Model (FFM) (sometimes called the "Big Five") is a theory intended to capture all the essential characteristics of personality in a set of five broad dispositions. Each disposition has six subscales or "facets." To characterize an individual completely requires knowing how that person rates on each of these 30 facets. The tool used to test the FFM is the Neuroticism-Extraversion-Openness Personality Inventory–Revised (NEO-PI-R), a questionnaire containing 240 items measuring the 30 facets (Costa & McCrae, 1992). Clinicians may use the NEO-PI-R to supplement other diagnostic instruments because it provides a measure of personality separate from psychopathology. Researchers use the NEO-PI-R to chart changes in personality over time or to study the relationship between personality and other behaviors, including those relevant to health status.

The five traits in the FFM are neuroticism, extraversion, openness to experience (or "openness"), agreeableness, and conscientiousness (you can remember these as spelling "OCEAN" or "CANOE"). Each trait name closely fits its meaning in everyday conversation—people high in neuroticism tend to worry a great deal, those who are extraverted are outgoing and sociable, being open to experience means that you are willing to entertain new ideas, having high agreeableness means you get along well with others, and being conscientious means that you attend to detail and tend not to procrastinate.

Within the trait categories, where you stand within the six facets can make a difference in how your personality is reflected in your behavior. For example, within the extraversion trait, people can be either high or low in the facet of warmth and high or low on the facet of gregariousness. Being high on both would mean you genuinely like to be around people and relate easily to others. Being low on warmth but high on gregariousness would mean that you seek out being with others but that people find it hard to get to know you very well.

Research on Aging and the Five-Factor Model

Studies based on the scales of the FFM and aging show a high degree of consistency over time throughout adulthood, with greater consistency among increasingly older

FIGURE 8.7

Five-Factor Model

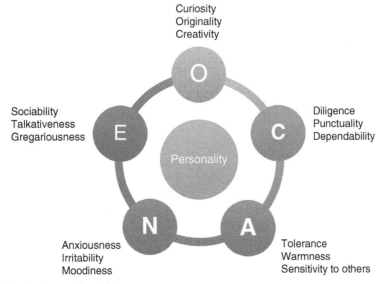

The Five-Factor Model, with key indicators of each factor.

groups of adults. However, the consistency between scores obtained at different measurement points becomes smaller the longer the time interval between them (Roberts & DelVecchio, 2000). This means that people maintain their relative positions along the traits in comparison to their age peers; the "highs" stay high and the "lows" stay low. If you had high neuroticism scores as a young adult, you would continue your high levels of worry, anxiety, and general malaise throughout your midlife years and beyond.

Although people may maintain their relative positions along each of the traits, their mean scores may undergo change across adulthood. In a meta-analysis of 92 longitudinal studies, Roberts (2006) reported that individuals increase in social dominance, conscientiousness, emotional stability (the opposite of neuroticism), social vitality (a facet of extraversion), and openness to experience through age 40. Social vitality and openness decreased after this point, but agreeableness increased. However, the meta-analysis also showed that four out of the six traits continue to change in middle and later adulthood. Specifically, agreeableness shows steady increases, as does conscientiousness. Emotional stability (the opposite of neuroticism) increases early in adulthood and then remains relatively stable. Openness to experience increases early in life and then remains stable, falling somewhat after the age of 60. Finally, there are increases in a trait called "social dominance," a component of extraversion referring to traits reflecting not only

dominance but also independence and self-confidence, especially in social contexts. These findings led the authors to conclude that "this meta-analysis clearly contradicts the notion that there is a specific age at which personality traits stop changing" (p. 14). A subsequent longitudinal study spanning the 50 years from ages 16 to 66 further supported the meta-analytic findings, with patterns of maturation evident among from 20% to 60% of the sample (Damian et al., 2018). The results of these findings led Roberts and his colleagues to regard the patterns as consistent with the "maturity principle" of adult personality development, which proposes that, for example, individuals become less impulsive as they develop into adulthood.

It is also important to understand how people's personalities influence their life choices, which in turn affect their personalities. According to the correspondence principle, people experience particular life events that reflect their personality traits; once these events occur, they further affect people's personalities (Roberts et al., 2013). Figure 8.8 illustrates the correspondence principle. As you can see here, a person high in conscientiousness would be more likely to work in an office environment with its constraints of space and time. That environment will continue to shape conscientiousness in its workers because lateness and slacking off are not rewarded. Conversely, people high in extraversion are more likely to be attracted to social environments, which, in turn, shape them to be even more

FIGURE 8.8

Examples of Correspondence Principle

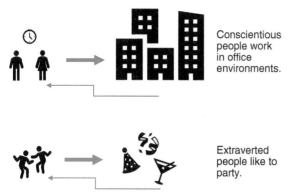

Conscientious people work in office environments.

Extraverted people like to party.

According to the correspondence principle, people seek environments consistent with their personalities, which further influences their personalities to conform to the environment.

outgoing. According to this principle, then, personality stability is enhanced by the active choices that people make rather than by any intrinsic likelihood of traits remaining static over time.

Support for the correspondence principle comes from an unusual 40-year longitudinal study spanning the years from ages 12 to 52 (Spengler et al., 2015). Adult career outcomes could be predicted from both questionnaire measures and teacher observations on personality-like qualities of adherence to school rules, inattentiveness, pessimism, and feelings of inferiority above and beyond the effects of parent SES and IQ. In a shorter-term investigation of changes in narcissism (extreme self-absorption and grandiosity), young adults who were high in this quality also experienced more stressful negative events, suggesting ways that personality influences life outcomes (Grosz et al., 2019). Thus, there can be significant consequences of personality characteristics emerging early in life whose effects persist throughout the adult years.

Health and Personality Traits

The idea that personality traits could be related to significant health problems and health-related behaviors originated when researchers discovered what became known as the **Type A behavior pattern**, a collection of traits that include being highly competitive, impatient, feeling a strong sense of time urgency, and highly achievement-oriented. First identified by cardiologists Meyer Friedman and R.H. Rosenman (1974), the Type A behavior pattern became known as a major risk factor for

heart disease, particularly when people high in the Type A behavior pattern also have high levels of hostility (Suarez et al., 1991).

Other negative emotions also appear to be important personality traits to add to the equation in predicting heart disease. In one study, researchers followed over 300 healthy men for a 10-year period, measuring their hostility, depression, and anger as well as physiological risk factors for heart disease (Boyle et al., 2007). The men higher in hostility and more prone to experience anger also showed increases in coronary heart disease risk.

Another personality risk factor for heart disease is the so-called **Type D personality** (where "D" stands for "distressed") characterizing people with high levels of anxiety, loneliness, and depression who try to suppress their feelings. People high in Type D qualities have a poor prognosis when they develop heart disease. A common feature underlying their negative emotions appears to be extreme social inhibition, or fear of new situations (Allen et al., 2018).

On the positive side, personality traits associated with favorable qualities appear to play a protective role in heart health, including agreeableness, as shown in a study of over 5,500 Danish adults, ages 49 to 63 (Christensen et al., 2019).

Another favorable personality trait with respect to health is conscientiousness. In a study of nearly 13,000 participants in a large longitudinal study, researchers found that conscientiousness facets of self-control, organization, industriousness, and responsibility were related to lower body fat, healthier metabolic, cardiovascular and inflammatory markers, and better performance on physical assessments. Individuals high in conscientiousness, who are also low in neuroticism and extraversion, are also less likely to smoke, as shown in a meta-analysis involving nearly 80,000 adults spanning nine cohorts (Hakulinen et al., 2015).

Conscientiousness continues to play a role in mortality in later adulthood as well. Among a sample of more than 1,000 Medicare recipients ranging from 65 to 100 years of age followed over a 3- to 5-year period, conscientiousness, particularly self-discipline (a facet of conscientiousness), predicted lower mortality risk over a 3-year period. As the study's authors point out, it is possible that high levels of self-discipline relate to a greater tendency to be proactive in engaging in behaviors that are protective of health and to avoid those behaviors that are damaging to health (Weiss & Costa, 2005).

Conscientiousness may exert its positive effect on health through its link with prevention-related behaviors. Lodi-Smith et al. (2010) used structural equation modeling to analyze the relationships among conscientiousness as rated by the participant and someone close to the participant ("observer-rated"), and self-reported engagement in preventive and risky health-related behaviors, education, and self-reported health. People higher in conscientiousness engaged in more preventive behaviors and fewer high-risk health behaviors (smoking, excessive drinking). Because self-report bias may lead people to rate themselves high in conscientiousness and positive health-related behaviors, the observer ratings were an important data source in this study. In fact, people high in observer-rated conscientiousness actually did engage in fewer risky health-related behaviors.

The favorable effects of high conscientiousness on health may also be traced to lower neuroendocrine and inflammatory responses. A longitudinal study conducted in England on over 2,300 adults showed lower stress levels as measured in hair cortisol concentration among individuals higher in conscientiousness, even after adjusting for health behavior and demographic factors. These findings suggest that conscientiousness plays a direct role in heart health through its relationship to stress (Steptoe et al., 2017).

Researchers are also gaining insight into the relationship between personality traits and cognitive functioning. In a study of over 90,000 individuals across 10 cohorts, Sutin et al. (2019) reported that, independent of age, gender, and education, individuals with lower neuroticism and higher extraversion, openness, and conscientious had higher verbal fluency scores. In part, this relationship may reflect the impact of cognitive functioning on personality changes in middle and later adulthood (Wettstein et al., 2017).

Clearly, personality factors are integral aspects of the biopsychosocial model of development in adulthood and old age. Traits and behavior patterns that have their origins in inherited predispositions or through early life experiences influence the health of the individual through a variety of direct and indirect pathways. However, although personality traits may be an inherent part of "who" you are, they can modulate and change over adulthood even as they influence some of the most basic components of your ability to remain healthy.

SOCIAL COGNITIVE APPROACHES

Personality psychologists, as you have just seen, focus on individual differences in such qualities as defense mechanisms, the structure of personality, and traits. Social cognitive approaches to personality and aging focus on how people's emotions and motivations change over time, and how these changes affect the way they see themselves and other people. Researchers in the social cognitive

tradition who study aging and emotions are also gaining an increased appreciation for the ways that older adults are able to focus their attention on the positive, rather than negative, aspects of their daily lives. Research on motivation and aging helps provide insight into people's goals, desires, and needs and how they change through life.

The desire to experience positive emotions forms the basis for socioemotional selectivity theory (SST), the view that people seek to maximize the positive emotions they experience in their relationships. SST is based on the premise that there are two types of rewards that relationships can provide. Informational rewards are those that give you new knowledge and emotional rewards give you positive feelings. As shown in Figure 8.9, as people perceive their time to be running out (as happens when people get older), emotional rewards gain in importance compared to informational rewards.

To understand the nature of informational rewards, consider how you felt when you began college. You probably sought out people who seemed to know the most about how to get started, and who could also guide you to the places you needed to find. In emotional rewards, you seek out people who help you feel good about yourself and your life. These are the people you turn to when you're feeling lonely, depressed, or stressed in hopes that they will make you feel better. In psychological terms, we would say that through this process you are engaging in affect regulation, or increasing your feelings of happiness and well-being.

Endings of any kind, whether the end of life or the end of a chapter in your life, bring out strong emotions and cause you to want to spend time with the people who have been closest to you. Think of times when significant life events have come to an end, such as when you graduated from high school and said goodbye to your classmates.

FIGURE 8.9

Socioemotional Selectivity Theory

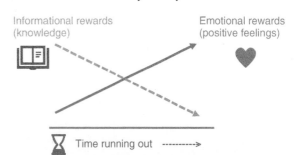

Socioemotional selectivity theory proposes that the perception of time running out leads individuals to seek to maximize emotional rewards in relationships and minimize informational rewards.

Knowing that you did not have much time left to spend with these people, you wanted to make the most out of the time you did have.

Similarly, the desire to maximize emotional rewards leads adults increasingly to prefer spending time with people who are familiar to them rather than seeking out new friends and acquaintances. Family and long-time friends are the people who will serve these positive emotional functions of self-validation and affect regulation. Older adults are less interested in meeting new people and broadening their social horizons than they are with deepening their ties to the people closest to them (Lang & Carstensen, 2002).

A number of studies have examined the propositions of SST and have arrived at varying degrees of support for the theory regarding whether older adults actually do seek to maximize positive affect by regulating their relationships. In one early study, Isaacowitz and colleagues (2006) showed that older adults were more likely than young adults to focus their attention on facial expressions suggesting positive rather than negative emotions. Later research showed, furthermore, that older adults with higher levels of cognitive functioning were particularly likely to show this bias toward positively valenced faces (Isaacowitz et al., 2009).

Even though older adults prefer emotionally positive stimuli, this preference may not be reflected in the way that they feel (Isaacowitz, 2012). Furthermore, the positivity effect in viewing happy faces may not translate to non-Western cultures. Research testing SST on a Chinese sample showed older adults to look away from, not toward, happy faces (Fung et al., 2008).

The so-called positivity effect may transfer to memory. According to this view, it is easier to remember words with positive associations than those with negative associations. Testing this approach within the context of SST, Barber et al. (2016) found that when prompted to think about a limited future, both younger and older adults showed better memory for pictures depicting positive than for those having negative content.

A most recent approach to testing SST examines the emotionally laden situations that individuals seek out. It may be one thing to show a preference to look at positive images, or even to remember them, but quite another to understand how people regulate the situations that could affect their emotions. Across a series of five experiments on individuals ranging from young to later adulthood, Livingstone and Isaacowitz (2019) found that the tendency to seek out happy experiences was not unique to older adults. In experimental versus natural settings, this desire to be exposed to positive emotional content may be more universal than SST implies (Isaacowitz et al., 2018).

COGNITIVE PERSPECTIVE

The cognitive perspective in personality views people as driven by the desire to predict and control their experiences. Emerging from this perspective are cognitive self theories, which propose that people regard events in their lives from the standpoint of how relevant these are to their own sense of self.

Specific theories about aging and personality based on the cognitive perspective place importance on the ways that people interpret their experiences and understand themselves over time. Figure 8.10 summarizes the three main approaches within the cognitive perspective. All focus on thoughts about experiences as the driving force for the ways in which people respond to those experiences.

Possible Selves Theory

The possible selves model proposes that the individual's view of the self, or self-schema, guides the choice and pursuit of future endeavors (Markus & Nurius, 1986). The possible self means literally just that: what are you now, and what *could* you be in the future? These thoughts about the self can motivate you to act in certain ways so that you achieve your "hoped-for" possible self, or the person you would like to be. These self-conceptions about the person you will be in the future continue to shift as you develop throughout adulthood. People can remain hopeful of change until well into their later years (Smith & Freund, 2002). Increasingly important as you get older is your health-related possible self, meaning your hope that you

Possible Selves	Coping and Control	Identity Process Theory
We are motivated to achieve a hoped-for self and avoid a feared self	Coping strategies work to reduce stress	Self-esteem maintained through use of identity balance

FIGURE 8.10

Cognitive Perspective

The three major cognitive approaches to adult personality.

will remain in good shape and free of disease (Frazier et al., 2002). A dreaded possible self is the opposite of the hoped-for possible self. With regard to health, most people would rather not become ill and so they will take action to avoid that outcome.

According to possible selves theory, people are motivated to strive for a hoped-for possible self and will attempt to avoid a dreaded or feared possible self. To the extent that they are successful in this process, positive feelings of life satisfaction are theorized to emerge. People think of themselves in a negative light and view their lives negatively when they are unable to realize a hoped-for possible self or to avoid the dreaded possible self. For instance, you probably feel better when your grades confirm your possible self as a good student and study harder to avoid the dreaded self of a person who fails out of college.

However, people have ways to protect themselves from these negative self-evaluations. One tactic is to revise the possible self to avoid future disappointment and frustration if experiences suggest that the possible self may not be achievable. You may realize that you will not be a straight A student if your grades include a mix of As and Bs (or lower grades), so you revise your possible self accordingly. You will probably feel better about yourself in the long run if you do so even though you may continue to strive for good grades. A similar process seems to be at play for older adults. In one study, those older adults who underestimated their future selves (in both the physical and social domains) had higher well-being a year later than those who overestimated their future selves (Cheng et al., 2009). By lowering their expectations, they evaluated more positively the outcomes they did achieve.

Coping and Control

Adult development researchers are interested in the field of aging and sense of personal control in part, based on a popular belief that adults undergo a loss of the feeling that they control what happens to them as they with age. Studies carried out within the National Survey of Midlife Development in the United States (MIDUS) showed that contrary to the popular myth, older adults retain the feeling of being in control of their lives despite being aware of the constraints they may encounter. They do so by viewing their resources and potential positively rather than focusing on losses (Plaut et al., 2003).

The cognitive approach to stress emphasizes the role of perceptions as determining whether an event will be viewed as a threat, which, in turn, determines whether it is viewed as stressful. The experience of stress occurs when you perceive that the situation overwhelms your ability to manage effectively in that situation. Coping refers to

the actions people take to reduce stress. There are two main forms of coping. In problem-focused coping, people attempt to reduce their stress by changing something about the situation. Conversely, in emotion-focused coping, people attempt to reduce their stress by changing the ways they think about the situation. Other methods of coping fall in between these two, such as seeking social support, a coping method that involves both taking action (by talking to other people) and attempting to feel better (which may result from talking to other people). Another way to distinguish between the two types of coping is approach (problem-focused) and avoidance (emotion-focused).

Cognitive theories of coping propose that the most effective coping strategy is one that matches the demands of the situation and its modifiability by actions the individual can take. If the situation is one that cannot be changed, people only become more stressed if they keep trying to use problem-focused coping, particularly as their efforts deplete their coping resources. For situations that can be changed, however, using emotion-focused coping would mean that you fail to take advantage of steps to improve the situation that would cause it to be less of a problem in the future. For example, if you have a number of pressing deadlines, simply wishing they would go away will not be an effective means of coping because by missing the deadlines, you create further problems for yourself.

When you cope successfully with a stressful situation, your mood improves and you have a higher sense of well-being. The process seems to be reciprocal—people who feel better also cope more successfully. One longitudinal investigation of coping in midlife adults followed over a 10-year period found that people who were less depressed are more likely to resolve problematic situations successfully (Lachman et al., 2009).

Some people seem to be characteristically better able to cope with challenging life events. These are the individuals said to be high in resilience or the ability to recover from stress. Resilient older adults are able to overcome negative emotions and adapt to new situations as these arise, even if those situations are objectively stressful (Ong et al., 2006). Social support and personality appear to play a role in promoting resilience (Montpetit et al., 2010). Belief in their own coping resources, furthermore, can help older individuals approach stressful situations in a more effective manner (Trouillet et al., 2009). These resilient individuals can take charge of potentially stressful situations before they become problem, leading to fewer health-related stressful situations (Fiksenbaum et al., 2006). Finally, religion can also serve as an important coping resource for promoting resilience in older adults (Van Ness & Larson, 2002).

Although some discussions of coping in later life regard older adults as passive rather than active copers, it is not necessarily given that as people get older they adopt a fatalistic approach to managing their fortunes or that they become ineffective copers. A study of the victims of the 2005 Hurricane Katrina that devastated New Orleans showed that older and younger adults were equally effective in engaging in coping strategies to manage their responses to the disaster (Cherry et al., 2009).

Identity Process Theory

According to identity process theory, the goal of development is optimal adaptation to the environment through establishing a balance between maintaining consistency of the self (identity assimilation) and changing in response to experiences (identity accommodation). The actions people take upon the environment reflect attempts to express their sense of self by engaging in the activities they regard as important and worthwhile. Through identity assimilation, people interpret events in a way that is consistent with their present identity. If an event occurs that is so discrepant a person cannot interpret it in terms of identity at the moment, identity accommodation comes into play.

Most people have fairly positive views of themselves, but as they get older, more and more experiences occur that can potentially erode self-esteem. However, research on identity processes shows that adults increasingly rely on identity assimilation, and this is how older people are able to maintain a positive self-esteem. The edge that assimilation has over accommodation is theorized to be just enough to maintain this positive view without leading individuals into self-views that are so off base as to be completely out of sync with experiences (Pilarska, 2014).

The multiple threshold model, which we described in Chapter 2, predicts that individuals react to specific age-related changes in their physical and psychological functioning in terms of the identity processes. This model was tested out in a study of nearly 250 adults ranging in age from 40 to 95 years (Whitbourne & Collins, 1998). Individuals who used identity assimilation with regard to these specific changes (i.e., they did not think about these changes or integrate them into their identities) had higher self-esteem than people who used identity accommodation (i.e., became preoccupied with these changes). A certain amount of denial, or at least minimization, seems to be important with regard to changes in the body and identity.

Later studies have examined the relationship between identity and self-esteem more generally and found self-esteem to be higher in people who use both identity balance and identity assimilation (Sneed & Whitbourne, 2003). Identity accommodation, by contrast, is related to lower levels of self-esteem throughout adulthood. However, men and women differ in their use of identity processes in that

women use identity accommodation more than do men (Skultety & Whitbourne, 2004). In addition, some women who use identity assimilation may claim that they use identity balance to appear as though they are flexible and open to negative feedback when in reality, they prefer not to look inward and perhaps confront their flaws (Whitbourne et al., 2002).

That there may be an advantage to identity assimilation in terms of health and mortality is supported by research on self-perceptions of aging and longevity (Levy et al., 2002). Older adults who managed to avoid adopting negative views of aging (which may be seen as a form of identity assimilation) lived 7.5 years longer than those individuals who did not develop a similar resistance to accommodating society's negative views about aging into their identities. Self-perceptions of being ill can further affect the way that individuals view their age, seeing themselves as "older" in a process similar to identity accommodation (Kundrat & Nussbaum, 2003). The advantage of denial against negative self-evaluations associated with aging (a form of identity assimilation) also was demonstrated in a long-term longitudinal investigation in which people who used denial had better psychological health (Cramer & Jones, 2007). Conversely, relying primarily on identity accommodation is associated with the experience of depressive symptoms (Weinberger & Whitbourne, 2010).

The tendency to use identity assimilation when thinking back on your life and how you have changed is a general bias that pervades the way people recall their previous experiences. The life story is the individual's inner personal narrative of the past events in his or her life (Whitbourne, 1985). This tendency was demonstrated in one study investigating retrospective reports of personality change in a sample of nearly 260 men and women in their early 60s. Men, in particular, were likely to see themselves as having gained in attributes such as "confident power" between their 20s and 60s (Miner-Rubino et al., 2004).

Identity assimilation may also serve a protective function in other contexts in which older adults are faced with potentially negative information about their abilities. One group of researchers used a novel opportunity to study this process among older drivers referred to driver education classes due to a history of auto accidents. Those older drivers who overestimated their driving abilities became less depressed after receiving feedback about their actual driving abilities than older drivers who took a more pessimistic view of whether their driving abilities had changed (De Raedt & Ponjaert-Kristoffersen, 2006).

However, there may be cultural biases in the tendency to use identity assimilation or identity accommodation. A cross-national study comparing Dutch and American older adults showed that maintaining a youthful age identity mediates the link between identity processes and self-esteem. However, this mediation effect was stronger in the Americans than in the Dutch, reflecting cultural differences in views of aging (Westerhof et al., 2012). People in the United States are more likely to be focused on maintaining a youthful identity compared to people living in the Netherlands, which has strictly enforced mandatory retirement at age 65.

As personality research, with its focus on individual differences, continues to be integrated into studies within the field on topics as diverse as health, cognition, reactions to life events, and physical changes, greater understanding will be gained about how people vary in their reactions to the aging process. Such work will help further the development of the field in terms of biopsychosocial processes, leading both to a richer theoretical understanding of aging and practical implications for intervention.

MIDLIFE CRISIS THEORIES AND FINDINGS

The midlife crisis refers to a period of self-scrutiny and reevaluation of goals triggered by the individual's entry into middle age. Derived from an age-stage approach to personality in adulthood, the midlife crisis had its origins in psychodynamic theory but has spread far beyond its original meaning to become a catch-all term for any changes that people experience between the ages of 30 to 60. In this section of the chapter, we'll examine the evidence, pro and con, to see whether the midlife crisis deserves its place in the scientific literature, if not popular lore.

Theory of the Midlife Crisis

It is safe to say that most people in contemporary American society are familiar with the term "midlife crisis." The topic of the midlife crisis has become a permanent fixture in popular psychology. A recent search of a popular commercial website revealed more than 100 books on the topic, and there is no sign of diminishing interest in the foreseeable future. It may therefore surprise you to learn that the concept is largely discounted in academic psychology.

The term midlife crisis was coined by psychoanalyst Elliot Jaques (1965) in a paper outlining the role of fear of mortality as prompting life crises in well-known historical figures. The term remained relatively obscure until it was picked up by journalist Gail Sheehy (1974), whose popular book called *Passages: Predictable Crises of Adult Life* placed it front and center in the psychological life of 40-something adults. Sheehy's book was based on research being conducted by others, including Yale

psychologist Daniel Levinson, who would later publish his own best-seller called *The Seasons of a Man's Life* (Levinson et al., 1978). The Levinson/Sheehy approach emphasizes strict age-based turning points in adulthood, of which the midlife crisis was just one. In his subsequent publication on women, which was greeted with far less attention in the popular press, Levinson claimed that similar alternations between change and stability characterize adult women (Levinson & Levinson, 1996).

Levinson's publication itself was based on interviews with a small sample of 40 men ranging in age from the mid-30s to mid-40s. The men in the sample were intended to represent men from diverse backgrounds, with 10 from each of the following occupations: business executive, academic biologist, blue-collar worker, and novelist. In addition to these interviews, the authors included informal analyses of the biographies of famous men and the stories of men portrayed in literature.

Although the midlife crisis was the common notion to emerge from Levinson's work, his study went beyond age turning points in proposing the changes that occur throughout the midlife years (see Figure 8.11). Levinson proposed that development involves primarily changes in the life structure, or the way that the individual's life is patterned at a given point in time. Your life structure includes your involvement in family, work, leisure, friendships, and religion and takes into account your ethnicity. It is influenced by your conscious and unconscious sense of self but also by the social and cultural environment in which you are living.

The idea of the life structure is certainly consistent with other views of development in midlife, including that of the life story and the identity process model. What distinguishes Levinson's theory was his proposal that the life structure evolves through an orderly series of universal stages in adulthood. He proposed that these stages alternate

FIGURE 8.11

Stages in Levinson's Theory

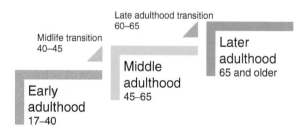

Levinson's theory of the midlife crisis is based on the idea that individuals experience transitions from one life structure to another between major periods of life.

between periods of tranquility and periods of transition, with each stage having a specific focus.

Levinson believed that during periods of stability, the man builds his life structure around the decisions he made in the previous stage. If he chose to pursue a certain career path, he continues in that path throughout the period of stability. However, as the period reaches its close, the man becomes driven by both internal and external factors to question his previous set of commitments. For the next 4 or 5 years, during the transitional period that ensues, he explores different alternatives and seeks a new life structure or a modification of the existing one. Levinson believed that these transitional periods are inevitable. Choices are always imperfect, and as the outcome of one set of choices plays itself out, the individual begins to experience regrets and a desire for change. As stated by Levinson (p. 200), "no life structure can permit the living out of all aspects of the self."

The period called the midlife transition has a special quality compared to other transitional periods because it involves the most significant shift, from early to middle adulthood. As shown in Figure 8.11, the period of the midlife transition ("crisis") is targeted as 40 to 45. However, its beginning can occur anywhere between 38 and 43, and its ending can occur anywhere between the years of 44 to 47.

The first theme of the midlife crisis is overcoming disillusionment due to failure to achieve the dreams of youth that inevitably cannot be fully realized. The individual must then establish a new set of more realistic aspirations. The second theme of the midlife crisis involves making decisions about how to pursue the life structure during middle adulthood. During this time, the man questions his marriage, comes to grips with the maturing of adolescent children, handles promotions or demotions at work, and reflects on the state of the nation and the world. He may begin to establish mentoring relationships with younger persons so that he may pass along the torch of what was handed to him during his early adulthood. Finally, the man must resolve the polarities of his personality involving masculinity and femininity, feelings about life and death, and the needs for both autonomy and dependence on others.

Although Levinson's theory predicts that the stage sequences are universal, it does allow for variations in progress through the late 30s that would affect the specific nature of the midlife crisis. In the most frequently observed pattern reported in the sample, a man advances steadily through a stable life structure but then encounters some form of failure. Usually, this need not be a catastrophic loss, such as getting fired or facing divorce, but it may be simply a perceived failure to achieve some particular desired goal by a certain age. For instance, he may not have won an award or distinction for which he was striving, such as the biologist who knows he will never win a Nobel Prize. Most people would not be distraught over such a "failure," particularly if they were generally well regarded in their profession or community. However, if this goal was part of an individual's "dream," it can lead to serious disappointment and self-questioning. Some men in the sample did in fact realize their dreams, others failed completely, and still others decided to change their life structures entirely out of boredom.

The characteristics of the midlife crisis are by now well known through their representation in contemporary literature, theater, movies, and song. For many people, they seem almost synonymous with the particular characteristics of the Baby Boomers, whom current society regards as being obsessed with aging, determined to stay young, and selfishly concerned with their own pleasure. However, this is not what Levinson believed. He regarded the midlife crisis to be a virtually universal process that has characterized human existence for at least 10,000 years.

Critiques and Research on the Midlife Crisis

Apart from the original investigation by Levinson and colleagues, little to no empirical support has been presented for the existence of the midlife crisis as a universal phenomenon (Lachman, 2004). Even before the data were available, however, psychologists in the adult development field expressed considerable skepticism about the concept of the midlife crisis based on what at the time appeared to be extrapolation far beyond the available evidence (Brim, 1976). Figure 8.12 summarizes the three main points of the midlife crisis critiques.

One of the most significant criticisms of the midlife crisis was the fact that Levinson (and Sheehy) relied too

FIGURE 8.12

Midlife Crisis Critique

 1   Age is not a marker of development.

 2   Levinson's book was highly subjective.

 3   The findings were never replicated.

The criticisms of the midlife crisis theory fall into three basic areas.

heavily on age as a marker of development. As you've already learned, chronological age is not necessarily an accurate indicator of an individual's psychological status or even physical functioning. However, adding to this problem is the fact that Levinson and other midlife crisis writers contradicted each other on exactly when this age was supposed to be. Some said 40 to 45, others 38 to 47, others exactly the age of 43. Because of this lack of clarity, the midlife crisis term can be used for any situation in which a person feels stressed, unhappy, or preoccupied with feelings of failure. We will return to this point shortly.

The Levinson study itself was also flawed in that the original sample was hardly representative enough to support claims of universality. Of the 40 men that Levinson and his team interviewed, half were from the highly educated and intellectually oriented strata of society. Another one-quarter of the sample consisted of successful business executives. The concerns of the men in this sample, such as running companies, publishing novels, and competing for Nobel Prizes, are hardly those of the average man (or woman).

The scientific basis for the Levinson model can further be criticized because Levinson himself seemed to lack objectivity, given his stated goal of writing the book: "The choice of topic also reflected a personal concern: at 46, I wanted to study the transition into middle age in order to understand what I had been through myself" (p. x). He speculated that perhaps the study's results reflected the "unconscious fantasies and anxieties" (p. 26) of himself and his middle-aged male colleagues. Compounding this problem was the fact that the study's investigators never clearly stated their procedures for conducting the ratings of life stages. They did not even publish the interview questions, would be typical for a study such as this one.

One of the first empirical challenges to the midlife crisis concept actually came from the laboratories of McCrae and Costa, who used their extensive database on personality at the time to test several specific predictions (McCrae & Costa, 2003). The easiest process was to plot the scores on the NEO scales by year across the supposed midlife crisis peak years. However, the scores were essentially flat; in fact, neuroticism was lower by a very small amount in the 43 year olds.

Having explored this indirect approach, McCrae and Costa created what they called a "Midlife Crisis Scale" and administered it to 350 men ages 30 to 60 years. Items on this scale asked participants to rate themselves on emotions related to the midlife crisis such as feelings of meaninglessness, turmoil, and confusion, job and family dissatisfaction, and fear of aging and death. If any questions had detected a midlife crisis, these surely would have. Yet they did

not, either on the initial sample or in a different group of 300 men tested with a slightly shorter version (Costa & McCrae, 1978). The most telling data of all, however, emerged in this second study on the Midlife Crisis Scale. The data were from men participating in the Department of Veterans Affairs Normative Aging Study, one of the longitudinal personality investigations that eventually became part of the basis for the FFM. Men who had received higher scores on the neuroticism factor 10 years earlier were the ones who received higher scores on the Midlife Crisis Scale. This finding suggests that people with chronic psychological problems are more likely to experience a phenomenon such as the midlife crisis. Other studies using a combination of interviews and questionnaires further call the midlife crisis concept into question.

One was a study conducted by the first author on nearly 100 adult men and women between the ages of 24 and 61 (Whitbourne, 1986). Among the extensive interview data collected on identity and life histories, none of the participants, even those in their 40s, fit the criteria for a midlife crisis even when they were asked specifically about the impact of aging on their identities. A second interview and questionnaire study conducted on another sample of more than 300 men ranging from age 38 to 48 ("prime time" for the midlife crisis) yielded similar findings (Farrell & Rosenberg, 1981).

The National Survey of Midlife Development in the United States (MIDUS) added another nail in the coffin to the midlife crisis concept (Wethington et al., 2004). Only 26% of respondents reported that they had experienced a midlife crisis, hardly the 100% that midlife crisis theory would predict. However, even this percentage is most likely an exaggeration because those who reported having a midlife crisis included the general experiences that everyone has in life of being aware that time is passing. Even so, when the researchers categorized these responses by age, they could detect no particular peak in the mid-40s. Some of the women in the sample even declared that the age of their midlife crisis was over 60, hardly considered "midlife" by any stretch of the imagination.

More recently, McFadden and Rawson Swan (2012) reviewed studies on midlife crisis versus midlife transition among women, including participants in the 10-year Melbourne Longitudinal Study. Their analysis showed that, once again, stages in midlife did not predict any of the well-being outcome measures, including self-esteem, life satisfaction, depression, and marital satisfaction.

Along similar lines, the findings of a study carried out in the United Kingdom asked participants ages 25 to 70 and older to recall a past crisis as occurring in the 20s, 30s, and 40s (Robinson & Wright, 2013). For each decade, about half the participants remembering back to that point in their lives recalled a crisis. Rather than being a broad existential crisis as predicted by theory, however, the issues participants reported related to problems involving relationships and finances. Additionally, people were more likely to report a crisis in the decade immediately prior to their own age. Supporting the idea that the midlife crisis (or those in the 20s and 30s) is not a universal phenomenon, the tendency to report a past crisis was more prevalent among people higher in empathy, or the sensitivity to feelings.

Related to the midlife crisis is the concept introduced by behavioral economists of the "U-shaped curve" claimed to show a steep dip in happiness during the broad swath of midlife (i.e., 35 to 60) (e.g., Blanchflower & Oswald, 2016). This idea has caught the popular imagination as support for a crisis in midlife but, like the original claims of universality, proves to be overly simplistic (Lachman et al., 2016). Data in support of the U-shaped curve fail to take into account important controls such as health, marital status, and income (Laaksonen, 2018). Looking at the supposed U-shaped curve across the world regions varying in wealth, Steptoe et al. (2015) reported that only in high-income countries could anything approaching a dip be observed. It is in these countries that income disparities lead the stressed-out and struggling lower-wage earners to make negative comparisons between themselves and the very wealthy.

The final criticism of the U-shaped curve pertains to the size of the "U." To obtain the data on age and happiness, the economists conducting these studies ask participants to answer this question on a 10-point scale: "Overall, how satisfied are you with your life nowadays?" scored from 0 to 10. When the "U" is reported, it involves a difference between 7.2 and 7.8. Displayed on a 10-point scale, the "U" turns into a slightly wavy line. Results showing relationships to age become significant because of the very large sample sizes involved in these economic analyses.

What keeps the midlife concept alive despite the evidence suggesting it is a myth? One view is that it makes a "good story" (Rosenberg et al., 1999). The idea of a "crisis" enhances its story appeal. As shown in Figure 8.13 with the emblematic red sports car, being able to blame your midlife excesses on a crisis can justify various forms of "naughty behavior." Because it is "one-size-fits-all" psychology, furthermore, the midlife crisis provides easy explanations for whatever problems an individual might be experiencing in midlife. Finally, it is quite likely at this point that the idea is far too popular to disappear from the media. Those hundreds of books and popular articles are unlikely to disappear soon.

The only virtue, perhaps, of having the midlife crisis become so prominent in the popular imagination is that it

FIGURE 8.13

Why Won't the Midlife Crisis Go Away? People for Trait Theory?

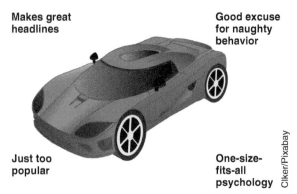

These four factors contribute to the continued belief in popular psychology of the validity of the midlife crisis, despite research that does not support it.

holds out the hope that change is possible in adulthood. This can be an important contrast to the "set in plaster" idea or even Freud's notion that change is not possible in adulthood. The "pathways" model suggests that continual evaluation and readjustment of an individual's identity and life commitments can prove to be adaptive. By making it permissible for midlife adults to undergo such occasional questioning, the concept of the crisis could have a beneficial effect on people's lives.

In summary, personality is characterized in multiple ways in psychology. Studying how personality develops over adulthood may lead to the realization that you need not become hardened into a rigid pattern of set dispositions. Change is possible throughout your life, if not in predictable stages, at least in ways that allow you to feel better about yourself as you grow older. As researchers explore relationships between health and personality, they will continue to provide greater understanding of how to maximize the chances of maintaining physical functioning as well.

SUMMARY

1. Studies of personality in adulthood are based on theories that attempt to define the nature and structure of personality. Within psychodynamic theory, the primary theories involve psychosocial development, attachment, and defense mechanisms. Several major longitudinal studies have provided tests of ego psychology theories. Psychosocial development from college to midlife was the focus of the Rochester Adult Longitudinal study

(RALS), which also examined the relationship of life experiences to personality among men and women. The RALS also identified five pathways of development in adulthood including the Authentic Road, Straight and Narrow, Meandering Way, Triumphant Trail, and Downward Slope.

2. Attachment theory proposes that the earliest interactions with caregivers involve adult personality and relationships. Studies on adult age differences in attachment style show that older adults are less likely to be anxiously attached and more likely to be dismissive compared with younger adults. Older adults may have fewer attachment figures in their social networks, but those they have fit into a wider range of roles.

3. Theories based on defense mechanisms differentiate among immature, intermediate, and mature defense mechanisms. In moving through adulthood, individuals become more likely to use the mature defense mechanisms to adapt to challenges.

4. Within the trait perspective, the Five-Factor Model (FFM) has stimulated a large body of longitudinal and cross-sectional studies on personality in men and women throughout the adult age range. The five traits in the FFM include neuroticism, extraversion, openness to experience, agreeableness, and conscientiousness.

There are also important individual differences in changes in personality over time: many of them are related to health and behavioral risk patterns, such as the Type A behavior pattern.

5. Socioemotional selectivity theory proposes that, over the course of adulthood, individuals select social interactions that will maximize the emotional rewards of relationships. Older adults appear to be better able than their younger counterparts to regulate negative affect.

6. Cognitive theories propose that individuals view the events in their lives from the standpoint of the relevance of these events to the self. Cognitive theories include possible selves, coping and control, and identity process theory.

7. According to the midlife crisis theory, there is a period in middle adulthood during which the individual experiences a radical alteration in personality, well-being, and goals. Subsequent researchers using a variety of empirical methods have failed to provide support for this theory, and it is generally disregarded within the field of adult development. Researchers believe that the midlife crisis makes a "good story" and may be too popular to disappear from the public imagination. Because it presents the possibility that change is possible in adulthood, however, the concept may have some value.

9

Relationships

By now you've probably realized how important staying physically and mentally active is for healthy aging. However, you can't overlook the importance of relationships! Here are some interesting facts about how social connections shape the lives of older adults.

AGEFEED

#trending

1. People with good social relationships have a **50% lower mortality risk** compared to those who don't.

2. Providing **support** to others can help lower one's **blood pressure**.

3. More older adults in long-term relationships are choosing not to live together or get married in a phenomenon known as **living apart together**.

4. **Strong friendships** play an important role in reducing the risk of developing chronic illness among older adults.

5. Positive relationships among **siblings** can offer protective support in older age, particularly for good health and positive mood.

6. **Older couples**, for better or for worse, often engage in the same types of health behaviors.

7. **Family relationships** promote physical health and well-being in older adults.

8. Older adults are increasingly using **online dating apps** and companies are taking note by creating apps specifically geared toward the 50-and-older market.

9. Increased TV watching among adults 65 and older (estimated to be around **47 hours/week**) is linked to social isolation.

10. **Volunteering**, especially at community-based events, positively impacts well-being for older adults.

Your relationships with others are essential to your existence throughout life. From your intimate partners to your family, friends, and the broader community, your social connections are a crucial part of who you are and how you feel on a day-to-day basis. It is difficult to capture the central qualities and complexities of these many relationships, and it is perhaps even more challenging to study the way these relationships interact with developmental processes within the individual over time. Yet researchers must be able to translate that intuitive sense of how important relationships are into quantifiable terms that can demonstrate the nature and impact of social processes in adulthood.

Changes in the broader society of the country and world heavily impact the nature of individual relationships. You can see from even brief glances at stories within your social media feed that patterns of marriage and family life change significantly with each passing year. In the United States at least, fewer people marry today, and those who do are waiting longer than previous generations. Family compositions are continually changing as people leave and reenter new long-term relationships, often involving their children and extended families as well. In this chapter, we examine these changing family patterns and try to provide an understanding of what theorists say about the qualities of close relationships and how they interact with the development of the individual.

MARRIAGE AND INTIMATE RELATIONSHIPS

The marital relationship has come under intense scrutiny in today's world. The union between two adults is thought to serve as the foundation of the entire family hierarchy that is passed along from generation to generation. You hear about the death of marriage as an institution, yet interest in marriage itself never seems to wane in the popular imagination, the media, and professional literature.

Marriage's centrality in people's lives stems in part from tradition as well as from the fact that many people define their own personal happiness in terms of their intimate relationships. There are also practical aspects of marriage, ranging from the financial benefits of having a spouse to the day-to-day needs of maintaining a household. Socially, marriage also plays a role in bringing families together, forming the basis for community ties, and becoming the basis for childrearing. All of these features serve to keep marriage a very relevant social institution.

Marriage

As a social institution, marriage is defined as a legally sanctioned union. People who are married are permitted to file joint income tax returns and are given virtually automatic privileges to share the rest of their finances as well as other necessities such as health care and housing. They often share a last name, usually the husband's, although many wives never change their names at least for professional purposes. In the 1970s, couples began to create a new hyphenated last name. Until 2013, homosexual couples could get married only within certain U.S. states until the Supreme Court ruled part of the Defense of Marriage Act to be unconstitutional in June 2013, making same-sex marriages legal throughout the country.

Generally, marital partners are entitled to retirement, death, and health insurance benefits as well as the entire portion of the estate when one partner dies. Although marriages need not legally conform to the statutes of a particular religion, they are often performed in a religious context.

The statistics on marriage provide important insights into the role of the marital relationship in people's lives. As you can see from Figure 9.1, the majority of adults 18 years

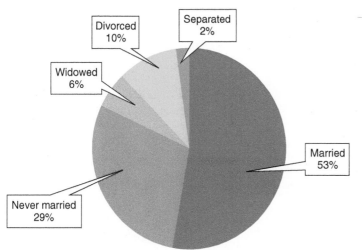

FIGURE 9.1

Marital Status, U.S. 2018

Distribution of the U.S. population ages 18 and older according to marital status.

of age and older choose to be married (U.S. Bureau of the Census, 2018c). However, as indicated above, the age of first marriage is on the rise in the United States, from lows in 1950 of about 20 for women and 23 for men to current median ages of nearly 28 for women and 30 for men (U.S. Bureau of the Census, 2019a). The reasons for the rise in age at first marriage, which currently refers to those in the millennial generation, reflect labor force characteristics, which seem to affect men and women to a similar extent (Gurrentz, 2018a).

Among individuals ages 65 and older, in the United States, a higher percentage of men than women are married and living with a spouse. As shown in Figure 9.2, the gender disparity in marriage rates grows wider with each progressively older decade past age 65. By the age of 85, over three times as many men as women are married and living with their spouse. Therefore, older women are at greater risk for some of the disadvantages that come with single status, including fewer financial resources, less access to health care, and potential loss of social support.

Although the age of first marriage is on the increase, by the age of 40, 84% of all women are married, a percentage that has not changed since 1995 (Copen et al., 2012). The highest percentage of married adults ages 20 and older are Asian Americans (60%) followed by Whites (56%), Hispanics (45%), and Blacks (32%) (U.S. Bureau of the Census, 2012). That income matters is shown by the fact that the highest percentages of men (77%) and women (66%) are in the highest income bracket of $100,000 USD and over (U.S. Bureau of the Census, 2018c).

Cohabitation

Living in a stable relationship prior to or instead of marrying is referred to as cohabitation. Since the 1960s, there has been a steady increase in the number of couples who choose this lifestyle at least for their first type of long-term, committed union and by 2019, over half of U.S. adults ages 15 to 44 have ever cohabited with a partner (National Center for Health Statistics, 2019). As you can see from Figure 9.3, among 25- to 34-year-olds in the United States, along with a drop in those living with a spouse, the percent living with an unmarried partner has risen in the 50 years between 1968 and 2018 (Gurrentz, 2018b). Estimates are that 17% of women and 16% of men ages 18 to 44 are currently cohabiting. Along with a rise in the overall numbers of couples who cohabitate is a parallel increase in the number of cohabitating adults with children under the age of 15. More births to unmarried women occur in a cohabiting than in a noncohabiting union (Nugent & Daugherty, 2018).

Most investigations of cohabitation involve younger adults, but middle-aged and older adults are also becoming increasingly likely to enter into cohabiting relationships. The percent cohabiting in the nearly 50 years between 1967 and 2017 has risen among adults 50 to 64 from 0.7% to 4.4%, with small but measurable increases in those 65 to 74 and 75 and older (Vespa, 2017).

The unions older adults form tend to persist longer than those formed by younger adults. Using data from the Health and Retirement Study, a longitudinal sample of

FIGURE 9.2

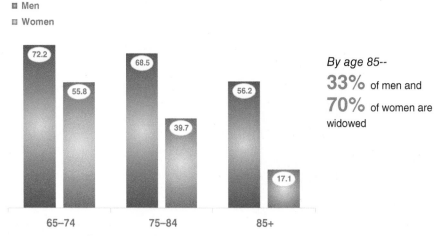

PERCENT BY AGE GROUP MARRIED WITH SPOUSE, U.S.

▣ Men
▣ Women

72.2 — 55.8 — 68.5 — 39.7 — 56.2 — 17.1

65–74   75–84   85+

By age 85--
33% of men and
70% of women are widowed

Percent within each age and sex group of those 65 and older who are currently married.

FIGURE 9.3

History of Cohabitation in the U.S., 1968–2018

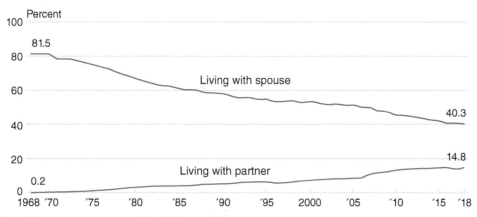

Living Arrangements of Young Adults Ages 25 to 34

Cohabitation is becoming more common among 25- to 34-year-olds.

Source: From U.S. Census Bureau, Current Population Survey, Annual Social and Economic Supplements, 1968 to 2018. Public Domain.

over 21,000 adults 50 and older followed from 1998 to 2006, Brown et al. (2012) reported that among the 4% who entered into cohabitation, only 18% ended in separation, and most people remained together either until one of them died or the study was over. Compared to younger adults, older adults seem to be more likely, then, to view cohabitation as an alternative to marriage.

Rather than sharing the same household, older adults also may enter into an arrangement known as living apart together (LAT). This is a living arrangement increasingly adopted by unmarried older adults in an intimate relationship who do not wish to share a residence. This arrangement may be prompted by concerns about finances (Lyssens-Danneboom & Mortelmans, 2015), a preference to remain in their separate households (Benson & Coleman, 2016), or a lack of interest in emotional commitment (van der Wiel et al., 2018).

Young adults may see cohabiting as a way to test the waters before committing to marriage, although only 40% of all cohabiting couples become married within 3 years, nearly a third do not get married, and about one-quarter break up (National Center for Health Statistics, 2019). Indeed, although the common sense wisdom is that the experience of living together contributes positively to the success of a marriage, the opposite seems to be true, at least in part. Data on divorce patterns show that there is a greater risk of marital breakup among people who cohabited before they became engaged. The greater likelihood of divorce among couples who cohabitate before becoming

engaged is referred to as the cohabitation effect (Cohan & Kleinbaum, 2002).

One explanation for the cohabitation effect is that couples who would not have gotten married "slide" into marriage through inertia; in other words, the fact that they were already living together becomes the basis for entering into marriage even if the fit between the two partners is not all that good. Eventually they divorce due to the fact that they were not well matched at the outset. Indeed, it appears that young adult cohabiting couples are more likely than other married or older cohabiting status groups to believe that divorce is the best solution if a couple's relationship is not working out (Nugent & Daugherty, 2018).

To try to tease out the causal links involved in the cohabitation effect, Lu and colleagues (2012) evaluated the likelihood of a cohabiting relationship's ending after controlling for demographic characteristics of the partners prior to their cohabitation. Rather than to compare cohabitating with noncohabitating partners, they separated out individuals who had engaged in "serial" cohabitation, meaning that they had lived with more than one partner in a cohabiting relationship. This turned out to be an important control. People who had cohabitated only with their spouse prior to marriage did not show the cohabitation effect. It was only those serial cohabitators who showed higher rates of marital disruption. However, trends in serial cohabitation may be changing, as among younger cohorts of women, those who have entered into multiple cohabitations appear to have less of an interest in marrying (Vespa, 2014).

Same-Sex Couples

Marriage of same-sex couples was first legalized in the United States by the Commonwealth of Massachusetts in 2004 and in 2013 was legalized at the federal level in the United States after the Supreme Court overturned the 1996 Defense of Marriage Act as unconstitutional. As of 2019, same-sex marriages are considered legal in 27 countries in at least some jurisdictions.

Estimates of the numbers of same-sex households in the United States are difficult to make. The Census Bureau's Current Population Survey, which is conducted on a yearly basis, reported errors prior to 2017 in its method of counting same-sex households. To correct this error, there are now separate opposite-sex and same-sex categories for the spouse and unmarried partner categories (Kreider & Gurrentz, 2019).

According to estimates based on the new reporting, there are 935,229 same-sex couples, divided about equally between male–male and female–female couples. The largest number live in California. The average age of the householder is 48 years, and the partner's average age is 46.4 years (U.S. Bureau of the Census, 2019b) (see Figure 9.4). Approximately 58% (547,000) are married. Of the 2 to 3.7 million children being raised by a parent identifying as LGBTQ (lesbian, gay, bisexual, transgender, and queer), 200,000 are being raised by same-sex couples (U.S. Bureau of the Census, 2017b).

Research on same-sex couples in marital relationships suggests that, compared to women in different-sex couples, both women and men in same-sex couples experience less strain on a daily basis (Garcia & Umberson, 2019). However, a 12-year follow-up study of same-sex couples showed higher rates of dissolution among female–female couples than different-sex married couples. In general, though, women are more likely to initiate divorce when they are dissatisfied in their relationship, whether in a same- or different-sex relationship (Balsam et al., 2017).

Sexual orientation discrimination stress may play a role in the dynamics of same-sex couples. People who believe that they are the targets of such discrimination are more likely to experience depression, especially if they cannot depend on their partners to help them cope with their feelings of stress (Randall et al., 2017). Such factors can affect both male–male and female–female couples, but seem to present a particular risk factor for women in same-sex relationships (Khaddouma et al., 2015). However, findings on same-sex relationships may be skewed by the relatively recent availability of data on those who have legalized their union. A short-term follow-up of those in legally sanctioned relationships showed that such formalization was a predictor of a relationship's stability and the satisfaction of both partners (Whitton et al., 2015).

Divorce and Remarriage

As of 2019, the divorce rate is 2.9 per 1,000, representing a continuous drop since 2000, when the rate was 4 per 1,000 (Centers for Disease Control and Prevention, 2019d). In fact, divorce rates have been declining steadily since reaching a peak in 1980. Contributing to the decline in divorce rates is the fact that young adults who fall in the millennial generation category are less likely to end their marriages. They are waiting longer to get married, meaning that they are older and more mature when they do decide

Massachusetts was first to legalize same sex marriage

The Supreme Court made same sex legal in 2013

The average age in same sex households is about 47 years old

FIGURE 9.4

Facts about Same-Sex Relationships

California has the highest number in the U.S.

Same sex marriage is legal in 27 countries

Legalization leads to longer-lasting relationships

to legalize their relationship. Furthermore, they are better educated, another factor that contributes to a relationship's longevity. Finally, their marriages are more likely to be first marriages, which statistically have a higher rate of success (Cohen, 2018). Ironically, then, although millennials are often stereotyped as unwilling to make commitments, it appears that their relationship decisions are made on the basis of strong and lasting commitments.

The dissolution of a marriage is ordinarily perceived by those involved as a disappointment and a sad if not tragic event. One or both of the partners may be relieved to see the end of an unsuccessful relationship, but they are nevertheless affected in many ways by the inevitable consequences of the divorce on their daily lives, the lives of children, and the lives of extended family members. The couple must resolve a range of practical issues, such as changes in their housing and financial affairs—but the greatest toll is the emotional one. For many couples, child custody arrangements present the most significant challenge caused by their altered status as a family.

Although technically divorce rates in the population as a whole have declined, the media frequently cite the disturbing statistic that one out of every two marriages will end in divorce. However, the divorce statistics are much more complicated than this simple formula would imply. Those who divorce in a given year are generally not the same people as those who have gotten married, so the number of divorces cannot simply be compared with the number of marriages to determine the odds of divorcing.

The probability of divorce is higher for people who are in their second marriage. In the United States, 13% of all marriages are second marriages, and 4% are third marriages (Lewis & Kreider, 2015). Remarried individuals may further inflate divorce statistics because they include those high in divorce proneness, the greater tendency to contemplate divorce when their marriage is in trouble (Whitton et al., 2013). Those high in divorce proneness may have a long history of difficulties in the area of intimacy. Data from the RALS (described in Chapter 8) showed that women who in college had low intimacy scores were more likely to have divorced by their late 50s; the same was not true for men (Weinberger et al., 2008).

Separated and divorced individuals often cite infidelity as the cause of their breakup. Data from a national U.S. survey conducted between 1991 and 2008 reveal that more than half of men and women who engage in extramarital affairs also become separated or divorced from their spouses (Allen & Atkins, 2012). People who are in a troubled marriage may become unfaithful because they are unhappy with their spouses. For these individuals, the extramarital affair provides the final push toward seeking a divorce, particularly if it is the other partner who has the affair. By the same token, people who engage in an affair and then say their marriage was unhappy may be using identity assimilation, seeking to protect their identities as good spouses.

Identity may also play a role in how individuals cope emotionally with divorce. There are a wide range of negative emotional outcomes associated with divorce. People who are divorcing experience such feelings as loss of trust, low self-esteem, anxiety, worry about being hurt in future relationships, anger, depression, and preoccupation with what other people think. For some individuals, however, divorce provides relief from a highly conflictual situation.

You might think that the initiator would have fewer negative emotions than the noninitiator, but the individual's role in the divorce does not clearly relate to the emotional outcome. Some divorced couples seem to transition well into postdivorce relationships in which they remain friends or share in parenting or operating a joint business. Examining these factors in divorce, Frisby et al. (2012) proposed that one of the most difficult aspects of divorce is loss of "face," meaning that divorce represents a threat to the individual's identity. Individuals divorced within the prior 2 years had more positive emotions if they were able to see the divorce as allowing them to gain independence and were supported by their partner in protecting their identities.

Of the nearly 74 million children under 18, approximately 8%, or 5.9 million, are living in the home of a divorced parent (U.S. Bureau of the Census, 2018c). As difficult as it is for children to be caught in between parents who are divorced, it may be just as hard, if not harder, to be caught in between parents who are in a high-conflict marriage. In one longitudinal study of marriage, children 19 years of age and older were asked to state whether they felt they had been caught in between parental arguments. The children of parents whose marriages were characterized by a high degree of conflict were most likely to feel caught in the middle. Not surprisingly, these feelings were related to lower subjective well-being and poorer relationships with their parents (Amato & Afifi, 2006). Poor relationships between parents and a child's step-parents (i.e., when one parent remarries) further accentuate the feeling of being caught when the child reaches young adulthood (Schrodt, 2016).

Among divorced couples, mediation is increasingly being seen as an effective means of reducing conflict and hence improving children's adjustment. Mediation is based on a model of cooperative dispute settlement rather than the more adversarial approach that occurs when lawyers become part of the scene. In one 12-year longitudinal study, divorced couples were randomly assigned to either mediation or legal assistance. Conflict significantly declined, particularly in the first year after divorce, among couples who participated in mediation (Sbarra & Emery, 2008). Involving the children in the remediation process can also help promote their ability to adjust to the divorce and its impact on the family (D'Onofrio & Emery, 2019).

Widowhood

The death of a spouse is regarded as one of the most stressful events of life, and for many older adults, widowhood involves the loss of a relationship that may have lasted 50 years or more. As we shall see, however, the effect of widowhood on the bereaved individual varies greatly according to the circumstances surrounding the spouse's death and the nature of the couple's relationship.

In the United States, there are currently approximately 15 million widowed adults ages 18 and older; 76% of them are 65 and older. The majority (78%) of the over-65 widowed adults are women. By the age of 85 and older, 70% of women are widows, compared to 33% of men. Widows are more likely than widowers to be living at low income levels (U.S. Bureau of the Census, 2018c).

The prevalence of depression among widows diminishes over time, from 38% in the month after the spouse's death to 19% from 12 to 18 months following widowhood, to 10.5% in the 2 to 5 years after the death of the spouse (Kristiansen et al., 2019a). Widows are also at risk for anxiety disorders, showing a 29.5% prevalence (Kristiansen et al., 2019b). Negative mental health outcomes are more pronounced when the spouse's death is not anticipated, in part because a partner caring for a terminally ill spouse becomes relieved of caregiver burden with the spouse's death (Siflinger, 2017).

In what is called the widowhood effect, there is a greater probability of death in those who have become widowed compared to those who are married (Williams et al., 2011). The mortality effects hold even after controlling for various health risks or causes of death, because widowed individuals have a higher risk of mortality than the nonwidowed. Contributing to the widowhood effect are factors such as depression, psychosocial stress, chronic economic hardship, and loss of social support and environmental resources.

There are variations in the pattern of adaptation to the loss of a spouse (see Figure 9.5). In a major prospective study of more than 200 widows, Bonanno and his collaborators (2002) followed women for 18 months after the death of their husbands. The majority showed relatively little distress following their loss, in a pattern called "resilient grief." However, some widows experienced

FIGURE 9.5

Levels of Depression in Five Types of Widows

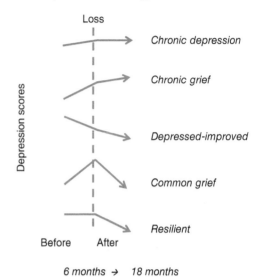

Research on widowhood shows there are five characteristic patterns with resilient being the most common.

chronic grief that did not subside during the study period, and some showed high levels of depression prior to and after the loss. Similar pathways exist among widowers, who like widows, are most likely to show patterns of resilience (Bennett, 2010). Studies such as these underscore the notion that widowhood is not a unitary process and that there are multiple factors influencing reactions to the loss of a spouse.

Psychological Perspectives on Long-Term Relationships

Throughout the vicissitudes of marriage, divorce, remarriage, and widowhood, most adults actively strive to maintain gratifying interactions with others on a day-to-day basis. Furthermore, for many adults, the feeling of being part of a close relationship or network of relationships is the most salient aspect of identity (Whitbourne, 1986). Whether this relationship is called "marriage," "family," "friendship," or "partnership" is not as important as the feeling that one is valued by others and has something to offer to improve the lives of other people.

Theories of long-term relationship dynamics attempt to understand the factors that contribute to successful relationships over the course of adulthood. Figure 9.6 summarizes the six main perspectives on long-term relationships that address issues relevant to adult development and aging.

FIGURE 9.6

Perspectives on Long-Term Relationships

Six prominent psychological perspectives on long-term relationships.

The earliest sociological explanations of relationship satisfaction across the years of marriage used a family life-cycle approach in which marital satisfaction among couples was charted in relationship to the ages of their children. As relationships in the real world have seemed to become more complicated, however, so have the theories, and there is now greater recognition of the multiple variations that are possible when adults form close relationships. The emotional factors involved in long-term relationships are also gaining greater attention, as it is realized that some characteristics of human interactions transcend specific age- or gender-based boundaries.

Looking first at socioemotional selectivity (introduced in Chapter 8), it very specifically predicts that older adults become more satisfied with their long-term partners as their awareness increases of the limited time they have left together with each passing year. Older adults should regard the long-term marital relationship as offering perhaps the most potential to serve emotional functions because their experience together over the years has allowed them to understand and respond to each other's needs. In what is called "positive sentiment override," older adults are more likely to keep sight of the positive aspects of their relationships even when they have disagreements (Story et al., 2007). In addition, if older adults are better able to control their emotions, particularly the negative ones, they should get along better with their partner because each is less likely to irritate the other one.

Social exchange theory attempts to predict why some relationships succeed and others fail in terms of whether the relationship's rewards exceed the costs of alternatives to that relationship. The rewards of marriage include love, friendship, and feelings of commitment. When considering a breakup, partners weigh these benefits against legal, financial, social, and religious barriers or constraints. Children will also factor into this equation, adding both to the perceived benefits such as co-parenting and to the costs, which include child custody. When the balance shifts

so that rewards no longer outweigh the costs, one or both partners will initiate a breakup. Over time, exchange theory predicts that the intrinsic rewards of being in the relationship, including the reliance the partners develop toward each other, increase to the point that the attractiveness of alternatives tends to fade.

Several studies support social exchange theory to explain some of the pragmatic factors that keep partners together. Some approaches focus on income as a factor in the exchange dynamics such that a partner's earning potential becomes part of what makes that partner attractive (Sweeney & Cancian, 2004). A study of same-sex couples showed, furthermore, that a partner's earning potential also influenced the division of household labor (Yabiku & Gager, 2009). Also in support of social exchange theory, a study of cohabiting versus married couples showed that cohabitors were more likely than married partners to end a relationship in which the partners only rarely engaged in sex (Yabiku & Gager, 2009).

Social exchange theory, then, proposes a cost-benefit approach to a relationship's formation and maintenance. In contrast, equity theory proposes that partners are satisfied in a relationship if they feel they are getting what they deserve (Walster et al., 1978). This means that they seek to get as much out of the relationship as they put into it (Hatfield & Rapson, 2012). Equity theory proposes, then, that partners will constantly try to adjust their efforts to match each other's contribution to the relationship according to principles of fairness. The couple's relationship quality will erode if the amount one partner puts in does not match what the other partner contributes (Hatfield et al., 2008). In a 20-year longitudinal study of married couples, DeMaris (2010) found that partners were able to gauge correctly the amount of effort each of them put into the relationship, but women tended to view themselves as putting more in than did their husbands.

Another set of theories examines the extent to which a matching of characteristics between partners helps to predict relationship satisfaction. The similarity hypothesis proposes that similarity of personality and values predicts both initial interpersonal attraction and satisfaction within long-term relationships (Gaunt, 2006). Sometimes, the similarity may be more apparent than real, however. In one 13-year longitudinal study of marital relationships, researchers found that couples who perceived each other as higher in agreeableness than they actually were in reality were more in love during the early stages of marriage and more likely to remain in love over time (Miller et al., 2006). Subsequent research supports the role of positive illusions about the spouse's personality as contributing to marital quality (Barelds & Dijkstra, 2011).

The need complementarity hypothesis proposes that people seek and are more satisfied with marital partners who are the opposite of themselves (Winch, 1958). Perceptions of complementarity could benefit relationships when partners regard themselves as being on the same "team" (Beach et al., 2001). People who are more introverted, for example, might prefer partners whose extraversion helps alleviate discomfort in social situations.

The behavioral approach to marital interactions emphasizes the actual behaviors that partners engage in with each other during marital interactions as an influence on marital stability and quality (Karney & Bradbury, 1997). According to this perspective, people will be more satisfied in a long-term relationship when their partners engage in positive or rewarding behaviors (such as expressing affection) and less satisfied with they are critical or abusive. Conflict increases when a partner either turns away from or turns against a partner who is trying to make an emotional connection (Gottman & Driver, 2005). Behavioral approaches to relationship satisfaction emphasize, then, that conflict need not be detrimental as long as it is constructive in nature (Ostensen & Zhang, 2014).

Finally, the latest approach to understanding marital satisfaction emphasizes the role of individual fulfillment within the context of the couple. According to Finkel et al.'s (2015) suffocation model of marriage, contemporary adults place more emphasis on marriage as a source of self-expression and fulfillment but have less time to devote to maintaining their marriages than ever before. Using the metaphor of "climbing Mount Maslow" (Finkel et al., 2014), the suffocation model proposes that the higher a couple attempts to move up the hierarchy of needs (from security to self-actualization), the more frustrated they will become with the quality of their relationship.

As you can see, theories of relationship satisfaction each have their own set of predictions about who will be happiest in a long-term relationship. From an empirical perspective, though, the key question remains whether research on long-term relationships bear out any of their predictions. As it turns out, there may be value to all of them because, as in personality development, there is more than one pathway in relationship development. A 13-year longitudinal study by University of Texas family psychologist Ted Huston and his collaborators (Huston, 2009) is based on the concept of pathways, showing the various routes that couples take as they navigate at least the first 13 years of their relationships (see Figure 9.7).

The surprising feature of Huston's work was his discovery that the seeds of marital bliss, or trouble, are sown even before the couple walk down the aisle. In the enduring dynamics pathway, the way a couple interacts early in their relationship will characterize the course of the relationship over time. They either get along well with each other and resolve conflict easily, or they don't.

There are, however, couples whose problems evolve over time. Those who fit the emergent distress pathway develop relationship problems over time as they find that they are unable to cope with the inevitable arguments that occur when people live together. Instead of resolving their problems with adaptive tactics such as communicating openly and working out compromises, they become defensive, withdraw, stonewall, and become blatantly vicious toward each other. It's not clear whether their distress causes these dysfunctional coping methods or whether their ineffective ways of handling problems leads to distress. The upshot is that these couples become increasingly unhappy over time until they finally decide to end things entirely.

Like couples who experience emergent distress, those who fit the disillusionment pathway start out happy and in love when they first tie the knot. Over time, they gradually fall out of love and start to develop mixed feelings about their partner. Part of what happens with these couples is that they take each other for granted.

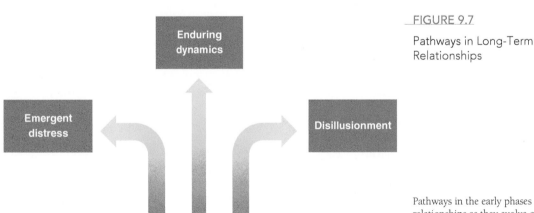

FIGURE 9.7

Pathways in Long-Term Relationships

Pathways in the early phases of committed relationships as they evolve over time.

They become less and less interested in seeking their partner's love and approval than they were at the beginning, and as the patina fades, they drift further and further apart.

Both the emergent distress and disillusionment models assume that couples start out as hopeful and optimistic that their relationship will work out; it is only after the months or years go by that they find themselves arguing constantly or just losing interest.

After following their couples 2 and 13 years after marriage, Huston and his team concluded that their data gave the most support to the enduring dynamics model of distress. Rather than newlyweds being head over heels in love, only to have the relationship unravel over time, the dynamics that characterize the beginning of a relationship persisted over time. Two key features seemed to differentiate the happy from the unhappy couples: positive expressions of affection and love, and negative behaviors of being critical, angry, and impatient toward the partner. The happy couples expressed their love through affectionate behaviors, enjoyed being together, and made sure that they spent time together. The unhappy ones created a negative emotional climate and avoided being with each other. The more in love the couple were, the more they expressed their positive feelings toward each other, including initiating sexual activity (Schoenfeld et al., 2012).

Such marital discord for unhappy couples takes its toll on well-being. Couples in their later years who are constantly in conflict are at risk of experiencing higher levels of depression and anxiety and lower levels of self-esteem and life satisfaction (Whisman et al., 2006).

For couples who want to work on a troubled relationship, couples therapy is a known effective method for promoting positive change (Davis et al., 2012). Although couples therapy shares many features of individual therapy, there are important differences. Couples therapists are trained to examine the types of interactive patterns that lead couples into conflict and then, more importantly, to help them break these dysfunctional patterns. They tend to be more "take charge" than individual therapists, actively intervening when they see problems unfolding before them during therapy sessions. As the couple learn to see their strengths and feel that change is possible, they can come to new understandings of themselves and their relationship (Benson et al., 2012).

Sexuality remains an important component of happy relationships throughout adulthood. Although you may imagine that older adults lose interest in sex, those who are in good physical health seem to maintain a virtually lifelong desire to engage in sexual relations (Lindau & Gavrilova, 2010).

Over 40% of women and men in the 75 to 84 age range engage in yearly (if not more) sexual intercourse. Furthermore, a considerable number were engaged in some form of sexual activity on a much more frequent basis, with over half of women and men (54%) in the 75- to 85-year-old age bracket having sex two to three times a month, or more. Approximately one-third in this age group also engaged in oral sex (Waite et al., 2009). It appears, then, that the majority of adults in their mid-50s and above find ways to incorporate sexuality into their lives on a regular basis, particularly if they are in an intimate relationship.

FAMILIES

The transformation of a marriage into a "family" traditionally is thought to occur when a child enters the couple's life on a permanent basis. However, with changing patterns of marriage, cohabitation, and decisions about children, the definition of "family" is expanding to include a wider variety of choices in living arrangements.

Despite these changing patterns of relationship dynamics, the large majority of households in the United States consist of people living together as a family. In 2018, there were 127.6 million households in the United States, of which 83.1 million described themselves as a "family" household. Of all family households, 61 million (74%) included married couples. There were 34.4 million households with children under the age of 18, and 23.8 million (69%) of these households included married couples. The average family household size was 2.53 (U.S. Bureau of the Census, 2018c).

Parenthood

The number of births in the United States in 2018 was 3.9 million, or 11.8 per 1,000 in the population. This figure represents a 2% drop from 2017, and was the fourth year of a decline. In fact, the number of births was the lowest it has been since 1986. However, this decline only applied to women ages 15 to 34, as women ages 35 to 49 (and older) actually have shown an increased birth rate (Hamilton et al., 2019).

Figure 9.8 summarizes the living arrangements of children under the age of 18. As you can see, the large majority live with two parents, with the next largest category including children living with their mothers. The figure also shows how many children live with other siblings and with grandparents.

The point when a couple has its first child ushers in the transition to parenthood (TtP), the period of adjustment to the new family status represented by the presence of a child in the home. From a biopsychosocial

FIGURE 9.8

Living Arrangements of Children under 18

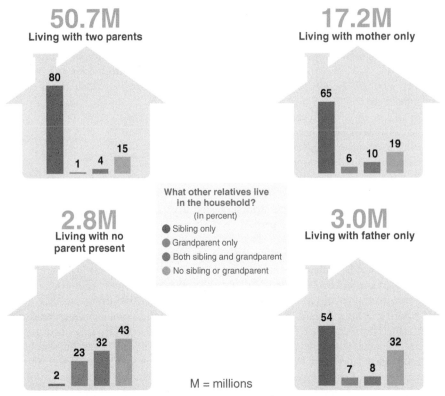

Census data provide information on living arrangements of children under the age of 18.

perspective, the TtP involves biological changes (when the mother bears the child) as her body adapts to rapid hormonal and other physiological alterations. Both parents experience psychological changes including the emotional highs and lows associated with this new status. At the same time, each individual's identity shifts as the parents begin to incorporate their new status in life into their sense of self. They also undergo social changes due to this new role that alter their status with other family members and the community. Their new role brings changes in what society expects of them, expectations that typically reflect social norms for men and women as fathers and mothers.

Researchers initially became interested in the TtP because they had consistently found (mainly through cross-sectional studies) that marital satisfaction dips during the child-rearing years, a drop-off particularly marked for women. Researchers now use a prospective design, studying couples before and after the child's birth.

The majority of these involve studies of the couple after the mother becomes pregnant.

In a meta-analysis of studies using this design, Mitnick and her collaborators (2009) identified 37 studies with sample sizes ranging from 23 to 400 on individuals who were, on average, in their late 20s. Although most of the studies they analyzed showed a slight decline in relationship satisfaction, this was comparable to that of nonparents together for similar lengths of time as the new parents.

There are, as you might imagine, individual differences in the way couples adapt across the TtP. The birth of a child can trigger difficult feelings for individuals who were themselves insecurely attached to their own caregivers (Simpson & Rholes, 2019). Couples must also negotiate the changes in their identities that accompany entry into parenthood if they are to maintain their well-being (Turner-Zwinkels & Spini, 2019). Their ability to adapt to the TtP can also affect each other's well-being, as was shown in a study of the contagious effects of a mother's depression late in pregnancy to the father's own levels of depression (Fredriksen et al., 2019).

As might be expected from the social equity theory of relationship satisfaction, the division of labor after the birth of the child becomes an important factor influencing the relationship of the new parents. Working women without children already perform more household duties than men do, but after becoming mothers, the situation is exacerbated (Coltrane, 2000). Mothers assume more of the stereotypically female roles of performing household duties such as laundry, cooking, and cleaning, in addition to providing the bulk of the child care. Men increase their involvement in paid employment outside the home after the child enters the family (Christiansen & Palkovitz, 2001).

This shift in family roles following the birth of the first child is called doing gender, a term that refers to the tendency of women and men to behave in stereotypically gendered ways. Parenthood sets up a dynamic which leads the parents to feel that they are now a "traditional" family (Vespa, 2009). For a couple who may have shared housework in a more egalitarian fashion before the child was born, this shift into gendered roles can place strain on the relationship (Grote et al., 2004). Even couples in commuter marriages, in which parents live apart together due to the demands of their jobs, may experience gendered role demands although it is possible that these situations also facilitate "undoing" of gender roles (Lindemann, 2017).

There are also variations in the TtP due to the availability of methods for same-sex married couples to have children through artificial insemination, adoption, or surrogacy. These couples share many of the experiences of heterosexual couples. However, the social context seems to have a significant impact on same-sex parents. Those who experience homophobia, live in states with unfavorable legal climates regarding adoption by gays, and receive less support from their friends and families are more likely to feel depressed and anxious (Goldberg & Smith, 2011). As their children grow older, lesbian parents may be able to find support through friendships with other mothers of similar-age children in same-sex relationships.

Fatherhood is increasingly being studied as an aspect of identity in adulthood, in part reflecting the increasing role of fathers in the raising of their children (Coles, 2015). Approximately 60% of the 121 million men age 15 and older in the United States are fathers; and 2% (1.7 million) are single fathers who raise their children with no spouse or partner present (U.S. Bureau of the Census, 2018d).

Becoming a first-time father can significantly influence a man's patterns of social interaction outside the home. A 7-year longitudinal study of nearly 3,100 fathers of children under the age of 18 described the "transformative"

process that occurs as new fathers become more involved with their own parents, grandparents, and other relatives. Fathers also become more involved with service-oriented groups and church. These effects occur along with the birth of each child but are particularly pronounced at the time of the first child's birth (Knoester & Eggebeen, 2006).

Men who feel that they will be better fathers during the TtP also become more involved in parenting. Moreover, the way that mothers perceive their husbands in the father role can help shape the way that fathers see themselves. A short-term longitudinal study of 183 Canadian couples studied over the first 18 months of first-time parenthood showed that the confidence that men had in their parenting was shaped by how competent their wives viewed them, which, in turn, shaped both their self-perceptions and their involvement with their infants (Tremblay & Pierce, 2011).

The extent to which a single father is able to adjust to the role of solo parent is affected by the characteristics of the children, including their age and gender, and his own characteristics, including his age and educational level. Overall, however, single fathers spend less time caring for their children than do single mothers but more than do married fathers (Hook & Chalasani, 2008).

Changes in the family living situation in recent decades are often discussed in terms of blended families, also known as reconstituted families. Within these family situations, at least one adult is living with a child who is not a biological child of that adult. Often, these family situations develop after a divorce and remarriage (or cohabitation), in which two adults establish a household together. The dynamics within these relationships, though the subject of many fictional accounts, are only beginning to receive empirical attention in the literature. Recent research suggests that stepmothers experience more stress than biological parents, but that a relaxing of gender roles and higher relationship adjustment within the couple (i.e., stepparent and biological parent) can facilitate their adjustment (Shapiro, 2014).

The Empty Nest

We have examined the factors that influence the transition of a couple that occur when their first child is born. Now we will take a look at what happens during the reverse process. The empty nest describes the period in a couple's life that occurs when their children permanently depart from the home.

For many years, the common belief was that the empty nest would be an unwelcome change, particularly for women. However, the reality that the empty nest may be a positive step in a couple's relationship is becoming more and more apparent. Much of the research on the empty nest dates back to earlier decades, when women were less likely to maintain continuous employment outside the home than is currently true. Furthermore, much of the earlier research was conducted at a time when children were more clearly launched, as compared to the present, in which children often take longer to leave the parental home and may "boomerang" back when their economic circumstances take a turn for the worse. Many parents then, if not now, regard their children's leaving to be a mark of their success in preparing them for adulthood.

With the children gone from the home, couples potentially have the opportunity to enjoy more leisure-time activities together, a change that should bring them closer together. Being able to spend time with each other may also allow them to enjoy greater marital satisfaction and also improved sexual relations. An intensive study of a small sample of Canadian women married after the age of 50 found a shift away from an emphasis on sexual intercourse to greater valuing of other expressions of intimacy, such as cuddling, companionship, and affection. These women still felt that they had strong sexual chemistry with their husbands, even though the expression of that chemistry had changed from the passion of youth (Hurd Clarke, 2006).

Perhaps for these reasons, the empty nest may have some advantages in helping keep a couple's sexual relationship alive. When children do return home for whatever reason, the quality of a couple's sexual relationship may decline at least in terms of frequency of sexual activities. A survey of more than 15,000 midlife Canadian women showed that the predictors of sexual activity within the past 12 months included age, marital status, race, income, alcohol use, smoking, and empty nest status (Fraser et al., 2004). Women whose children were still living in the home were less likely to have intercourse than women who were empty nesters.

However, among certain couples, the empty nest can pose challenges. Mitchell and Lovegreen (2009) identified a pattern they called the "Empty Nest Syndrome" (ENS) in an interview study they conducted of 300 empty nest parents from four cultural groups living in Vancouver, British Columbia. The interviews showed that mothers were slightly more likely than fathers to report ENS; however, the percentages of despondent parents were very low overall, ranging from 20% to 25% in most of the groups studied. Parents of Indo/East Indian ethnicity, whose culture emphasizes continuing bonds between parents and adult children, had far higher rates of ENS (50% and 64% for fathers and mothers) than the parents of Chinese or Southern European or British ancestry.

In addition to the role of culture, the Vancouver study identified key social psychological factors that seemed to place these midlife parents at risk of experiencing ENS. These include having an identity that is wrapped up in their parent role, feeling that they are losing control over their children's lives, having few or only children, and lacking a support network. Parents who worried about their children's safety and well-being in the world outside the home also were more vulnerable to ENS. For the most part, however, it's important to remember that the parents in this study were more likely than not to adapt well to the empty nest transition.

Although the empty nest is viewed as the norm when discussing adult children and their parents, there are a growing number of adult sons and daughters living with their parents (ages 25 to 34 years), a situation referred to by the slang term "boomerang" children in the United States and "kids in parents' pockets eroding retirement savings" (KIPPERS) or "kidults" in the United Kingdom. In 2016, more young adults lived with a parent (22.9%) than with a spouse (19.9%), as you can see from Figure 9.9.

As is true for the empty nest, there is surprisingly little research on the dynamics of young adults who live in the home of their parents. One Canadian survey reported cultural differences in the tendency of parents and young adult children to live together, with Asian and Latin American born parents most likely to host their 20-to-24-year-old children (Turcotte, 2006). Parents with live-in children were more likely than parents whose children did not live at home to experience feelings of frustration over the time spent taking care of their adult children, but the percentage of these negative feelings was very low. The financial situation for college graduates who return home varies considerably from family to family and seems to play a role in the way parents and adult children renegotiate their relationships in view of these variations (West et al., 2017). One qualitative investigation suggests that these negotiations are successful and perceived as beneficial to both the boomerang children and their parents (Casares & White, 2018).

Parents and children transition together, then, over the course of their relationship, from the children's entrance into the home until their eventual exit, whether permanent or not. The dynamics of these relationships over time may be understood both in terms of identity and in terms of sociocultural factors. Many parents highly value their identities as parents and therefore see the development of their children as reflections of their own competence. At the same time, children try to dissociate from their parents in order to establish their own identities. All of these changes happen in a sociocultural context which, as we have

FIGURE 9.9

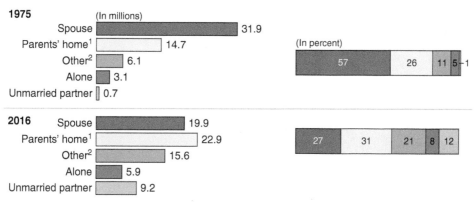

More Young Adults Lived with Parents than a Spouse in 2016
Living arrangements among adults aged 18 to 34: 1975 and 2016

As shown here, young adults are now more likely to live with their parents than with a spouse compared to 1975.

[1] College students who are living in dormitories are counted as living in the parents' home.
[2] "Other" includes people who are living with relatives besides a spouse, such as siblings or grandparents, and nonrelatives such as roommates.
Source: From U.S. Census Bureau, 1975 and 2016 Current Population Survey Annual Social and Economic Supplement. Public Domain.

seen in the empty nest research, may affect the normative expectations that parents and children have regarding their positions in the family. We will see later that the dimensions of intergenerational relationships are complex and multifaceted, reflecting these intersecting forces.

Parent–Adult Child Relationships

As children move through the years of adulthood, many facets of their relationships with their parents undergo change. For example, as children have their own families, they begin to gain greater insight into the role of being a parent. On the one hand, the children may now appreciate what their parents did for them; on the other hand, they may resent their parents for not having done more. Another changing feature of the relationship stems from the child's increasing concern that parents will require help and support as they grow older. Adult children and their parents may also find that they do not agree on various aspects of life, from an overall philosophy and set of values (such as in the area of politics) to specific habits and behaviors (such as how to eat and dress). Whether parents and their adult children live in the same geographic vicinity and actually see each other on a frequent basis must also be added into the equation.

There are several key concepts that can help you gain insight into parent–adult child relationships. **Filial**

maturity occurs when children reach the age of relating to their parents as equals. Achieving filial maturity means that you can share thoughts and feelings with your parents, think of your parents as friends, and see yourself as having much in common with your parents (Birditt et al., 2008). **Filial anxiety** is the fear of having to take care of an aging, infirmed parent (Cicirelli, 1988). **Filial obligation** describes the cultural values that adult children are expected to care for their parents, including having them live in their homes. Adult children who adhere to the value of filial obligation may believe that they can maintain both their work and family demands, but as caregiving hours increase, they find that they must reduce their time at work (Paulsen et al., 2017). Filial obligation is also known as **filial piety** in China, represented by the character 孝 (*xiao*).

An overarching framework for understanding parent–adult child relationships comes from the **Intergenerational Solidarity Model (ISM)**, which proposes that six independent dimensions of solidarity characterize adult family relationships: associational (frequency of interaction), affectual (feelings), consensual (agreement in values, beliefs, and lifestyles), functional (help exchange), normative (commitment to fulfill family obligations), and structural (availability in terms of distance and health) (see Figure 9.10).

Each of the ISM dimensions runs along a continuum from positive to negative. For example, the positive pole of the affectual dimension would describe families high

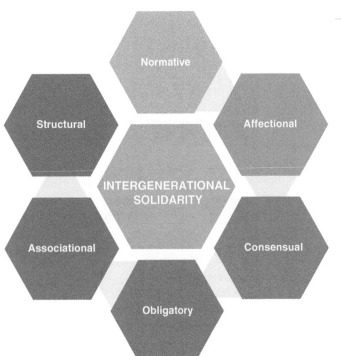

According to the intergenerational solidarity model, relationships can be defined along six dimensions.

in intimacy, and the negative pole would capture families that are emotionally distant. These poles apply to the family as it exists, not to the satisfaction or dissatisfaction that the family may have with where their family ranks on the dimension. A family may see each other only relatively infrequently (i.e., be low on the associational dimension) but not be dissatisfied if they prefer not to see each other very often (Bengtson et al., 2002). Think about your family and how you would rate the way you get along with parents, siblings, cousins, or others you include as relations. Do you feel emotionally connected (affectional) or are your bonds limited to the minimum that's expected of you (obligatory)? Is it important for you to act like the "perfect" son, daughter, niece, or nephew (normative)? How do you and your family get along when you sit down to a holiday meal? Do you all avoid talking about politics to avoid disagreements (consensual)? As you can see, the ISM provides a useful way to understand families not only in a theoretical sense but also in a way that applies to your own everyday experiences.

As you thought about your family, it might make sense that as your family changes, so does the way you relate to each other. However, some of those basic structural factors seem to be enduring. Indeed, an 18-year study of families showed that there is more continuity than change in the dynamics of intergenerational relationships over time (Hogerbrugge & Silverstein, 2015).

Although it is possible that your family relationships are always harmonious, it is more likely that there are occasional rifts or bad feelings. Some of these difficulties stem, according to the family relations literature, from a lack of clear norms to guide your interactions. Structural ambivalence in family relations means that society's structures do not make clear how family members should behave (Connidis & McMullin, 2002). Family members then face contradictory sets of expectations based on such factors as their age and their gender. The uncertainty they face may then produce psychological ambivalence, in which an adult child feels both love and annoyance at a parent.

Tensions between parents and their adult children can increase the extent to which they experience ambivalence, which, in turn, lowers their affectual solidarity (Birditt et al., 2009a). According to some researchers, these tensions are almost automatically built into the parent–adult child relationship by virtue of the fact that the parents are more emotionally invested in their children than children in their parents. The intergenerational stake hypothesis proposes that parents are higher in affectual solidarity toward their children than children are toward their parents. In other words, parents feel more positively about their children than do their children about them. Consequently, parents are likely to try to resolve conflicts with their children through methods that are as constructive as possible (Birditt et al., 2009b).

Although originally proposed as a feature of parents and their adult children only, the intergenerational stake also applies to three-generation families. Grandmothers report lower negative quality in their relationship than do their middle-aged children, who, in turn, report lower negative quality in the relationship than do their own children (Birditt et al., 2012).

Parents and their adult children also differ in their developmental needs resulting, in some cases, in another set of intergenerational tensions. The developmental schism occurs when there is a gap between the two generations in how much they value the relationship and whether they wish to be independent (Fingerman, 2001). One manifestation of the developmental schism is the mother's tendency to regard her daughter as more important than the daughter does the mother and for the daughter to regard the mother as more intrusive than the mother does the daughter. Mothers are also more likely to regard their daughters as confidants than daughters do their mothers.

Another contributor to the developmental schism occurs when the daughter still seeks the approval of the mother and feels guilty when she feels that she is not living up to her mother's expectations for her. Because of intergenerational stake, when conflicts occur, parents are more likely than are their children to try to resolve conflicts using constructive strategies in which they attempt to maintain and build a positive relationship (Birditt et al., 2009b). Despite these problems, the majority of adult children (56%) state that they feel close to their parents. Another large group (38%) see their relationships as ambivalent. Fortunately only a small minority (6%) see them as problematic (Fingerman et al., 2004).

For older adults, adult parent–child relationships can play a vital role in well-being, particularly with regard to the development of generativity, and particularly for women (An & Cooney, 2006). Aging parents who have good relationships with their adult children are less likely to feel lonely or depressed (Koropeckyj-Cox, 2002). Interestingly, perceptions of relationships with adult children may even influence the exercise and smoking habits of parents (Thomas et al., 2019).

Part of the intergenerational stake involves concern over the welfare of one's children. When their children succeed, parents can benefit in life satisfaction and well-being; when problems befall their children, parents can suffer ill consequences as well. In a longitudinal study carried out in the Netherlands, Kalmijn and colleagues (2012) found that the divorce of children produced an increase in depressive symptoms among parents, particularly for mothers. On the other hand, when children married and became parents, their own parents also showed a boost in feelings of well-being.

The intergenerational stake hypothesis proposes the opposite to the concept of role reversal, which refers to the family situation in which adult children take over in the role as parent because the parents are unable to care for themselves. Although this is a term we hear about in the popular literature, the data on intergenerational support present a more complicated picture (Blieszner, 2006), suggesting that much of the flow is downstream from parents to children.

Further reinforcing the inaccuracy of role reversal is contingency theory, which proposes that parents help their adult children who need it most, particularly in a financial sense. A survey of over 600 middle-aged adults showed that most were likely to provide help when their adult children experienced a crisis. Fewer middle-aged adults reported assisting their own parents, again primarily in crisis situations (Fingerman et al., 2010). Moreover, when parents do experience declines in health, it seems that the norms of filial responsibility lead to mutual adaptations between children and parents (Silverstein et al., 2006).

It appears that the majority of middle-aged adults are able to balance the need to help both their own children and their parents. Another popular idea regarding middle-aged adults is that they are in the sandwich generation, meaning they are sandwiched between their aging mothers and teenaged children. However, because disability rates of older adults are declining, less than 20% of families in the United States are involved at any one point in time in providing care for a parent (Grundy & Henretta, 2006). Moreover, despite the belief that one child (the daughter) has sole responsibility for caregiving, spouses tend to share caregiving roles even when in dual-earner situations (Henz, 2010).

There can be risks, however, experienced by middle-aged adults who serve as caregivers, at least for the time that they are engaged in these roles. In a large longitudinal study of nearly 5,000 Midwest adults, researchers found that both men and women were less likely to engage in a range of healthy behaviors, from using a seat belt, to choosing healthy foods based on their content, to smoking (Chassin et al., 2010).

A relatively recent trend in parenting literature describes the behavior of helicopter parents, those who supposedly smother and overprotect their overly dependent children (regardless of the age of the child). As we have seen, middle-aged parents are likely to provide whatever support they can to adult children who are in need of financial help. Moreover, parents benefit from their relationships with their adult children as do children from their relationships with parents. The question is: How much is too much?

Fingerman and colleagues (2012) interviewed middle-aged parents with at least one child over the age of 18 and also interviewed up to three of their children. Both parents and children rated the extent of support and indicated whether the amount provided was too little or too much. Approximately one-fifth of children and nearly 30% of parents reported "intense" support (i.e., too much). However, rather than being detrimental to the child's well-being, young adults whose parents provided a wide range of support ranked higher in life satisfaction. Their parents did not particularly suffer from the support they provided unless they thought their children needed "too much" support, perhaps reflecting what they perceived as their own failure to live up to the ideal identity of a parent.

Clearly, the area of parent–adult child relationships reflects many complex and interacting factors. From a biopsychosocial perspective, we can understand these relationships as involving biological processes pertaining to the aging and health of parents; psychological processes relating to areas such as emotions, identity, and closeness; and social expectations for normative parent–child relationships in one's culture and historical era.

Siblings

The sibling relationship has many unique features within the constellation of family interactions (Van Volkom, 2006). Those who are siblings by birth share a genetic background; those who have been raised together share many experiences dating to early childhood. By the time siblings reach later adulthood, it is quite possible that they are the only remaining members of their original family and have known each other longer than anyone else they have known in their entire lives. As is true for adult child–parent relationships, the sibling relationship is not one of choice; to be sure, many people allow their connections with brothers and sisters to fall by the wayside. However, even if they do not stay in frequent contact, they may still maintain the relationship and tend to value it in a positive manner (Bedford et al., 2000).

The potential exists for the sibling relationship to be the deepest and closest of an adult's life and to bring with that closeness both shared joy and shared pain. On the negative side, individuals can carry into adulthood long-standing resentment toward the sibling or siblings they felt received more attention from the parents (Suitor et al., 2009). They will feel better toward each other if their parents fostered warm and affectionate relationships that included equal

treatment of the siblings (Volling, 2003). In contrast, if their parents were equally unsupportive, the siblings may turn to each other to compensate for the poor treatment they received as children (Voorpostel & Blieszner, 2008).

Though obviously important to well-being throughout adulthood, the sibling relationship remains poorly understood in part because there are so many variations to factor into the findings, including age differences, gender, and, most recently, the complex relationships that can exist among blended families.

Grandparents

For many older adults, the rewards of family life begin to grow much richer when they reach the status of grandparents. At this point, they are in a position to be able to enjoy the benefits of expressing their generativity through interacting with the youngest generation. At the same time, grandparents can avoid the more arduous tasks of parenthood.

Many people still think of grandparents as the warm, generous, older adults portrayed in storybooks: kindly relatives who have ample time to spend with their families and want to do so. However, variations in patterns of grandparenting, along with a rapidly increasing growth in the number of grandparents in the population, may require a change in this image.

Estimates place the number of grandparents in the United States at 65 million (Ellis & Simmons, 2014); as many as 8.8 million are responsible for grandchildren with whom they reside. As you can see from Figure 9.11, of these grandparents, nearly half are still in the labor force, including a sizable number (368.3 thousand) who are 60 years and older (U.S. Bureau of the Census, 2017c).

The term skip generation family refers to the family living situation in which children live with their grandparents and not their parents. The skip generation family may occur when there is substance abuse by parents; child abuse or neglect by parents; teenage pregnancy or failure of parents to handle children; and parental unemployment, divorce, AIDS, or incarceration. The opioid crisis is creating the need for grandparents to step in to raise their grandchildren, a problem most prevalent in the states of Alabama, Arkansas, Louisiana, and Mississippi (Anderson, 2019).

Grandparents vary in the extent to which they become involved in the lives of their grandchildren. The classic study of grandparenting conducted by Neugarten and Weinstein (1964) identified five types of grandparents. The first type, the formal grandparent, follows what are believed to be the appropriate guidelines for the grandparenting

FIGURE 9.11

Grandparents Still Work to Support Grandchildren

Nearly 1.5 Million Grandparents in the Labor Force Are Responsible for Most of the Basic Care of Coresident Grandchildren Under Age 18

Grandparents in labor force (Total: 3,484,140)	Responsible for care of coresident grandchildren	Grandparents not in labor force (Total: 3,807,876)
368,348	60 years old and over	654,524
1,091,189	30 to 59 years old	458,085

Note: Among grandparents not responsible for care of coresident grandchildren, 2,024,603 were in the labor force and 2,695,267 were not.

Grandparents caring for grandchildren according to their labor market status and age.

Source: From U.S. Department of Commerce Economics and Statistics Administration. U.S Census Bureau. Public Domain.

role. Formal grandparents provide occasional services and maintain an interest in the grandchild but do not become overly involved. By contrast, the second type, the fun seeker, prefers the leisure aspects of the role and primarily provides entertainment for the grandchild. The surrogate parent is the third type; as the name implies, takes over the caretaking role with the child. Fourth, the reservoir of family wisdom, which is usually a grandfather, is the head of the family, who dispenses advice and resources but also controls the parent generation. Finally, the distant figure is the fifth type of grandparent; he or she has infrequent contact with the grandchildren, appearing only on holidays and special occasions.

Other attempts to characterize or delineate styles or categories of grandparenting have followed a similar pattern, with distinctions typically being made among the highly involved, friendly, and remote or formal types of grandparents (Mueller et al., 2002). The "remote-involved" dimension is one that seems to resonate in the attitudes that grandchildren have toward their grandparents as well (Roberto, 1990). The symbolic value of the grandparent in the family lineage, or the "family watchdog" (Troll, 1985), is another central component identified in several classifications.

Although these variations may exist in patterns of grandparenting, it is safe to say that the role of grandparent is an important one for the older adult and that grandparent identity is an important contributor to well-being (Sheppard & Monden, 2019). Grandparents feel a strong sense of connection to the younger generation (Crosnoe & Elder, 2002) and may play an important role in mediating relationships between parents and grandchildren during conflicts (Werner et al., 2005). Spending some time watching grandchildren may also help improve an older adult's executive functioning (Burn & Szoeke, 2015). Think about the times you introduced a grandparent to new technology or shared the latest news from the entertainment world. Through younger generation family members, grandparents can gain an understanding of everything from the latest music to the newest video games.

As you can probably attest to from your own life, contact with grandchildren declines steadily through the grandchildren's early adulthood, particularly when they leave the home of their parents and start an independent life of their own (Geurts et al., 2009). Those grandparents who get along with their own children are more likely to maintain contact with their grandchildren throughout this period (Dunifon & Bajracharya, 2012). Research shows that such contact may be important to the mental health of the older generation. Grandparents who are unable to maintain contact with their grandchildren due to parental divorce or disagreements within the family are likely to suffer a variety of ill consequences, including poor mental and physical health, depression, feelings of grief, and poorer quality of life (Drew & Smith, 2002). However, as their grandchildren get older, many grandparents are able to stay in touch and even to consider their grandchildren as part of their social network (Geurts et al., 2012).

FRIENDSHIPS

Of the areas of relationships examined in this chapter, oddly enough, friendship has probably received the least attention regarding its function, meaning, and changes over the course of adulthood. Yet, everyone can attest to the importance of friends in their own life, and the many roles that friends play in providing many forms of support and boosting one's emotional well-being.

Theoretical Perspectives

From a life course perspective, the major dimension that underlies close friendships is reciprocity or a sense of mutuality (Hartup & Stevens, 1997) (see Figure 9.12). The fundamental characteristic of reciprocity is that there is give and take within the relationship at a deep, emotional level involving intimacy, support, sharing, and companionship. At the behavioral level, reciprocity is expressed in actions such as exchanging favors, gifts, and advice.

Close friends in adulthood confide in each other, help each other in times of trouble, and attempt to enhance each other's sense of well-being. Although there may be developmental differences across the life span in the expression of reciprocity, the essence of all friendships remains this

FIGURE 9.12

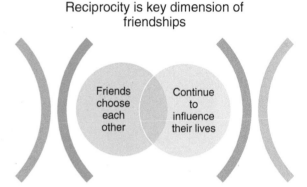

Friendships are characterized by reciprocity throughout life.

sense of deep mutuality. Another important function of friendships is socializing, or helping each other through life transitions in other spheres, such as changes in health, marital relationships, residence, and work.

Patterns of Friendships

Although people's lives change substantially throughout the vicissitudes of adulthood, many people remain close to their "best" friends. According to a 2002 survey (Fetto, 2002), 65% of American adults have known their best friends for at least 10 years and 36% for 20 years or more. Nearly, all (91%) said they would take a vacation with their best friend.

This tendency to stick with their best friends occurs despite the pressures of people's jobs, children, and romantic partners. In fact, as people enter long-term intimate relationships, many engage in dyadic withdrawal, which is the process of reducing the individual friendships of the couple and increasing the joint friendships (Kalmijn, 2003). Overall, this means that a decline will occur in a person's total number of friends. On the other hand, as couples share social networks, they expand their own friendship circles and also strengthen their own relationship (Cornwell, 2012). Part of this may occur through "platonic couple love" in which couples who are best friends also emulate the desirable qualities of the other couple (Greif & Deal, 2012).

Friendship patterns at any age may be seen as following a developmental trajectory from formation to dissolution (Adams & Blieszner, 1994). You have probably experienced this trajectory with your own friends. The stage of friendship formation involves moving from being strangers to acquaintances to friends. The maintenance phase encompasses what is usually thought of as "friendship," during which friends sustain an active interest and involvement with each other. They may evaluate the quality of the friendship periodically during this phase, deciding to increase or decrease their level of involvement. In terms of Hartup's framework, it would be during the maintenance phase that reciprocity levels are highest. Friendships may remain in the maintenance phase for years, even decades, at varying levels of closeness. The end of a friendship, which occurs during the dissolution phase, may be hard to identify. A friendship may end gradually over a period of time as feelings of reciprocity dwindle and the relationship essentially falls by the wayside. Friendships may also end through a conscious decision based on insurmountable disagreements and conflict.

Friendships in adulthood may also be distinguished in terms of the closeness of the relationship, which may or may not change over time. People may maintain peripheral ties, which are not characterized by a high degree of closeness, for many years (Fingerman & Griffiths, 1999). Peripheral ties include people such as neighbors, coworkers, professional contacts, gym buddies, friends of friends, or the parents of one's children's friends. These relationships may be amicable and cordial but never progress beyond this level. Other peripheral ties may be those that are in the friendship formation stage and will later progress to close friendships. A third type of peripheral tie is one that was formerly a close friendship and has now moved to the dissolution/disinterest stage.

There may also be variations in friendship patterns in adulthood based on individual differences in approaches toward friends, called friendship styles (Miche et al., 2013). Individuals who have an independent friendship style may enjoy friendly, satisfying, and cordial relationships with people but never form close or intimate friendships. The type known as discerning individuals are extremely selective in their choice of friends, retaining a small number of very close friends throughout their lives. Finally, people with an acquisitive friendship style are readily able to make and retain close friendships throughout their lives and therefore have a large social network.

Throughout adulthood, close social ties serve as a buffer against stress and are related to higher levels of well-being and self-esteem. Relationships with friends may also serve as important buffer against late-life stresses (Huxhold et al., 2014). Having frequent contact with friends may even help older adults maintain better memory (Zahodne et al., 2019). Moreover, friendships play a particularly important role in the lives of older gay men and lesbians, who have considerably more elaborated conceptions of their

friendship ties than do heterosexual individuals (De Vries & Megathlin, 2009).

Friends are an important influence on you throughout your life. Although you may not realize it, they contribute to our personal narratives, sense of self, and even important life choices (Flora, 2013). The nature of your friendships may change over time, but they continue to serve as a source of self-definition and support.

As you have learned in this chapter, close social ties play an important role in development. Even as relationships respond to a changing social context, they continue to influence people's well-being and adaptation. There continue to be areas of research that need further work, however, particularly in the areas of grandparenting, siblings, and friendships. From a biopsychosocial perspective, this research will provide greater understanding of the interactions among health, personality, and social context.

SUMMARY

1. Close relationships form an important component of adult life. Development in adulthood and later life interacts in important ways with the ties that people have with others. Societal changes impact the nature of individual relationships. The large majority of adults get married. Although marriage rates are decreasing and people are waiting longer to get married than in previous decades, the majority of adults are living in a marital relationship.

2. Cohabitation rates have been increasing in recent decades. According to the cohabitation effect, people living together before marriage are more likely to divorce unless they had become engaged prior to cohabitation.

3. With the legalization of same-sex marriages, there has been increased attention to the nature of same-sex families. Not only are the numbers of marriages increasing but so are the numbers of children of LGBTQ parents.

4. Birthrates in the United States are decreasing in women younger than 35 years, but have increased slightly in older mothers.

5. Widowhood is a stressful event for men and women; although increased mortality is associated with widowhood, the majority of those who are widowed maintain their resilience. The widowhood effect refers to the higher rates of mortality in widowed individuals.

6. Studies of the TtP indicate that decreases in marital satisfaction are especially likely to occur when the division

of labor assumes more traditional lines in the household. The study of adult child–parent relationships reveals a number of important phenomena related to changes in roles and their altered views of each other. Important concepts in adult child–parent relationships include filial maturity, filial anxiety, and filial obligation as well as developmental schism and intergenerational stake. The intergenerational solidarity model proposes six dimensions to characterize the cohesiveness of these relationships.

7. Siblings are another important family tie in adulthood. Closeness between siblings varies over the adult years and can be affected by the way the siblings were raised by their parents.

8. The majority of older adults are grandparents, a relationship that tends to be positive. There is a trend toward grandparents raising grandchildren in a "skip generation" (no parents present) household. Theoretical explanations of grandparenting focus on the remote-involved dimension, and various categorization schemes are based on this concept. Grandparenthood is an important source of life satisfaction.

9. Friendships are another source of important close relationships in adulthood. Even if individuals are not involved in tight-knit friendships, they may have many important peripheral ties. Friendships can potentially have positive benefits on cognition.

10

Work, Retirement, and Leisure Patterns

What are older workers really like? See whether these statements are fact or myth! Check your answers on the next page.

OLDER WORKERS:

1. take more sick days than younger workers.

2. try hard to get a task done right the first time.

3. are less flexible than younger ones.

4. can be easily replaced by younger ones.

5. learn new skills to stay competitive in the workplace.

6. are not as productive as younger ones because they're just waiting to retire.

7. are a good fit to start-up companies.

8. aren't worth hiring because they'll just retire soon after starting.

9. are team players.

10. are more expensive than younger ones.

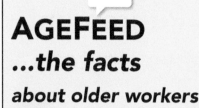

AGEFEED
...the facts
about older workers

1. take more sick days than younger workers.
   Myth! Older workers tend to have better regular job attendance than younger ones.

2. try hard to get a task done right the first time.
   Fact! While older workers may not work as quickly, they strive to get the tasks done right the first time without any mistakes. Speed does not always produce the best results!

3. are less flexible than younger ones.
   Myth! Older workers may be more likely to question changes, but they are just as likely as younger workers to adapt if the changes are well reasoned.

4. can be easily replaced by younger ones.
   Myth! The workplace knowledge and expertise gained by older workers is often very difficult to replace and can take years to develop.

5. learn new skills to stay competitive in the workplace.
   Fact! Many take courses to enhance their skills helping to keep up with changing technologies or practices.

6. are not as productive as younger ones because they're just waiting to retire.
   Myth! Evidence suggests that older workers are just as productive as younger ones.

7. are a good fit to start-up companies.
   Fact! The experience older workers bring to new companies can be valuable, particularly in times of uncertainty.

8. aren't worth hiring because they'll just retire soon after starting.
   Myth! Older workers stay at a job longer than younger ones, who may view jobs as stepping stones.

9. are team players.
   Fact! With experience comes a better understanding of one's strengths and weaknesses, which can be invaluable in a team setting.

10. are more expensive than younger ones.
    Myth! With older workers, costs are lower for hiring, retention, training, and on the job accidents.

The majority of adults are involved in productive activities in some form of paid employment. For people who are fortunate enough to be in a job they enjoy, the experience of work is positive and fulfilling and allows them to express their personal interests and abilities. Other workers view their job primarily as a means of supplying income that enables them to support themselves and most likely their families. Yet others struggle to balance their worklives with family obligations, perhaps requiring two jobs to stay afloat.

Whatever a person's current job situation, work provides the primary focus of his or her life. Work will dominate your life from your 20s onward, until either you retire or become too ill to continue. The type of job you have, the amount of money you make, and the conditions in which you work carry over to virtually every other area of your life. If you're like most people, you will come to define your identity in terms of your job title, prestige, security, and status.

In this chapter, we will talk about work in terms of vocational development, satisfaction, and performance. We will conclude the chapter with an extensive look at how retirement affects people in terms of their finances, life satisfaction, and leisure pursuits. Although the thought of retirement may seem very far away to you now, as you will learn, it's never too early to start planning for it. Before we get to that section, however, we'll explore the ways that you can lead a fulfilling work life.

WORK PATTERNS IN ADULTHOOD

We will start with some basic concepts and statistics about work before we explore the psychological aspects of work in adulthood. The labor force includes all civilians in the over-16 population who live outside of institutions (prisons, nursing homes, and residential treatment centers) and have sought or are actively seeking employment. They are not necessarily the people who are employed.

In 2018, the total size of the civilian labor force 16 years of age and older was 162 million. The unemployment rate in 2019 was 3.7%, reflecting a continued improvement in the economic situation of the United States since the most recent time of high unemployment (10%) in late 2009. There remain 1.3 million unemployed for 27 weeks or longer, but this figure is down from the peak of 6.6 million reached in mid-2010. There are at least 7.5 million multiple job holders, equally divided by sex.

As you can see from Figure 10.1, the labor force participation rate, or the percent of the civilian population who are in the labor force, will more than double for the oldest workers (75 plus). From ages 55 and older, the labor force participation will also show steady increases through 2028 (Bureau of Labor Statistics, 2019a). These shifts reflect the continued aging of the Baby Boomer generation who were between 36 to 53 in 1998 and 66 to 83 in 2028. In 2019, 63% of the civilian noninstitutionalized population was in the labor force. The overall unemployment rate

FIGURE 10.1

Percent of Civilian Labor Force by Age, United States 1998–2028

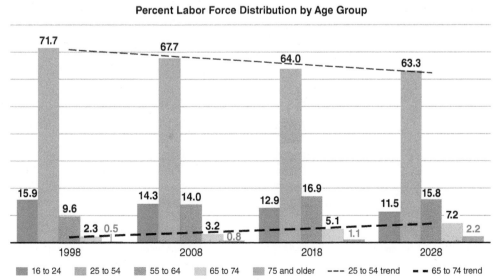

As is shown here, there will be increasing percentages of older workers by 2028 (percentages represent percent of respective age groups).

was 3.9% (i.e., the percent not employed but in the labor force). Among those 65 to 69, 31% of the labor force in that age group were employed; these numbers decrease to 19% of those 70 to 74 and 8.4% 75 and older. By race and ethnicity, Asians have the highest employment rate (61%) followed by Whites, 58% for Blacks, and 58% for the Hispanic or Latino population (Bureau of Labor Statistics, 2019c).

People with a college education are far more likely to be employed than people with a high school education or less. As you can see from Figure 10.2, education level is directly related to unemployment rate as are weekly earnings (Bureau of Labor Statistics, 2019d). However, there remain racial disparities among the college-educated, with a 5.2% unemployment rate for Blacks compared to the overall unemployment rate for all college graduates of 2.2% (Bureau of Labor Statistics, 2015).

Women have lower labor participation rates than men, with 57% compared to the male participation rate of 69%. Of all women in the civilian noninstitutionalized population, never-married women have the highest participation rates (64.3%). However, 62% of women living with a spouse with children under 3 years old are in the labor force, which is higher than the 53% among married women with no children under 18 in the home (Bureau of Labor Statistics, 2018).

Despite their increasing involvement in the labor force, however, women still earn less than men. We call this the gender gap: it is expressed as a proportion of women's to men's salaries. The overall gender gap in 2017 was reported as 82%, or $770 per week for women compared to $941 for men. As you can see from Figure 10.3, an important contributor to the gender gap is the fact that women tend to cluster in the lower-paying occupations of office workers, teaching assistants, and childcare workers. For jobs with 80% or more men, more jobs are highest-paying, with men in computer-related fields receiving the highest average pay (U.S. Bureau of the Census, 2018e).

The gender gap can be explained in part by women's lower representation in higher occupational groupings. For example, there are almost twice as many men in high-earning management, professional, and related occupations. However, the gender gap in actual pay remains high at 71% (larger than the overall rate of 82%). The lowest

FIGURE 10.2

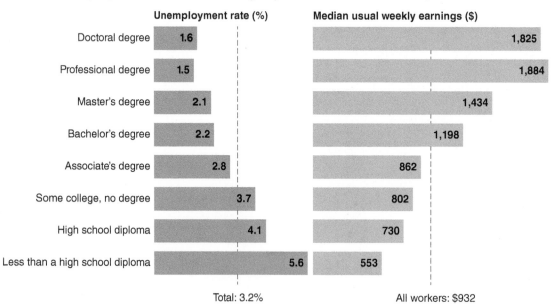

Unemployment rates and earnings by educational attainment, 2018

	Unemployment rate (%)	Median usual weekly earnings ($)
Doctoral degree	1.6	1,825
Professional degree	1.5	1,884
Master's degree	2.1	1,434
Bachelor's degree	2.2	1,198
Associate's degree	2.8	862
Some college, no degree	3.7	802
High school diploma	4.1	730
Less than a high school diploma	5.6	553
	Total: 3.2%	All workers: $932

Note: Data are for persons age 25 and over. Earnings are for full-time wage and salary workers.

The unemployment rate decreases and earnings increase with each increase in educational level.

Source: Data from U.S. Bureau of Labor Statistics, Current Population Survey. Public Domain.

FIGURE 10.3

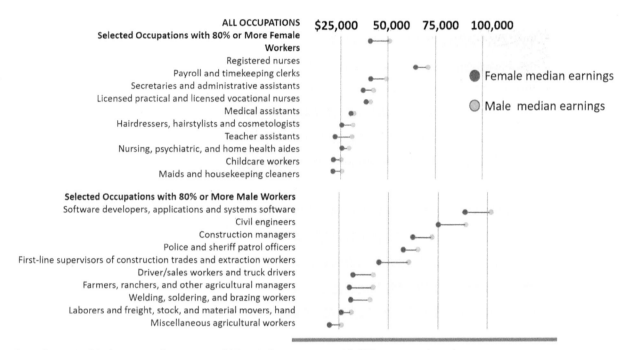

As can be seen in this chart, women's earnings are highest in the occupations with 80% or more male workers.

Source: From American Community Survey. U.S. Department of Commerce Economics and Statistics Administration, U.S. Census Bureau, 2016. Public Domain.

gender gap (92%) is in office and administrative support positions, where women slightly outnumber men. Weekly earnings in the top occupations for men average $1,559 compared to $779 in office and administrative support jobs (Bureau of Labor Statistics, 2019e).

Related to occupational attainment is education. In general, there has been an increase over the past 40 years in the number of older adults with a college diploma. Those 65 years of age and older are more likely to have graduated from college (26.7%) than was true in 1985 (9.4%). Among the 65 year and older group, 11% have an advanced degree (Ryan & Bauman, 2016). The trends toward increased education among the U.S. population is likely to continue as is evident by a steady rise of college graduates in the 25-to-34-year-old age group (32.5%) since the 1940s, along with a steady increase in high school graduates (90.5%).

U.S. military veterans represent a population of concern from the standpoint of employment statistics. As of 2018, there were 19.2 million adults (8% of the civilian population 18 and older) who had served in the U.S. Armed Forces, with women representing 10% of all veterans. The unemployment rate in Gulf War-era II veterans

(September 2001 to the present) was 3.5%, and 3.9% for men. Veterans with a service-related disability had a higher unemployment rate of 5.2%, and about one-third of these worked in public service sector industries. Veterans between the ages of 18 and 24 were least likely of all veterans to be unemployed (6%); the largest percentage of unemployed veterans (54%) were those between 25 and 54 years of age (Bureau of Labor Statistics, 2019f). Thus, the situation for veterans varies tremendously by age group, although the lower unemployment for younger veterans suggests a better outlook as they move through their adult years.

VOCATIONAL DEVELOPMENT

Vocation is a person's choice of occupation. It reflects the individual's personal preferences and interests. Theories of vocational development propose that vocational choices and experiences change over time, reflecting their own interests and desires within the workplace.

Thinking about your own desire to enter a given field, it is likely that you chose your career path and hence college major because of your vocational interests. You decided at an earlier point in your life that you wanted to pursue a given field, whether it was music, psychology, nursing, or social work because it suited your personality, values, and skills. These are the factors that vocational development theories take into account when they attempt to explain the career choices that people make and determine people's levels of happiness and productivity once they have acted on those choices.

The basis of vocational development theories is the concept of career, which is the term that captures the unique connection between individuals and social organizations over time. Many factors shape the individual's career, including personal development, the specific organization for which the person works, and the profession or occupational category that describes the individual's occupation.

Holland's Vocational Development Theory

According to Holland's vocational development theory (Holland, 1997), people express their personalities in their vocational aspirations and interests. Holland proposed that there are six fundamental types (also called codes) that represent the universe of all possible vocational interests, competencies, and behaviors. Each of the six types is identified by its initial letter: Realistic (R), Investigative (I), Artistic (A), Social (S), Enterprising (E), and Conventional (C). The theory is also referred to as the RIASEC model, referring to the six basic types that characterize an individual's vocational interests (see Figure 10.4).

The RIASEC types also apply to the occupational environment because they reflect particular patterns of job requirements and rewards. For example, social occupations involve work with people, and realistic occupations involve work with one's hands. Occupational environments, then, are the settings that elicit, develop, and reward specific interests, competencies, and behaviors of the individuals who work in those environments. If you are working in a realistic environment, you will be expected to complete activities that make use of your ability to work with things rather than your ability to work with people.

Vocational psychologists typically combine two or three of the codes in the RIASEC model to describe people and occupations. The first letter reflects the primary code into which a person's interest or occupation falls ("S" for Social, for example). The second and third codes allow for a more accurate and differentiated picture of the individual or

FIGURE 10.4

RIASEC Model

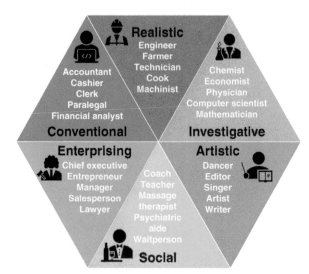

Holland's RIASEC model proposes that all occupations are organized according to six basic types.

occupation. Both a construction worker and a corrections officer are R code occupations, and both have the RE code designation. They differ in their third code, which is C for the construction worker and S for the corrections officer.

In one variant of the RIASEC model, two underlying dimensions of the six types are identified: interest in people versus things and preference for data versus ideas (Prediger & Vansickle, 1992). The R code reflects the extreme of interest in things, the S the extreme of interest in people, the combination of I and A is at the extreme of ideas, and the combination of E and C is at the extreme of data. Although meant to be comprehensive, the RIASEC model appears to benefit from including these additional dimensions (Deng et al., 2007).

From a personality perspective, the RIASEC types as applied to individuals are very much like traits (Armstrong & Anthoney, 2009). Putting the two together, researchers have suggested that there are three underlying dimensions: interest in people versus things, preference for abstract versus concrete ideas, and striving for personal growth versus striving for accomplishment.

As you can see, the six RIASEC types are organized within the individual in a hexagonal structure. This structure implies that the types have a relationship to each other based on their distance from each other on the structure. Types that are most similar (such as R and C) are closest;

those that are the most dissimilar (such as C and A) are farthest away from each other.

The notion of the hexagon is an important one because it helps define the way that your interests correspond to your environments. You will be the most satisfied in your job if you are in an environment that fits your personality type. Congruence or "fit" occurs when your vocational type matches your occupational environment.

When your personality and work environment are congruent, you will be more satisfied and, as a result, more productive in your job. Supporting this idea, researchers have found that individuals who fit the Artistic type working in Realistic environments have lower work quality, at least in part because they feel dissatisfied (Kieffer et al., 2004). Lack of congruence can also lead people to become bored, if not outright dissatisfied (Phan & Rounds, 2018). The Artistic type in the Realistic job may wait out the hours until the workday is over and then rush home to work on crafts, play a musical instrument, or go to a pottery studio.

The RIASEC theory is empirically derived from the responses of many thousands of individuals who have been tested over the years of its development. Many of the studies on the RIASEC model used the Strong Vocational Interest Inventory (SVII), which asks respondents to rate their top interests based on their preferences regarding work and leisure activities, areas of study (i.e., college courses), specific occupations, and preferences regarding their own work style, learning environment, leadership style, desire to take risks, and team orientation. The SVII must be administered by a trained and certified practitioner. To assess yourself, you can take Self-Directed Search (SDS), a self-administered questionnaire that allows you to assess where you fit on the RIASEC dimensions; it also asks you to rate your strengths.

The RIASEC codes now have become fully integrated into O*NET, the Occupational Information Network, which consists of an interactive national database of occupations. O*NET (also called ONET) was established in 1998 by the U.S. Department of Labor, Employment, and Training Administration. You can go to the O*NET website (onetonline.org) and explore the options it provides, including lists of jobs that match your interests along with their RIASEC profiles and other vocational features as well as salary ranges, future outlooks for hiring, and prospects in your state of residence.

Consider the occupation of dental hygienist, which O*NET lists as having a "bright outlook." The RIASEC code is SRC, and in addition to the obvious tasks, requires technology skills in various software applications (mail, medical instruments, and spreadsheet). As a hygienist, you would be expected to maintain contact with others and use your hands to operate the cleaning equipment. There are slightly over 200,000 dental hygienists in the United States, and the projected growth is much faster than average. This information could be very useful to you in comparing this occupation with, for example, radiologic technologist, whose RIASEC code is similar but not identical (R and S, but no C).

The notion of congruence between people and jobs has received considerable empirical support, not only in terms of job ratings but also in terms of career change behavior. All other things being equal, people will tend to move out of incongruent jobs and into positions more suited to their interests (Donohue, 2006). At the same time, their vocational interests and perhaps even their personality traits may change in response to socialization in their workplace (Wille & DeFruyt, 2014).

Unfortunately for many people, factors outside their control, such as discrimination due to gender, race, and ethnicity, limit these choices (Eshelman & Rottinghaus, 2015). For individuals whose vocational situations are affected by such constraints, the role of identity and the possibility for realizing one's true vocational interests are far less significant than the reality of these sociocultural factors.

Conversely, the RIASEC congruence model does not take into account another key feature of occupations, their level of prestige. You may be very attracted to a job involving the use of your hands, but all things being equal, a career as a neurosurgeon (which has a high prestige rating) would appeal to you more than a career in a less prestigious field (Guntern et al., 2016).

Super's Life-Span Life-Stage Theory

As individuals traverse the various stages of their vocational development, their sense of self also undergoes changes. Super's life-span life-stage theory focuses on the role of the self and proposes that people attempt to realize their inner potential through their career choices (Super, 1990). If you see yourself as an artist, then you will desire work in which you can express that view of yourself.

In contrast to Holland's theory, which emphasizes vocational preferences (the fact that you prefer artistic work), Super's theory places the focus on the occupation that you see as most "true" to your inner self. Super's theory also takes into account the fact that the constraints of the marketplace mean that people are not always able to achieve full realization of their self-concepts. In a society with relatively little demand for artists, the person with the artistic self-concept will need to seek self-expression in a job that allows for a certain degree of creativity but will also bring in a paycheck. Such an individual may seek a career in computer graphic design, for example, because that is a more viable occupation than that of an oil painter.

According to Super, the expression of self-concept through work occurs in a series of what he called "life-space life-stages." In this model, there are three "lifestyle factors" that include environmental determinants (e.g., labor market), situational determinants (e.g., period of history), and personal determinants (biological and psychological). In a sense, this model is very similar to Bronfenbrenner's ecological model and is compatible with the biopsychosocial approach. However, Super goes on to propose that these influences intersect with such life roles as student, "leisurite," citizen, worker, and homemaker or parent. Dividing the life course into stages from childhood through later life completes the life-space, life-stage model. Super's theory, then, views career development as occurring within a larger context.

From the standpoint of career development, four of the six stages proposed by Super are of greatest relevance, as shown in Figure 10.5. In the exploration stage (teens to mid-20s), people explore career alternatives and select a vocation that they will feel to express their self-concept. By the time they reach the establishment stage (mid-20s to mid-40s), people are focused on achieving stability and attempt to remain within the same occupation. At the same time, people seek to move up the career ladder to managerial positions and higher. In the maintenance stage

(mid-40s to mid-50s), people attempt to hold onto their positions rather than to seek further advancement. Finally, in the disengagement stage (mid-50s to mid-60s), workers begin to prepare for retirement, perhaps spending more time in their leisure pursuits.

When Super first wrote about career development, people often stayed in the same job with the same company for years, if not their entire employed life. At the same time, people had no choice but to retire and they saw their last decade of employment as a winding-down period. Combined with shorter life expectancies, this meant that many people employed in a career started to change the way they viewed their trajectories. This model began to change substantially in the 1980s, when large corporations began programs of downsizing, particularly after the advent of computerized technology. Moreover, as you will learn later, mandatory retirement was no longer legal for the majority of occupations, so that people could keep working longer, perhaps even starting second careers.

Changes in the dynamics of the labor force and retirement since the time of Super's original writing are now reflected in a more flexible view of career development. Workers now may consider recycling, in which they change their main field of career activity partway into occupational life (Duys et al., 2008). In recycling, middle-aged workers may find themselves once again in the establishment stage they thought they had left behind in their late 20s. Indeed, with constant changes in the demands of the labor market along with the greater labor force participation of midlife and older workers, recycling is likely to become increasingly normative.

FIGURE 10.5

Super's Life-Space Life-Stages Career Develoment Model

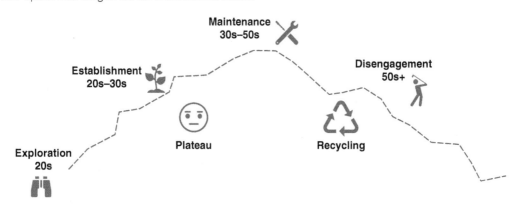

Super's life-space life-stages model of vocational development along with the variations of plateau and recycling for the period from the 20s to the 50s and beyond.

On the other hand, people may also experience career plateauing, in which they remain static in their vocational development. They may experience structural plateauing, in which they do not advance up to higher-level positions, or content plateauing, in which they feel that they have mastered their work and no longer see it as a challenge (Lapalme et al., 2009). People may reach their plateau at a young age if they enter a so-called dead-end job, or if their moves within or between companies involve lateral changes rather than vertical advancement. At that point, the individual may decide that it is time to seek another job (Heilmann et al., 2008). However, some employees are content to remain in the status quo, particularly if they have achieved success and are satisfied with their current positions (Smith-Ruig, 2009).

There are strategies for those workers who wish to combat plateauing. A study of more than 300 government employees showed that workers who reported serving as a mentor were less likely to experience the negative effects of plateauing (Lentz & Allen, 2009). In line with Erikson's concept of generativity, such mentoring activities can help middle-aged and older workers with their own psychosocial development. Additionally, companies can help guard against plateauing by devising ways for workers who are not on track for promotion to benefit instead from job variety, job rotation, and job enrichment. Showing plateaued employees respect and appreciation can also help these individuals feel connected to their employer (Yang et al., 2019).

Occupation as Calling

The role of the self in vocational development forms the core of theories that emphasize people's desires both to achieve self-expression through their work and to contribute to the larger good. A calling is an individual's consuming passion for a particular career domain that serves people in some capacity and contributes to a sense of personal meaning and purpose. Whether it serves your own desire for fulfilling your potential or because you want to help others is less important than the fact that the calling is integral to your sense of identity (Michaelson & Tosti-Kharas, 2019). People can live a calling for a career that is not necessarily altruistic in nature.

Some of the features of a career that represents a calling include that you feel passionate about it, enjoy this work more than anything else, are willing to make sacrifices to get into this field, have it on your mind in some way at all times, and find the actual work to be deeply gratifying (Dobrow & Tosti-Kharas, 2011).

The idea of work as calling is becoming increasingly recognized within vocational and counseling psychology, generating a rapidly growing area of research. The factors that predict whether people will be able to achieve their callings include person–environment congruence, career commitment, and sense of meaning in work. All of these are critical in helping individuals translate their perceived callings into one that they can actualize in their occupations. Personal motivation, support from the individual's organization, and the ability to engage in "job crafting" can help individuals realize their calling within their work environments (Duffy et al., 2019).

However, it might strike you that your calling might be a completely unrealistic aspiration. What if you always wanted a career as a professional musician but you're not good enough to break into the field? Your calling may still be in the musical field, but you will instead need to fulfill that desire through being a music teacher. It's also possible that you have to switch gears altogether because even music teaching is not a realistic goal. Instead, you might fulfill that calling by either playing on your own as a hobby or subscribing to a concert series in your local community. People who cannot find a job in the area of their calling may, therefore, find satisfaction through their leisure pursuits (Berg et al., 2010).

Variations in Vocational Development

Views of vocational development in which individuals guide their own paths contrast with the more passive career stage concept such as that proposed by Super's theory. The changing environment in which career development occurs increasingly is being viewed as providing workers with more opportunities to shape their own vocational development pathways. One idea within this new framework is that of the boundaryless career, or a career that crosses the boundaries of an employer or organization. People who adhere to the boundaryless mindset would agree with statements such as "I enjoy jobs that require me to interact with people in many different organizations" (Briscoe et al., 2006, p. 35).

The boundaryless career is, then, a frame of mind that allows workers to think more flexibly about their commitment to a particular employer. Although they may remain committed to working for the same organization, they may seek out horizontal connections to people in other companies who hold the same job or have similar interests as they do. Professional organizations, whether unions or scientific societies, tap into this boundaryless framework. People who belong to these organizations do not see themselves as competing with their fellow members, but instead as benefiting from the opportunity to share experiences and perspectives.

The second form of self-directed vocational development is the protean career, in which individuals are both self-directed and driven internally by their own values. In the protean career, the individual seeks personal growth through self-reflection and self-learning. Instead of focusing on external criteria for success, the individual following the protean career has internal standards for success that will enhance his or her identity. A strong protean career orientation is indicated by, for example, agreement with an item such as: "I am in charge of my own career" (Briscoe et al., 2006, p. 34).

Examining data from 135 samples representing 35 countries (with over 45,000 participants), Wiernik and Kostal (2019) conducted a meta-analysis to determine the relationship between boundaryless and protean career orientations. Rather than the two concepts being distinct, it appears that they both tap what the authors call a proactive career orientation. People high on this overall factor are more likely to take their career management into their own hands in order to maximize their job satisfaction.

Individuals who believe that they can shape their careers appear to be high in the quality known as core self-evaluation, which represents a person's appraisal of people, events, and things in relation to oneself. The core self-evaluation is composed of self-esteem, generalized self-efficacy, high emotional stability, and the belief that you control your fate. Research on recent college graduates shows that people whose core self-evaluation includes the perception that they are highly employable will feel that they will have the power to determine the shape of their careers (Rodrigues et al., 2019).

These findings regarding the importance of variations in vocational development reinforce the value of flexible careers. Additionally, they suggest the potential for organizations to create a culture in which individuals can seek the variations that best suit their particular developmental pathways (Tomlinson et al., 2018).

VOCATIONAL SATISFACTION

As we have just discussed, people find the most fulfillment from their jobs in terms of personal development when they can express their identities. The concept of vocational satisfaction refers to the extent to which people find their work to be enjoyable. For our purposes, we will consider vocational satisfaction to be equivalent to job satisfaction, as both terms are used in the literature. Vocational satisfaction is important to the individual as well as to the

employer because workers who are satisfied show higher commitment to their jobs (Hoffman & Woehr, 2006).

Intrinsic and Extrinsic Factors

People can be satisfied with their jobs either because they love the work that they perform, they value the salary and other perks it provides, or some combination of the two. The distinction between intrinsic and extrinsic factors in vocational satisfaction, shown in Figure 10.6, represents the difference between those factors unique to the job itself and those which involve contributions to satisfaction that can come from any job, not that specific one.

Intrinsic factors in vocational satisfaction refer to the tasks required to perform the work itself. The central defining feature of an intrinsic factor is that it cannot be found in precisely the same fashion in a different type of job. For example, the sculptor engages in the physical activities of molding clay or stone, and the accountant must perform the mental activities of manipulating numbers. Although each job involves other activities, these are the ones that serve to define the work required to perform each.

Intrinsic factors involve or engage your sense of identity in that the work directly pertains to your feelings of competence, autonomy, and stimulation of personal growth. Your ability to express autonomy and self-direction in the daily running of your job are also part of the intrinsic aspects of work because these factors are directly tied to your sense of self. Having work that is a calling fulfills your intrinsic motivation, but you can have intrinsic motivation for your work without feeling that it is a calling.

FIGURE 10.6

Intrinsic and Extrinsic Factors in Vocational Satisfaction

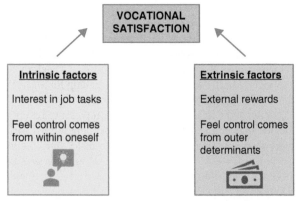

Two basic categories of factors that influence vocational satisfaction are intrinsic and extrinsic.

Extrinsic factors in vocational satisfaction are the features that accompany the job but are not central to its performance. You can receive extrinsic satisfaction from many different jobs regardless of the work tasks they require. The easiest extrinsic factor to understand is salary. Although some jobs earn more than others, you can earn the same amount of money by performing very different work tasks. A professional athlete and a real estate magnate may earn the same six- or seven-figure paycheck for performing a very different set of job activities. Therefore, salary is not intrinsic to work.

There are a number of additional extrinsic factors associated with the conditions of work, such as the comfort of the environment, demands for travel, convenience of work hours, friendliness of coworkers, amount of status associated with the job, and adequacy of the company's supervision and employment policies. These aspects of work are "psychological," in a sense, but they do not directly engage your sense of personal identity and competence. Although a high salary may certainly reinforce your sense of worth (particularly in Western society), you can earn that high salary in many ways that are not necessarily tied to your true vocational passions. Other extrinsic but important factors for vocational satisfaction involve the emotional climate of the workplace and attitudes toward individuals of diverse races (Lyons & O'Brien, 2006) and sexual orientations (Velez & Moradi, 2012).

At this point in your life, you may or may not have had a job yet that you felt was intrinsically satisfying. However, you can probably think of people you know who do feel connected to their work at an intrinsic level. Perhaps you have encountered a customer service representative who seemed genuinely interested in helping you solve a problem and was willing to work with you until you found the satisfactory solution. This may have been an employee who found the job to be intrinsically rewarding, feelings that she expressed in the apparent pride that she took in helping you with your situation.

Intrinsic factors give you a sense of active engagement in your work and contribute to your sense of self. The customer service representative who provided you with such kind and gracious help may not see her job as one that represents her life's work; however, she may nevertheless enjoy the part of her job that allows her to get people what they need.

Intrinsic and extrinsic factors are also the basis for understanding the role of motivation in vocational satisfaction. According to the two-factor motivational theory intrinsic factors are job "motivators," and extrinsic factors are the "hygiene" conditions present in the workplace. When people work for intrinsic reasons, according to this theory, they will be more likely to achieve self-actualization.

Favorable hygiene factors can prevent people from becoming dissatisfied, but they do not serve as the sole motivator for work. Growth, self-fulfillment, and feelings of achievement can only come from the fulfillment of job motivators not from the hygiene factors (Herzberg et al., 2005).

Expanding upon the two-factor motivational theory, self-determination theory proposes that workers attempt to fulfill their needs for competence, autonomy, and relatedness (Deci & Ryan, 2008). When workers fulfill their competence needs, they are able to feel a sense of mastery. Autonomy needs include the worker's desire to feel in control over the conditions under which the job is performed. Relatedness refers to the need to feel connected to others. In the ideal situation, workers experience a sense of self-determination, in which they are expressing their true interests and abilities (similar to intrinsic factors), are able to have a voice in what happens to them at work (similar to extrinsic factors), and share a sense of belongingness with their fellow workers. Conversely, when these conditions are not met, workers are more likely to seek other employment or if they cannot, to experience burnout and poor health (Olafsen et al., 2017).

One of the assumptions of self-determination theory is that people will work harder when they feel they are in control of what they do (autonomy) and also that they are able to satisfy their needs for mastery. As you can attest from your own experiences, however, you cannot have complete freedom over every aspect of your job because you do need to answer to your supervisor or employer's requests for you to complete the job tasks. The point of self-determination theory is that you have as much autonomy as is feasible or at least feel that you can work within your employer's requirements. Your boss may ask you to complete "x" numbers of tasks in a given day; ideally, you feel that this is a reasonable demand so this becomes an internal goal that you also adopt.

Early in the development of self-determination theory, its originators identified the process of motivation crowding out, in which people's intrinsic motivation decreases when they receive extrinsic rewards for completing the work they enjoy. This idea began to become implemented in the workplace though with the caveat that people will not, or cannot, work for free. In a meta-analysis of 183 studies on nearly 213,000 individuals, Cerasoli et al. (2014) found that across a variety of domains, intrinsic motivation predicted the quality of work while incentives or extrinsic rewards predicted quantity.

Positive and Negative Moods

Job satisfaction can be affected not only by the motivation to work but also by people's feelings about their jobs. You can

Rawpixel Image/Pixabay

Having an enjoyable workplace environment can be an important contributor to job satisfaction.

have feelings on the job (such as being excited about the upcoming weekend) and feelings about the job (such as liking your job activities). According to affective events theory, events at work lead individuals to experience affective reactions, and these in turn influence attitudes toward work and performance (Weiss & Cropanzano, 1996).

There are many factors that can affect your mood, and ultimately your satisfaction at work. For example, if you experience positive events at work, such as being complimented by a supervisor, you will have a positive emotional experience; if you experience negative events, such as conflict with a coworker, your emotions will be negatively affected. By the end of the day, your negative mood will affect the way you feel when you return home (Kempen et al., 2019).

Your mood when you wake up in the morning can become an important influence on the way you feel about your work as you go through the day. This was the finding of a study of 29 customer service representatives employed at a call center of an insurance company. Researchers tracked mood changes throughout the day, the affective display of their customers, and the employee's affect subsequent to the call. The organization measured the productivity of the employees. The call center employees who started the day in a bad mood rated their customers more negatively. After talking to a customer who displayed positive affect, the employees themselves felt better. In contrast, after talking to a customer who displayed negative affect, the employees felt no worse themselves, but their productivity suffered in that they were more likely to take a break after such a call. The findings suggest that

start-of-the-day mood plays an important role in affecting how employees feel throughout the day and, ultimately, how well they perform (Rothbard & Wilk, 2011).

From your own job experiences, you can probably also relate to the ways that positive emotions can be boosted under the right conditions at work. Employers who provide an environment in which employees can engage in a shared pleasant activity can help boost overall productivity through such activities as outings, team building activities, relaxing, and sharing jokes (Tang et al., 2017).

Fortunately, the fluctuations across the day, or "affect spin," do not seem to have effects that carry over to the next day at work. Changes in affect seem responsive to the events that actually take place during the day, such that positive events can make up for prior negative workplace-related events (Clark et al., 2018).

Personality traits can also influence the ways in which people interpret what happens to them at work. Affective events theory predicts that people will differ in their reactions to daily work experiences on the basis of their personality traits. You might think that people high in agreeableness would be better able to bounce back from negative interactions at work. However, in a study of university employees, researchers found that those high in agreeableness actually had more negative affect following interpersonal conflict than those low in agreeableness. Highly agreeable employees were also more likely to experience negative affect when they perceived their work environments to be low in social support (Ilies et al., 2011). By the same token, the personality of supervisors can also affect the way they are affected by their own work overload. Supervisors high in agreeableness will be less likely to take out their frustrations on their employees (Eissa & Lester, 2017).

In general, it appears that high subjective well-being predicts job satisfaction. In a meta-analysis testing the relationship over time between overall well-being and job satisfaction, researchers found more support for the direction from subjective well-being to job satisfaction than vice versa. Consistent with other research on overall mood, it appears that people high in subjective well-being tend to experience more positive emotions that carry over into their work lives (Bowling et al., 2010).

Personality traits may also interact with changes in job satisfaction over time. Looking at the intrinsic–extrinsic dimension of vocational satisfaction, researchers have found that people with high neuroticism scores are less likely to feel that their jobs are intrinsically rewarding. Perhaps for this reason, neuroticism is negatively related to job satisfaction; by contrast, people high in the traits of conscientiousness and extraversion are more satisfied in their jobs (Furnham et al., 2009). By the same token, people's personalities may be affected by their levels of work satisfaction. In one longitudinal study, workers who were more satisfied with their jobs showed moderate increases in extraversion (Scollon & Diener, 2006).

Person–Environment Correspondence

We have seen that Holland's vocational development theory proposes that people seek to find congruence between their personalities and the characteristics of the job. According to person–environment correspondence theory, people are most satisfied when their workplaces respond to their needs. In contrast to Holland's congruence model, person–environment correspondence theory focuses on values and needs rather than interests (Dawis, 2002). Person–environment correspondence theory stresses the role of values in promoting job satisfaction. Occupational reinforcement patterns (ORPs) are the work values and needs likely to be reinforced or satisfied by a particular occupation. The six ORPs are (1) achievement: using one's abilities and feeling a sense of accomplishment; (2) altruism: being of service to others; (3) autonomy: having a sense of control; (4) comfort: not feeling stressed; (5) safety: stability, order, and predictability; and (6) status: being recognized and serving in a dominant position.

As you think about your own values and needs, contrast the extent to which you focus on achievement with your desire to be of service to others. Reflecting the importance of ORPs, O*NET incorporates ORPs into its job search system. The original six value dimensions are now labeled achievement, working conditions, recognition, relationships, support, and independence. Occupations high in achievement range from veterinarian to actor; those high in relationships include rehabilitation counselor and human resource specialist. Research continues to support the role of person–environment correspondence to workplace adjustment suggesting that, over time, workers attempt to fit the demands of the job to their own work styles (Bayl-Smith & Griffin, 2018).

Work Stress

Work stress can be a major threat to people's feelings of well-being and can eventually take its toll on physical health as well. There are many forms that work stress can take, as we have already seen, ranging from negative interactions with coworkers to difficulties dealing with clients, customers, and supervisors. People may also experience stress when they feel that their job is not compatible with their needs, interests, values, and personal dispositions. Therefore, work stress is a very broad category. For our purposes, we will turn here to studies that specifically examine ratings of stress as reported by employees in specific situations.

Emotional labor is the requirement of service-oriented jobs in which workers must smile and maintain a friendly attitude regardless of their own personal feelings or emotions. Performing emotional labor can be stressful to those service employees who feel that they must constantly put on an act in order to carry out their job successfully. This component of emotional labor, or "surface acting," puts stress on the employees who feel constantly that they have to simulate emotions they truly do not feel. Even though people who like jobs in which they are required to interact with the public may gravitate toward those jobs, the disconnect between the way they are feeling and the constant pressure to put on a false front can erode their vocational satisfaction (Bhave & Glomb, 2016).

Workers can help to alleviate emotional labor by engaging in a deeper level of identification with the emotions they are expected to portray (Chu et al., 2012). Emotional labor can also take the form of needing to cover up a stigmatized but concealable identity in the workplace, such as sexual orientation or a nonnormative family situation. When they feel they can reveal this hidden aspect of their identities, their productivity can benefit as can the atmosphere in the workplace (Berkley et al., 2019).

Workplace bullying is another form of stress in which individuals are exposed over a lengthy period to negative interpersonal acts on the job which they cannot cope with or control. Some forms of workplace bullying include social isolation, direct harassment, intimidating behavior, work-related criticism, and physical violence. A large study carried out in Denmark on over 1,000 workers from 55 workplaces showed that all forms of workplace bullying were stressful, particularly direct harassment and intimidating behavior (Hogh et al., 2012). Thus, individuals exposed to work-related bullying become traumatized in ways that can lead to both psychological and physiological consequences.

Work-related stress can take its toll on physical functioning as shown by studies conducted within Whitehall II. Holding all other factors constant and excluding participants who were initially obese, men under high levels of work stress over the course of the study had twice the risk of subsequently developing metabolic syndrome. Women with high levels of stress had over five times the risk of developing this condition (Chandola et al., 2006).

Lack of job fairness can be another workplace stressor, and as shown by Gimeno et al. (2010) in Whitehall II, men who reported higher justice at work were less likely to have metabolic syndrome than those who felt their job conditions were unfair. For women, stress encountered at work independently predicted type 2 diabetes, even after controlling for socioeconomic position and stressors unrelated to work (Heraclides et al., 2009).

Physiological data obtained in the form of cortisol levels from Whitehall II also illustrate the impact of employment grade on health. People in lower employment grades have less control over their work conditions and, as a result, can experience greater stress. Daily assessments of cortisol, the hormone involved in the response to stress and anxiety, were taken from an older Whitehall cohort six times throughout the day. Men in lower employment grades showed higher cortisol levels early in the morning, levels that remained higher throughout the day than for men in higher employment grades. These higher levels could be explained not only by higher levels of stress during the day but also by poorer quality of sleep at night (Kumani et al., 2010). This differential level of workplace control on cortisol patterns can even carry through to the retirement years (Chandola et al., 2018).

Thus, maximizing workplace satisfaction, in addition to helping maintain worker productivity, can make a key difference in promoting the health and long-term well-being of the individual.

Relationships Between Work and Family Roles

One of the great challenges of adult life is dividing your time, energy, and role involvement across your many commitments. The two areas that many people find most difficult to integrate in terms of competing demands are occupation and family life. Both carry with them major obligations and responsibility, and both contribute heavily to the individual's sense of identity. However, they do not necessarily need to be in conflict, as research is increasingly demonstrating.

According to the work–family enrichment model, experiences in one role improve the quality of life in the other. This model is based on the theory of conservation of resources, which proposes that organizations can protect their workers against stress by providing them with support to maintain both their work and family roles (Hobfoll, 2002).

As shown in Figure 10.7 (top half), enrichment can take the form of development, in opportunities for growth, and affect, or levels of happiness. The need to balance work and family life can lead the worker to become more time-efficient, a benefit that carries over to the job. Conversely, apart from supplying a salary, work provides individuals with social capital in the form of feeling a sense of accomplishment. Researchers also use the term "positive spillover" to describe this transfer of skills from one domain to the other (Masuda et al., 2012). There can also be crossover effects onto the spouse who not only feels better about the relationship but also about the spouse's workplace (Carlson et al., 2019).

Alternatively, the work–family conflict model proposes that people have a fixed amount of time and energy to spend on their life roles. This model is based on a scarcity perspective (Edwards & Rothbard, 2000) according to which the more time and energy people invest in one area, the less they have for the other set of demands and activities. The workaholic, according to this view, has little energy or time for family relationships. Conversely, high involvement with family should preclude total commitment to the job.

As shown in the bottom half of Figure 10.7, conflict can take a variety of forms including lack of time and emotional exhaustion (van Hooff et al., 2005). At an extreme, work–family conflict can take the form of counterproductive behaviors on the part of the employee (such as leaving early, taking office supplies home) as retaliation for a perceived lack of support (Morgan et al., 2018).

There are variations in the extent and impact of work–family conflict, however, and not all workers feel the same degree of conflict. Conflict is most likely to occur among mothers of young children, dual-career couples, and those who are highly involved with their job. Additionally, work–family conflict is higher for workers employed in the private sector than those employed in the public sector (Dolcos & Daley, 2009).

From the perspective of affective events theory, positive experiences at home should translate into better

FIGURE 10.7

Two Models of Work–Family Relationships

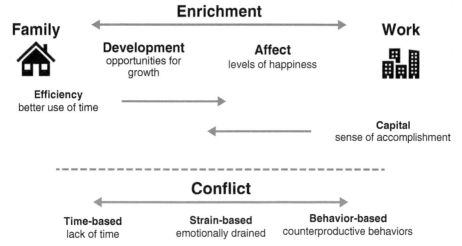

Relationship between work and family roles can be conceived in terms of enrichment or conflict.

moods at work, and vice versa (Kempen et al., 2019). Conversely, people who experience exhaustion as a result of work–family conflict may perceive the work–family trade-off as more stressful, which only increases their exhaustion (Rubio et al., 2015).

With all of the possibility for unfavorable outcomes posed when work and family demands do become mutually exclusive, organizations are increasingly recognizing the importance to their workers of providing a "family-friendly" environment, which may include support and schedule control. As shown in a study in the banking sector conducted in Spain, even if family-friendly work policies do not alleviate all forms of stress, the fact of their existence can generate positive effects by showing that the organization cares about the well-being of its workers (Medina-Garrido et al., 2019). Ultimately, for these measures to be effective, workers need to feel that they can take advantage of them without worrying they will give up opportunities for promotion or other rewards from their supervisors (Moore, 2018). Perhaps for this reason, benefits that help employees fulfill their childcare arrangements are more important than flexible work schedules (Pailhé & Solaz, 2018).

Age and Vocational Satisfaction

The question of whether job satisfaction increases, decreases, or stays the same over adulthood is a surprisingly difficult one to answer. Age interacts with other factors, including gender, level of employment, salary, and the nature of the work environment. In addition,

workers of the same age may differ in job tenure, the length of an individual's employment. Separating age from tenure becomes particularly important in understanding vocational satisfaction as individuals grow older.

Taking into account the differences between age and job tenure turns out to be an important consideration in examining changes in vocational satisfaction over time. In a longitudinal study of nearly 22,000 employees across two studies spanning 40 years, Dobrow Riza and colleagues (2018) found that tenure is associated with a decrease in vocational satisfaction. However, older employees who switched jobs actually increased in satisfaction. At the same time, those employees who did change jobs also received higher pay, which was positively related to their vocational satisfaction.

The finding that salary is tied to increased job satisfaction in older workers who change employers might suggest that, as people age, salary may come to represent a token of worth in addition to providing extrinsic rewards. However, it is also possible that the employees who are offered new jobs at higher pay have more job skills than those who remain in the same position throughout their careers.

Passage of the Age Discrimination in Employment Act (ADEA) in 1967 made it illegal to fire or not employ workers on the basis of their age. This legislation was intended to provide protection for older workers (over 40) from discrimination by employers who would otherwise seek to replace them with younger, cheaper, and, presumably, more productive employees. For example, potential employers in most jobs cannot ask a job seeker for his or her age or even questions that would give away the job seeker's age, such as year of college or high school graduation. However, the ADEA does not protect workers in occupations in which age has a presumed effect on the performance of critical job tasks, including firefighters, police officers, and airline pilots.

Employers nevertheless may try to skirt around the ADEA by using criteria other than age in hiring and retention decisions. In a landmark case in November 2015, a U.S. appeals court ruled in favor of Richard Villarreal, a Georgia man who, at the age of 49, completed an online application for a job as a regional sales representative for R. J. Reynolds, the tobacco company. Not hearing a response, he continued to apply for the job for a total of six times, and each time was unsuccessful. As it turned out, Reynolds used a set of "resume review guidelines" to screen potential employees not on the basis of age (which would have clearly been prohibited) but on the basis of years out of college (2 to 3) and number of years previously working in sales (no more than 10). In fact, of the over 1,000 job applicants hired over a 3-year period, only 19 were over the age of 40. Villarreal sued successfully and therefore set a precedent for applicants to be affected by discrimination, not only current workers.

Despite the reach of ADEA not only to the workplace, but also to hiring, ageism still exists and can take many forms, ranging from biases against the abilities of older workers to stereotyped beliefs about their personalities and work attitudes (O'Laughlin et al., 2017). One study found that 29% of older workers experienced the "soft" form of age discrimination involving the interpersonal sphere. Women and workers whose jobs were precarious seem particularly likely to be targets of this more subtle form of age discrimination (Stypinska & Turek, 2017).

Social cognitive career theory helps to explain why older workers who experience age discrimination, particularly the interpersonal variety, are likely to become dissatisfied. Older workers who feel that their contributions are not valued, or who experience ageism on the job, will have lower vocational satisfaction as their core self-evaluations erode in the face of an unsupportive work environment (Foley & Lytle, 2015). The potential for the older employees to feel negative emotions is also heightened if their supervisors are considerably younger than they are (Kunze & Menges, 2017).

Level of occupation is yet another factor to be considered in vocational satisfaction, as a person in a managerial position who is earning a high salary has the resources to invest time and energy in nonwork options. Of course, a higher level of employment may involve higher daily job demands, leading to less time for leisure pursuits. Individual differences in the extent to which an adult believes

in the "work ethic" may also interact with the age–job satisfaction relationship. Older employees who continue to feel engaged in their work will be more likely to be able to fend off perceived age discrimination, even putting off their retirement age (Bayl-Smith & Griffin, 2014). Identifying oneself as an "older worker" may not, therefore, negatively impact the individual's perceived involvement in the job.

AGE AND VOCATIONAL PERFORMANCE

We've seen how individuals feel about their jobs throughout the years of adulthood. Now it's time to evaluate how well people perform in these jobs. As you might imagine, there are a host of variables to consider in addition to age, including education, occupational status, health, cognitive functioning, and personality. The core components of the job, or the tasks that employees need to have to perform successfully, serve a major role in determining the quality of older workers' performance. Additionally, workplace behaviors influence older workers' ability to contribute to the organizational environment, which, in turn, influences the productivity of all employees.

Figure 10.8 provides a "scorecard" for evaluating older workers' performance. On the loss side, older workers will encounter difficulty in jobs that require strength or

FIGURE 10.8

Age and Work Performance Scorecard

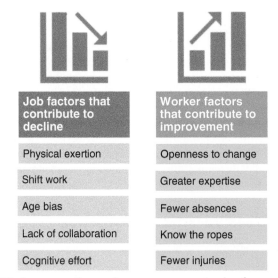

Job factors that contribute to decline	Worker factors that contribute to improvement
Physical exertion	Openness to change
Shift work	Greater expertise
Age bias	Fewer absences
Lack of collaboration	Know the ropes
Cognitive effort	Fewer injuries

Whether age contributes to better or poorer vocational performance depends on the balance between the factors that contribute to decline and those that contribute to improvement.

agility beyond their capability. Jobs that require a great deal of exertion such as stooping, physical effort, kneeling, crouching, and lifting present more injury risks for older workers (Fraade-Blanar et al., 2017). Shift work requiring changing work hours is a second job factor that will make the job more difficult for older workers due to age changes in circadian rhythm (Bonnefond et al., 2006).

From the employee's perspective, a corporate culture that fails to guard against biases toward older employees can also create a work environment that negatively affects their job performance. In a simulation of a mail-sorting task on a desktop computer, workers who were primed with negative age stereotypes performed with less accuracy than those who received positive unconscious priming (Kirchner et al., 2017).

In a similar vein, employers who exclude older workers from opportunities to collaborate may also ensure that the "age handicap" remains in the way these employees are able to contribute. When older employees are able to meet in a collaborative fashion with other workers, they are able to be more productive (Guillén & Kunze, 2019).

Finally, job tasks that require speeded performance, attention, working memory, and flexibility can present a greater challenge to older workers, as was shown in a flight simulator study of pilots. However, pilot expertise was found to compensate, to some extent, for those cognitive changes (Van Benthem & Herdman, 2016).

In looking at other positive attributes of older workers, tenure becomes more important than age (Ng & Feldman, 2013). Thus, workers who have been in the job longer are better able to navigate the system, because they know whom to consult when something needs to be done. Having learned the ropes is also valuable in helping employees with longer tenure to understand the negative consequences of taking involuntary absences. Finally, their tendency to be more careful can also help older workers avoid injury and therefore have better safety records.

Willingness to consider change is another characteristic of older workers that can contribute to better job performance. Countering the stereotype that older workers are resistant to change, researchers have found that not only is this untrue, but also that higher openness to change is related to the better job performance of older workers (Kunze et al., 2013).

The findings on age and job performance, like those in the area of vocational satisfaction, point to the importance of applying knowledge about adult development and aging in general to specific questions relating to older workers. From a human resources perspective, managers need to attend to the varying capabilities of workers of different ages and also to take into account age dynamics as they play out in the workplace, balancing the complementary strengths of workers of younger and older ages. In such environments, all workers can achieve their maximum performance while also feeling that they have something worthwhile to contribute in the workplace.

RETIREMENT

Retirement may be the furthest thing from your mind if you are a college student in your late teens or early 20s. You are most likely concentrating on finding a job rather than retiring from one. Ideally, you will find a job that you enjoy and that will also give you a solid basis for being able to spend 10 or 20 years (or more!) enjoying your retirement years.

Many people think of retirement as an event that is marked by a ceremony such as the proverbial "gold watch" given to the retiree as thanks for years of loyal service. This traditional image of retirement was never really true, however. Even when careers had more predictable trajectories, people often continued to maintain some type of employment after they had retired from their primary job. The definition of retirement is becoming even murkier with current changes in labor force participation by individuals in their middle and later years, as you will soon learn.

The economy's health affects not only the financial security of the employed, but also the financial security of the retired. Interest rates, tax policies, inflation, and the overall growth of the economy are some of the factors that determine the amount of money that retired individuals receive from their various sources of income. Policies being decided upon now by governments around the world will affect billions of older individuals in the decades to come. You might feel as though you are years away from retirement and therefore are not affected by these debates, but they are affecting your current paycheck now and will continue to have an impact on your financial stability throughout the rest of your life.

Definitions of Retirement

Retirement is defined simply as the withdrawal of an individual in later life from the labor force. However, for most workers, retirement occurs in a series of phases through which they progress at least once, if not several, times throughout their lives.

Because retirement is not simply an event with a defined start and end point, it is best conceptualized in terms of a period of adjustment (Wang & Shultz, 2010). The retirement process occurs over five phases, as shown in Figure 10.9. People experience an anticipatory period that may last for decades. Eventually, they make the decision

FIGURE 10.9

Retirement Process

Anticipatory period
Changes in work attitudes
Financial assessment

Decision to retire
Announcement of
retirement date
Financial preparation

Official retirement
Final day of work
Recognition by employers
and coworkers

Initial adjustment
Shifts in use of time
Financial adaptation

Stabilization
Adaptation to
nonworking role

Bridge employment
Blurred retirement
Continued involvement in
labor force

Retirement is best thought of as a process that evolves over stages until stabilization is achieved.

to retire. After their last day of work in the particular job (the act of retirement), workers go through an initial adjustment period followed, ultimately, by a more or less final restructuring of their activity patterns.

Complicating this picture is the fact that fewer and fewer workers are showing the crisp retirement pattern, in which they leave the labor force in a single, unreversed, clear-cut exit. More typically, retirees show the blurred retirement pattern, in which they exit and reenter the labor force several times. Some accept bridge employment, which is when retirees work in a completely different occupation than they had during most of their adult life. For example, an insurance agent may retire from the insurance business but work as a crossing guard or server at a fast-food restaurant. Other workers may retire from one job in a company and accept another role in the same company.

In general, involvement in bridge employment is strongly related to financial need. Workers who have a long, continuous history of employment in private sector jobs tend not to seek bridge employment because they typically have sufficient financial resources (Davis, 2003).

Ultimately, the criteria for retirement are met when an individual in later life with a cohesive past work pattern has not worked for a sustained period of time and is not psychologically invested in work any longer (Beehr et al., 2000).

Facts About Retirement

Retirement is in many ways a 20th-century phenomenon (Sterns & Gray, 1999). Throughout the 1700s and mid-1800s, very few people retired—a trend that continued into the 1900s; in 1900, about 70% of all men over 65 years were still in the labor force. The jobs held

by older workers often held high status and prestige. The wisdom and experience of older workers were valued, and it was considered a benefit to society to have them continuing to contribute to the workplace. However, by the early 1930s, pressures on the economy in combination with the growth of unions led to the first instance in the United States of compulsory retirement (in the railroad industry). Because older workers were forced to retire but did not receive retirement benefits, they lived in poverty.

In 1935, spearheaded by President Franklin D. Roosevelt, the U.S. Congress passed the Social Security Act, federal legislation that guarantees income for retirees and others who are unable to work as well as a lump sum in death benefits for survivors. By 1940, the number of older workers in the labor force had dropped to slightly over 40%; this number has continued to decrease. Social Security payments are divided into Old-Age and Survivors Insurance (OASI) and Disability Insurance (DI). Old Age and Survivors Disability Insurance (OASDI) combines OASI and DI.

As of 2019, 46.4 million people in the United States over the age of 65 were receiving Social Security benefits (Social Security Administration, 2019a). Social Security benefits represent about one-third of the income of people 65 and older. Half of married couples and 70% of unmarried persons receive 50% or more of their income from Social Security (Social Security Administration, 2019b).

U.S. political leaders are struggling with the economic ramifications brought about by the growth of the older population. Social Security benefits continue to rise, placing greater strain on the economy as a whole. Medical insurance, which is also paid out by the Social Security Administration, is also rising at astronomical rates. To understand how this crisis came about, you need to know how Social Security is funded.

The OASDI trust fund receives its income from Social Security payroll taxes on current U.S. workers. It is a "pay-as-you-go" system, meaning that, like a pay-as-you-go phone, Social Security can only pay out what is paid into it; in other words, it is not pre-funded as is true for a retirement pension plan. However, OASDI invests whatever excess payments it receives, including interest, into the OAS and DI trust funds (asset accounts). Figure 10.10 answers the question that is probably on your mind, which is whether there will be any funds left to pay your own Social Security when you reach the age of 65. The answer appears to be "yes," but only 79% of what is due to you. Therefore,

FIGURE 10.10

The Future of Social Security

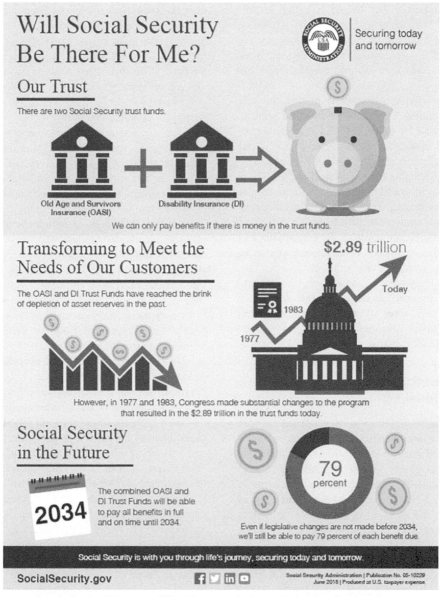

Many younger workers wonder whether Social Security will be able to provide them with their benefits when they retire.

Source: From U.S. Social Security Administration. Public Domain.

it is important as you plan for retirement that you look into funding other options for yourself such as private Investment Retirement Accounts (401K's).

Other Western countries are also facing questions about the future of their government pension programs. The European Union (EU) countries such as France, Germany, Italy, and Greece are grappling with an aging population that will need to be supported by a smaller workforce. As a result, EU nations are beginning to examine stronger incentives to reduce early retirement and keep more older workers in the labor force (European Union, 2019). Indeed, a group of researchers in the United Kingdom recommended that, to keep older workers in the workforce longer, employers should more consciously recognize the contributions of older workers and create a less toxic work environment that leads them to exit prematurely (Carr et al., 2016).

Changing demographics are clearly putting pressure on the global economy to ensure the financial security of retired individuals. It is likely that a combination of later retirement, longer involvement in the workforce, and difficult decisions by policy makers will be needed sooner rather than later. Changing the norms in countries whose pension systems support early retirement or retirement at age 65 may require putting more efforts into making continued employment seem more attractive such as making work more challenging, appreciating the contributions of older workers, reducing physical demands, and, of course, providing financial incentives (Rijs et al., 2012).

Now that you know some of the scope of the problem, you can see why we stated at the outset that knowledge about retirement even while you are in college may help you as you think about your own future and that of your family.

The Effects of Retirement on the Individual

Until the 1960s, most American workers resisted the idea of retiring because they believed that retirement would place their financial security at risk. However, succeeding generations of workers are viewing retirement more positively. In part, this is true because their retirement earnings are higher than that was for past older Americans. Just as importantly, with the abolition of mandatory retirement for most jobs, older workers no longer feel forced out of the labor market.

Furthermore, retired individuals no longer necessarily experience the poor health, low income, and loss of status that was associated with exit from the labor force earlier in the 1900s. Many older individuals can also look forward to

a healthy period of retirement in which they can continue to pursue part-time work as desired, travel, spend time with family, and move to more comfortable climates or housing situations.

The increasingly outdated view of retirement as an unwanted life change fits most closely with the role theory of retirement, which proposes that retirement has deleterious effects because the loss of the work role loosens the ties between the individual and society.

The continuity theory of retirement proposes that retired individuals maintain their self-concept and identity over the retirement transition. Even though they are no longer reporting for work on a daily basis, they are able to engage in many of the same activities they did when they were working. In addition, a retired person remains a retired "X" in his or her community, a status conferred officially in some professions as in retired professors who are referred to as "emeritus." These two theories focus on retirement as an isolated event.

The life course perspective on retirement proposes that changes in the work role in later life are best seen as logical outgrowths of earlier life events. The factors that shaped the individual's prior vocational development will have a persisting influence throughout retirement.

According to the resource model of retirement, the individual's adjustment to retirement reflects his or her physical, cognitive, motivational, financial, social, and emotional resources; the more resources, the more favorable will be the individual's adjustment at any one point through the retirement transition (Wang & Shi, 2014). Indeed, the resource model is a form of continuity theory, in that an individual's resources prior to retirement also predict the resources that will be available through the retirement years (Wetzel et al., 2019).

The resource model fits well with the biopsychosocial perspective, as shown in Figure 10.11. As you can see from Figure 10.11, physical changes and health are important biological contributions to retirement adjustment. Individuals with higher levels of physical functioning, and those in good health, are better able to enjoy retirement pursuits, and may also be better able to take advantage of bridge employment opportunities. From a psychological perspective, retirees who view retirement with a positive set of expectations will be able to adapt better to retirement, perhaps invoking a sense of mastery about their ability to make the transition work for them (Muratore & Earle, 2015).

Related to expectations, the timing of the retirement decision is another key factor influencing the individual's ability to adapt, easing the transition to retirement can be helped by invoking a sense of mastery, or the belief in one's ability to adapt successfully (Muratore & Earl, 2015).

FIGURE 10.11

Biopsychosocial Model of Retirement

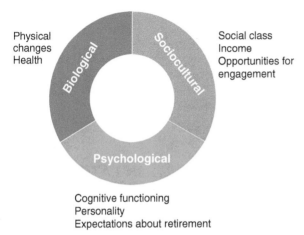

Physical
changes
Health

Social class
Income
Opportunities for
engagement

Cognitive functioning
Personality
Expectations about retirement

Retirement is best thought of as a biopsychosocial process.

Voluntarily retiring, instead of being forced to retire through downsizing, also promotes better adaptation (Clarke et al., 2012). The amount of time allowed for retiring is another related factor. A minimum planning time of 2 years prior to retirement is related to a positive retirement experience compared with a decision made 6 months or less prior to retirement (Hardy & Quadagno, 1995). As important as length of time, however, is the quality of retirement planning, which should include not only financial planning but also adequate discussion with the individual's spouse or partner (Noone et al., 2009).

From a sociocultural perspective, individuals with more disposable income or higher income security can, for example, support a more active retirement lifestyle including travel and recreation. People at the high end of the social class scale are less likely to retire than people at the lower end and the higher-SES individuals tend to retire at a later age. When they do retire, those higher in social class tend to be in better health than are people at lower socioeconomic levels and also have longer life expectancy (Majer et al., 2011). Their advantaged economic security also means that they are better able to take advantage of the opportunities that retirement offers them to engage in productive and enjoyable leisure activities, such as involvement in retirement learning communities and the opportunity to travel. Individuals with higher levels of education and previous experience in managerial or professional positions may be better able to find part-time employment after retirement if they desire it. Past experience in community organizations and activities may

also make it easier for such individuals to find rewarding opportunities for unpaid volunteer work and participation in clubs, organizations, and informal networks.

Compared to blue-collar workers, then, individuals in middle-class and higher jobs appear to have greater discretion in retiring when they want to, rather than when they are forced to do so by factors outside of their control (Solem et al., 2016). The dilemma is particularly pressing among European workers with unstable work histories, who may have difficulty remaining employed so they can ensure a comfortable standard of living postretirement (Hofäcker, 2015).

Thus, the continuity of an individual's work career is a further influence on the impact of retirement. Those in orderly careers spend the majority of their employed years in a series of related occupations. The higher the extent of orderliness in people's careers, the higher their attachments to their communities, friends, and social activities. The social integration that these individuals maintain during their careers eases their retirement transition and means that they are likely to be in better physical and psychological health. Individuals with more continuous work histories also have higher socioeconomic status and income than those in disorderly careers, and these are factors generally related to greater satisfaction with retirement.

A final factor to consider when examining variations in preretirement characteristics of older workers relates to the role of intrinsic factors in work motivation. As identified in a study of French-Canadian teachers (Houlfort et al., 2015), there is a type of passion that is beneficial for retirement adjustment and one that is not. In "harmonious" passion, work becomes part of an individual's identity and fits, most closely, the idea of autonomous work motivation. In "obsessive" passion, the individual needs work to validate his or her self-esteem. Having harmonious passion for work, among these teachers, positively predicted retirement adjustment; the converse was true for obsessive passion. Thus, the ways in which work satisfies an individual's needs seems to play an important role in influencing the impact that retirement has on that individual's sense of well-being. When work is seen as important for maintaining self-esteem, then, the loss of the role will be more devastating than when work is seen as an expression of personal identity.

There has been somewhat of a debate in the literature concerning the effect of retirement on a married couple's relationship. One school of thought describes the "spouse underfoot syndrome," whereby partners are more likely to experience conflict now that they are in each other's presence for most of the daytime and nighttime hours (the spouse who is underfoot is typically the husband).

However, there is a contrasting view of retirement as a second honeymoon, in which couples are now free to enjoy each other's company on a full-time basis, without the constraints presented by having to leave home for 8 or more hours a day. The couple may benefit from improved health of the retired spouse, although there is no evidence that this improved health has a spillover effect on the partner (Messe et al., 2019).

Shedding light on this debate, there is evidence that men and women engage in more equitable division of household tasks than they did prior to retirement. The convergence of the gender gap in everyday chores after retirement may be one of the factors that helps to promote a couple's feelings of satisfaction with retirement as a whole (Leopold & Skopek, 2015).

The factors that influence retirement adjustment do appear to differ between women and men. Men operate according to the "usual" mode of retirement view, in which decisions regarding retirement do not involve the family. According to the new mode of retirement perspective, the characteristics of the person's spouse and lifelong family responsibilities play a role in retirement decisions and adjustment. Current cohorts of older women are more likely to operate according to the new modes of retirement; they are more likely than men to be influenced by the health, financial security, and work status of their spouses. However, among couples raised with more egalitarian values, both are likely to be influenced increasingly by the work status of their spouses (Pienta, 2003).

Given the increase in the size of the retirement population and the increase in life expectancy, there is reason to expect that the field of retirement planning will continue to show strides. The resource model provides an excellent framework for such developments, as retirement planners must take into account not only an individual's financial situation but also the intersection of health, psychological, and sociocultural factors (França & Hershey, 2018). Retirees still wish to "matter" even though they may have given up their role in the workplace (Froidevaux et al., 2016).

LEISURE PURSUITS IN LATER ADULTHOOD

Throughout adulthood, people express themselves not only in their work lives but also through their hobbies and interests. Occupational psychologists and academics studying the relationship between job characteristics and satisfaction often neglect the fact that, for many adults, it is the off-duty hours rather than the on-duty hours that contribute the most to identity and personal satisfaction. In contrast, marketers recognize the value of developing promotional campaigns that appeal to the aging Baby Boomers who potentially have resources to spend on leisure pursuits (Ferguson & Brohaugh, 2010).

As people move through adulthood and into retirement, it becomes more crucial for them to develop leisure

FIGURE 10.12

Functions of Leisure Pursuits in Adulthood

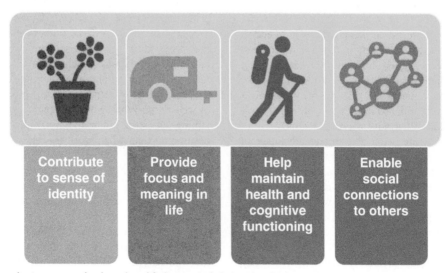

| Contribute to sense of identity | Provide focus and meaning in life | Help maintain health and cognitive functioning | Enable social connections to others |

Leisure pursuits can play important roles throughout life, but particularly in retirement.

interests so that they will have activities to engage in during the day to provide focus and meaning to their lives. In addition, leisure pursuits can serve important functions by helping older adults maintain their health through physical activity and their cognitive functioning through intellectual stimulation. The social functions of leisure are also of potential significance, particularly for people who have become widowed or have had to relocate due to finances, a desire for more comfortable climates, or poor health. These functions are summarized in Figure 10.12.

That regular leisure-time physical activity can have important health consequences was shown in a longitudinal study in Sweden that followed men over five time points (Byberg et al., 2009). Participants were asked about their level of physical activity with questions such as, "Do you often go walking or cycling for pleasure?" People who engaged in physical activity in their leisure time died at later ages than those who did not over the 35-year period of the study. Another follow-up in Sweden of over 1,800 men and women ages 75 and older showed that the protective effect of physical activity on mortality continued into the 90s, an effect enhanced by engaging in other healthy lifestyle behaviors, particularly not smoking (Rizzuto et al., 2012).

The impact of leisure activities on health also extends to a reduced risk of neurocognitive disorder, including Alzheimer's disease (Tolppanen et al., 2015). These benefits also include stress reduction, thus helping to support immune functioning (Lin et al., 2012).

Another approach to understanding the satisfaction older adults can obtain from leisure activities comes from "Innovation Theory." According to this view, older adults who become involved with a new leisure activity may experience a range of psychological benefits, including enhanced sense of meaning in life and well-being and even a feeling of self-reinvention.

Travel is a leisure activity that often takes people out of their comfort zone and can therefore stimulate these benefits. Using responses from Israeli participants in a mail-in survey reporting on their most recent vacations involving travel, Nimrod and Rotem (2012) defined a group of "absolute" innovators (the most extreme) who were most likely to say that they took the trip in order to participate in new activities, try new food, learn something new about their relationships, gain a new skill, and learn something new about themselves and life in general. This group, comprising about one-fifth of the sample, shared many similarities with the noninnovators in the activities engaged in while traveling. However, the groups differed in some of the activities they engaged in while on vacation. The innovators were more likely to visit small towns and villages rather than big cities, getting to know the local people, gambling, and engaging in physical exercise,

and using travel to find opportunities for growth and self-expression. Unlike the noninnovators, the absolute innovators used travel to find opportunities for growth and self-expression. Clearly, retirement involving such active leisure-time pursuits can facilitate the individual's overall well-being even long after the vacation is over.

Harkening back to activity theory, maintaining an active social life in retirement seems to have a variety of benefits in promoting retirement adjustment. Among a sample of Australian retirees, those who participated in a wider variety of social activities had higher levels of positive affect and, importantly, were higher in their self-efficacy and feelings of mastery (Earl et al., 2015).

In conclusion, changes in the labor force, the meaning of work, and the economic realities of an aging population all affect the nature of work and the workplace. As you contemplate your future career, your top priority should be thinking about what you will find to be most fulfilling.

SUMMARY

1. Work is a major focus of adult life from the 20s until retirement and beyond. Labor force age dynamics have shifted with movement of the Baby Boom generation and the aging of the labor force. There are disparities by race and gender in income levels, even controlling for educational attainment.

2. Contemporary vocational psychology is oriented primarily around Holland's RIASEC theory of vocational development, which is the basis for O*NET, a comprehensive catalog of occupations. The highest level of worker satisfaction and productivity is theorized to occur when there is congruence between persons and their environments. Super's self-concept theory proposes that individuals move through several stages of career development, in which they attempt to maximize the expression of their self-concept in their work. Rather than proceed straight through these stages, however, individuals may plateau at the maintenance stage or recycle through earlier stages after a career change. The ideas of vocation as a calling and the boundaryless and protean careers provide support for the need to view career development from more than a life-stage perspective.

3. Theories and research on vocational satisfaction attempt to determine the relative influence of intrinsic and extrinsic factors on a worker's happiness and productivity in a job. Occupational reinforcement patterns are the work values and needs that are likely to be satisfied in a job, and if these are present, the individual will be more satisfied. Self-determination theory proposes

that the greatest job satisfaction occurs when needs for competence, autonomy, and relatedness intersect. Conflict between work and family is a source of potential vocational dissatisfaction. There is not a clear-cut relationship between age and job satisfaction but job tenure appears to play an important role as do factors related to the nature of the work environment.

4. The question of whether older workers are as productive as younger workers is another focus of occupational research. There is a balance between the factors that predict improved performance and those that predict declines in performance. In general, older workers are disadvantaged when a job places heavy demands on speed and physical strength, and perform better when their organization's culture allows them to collaborate and use their expertise.

5. Retirement is defined as the individual's withdrawal from the labor force in later life. Rather than being a discrete event, however, for most people, it spans a process that may last for years. Most retired people do not suffer a loss of health, either mental or physical, but some do experience the transition as stressful. The resource model of retirement proposes that people will be most satisfied in retirement if they can draw on physical, psychological, and social sources of support.

6. Leisure activities can serve a variety of important functions for adults throughout their working lives, but particularly in later adulthood after retirement. Researchers have identified positive effects of leisure involvement on physical functioning, well-being, and ultimately mortality.

11

Mental Health Issues and Treatment

Recognizing mental health issues in older adults can be difficult since the symptoms are often attributed to the aging process. Here are some warning signs to watch out for indicating that older adults may need to seek mental health treatment.

AGEFEED

#warningsigns

1. Changes in **mood**
2. **Memory** loss
3. Change in **sleep habits**, such as difficulty sleeping or sleeping too much
4. Sudden decrease or increase in **appetite**
5. **Anger** or **irritability**
6. Inability to experience **positive emotions**
7. Feelings of **restlessness**
8. **Withdrawal** from family and friends
9. Engaging in **risky** behaviors
10. Difficulty maintaining **daily routines**

Up until this point in the book, we have focused primarily on people who fit the definition of "normal" as they navigate the adult years. We will now turn our attention to psychological disorders and how they affect individuals throughout their lives. By some accounts, over half of the entire adult population struggle with the symptoms of one or another disorder. However, it is important to keep in mind that the difference between normal and abnormal is often a matter of degree. Furthermore, psychological disorders reflect developmental processes that continue throughout life. Researchers are beginning to identify the roots of later life psychological disorders in early childhood traumatic experiences. Approximately one-third of older adults report some form of early trauma, such as parental psychopathology, physical or psychological abuse, and other traumatic life events. Having just one of these experiences increases significantly the odds of developing a psychological disorder, including substance use disorder (Rhee et al., 2019). From a biopsychosocial perspective, then, the balance of risk and protective factors as they evolve earlier in life have a cumulative impact in later adulthood (Whitbourne & Meeks, 2010).

PSYCHOLOGICAL DISORDERS IN ADULTHOOD

The criteria used to judge behavior as "abnormal" include feeling personal or subjective distress, being impaired in everyday life, causing a risk to the self or other people, and engaging in behavior that is socially or culturally unacceptable (Whitbourne, 2019). Psychological disorders include the range of behaviors and experiences that fall outside of social norms, create adaptational difficulty for the individual on a daily basis, and put the individual or others at risk of harm. People who have a hobby of collecting coins would not be considered abnormal, for example, because they are engaging in a behavior that does not hurt them or others and is culturally acceptable. By contrast, consider people known as "hoarders," who

collect old newspapers, magazines, and cereal boxes to the point that their homes become virtually uninhabitable. These individuals might very well be considered to have a psychological disorder: they are not only engaging in behavior that is outside the norm but may also be putting themselves and others at risk for fire, injury, or disease due to the dirt and debris that have accumulated in their home.

Clinicians diagnose people with psychological disorders using criteria set forth in the Diagnostic and Statistical Manual (DSM), which is the major reference used by mental health professionals in the United States and Canada to diagnose people with psychological disorders. Outside the United States and Canada, clinicians and researchers use the International Statistical Classification of Diseases and Related Health Problems (ICD), the reference guide to all medical illnesses, including psychological disorders.

The DSM has undergone numerous revisions since first introduced in 1952. The most recent version is the DSM-5 (American Psychiatric Association, 2013). As thorough as this manual is, it unfortunately does not address the fact that a number of psychological disorders are expressed differently in older adults, particularly those who also have medical conditions. Consequently, older adults may not receive treatment that reflects state-of-the-art approaches based on research on mental health and aging.

Lacking specific guidance from the diagnostic manual, health care professionals working with older adults may be caught up in ageist attitudes that affect their work (Whitbourne & Martins, 2020). As we summarized in Figure 11.1, one misguided assumption service providers may hold is that aging is automatically associated with poor mental health, particularly depression. Consequently, when older adults express symptoms of depression, a mental health professional may not regard these as either unusual or treatable. Second, it is likely that mental health professionals are younger than the older adults they serve, leading to the possibility that they react to their clients in the same way, for better or worse, as they do to their own family members. As a result, older adult mental health

FIGURE 11.1

Ageism and Its Effect on Service Provision

Prior to considering specific psychological disorders, it is worth pointing out these general biases that can limit mental health interventions with older adults.

patients may not get the benefit of the objectivity required of a treating professional.

Another way that ageism may affect service providers, as shown in Figure 11.1, is that they believe that older adults are no different than their other patients. As a result, the clinicians may fail to take into account special considerations relevant to aging, such as the co-occurrence of mental health issues with physical changes or chronic diseases.

Finally, the ageism that can affect service providers can also affect older adults with mental health needs. The patients themselves may feel that symptoms of depression or anxiety are a natural part of the aging process, and so they do not seek treatment when they develop what would otherwise be treatable conditions (Wuthrich & Frei, 2015).

Apart from the problems involved with ageism in service provision, affecting both older adults and treatment professionals, diagnosis of psychological disorders in older adults can be made more complicated by inaccurate symptom reporting by older adults. Their disorders may also be misdiagnosed because the symptoms of a psychological disorder occur in conjunction with a medical condition. Finally, adding to the problem, health professionals conducting the annual wellness visits allowed by Medicare may fail to conduct the recommended screening for psychological disorders (Pfoh et al., 2015).

Major Depressive Disorder

Individuals who experience prolonged and extreme sadness may be diagnosed with a form of depressive disorder, depending on the length and nature of the symptoms. In major depressive disorder, the major symptom is an extremely sad mood that lasts most of the time for at least 2 weeks and is not typical of the individual's usual mood. The individual may also experience other symptoms including appetite and sleep disturbances, feelings of guilt, difficulty concentrating, and a low sense of self-worth.

Though the prevalence of a diagnosable mood disorder is lower in older than in younger adults, many older adults report symptoms of depressive disorders. Among a sample of nearly 2,000 women aged 60 to 91 years, the rates of subclinical depression were estimated at 20%. However, among those seen in medical settings, such as inpatient hospitals or clinics, the rates of depressive symptoms can reach as high as 30% (Whitbourne & Meeks, 2010). Moreover, although women are more likely to experience the diagnosable condition of major depressive disorder, depressive symptoms are higher in men between the ages of 60 and 80. By that point, the rates of depressive symptoms in women and men are roughly equal (Patten et al., 2016).

There are age differences in the symptoms of depression, and what appears as a depressive symptom for a younger adult may not appear as one in an older adult. The traditionally recognized "psychological" symptoms of depression, such as dysphoria (sad mood), guilt, low self-esteem, and suicidal thoughts are less likely to be acknowledged by older adults.

When trying to determine the cause of an older adult's depression, it is important for health care workers to look for possible contributing factors (see Figure 11.2). These can include mobility limitations and pain due to musculoskeletal-related illnesses, including arthritis (Rathbun et al., 2019) and hip fracture (Liu et al., 2018). The chronic conditions of metabolic syndrome, diabetes, and hypertension can also increase the risk of depression in older adults (Kokkeler et al., 2019), as can stroke (Xekardaki et al., 2012). Sensory impairments, sleep disturbance, tooth loss (Rouxel et al., 2017), and deficiency in vitamins D and K are additional risk factors for depression in older adults (Bolzetta et al., 2019). Finally, individuals living in long-term care institutions are also at greater risk for depression (Chau et al., 2019).

Not only do physical conditions increase the risk of major depressive disorder, but older adults become more

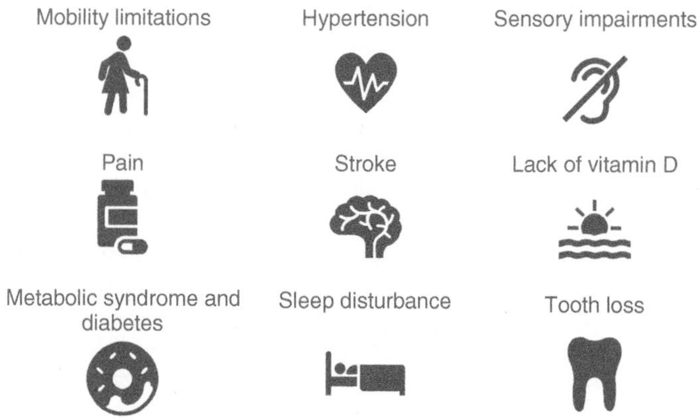

FIGURE 11.2

Contributors to Depression in Later Adulthood

A variety of physical conditions can contribute to the experience of depression in older adults.

likely to suffer further impairments in physical and cognitive functioning when their psychological symptoms are untreated (Olaya et al., 2019). Depressive symptoms predict mortality in older adults (Saeed Mirza et al., 2018). In one large-scale study of older adults living in the community followed for over 13 years, those with both depressive symptoms and diabetes had higher rates of mortality, reflecting higher levels of C-reactive protein (Castro-Costa et al., 2019).

Bipolar Disorder

Bipolar disorder is diagnosed in people who have experienced one or more manic episodes during which they feel elated, grandiose, expansive, and highly energetic. Formerly called manic depression, people with bipolar disorder may or may not have experienced a period of significant depression along with being manic for at least a week (bipolar I) or may have experienced depression and at least one "hypomanic" episode, in which their manic symptoms lasted for less than a week (bipolar II).

Researchers know considerably less about bipolar disorder in later life than they do about major depressive disorder (Dols et al., 2016). Estimates are that rates of bipolar disorder are relatively low in older adults, affecting 0.5% to 1.0% of the over-65 population (Sajatovic et al., 2015). Older adults with bipolar disorder have shorter life expectancies due to the higher co-occurrence, in this population, of other physical illnesses but the cause for this association is not yet known (Colpo et al., 2015).

Bipolar disorder exacts a high psychosocial cost on those who have experienced its symptoms throughout their lives. For example, older adults with a lifetime history of "rapid cycling," in which their symptoms alternate frequently between depression and mania, feel that their life goals were significantly interfered with if not entirely derailed (Sajatovic et al., 2008). Fortunately, lithium carbonate, the treatment of choice in bipolar disorder, appears highly effective in older adults (Fotso Soh, 2019). Additionally, older adults with bipolar disorder can benefit from a "prudent" lifestyle in which they avoid alcohol and smoking while also maintaining healthy weight and levels of physical activity (Almeida et al., 2018).

Anxiety Disorders

The main characteristic of an anxiety disorder is anxiety, a sense of dread about what might happen in the future. In addition to having the unpleasant feelings associated with anxiety, people with anxiety disorders go to great lengths to avoid anxiety-provoking situations. As a result, they may have difficulty performing their jobs, enjoying their leisure

FIGURE 11.3

Forms of Anxiety Disorder

- Generalized Anxiety Disorder
- Panic Disorder
- Agoraphobia
- Specific Phobia
- Social Anxiety Disorder

These are the five major forms of anxiety disorder, with specific phobia having the highest prevalence followed by social anxiety disorder.

pursuits, or engaging in social activities with their friends and families. The forms of anxiety disorder are shown in Figure 11.3. The implications of failing to diagnose anxiety disorders can be serious, as older adults with anxiety symptoms have higher rates of mortality, particularly among African American older adults (Brenes et al., 2007).

In the anxiety disorder known as generalized anxiety disorder, the individual experiences an overall sense of uneasiness and concern without a specific focus. People who have this disorder are very prone to worrying, especially over minor problems. They may also have additional symptoms, such as feeling restless and tense, having trouble concentrating, being irritable, and having difficulty sleeping.

The form of anxiety disorder known as panic disorder involves the experience of panic attacks, in which people have the physical sensation that they are about to die (e.g., shortness of breath, pounding heart, and sweating palms). People who suffer from a panic disorder may have these episodes at unpredictable times. Individuals may also experience agoraphobia, the fear of being in an open or crowded space, or of being in a space from which escape is difficult. People with agoraphobia avoid places such as elevators, shopping malls, or public transportation, where escape during an attack would be difficult.

The diagnosis of specific phobia is based on the individual's having an irrational fear of a particular object or situation. Almost any object or situation can form the target of a specific phobia. People can have phobias of anything from driving to syringes. The four categories of specific phobias include animals, the natural environment (storms, heights, and fires), blood-injection-injury (seeing blood, having an invasive medical procedure), and engaging in activities in particular situations (driving, flying, and being in an enclosed space). A fifth category of specific phobias includes a variety of miscellaneous stimuli or situations, such as a child's fear of clowns or an adult's fear of contracting a particular illness. You may have your own particularly bothersome situations or organisms, but to be diagnosable, they must be severe enough to interfere with your everyday functioning.

In social anxiety disorder, the individual experiences extreme anxiety about being watched by other people. The term, which was formerly called social phobia, is somewhat misleading in that it is not literally a fear of other people but a fear of being publicly embarrassed or made to look foolish. People with social anxiety disorder not only have difficulty in situations where they are actually being judged but also in situations that they believe involve the potential for judgment such as eating in the presence of other people.

Estimates are that anxiety disorders have a 12-month prevalence rate of 17.2% among those 65 and older. Agoraphobia is the most frequently reported anxiety disorder (4.9%), followed by panic disorder (3.8%), animal phobia (3.5%), general anxiety disorder (3.1%), and social anxiety disorder (1.3%). Women are twice as likely to be diagnosed with agoraphobia or general anxiety disorder compared to men (Canuto et al., 2018).

As is true for mood disorders, older adults may be reluctant about reporting their symptoms, or they may genuinely not realize that their symptoms are due to anxiety. Thus, they may report having somatic complaints rather than the experience of anxiety. Furthermore, as is true for mood disorders, older adults with anxiety disorders may actually have a medical condition that masks the anxiety symptoms or, conversely, exacerbates them. Furthermore, it is important to distinguish between disorders that first appear in later life and those that have persisted for years, if not decades. For example, an older adult living in a high-crime neighborhood may develop anxiety based on the fear of being victimized. As is true with depression, furthermore, health-related conditions can contribute to the experience of anxiety.

Obsessive-Compulsive and Related Disorders

People who experience obsessive-compulsive disorder suffer from obsessions, or repetitive thoughts (such as the belief that one's child will be harmed) and compulsions, which are repetitive behaviors (such as frequent hand washing). The obsessions and compulsions are unrelenting, irrational, and distracting. The most common compulsions involve repeating a specific behavior, such as washing and cleaning, counting, putting items in order, checking, or requesting assurance. Compulsions may also take the form of mental rituals, such as counting up to a certain number every time an unwanted thought intrudes.

Among older adults, the 1-month prevalence of obsessive-compulsive disorder is estimated to be 2.9%, but another 21% have obsessive-compulsive symptoms. Older adults with obsessive-compulsive disorder also appear to be more likely to be diagnosed with depression. Individuals whose symptoms include checking appear to have poorer memory than those with other symptoms, suggesting that there may be a cognitive component to this form of the disorder (Klenfeldt et al., 2014).

In the related disorder known as hoarding, people collect and store seemingly useless items that they cannot discard. You may have older adult relatives or neighbors who have a large number of items stored away in closets, garages, basements, or attics. People who have a lifetime of accumulated objects may very reasonably run out of room for their belongings, mementos, tools, or cooking-related objects. In hoarding disorder, the items can be as insignificant as outdated newspapers, mail, shopping bags, empty food containers, and even food remnants. People with hoarding disorder cannot dispose of these items because they are convinced that they will need them later, even though they have no clear utility. Their hoarding goes beyond a mere collecting or inability to dispose of precious mementos when accumulation of these objects threaten their health and safety.

The symptoms of hoarding disorder appear to worsen over the years of adulthood. Although some individuals begin to show evidence of hoarding in their teenage years, nearly one-quarter first become hoarders after the age of 40. Regardless of when the symptoms appear, the severity of the hoarding become worse over time (Dozier et al., 2016).

Trauma and Stress-Related Disorders

Exposure to trauma such as an earthquake, fire, physical assault, and war can lead individuals to experience symptoms that may last for a prolonged period of time, even after the trauma subsides. These symptoms include intrusion of distressing reminders of the event, dissociative symptoms such as feeling numb or detached from others, avoidance of situations that might serve as reminders of the event, and hyperarousal, including sleep disturbances or irritability. People are diagnosed with acute stress disorder if they experience these symptoms for up to a month after the trauma. The diagnosis of post-traumatic stress disorder (PTSD) is given to people whose symptoms persist for more than a month.

The symptoms of PTSD and related disorders, such as depression, can persist for many years. Survivors of the North Sea oil rig disaster in 1980 continued to experience symptoms of PTSD along with anxiety disorders (not including PTSD), depressive disorders, and substance use disorders that were significantly higher than those of a matched comparison group. Estimates are that at the age of 19, the prevalence of PTSD among Vietnam soldiers was 15%. It is likely that the rates of PTSD among the older adult population will grow in future years due to the aging of Vietnam veterans.

In a study of nearly 5,600 male veterans, those 60 years and older who were in the theater of operations were found to have a lifetime prevalence of 17%, compared to 6% who were not exposed to combat (Goldberg et al., 2016). As they age, combat veterans may be more vulnerable to current stressors suggesting that prior exposure to traumatic events sensitizes older adults to difficulties they encounter in later life (Sachs-Ericsson et al., 2016). Supporting the value of a lifespan perspective, findings from the Veterans Administration Normative Aging Study suggest that veterans with supportive environments in their childhood are less likely to experience PTSD symptoms after exposure to combat (Kang et al., 2016).

PTSD may also develop in older adults exposed to other forms of trauma including motor vehicle collisions (Platts-Mills et al., 2017), imprisonment (Flatt et al., 2017), and employment in emergency services such as firefighting (Milligan-Saville et al., 2017). Natural disasters present another risk for PTSD among older adults, as was the case in a study of Hurricane Sandy (New Jersey) survivors, although high levels of social cohesion were found to buffer against the development of symptoms.

Older adults with PTSD are at risk not only for the psychological consequences of the disorder but also for poorer physical health, including metabolic syndrome (Wolf & Schnurr, 2016). PTSD may also be associated with accelerated aging as indicated by shorter telomere length (Lohr et al., 2015) as well as with increased risk for developing neurocognitive disorders (Clouston et al., 2019).

The symptoms of PTSD may take decades to emerge after an individual has been exposed to trauma. **Late-onset stress symptomatology (LOSS)** refers to a phenomenon observed in aging veterans who were exposed to stressful combat situations in young adulthood and are now reexamining their past wartime experiences (Brady et al., 2019). Symptoms related to the combat experiences (such as an increase in memories about the trauma) begin to emerge in later life, perhaps as a function of exposure to stresses associated with aging, such as retirement and increased health problems (Davison et al., 2006). Symptoms of LOSS

are similar to those of PTSD, but the progression is distinct in that it develops later in life and may exist at levels below the threshold for a PTSD diagnosis (Potter et al., 2013).

Schizophrenia and Other Psychotic Disorders

The term schizophrenia refers to a disorder in which individuals experience distorted perception of reality and impairment in thinking, behavior, affect, and motivation. Individuals with schizophrenia do not experience these symptoms continuously, but to receive the diagnosis, they must have displayed them for a significant period of time during a 1-month period.

The types of symptoms people with schizophrenia experience include delusions (false beliefs), hallucinations (false perceptions), disorganized and incoherent speech, very unusual motor behavior, and what are called the "negative" symptoms of apathy, withdrawal, and lack of emotional expression. While their symptoms are active, they are unable to get or hold onto a job, remain in a relationship, or take care of themselves. These symptoms must have lasted for 6 months or more, and the individual must not have another diagnosis (such as drug or alcohol abuse) that could better explain the symptoms. In addition to providing the overall diagnosis, clinicians use rating scales that are new to the DSM-5 in which they evaluate the severity of each of these types of symptoms.

Schizophrenia is relatively rare, affecting 0.28% of the population at any one time. However, the global disease burden is increasing as a result of population growth and aging (Charlson et al., 2018).

Lifestyle factors lead individuals with schizophrenia to have higher rates of mortality. In a 6-year longitudinal study of over 1 million patients with schizophrenia between the ages of 20 and 64, mortality rates were more than 3.5 times the rate for adults in the general population. The majority of these deaths were related to use of tobacco, alcohol, and other drugs that led to cardiovascular and respiratory diseases as well as higher rates of accidental deaths (Olfson et al., 2015). Additionally, 15% of individuals with schizophrenia die as a result of suicide, and up to 50% make a suicide attempt at some point in their lives (Harvey & Bowie, 2013).

Compared to other psychological disorders, the course and outcome of schizophrenia are poorer (Jobe & Harrow, 2010). During the first 10 to 15 years, people with schizophrenia have more recurrent episodes and their chances of completely recovering, even after the first 10 years, are worse than those of people with other disorders. Most people continue to experience psychotic symptoms and disordered thinking, as well as negative symptoms. They are less able to obtain or keep a job. On the positive side, however, if they receive treatment during their acute phase, as many half may recover or experience significant improvement (Vita & Barlati, 2018). The long-term outcomes are somewhat poorer for individuals whose symptoms are considered "negative," in that they involve apathy and lack of ability to experience emotions (Ventura et al., 2015).

A debate in the literature involves a condition known as late-onset schizophrenia, a form of the disorder originating in adults over the age of 45 years. Individuals who develop symptoms of schizophrenia late in life appear to be influenced less by the factors that lead to schizophrenia in younger adults, including heredity, and more by psychosocial stressors such as unemployment (Chen et al., 2018). The question remains, however, as to whether the schizophrenia that develops late in life is a fundamentally different subtype than earlier onset schizophrenia (Cohen, 2018).

Substance-Related Disorders

The majority of adults who abuse or are dependent on alcohol or illicit drugs are in their late teens and early 20s; however, the overall numbers and percentages of older adults are on the rise with the aging of the Baby Boom generation. The legal use of both recreational and medical marijuana may also change patterns of substance use among middle-aged and older adults in the coming years.

Substance use disorders involve the use of alcohol and/or drugs to a degree that causes clinically significant impairment, including health problems, disability, and failure to meet major responsibilities at work, school, or home. In 2017, as estimated by the Substance Abuse and Mental Health Services Administration (SAMHSA, 2018), 30.5 million people aged 12 or older had used an illicit drug in the past 30 days (considered to represent current use), which corresponds to an overall rate of 11.2%. Among the 30.5 million people aged 12 or older who were current illicit drug users, 26.0 million were current marijuana users and 3.2 million were current misusers of prescription pain relievers. Smaller numbers of people were current users of cocaine, hallucinogens, methamphetamine, inhalants, or heroin or were current misusers of prescription tranquilizers, stimulants, or sedatives.

Although illicit drug use does not necessarily constitute a substance use disorder, data from SAMHSA's yearly reports provide indications of the extent to which the risk exists in the population. Figure 11.4 shows the age distribution of illicit drug use within the past year. As you can see, young adults between 25 and 34 years of age have the highest use of all illicit drugs (34.3%), and the percentages drop with each succeeding decade until age 65 and older (5.7%) (SAMHSA, 2018).

Figure 11.5 summarizes SAMHSA's 2018 data on types of illicit drugs used by Americans 65 years of age and older. As you can see, marijuana use is the highest among this age group, a percent that might change as marijuana use becomes legalized. After marijuana, prescription drugs,

FIGURE 11.4

Illicit Substance Use by Age

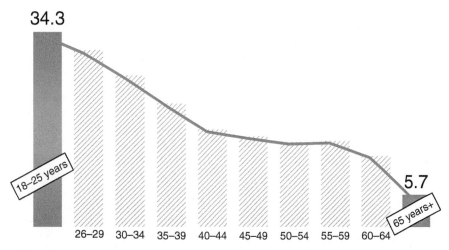

As shown here, illicit substance use decreases across success age groups. The data represent the percent of those in each age group who are users of any illicit substance within the past year.

FIGURE 11.5

Illicit Drug Use in Adults 65 and Older, U.S. 2017

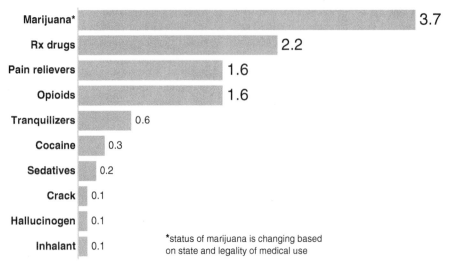

This figure shows the percent of individuals 65 and older in the United States who use each of the above substances.

pain relievers, opioids, and tranquilizers become the second largest category of drugs misused by older adults. The percentages of users of these medications are far higher, with almost half of those 65 and older using a prescription psychotherapeutic in the past year, and 36% having used pain relievers. Thus, older adults are at greatest risk from the abuse of prescription pain relievers.

You may not associate excessive drinking with older adults, but as the SAMHSA data show, there is a substantial number of people 65 and older who engage in binge or heavy alcohol use (see Figure 11.6). Older individuals who abuse alcohol are at risk of developing cirrhosis of the liver (a terminal condition) as well as higher rates of injury due to hip fractures and motor vehicle accidents. Alcohol use is also associated with greater risk of adverse reactions from both psychotherapeutic medications and over-the-counter pain and allergy medications. Individuals with a lifetime history of alcohol use are also at increased risk of developing diabetes, congestive heart failure, osteoporosis, and mood disorders (National Institute on Alcohol Abuse and Alcoholism, 2013).

Again, going against what is most likely your view that alcohol abuse is a problem of younger individuals, including those living in college communities, there appear to be relatively high rates of alcohol use in settings in which only older adults live, such as nursing homes and retirement communities (Fishleder et al., 2016). People with a history of problem drinking and those who retired involuntarily seem most likely to abuse alcohol after they enter retirement (Kuerbis & Sacco, 2012).

Long-term alcohol abuse may lead older adults to develop neurocognitive disorders, as we discussed in Chapter 5. However, among otherwise neurocognitively healthy older individuals, the long-term effects of alcohol use may depend on other factors as well, particularly education, sex, age, race, and smoking history (Kalapatapu et al., 2017). As we have seen before, smoking is a lifestyle factor that interacts with other threats to the health of older adults. Alcohol use still involves risks for older adults, but the role of smoking must be taken into account when examining effects on cognition (Figure 11.6).

Personality Disorders

A personality disorder is a long-standing pattern of inner experience and behavior that has maladaptive qualities. The DSM-5 includes diagnostic criteria for 10 personality disorders, all of which are characterized by significant and chronic difficulties in everyday life. Clinicians diagnosing individuals with personality disorders may also use an optional system in the DSM-5 based on personality traits similar to those in the Five-Factor Model.

Several personality disorders are of particular relevance with regard to aging. Antisocial personality disorder is characterized by psychopathy, a set of traits that include lack of remorse and an impulsive lifestyle. The traits associated with psychopathy fall into two dimensions (Hare & Neumann, 2006). Factor 1 is a cluster of traits that represent disturbances in the capacity to experience emotions

FIGURE 11.6

Alcohol Use by Age

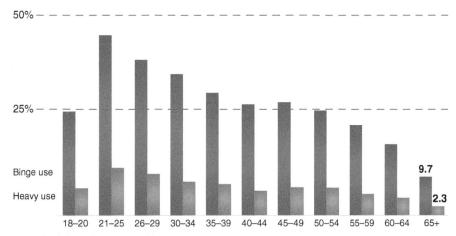

Alcohol use by age group, divided into binge use and heavy use.

such as empathy, guilt, and remorse. This cluster also includes manipulativeness, egocentricity, and callousness. Factor 2 incorporates the unstable and impulsive behaviors that contribute to the socially deviant lifestyle of the individual with this disorder.

Older adults diagnosed previously in life with antisocial personality disorder are less likely to exhibit the symptoms associated with the socially deviant and impulsive component of psychopathy (Boudreaux et al., 2019). Rates of criminal offending are known to be lower among older adults (Matthews & Minton, 2018). Figure 11.7 illustrates, among a Canadian population, the lower probability of criminal offenses across adulthood, which is most pronounced for the most frequent crime of criminal assault (Allen, 2016).

The majority of men showing antisocial behavior are the so-called "adolescence-limited." Less common are the "life-course persistent" offenders whose antisocial behavior continues throughout adulthood (Moffitt et al., 2018). These findings support the view that the developmental course of antisocial personality disorder is to show at least some improvement over time.

Changes over adulthood in the impulsive and antisocial element of psychopathy may reflect a number of influences other than changes in the personality disorder itself, however. Once again, we return to an explanation involving survivor or attrition effects. The apparent decrease in antisocial behavior may reflect the fact that people who were high on Factor 2 (impulsivity) of psychopathy are no longer alive. In addition to having been killed in violent crime or due to drug or alcohol abuse, people with antisocial personality disorder have a higher rate of mortality due

to suicide, HIV infection (reflecting substance use, needle sharing, and multiple sex partners), cancer, COPD, and (Krasnova et al., 2019).

Another personality disorder studied in later adulthood is borderline personality disorder (BPD), a diagnosis given to people who show symptoms that include extreme instability in sense of self and relationships with others, sexual impulsivity, fear of abandonment, repeated suicide attempts, and difficulties controlling their emotions.

The majority of individuals with BPD describe their symptoms as first manifesting in adolescence, if not before the age of 13. The factors associated with increased risk of developing BPD include family adversity, limited social resources (wealth and education), psychopathology in the mother, harsh parenting, sexual abuse or neglect, and symptoms of other disorders such as substance abuse.

The symptoms of BPD gradually shift from early to middle adulthood from inability to control emotions, impulsivity, and suicidality to problems in relationships and occasional periods of improvement.

Later adulthood is the least well-investigated period of life with regard to BPD. The results of cross-sectional studies suggest improvements occur in the symptoms relevant to suicidality and impulsivity. However, people who do not recover from BPD are at risk of dying younger and therefore are not part of later life samples. Older individuals with BPD retain the underlying qualities of fear of abandonment, selfishness, lack of empathy, and a tendency to manipulate others. They are also at higher risk for arthritis and heart disease, primarily as a result of increased obesity. Moreover, older adults who remain impulsive, as well as those who are experiencing chronic feelings of emptiness and

FIGURE 11.7

Selected Offenses Which Peak During Young Adulthood and Decline Gradually with Age, Canada, 2014

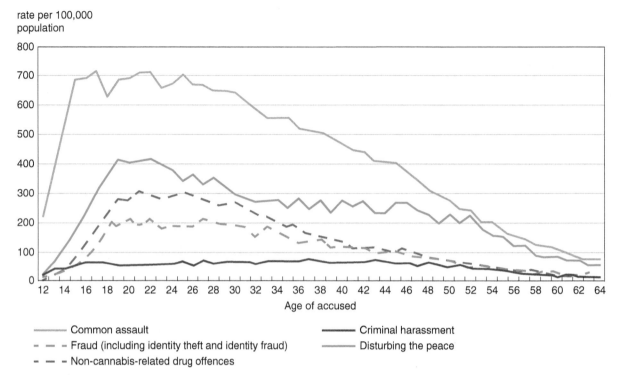

Common assault

- - - Fraud (including identity theft and identity fraud)

- - - Non-cannabis-related drug offences

Criminal harassment

Disturbing the peace

Note: Rates are calculated on the basis of 100,000 population at each age in 2014. Populations are based upon July 1st estimates from Statistics Canada, Demography Division. Accused under age 12 cannot be charged with an offence under the *criminal code*.

Criminal offenses, as based on reporting from Canada, peak in early adulthood.

Source: From Statistics Canada, Canadian Centre for Justice Statistics, Incident-based Uniform Crime Reporting Survey, 2014. Public Domain.

having unstable relationships, are also at risk for a higher frequency of stressful life events (Videler et al., 2019).

In obsessive-compulsive personality disorder, individuals show patterns of behavior that include excessive rigidity, preoccupation with details and rules, excessive perfectionism, and workaholism. In contrast to the diminution of antisocial and borderline personality disorders in later life, obsessive-compulsive personality disorder shows greater prevalence in older adults (Schuster et al., 2013). Despite what might seem to be a natural link between the personality trait of conscientiousness and this personality disorder, it appears that some of the perfectionistic symptoms of obsessive-compulsive personality disorder can interfere with the component of conscientiousness involving the ability to get things done (Mike et al., 2018). Older adults with this disorder, rather than being healthier due to their sticking to routines, are more likely to suffer from disability and lower quality of relationships as well as depression (Cruitt & Oltmanns 2018).

Overall, having a personality disorder in later life does not bode well for the individual's ability to navigate the aging process. Even when controlling for current health problems, depression, and health-related behaviors, people in their late 50s and early 60s with personality disorders are more likely to require more medical care. People with borderline personality, in particular, reported experiencing higher levels of pain and fatigue and more negative perceptions of their general levels of physical health (Powers & Oltmanns, 2012).

It is also important to distinguish between the older adult's perception of personality disorder symptoms and the way the individual is actually regarded by other people. Older adults with personality disorders may regard their symptoms as improving, but when others rate their personalities, they provide a more negative and, presumably, realistic assessment (Cooper et al., 2014). One possible explanation for this is a positivity bias also seen in the autobiographical memories of older adults in which they prefer to view themselves and their past in more favorable terms than is warranted (Isaacowitz, 2014).

ELDER ABUSE

A condition that may become one of serious clinical concern is the abuse of an older adult through the actions taken by another person. The term elder abuse is used to refer to a large category of actions taken directly against older adults that inflict physical or psychological harm. To protect vulnerable adults, Adult Protective Services (APS) were mandated by Title XX of the Social Security Act in 1975. Although a federal program, there is little or no funding attached to it. This means that the states are responsible for enforcing the regulations, and as a result, there is considerable variation in the definitions and reporting mechanisms for abuse.

Elder abuse is a notoriously difficult behavior to document because it is one surrounded by guilt, shame, fear, and the risk of criminal prosecution. Victims are afraid to report abuse because they are afraid of being punished by their abusers, and the perpetrators obviously do not wish to reveal that they are engaging in this socially unacceptable if not criminal activity. The most prominent signs of elder abuse are depression, confusion, withdrawn behavior, isolation from friends and family, unexplained injuries (bruises, burns, or scars), appearing in need of care (dirty, undermedicated, or dehydrated), having bed sores, and

making changes in banking or spending patterns (National Institute of Aging, 2019).

There are five types of elder abuse: physical abuse, psychological abuse, financial exploitation, neglect, and sexual abuse (National Institute of Aging, 2019). In physical abuse, the older adult is the victim of harm due to slapping, pushing, or hitting. Psychological abuse, also called emotional abuse, involves yelling, threatening, or shunning the older adults, and may also include preventing the older individual from contact with close friends and family members. Financial abuse involves the exploitation of older adults through such tactics as scamming, selling overpriced products, or taking over and draining credit cards or savings accounts (see Figure 11.8). Neglect is the form of elder abuse in which the individual does not attempt to respond to the older adult's needs such as food, water, clothing, shelter, medicine, and safety. Finally, sexual abuse occurs when a caregiver forces an older adult to watch or be part of a sexual act.

Given its potential to cause significant psychological and physical harm to older adults, there is surprisingly little research on the topic of elder abuse. According to a survey in the United States of nearly 5,800 respondents 60 and older, 14.1% experience some form of abuse with 4.6% suffering emotional abuse, 1.6% being victimized by physical abuse, and 5.2% being financially exploited (Acierno et al., 2010). Estimates of neglect, most often by a relative or professional caregiver, were 11% in a New York State sample (Burnes et al., 2015). Older adults most at risk of

FIGURE 11.8

Forms of Financial Abuse for Which Older Adults are at Risk

Lottery scams   Grandparent scams   Romance scams   Internal Revenue Service imposter scams

Tech support scams   Securities fraud   Health care fraud

Source: From GAO analysis of information from the U.S. Senate Special Committee on Aging, Department of Justice, Department of State, and Department of Treasury. | GAO-19-365. Public Domain.

fraud are ones who have experienced cognitive decline, difficulties in emotion regulation, social isolation, a tendency to be too trusting, and lack of knowledge regarding fraud protection (Shao et al., 2019). Individuals who are victims of financial abuse have higher mortality rates and tend to be in poor physical and mental health (Burnes et al., 2017).

In general, women are more likely to be victims of abuse, particularly women in the young–old age range because they are most likely to be living with spouses and children and these are the most frequent perpetrators (Lachs et al., 2015). Older adults living in rural settings, particularly those with psychiatric diagnoses, also are more likely to be targets of abuse (Mehra et al., 2019).

Researchers agree that there are, as yet, few evidence-based approaches to prevent elder abuse and treat its victims, though it appears that a focus on caregivers will be key to successful interventions (Baker et al., 2016).

It is also clear that if elder abuse is to be stemmed, changes must occur at the larger societal level. The U.S. Government Accountability Office recommends that the Department of Justice increase its efforts to achieve elder justice, and that the U.S. Attorney General should develop and document outcome measures to track progress in achieving these goals (Government Accountability Office, 2019) as mandated by the U.S. Elder Abuse Prevention and Protection Act (EAPPA) of 2018. Additionally, the

Administration for Community Living (ACL), a branch of the U.S. Department of Health and Human Services, funds community-based organizations to help improve local Adult Protective Services agencies. ACL also provides information that can be of use to individuals and families coping with elder abuse (Administration for Community Living, 2019).

SUICIDE

Although suicide is not a diagnosis in the DSM-5, suicide is related to psychological disorders that are diagnosable (National Institute of Mental Health, 2019). Figure 11.9 shows rates of suicide in the United States by age and sex (National Institute of Mental Health, 2019). As you can see from this figure, men have higher suicide rates at all ages; the highest suicide rate for men is 65 years and older. The majority of suicides involve firearms (56%) followed by hanging (27.7%).

Although statistically it is difficult to predict who will commit suicide at any age because the rates in the population are so low, there are several known risk factors for older adults. Older adults at greater risk of suicide suffer from higher rates of physical illness including cancer, epilepsy, cardiovascular disease, cataracts, COPD, liver disease, osteoarthritis, prostate disorders, and spinal fracture (Erlangsen et al., 2015). Higher suicide rates are also

FIGURE 11.9

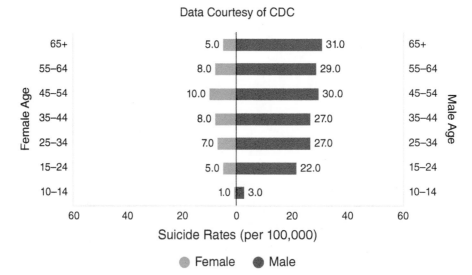

Suicide rates for men are higher than for women throughout life; highest rates are for those 65 and older, but midlife rates are also high (these are per 100,000 in the specific age group).

Source: From Suicide-National Institute of Mental Health. U.S. Department of Health and Human Services. Public Domain.

associated with poverty status in older men (Choi et al., 2019) and those with food insecurity (Cabello et al., 2019).

One key symptom to identifying an older person at risk of suicide is a history of previous suicide attempts (Murphy et al., 2012). However, the older adult contemplating suicide may not appear, even to a trained clinician, to be severely depressed. The majority of older adults who commit suicide have visited their primary care physician in the year before suicide (Raue et al., 2014). Greater sensitivity to symptoms of mood disorders in conjunction with more thorough evaluation of the additional psychological and medical risk factors through multidisciplinary training can prove helpful in identifying and managing suicide risk in older adults (Okolie et al., 2017). It is also important for health care providers to monitor prescriptions given to older adults who have a high suicide risk as well as to their families (Cobaugh et al., 2015).

TREATMENT ISSUES IN MENTAL HEALTH CARE

With the aging of the Baby Boom generation, mental health researchers are turning their attention with great concern toward the need for more research and training in providing services to older adults. Clearly, more training will be needed both for practitioners currently in the field and those who will be entering the ranks of therapists and other mental health care workers.

The publication of the *APA Guidelines for Psychological Practice with Older Adults* (American Psychological Association, 2014) has led to the development of training models in the emerging field of professional geropsychology, the application of gerontology to the psychological treatment of older adults. Geropsychologists are expected to be aware of their attitudes and beliefs about aging, to have general knowledge about the aging process, understand psychopathology in older adults, learn to use and interpret appropriate assessment tools, and be aware of the best practices in service provision. As is true for all licensed psychologists, geropsychologists are also expected to gain continuing education in the field to stay abreast of the latest developments.

Clinicians are increasingly being trained according to these guidelines, following what is known as the Pikes Peak Model of Geropsychology, a set of competencies that professional geropsychologists are expected to have when working with older adults (Karel et al., 2010). Those who wish to gain further credentials can earn board certification from the American Board of Professional Psychology once they have met their state's criteria for licensure.

Providing psychotherapy to older adults therefore requires that the mental health professional be aware of the specific needs and concerns associated with psychological disorders in later life. Demographic factors must also be taken into account in providing psychological services to older adults, including race, ethnicity, gender, socioeconomic status, and the availability of family and other social supports (Whitbourne & Martins, 2020).

Assessment

A psychological assessment is a procedure in which a clinician provides a formal evaluation of an individual's cognitive, personality, and psychosocial functioning. An older adult may see a clinician for an assessment as part of a formal diagnostic process. The assessment may instead be used for the purpose of determining an older adult's legal competence or for planning appropriate levels of care for the older individual.

Clinicians should tailor each assessment they conduct to the physical and cognitive needs of their clients which, in the case of older individuals, should take into account certain accommodations. Clients should be made to feel comfortable and relaxed and given sufficient time to ask questions about the procedure, which may be unfamiliar and hence stressful. There are also practical concerns that psychologists should address, such as making sure that the people they are testing have the correct eyeglasses and hearing aids, if necessary. The clinician may also have to take into account physical limitations due to arthritis and the potential for older adults to require rest periods or breaks during lengthy testing sessions.

As is true in general for communicating with older adults, clinicians conducting assessments should speak in a clear voice, make sure there is adequate lighting, and clear the room as much as possible of distractions from outside noise. Finally, it is also important to be sensitive to cultural or language differences between clinician and client, regardless of the age of the client (Edelstein et al., 2013).

A typical assessment incorporates multiple approaches, allowing the clinician to get a full picture of the individual's psychological functioning. Many clinicians begin their assessment with a clinical interview, a series of questions that they administer in face-to-face interactions with the client. The clinical interview has the advantage of being somewhat flexible as well as providing clinicians with insights they could only gain by directly observing how the client behaves.

The second component of assessment that is particularly important in working with older adults is a mental status examination, which assesses a client's current state of mind. In conducting a mental status examination, the clinician assesses such qualities of the client as appearance, attitudes, behavior, mood and affect, speech, thought processes, content of thought, perception, cognition, insight, and judgment. The outcome of the mental status examination is a comprehensive description of how the client looks, thinks, feels, and behaves. The mental status examination also typically includes a measure of orientation, which reflects whether examinees know where they are (orientation to place), what time it is (orientation to time), and who they are (orientation to person).

The Mini-Mental State Examination (MMSE) is a brief structured tool that clinicians use as a screening device to assess dementia (Folstein, 1975). The questions on the MMSE include orientation to time, visuospatial skills (copying a simple design), and the ability to remember three words. Because the MMSE is so brief, it is widely used in primary care (Pelegrini et al., 2019), but it provides only a snapshot of an individual's mental state. If a patient receives a low score, the health professional would most likely recommend a more thorough neuropsychological assessment.

Researchers and clinicians alike also make use of measures targeted toward specific symptoms in older adults. Several of these focus on depression, which, as we discussed in Chapter 5, may coexist, mask, or be the result of a neurocognitive disorder. The Geriatric Depression Scale (GDS) is a screening tool that asks individuals to answer a true–false set of questions about their symptoms and is well established for use with older adult populations, although its accuracy can be improved if family members are interviewed as well (Davison et al., 2009). The Center for Epidemiological Studies Scale for Depression (CES-D) is a 20-item questionnaire that screens for depressive symptoms (Radloff, 1977), which is also widely used in research settings.

A key area of differential diagnosis is distinguishing between a neurocognitive and other psychological disorders, particularly depression. As we saw in Chapter 5, depression can cause pseudodementia and can lead the clinician to inaccurately diagnose a neurocognitive disorder when the client's symptoms represent a disturbance of mood. However, there are important differences in the symptom pattern of individuals with these disorders. In depression, the symptoms of dysphoria are more severe, and the individual is likely to exaggerate the extent to which he or she is experiencing memory loss. People who have neurocognitive disorders tend, in contrast, to be overconfident about their cognitive abilities. They may show very wide variations in performance from one test to another; however, older adults with neurocognitive disorder show a progressive loss of cognitive abilities that tends to affect them across the board.

Differences between depression and dementia are important for clinicians to note in their assessment of older adults. As we pointed out in Chapter 5, if the depression is caught in time, there is a good chance of successful treatment, whereas if the individual's symptoms are due to a neurocognitive disorder, the clinician will take another approach to intervention. Conversely, if their depression is not treated, older adults with pseudodementia may go on to develop an irreversible neurocognitive disorder (Connors et al., 2018).

In addition to psychological assessment tools, clinicians evaluating older adults also measure their ability to perform activities of daily living (ADLs) and instrumental ADLs (IADLs). These provide important information that can be used in treatment planning, especially if it appears that the client might be best served in an institutional setting. Moreover, clinicians also track changes in the ADLs and IADLs over time to determine whether changes are needed in the client's placement status, perhaps corresponding to changes in cognitive functioning.

Clinicians typically complete their assessment of a client before they go on to adopt a treatment strategy, although they continue to assess their clients throughout the course of therapy. Ongoing evaluations allow clinicians to use information gathered from treatment to help refine their initial diagnoses and monitor the progress of their clients as they proceed through treatment.

Treatment

Following the assessment phase, clinicians embark on a program of treatment intended to provide the client with relief from his or her symptoms. The best mental health treatment follows a biopsychosocial model in which clinicians take into account the complex interactions among the client's physical symptoms and health, cognitive abilities, emotional strengths, personality, sense of identity, and social support network.

As is true for medical care, clinicians in the field of mental health also strive to work with professionals in other disciplines, allowing the older client to benefit from an integrated approach that brings together nursing, physical therapy, occupational therapy, psychotherapy, medical care, and input from family. Models other than the traditional provision of psychotherapy are clearly becoming seen as viable alternatives for work with older adults. Care managers can be used to coordinate services to individual clients, offering services through primary care physicians to ensure that the clients maintain their involvement in treatment.

Interventions with older adults are increasingly following the standard of evidence-based practice, meaning that clinicians should integrate the best available research evidence and clinical expertise in the context of the cultural background, preferences, and characteristics of their clients (American Psychological Association Presidential Task Force on Evidence-Based Practice, 2006). Consequently, mental health professionals need to be able to adapt their treatment modality that provides the best fit to the patient's diagnosis. Aiding in this effort are the continuing publications of clinical guidelines by the American Psychological Association that psychologists and other mental health professionals are able to use to ensure they are providing the best treatment to their clients.

Medical Interventions.   Treatment offered from the perspective of the medical model focuses primarily on the physiological causes of a psychological disorder. In the medical model, the primary line of defense against psychological disorders involves using psychotherapeutic medications, which attempt to reduce an individual's psychological symptoms. These medications cannot cure the disorder, but they can alleviate the client's distress from its most prominent symptoms.

The major categories of medications used to treat psychological disorders in older adults are antidepressants, anxiolytics (used to treat anxiety), and antipsychotics (used for schizophrenia and related disorders). Individuals with bipolar disorder receive mood stabilizers, primarily lithium carbonate.

Additionally, for older adults with severe depression, another medical intervention involves electroconvulsive therapy (ECT), in which an electric current is applied through electrodes attached across the head. Although it can be effective when no other treatment has proven to alleviate an older adult's depression, ECT carries the risk of short-term memory loss, which makes it a less than desirable treatment for older adults.

The prescribing of psychotherapeutic drugs may involve a process in which alternate medications are prescribed until one, or a combination, is found that helps the client's symptoms subside. For older adults, this process may be a challenge because many psychotherapeutic medications interact with other medications that these clients take for their chronic diseases. Moreover, because older adults typically see multiple health professionals, they are great risk for these unintended consequences. A physician might prescribe a sleeping medication to an older adult patient who is already taking an antianxiety or cardiac medication, potentially causing the older adult to become suicidal due to the interaction of the medications. Consequently, clinicians who work with older adults must take detailed and careful histories. The need to avoid dangerous interactions among medications is another reason that integrative health care is so important for older adults.

In addition to taking precautions against drug interactions, clinicians must be familiar with the medication's side effects for older adults, which may differ from those seen with younger adults. Unless the clinician prescribes them in lower doses, older adults are at risk of accumulating toxic levels in the blood because aging increases the time that medications take to clear the excretory system of the kidneys.

Psychotherapy.   Research on evidence-based treatments for older adults with psychological disorders increasingly supports the use of psychotherapy alone. Medications may also be prescribed by a treating professional. However, the risks of overmedication or harmful drug–drug interactions (Kok & Reyolds, 2017), along with empirical support for psychotherapy make it more likely to be the first line of intervention with older adults (Raue et al., 2017).

In cognitive-behavioral therapy (CBT), the clinician encourages clients to develop more adaptive behaviors and ways of thinking about their experiences. There is increasing support for CBT in treating older adults (Conti et al., 2017) (see Figure 11.10). CBT's advantages include being relatively short term (as few as seven sessions) and deliverable via audio therapy (delivered with audio CDs) and computer-based teletherapy (Shah et al., 2018). These approaches are advantageous to patients who live in rural areas or are unable to be transported to a therapist's office.

For older adults with depression, CBT involves helping clients understand the relationship between their mood and their involvement in pleasant and unpleasant events. The cognitive piece, further, involves therapists teaching their clients to be alert to and then try to change their negative thoughts about themselves. CBT has also shown to be an effective intervention for suicidal older adults (Bhar & Brown, 2012). For older adults with insomnia and depression, CBT can aid in promoting better sleep habits (Tanaka et al., 2019).

The relaxation component of CBT, in which patients learn to achieve physical and mental relief from stress (Klainin-Yobas et al., 2015), can also benefit older adults with anxiety as well as those with depressive disorders. For older veterans with PTSD, relaxation therapy also can be effective, at least for the short term, when combined with exposure therapy, a behavioral method in which patients mentally reenact the trauma (Thorp et al., 2019).

Although not a psychological disorder, fear of falling is a significant risk factor that can impact the health of older adults. CBT can be targeted to fear of falling as one component of intervention along with exercise training (Chua et al., 2019).

Exercise also appears to have potential in treating depression in older adults. A meta-analysis of studies using randomly assigned experimental and control groups

FIGURE 11.10

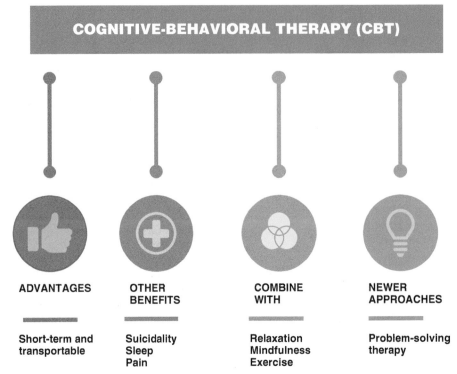

Summary of cognitive-behavioral therapy with older adults.

showed beneficial effects of even moderate intensity (aerobic) exercise even for individuals assigned to group exercise conditions (Schuch et al., 2016). There is also evidence from the "Warrior Wellness Study" that older veterans with PTSD can benefit from exercise training, both in terms of their PTSD symptoms and in treating insomnia, depression, and health-related quality of life (Hall et al., 2019).

Another approach extends CBT to incorporate principles of mindfulness, in which patients learn to attend to the details of their experiences as they become guided in "living in the moment." Mindfulness therapy is effective in improving positive affect, reducing anxiety, and also having the added benefits of improving cognition as well as reducing insomnia and lower back pain (Hazlett-Stevens et al., 2019).

Related to CBT is a relatively newer approach of problem-solving therapy (PST), in which patients are taught systematic ways of identifying and solving their actual life problems. The theory behind PST is that as individuals reduce their sources of stress, their mood and well-being will improve. Promising results from controlled studies with randomized designs support PST's utility in reducing disability due to depressive symptoms in older adults (Kirkham et al., 2016).

Psychosocial issues involving relationships with family may also confront an older adult and should be taken into account by clinicians providing psychotherapy (Knight & Kellough, 2013). These issues include death of family and friends, changes in relationships with children and spouses, and the need to provide care to a spouse or parent. Along these lines, older adults with higher levels of social support seem to benefit more from CBT in terms of improved quality of life following treatment (Shrestha et al., 2015). By addressing issues involving family and other social relationships in therapy, it may be possible to augment the impact of treatment on the older adult's symptoms.

Although therapy can have many beneficial effects, equally important as treatment is prevention. Targeting specific older adults at risk, such as those who have become bereaved and have experienced illness or disability, can help not only to reduce the need for treatment but also to maximize the functioning of older adults who might otherwise be at risk of developing psychological disorders.

FIGURE 11.11

Rates of Serious Mental Illness in Adults by Age, U.S., 2017

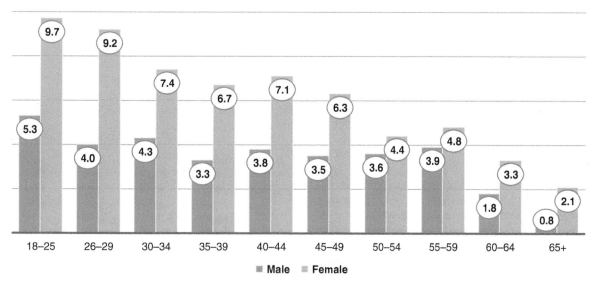

As can be seen here, the rates of serious mental illness are consistently lower across adulthood.

SERIOUS MENTAL ILLNESS

Though we have focused in this chapter on psychological disorders in older adults, it is important to remember that despite the presence of chronic physical health conditions, the majority of older adults do not experience significant distress. This fact is borne out by the Substance Abuse and Mental Health Services Administration (SAMHSA), which tracks the incidence of serious mental illness. Survey after survey in this series consistently reports lower rates of serious mental illness within the past year for adults 65 and older (see Figure 11.11). As you can see, women have higher rates of serious mental illness than do men at all ages, particularly in emerging adulthood and less so at later ages. With the exception of a slight rise among women 55 to 59 years, all other indications are that older adults are in better mental health than are younger aged adults (SAMHSA, 2018).

Clearly, although older adults are at higher risk in an objective sense for experiencing psychological disorders, a combination of selective survival, enhanced use of coping mechanisms, and an ability to maintain an optimistic attitude toward adversity seem to offer significant protective factors against psychological problems in later adulthood. Increasingly, new methods of treatment are becoming available to provide services to those older adults who need assistance in these adaptive processes.

In summary, when you think of the aging process, you are likely to anticipate a number of negative changes that would have adverse mental health effects. By contrast, the facts reveal that older adults are highly resilient to the physical, psychological, and social changes involved in the aging process. It is nevertheless true that there will be an increasing need for mental health workers in the coming decades trained in diagnosis, assessment and treatment, and there will also be an increased need for research on effective treatment methods for aging individuals in need of intervention.

SUMMARY

1. Psychological disorders are those behaviors that significantly alter the individual's adaptation. The DSM-5 contains descriptions of the disorders that can affect children and adults and is used by clinicians to assign diagnoses based on specific criteria. Ageism may affect the quality of services provided to older adults for the treatment of psychological disorders.

2. Although the prevalence of a diagnosable mood disorder is lower in older than in younger adults, many older adults report symptoms of depressive disorders. Health care professionals may not be attuned to diagnosing depressive symptoms in older adults. Medical conditions increase the risk for depression, including hip fracture, stroke, hypertension, and diabetes. A diagnosis of bipolar disorder occurs in individuals who have experienced one or more manic episodes during which they feel elated, grandiose, expansive, and highly energetic. Rates of bipolar disorder are lower among older adults compared with younger adults. Individuals diagnosed with anxiety disorders experience a sense of dread about what might happen in the future and will avoid anxiety-provoking situations. Anxiety disorders are more common in younger rather than older adults as well as among women. Types of anxiety disorders include generalized anxiety disorder, panic disorder, agoraphobia, specific phobias, and social anxiety disorder. People who experience obsessive-compulsive disorder suffer from unrelenting, irrational, and distracting obsessions and compulsions. Although the lifetime prevalence among older adults is extremely low, rates of detection may also result in lack of treatment.

3. Exposure to traumas can lead individuals to experience a variety of symptoms that may last for a prolonged period of time and can include acute stress and PTSD. Combat exposure appears to put older adults who served as veterans in the theater of war at risk for PTSD and the related condition of LOSS. Individuals diagnosed with schizophrenia experience distorted perception of reality and impairment in thinking, behavior, affect, and motivation. Substance-related disorders are more likely to occur in younger adults. However, alcohol abuse and dependence are becoming an area of concern for the over-65 population, as are disorders related to the use of prescription medications. Personality disorders are characterized by a long-standing pattern of inner experience and behavior that has maladaptive qualities. Older adults are less likely to exhibit antisocial and borderline personality disorder symptoms, although selective survival may affect the rates of antisocial behaviors by older adults.

4. Two additional topics of concern in the area of mental health and aging are elder abuse and suicide. Elder abuse includes physical, sexual, emotional, financial, and neglect. Risk factors for suicide among older adults include the presence of a psychiatric illness, physical illness, and limitations in functioning, chronic pain, and cognitive functioning deficits.

5. The field of clinical geropsychology involves the provision of psychological services to older adults. Treatment begins with a thorough assessment. A number of tools are available that can be applied specifically to persons in later life. These tools range from clinical interviews to structured self-report inventories. Assessment of people within this age group requires that the clinician adapt the test materials and the testing situation to the specific needs and cognitive or sensory limitations of the older adult. CBT is regarded as having considerable value in the treatment of older adults with depression, anxiety, and PTSD. Enhancements to CBT can have additional benefits to physical health.

6. Despite the many threats to positive mental health, the majority of older adults do not report elevated levels of serious mental illness suggesting that there is considerable resilience among individuals in later adulthood.

12

Long-Term Care

Compassionate and respectful care of older adults living in long-term care facilities is incredibly important for families, friends, and, of course, the residents who live there. Here are the top 10 ways that facilities truly stand out!

AGEFEED

#top10facts

1. Keeping family members up-to-date on day-to-day activities through blogs, social media, or electronic communication.

2. Having sing-alongs with local daycares and schools.

3. Encouraging residents to eat together to foster a sense of community.

4. Getting residents to engage in physical activity such as through dance or fitness classes.

5. Having communal kitchens so residents can cook together and with loved ones.

6. Offering lectures on topics such as literature, art, and music.

7. Engaging residents to plant and tend to vegetable or herb gardens that provide fresh foods.

8. Celebrating holidays and birthdays as a community.

9. Having regular social activities, such as game, movie, and trivia nights.

10. Allowing residents to make their living quarters feel like home, such as by hanging treasured artwork or bringing in their favorite furniture.

Have you ever lived in an institution? Your first response may be to answer "no," unless you have ever spent time in a hospital. However, think about the question in a slightly different way and you might realize that it's more accurate to say "yes." If you live in on-campus housing, then it's fair to regard the situation as involving institutional living. Dormitory residents live under one roof, are not related to each other, and are there because they share a similar position in life. In a dormitory, as in a hospital setting, residents must deal with problems that come with communal living, such being unable to control many aspects of the environment, needing to answer to people in charge, eating food prepared for a large number of people, and being assigned to live with a stranger.

In this chapter, we define an institutional facility as a group residential setting that provides individuals with medical or psychiatric care. Hospitals are short-term institutional facilities to which people are admitted with the understanding that they will be discharged when they no longer need round-the-clock treatment. At the other end of the spectrum are long-term institutional facilities into which an individual moves permanently after losing the ability to live independently.

Closely related to the issue of institutional care is that of the funding for health care, another topic we cover in this chapter. Individuals hospitalized for physical and psychological problems in later life are increasingly confronting the rising cost of health care as a barrier to the effective resolution of their difficulties. In addition to the problems that result from the failure to receive proper treatment, this situation creates considerable stress and anguish for the older individual and that individual's loved ones.

Although you may not spend much time thinking about the health care coverage available to you in your later years, as is true for Social Security, you are surely aware of the hotly debated discussions about the politics of health care. From offering public options for health insurance to making prescription medications more affordable for older adults, health care is one of the most crucial issues facing the United States as well as many other countries. From a biopsychosocial perspective, these large-scale social factors can have significant impacts on the health and well-being of the older population.

INSTITUTIONAL FACILITIES FOR LONG-TERM CARE

Traditionally, the term "long-term care" has been used to refer to services and supports designed for older people in poor health and younger persons with disabilities who require assistance in living to be able to maintain their daily lives. Alternative terms are now gaining wider use, including "long-term services and supports," the terminology used in the Patient Protection and Affordable Care Act (ACA, P.L. 111–148, as amended) to include both institutionally and noninstitutionally based long-term services and supports.

Figure 12.1 illustrates the continuum of long-term care facilities for older adults and shows the patterns that may characterize the living arrangements as individuals move along the continuum of care from fewer to more supports, moving back to lesser care if they are able to do so. The process begins with older individuals living on their

FIGURE 12.1

Continuum of Long-Term Care

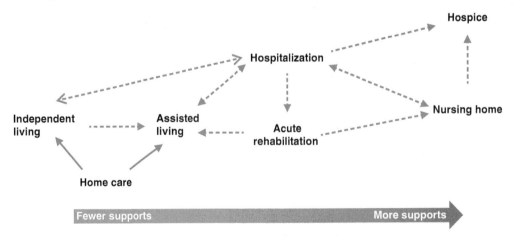

This continuum of care shows the trajectory that care for older adults takes as individuals progress from independent living to nursing homes, and ultimately to a hospice for end-of-life care.

own, or in a group setting such as an assisted living facility. In either case, they may receive home care. When there is an acute health event (such as broken hip or stroke), they will then require hospitalization. From there, they will be placed in an acute rehabilitation facility and either return home or to the assisted living facility. However, if they require more care than they can receive in these settings, they will be transferred to a nursing home. The process may continue through cycles if the individual experiences a health event, potentially culminating in death in a hospice (which we discuss in Chapter 13). As you can see, the progress of individuals through institutional living can become quite complex.

Nursing Homes

As we have just explained, older adults may progress through various institutional care facilities depending on their health status. We will begin describing in more detail each of these facilities with a discussion of the institutions that provide active nursing care. A nursing home is a type of medical institution that provides a room, meals, skilled nursing and rehabilitative care, medical services, and protective supervision. The care provided in nursing homes includes treatment for problems that residents have in many basic areas of life, including cognition, communication, hearing, vision, physical functioning, continence, psychosocial functioning, mood and behavior, nutrition, and dental care. To manage these problems, residents typically need to take medications on a regular basis. Residents of nursing homes may also receive training in basic care as

well as assistance with feeding and mobility, rehabilitative activities, and social services.

A nursing home may also have a rehabilitation unit in which residents receive intensive treatment to restore previous levels of functioning. Rehabilitation units typically include occupational and physical therapy services in addition to medical care. Referring back to Figure 12.1, acute rehabilitation typically follows hospitalization.

Nursing homes are certified by state and federal government agencies to provide services at one or more levels of care. A skilled nursing facility is a type of nursing home that provides the most intensive nursing care available outside of a hospital. Nurses and other health care workers in this type of facility can apply dressings or bandages, help residents with daily self-care tasks, and provide oxygen therapy. They are responsible for taking vital signs of their patients, including their temperature, pulse, respiration, and blood pressure.

In an intermediate care facility, individuals who do not require hospital or skilled nursing facility care but do require some type of institutional care receive health-related services. These facilities provide health and rehabilitative services as well as food but do not have intense nursing care services available.

Nursing home services have become a big business in the United States. In the year 2017, expenditures for nursing homes (including those attached to retirement communities) totaled 166.3 billion dollars or about 4.7% of total expenditures (Centers for Medicare & Medicaid Services, 2019d). Figure 12.2 shows the cost breakdown

FIGURE 12.2

Costs of Long-Term Care in the U.S., 2017

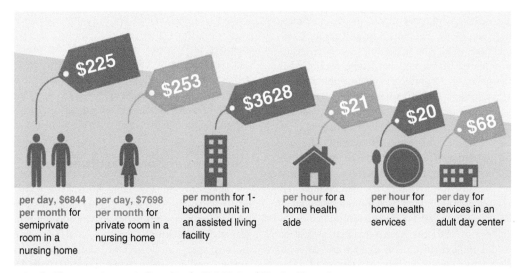

The costs associated with care settings, as indicated in the U.S. National Nursing Home Survey.

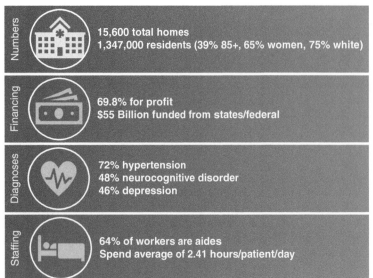

Numbers
15,600 total homes
1,347,000 residents (39% 85+, 65% women, 75% white)

Financing
69.8% for profit
$55 Billion funded from states/federal

Diagnoses
72% hypertension
48% neurocognitive disorder
46% depression

Staffing
64% of workers are aides
Spend average of 2.41 hours/patient/day

FIGURE 12.3

Characteristics of Nursing Homes and Their Residents

These figures show the key features of nursing homes.

for nursing home compared to other types of long-term care. As you can see, the yearly average private-pay facility is approximately $82,000 USD for a semiprivate room (U.S. Department of Health and Human Services, 2017).

Figure 12.3 provides a snapshot of the major characteristics of nursing homes and their residents. As of 2016, there were approximately 15,600 nursing homes in the Unites States with a total of 1.37 million patients (Harris-Kojetin et al., 2019). Half of all nursing homes have 100 beds or more, and 81% have between 50 and 199 beds (Centers for Medicare & Medicaid Services, 2015). The majority (69.8%) of all nursing homes fall into the category of "for-profit" facilities, meaning that their revenue exceeds their expenses. Nonprofit facilities, which include primarily those run by religious organizations, constitute the second largest group (24%), and government-owned facilities, primarily those run by the Veterans Administration, compose the remainder (6%). The majority of nursing homes (57.6%) are affiliated with a national chain. As of 2015, nursing homes received $55 billion from a combination of state and federal funding (Harris-Kojetin et al., 2019).

Perhaps because they are less oriented toward the "bottom line," not-for-profit nursing homes have higher quality ratings than their for-profit counterparts (Ronald et al., 2016). Related to this issue is the payment mode of residents. When nursing homes have more private-pay patients, they are able to provide better care because the rates for these patients are higher than the reimbursement rates that facilities receive from governmental subsidies.

The numbers of residents have remained steady at about 1.3 to 1.4 million since 1995 despite increases in the older adult population. Thus, the percentage of older adults in nursing homes has continued to decline to its present point of 2.6% of the 65 and older population. Among current nursing home residents, 84.5% are 65 and older and 41.6% are 85 and older (Centers for Medicare & Medicaid Services, 2015). As you can see from Figure 12.3, the most common diagnosis among nursing home residents is hypertension, followed by neurocognitive disorder and depression. Almost all (97%) require help with bathing, but high percentages require assistance with other activities of daily living (ADLs); the ADL least likely to require help for these residents is eating (60%).

The majority of employees in nursing homes (64%) are aides rather than nurses (12%) or licensed practical or vocational nurses (22.3%) who spend approximately 2.41 hours with each resident. Although almost all nursing homes employ some form of nursing assistance and activities, only three-quarters have full-time equivalent social workers who spend approximately 10 minutes or less per day interacting with residents. However, the majority (87%) provide some type of mental health or counseling. A small percentage (15%) provide a separate unit for the housing of patients with a neurocognitive disorder (Harris-Kojetin et al., 2019).

Residential Care Facilities

An alternative to a nursing home is a residential care facility, which provides 24-hour supportive care services and supervision to individuals who do not require skilled nursing or health-related care. Residents receive meals, housekeeping, and assistance with personal care such as bathing and grooming. Some residential care facilities may provide other services, such as management of medications and social and recreational activities.

As of 2016, there were approximately 811,500 people living in residential care facilities in the United States. Their median length of stay was just under 2 years. The majority were non-Hispanic white, female, and ages 85 and older. Over half (51%) had a diagnosis of hypertension and 42% had arthritis, roughly the same as the percentage of residents with a neurocognitive disorder. The diagnosis with the next highest prevalence was depression (31%). Compared to nursing home residents, residential care facility residents were less likely to require assistance with ADLs, but over half required assistance in bathing (64%) and walking (57%). The majority of care residents receive was provided by aides (83%). Very few (0.8%) employed social workers (Harris-Kojetin et al., 2019).

A board and care home is a group living arrangement designed to meet the needs of people who cannot live on their own in the community and who also need some nursing services. Typically, these homes provide help with ADLs such as bathing, dressing, and toileting. Although the name may imply that these homes provide a "homelike" setting, research refutes this idea. A survey conducted by the Institute of Medicine determined that board and care homes are typically understaffed by workers who are not required to receive training (Wunderlich et al., 2001).

Housing complexes in which older persons live independently in their own apartments are known as assisted living facilities. The residents of these facilities pay a regular monthly rent that usually includes meal service in communal dining rooms, transportation for shopping and appointments, social activities, and housekeeping services. These facilities are professionally managed and licensed and may represent one of several levels of care provided within the same housing community, including health care services, in some cases. The cost for living in an assisted living facility may range from hundreds to thousands of dollars a month. In some states, funds may be available through government support programs for those who cannot afford to live in these facilities on their own. However, most residents pay the rental and other fees out of their own funds.

The philosophy of assisted living is to allow residents to live in private apartments but to receive high levels of service so that they can continue living in the same facility even if they experience changes in their physical or cognitive functioning. However, many facilities do not achieve the goal of providing high levels of service, particularly those facilities that are on the lower end of the cost spectrum (Wunderlich et al., 2001).

Older adults may also choose to live in group homes, where they can share a house and split the cost of rent,

housekeeping services, utilities, and meals, sometimes under the supervision of a manager who assists them in some home maintenance tasks. Another arrangement involves adult foster care, in which a family provides care in their home for one or more older adults. The foster family may provide the older adult with meals and housekeeping and help with dressing, eating, bathing, and other personal care. These settings offer some advantages because of their homelike feeling, but because they are small and rely on a live-in caregiver for help with personal care, cooking, housekeeping, and activities, that caregiver's resources may be spread thin. If one resident becomes ill and requires more nursing care, other residents may suffer from lack of attention. Another problem in adult foster care is lack of privacy compared to a residential care setting (Wunderlich et al., 2001).

COMMUNITY-BASED FACILITIES AND SERVICES

Older adults who choose not to live in a residential facility but still need some type of care can take advantage of a number of support services that allow them to live independently in their own homes. Some of these services are offered by volunteer groups at no cost to the individual. Others are fee-based, some of which may be paid for by Medicare.

The residential environment of the older adult can be conceptualized along four dimensions, including the aesthetics and safety of the local area, convenience of access to shops and services, positive regard and mutual help among neighbors, and the attractiveness and ease of accommodation within the home. Each of these represents qualities of the physical environment, rather than the perceived environment. Research evaluating their contribution to the older adult's adaptation to the community suggests that the reality of the environment plays a crucial role in influencing well-being and satisfaction (Rioux & Werner, 2011).

The concept of aging in place refers to the principle that with appropriate services, older adults can remain in their own homes, or at least in their own communities (Gillsjö et al., 2011). Taking advantage of the same multidisciplinary focus so important for institutional care, older adults can benefit from interventions that allow them to maintain their autonomy and previous patterns of living (Szanton et al., 2019). The aging in place movement should also be bolstered by advances in digital technology that can supplement the services provided to older adults by connecting them to online sources of support. Other assistive technology advances can also benefit older adults living at home, including adaptive toilets that allow height and

Reduce fire hazards

Stay connected

Move items to easy reach

AGING IN PLACE

Remove tripping hazards

Put grab bars on shower

Open space between rooms

Improve lighting

Lower water heater temperature

FIGURE 12.4

Key Elements of the Aging in Place Model

According to the model of aging in place, older adults should be able to remain in their own homes as long as possible with the supports shown here.

tilt adjustment, as well as emergency notification (Mayer et al., 2019).

Figure 12.4 shows suggestions for modifications to the home that can help facilitate aging in place. The lowering of water temperature is intended to reduce burn risks. Maintaining a smart home will also permit older individuals to be able to not only call in the case of emergencies but also to stay on top of weather or other community alerts.

Home Health Services

Bringing services into the home is the focus of home health services, which provide assistance to older adults within their own private residences. Some of these services are free, or offered at a minimum price. These include "Meals on Wheels," the provision of a hot meal once a day; so-called "friendly visiting," in which a volunteer comes to the home for a social visit; and assistance with shopping. Other home-based services provide assistance with light housekeeping, such as laundry, cooking, and cleaning.

Home health care services may also include the types of restorative services that nursing homes provide, such as physical therapy, speech therapy, occupational therapy, rehabilitation, and interventions targeted at particular areas of functional decline. The home health care worker comes right into the individual's home, bringing along equipment as necessary. The advantage to home health care over institutional care is that the older adult can remain at home, staving off institutionalization or emergency room care. Moreover, home health care workers can teach older adults in their care how to maximize their mobility through such measures as fall prevention, muscle strength training, and home safety (Gitlin et al., 2009). However, home health care workers cannot provide skilled nursing to their clients nor can they perform heavy maintenance or assistance in areas outside of health services, such as paying bills.

Because they promote aging in place, and are becoming increasingly available, the number of older adults who receive home health services has increased substantially within the last decade. In the early 2000s, there were approximately 1 million older adults receiving these services; by 2015, the number rose to 4.5 million. The large majority of individuals needing home health services have hypertension (89%); arthritis (60%) and heart disease (55%) are the two other prominent diagnoses. Home health agencies are nearly equal to nursing homes in the assistance individuals receive in bathing (97%) and walking (85%) but fewer receive help in toileting (81% vs. 89%). Perhaps reflecting the fact that the majority of care they receive involves visits from health care professionals, home health agencies have the largest percentage of all long-term health care sectors who are registered nurses (53%) (Harris-Kojetin et al., 2019).

As is true for institutions providing long-term care for older adults, the majority of home health agencies are for-profit (80%). In the year 2017, $97 billion was spent in the United States on home health care; 76% of these costs were publicly funded (Centers for Medicare & Medicaid Services, 2019).

Day Treatment Services

Older adults who do not need to be in an institution on a 24-hour basis can receive support services during the day from community services specifically aimed at their needs. A geriatric partial hospital provides older adults living in the community who need psychiatric care with a range of mental health services. In adult day services, older adults who need assistance or supervision during the day receive a range of services in a setting that is either attached to another facility, such as a nursing home, or is a standalone agency. Depending on the site, the services provided can include medication management, physical therapy, meals, medical care, counseling, education, and opportunities for socialization. There are 4,600 adult day services centers, of which 45% are privately owned and operated. On any given day, an estimated 286,000 individuals receive services, of whom 63% are 65 years and older (Centers for Medicare & Medicaid Services, 2019a).

These services may fall into the category of respite care, which provides family caregivers with a break while allowing the older adult to receive needed support services. Being able to bring their relatives to these services for help during the day allows caregivers to maintain their jobs or spend time taking care of their own household or personal needs.

Community Housing Alternatives

Other alternatives in community care involve the provision of housing in addition to specialized services that can maintain the person in an independent living situation. Government-assisted housing is provided for individuals with low to moderate incomes who need affordable housing or rental assistance. People using government-assisted housing typically live in apartment complexes and have access to help with routine tasks such as housekeeping, shopping, and laundry.

An accessory dwelling unit, also known as an "in-law apartment," is a second living space in the home that allows the older adult to have independent living quarters, cooking space, and a bathroom. People living in these units may also take advantage of day treatment services to receive support when the rest of the family is at work or school.

A continuing care retirement community (CCRC) is a housing community that provides different levels of care adjusted to the needs of the residents. Within the same CCRC, there may be individual homes or apartments in which residents can live independently, an assisted living facility, and a nursing home. Residents move from one setting to another based on their needs but continue to remain part of their CCRC complex. CCRCs typically are on the expensive side. Many require a large down payment prior to admission and also charge monthly fees. Some communities, however, allow residents to rent rather than buy into the facility.

Residents moving into CCRCs typically sign a contract that specifies the conditions under which they will receive long-term care. One option provides unlimited nursing care for a small increase in monthly payments. A second type of contract includes a predetermined amount of long-term nursing care; beyond this the resident is responsible for additional payments. In the third option, the resident pays fees for service, which means full daily rates for all long-term nursing care.

If the older adult can afford this type of housing, there are definite advantages to living in CCRCs. In addition to the relative ease of moving from one level of care to another, the CCRCs provide social activities, access to community facilities, transportation services, companionship, access to health care, housekeeping, and maintenance. Residents may travel, take vacations, and become involved in activities outside the community itself.

Returning now to Figure 12.1, you can see how the institutional care system can function to place older adults into the level of care their current health requires. Ideally, individuals are able to move in and out of these different levels of care without undue difficulty and are also able to be placed in settings that allow them to live as independently as possible for as long as possible.

THE FINANCING OF LONG-TERM CARE

Long-term care is becoming big business, financed in the United States and many other countries by government agencies. Because of the huge expenditures involved, the financing of long-term care is currently undergoing intense scrutiny in every nation of the world. The current U.S. health care financing crisis is a function of the huge expenses associated with the long-term care of older adults. Insecurity over the financing of health care can constitute a crisis for adults of any age, but particularly so for older persons with limited financial resources or those who fear losing their savings in order to pay for long-term care. The ability to receive proper treatment for chronic conditions is therefore a pressing social and individual issue.

Long-term health care financing has a history dating back to the early 1900s and the first attempts in the United

States to devise government health insurance programs. In the ensuing century, as these programs became established, their benefits structure and financing grew increasingly complex and diversified. Throughout this process, the developers of these plans, which involve state and federal agencies along with private insurance companies, have attempted to respond to the rapidly changing needs of the population and the even more rapidly changing nature of the nation's economy. Outside the United States, developed countries such as Canada and many European nations have worked out different solutions than those existing in the United States and are also encountering challenges to their economy as their populations grow older.

As you will see shortly, the nursing homes and other facilities in which older adults receive treatment that we just described are subject to strict federal and state requirements to ensure that they comply with the standards set forth in the legislation that created the funding programs. The intimate connection between financing and regulation of these long-term care facilities has provided the incentive for nursing homes to raise their level of care so that they can qualify for this support.

Medicare

Title XVIII of the U.S. Social Security Act, passed and signed into law by President Lyndon B. Johnson in 1965, created the federal health care funding agency known as Medicare, designated as "Health Insurance for the Aged and Disabled." The four basic components of Medicare are summarized in Figure 12.5.

Structure of Medicare   Medicare Part A (Hospital Insurance, or HI) coverage includes all medically necessary

FIGURE 12.5

Components of Medicare

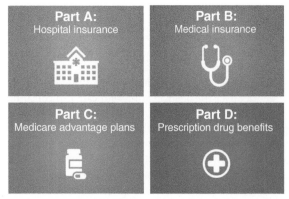

Medicare has four basic parts.

services and supplies provided during a patient's stay in the hospital and subsequent rehabilitation in an approved facility. This includes the cost of a semiprivate hospital room, meals, regular nursing services, operating and recovery room, intensive care, inpatient prescription drugs, laboratory tests, X-rays, psychiatric care, and inpatient rehabilitation. Luxury items, cosmetic surgery, vision care, private nursing, private rooms (unless necessary for medical reasons), and rentals of television and telephone are not included in coverage.

Coverage in a skilled nursing facility is included in Part A if it occurs within 30 days of a hospitalization of 3 days or more and is certified as medically necessary. Part A of Medicare covers rehabilitation services and appliances (walkers and wheelchairs) in addition to those services normally covered for inpatient hospitalization. Patients must pay a copayment for days 21 to 100 of their care in this setting. Home health services are also included in Part A of Medicare for the first 100 days following a 3-day hospital stay. Respite periods are also covered for some forms of end-of-life care to allow a break for the patient's caregiver.

Medicare's costs are updated on a yearly basis on their website (Medicare, 2019a), allowing patients and their advocates to calculate precisely how much they will pay and what their benefits will be during the current calendar year. If you are helping an older adult with health care plan costs, this website can be a very useful starting point.

For most people, Medicare Part A is free, but people who were self-employed or paid Medicare taxes for less than 10 years combined must pay a monthly fee. In 2019, the maximum monthly fee was $437. Hospital stays are free for the first 60 days (the "benefit period") and then from 61 to 90 days are $341 per day. After 90 days, the amount goes up to $682 per day. After 91 days, the individual pays $682 per day within that benefit period. However, if the individual does not use up the entire 90 days, the benefit period resets as long as the individual has stayed out of the hospital for 60 consecutive days. The deductible for that benefit period is a total of $1,364. If individuals require hospital insurance beyond the 90 days, they have a "lifetime reserve" of 60 days during which they can receive insurance payments from Part A, but when that is depleted, they are responsible for all costs.

Medicare Part B provides benefits for a range of medical services available to people who receive Medicare Part A. The amount an individual pays varies according to his or her income. Part B services include preventive treatments, including glaucoma and diabetes screenings as well as bone scans, mammograms, and colonoscopies. Other covered services include laboratory tests, chiropractor visits, eye exams, dialysis, mental health care, occupational therapy, outpatient treatment, flu shots, and home health services. A one-time physical examination is also included in Part B.

The premium for Medicare Part B varies by a person's yearly income, with those earning $85,000 or less paying $135.50 per month rising up to $460.50 for couples earning $750,000 or more and individuals earning $50,000 or more. The deductible is $185 per year, and after the deductible amount is reached, those with Part B insurance pay 20% of the Medicare-approved amount for their services.

Part C of Medicare, also called Medicare Advantage, provides coverage in conjunction with private health plans. Individuals who have both Parts A and B can choose to get their benefits through a variety of risk-based plans, including health maintenance organizations (HMOs), preferred provider organizations (PPOs), private fee-for-service plans, and a health insurance policy administered by the federal government.

Established by the Balanced Budget Act of 1997 (Public Law 105-33), Part C first became available to Medicare recipients in 1998. Beginning in 2006, PPOs began to serve beneficiaries on a regional basis. HHS identified 26 regions across the nation in which PPO plans compete to provide services in order to ensure that all Medicare beneficiaries, including those in small states and rural areas, would have the opportunity to enroll in a PPO as well as to encourage private plans to participate.

Part D of Medicare is a prescription drug benefit plan that provides coverage for a portion of the enrollee's costs. First available in 2006, through passage of the 2003 Medicare Modernization Act (MMA), by the end of 2018, there were 45.8 enrollees in Part D according to the Social Security Trust Fund report. People who wish to receive Part D coverage pay a monthly premium that varies by plan and income. In 2019, the average monthly premium was $33.19, but higher-income plan members pay premiums of up to $77.40 per month on top of this.

Part D has four phases of coverage over the course of the calendar year (see Figure 12.6). At the beginning of the year, the enrollee is responsible for a deductible of up to $415. After that point, the initial coverage period begins when recipients pay a reduced amount for their prescriptions of 25%. Part D will count the total value of the drugs (not what plan members pay) until a limit is reached of $3,820 for the actual drug costs. This is when the coverage gap, or donut hole, begins in which recipients pay more for generic drugs (37% instead of 25%); brand name drugs remain the same (25%). Once their drug costs total $5,100, out-of-pocket payments for enrollees become reduced to 5% of the drug's costs (or $3.40 for generic and $8.50 for brand name). The donut hole has shrunk considerably since 2006, when participants in the plan paid 100% of all drug costs before reaching catastrophic coverage.

Total drug spending in the United States was $334 billion in 2018. As reported by the trustees of the Medicare Trust Fund, Part D of Medicare paid out nearly one-third of these costs, or $95 billion. The costs of prescription drugs continue to rise at rates greater than inflation with,

FIGURE 12.6

Structure of the Medicare "Donut Hole"

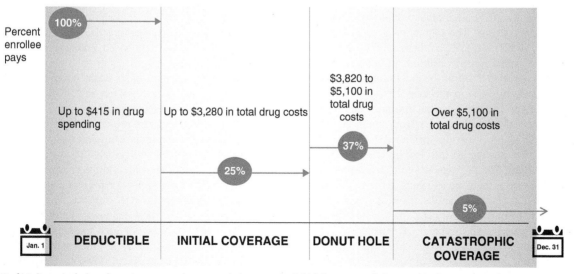

Part D of Medicare includes a lapse in coverage that occurs in between the Initial Coverage and Catastrophic Coverage periods.

for example, the cost of polyethylene glycol (used to treat constipation), prescribed for over 1.3 million Medicare recipients, rising 20% between 2013 and 2017. The Centers for Medicare & Medicaid Services (CMS) released a drug search portal that provides detailed information on the costs associated with each of the drugs (Centers for Medicare & Medicaid Services, 2019b).

CMS is striving to increase the transparency of drug costs as part of a government effort to rein in the rising price tag of healthcare. These measures could potentially contribute to a greater competition in the prescription drug marketplace by allowing consumers and their healthcare professionals make more informed choices.

Facts About Medicare   The government organization overseeing federally-funded health care programs is CMS, which is responsible for the formulation of policy and guidelines, oversight and operation of contracts, maintenance and review of records, and general financing.

Medicare, like OASDI, is funded by a pay-as-you-go system, meaning that revenues from taxes on employees and employers must be able to fund benefits paid out to Medicare recipients. Like Social Security, there is a Medicare Trust Fund which can be used to make up the gap between revenues and expenses. Unlike OASDI, Medicare recipients pay premiums and co-payments for services they receive, The Medicare Trust Fund is divided into the Hospital Insurance Trust Fund (HI), which covers Part A, and the Supplemental Medical Insurance Trust Fund (SMI), which funds Parts B and D. Part C of Medicare is paid for through premiums by the insured through their individual Medicare Advantage plans.

Medicare has grown enormously since its inception. In 1966, Medicare covered 19.1 million people at a cost of $1.8 billion. By 2018, 51.2 million adults 65 and older had Medicare coverage. The amount paid out by Medicare (Parts A, B, and D) was $740.6 billion. Of this, $28 billion was paid to skilled nursing facilities. Total Medicare Part A spending equaled 2.1% of the gross domestic product, and will grow to 3.8% in the next 25 years (Boards of Trustees of the Federal Hospital Insurance and Federal Supplementary Medical Insurance Trust Funds, 2019).

The Affordable Care Act (ACA) (P.L. 111–148) is legislation that was signed into law by President Barack Obama in 2010. The ACA has served to reform Medicare spending. Because there are still gaps in the health insurance of millions of younger adults, politicians in 2020 have proposed a "Medicare for All Plan" that would replace or augment private health insurance. It remains to be seen whether this proposal will become the basis for future health care reforms.

Medicare's future is a topic of great concern among policy makers and analysts. At the beginning of 2018, Medicare's Trust Fund assets were nearly $202 billion. Revenues, including $268 billion in taxes, amounted to nearly $307 billion. Its expenditures were $308 billion, meaning that the gap had to be met by $1.7 billion from the Trust Fund, which took the Trust Fund down to just about $200 billion. Part of the reason for the depletion of the Trust Fund, in addition to rising health care expenditures, is the decline in the ratio of workers to beneficiaries from 4 to 5 in 2000 to 2 to 5 starting in 2030.

Expenditures will continue to outpace revenues over the coming decade, and so by 2026 the Medicare Trust Fund will be brought to, or close to, zero. According to the pay-as-you-go principle, this means that Medicare could pay health plans and providers of Part A services only to the extent allowed by ongoing tax revenues. Because these revenues would be inadequate to fully cover costs, beneficiary access to health care services could rapidly be curtailed. In other words, people who rely on Medicare would lose some coverage for their acute care costs. Parts B and D are protected because the law permits premiums to rise in order to cover expenses.

Medicaid

Title XIX of the Social Security Act of 1965, known as Medicaid, is a federal and state matching entitlement program that provides medical assistance for certain individuals and families with low incomes and resources. Initially, Medicaid was formulated as a medical care extension of federally funded programs providing income assistance for the poor, with an emphasis on dependent children and their mothers, the disabled, and the over-65 population. More people are now eligible for Medicaid, including low-income pregnant women, children living in poverty, and some Medicare beneficiaries who are not eligible for any cash assistance program. Legislative changes are also providing increased and better medical care, enhanced outreach programs, and fewer limits on services.

Medicaid services for older adults cover inpatient and community health care costs not included in Medicare, such as skilled nursing facility care beyond the 100-day limit covered by Medicare, prescription drugs (without a premium), eyeglasses, and hearing aids. Although intended to provide support for individuals living at, close to, or below the poverty level, older adults receiving long-term care who are not otherwise poor may be eligible for Medicaid when their benefits have run out and they cannot afford to pay their medical expenses. Many states have a medically needy program for such individuals, who have too much income to qualify as financially needy. This program allows them to spend down their assets to the point of being eligible for Medicaid by paying medical expenses to offset their excess income. Medicaid then pays

FIGURE 12.7

Medicaid Expenditures as Percent of Total U.S. Health Expenditures, 2016

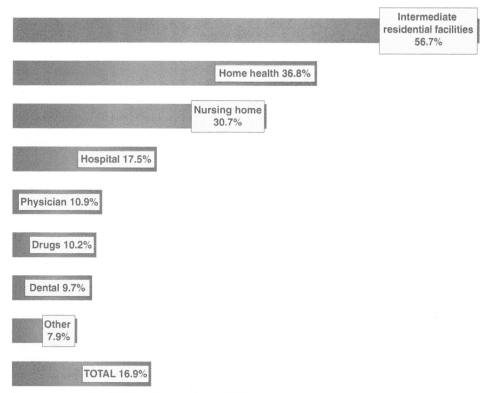

Medicaid expenditures as percent of total U.S. health expenditures, 2016.

the remaining portion of their medical bills by providing services and supplies that are available under their state's Medicaid program. This means that individuals will not go into debt in order to pay their medical bills.

Each state has different regulations governing Medicaid eligibility, including those that govern the spend down clause. Couples may also have different rules governing spend down requirements than individuals. Prior to becoming in need of services, then, individuals who wish to protect their assets should receive financial counseling in order to determine the best plan for their situation. For example, older adults with assets in their homes, savings, and long-term investments can benefit from shielding those assets in trust funds.

The largest source of funding for medical and health-related services for those in need of assistance, Medicaid provided health care assistance to 5.7 million older adults in 2016, or 8% of all Medicaid enrollees (Wolfe et al., 2017). In 2016, the combined shares of federal and state Medicaid outlays totaled $115.8 for long-term care benefits, which was 21% of all health care expenditures making Medicaid the largest contributor to the funding of long-term care

(Wolfe et al., 2017). Medicaid is the primary source of pay for 62% of all nursing home residents, 66% of all adult day services centers, and 17% of all those living in residential care facilities (Harris-Kojetin et al., 2019).

Figure 12.7 shows the percentages paid by Medicaid in 2016 of all U.S. spending on health care by category. The intermediate care facilities category includes residents for adults with intellectual disabilities and home and community based services. The "other" category includes other professionals. As you can see, Medicaid accounts for a significant percentage of care for older adults based on the two categories of home health and nursing home services (Wolfe et al., 2017).

Medicaid has grown significantly since 1966, in part because of the new eligibility provided for adults through the ACA. The number of enrollees is expected to increase to 81.6 million by the year 2025, with the total cost rising from $592 billion in 2017 to $938 billion by 2025. Medicaid accounts for 9.3% of the federal budget and 28.7% of all state budgets (Wolfe et al., 2017). Since all of Medicaid's funding comes from federal and state taxes, rather than a payroll tax as is true for Medicare, this growth must be paid for from general revenues. Consequently, there will be increasing pressure on policy makers to find ways to offset the effect of Medicaid on the economy. Countering the growth of health care spending, however, we can hope will be improved health in the older adult population, better health habits in the young, and perhaps greater adoption of alternatives to prescription medications for treatment of conditions amenable to behavioral health measures.

LEGISLATIVE LANDMARKS IN THE LONG-TERM CARE OF OLDER ADULTS

The regulation of nursing homes and community-based services for older adults and the disabled is a major focus of U.S. health policy and legislation in the United States. It is only through such legislation that quality standards for health care facilities can be enforced. Unfortunately, the process of ensuring quality long-term care has been a difficult one marked by a series of regulatory efforts that failed because they were not properly enforced. The system only now seems to be coming under control after over 30 years of active reform efforts.

Figure 12.8 highlights the major legislative actions affecting the long-term care provided to older adults in the United States. Following the signing into law of Medicare and Medicaid in 1965, continued developments in the regulation of long-term care have included both new legislation and consumer-led movements for improved services.

1987 Nursing Home Reform Act (NHRA)

The current U.S. laws governing the operation of institutional facilities have their origins in a report completed by the prestigious Institute of Medicine in 1986 called "Improving the Quality of Care in Nursing Homes." This report recommended to Congress major changes in the quality and nature of services provided to nursing home residents. The outcome of the report was passage of the Omnibus Budget Reconciliation Act of 1987 (OBRA, 1987). This budget bill included a number of pieces of legislation, including the Nursing Home Reform Act (NHRA), a U.S. federal law that mandated that facilities must meet physical standards, provide adequate professional staffing and services, and maintain policies governing their administrative and medical procedures.

The conditions of NHRA specify that nursing homes must be licensed in accordance with state and local laws, including all applicable laws pertaining to staff, licensing, registration, fire, safety, and communicable diseases. They must have one or more physicians on call at all times, 24-hour nursing care services (including at least one full-time registered nurse), a range of rehabilitation and medical services, and activity programs. In terms of administration, they must have a qualified administrator, a governing body legally responsible for policies, and confidential record-keeping procedures. The facility must admit eligible patients regardless of race, color, or national origin.

In addition to specifying requirements for nursing homes to be licensed, NHRA mandated a set of resident rights (Medicare, 2019c). These are summarized in Figure 12.9. These resident rights are now used as part of the ratings of quality of care in nursing homes.

NHRA also established procedures to ensure that all conditions are met for maintaining compliance with the law. These procedures included monitoring of the performance of facilities by outside survey agencies to determine whether they comply with the federal conditions of participation. Unfortunately, 10 years after the NHRA

FIGURE 12.8

Timeline of Long-Term Care Legislation

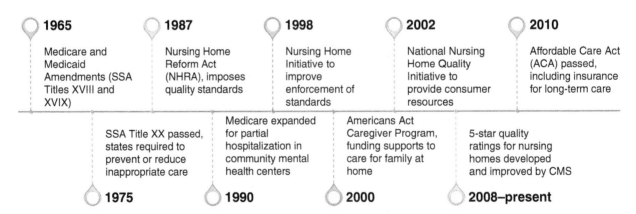

This is the abbreviated timeline of major events in long-term care legislation.

regulations were put into effect, it became clear that there were still serious problems with nursing home quality. Some regulations were never implemented, and others were not enforced.

In 1997, the U.S. Senate Committee on Aging received reports that documented inadequate care in California nursing homes had caused widespread death and suffering of residents. These reports triggered a hearing in 1998 by the U.S. Senate Special Committee on Aging regarding the substandard quality of care in California nursing homes. The report's title was "Betrayal: The Quality of Care in California Nursing Homes." This report revealed that 98% of nursing homes had minimal (35%), substandard (33%), or serious (30%) deficiencies.

1998 Nursing Home Initiative

In response to the Senate Committee on Aging's 1998 hearing, President Bill Clinton's administration announced the 1998 Nursing Home Initiative. This was intended to improve enforcement of nursing home quality standards, including altering the timing of nursing home inspections to allow for more frequent inspections on weekends and evenings as well as weekdays (when many of the abuses occurred); conducting background checks on workers; and establishing a national registry of nursing home aides. States were given the authority to impose immediate sanctions and monetary penalties on nursing homes that continued to violate the rights of residents.

Despite the best intentions of the Nursing Home Initiative, hearings on nursing home quality held by the Senate Committee on Aging just a short time later, in 1999 and 2000, revealed that nursing home abuse was still rampant. Nationwide, 27% of nursing homes were cited with violations causing actual harm to residents or placing them at risk of death or serious injury; another 43% were cited for violations that created a potential for more than minimal harm.

The Senate hearings also revealed flaws in the surveys. Inspectors often missed significant problems such as pressure sores, malnutrition, and dehydration. In some cases, nursing homes were cited because a member of the nursing staff had committed acts of physical, sexual, or verbal abuse against residents. Formal complaints made by residents or families were uninvestigated.

Making the problem worse was the fact that the state governmental agencies discouraged the filing of complaints because they did not have the resources to follow through on them. The Senate Committee also found that the majority (54%) of nursing homes were understaffed, putting residents at increased risk of hospitalization for avoidable causes, pressure sores, and significant weight loss months (Minority Staff Special Investigations Division

Committee on Government Reform U.S. House of Representatives, 2001).

2002 National Nursing Home Quality Initiative

In November 2002, the federal government introduced another initiative intended to correct the problems identified in the 2000 reports. The 2002 National Nursing Home Quality Initiative combined new information for consumers about the quality of care provided in individual nursing homes with resources available to nursing homes to improve the quality of care in their facilities. Quality improvement organizations (QIOs) were contracted by the federal government to offer assistance to skilled nursing facilities to help them improve their services. The 2002 initiative also included a provision to train volunteers to serve as ombudspersons. The role of the ombudspersons is to help families and residents on a daily basis to find nursing homes that provide the highest possible quality of care and to give consumers the tools they need to make an informed, educated decision on selecting a nursing home.

The 2002 initiative should have done a considerable amount to improve the quality of care in nursing homes, but like its predecessors, it was ineffective in achieving its goals. In 2007, the GAO issued a major report analyzing the effectiveness of the online reporting system based on data from 63 nursing homes in California, Michigan, Pennsylvania, and Texas, institutions that had a history of serious compliance problems. From this analysis, the GAO concluded that, once more, efforts to strengthen federal enforcement of sanctions had not been effective.

The 2007 report showed that nursing homes that committed violations of patient care or rights were often given leeway, either in terms of the amount they were penalized or the length of time they were granted before being required to pay the penalty. Even those that were penalized simply made temporary changes—only to slide back down until they were sanctioned again. Meanwhile, the residents of these homes continued to suffer abusive treatment because the administrators did not correct the fundamental problems (Government Accountability Office, 2008).

2008 (to Present) CMS Five-Star Quality Ratings

In 2008, CMS created a set of five-star quality ratings intended to help consumers, their families, and caregivers to make educated comparisons among nursing homes in their areas. Each nursing home receives a rating of between one and five stars. In addition to an overall rating, nursing homes receive specific ratings in the areas of health inspections, staffing, and quality measures. In 2019, the rating guidelines were revised by CMS (Centers for Medicare & Medicaid Services, 2019c). The website Nursing Home Compare (Medicare, 2019b) uses the five-star system as the basis for its searchable database of all nursing homes certified by Medicare or Medicaid, organized by location.

THE QUALITY OF LONG-TERM CARE

Information about nursing homes and nursing home residents comes from the Online Survey, Certification, and Reporting system (OSCAR). The OSCAR system collects information from state surveys of all the certified nursing facilities in the United States, which is entered into a uniform database. Surveyors assess both the process and the outcomes of nursing home care in 15 major areas. Each of these areas has specific regulations, which state surveyors review to determine whether facilities have met the standards. When a facility fails to meet a standard, a deficiency or citation is given. The deficiencies are given for problems that can result in a negative impact on the health and safety of residents. Similarly, home health agencies are mandated to submit data on their effectiveness through a survey tool called the Outcomes Assessment and Information Set (OASIS). Unfortunately, as reported by CMS, nursing homes are becoming more and more likely to receive at least one health deficiency in these annual surveys, although these deficiencies are becoming less likely to involve serious harm to residents.

Figure 12.9 shows the ratings grid that inspectors use to rate a nursing home's adherence to each of 15 areas of evaluation (Centers for Medicare & Medicaid Services, 2019d). There are two dimensions along which ratings are made: Scope, signifying the amount of potential harm, and severity, signifying how widespread the raters find the harm to be. A nursing home is cited for having a deficiency if it rates a "G" or higher in a particular area.

Figure 12.10 summarizes the top four deficiencies identified in the most recent survey (Harrington et al., 2018), listing those that, across the United States, received a rating of "G" or higher on the OSCAR scale. Infection control program deficiencies include failure to protect residents from

FIGURE 12.9

OSCAR Rating System

SEVERITY

SCOPE

	Isolated	Pattern	Widespread
Immediate jeopardy to resident health or safety	J	K	L
Actual harm that is not immediate jeopardy	G	H	I
No actual harm with potential for more than minimal harm that is not immediate jeopardy	D	E	F
No actual harm with potential for minimal harm	A	B	C

The "scorecard" used in OSCAR rating systems of nursing homes.

Poor infection control

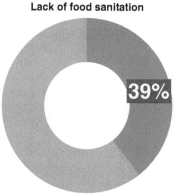

Failure to protect from accidents

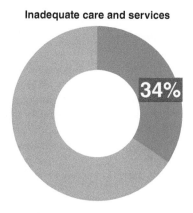

FIGURE 12.10

Top 4 Deficiencies in Nursing
Homes, 2018

Lack of food sanitation

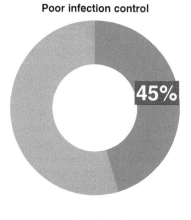

Inadequate care and services

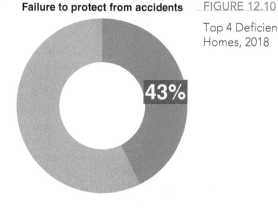

As shown here, high percentages of
nursing homes in the U.S. are rated as
having serious deficiencies.

the spread of disease such as failing to provide antiseptic hand wash. Failure to protect residents from accidents means that the environment presents hazards that could cause unexpected and unintended injury, such as hallways cluttered with furniture. Lack of food sanitation means that the institution does not maintain sanitary conditions in storing, preparing, distributing, and serving food to prevent food-borne illness, such as ensuring proper refrigeration of perishable items. Finally, inadequate care and services means that residents do not receive the proper treatment to attain or maintain the highest practicable physical, mental, and psychosocial well-being. Other deficiencies included lack of protection from overmedication (25%), improper maintenance of hospital records (23%), and lack of treatment with dignity (21%).

Returning to the rights of nursing home residents, as established by the NHRA, it is clear that residents are not receiving the care that they deserve, particularly in areas that can prove life-threatening to at-risk older adults. For example, older adults who are institutionalized may have compromised immune systems as well as mobility issues. The problem of lack of dignity further exacerbates the

problems that can face nursing home residents, limiting their ability to maintain their autonomy even in basic areas of living, such as bathing and dressing. Additionally, the NHRA mandated that residents are involved in their care, but 25% of nursing homes do not engage residents in their planning process.

These data led Harrington, the report's author, to issue several cautionary warnings. Having conducted each of the nursing home deficiency reports dating back to 2003, Harrington believes that some areas have shown improvement in response to federally mandated attempts to ensure compliance by nursing homes with CMS regulation. Against this backdrop, she expresses concern that attempts to limit funding of Medicaid will put at risk the millions of people needing assistance for whom this program provides a "long-term safety net" (p. 17). Cuts in Medicaid would both limit the quality of service and the mechanisms now in place to enforce standards of quality and performance. Additionally, the growth of for profit large chains, which we observed at the outset of this chapter, could exacerbate the situation, given their link to poorer quality care.

PSYCHOLOGICAL ISSUES IN LONG-TERM CARE

As you have just learned, over one-third of facilities in the Harrington et al. (2018) report fail to help residents achieve the highest quality of well-being not only by being deficient in providing for their medical needs but also for their psychosocial. Yet, not all facilities fall short of the mark. Models of adaptation to the institutional environment attempt to explain the factors that contribute to a facility's ability to meet the psychosocial needs of its residents.

The basic problem that institutions face in providing for the needs of its residents is that, as institutions, they must try to meet the need of the "average" resident. Consider the case of temperature. It is more cost effective for institutions to be built with one heating and cooling system rather than to be able to provide individualized thermostats within each room. Other features of the environment, from lighting to dining menus, similarly, cannot be individually tailored to each resident's needs.

Add to this problem of meeting the average resident's needs is the fact that people will differ considerably in the ways they perceive the same physical features of the environment. How many times have you told another student that you dislike the seats in the classroom, only to have the other students say they are fine? When it comes to temperature, you have probably been in classes in which one student is wearing an overcoat and another is wearing shorts and a tee shirt. The subjective environment, then, becomes an added complication for institutions to take into account when designing and maintaining a facility.

As you can see from this example, in predicting adaptation to the institution, the actual qualities of the environment are only part of the equation. Researchers are interested in learning how residents perceive the institution's physical qualities and relating these perceptions to their adaptation (Sloane et al., 2002).

The ability to control your environment is another factor that will determine how well you are able to adapt to it. In your own home, you make your own decisions about how your environment looks and feels. You set your own hours for eating, sleeping, waking, and bathing. In an institution, you may have these decisions made for you by the staff. A study of nursing home residents in Victoria (British Columbia) revealed that the ability to control the environment was indeed important to certain residents. Interviewers presented the residents with vignettes asking them to make decisions such as what time to go to bed, what medicines to take, whether to move to a different room, and what type of end-of-life care to receive. The researchers found that, perhaps unexpectedly, not everyone wanted to have this type of control over their health care decisions. Older adults with more years of education and a greater number of chronic illnesses were likely to state that they wished to be able to make these decisions themselves rather than have them made for them by nursing home staff (Funk, 2004).

As you can see, institutions present residents with environments that meet their needs to varying extents. In the ideal situation of maximum adaptation, residents feel that they are a good fit in their environment. This principle of person-environment fit underlies the competence–press model (Lawton & Nahemow, 1973), which predicts an optimal level of adjustment that institutionalized persons will experience when their levels of competence match the demands, or "press," of the institutional environment.

Figure 12.11 illustrates the competence–press model. The qualities of the individual, psychological and physical, can range from low to high in competence. A highly competent resident will be able to get around easily, is cognitively intact, and is relatively free from depression. Institutions, for their part, can range from low to high in press. An environment low in press will be relatively low in stimulation. One that is high in press will have high expectations for residents to be active.

As you can see, there is a boundary around the perfect fit between competence and press (dashed line). That zone incorporates maximum comfort and maximum performance potential, or ability to be as satisfied and independent as possible. Adaptation, in this middle zone, will be high. As you move toward the edges, adaptation drops and individuals express negative affect and engage in maladaptive behavior such as, in the extreme, being aggressive toward staff. The individual who is intellectually competent is best adapted, then, in a highly stimulating environment and residents who have diminished capacity will be best adapted in a less stimulating environment.

Looking now at the range of maximum adaptation, it is clear that residents low in competence have a narrower band that will define their feelings of comfort and ability to perform. Cognitively and physically more competent residents may be bored in a less stimulating environment than in one suited toward their abilities, but they will have the capacity to find ways to keep from getting bored.

By considering the interaction between the individual and the environment of the institution, the competence–press model makes it possible to provide specific recommendations to institutions about how best to serve the residents. The model also predicts the adaptations individuals might make to changes in health as they seek environments that will best support their ability to maintain their independence (Perry et al., 2014).

FIGURE 12.11

Competence–Press Model

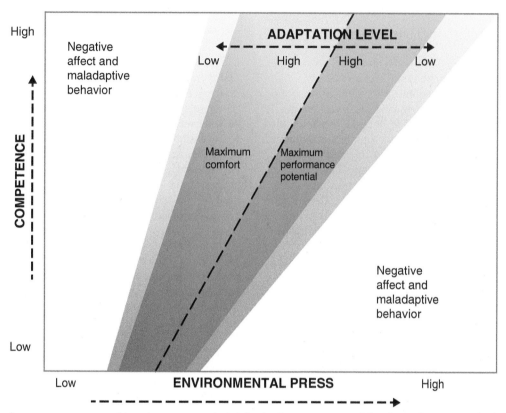

According to the competence–press model, environments vary in their levels of press, or stress, and therefore in the maximum level of affect and adaptation they provide.

Environments can also adapt to the competence of residents whose cognitive abilities are diminished by neurocognitive disorder. Specifically, such environments should meet the criteria of being safe and secure, be visually accessible, minimize memory requirements, provide opportunities for a range of social interactions, and support the values and goals of care (Fleming & Bennett, 2015). Cognitive supports, furthermore, can help promote the social well-being of residents by enhancing their ability to navigate the environment (Nordin et al., 2017a).

Suggestions for Improving Long-Term Care

Clearly, the environment plays an important role in affecting the individual's health, both inside and outside an institutional environment. Within the institutional setting, the implications of the competence–press model are that

the needs of individuals should be met to the greatest extent possible. For example, one approach to intervention for patients with neurocognitive disorder who exhibit agitation is to develop an individualized "algorithm" that matches interventions with the abilities and preferences of the residents. Rather than treating this behavior with medications, which is the typical route of treatment, the nonpharmacological approach can better preserve the resident's ADLs, speech, communication, and responsiveness (Cohen-Mansfield et al., 2014).

Nurses aides, who increasingly are managing many of the daily living activities of residents (Seblega et al., 2010), can be taught to use behavioral methods to help residents maintain self-care and, hence, independence (Burgio et al., 2002). Such interventions can also benefit staff–resident relationships. Because satisfaction with treatment by staff is such a significant component of satisfaction with the institution (Chou et al., 2002), any intervention that maximizes positive interactions between staff and residents is bound to have a favorable impact on the sense of well-being experienced by residents. Such training, even with patients who have severe neurocognitive disorder, can help reduce dependence on psychotropic medications (Fossey et al., 2006).

The size of the institution can also affect the adaptation of residents. The typical long-term care facility design is similar to that of a hospital, with long hallways and centralized lounge areas and nursing stations. New models for nursing home design attempt to break up the monotony to create a heightened feeling of a community or neighborhood. Nursing stations are removed from view, allowing residents and staff to share lounges. Hallways have alcoves that can store medicine carts and nursing stations. Small group living clusters, improved interior design, and access to gardens can help maintain independence in residents whose autonomy would otherwise be threatened (Regnier & Denton, 2009). Even if the rooms themselves are well designed, then, the overall layout becomes an important factor in determining how easy or difficult it is for residents to benefit from social interactions among themselves (Nordin et al., 2017b).

Other models of change stress new ways of allocating staff to meet the care needs of residents. In one such model, rather than basing staff assignments on the completion of specific tasks for all residents (bathing, changing dressings, and administering medications), staff are assigned to meet all the needs of a particular group of residents. Although such a system increases the staffing requirements, overall the institutions reduce their expenses in the areas of restraints and antipsychotic medications. Hospitalization rates, staff turnover, and success in rehabilitation also improve as does the satisfaction that residents express about their care (Bartels et al., 2002). Another improvement involves the use of a team approach to providing mental health services. Residents with chronic physical illnesses or neurocognitive disorders who also have psychiatric conditions can benefit from a multidisciplinary approach that involves thorough assessment of psychiatric, medical, and environmental causes as well as programs for teaching behavioral management skills to nurses (Collet et al., 2010).

Another factor to consider in understanding the psychological adaptation of the older adult to the institutional environment is the possibility that a nursing or residential care home may represent an improvement over a private residence. Researchers in Finland found that nursing home residents were higher in sense of well-being than those living at home, many of whom were no longer able to care for themselves. Because many residential facilities for older adults have long waiting periods, particularly the better

ones, older adults may be relieved to be admitted where they know they will no longer suffer the burden of living on their own (Böckerman, Johansson, & Saarni, 2012).

The Green House model offers an alternative to the traditional nursing homes by offering older adults individual homes within a small community of 6 to 10 residents and skilled nursing staff. Figure 12.12 shows the outlines of a typical Green House residence. A key feature of this design is the open-plan layout of shared spaces, with the centerpiece being the hearth and surrounding seating area. As you can see, the Green House residence is designed to feel like a home; medical equipment is stored away from sight, the rooms are sunny and bright, and the outdoor environment is easily accessible. Data from longitudinal studies of the Green House model have recently become available. As you might expect from seeing the layout of a typical Green House design, residents in these facilities are more likely to engage in social interaction than residents of traditional long-term care facilities. Somewhat surprisingly, though, one study identified along with this increase in social interaction an increase in depressive symptoms as well, perhaps due to greater recognition of these symptoms in the open-plan setting (Yoon et al., 2015).

The Green House model is consistent with principles of the Culture Change Movement in services for older adults (Bowers et al., 2016), which promotes person-centered care, allowing individuals to feel "at home" despite living in institutional settings. The goal of the Culture Change Movement is to transform services for older adults by adopting care to the needs of the individual in innovative ways (Briody & Briller, 2017). However, researchers caution that despite its obvious appeal, the Culture Change Movement still requires more rigorous testing before it becomes translated into a more widespread policy (Shier et al., 2014).

Clearly, new ideas are needed to revamp the current health care system for the aging Baby Boomers, whose numbers, lifestyles, and values will almost invariably lead to challenges of the status quo of care now being offered in the typical long-term care facility.

In conclusion, the concerns of institutionalized older adults are of great importance to individuals and to their families, many of whom are involved in helping to make long-term care decisions for their older relatives. The dignity and self-respect of the resident, which is fortunately now being regulated by state and federal certification standards, can best be addressed by multidimensional approaches that take into account personal and contextual factors. Interventions based on these approaches will ultimately lead to a higher quality of life for those who must spend their last days or months in the care of others.

FIGURE 12.12

Green House Design

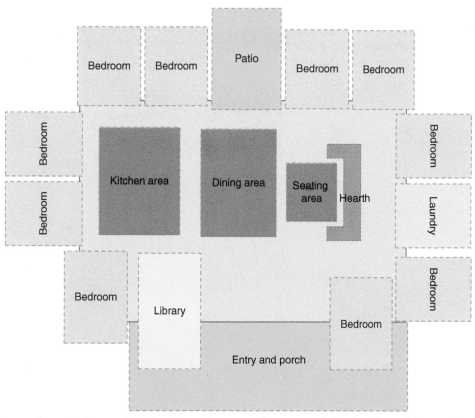

This is a sample layout of a nursing home with the Green House design. Note the presence of a hearth and central dining and kitchen areas.

SUMMARY

1. A wide range of long-term care settings are available that are specifically designed for older adults. These include residential care facilities that provide medical and nursing care, and community-based treatment in which residents live in a range of group settings. Home health care is increasingly becoming available to allow older adults to "age in place." Other facilities offer a range of services, such as assisted living facilities that are attached to nursing homes. Care for older adults in these facilities is best thought of as spanning a continuum from home to acute care facilities, with the last phase being end-of-life care in a hospice.

2. Medicare, a pay-as-you-go system, is designed to provide hospital insurance and supplemental medical insurance. Other forms of insurance attached to Medicare are becoming increasingly available to older

adults. Medicaid is intended to reduce the burden of health care costs among those who need help paying for medical services, but individuals receiving this assistance must "spend down" to eliminate their assets. The cost of Medicare is expected to skyrocket over the coming decades; this will lead to the bankruptcy of the Medicare Trust fund unless preventive measures are taken.

3. The rights of nursing home residents became protected with the passage of the Nursing Home Reform Act in 1987. Since then, there have been major landmarks involving increasing regulation of the nursing home industry. Rating systems are now mandated by certification agencies, and these are available to help consumers make decisions about care for themselves or their family members. Despite the attempts by federal and state governments to ensure higher quality of care, there remain significant deficiencies, particularly in the

areas of infection control, accident protection, and food sanitation.

4. Psychological issues in long-term care focus on the provision of an adequate environment that will maximally meet the needs of residents. The competence–press model proposes an ideal relationship between how demanding an environment is and the abilities of the resident to meet those demands. New approaches in institutional care include the Green House model, in which residents share living spaces around common eating, dining, and relaxing areas. The Culture Change Movement promotes person-centered care and may become the basis for improved long-term care facilities in the future.

13

Death and Dying

Saying goodbye to loved ones is never easy, but there are ways to help with grief. Here are different strategies people use to remember and honor important people who have passed away:

AGEFEED

#TIPS

1. Starting new traditions for dates for holidays or anniversaries, such as a family gathering to commemorate those who have passed away.

2. Planting trees or gardens as a memorial.

3. Writing down memories about loved ones and referring to them during difficult times. Even the small, simple memories will have meaning for years to come.

4. Reading their favorite books.

5. Turning keepsakes into special mementos. Some opt to make favorite items into blankets, stuffed animals, or even artwork.

6. Encouraging others who knew the loved one to share their memories with you—you may learn things you never knew!

7. Playing their favorite music. Music has a way of bringing memories back to life and can help keep a connection.

8. Living life in a way that would make them proud.

9. Dedicating a bench, section of the highway, or other location meaningful to the loved one.

10. Finding meaning in lyrics to songs or seeing objects or animals and thinking of the loved one (cardinals, for example, are very common).

For many people, the concept of death is as fascinating as it is frightening. By definition, death remains the great unknown; even individuals who have had so-called near-death experiences cannot claim with certainty that what happened to them is an accurate prediction of what is to come in the future.

You may think occasionally about what death means to you, and how you would approach the ending of your life. As people age, the concept of death takes on greater reality. Perhaps what most people wish for is to live a maximum health expectancy, which is the length of time an individual can live without significant disease and disability. In keeping with Erikson's concepts of generativity and ego integrity, many people also wish to leave something behind to be remembered by and to have made an impact on other people's lives.

From the biopsychosocial perspective, death and dying are best understood in a multidimensional manner. Death is, of course, a biological event, as it is the point in time when the body's functions cease to operate. However, this biological fact of life is overlaid with a great deal of psychological meaning, both to the individual and to those in the individual's social network. Socioculturally, death is interpreted in multiple ways varying according to time, place, and culture.

WHAT DO WE KNOW ABOUT DEATH?

The technical definition of death is the irreversible cessation of circulatory and respiratory functions, or when all structures of the brain have irreversibly ceased to function (President's Commission for the Study of Ethical Problems in Medicine and Biomedical and Behavioral Research, 1981). The 1981 report was the basis for the Uniform Determination of Death Act, a model state law that was adopted by most U.S. states. The term dying refers to the period during which the organism loses its vitality. These terms, as you will learn, are not always clear-cut, particularly with advances in life support technology that allow people to be kept alive almost indefinitely after an organ vital to survival has failed. In fact, in 2019, Nova Scotia passed an act "Respecting Human Organ and Tissue Donation," which alters the definition of brain death to state "irreversible loss of the brain's ability to control and co-ordinate the organism's critical functions" instead of the U.S. law's terminology of "irreversible cessation" (Nova Scotia Legislature, 2019).

Medical Aspects of Death

Although the death experience varies from person to person, there are some commonalities in the physical changes shown by a person whose functions are deteriorating to the point that death will occur within a few hours or days. In a dying person, the symptoms that death is imminent include being asleep most of the time, being disoriented, breathing irregularly, having visual and auditory hallucinations, being less able to see, producing less urine, and having mottled skin, cool hands and feet, an overly warm trunk, and excessive secretions of bodily fluids (Gavrin & Chapman, 1995). An older adult who is close to death is likely to be unable to walk or eat, recognize family members, suffer constant pain, and feel that breathing is difficult.

There are many variations in the dying process, which can make it difficult for health professionals to diagnose whether a patient is dying or not (Kennedy et al., 2014). However, there do appear to be some patterns in the dying process that can serve as guidance. These patterns are captured in the concept of the dying trajectory, which is the temporal pattern of the disease process leading to a patient's death (Glaser & Strauss, 1968). Although originally identified through qualitative interviews, subsequent epidemiological data support the validity of the dying trajectories (Lunney et al., 2003). Figure 13.1 illustrates the four types of dying trajectories. As you can see, they vary in their duration and their shape, and are associated with different causes of loss of function and death.

In sudden death, the individual is at a high level of functioning until the death suddenly occurs. The sudden death trajectory applies to people in good health whose death is due to an accidental cause. The sudden death trajectory can also apply to people who die due to an unanticipated medical event, such as heat stroke or sudden cardiac failure.

Moving now to the terminal illness trajectory, this applies to people who have advance warning of a terminal illness such as cancer. They were functioning at a high level until the disease progressed to the point at which the body could no longer sustain life (Teno et al., 2001). The third dying trajectory occurs in cases of death due to the progressive failures of organs as in COPD and chronic heart failure, as well as in other conditions such as kidney failure. The individual's death will occur over a prolonged period with a series of dips and recoveries until the organ failure completely compromises life.

Finally, the trajectory reflected by declines in functioning among frail individuals applies to people who have limited physical reserves. The pattern characterizes individuals in the later stages of Alzheimer's disease, for whom the immediate cause of death may be an acute illness such as pneumonia developing against a backdrop of general loss of function.

A common syndrome observed at the end of life is the anorexia-cachexia syndrome, in which the individual loses appetite (anorexia) and muscle mass (cachexia).

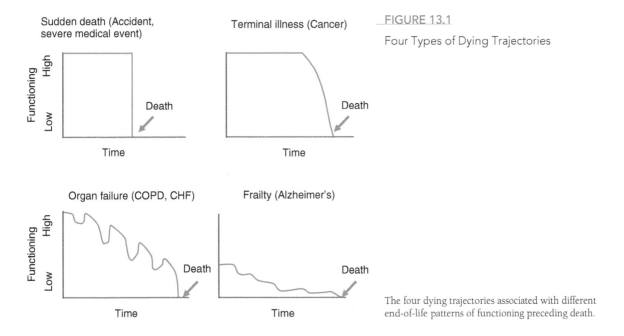

FIGURE 13.1

Four Types of Dying Trajectories

The four dying trajectories associated with different end-of-life patterns of functioning preceding death.

The majority of cancer patients experience cachexia, a condition also found commonly in patients who have AIDS and neurocognitive disorder. Patients who are dying are also likely to experience nausea, difficulty swallowing, bowel problems, dry mouth, and edema, or the accumulation of liquid in the abdomen and extremities that leads to bloating. Anxiety, depression, confusion, and memory loss are also common psychological symptoms that people experience in their final days and hours.

These symptoms at the very end of life clearly create discomfort for the dying patient. Families also are affected by watching their loved ones suffer, as you may be able to attest from your own experience. Psychologists and other health care providers have become increasingly attuned to the need to provide services to assist patients and their families during the final stages of dying, as you will learn later in the chapter.

Death by the Numbers

Mortality data provide a fascinating picture of the factors within a given population that influence the course of human life. By knowing how to interpret statistics about death, you can gain a great deal of insight into the factors that contribute to living a long life.

The quickest way to gauge the health of a given region of the world or period in history is to find out who dies and when. The crude death rate is simply the number of deaths divided by population alive during a certain time period. An age-specific death rate is the crude death rate for a specific age group. The age-specific death rate only

discloses the likelihood of people dying within their own age group. This statistic is calculated by dividing the number of deaths within a particular age group by the number of people in that age group in the population. The third mortality statistic is the age-adjusted death rate, a mortality rate statistically modified to eliminate the effect of different age distributions in the different populations. The age-adjusted death rate is based on a weighted average of the age-specific mortality rates, eliminating the effect of different age distributions among the different populations (Centers for Disease Control and Prevention, 2012).

Figure 13.2 illustrates the difference between the crude death rate (red line) per age group and the age-specific death rate (blue line). As you can see, the most number of deaths occur for people in their 70s and 80s. The age-specific death rate is far higher in the later decades than in earlier decades of life, reflecting the fact that they are not only smaller segments of the total population but also the most likely to die. Indeed, those 75 and older make up over half the number of deaths in the United States.

In 2017, there were 2,813,503 deaths in the United States, which translates to a crude death rate of 863.8 per 100,000 in the population, and an age-adjusted death rate of 731.9 (Kochanek et al., 2019). The age-adjusted death rate is lower than the crude death rate because more of the deaths occurred disproportionately to that smaller population base of people 75 and older. Just 10 years earlier, fewer Americans had died (about 2.4 million). The age-adjusted death rate at that time was 760.2. As you can see, then, although fewer people died in 2007, the United States was statistically unhealthier then because the

FIGURE 13.2

Mortality Statistics by Age Group, U.S.

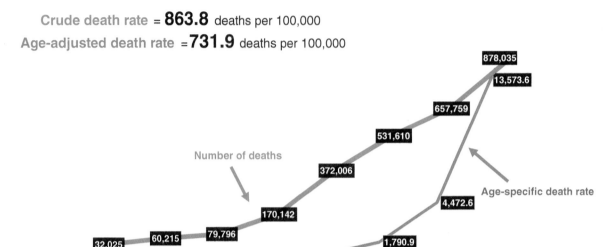

Crude death rate = **863.8** deaths per 100,000
Age-adjusted death rate = **731.9** deaths per 100,000

These statistics on death rates show that the majority of deaths in the United States occur in people 75 years of age and older.

age-adjusted death rate was so much higher than it was 10 years later. In general, the age-adjusted death rate in the United States has been declining steadily.

Figure 13.3 shows the leading causes of death (excluding "other") in the age groups of 25 to 44, 45 to 64, and 65 and older. The charts highlight the number one cause of death for each group. The youngest group of adults is most likely to die due to unintentional injuries, primarily motor vehicle accidents. In the middle-aged group of adults, cancer becomes the primary cause, and the oldest age group is most likely to die from heart disease.

Remember that the actual numbers of deaths are lower for progressively younger age groups. This means that, for example, people 25 to 44 years of age have lower rates of death in general. This is the age group least likely to have heart disease or cancer. When you hear that "heart disease is the number one killer" in the United States, you can see that this is because the majority of deaths occur in people 65 and older, and it is only in this age group that heart disease is the number one cause of death. From a public health perspective, younger adults need to prevent the development of heart disease and cancer, but to avoid an early death, they need to prevent accidental injuries.

Another way to look at mortality patterns is to compare life expectancy, which, as you will recall, is the average number of years of life remaining to people born within a similar period of time. Currently, the U.S. life expectancy is 78.6 years (Kochanek et al., 2019). As you can see from

Figure 13.4, life expectancy varies by sex and race/ethnicity. Epidemiologists regard the higher life expectancy for Hispanic males as paradoxical, given that in the United States, individuals of Hispanic (and Latino) ethnicity live in harsher economic conditions. The phenomenon is termed the Hispanic mortality paradox. However, this paradox may apply to immigrant populations in general (Teruya et al., 2013). Individuals who immigrate to the United States may be a healthier group. Additionally, they are less likely to smoke and may have more robust social support networks. It is also possible that the mortality advantage is conferred to working-age individuals, and not to children or older adults (Shor et al., 2017).

Figure 13.5 shows other important demographic factors related to mortality within the United States as well as variations by region of the world and country. People who are married have lower mortality rates as do those with higher education. Within the United States, as you might expect from regional variations in heart disease and stroke, the mortality rates are highest in the southeast. Oklahoma's high mortality rates are due to the prevalence of high BMIs (The U.S. Burden of Disease Collaborators, 2018). Furthermore, within each state, there are variations by county in mortality rates as well as in causes of death (Dwyer-Lindgren et al., 2016).

The bottom half of Figure 13.5 presents facts about worldwide mortality rates (United Nations, 2019). Due to poorer quality information on age group variations in

FIGURE 13.3

Top 10 Causes of Death by Age Group, U.S.

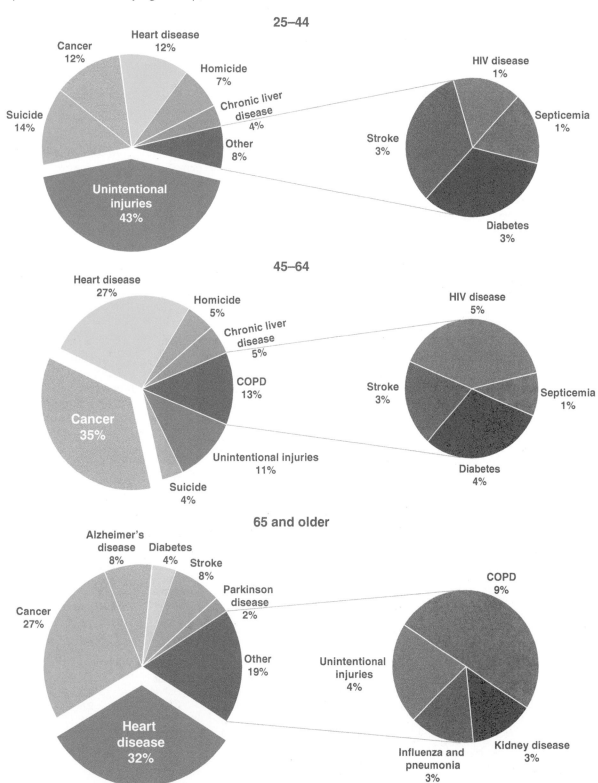

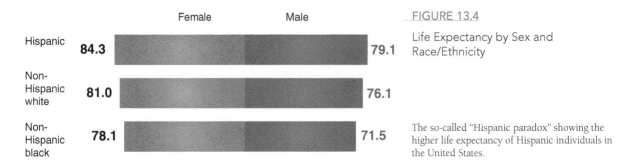

FIGURE 13.4

Life Expectancy by Sex and Race/Ethnicity

The so-called "Hispanic paradox" showing the higher life expectancy of Hispanic individuals in the United States.

death rates, these data are presented in terms of crude mortality rates (per 1,000 in the country's population). Overall, mortality rates were higher in the less developed regions of the world, reflecting higher mortality at lower ages in countries with high incidence of communicable diseases and less access to health care. Among the top five countries in mortality rates are several from Central and Eastern Europe which are characterized by unhealthy diets. Central African Republic's high mortality rate is due to high rates of infectious and parasitic disease (Green, 2012).

The low mortality rates in the Middle Eastern countries shown in the bottom of Figure 13.5 reflect an influx of "healthy migrants" (Chaabna et al., 2018), similar to that observed in the United States. The low mortality rates in Maldives appears to be due, instead, to a lowering in maternal mortality rates, reflecting a concerted effort by the government to improve health care to expectant mothers (United Nations Population Fund, 2016).

Mortality statistics show how the numbers differ according to key demographic factors. However, the numbers only tell part of the story. Researchers are interested in determining how mortality patterns also reflect the psychosocial factors represented in such indicators as education, marital status, and geography that can influence longevity. These factors are summarized in Figure 13.6.

Beginning with education, as you learned earlier, mortality rates are lower for people with a college education. The health habits associated with educational level account, at least in part, for this effect. A 30-year retrospective study conducted on nearly 180,000 individuals ages 20 to 65 identified alcohol consumption and smoking as the two key factors that contributed to higher death rates among the less educated (Doniec et al., 2019).

Related to education, but distinct in its effect on mortality is occupational status. Whitehall II established some years ago that men and women in lower socioeconomic

FIGURE 13.5

Key Facts About Mortality Statistics

Demographic factors as they relate to death rates in the United States and around the world.

FIGURE 13.6

Summary of Mortality Predictors

Education	Occupational status	Political economy
Air pollution	Loneliness	Religious involvement
Moderate exercise	Chronotype	Hip fracture

Top psychosocial factors related to mortality.

positions died at younger ages than did their counterparts from higher status occupations. At least some of this differential reflected differences in eating habits and smoking (Marmot et al., 2008) as well as obesity (Hart et al., 2011).

Further support for the role of occupational status as a contributor to mortality independent of education are findings showing that upward mobility in socioeconomic status predicts a lower risk of mortality due to cardiovascular disease (Sung et al., 2019). However, individuals in jobs with higher prestige may suffer health setbacks under certain conditions. A large cross-national study of workers in Japan, South Korea, and eight European countries conducted between 1990 and 2015 supported the overall social class and mortality relationship for Europe. For the two Asian countries, however, the economic downturns of the late 1990s and 2000s took their toll on workers in higher-level managerial and professional positions, who were more likely to die from cancer and suicide (Tanaka et al., 2019).

The political, economic, and social climates, then, may interact with the individual's own risk factors for higher mortality. An analysis of 58 articles reviewing the available literature on health risks and type of economy showed that the populations in countries with greater support for health care and fewer income inequalities benefited in terms of health and mortality (McCartney et al., 2019).

Health risk factors also contribute to increased mortality due to forces outside the individual's control. One of these is exposure to air pollution. Among a large national cohort of over 635,000 U.S. adults, across subgroups identified on the basis of sex, age, race/ethnicity, social class, and region, the presence of fine particulate matter in the local area predicted early mortality. Lack of feelings of social connection can also contribute to mortality risk.

The Whitehall II cohort provided some of the first evidence for job status and mortality. More recent analyses suggest that, at least for men, social support becomes an additional factor in the equation. Social network size predicted 27% of the relationship between job status and cardiovascular mortality; marital status predicted an additional 25% (Stringhini et al., 2012). Older adults who live alone and feel emotionally isolated were found, in the Berlin Aging Study, to have a higher risk of mortality (O'Suilleabhain et al., 2019).

Understanding the role of social support in mortality risk can also help explain the longstanding observation that people who are active in organized religion live longer than those who are not. Attendance at religious services appears to be the key protective factor against mortality due to cancer and cardiovascular disease (Li et al., 2016). Social status and lifestyle factors also play a role in affecting this relationship (Wen et al., 2019).

Exercise is known to affect mortality, primarily through its role in protecting against cardiovascular disease. In an innovative study linking steps walked per day to mortality, the "myth of 10,000 steps" was "busted" by showing a mortality benefit, among women, from walking 4,400 daily steps compared to walking only 2,700. For the women in this study, averaging 72 years, a step count of over 7,500 proved no more effective in lowering mortality than 4,400, and rate of walking seemed to make no difference (Abbasi, 2019).

Hip fracture presents another well-known risk to mortality, as it is known to initiate a cycle of institutionalization that can create its own adverse health consequences. However, even before leaving the hospital, 13% of hip fracture patients requiring surgery developed a systemic septic (blood) infection that more than doubled the risk of mortality within 30 days of admission (Kjorholt et al., 2019).

Finally, a chronotype in which an individual shows a lifetime of being an "evening person" seems to contribute to mortality in later life, as shown in a 35-year longitudinal study of over 6,000 British adults. People with the evening chronotype tend to engage in unhealthier habits, such as exercising less, eating later, smoking more, and drinking more alcohol than those with the morning chronotype. Even after taking these unhealthier habits into account, those with an evening chronotype had elevated mortality risk (Didikoglu et al., 2019).

Mortality statistics provide valuable insights into patterns of health and well-being in later life. Analyzing the causes of mortality requires taking many related factors into account, and with the availability of more and more longitudinal datasets, and the techniques to analyze them, there should be even more valuable lessons to learn from future studies.

SOCIOCULTURAL PERSPECTIVES ON DEATH AND DYING

According to the sociocultural perspective, people learn the social meaning of death from the language, arts, and death-related rituals of their cultures (see Figure 13.7). A culture's death ethos, or prevailing philosophy of death, can be inferred from funeral rituals, treatment of those who are dying, belief in the presence of ghosts, belief in an afterlife, the extent to which death topics are taboo, the language people use to describe death (through euphemisms such as "passed away"), and the representation of death in the arts.

Throughout the course of Western history, cultural meanings and rituals attached to the process of death and to the disposition of dead bodies have gone through remarkable alterations. The ancient Egyptians practiced what are perhaps the most well known of all death rituals. They believed that a new, eternal life awaited the dead and that the body had to be preserved through mummification in order to make it the permanent home for the spirit of the deceased. The mummies were buried in elaborate tombs, where they were decorated and surrounded by valued possessions. Family members would visit the tombs to bring offers of food to sustain the dead in the afterlife. The *Book of the Dead* contained magic spells intended to guide the departed through the underworld and into the afterlife.

Mummification was practiced in many cultures, including South America, where the Incans were known to have preserved their dead until as recently as 500 years ago. People can still request that their bodies be mummified today, with services provided by a firm in Salt Lake City for the cost of $35,000 to $60,000 (Dickinson, 2012).

Cultural views within Western society toward death and the dead have undergone many shifts from ancient times to the present (Ariès, 1974, 1981). Throughout the Middle Ages, the prevailing view was of tamed death, in which death was viewed as familiar and simple, a transition to eternal life. Death and dying were events that involved the entire community, supported by specific prayers and practices that "tamed" the unknown.

Over the next several centuries, this view of death as a natural process began to be replaced in a cultural shift to a view of death as the end of the self, something to be feared and kept at a distance. For a period in the 1800s, death and dying became glorified, and it was considered noble to die for a cause (the "beautiful death"). Gradually, Western attitudes have shifted once again into what Ariès called invisible death, the preference that the dying retreat from the family and spend their final days confined in a hospital setting. These attitudes become translated into social death, the process through which the dying become treated as nonpersons by family or health care workers as they are left to spend their final days in the hospital or nursing home.

As death has become removed from the everyday world, it has acquired more fear and mystery. Instead of developing our own personal meanings, we are at the mercy of the many images of death we see in the media. News sources expose us to stories of death from the massive scale of natural disasters to school shootings and terrorist attacks. The death of one famous person may preoccupy the American or European media for weeks, as was the case in the deaths of such celebrities as Princess Diana (1997), John F. Kennedy, Jr. (1999), Michael Jackson (2009), Whitney Houston (2012) and Prince (2016). Some of the most popular movies and television shows focus exclusively on homicide, often taking us step-by-step through the grisliest of tales involving serial killers and the work of forensic scientists.

Amid the growing institutionalization of death and the attempts by the medical establishment to prolong life, a small book published in 1969 was to alter permanently Western attitudes toward and treatment of the dying. This book, by Elisabeth Kübler-Ross (1969), called *On Death and Dying*, described five stages of dying considered to occur universally among terminally ill patients: denial, anger, bargaining, depression, and acceptance.

Rather than being discrete step-like stages, as is often portrayed in the lay literature, the five stages of dying may

FIGURE 13.7

Components of a Society's Death Ethos

Funeral rituals

Treatment of the dying

Representation in the arts

Belief in the afterlife and ghosts

Social conventions regarding talk of death and dying

These are the key indicators of a society's death ethos.

FIGURE 13.8

Kübler-Ross Change/Five Stages/Curve

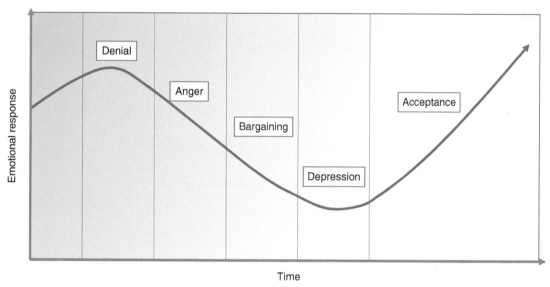

Stages in the Kübler-Ross model of death and dying shown as a curve instead of discrete steps.

be more accurately regarded as points along a progression (see Figure 13.8). Indeed, the "change curve" as shown here is now used in a variety of contexts outside of the death and dying literature, such as in helping individuals cope with change more generally. If you think about the last change you had to endure, such as being let go from a job, it is possible you can relate to your own progression until you finally had no choice but to accept the firing and move on.

Unfortunately, the original views of Kübler-Ross became distorted as the book's popularity grew. The five stages began to be interpreted as a series of steps that must be followed by each dying patient. If a patient refused to engage in "bargaining," for instance, then it must mean something was wrong with the way that person was handling the terminal illness. The Kübler-Ross formulation also ignores other emotions that dying individuals may experience, such as curiosity, hope, relief, and apathy.

The critical point that Kübler-Ross attempted to make in her writing is that to reach acceptance of a fatal illness, the dying person must be allowed to talk openly with family members and health care workers. Rather than hide the diagnosis or pretend that everything will be all right, those who interact with the dying individual need to give that person a chance to express the many emotions that surface, ranging from fury to dejection. Along with the work of cultural anthropologist Ernest Becker, whose book *The Denial of Death* (Becker, 1973) drew attention to Western culture's unwillingness to face the reality of

mortality, these writings set the stage for a major shift in cultural attitudes and medical practice for the dying.

Most importantly, the idea of death with dignity proposed that the period of dying should not subject the individual to extreme physical dependency or loss of control of bodily functions (Humphrey, 1991). This idea now lies behind efforts in the medical community for dying patients and their families to bring death back into the home. Similarly, patients are being offered the opportunity for a good death, in which they can have autonomy in making decisions about the type, site, and duration of care they receive at the end of life (Carr, 2012).

The shifts away from invisible death in the mid-20th century to more contemporary approaches allow dying patients to receive support in the final stages of a terminal illness. Patients and their loved ones are increasingly finding ways to make death once again a more natural way to bring those lives to a humane ending.

PSYCHOLOGICAL PERSPECTIVES ON DEATH AND DYING

From a psychological standpoint, death and dying carry many layers of meaning. Toward the end of their lives, individuals may begin to shift their identities to incorporate the reality that faces them. As with changes they experience throughout life, people use identity assimilation to minimize if not deny, as much as possible, this coming reality. At some point, however, they must accommodate the fact that their life will be ending, at which point the process of identity balance may start to allow them to face this fact with equanimity. Indeed, these shifts in identity as the individual adapts to the reality of death fit well with the Kübler-Ross change curve, which also begins with denial and ends with acceptance.

The way that people die can also come to define their identities in ways that no other life changes can. Think about the way your views changed about one of those celebrities whose life came to a premature ending. Your memory of them is forever altered by the timing, if not cause, of their death. That same process can apply to the way you think about the death of people who were close to you. Similarly, the ending of your life will alter your identity in the way that close ones will remember you.

When you reach the point of thinking about your own life's ending, you may wish to take steps to leave a legacy that will continue to define you after you are gone, a process called legitimization of biography. Through this process, people attempt to see what they have done as having meaning, and they prepare the "story" of their lives by which they will be remembered in the minds of others (Marshall, 1980). Some individuals may put their memoirs in writing, and others achieve an internal reckoning in which they evaluate their contributions as well as their shortcomings.

Psychologically, the dying process can begin well before the individual is in any real physical jeopardy. People first start to think about their own mortality when they reach the point called awareness of finitude, which is when they pass the age when other people close to them had themselves died (Marshall, 1980). For example, if a man's father died at the age of 66, a kind of counting-down process begins when the son reaches that age. He anticipates the end of life and understands that life really will end.

The notion that the awareness of life's end triggers an intense period of self-evaluation is also an important component of Erikson's concept of ego integrity, as we discussed in Chapter 8. Erikson emphasized that during this period of life, individuals deal with mortality and questions related to the ending of their existence by attempting to place their lives into perspective. Presumably, this process may occur at any age, as the dying individual attempts to achieve a peaceful resolution with past mistakes and events that can no longer be made up for or changed.

Terror management theory also proposes that when people's thoughts of death are activated, either consciously or unconsciously, they can experience a wide range of beneficial effects. They may adopt better health habits, be more focused on intrinsic rather than extrinsic goals, show more compassion, and be more motivated to have

close interpersonal relationships. People may even be more creative, less likely to hold stereotypes, and feel greater attachment to their community. On the other hand, the "terror" part of terror management suggests that heightened awareness of death can come at a price. Awareness of mortality can be beneficial to people who are able to cope with stressful situations (Kelley & Schmeichel, 2015). Others who lack this ability may experience greater levels of anxiety and lower well-being (Juhl & Routledge, 2016).

ISSUES IN END-OF-LIFE CARE

Improvements in medical technology along with changes in attitudes toward death and dying are leading clinicians to become far more sensitive to the emotional and physical needs of dying patients. At the same time, legislation and social movements that advocate for the rights of dying patients are making progress in allowing them to preserve their dignity and autonomy.

Advance Directives

One of the most significant changes to take place in medical treatment of the dying, the Patient Self-Determination Act (PSDA) of 1990 guarantees the right of all competent adults to have an active role in decisions about their care. The PSDA guarantees that prior to becoming ill, an individual can put in writing his or her wishes regarding end-of-life treatment.

A patient can express these wishes in a legally binding document known as an advance directive. There are two components of the advance directive. A living will stipulates the conditions under which a patient will accept or refuse treatment. Figure 13.9 shows the components of an advance directive. The second component of an advance directive is a durable power of attorney for health care (DPAHC) appointment, also known as a health care proxy, to make decisions to act on their behalf should the patient become incapacitated. Not only are advance directives useful in ensuring that patients play an active role in deciding on their treatment but they also facilitate communication among patients, health care staff and families, protect an individual's resources, alleviate anxiety, and reduce the chances of the patient's being maltreated (The President's Council on Bioethics, 2005).

Advance directives specify the code status, or the conditions under which dying patients wish to be treated. Full code means that there should be no limit on life-sustaining treatment; in other words, the patient requests to be intubated or ventilated and resuscitated with cardiopulmonary resuscitation (CPR) after fatal cardiac or pulmonary

FIGURE 13.9

Components of Advance Care Planning Decisions

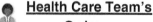

Life Support Orders

Heartbeat
Restoring heartbeat by pushing on the chest, medication, or defibrillation (electric shocks).

Breathing
Bringing air into the lungs by a tube pushed into the windpipe connected to ventilator.

Digestion
Providing nutrition with a tube inserted into the stomach or by hand feeding.

Health Care Proxy

Proxy
Someone to make treatment decisions if the patient is unable to do so such as relative, friend, lawyer, or in social or spiritual community.

Instructions
Specific life-sustaining treatments including blood transfusion, kidney dialysis, and organ and tissue donations.

Health Care Team's Orders

MOLST
Medical orders for life-sustaining treatments to be acted on immediately, intended for nurse practitioner or physician assistant.

POLST
Physician orders for life-sustaining treatments to be acted on immediately, intended for the physician.

Advance care planning decisions

Decisions that must be made in advance care planning.

arrest. A do not resuscitate (DNR) order directs health care workers not to use resuscitation if the patient experiences cardiac or pulmonary arrest. Overtreatment occurs when patients receive active life support that includes resuscitation do not have their DNR orders respected but instead.

Another component of an advance directive includes direct orders to be followed in case of an emergency. A Medical Order for Life-Sustaining Treatment (MOLST) contains orders for a physician's assistant or nurse practitioner, and a Physician's Order for Life-Sustaining Treatment (POLST) contains orders for physicians.

The PSDA mandates that health care professionals receive education about advance directives as well as provide information to patients as they are being admitted to the hospital. The existence of an advance directive must be documented in the medical record. Each state is permitted to establish and define its own legislation concerning advance directives, but the basic federal requirements must be met in all Medicare- and Medicaid-funded facilities in order for them to continue to receive funding.

Various safeguards are in place to protect against abuse of the process, such as the requirement for witnesses and the requirement that more than one physician provide a diagnosis for a condition. In addition to documenting the patient's wishes, the PSDA was intended to ensure more active involvement in planning and treatment by patients and to uphold the principles of respect for their dignity and autonomy.

Studies on the effectiveness of the PSDA show that health care providers do not always communicate or do not communicate enough with dying patients or alleviate their pain (Yuen et al., 2011). Nursing home residents may also complete a DNH, or do not hospitalize order. Those who do are less likely to be hospitalized or to die in the hospital, but nevertheless hospitalization may occur regardless of their wishes (Tanuseputro et al., 2019). Hospital patients themselves do not consistently receive the opportunity to complete an advance directive, although standard forms that involve a MOST can improve the rates of implementing DNRs (Kohen & Nair, 2019). Nevertheless, only about one-third of adults including those with chronic diseases actually do have advance directives (Yadav et al., 2017), meaning that there is still a considerable need for education for older adults, their families, and health care providers.

Physician-Assisted Suicide and Euthanasia

Patients can write an advance directive in order to specify the level of care they want to receive at any point in time, including well before they become terminally ill. In physician-assisted suicide (PAS), terminally ill individuals make the conscious decision, while they are still able to do so, that they want their lives to end before dying becomes a protracted process. When the time comes, patients themselves receive from their physicians the medical tools necessary to end their lives. In contrast, physicians performing euthanasia take the actions that cause the patient to die, with the intention of preventing the suffering associated with a prolonged ending of life.

The leading proponent of PAS was Dr. Jack Kevorkian. In 1989, he built what he called a "suicide machine," which he then used in 1990 on his first patient, a 54-year-old woman with Alzheimer's disease. Throughout the 1990s, he conducted more than 100 assisted suicides. In a highly controversial televised segment on the program *60 Minutes*, aired in November 1998, Kevorkian ended the life of a 52-year-old Michigan man suffering from a terminal neurological disease. Because this procedure was illegal (and was flagrantly performed in front of millions of TV viewers), Kevorkian was arrested and subsequently convicted on second-degree murder charges. In 2007, Kevorkian was released from prison after serving 8 years of a 10-to-25-year sentence; he died in 2011 shortly after the release of an award-winning HBO documentary about his life called *You Don't Know Jack*.

Physician-assisted suicide is legal in nine U.S. states (with two requiring a case-by-case court review), and the District of Columbia, meaning that physicians can prescribe medications to hasten death without being subject to prosecution. The individuals must have a terminal illness and a prognosis of 6 months or less to live. In these states, euthanasia is considered equivalent to PAS. Physician-assisted suicide and euthanasia are also legal in Canada, Belgium, the Netherlands, Luxembourg, Colombia, Switzerland, and some parts of Australia.

Physicians themselves appear to have very mixed reactions to following the request by their patients to end their lives. There is little empirical research on the subject but what exists suggests that these reactions persist long after physicians' assistance with the death of their patients. One review of the available data suggest that 30% to 50% feel emotionally burdened about participation, and 15% to 20% reported ongoing, adverse personal impacts despite recognizing that they were following the wishes of the patient (Kelly et al., 2019).

To clarify and refine the approach to patients who seek to end their lives, an international collaborative group established a definition of the "wish to hasten death (WTHD)," which they define as "a reaction to suffering, in the context of a life-threatening condition, from which the patient can see no way out other than to accelerate his or her death. This wish may be expressed spontaneously or after being asked about it, but it must be distinguished from the acceptance of impending death or from a wish to die naturally, although preferably soon" (Rodriguez-Prat et al., 2017). The factors that may prompt WTHD, according to the group's consensus statement, include physical symptoms being experienced or foreseen, psychological distress, a feeling of that one's life has lost its meaning, or social circumstances, such as the belief that one is a burden to others. In all cases, the WTHD is a reaction to suffering and it is not suicidal ideation in the absence of physical diseases or incapacity.

Hospice Care

Increasingly, the provision of end-of-life care is the domain of a hospice, a site or program that provides medical and supportive services for dying patients. Within the hospice environment, dying patients are attended to with regard to their needs for physical comfort and psychological and social support and given the opportunity to express and have their spiritual needs met. The care is palliative, focusing on controlling pain and other symptoms, and it is likely to take place within the home, beginning when the patient no longer wishes to receive active disease treatment. Physicians supervise the care of the patients, working closely with spiritual and bereavement counselors. Hospice services fit closely with expressed patient needs of obtaining adequate pain control and symptom management, avoiding an extended period of dying, achieving a sense of personal control, relieving the burden they place on others, and strengthening ties with those who are close to them.

Figure 13.10 illustrates a model showing how hospice care falls in the continuum of an individual's illness timeline. At the beginning of the illness, the patient is treated entirely with active care in a hospital. As the illness progresses, the ratio of palliative to active care increases steadily until by the end, the patient receives palliative care only.

The first well-known hospice was St. Christopher's in London, which opened in 1967. The hospice movement spread to the United States in the 1970s. In 1982, hospice benefits were made available to persons on Medicare who had a life expectancy of less than 6 months. By 2016, there were 4,300 hospices in the United States caring

FIGURE 13.10

Continuum from Hospital to Hospice

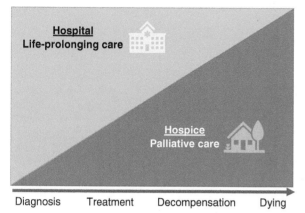

Life-prolonging to palliative care can be thought of as occurring on a continuum.

for an estimated 1.4 million individuals (Harris-Kojetin et al., 2019).

Improving Health Care and Mental Health Services to Dying Patients

Research on end-of-life care, including studies of the needs of and services preferred by dying patients and their families now provides the basis for improved training of health care professionals. One of the largest research projects carried out on the effectiveness of advance directives was known as "SUPPORT" ("Study to Understand Prognoses and Preferences for Outcomes and Risks of Treatments") (Lynn et al., 1997). Its authors concluded that the best end-of-life care is adapted to the nature of the patient's needs, rhythms, and situations as these vary over the dying trajectory.

Professional organizations are increasingly incorporating principles of good end-of-life care into their policy as well as providing suggested training curricula. The American Medical Association guidelines to establish quality care for individuals at the end of life include providing patients with the opportunity to discuss and plan for end-of-life care, assurance that attempts will be made to provide comfort and respect the patient's end-of-life wishes, assurance of dignity, and attention to the individual's goals. These rights also include minimizing the burden to the family and assisting the bereaved through the stages of mourning and adjustment. Additionally, the American Medical Association's Code of Ethics addresses organ procurement and transplantation, which are intended to protect the interests of living and deceased donors.

In 2014, the Institute of Medicine published a consensus report outlining the core components of quality end-of-life care (Institute of Medicine, 2014). These include adopting a person-centered, individualized approach along with involvement of family in end-of-life care planning. Key to the success of this care is communication between clinicians, their patients, and families. Additionally, the report also called for improved education and opportunities for professionals. Finally, the report stresses the need for policies and payment systems to support high-quality care (see Figure 13.11).

Some of the core recommendations for care include managing emotional distress, providing round-the-clock access to coordinated care and services, counseling and caregiver support, and attention to the patient's religious and spiritual needs. Finally, in keeping with a key study on getting services for the dying "right" (Dy & Lynn, 2007), to take the patient's specific dying trajectory into account, the report advocates continued personalized revisions to the patient's care plan.

BEREAVEMENT

Bereavement is the process during which people cope with the death of another person. A process that can affect anyone, regardless of age, bereavement is more likely to take place in later adulthood when people have an increased risk of losing their spouse, siblings, extended family, friends, colleagues, and neighbors.

Like the processes of death and dying, we can best understand bereavement as a biopsychosocial process. Physiologically, bereavement places stress on the body, leading to a series of physical symptoms, such as tightness in the chest, shortness of breath, loss of energy and strength, sleep problems, digestive symptoms, and decreased immune system resistance. As we saw in Chapter 9, these symptoms can be severe enough to increase risk of dying in widowed spouses. Emotionally, bereaved individuals experience a range of feelings including anger, depression, anxiety, feelings of emptiness, and preoccupation with thoughts of the deceased. Cognitive changes can also occur in some bereaved individuals, including impaired attention and memory, a desire to withdraw from social activities, and increased risk of accidents. Socioculturally, the loss of a spouse alters the individual's position in the family and community and status within society and may also place the individual at risk of an increasing financial burden. Loss of other family members, friends, and neighbors can dramatically change the individual's support network.

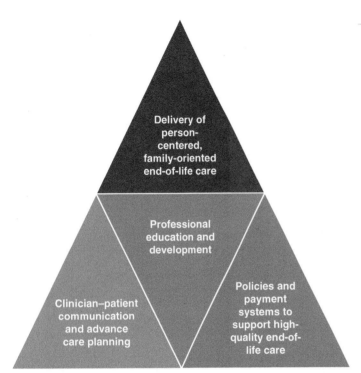

FIGURE 13.11

Components of End-of-Life Care

Principles of end-of-life care supported by the Institute of Medicine.

Of all forms of bereavement, the loss of an adult child is perhaps the most devastating, even more so than the loss of a spouse (Maccallum et al., 2015). The grief a parent experiences over a child's death is highly intense and is associated with increased risk of depression, guilt, and health complaints lasting for many years (Rogers et al., 2008). The loss of a child through stillbirth, moreover, can be associated with stigma, which further exacerbates the bereavement reaction (Pollock et al., 2019).

Moreover, bereaved parents are themselves at higher risk of mortality. A longitudinal study carried out in Sweden showed that mothers of children 18 and under were themselves at greater risk of dying than their nonbereaved counterparts. In this study, although the risk of dying was lower in mothers of children 18 and older, it remained elevated for at least 8 years following the child's death (Rostila et al., 2012). An Israeli study on an older sample of adults between 75 and 94 years of age showed the effects of parental bereavement can continue for as long as 20 years, even after controlling for age, gender, education, and widowhood status. The effect was more pronounced for mothers than fathers (Cohen-Mansfield et al., 2013), replicating the findings of the Swedish study.

Religious teachings can provide comfort to the dying and bereaved through their emphasis on the existence of an afterlife and the belief that human events occur because of some higher purpose. The loss of a loved one, particularly when it occurs "prematurely" (i.e., before old age), may be seen as a test of one's faith. Grieving families and friends comfort themselves with the knowledge that they will be reunited in heaven with the deceased, where they will spend eternity together. Another belief in which people may find comfort is that death is a blessed relief from a world of trouble and pain. Bereaved individuals may also seek solace in the belief or perception that they can sense the presence of departed loved ones. As the bereaved or terminally ill attempt to come to grips with the ending of a life, they rely on these beliefs to make sense out of the death or achieve some kind of understanding of its meaning.

One belief held about people who are engaged in caregiving prior to their loved one's death is that they could benefit from anticipatory grief, in which they begin to work through the loss before it occurs. Although such pre-loss grief work does not seem to reduce the bereavement reaction in caregivers, there are advantages to being prepared for the impending death, both emotionally and in practical terms (Nielsen et al., 2016).

Conventional and professional wisdom regarding bereavement was based on the assumption that the survivor must "work through" the death of the deceased. According to this view, the individual must experience a period of mourning, but after that, it is time to move on and seek new relationships and attachments. In part, this view was based on the assumption within psychodynamic theory that to resolve grief normally, emotional bonds to the loved one must be broken.

Researchers and theorists now recognize that the bereaved can benefit from the continuing bond they feel toward those they have lost. In the attachment view of bereavement, the bereaved can continue to benefit from maintaining emotional bonds to the deceased individual. This means that the survivor can hold onto at least some of the spouse's possessions because of their symbolic value without ever having to dispose of them. Similarly, the bereaved individual can benefit from holding onto thoughts and memories of the deceased (Field et al., 2003). In some ways, the deceased person becomes a part of the survivor's identity.

In the dual-process model of coping with bereavement, the practical adaptations to loss are regarded as important to the bereaved person's adjustment as the emotional (Stroebe et al., 2010) (see Figure 13.12). The practical adaptations include the set of life changes that accompany the death, including taking on new tasks or functions, called the "restoration-oriented". The "loss-oriented" involves coping with the direct emotional consequences of the death.

One memorable example of restorative coping comes from the main character in the movie *Up*. The main character, Carl Fredericksen, has lost his beloved wife of many years, Ellie. He is embittered and miserable, though determined to go through on his plans he had with Ellie to revisit South America. However, he becomes transformed through his relationship with Russell, a boy scout who literally wanders into his life and helps Carl to learn once more how to experience positive emotions.

According to the dual-process model, people are able to adjust to bereavement by alternating between the two dimensions of coping. At times, it is best to confront the emotional loss of the individual; at other times, it is most advantageous to avoid confronting these emotions and instead attempt to manage the practical consequences. People seem to vary in their response to loss, according to this model, on the basis of their attachment style. Securely and insecurely attached individuals show different patterns of mourning and require different types of help to be able to adapt to the loss.

Focusing specifically on personality factors as predictors of reactions to bereavement, Mancini and Bonanno (2009) propose that people who are best able to cope with loss are able to use flexible adaptation—the capacity to shape and adapt behavior to the demands of the stressful event. At other times, though, it is more beneficial to use "repressive coping," in which the painful event is expunged from conscious awareness. Other personal qualities that can help people cope with significant losses, such as widowhood, include optimism, the capacity for positive emotions, and ability to maintain a sense of continuity over time.

FIGURE 13.12

Dual-Process Model of Bereavement

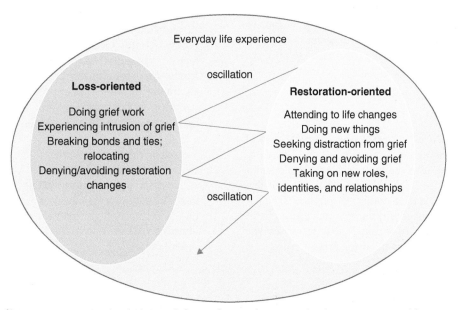

The dual process of bereavement proposes that the bereaved alternate between loss-oriented and restoration-oriented functions.

The idea that denial may be adaptive, at least for a time, fits well with identity process theory. Let us consider the example of widowhood. Identity assimilation may be a preferable approach during the early days and weeks after the loss of the spouse. Being able to avoid focusing on or ruminating over the loss, as in the healthy denial component of assimilation, may allow individuals to remain optimistic and feel a greater sense of personal control. They may also be better able to carry out the restoration dimension of adapting to the practical changes in their living situation, as stated in the dual-process model.

For example, widows who wear their wedding rings and refer to themselves as "Mrs. X" for a time after their husband's death are displaying this type of adaptation. Continuing to identify with their role as wife may help them retain this valued part of their sense of who they are within their families and communities. Over time, through identity accommodation, they may be able to establish greater identity balance by gradually incorporating the notion of themselves as widows into their sense of self.

There are lessons to be learned from the experience of people as they cope with death, dying, and bereavement. In particular, older adults have a remarkable ability to manage the fear of death that causes younger people to react with anxiety and efforts at denial. It may be the ability to move ahead without losing the memory of the departed individuals in one's life that long-lived individuals possess and make it possible for them to survive repeated losses in later adulthood. These individuals have developed ways of integrating the pain of multiple losses into their lives and are able to take their lives in positive new directions. In the future, this process may be made that much less painful by the understanding among mental health professionals of the need that the bereaved have to retain rather than abandon the emotional ties of attachment.

SUMMARY

1. Death is defined as the point of irreversible loss of bodily functions, although this state may be difficult to determine as a result of the advent of life support systems that can keep people alive longer. At the end of life, individuals experience a number of physical changes, many of which are physically uncomfortable, in addition to involving a great deal of pain. Dying trajectories take into account variations in the dying process.

2. Mortality data provide insight into the variations by age, sex, and race in the causes of death. Mortality rates differ according to demographic variables such as ethnicity, geographic variations, marital status, education, and occupation. Additionally, predictors of mortality include education (reflecting better health habits), occupational status, political economy, amount of clean air in the environment, loneliness, religious involvement, amount of exercise, chronotype, and infection following hip fracture.

3. A culture's death ethos is reflected in the traditions established by that culture in funeral rituals, belief in the afterlife, and the language used to describe death. Western attitudes toward death have undergone major shifts throughout history. Contemporary American attitudes regard death in a sensationalistic way, but there is a predominant tendency to institutionalize death and make it "invisible." The death with dignity movement has attempted to promote the idea that the individual should have control over the conditions of death. The work of Elisabeth Kübler-Ross was important in shaping contemporary approaches to care of the dying.

4. Issues in end-of-life care focus on the extent to which dying patients can exert control over their medical care. As a result of the Patient Self Determination Act, individuals can establish advance directives that indicate whether they wish to receive life support and also to name a health care proxy as well as to provide specific orders to physicians and other health professionals. Physician-assisted suicide is a controversial issue that is now legal in the states of Oregon and Washington. Hospices are settings that provide medical and supportive services for dying patients, allowing them to receive personal attention and maintain contact with family. There are also changes in end-of-life care based on employing ways to help patients and their families have their wishes heard.

5. Bereavement is the process of mourning the loss of a close person. In the past, theories of grief resolution focused on the need to "work through" a death. Current views emphasize an alternative in which the bereaved are more accepting of the sad feelings accompanying the loss. The dual-process model of bereavement proposes that both practical (restorative) and emotional (loss) dimensions describe the period of adaptation to the loss of a loved one.

14

Successful Aging

Can you guess what it takes to age successfully? See which of these criteria apply to successful agers and check your answers on the next page:

AGEFEED

? test yourself

1. Focus on positive past achievements.
2. Express creativity.
3. Try to look as young as possible.
4. Receive and offer social support.
5. Remain physically active.
6. Avoid believing in stereotypes about aging.
7. Be free of any chronic diseases.
8. Be resilient in the face of challenges.
9. Live in one's own home.
10. Have adequate financial resources.

AGEFEED

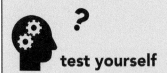

? test yourself

Now see how well your answers measure up to what the experts say about successful aging. Each of the check marks shows which qualities are found in successful agers:

✓ Focus on positive past achievements.

✓ Express creativity.
　Try to look as young as possible.

✓ Receive and offering social support.

✓ Remain physically active.

✓ Avoid believing in stereotypes about aging.
　Be free of any chronic diseases.

✓ Be resilient in the face of challenges.
　Live in one's own home.
　Have adequate financial resources.

Keep reading the chapter to learn more about successful aging!

Many people assume that at the end of life, people experience a precipitous drop in their well-being and adjustment. However, as you have learned by now, survival into the later years of adulthood requires that individuals can negotiate the many threats presented to living a long life. As we stated at the outset of this book, to get old you have to not die; to age successfully requires additional adaptive qualities. Because older adults have managed to avoid so many threats that could have ended their lives at a younger age, there may be some special quality about increasingly older individuals that can account, in part, for their having reached this point in their lives.

In this final chapter, we will explore the topics of psychological growth and creativity in the later adult years. Successful agers not only "survive" but also achieve heightened levels of personal expression and happiness. We hope that these inspirational qualities can guide and sustain your optimism and hope about your own future adult years.

WHAT IS SUCCESSFUL AGING?

As we discussed in Chapter 1, the process of optimal aging refers to age-related changes that improve the individual's functioning. Throughout this book, we have identified many ways in which older adults can maximize their abilities and well-being. Here we will try to pinpoint the factors that coalesce in certain older adults to give them an edge and permit them to hold onto their abilities until the very end of their lives.

An Overview of Successful Aging

Let us begin by asking you to think of people you would nominate as successful, or optimal, agers. Do you have a grandmother who you have difficulty keeping up with when the two of you go for a walk? Is there a great-uncle in your family who can beat everyone at word games? How about your mother's cousin, who backpacks around the world for 3 or 4 weeks a year? Perhaps your 80-year-old neighbor has never worn glasses and can hear better than you can. Now, think about well-known older individuals who became cultural icons. Perhaps you have come up with Betty White, the American television comedian and star of television's legendary sitcom about older women, *Golden Girls*. White skyrocketed to popularity in 2010 when a Facebook-inspired movement led the producers of *Saturday Night Live* to invite the 88-year-old to host the show, a performance that garnered her an Emmy Award. She remains an inspiration to people of all ages, both for her sense of humor and her indefatigable approach to life.

The most widely researched model of optimal aging, proposed by Rowe and Kahn (1998), serves as the theoretical foundation of their work on the MacArthur Foundation Study of Aging in America. As distinct from "usual" aging (i.e., primary), the Rowe and Kahn definition of successful aging regards the optimum state to be the absence of disease and disability, high cognitive and physical functioning, and engagement with life. You can see this model of successful aging in Figure 14.1, showing it as the combination of these three contributing factors.

The Rowe and Kahn model of successful aging served to highlight the growth that can occur in later life, but subsequent researchers find it to be incomplete or flawed, as summarized in Figure 14.2 (Martinson & Berridge, 2015). These critiques focus around the common theme that the model is overly "normative," meaning that it excludes the many variations that exist among successful agers who do not meet every single criterion. Those who come from disadvantaged backgrounds, moreover, may not have the ability to achieve all three of these conditions due to stressful early lives or lack of access to health care and other resources in later life. The qualities it takes to be a successful ager, furthermore, are not well specified in the model. Finally, the model does not take into account the subjective meanings that older adults themselves have about the extent to which they feel they have aged successfully.

These criticisms make sense; even when you think of the successful agers you have either known or seen in the media, some may very well have one or more age-related limitations. That sprightly grandmother may have a few memory lapses now and then, or perhaps she has had

FIGURE 14.1

Rowe and Kahn Model of Successful Aging

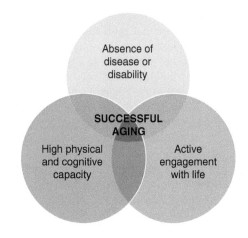

FIGURE 14.2

Critiques of Rowe & Kahn Model of Successful Aging

Overly normative, not inclusive or those who fail to meet each criterion

Fails to take into account sociocultural factors

Does not take into account subjective meanings by older adults

Criteria are not well specified in the model

Criticisms of the Rowe and Kahn model of successful aging.

cataract surgery. That backpacking mother's cousin may need to use a cane as she navigates her way around the world. You may also know other individuals who have an age-related physical disability that severely limits their mobility, but whose sense of optimism and hope rivals yours, even on your best days.

The World Health Organization (WHO), in its report on Active Ageing (2002a), defined active aging as the process of optimizing opportunities for health, participation, and security in order to enhance quality of life as people age (World Health Organization, 2002). Figure 14.3 shows the WHO model of active aging which, in many ways, is like that of the Bronfenbrenner (1994) ecological perspective in that it specifies a role for social, health care, and economic determinants as well as pointing to the importance of the physical environment. Noteworthy is the fact that WHO makes explicit the role of autonomy and independence, placing greater emphasis on the individual's ability to get around in the environment, rather than on whether the individual needs physical accommodations due to disability.

Building on the concept of active aging, the World Health Organization subsequently released its World Report on Ageing and Health (2015), noting that a comprehensive public response is needed if older individuals around the globe are able to achieve active aging, or what they now refer to as active and healthy aging (AHA). The challenges for this effort are to understand diversity

in later life and the fact that "the diversity seen in older age is not random" (p. 8). Ageism further creates policy challenges, because stereotypes about older adults, for example, as draining social and health resources need to be overcome. Finally, social safety nets may be disappearing with changes in the economy as well as in the family.

Combining the WHO definition of active and healthy aging with the original Rowe and Kahn criteria, researchers involved with the Survey of Health, Ageing and Retirement in Europe (SHARE) provided support for expanding the definition of successful aging beyond the original three criteria (Bosch-Farré et al., 2018). The SHARE dataset used to assess active and healthy aging included nearly 53,000 individuals aged 50 and older living in 14 European countries. The Rowe and Kahn criteria were operationalized into measures of no previous diagnosis of a major disease or activities of daily living limitation, high scores on cognitive and physical functioning measures (e.g., memory scores, ability to climb a full set of stairs), and social engagement (e.g., paid work or caring for grandchildren and social support).

The SHARE study then assessed AHA with the additional criteria of physical well-being (frailty and age-adjusted cognitive performance), mental well-being (satisfaction with life and no depressive symptoms) and social well-being, consisting of satisfaction with social activities (e.g., work, grandparenting, religion, politics), and low scores on a standard measure of loneliness in addition to actual social support. Thus, SHARE provides a broader definition of successful aging than does the original Rowe–Kahn model and also takes the individual's subjective ratings into account.

With this expanded definition, the SHARE findings revealed that although only 19% of the sample fit the more restrictive Rowe–Kahn criteria for successful aging, 57% met the AHA-based criteria. In other words, 38% more SHARE participants fit the definition of successful aging than would have with the original three criteria.

The SHARE findings, then, support the criticisms of the original successful aging model. Furthermore, the methods used to obtain those results are defined in clear enough terms to be applied by other researchers.

Successful Cognitive Aging

A number of investigators are exploring the notion that successful aging in the cognitive sense remains an important topic in its own right. As we have explored in earlier chapters, there are large interindividual differences in cognitive functioning, so we know that some people maintain higher levels of performance than do others. Moreover, an individual's cognitive functioning plays an important

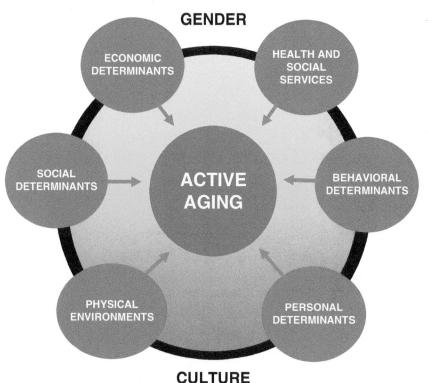

FIGURE 14.3

WHO Model of Active Aging

The WHO model of active aging proposes a wide range of influences that contribute to active, or successful, aging.

role in the ability to adapt to the demands of everyday life, as we saw in Chapter 7. Many older adults, as we have also seen, regard cognitive functioning as central to their identities; this is one reason that they so greatly fear developing Alzheimer's disease and other forms of neurocognitive disorder.

In keeping with this focus, then, successful cognitive aging can be defined as cognitive performance that is above the average for an individual's age group as objectively measured (Fiocco & Yaffe, 2010) (Figure 14.4). Superagers, in turn, are defined as individuals 80 years and older with episodic memory that is comparable to, or superior than, that of middle-aged adults.

The search for factors that contribute to successful cognitive aging can engage individuals, families, and policy makers in discussions of the factors that promote health, rather than those that focus solely on diagnosis and treatment of neurocognitive disorders (Institute of Medicine; Board on Health Sciences; Policy Committee on the Public Health Dimensions of Cognitive Aging, 2015).

Factors that might contribute to the superior cognitive performance of superagers appear to include cortical thickness (Harrison et al., 2012), greater brain plasticity (Greenwood, 2007), an activated inflammatory response that protects the brain's white matter (Gefen et al., 2019),

improved connectivity in the default mode and information filtering networks in the brain (Zhang et al., 2019), faster electrophysiological encoding (Dockree et al., 2015), and a "super-aging" phenotype (Huentelman et al., 2018). Perhaps related to the AHA model, cognitive superagers may also experience more rewarding social relationships (Cook Maher et al., 2017).

Factors That Promote Successful Aging

As we have just seen, people may age successfully even if they have a number of chronic health conditions. Older adults are also less likely to experience serious mental illness, as you learned in Chapter 12.

Interest in successful aging fits more generally within the larger field of positive psychology, which seeks to provide a greater understanding of the strengths and virtues that enable individuals and communities to thrive. Within this tradition, life satisfaction is the overall assessment of an individual's feelings and attitudes about one's life at a particular point in time. Subjective well-being is the individual's overall sense of happiness. These two terms clearly are related; however, somewhat separate research traditions have developed around their use, so it is helpful to treat them as distinct. One difference is

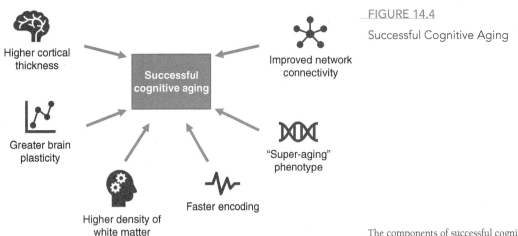

FIGURE 14.4

Successful Cognitive Aging

The components of successful cognitive aging.

that life satisfaction may be more of a cognitive evaluation, but subjective well-being is more affective or emotional. Research on the factors that contribute to successful aging emphasizes both the affective and cognitive components, as shown in Figure 14.5.

One of the great puzzles for researchers who study successful aging is to explain why, as you saw in research from the SHARE study, so many older adults are able to remain positive in their approach to life despite their accumulating chronic health conditions, normal age-related changes, and alterations in their social roles and financial security. The paradox of well-being refers to the findings from research on successful aging that older adults maintain high subjective well-being despite facing challenges from their objective circumstances.

FIGURE 14.5

Psychological Components of Successful Aging

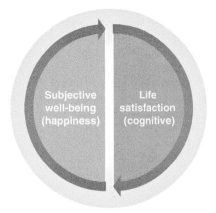

Factors that promote successful aging include cognitive and affective components.

The paradox of well-being exists, at least in part, because it contradicts the belief that well-being is determined by social indicators, or objective measures of social and economic welfare. According to the social indicator model of well-being, these demographic and social structural variables account for individual differences in levels of well-being. Because by demographic standards older individuals are in a disadvantaged position on these indices, they should therefore be less happy than the young. When an older adult is able to avoid becoming depressed by the potentially disturbing circumstances of poor health, widowhood, and low income, then that person seems deserving of some kind of special recognition.

Where do you stand on the social indicator model as an approach to understanding changes in later life? Do you believe that the changes associated with the aging process should have detrimental effects on the older adult's life satisfaction and subjective well-being? According to a national survey conducted by the Pew Research Center (2009) on almost 3,000 Americans, most older adults manage to enjoy relatively high subjective well-being on a variety of indices. Among respondents 75 and older, 81% said they were "very" or "pretty" happy, and only 19% rated themselves as "not too happy." Supporting the paradox of well-being model, as shown in Figure 14.6, most older adults rated their own experience of aging more favorably than younger adults would expect along a variety of dimensions from extent of memory loss to the feeling of being a burden on others.

The question is whether older adults have developed a set of coping skills over their lifetimes that allow them to frame events that younger adults would consider detrimental to their own well-being or even that the older adults would have found challenging when they themselves were

FIGURE 14.6

Expectation of Aging versus Experience of Aging among American Adults

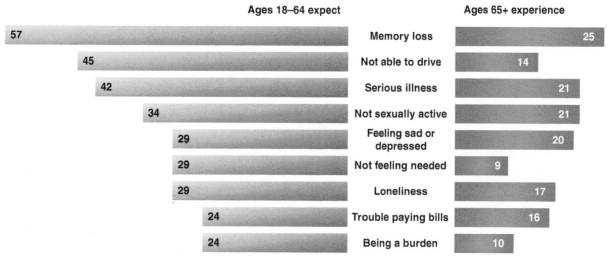

Ages 18–64 expect		Ages 65+ experience
57	Memory loss	25
45	Not able to drive	14
42	Serious illness	21
34	Not sexually active	21
29	Feeling sad or depressed	20
29	Not feeling needed	9
29	Loneliness	17
24	Trouble paying bills	16
24	Being a burden	10

The difference between expectations of aging and reality of aging as shown in a Pew survey of American adults.

younger. It is also possible that cohort effects lead current generations of older adults to feel higher levels of subjective well-being because they grew up with different expectations about what their lives would be like than is true for current cohorts of young adults. Another possibility is that the paradox of well-being reflects a survival effect and that the older adults who are still alive and available to be tested are hardier and more optimistic than those who are either no longer in the population or unwilling to be sampled. Perhaps these individuals were always inclined to view the world in a positive way, and the fact that they are the ones left standing at the end of life reflects their particular optimistic bias.

The idea that optimists are the ones that remain alive is consistent with the set point perspective, which proposes that people's personalities influence their level of well-being throughout life. However, research on happiness as a predictor of longevity does not support this approach. Data from two large longitudinal panels studied in Germany and Australia showed that unhappy people are more likely to die relatively early in life, perhaps because they are more likely to engage in risky behavior. Beyond that point, there appeared to be no relationship between longevity and subjective well-being (Headey & Yong, 2019).

Figure 14.7 summarizes the three contrasting models of subjective well-being and aging. The paradox of well-being model, as you have just seen, appears to provide a better explanation of the phenomenon of successful aging than either the social indicator or set point perspective models.

These three models suggest, then, that the way individuals perceive their circumstances in later life appears more important than the objective circumstances in which they live or even their levels of personal optimism. The WHO model of AHA suggests, though, that sociocultural factors must also be taken into account. It becomes more difficult to maintain that positive perception of life when aging takes place against the backdrop of negative stereotypes toward, and discrimination against, older adults.

These challenges toward successful aging are being addressed by WHO (2018f), in conjunction with the United Nations Sustainable Development Goals (2015) to ensure healthy lives and promote well-being for all at all ages. The concept of the age-friendly environment, as defined by WHO, enables people of all ages to participate in their communities, treats everyone with respect, regardless of age, makes it easy for older people to maintain their social connections, and helps people maintain their health and activity even at the oldest ages (see Figure 14.8).

In practical terms, an age-friendly environment, according to WHO, is free of physical and social barriers and is supported by programs, services, and technologies that promote mental and physical health and enable even people with capacity loss to continue to engage in the activities they value.

The age-friendly network has grown from 11 membership cities in 2010 to 760 communities and cities by September of 2018, covering 39 of the 194 WHO member states. Some of the age-friendly initiatives reported by

Social indicator model

Older adults have less and so should be unhappier

Paradox of well-being

Older adults are able to overcome objective circumstances

Set point perspective

Personality determines happiness levels

FIGURE 14.7

Models of Subjective Well-Being

Three approaches to explaining subjective well-being in later adulthood.

WHO (2018g) include Ottawa, Canada, adding modified fitness equipment to recreation areas, removing tripping hazards from sidewalks, and adding outdoor benches. Intergenerational exchange is promoted in the educational plan of Loncoche, Chile. In Melville, Australia, cafes are dedicating spaces for individuals with dementia to meet with friends and family members.

WHO's definition of an age-friendly environment has stimulated an area of research that includes the age-friendly community as well as the age-friendly university (Silverstein et al., 2019). Such an educational environment would not only reduce institutional ageism directed against older members of the community (Whitbourne & Montepare, 2017) but also promote intergenerational learning. The course you are taking now, particularly if it includes contact with older learners or members of the community, would be an example of the type of effort that can produce more age-friendly learning environments.

One manifestation of ageism that could be addressed by an age-friendly environment is the way in which older adults come to view themselves. According to the communicative ecology model of successful aging (CEMSA), their own ways of seeing, and talking about, themselves can influence the way older adults feel about aging and, ultimately, their actual ability to age successfully (Fowler et al., 2015). According to CEMSA, people have great uncertainty about aging, which influences the way they talk about their own aging. The communication strategies they use in response to this uncertainty can alter their levels of self-efficacy about aging. The higher their self-efficacy, the more likely they will, as predicted by CEMSA, be able to age successfully (Figure 14.9).

FIGURE 14.8

Model of Age-Friendly Environments

World Health Organization Age-Friendly Environments

DOMAINS
Health
Long-term care
Transport
Housing
Labor
Social protection
Education
Information and communication

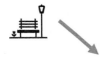

ACTED ON BY
Government
Service providers
Civil society
Older people and their organizations, families, and friends

GOALS
Combat ageism
Enable autonomy
Support *Healthy Ageing* in all policies at all levels

The World Health Organization's criteria for age-friendly environments.

FIGURE 14.9

Communication Ecology Model of Successful Aging

Express	optimism about aging
Don't use	aging as reason for problems
Avoid	applying age stereotypes to self and others
Plan	for the future
Don't	give up on new technology
Let	others know ageism isn't acceptable
Don't	be tempted by antiaging products

According to the CEMSA model, these are the strategies that older adults should use to be able to avoid the limitations of ageism.

The communication strategies specific to CEMSA include expressing optimism about the aging process, not using age as a reason for general problems or limitations (i.e., not using the term "senior moment"), avoiding use of age stereotypes when referring to or thinking about other older adults, planning for the future with the assumption that one will be there to enjoy it, and not giving up on trying to use new technology strategies such as social media and cell phones. Older adults can also change the context in which they age by effectively managing ageist treatment by others to let them know that this sort of language is not acceptable. Finally, CEMSA advocates that older adults not allow themselves to be swayed by "peddlers of anti-aging products ... to recognize and resist the images propagated by an industry whose profitability rests on inducing their self-loathing" (p. 437).

Successful aging is a complex process involving many moving parts. Older adults are able to develop a sense of high subjective well-being even in the face of daunting challenges. Although researchers are beginning to view subjective well-being as subject to potential threats very late in life, the vast majority of older adults avoid becoming depressed or even dissatisfied with their life situations. New approaches that can alter the environment in which individuals age can further take advantage of the strengths already evident in these aging individuals.

CREATIVITY AND AGING

You do not have to be a creative genius to age successfully, but the older adults who have become the creative geniuses of the past and present seem, to many, to represent the most successful agers of all. Understanding the factors that contribute to their ability to retain their creativity can provide new pathways to promote the successful aging of ordinary individuals (Palmiero et al., 2016a).

What Is Creativity?

A creative person is conventionally thought of as someone who has the ability to produce a notable or extraordinary piece of work; however, more generally, researchers define creativity as the ability to generate products or ideas that are original, appropriate, and have an impact on others. The originality inherent in creativity means that the idea or products are novel rather than being copies, precise renderings from a set of instructions, or mass-produced. In terms of appropriateness, this might be considered a subjective quality, but in the context of creativity, it implies that other people appreciate the work and may want to purchase or use it (Runco & Beghetto, 2019).

That creative products have an impact on others is a quality that you might be able to attest from your own experience. You may listen to a piece of music and feel that it expresses the way you are feeling or have felt in the past. That music will stay with you more than will the notes of a piece that seem to have less personal meaning.

Think about the people you would nominate as most creative. Some of them may be eminent or popular artists, musicians, or writers, but some may be people you interact with in your family or among your friends. Perhaps you have an aunt who can take an ordinary room and with just a little rearrangement make it more inviting and comfortable. A grandmother who cooks for family celebrations may seem to have an endless set of new ideas for decorating cupcakes, never repeating the same recipe or finishing touches from holiday to holiday. To distinguish eminent creativity from everyday creativity, researchers talk about "Big C" (eminent) and "little c" (everyday); individuals may also show "mini-C" creativity, which refers to creativity in constructing personal, or self, understanding (Beghetto & Kaufman, 2007).

Among your list of highly creative people, there are undoubtedly not only older relatives with talent at various feats of homemaking but also famous painters or musicians with long and highly successful careers, ranging from the singer Cher to the painter Pablo Picasso. What factors do you believe might support their continued ability to deserve acclaim?

Experimental studies of creativity linking the ability to generate novel ideas with cognitive abilities suggest that older creative adults appear to have greater cognitive reserve (Palmiero et al., 2016b). Personality may also play a role in promoting creativity in later life as indicated by the finding that older individuals higher in openness to experience show greater activation of brain regions involved in maintaining cognitive flexibility (Sutin et al., 2009).

Personality openness may, in turn, be a protective factor against mortality. In a longitudinal study of aging veterans, Turiano and colleagues (2012) found a positive association between scores on the creativity facet of openness to experience and lower risk of mortality. The protective effects of personality creativity remained statistically significant even after the researchers controlled for other correlates of mortality including age, education, health status, and health risk behaviors.

One approach to understanding the neuroscience of creativity in older adults involves studying the connections between the brain's default brain network and the executive functions carried out in the prefrontal cortex. As mentioned earlier, pathways involved in the default network may be involved in successful cognitive aging. The default network would support creative thinking in the stage at which individuals come up with new ideas. Evaluating the quality of these ideas would be the task of the executive control network. Older adults with higher scores on divergent thinking task performance (e.g., coming up with as many uses of a common object as possible) showed stronger connections between these two brain regions than was true for younger adults (Adnan et al., 2019). This finding suggests that older adults may be better to take advantage of the greater storehouse of knowledge they have accumulated over their lifetimes.

Creative Older Adults

This conceptual background to understanding creativity shows that creativity may involve many of the same features as successful aging. Among the ranks of the eminently creative (who are creative with a "capital C") are highly successful artists, musicians, writers, and performers who continued to produce highly acclaimed works well into their later decades. Outside of the arts, older adults continue to make important contributions to the world in everything from politics to science.

The first systematic effort to identify age trends in productive accomplishments was the book by Harvey Lehman, *Age and Achievement* (1953). Lehman analyzed the quantity and quality of creative products by age and discipline and concluded that the peak of productivity in the adult years tends to occur prior to the age of 40, often between 30 and 35. However, Lehman found that earlier peaks are reached in the sciences and in fields in which success was dependent on intellectual imagination and physical ability. Later this observation was dubbed the Planck hypothesis after the brilliant German scientist Max Planck, to refer

to the tendency of peak scientific productivity to occur in early adulthood (Dietrich, 2004).

Lehman claimed that older adults are most likely to retain their productivity in fields that rely on experience and judgment, such as politics and diplomacy. Authors write their "best books" in between these extremes, for an author's success involves imagination, discipline, and the philosophical perspectives gained from experience. He also noted that some artists who lived until very old age produced their best works very late in life, as did other notable individuals in virtually every field of accomplishment.

Rather than take quality into account, a judgment that can involve subjectivity (which is "better," an early or a late Picasso?), the approach adopted by Dennis (1966) relied only on total output by age of productions by artists and scientists. This analysis yielded a pronounced peak age of productivity for artists in the decade of the 40s, followed by a steep drop-off thereafter. Scientists also showed a peak in the 40s, but their productions were more likely to be spread across the 40s, 50s, and 60s. Noting that Lehman's analysis was limited by the fact that those who died before old age could not be counted (the survivor effect once again), Dennis limited his sample to people who lived to be at least 80 years old. This approach, however, eliminated such creative individuals as Mozart, Van Gogh, and even Shakespeare, all of whom died well before late adulthood.

More recently, the work of Simonton takes into account factors other than simple chronological age as a way to characterize the age–creativity relationship. Figure 14.10 summarizes the key elements of this model. **Creative potential** is the total number of works that a person could hypothetically produce in a life span with no upper limits. The grandmother with a seemingly infinite supply of cupcake ideas would, in this model, be high in creative potential. On the other hand, a person with low creative potential may continue to bake the very same cake, year in and year out, without variation. In the musical world, such individuals are called "One-Hit Wonders."

Creative potential becomes the inspiration, then, for the number of ideas an individual can generate. Next, however, the task becomes one of turning those ideas into products, also known as elaboration. Successful creative individuals are able to put their ideas into words, pictures, notes, or published research papers. An individual's creative career, according to Simonton, will reflect the combination of all three factors.

Simonton also tackled the question of how best to take age into account, including not only age at death but also career age, or the age at which an individual began to produce creative works. People with similar high degrees of creative potential (or total number of ideas) who start out early in life will peak earlier than those who start out later.

FIGURE 14.10

Simonton's Model of Creative Productivity

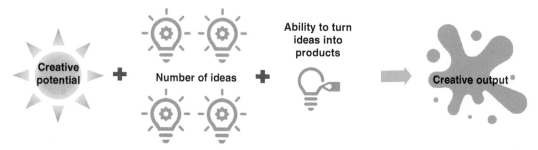

Simonton's model of creativity predicts creative output from these three components.

You can see these relationships in Figure 14.11, in the distinction between early and late bloomers.

Of course, those who die prematurely can never be evaluated even with this model. For example, Margaret Mitchell wrote *Gone with the Wind*, her only published novel, at the age of 35 after spending the early years of her career as a journalist. Because she died at the age of 48, she can only be considered a One-Hit Wonder rather than a late bloomer, though she may have produced more if she had survived past middle age.

The age at death is not factored into Simonton's calculations, meaning that the model still suffers from the problem of not counting the works of people who might have been productive into later adulthood. The general curve that characterizes productivity averages across a large enough number of creative individuals, however, was based on mathematical formulas that could take this problem into account to a certain extent.

Simonton's model does not take the quality of an individual's productions into account. However, according to his equal odds rule, creative individuals who produce more works are more likely to produce one or more of high quality than those who produce fewer works.

If this sounds familiar, it is because it is the same as the law in sports that "If you don't shoot, you can't score." The equal odds rule implies that people are most likely to produce their best work during their peak period of productivity on the basis of probability alone. Verdi composed his first operatic masterpiece at the age of 29 and his last at the age of 80. He had a relatively high probability of creating a masterwork during his late career because he continued to produce such a large number of pieces of music right up until the end.

A variant of the equal odds rule is the blind variation and selective retention (BVSR) theory, which proposes that true creativity requires producing a large number of ideas in trial-and-error fashion, the best (most creative)

of which will remain in the wake of all the failed ones (Simonton, 2015).

Contemporary older adults have an even better chance of remaining productive throughout their later years than those living in previous centuries (Simonton, 2012). As life expectancy continues to increase with improvements in health care and other living conditions, older adults are likely to have a longer empty nest period after their children leave the home. Modern technology also makes more resources available on the Internet so that the artist need not be the "lone genius" of years past. With more leisure time, the older artist also has the chance to pursue multiple interests, making it possible to continue to develop the personality openness that fosters creativity. Improved communication also means that artists, scientists, writers, and creative individuals from many fields can collaborate to cross-foster new ideas and projects. Older and younger collaborators can further enhance each other's productivity, leading both to improve the quality and quantity of their output.

Characteristics of Last Works

However many creative works that older artists and writers produce, and however old they are when they produce them, the old age style is a special quality common to their work.

The art critic Kenneth Clark (2006), in characterizing the paintings of late-life artists (see Figure 14.12), notes that they are "pessimistic and not concerned with the imitation of natural appearances" (p. 80). The themes that emerge in the works of late-life artists are more likely to express tragic rather than uplifting themes, and they may stem from feelings of social isolation and the need to deal with physical limitations. Consider the amount of stamina required to produce a sculpture or an oil painting. Interestingly, in contrast to what you might expect from

FIGURE 14.11

Creativity by Age and Career Age

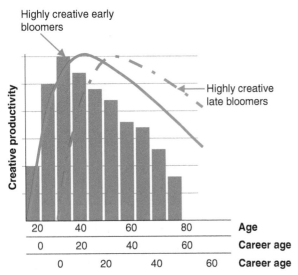

Age, levels of creativity, and career age must be considered in predicting whether individuals will retain their creativity into later life.

socioemotional selectivity theory, these older artists feel frustrated that their time is running out, what Clark calls a sense of "imminent departure."

On the positive side, and perhaps because of that sense of time running out, older artists are less preoccupied with realism, and their work becomes more expressive. They even show a greater freedom in their use of paint and the strokes appear to stand out more from the canvas. The meanings that older artists attempt to convey, additionally, appear to be deeper and more symbolic.

Aging artists may also confront limitations due to changes in vision. Claude Monet, famous for his impressionistic paintings of water lilies, developed cataracts at a time when cataract surgery was far less common and more complicated than today. However, at the age of 85, he had successful cataract surgery and went on to complete an enormous water lilies project that was installed in a Paris museum after his death. Other artists such as Georgia O'Keeffe and Henri Matisse faced sensory and physical limitations at the end of their lives, which they overcame by changing their mediums from painting to sculpture (O'Keeffe) and collages (Matisse).

Thus, when you see a creation produced by an older artist showing the old age style, you are likely to have a strong emotional reaction rather than be as focused on the details of the work's rendering. Although many of the artists showing old age style were painters, the old age style can also characterize sculptures. Rather than carve out each detail, the sculptor will have concentrated more on the form and underlying emotion of the piece.

The emergence of an old age style can be seen in the works of history's most famous artists, including Michelangelo, Rembrandt, Renoir, Matisse, Degas, Georgia O'Keeffe, and Picasso. Henri Matisse explicitly talked about this change in his own perspective as a "distillation of form. I now keep only the sign which suffices, necessary for its existence in its own form, for the composition as I conceive it" (Brill, 1967). Another excellent example of the old age style is provided by the work of Michelangelo, who sculpted a Pietà late in his life (the Pietà Rondanini), less detailed than the more meticulously sculpted iconic Pietà in the Vatican for which he is much more famous. Some art historians regard the later work as more emotionally charged and hence effective (on page 292).

It is likely that, even without knowing the age of artists when you study their creations, you could guess which ones were from early and which were from later periods of their lives. Lindauer (1993) presented undergraduate students with pairs of images from artists at younger and older ages and had them rate which were completed in late life. Nearly two-thirds of the students were able to make the correct identifications, using the criteria of style differences, age, and detail. The artists represented in the study ranged from classic to contemporary and included both realistic and abstract themes.

Lindauer also surveyed artists who were between 60 and 80 years to find out about their own perceptions of age-related changes in their work. Although they did not perceive their own styles to have changed drastically, they did acknowledge changes due to physical and sensory limitations. On the positive side, though, they felt that their accumulated experience caused them to produce work that was steadily and consistently better.

As a preface to the old age style, creativity may be expressed in midlife as "paring down life to the essentials." Midlife may bring with it not a crisis involving confrontation with mortality, but a heightened sense of urgency to create a lasting legacy. Strenger (2009), from this vantage point, analyzed the productive works of a 20th-century educator in the business field, Charles Handy. At the age of 49, Handy left behind a prestigious position in industry because he felt that he had lost touch with his sense of inner purpose. He started a new life as an author and, having written 17 books between the ages of 50 and 75, sought and eventually found new meaning in life.

FIGURE 14.12

Characteristics of Old Age Style

Negative features	Positive features
More pessimistic view of life	More expressive, less realistic
Sense of isolation	Accumulation of symbolism
Choice of tragic themes	More freedom in use of paintstrokes
Feeling of imminent departure	Richer in meaning

The negative versus positive features of the work of older artists, called the old age style.

Clark (2006) also took on the question of old age style in literature and music. The last play of Shakespeare, who died at about age 50, was *The Tempest*. The lines and theme of this play convey, according to Clark, "characteristics that only an artist who has lived his life could give ... (and more than) the earlier plays it creates a private world of the imagination" (p. 88).

There is some debate about whether older musicians show the old age style. Termed the swan song, the musical form of old age style was defined as the last burst of creativity of an older musician (Simonton, 1989). The melody of the swan song, by definition, should be more compelling than earlier compositions because it is shorter and simpler. However, in a reanalysis of data from 2,270 works by 57 composers using hierarchical linear modeling, not a single case of a swan song could be reliably identified. Even so, the authors of this critique note the value of studying creativity in aging musicians as they cope with age-related changes. For example, Beethoven became deaf, and Bach became blind in their later years (Meredith & Kozbelt, 2014).

Another quality that the work of older artists may demonstrate is lastingness in that they persist over time; "that which does not end" (Delbanco, 2011, p. 244). Creative older adults experience a deep sense of gratification and experience the process as rewarding regardless of the result. However, works that endure nevertheless resonate and touch the lives of others.

The work of scientists and academicians may show a different set of changes as they age. According to the Planck hypothesis, the work of young scientists is more innovative than that of older scientists. Perhaps reflecting in part the nature of scientific discovery, and in part the greater experience they gain in their field, older scientists shift their priorities. The aging scientist may become more involved in the writing of texts and integrative review articles rather than in conducting research to produce new scientific discoveries. If scientists work in academic settings, they may move up the administrative hierarchy to a position of authority, meaning that they have less time for their own research.

Some aging academicians turn to the subject of aging; this was true for B. F. Skinner, who wrote *Enjoy Old Age: A Practical Guide* (Skinner & Vaughan, 1983) toward the end of his life. In fact, the first geriatrics text was written by Sir John Floyer in the early 1700s when he was 75 years old. An aging inventor may start to address age-related concerns, as was the case for Benjamin Franklin, who fabricated the first known pair of bifocals when he was 78 years old, well past the age when most people start to need them.

Biopsychosocial Perspectives on Creativity and Aging

From a biopsychosocial perspective, it is clear that creativity in later life may reflect the physical changes that individuals experience as they age. In addition, returning to the earlier discussion of the neuroscience of creativity, older artists, writers, and scientists may be able to draw from a deep reservoir of past experiences that informs their work.

©National Trust Images/Chris Titmus

Rembrandt (1606–1669). https://commons.wikimedia.org/ wiki/File:Rembrandt,_Self-portrait,_1668%E2%80% 931669,_Galleria_degli_Uffizi,_Florence.jpg

Rembrandt's self-portraits (30 years apart) provide an excellent example of the difference between art produced early in life (as shown on the left) with that produced later in life (shown on the right).

Personality flexibility also appears to play a role in the approach to their work taken by highly creative individuals even into their 90s and 100s (Antonini et al., 2008). Rather than dwell on their past accomplishments, these individuals continue to look forward to new goals and new creative enterprises. They maintain their curiosity, keeping up with the times and adapting to changing circumstances.

Cognitive flexibility and personality also appear to play a role in the productivity of less well-known individuals as they age. A 45-year longitudinal study of men originally tested in graduate school showed that those with the highest number of awards and notable publications at age 72 were higher on measures comparable to openness to experience, namely tolerance and psychological-mindedness (Feist & Barron, 2003). Creative accomplishments in the sciences, then, may reflect the role of personality in lowering behavioral inhibitions (Grosul & Feist, 2014).

Creativity can also be understood from a sociocultural perspective. Socioeconomically and racially disadvantaged individuals have a much lower chance of ever reaching old age, much less "successful" old age, as traditionally defined within psychology or the arts. Certain sectors of the population, particularly minorities from low-income backgrounds, do not have the opportunity to achieve good health and full expression of their innate abilities. Everyone we have talked about up to now came from a relatively advantaged background or at least achieved material success. For many talented individuals who are not afforded the benefits of higher levels of education and income, the creative process faces more challenges.

A second critical fact in the analyses of successful aging regards the definition of eminence as used in studies of aging and creativity. Women are far less likely than would be expected on the basis of chance to appear in lists of the creative and productive at any age. For example, it is only within the area of children's literature that Lehman (1953) listed women as constituting anywhere near 50% of the notable contributors. A total of only 20 women were listed in the Lehman work as "worthy of mention" (p. 91).

Little, if any, mention in the analysis of productivity is also made of members of ethnic or racial minorities. Simonton (1998) explored the question of whether assessments of creative output among historical figures would show evidence of bias against members of minority cultures. Specifically, he examined whether African Americans who had achieved recognition within reference works specific to Black scholarship would also be mentioned in reference works of the White majority culture. Although there was considerable convergence between the minority and majority reference works, one-fifth of African Americans who had achieved eminence in the minority reference works were not mentioned in any of the majority indices of eminence. Furthermore, certain areas of accomplishment within Black culture were not recognized within the majority reference works, including law, education, religion, classical music, and the sciences. White reference works gave higher ratings to African Americans in the fields of athletics and in jazz and blues music, but African American sources gave greater recognition to those who achieved eminence in the civil rights movement.

These differential patterns of recognition point to distinct opportunities that affect an individual's ability to achieve career recognition, if not personal fulfillment. Clearly, differences in educational opportunities as well as cultural values play a role in determining the ultimate

Activation of
relevant brain
regions

Physical changes
and diseases

Biological

Sociocultural

Psychological

Educational background

Definitions of eminence that
exclude women and
minorities

Personality flexibility and
openness

Ability to draw from
experience

FIGURE 14.13

Biopsychosocial Model of Creativity
in Later Life

Creativity is best understood from the
biopsychosocial perspective.

achievements of people from nonmajority backgrounds. Those who do manage to break through cultural barriers are likely to receive considerable recognition within their own as well as the majority culture.

Some examples of eminent minority productive agers are Jackie Robinson, the first African American to play major league baseball; Booker T. Washington, the first to receive an honorary degree from Harvard; and William Grant Still, the first to conduct a major symphony orchestra and to have his own composition performed by a major American orchestra. These "famous firsts" seem particularly important within African American reference works of eminence because they attest to the ability of highly talented and persistent individuals to overcome the effects of discrimination. That their work has until recently been overlooked in studies of aging and creativity limits the generalizability of current models of successful aging.

Figure 14.13 summarizes the biopsychosocial approach to understanding creativity in later life. Physical changes and disease as well as the neuroscience underpinnings of creativity interact with personality and the ability to draw from experience. Limitations due to lack of educational opportunities and biases against women and minorities in counts of eminence play a role in determining which older individuals are recognized as creative.

SUCCESSFUL AGING: FINAL PERSPECTIVES

People in later life appear not only to manage to feel satisfied with their lives but also to be able to achieve new forms of creative expression. Although not contained within any of the existing definitions of successful, healthy, or active

and healthy aging, the ability to enjoy creativity, even with a "mini-C," can enhance individuals' lives throughout their later years.

Throughout this course, you have learned about the qualities that can influence your life as you grow older, as well as the many opportunities for change and growth that your life experiences will present to you. Becoming a "survivor," as we pointed out at the beginning of the book, is the key to reaching your later years. As you continue to develop and navigate through your adult years, we hope that you will find your personal sense of meaning to accompany a long and successful life.

SUMMARY

1. The process of successful aging involves being able to overcome the threats to physical and psychological well-being presented by the aging process. Successful aging also involves the ability to become engaged with life in terms of both relationships and productive activity; successful cognitive aging refers to individuals who perform above average compared to their age group. Subjective well-being, a component of successful aging, is higher in older adults, a phenomenon referred to as the paradox of well-being. The WHO's movement to foster global age-friendly environments will make it possible for more individuals to feel connected to their communities and be able to fulfill their personal goals, regardless of age.

2. Creativity includes the work of geniuses as well as everyday behaviors. Research on productivity and creativity has involved attempts to determine whether older individuals are more or less able to maintain the quality and

quantity of works produced when younger. Simonton's model of creative productivity describes the relationship between age and production of creative works using a mathematical formula that incorporates creative potential, ideation, and elaboration based on the career age of an individual rather than chronological age. In this model, highly productive individuals begin early and maintain a high production rate long into their careers. Those who are more productive are also more likely to produce works of high quality.

3. The old age style characterizes the works of older artists and musicians. One component of the old age style is simplification of detail and increasing subjectivity. Among scientists and academicians, the old age style refers to a tendency to synthesize, producing works such as texts and reviews that integrate existing knowledge. The old age style may be a reaction to increasing proximity to death or to the presence of age-related changes or health problems.

4. Creativity is best understood from a biopsychosocial perspective, incorporating the activity of the brain, physical changes and diseases, personality openness and ability to draw on past experiences, and sociocultural factors that limit opportunities and recognition.

GLOSSARY

1998 Nursing Home Initiative: program developed by President Clinton intended to improve enforcement of nursing home quality standards.

2002 National Nursing Home Quality Initiative: federal program that combined new information for consumers about the quality of care provided in individual nursing homes with resources available to nursing homes to improve the quality of care in their facilities.

Accessory dwelling unit: also known as an "in-law apartment," this second living space in the home allows the older adult to have independent living quarters, cooking space, and a bathroom.

Accommodation: when people change their schemas in response to new information about the world.

Acetylcholinesterase: the enzyme that normally destroys acetylcholine after its release into the synaptic cleft; also called cholinesterase.

Activities of daily living (ADL): an individual's ability to complete the tasks of bathing, dressing, transferring, using the toilet, and eating.

Active aging also called **active and healthy aging (AHA):** according to the WHO, the process of maximizing opportunities related to health, participation, and safety in order to improve quality of life.

Activity theory: the view that older adults are most satisfied if they are able to remain involved in their social roles.

Acute stress disorder: the diagnosis given to an individual whose symptoms persist for up to a month after a trauma and include the intrusion of distressing reminders of an event; dissociative symptoms, such as feeling numb or detached from others; avoidance of situations that might serve as reminders of the event; and hyperarousal, including sleep disturbances or irritability.

Adrenopause: the phenomenon where DHEA, which is higher in males than females, shows a pronounced decrease over the adult years.

Adult attachment theory: proposal that the early bond between the infant and caregiver set the stage for all of the individual's later significant relationships.

Adult day services: services given to adults who need assistance or supervision during the day in a setting that is either attached to another facility, such as a nursing home, or is a standalone agency.

Adult-onset diabetes or type 2 diabetes: a disease that develops over time and gradually reduces the individual's ability to convert dietary glucose to a form that can be used by the body's cells.

Advance directive (AD): a legally binding document in which patients express their wishes for end-of-life care.

Aerobic capacity: the maximum amount of oxygen that can be delivered through the blood.

Affect regulation: the ability to increase a person's feelings of happiness and well-being.

Affective events theory: proposal that events at work lead to affective reactions; these in turn influence attitudes toward work and performance.

Affordable Care Act (ACA): legislation signed into law by President Barack Obama in the spring of 2010 intended to expand health care insurance to all Americans.

Age Discrimination in Employment Act (ADEA): legislation passed in 1967, makes it illegal to fire or not employ workers on the basis of their age.

Age: an objectively determined measure that indicates how many years (and/or months or days) a person has lived up to the present moment.

Age-adjusted death rate: a mortality rate statistically modified to eliminate the effect of different age distributions in the different populations.

Age-as-leveler view: proposal that as people become older, age overrides all other "isms."

Age-complexity hypothesis: proposal that through a slowing of the central processes in the nervous system, age differences increase as tasks become more complex and the older adult's processing resources are stretched more and more to their limit.

Age-friendly environment: as defined by WHO, enables people of all ages to participate in their communities, treats everyone with respect, regardless of age, makes it easy for older people to maintain their social connections, and helps people maintain their health and activity even at the oldest ages.

Ageism: a set of beliefs, attitudes, social institutions, and acts that denigrate individuals or groups based on their chronological age.

Age-related macular degeneration (ARMD): a condition caused by damage to the photoreceptors located in the central region of the retina known as the macula.

Age-specific death rate: the crude death rate for a specific age group.

Aging in place: the principle that older adults can remain in their own homes, or at least in their own communities, with appropriate services.

Agnosia: the loss of the ability to recognize familiar objects.

Agoraphobia: the fear of being in an open or crowded space, or of being in a space from which escape is difficult.

Alveoli: tiny air sacs in the lungs where exchange of gases takes place.

Alzheimer's disease: a form of neurocognitive disorder in which the individual suffers progressive and irreversible neuronal death.

Amnesia: a condition where the individual has as the main symptom profound memory loss.

Amyloid plaque: a formation of abnormal deposits of protein fragments.

Amyloid precursor protein (APP): protein found in the normal brain.

Androgenetic alopecia: male and female pattern hair loss.

Andropause: age-related declines in the male sex hormone testosterone.

Anorexia-cachexia syndrome: a syndrome observed at the end of life in which the individual loses appetite (anorexia) and muscle mass (cachexia).

Anticholinesterase: treatments that inhibit the enzyme acetylcholinesterase.

Antioxidants: chemicals that prevent the formation of free radicals.

Anxiety disorder: disorder in which the main characteristic includes anxiety, a sense of dread about what might happen in the future.

Anxious attachment style: pattern in which individuals imagine that their adult partners will abandon them.

Aphasia: the loss of language ability.

ApoE: a protein that carries cholesterol throughout the body but also binds to beta-amyloid, possibly playing a role in plaque formation.

Apolipoprotein E (ApoE) gene: one of the prime genes thought to be involved in late-onset familial Alzheimer's disease.

Apoptosis: process that results in the destruction of neurons.

APP gene: gene that appears to control the production of APP, the protein that generates beta-amyloid.

Apraxia: the loss of the ability to carry out coordinated movement.

Archival method: type of research in which investigators use available records to provide data on the hypotheses they wish to test.

Arteriosclerosis: a general term for the thickening and hardening of arteries.

Arthritis: a general term for conditions affecting the joints and surrounding tissues that can cause pain, stiffness, and swelling in joints and other connective tissues.

Assimilation: process in which people use their existing schemas in order to understand the world around them.

Assisted living facilities: housing complexes in which older persons live independently in their own apartments.

Atherosclerosis: a form of cardiovascular disease where fatty deposits collect at an abnormally high rate within the arteries, substantially reducing their width and limiting the circulation of the blood.

Attachment styles: mental representations or frameworks about what to expect in a relationship.

Attachment view of bereavement: the view that the bereaved can continue to benefit from maintaining emotional bonds to the deceased.

Attention: the ability to focus or concentrate on a portion of experience while ignoring other features of that experience, to be able to shift that focus as demanded by the situation, and to be able to coordinate information from multiple sources.

Attentional resources: a theory that regards attention as a process reflecting the allocation of cognitive resources.

Autobiographical memory: the recall of information from a person's own past.

Autoimmune theory: proposal that aging is due to faulty immune system functioning in which the immune system attacks the body's own cells.

Autonomy versus shame and doubt: stage in Erikson's theory when young children learn ways to be able to act independently from their parents without feeling afraid that they will venture too far off on their own.

Avoidant attachment style: a fear of abandonment so intense that individuals stay away from close relationships altogether.

Awareness of finitude: thoughts about mortality that occur when individuals pass the age when other people close to them had themselves died.

Baby Boom generation: the term used to describe people born in the post-World War II years of 1946–1964.

Basal metabolic rate (BMR): the rate of metabolism.

Basic trust versus basic mistrust: stage in Erikson's theory that involves the infant's establishing a sense of being able to rely on care from the environment (and caregivers).

Behavioral approach to marital interactions: emphasizes the actual behaviors that partners engage in with each other during marital interactions as an influence on marital stability and quality.

Bereavement: the process during which people cope with the death of another person.

Berlin Wisdom Paradigm: proposal that wisdom is a form of expert knowledge in the pragmatics of life.

Beta-amyloid-42: the form of amyloid most closely linked with Alzheimer's disease which consists of a string of 42 amino acids.

Biological age: the age of an individual's bodily systems.

Biopsychosocial perspective: a view of development as a complex interaction of biological, psychological, and social processes.

Bipolar disorder: disorder in which people who have experienced one or more manic episodes during which they feel elated, grandiose, expansive, and highly energetic.

Blended families: also known as reconstituted families, family situations where at least one adult is living with a child who is not a biological child of that adult.

Blind variation and selective retention (BVSR) theory: proposal that true creativity requires producing a large number of ideas in trial-and-error fashion, the best (most creative) of which will remain in the wake of all the failed ones.

Blurred retirement pattern: a pattern of retirement in which workers exit and reenter the workplace several times.

Board and care home: a group living arrangement designed to meet the needs of people who cannot live on their own in the community and also need some nursing services.

Body mass index (BMI): an index of body fat calculated by dividing weight in kilograms by (height in meters) squared.

Bone remodeling: a process in which old bone cells are destroyed and replaced by new cells.

Borderline personality disorder: a set of symptoms that include extreme instability in sense of self and relationships with others, sexual impulsivity, fear of abandonment, and difficulties controlling their emotions.

Boundaryless career: a career that crosses the boundaries of an employer or organization; people with this mindset seek opportunities for development in their jobs.

Bridge employment: retirement pattern in which retirees work in a completely different occupation than they had during most of their adult life.

Brinley plot: plot in which reaction times of older adults are graphed against those of younger adults.

Calling: the choice of occupation based on a combination of factors related to career development, job satisfaction, well-being, and personal growth.

Caloric restriction: the view that they key to prolonging life is to restrict the number of calories that individuals consume.

Cardiac output: the amount of blood that the heart pumps per minute.

Cardiovascular disease: a term that refers to a set of abnormal conditions that develop in the heart and arteries.

Career age: the age at which an individual begins to embark on his or her career.

Career plateauing: term that refers to static period of vocational development.

Career: the term that captures the unique connection between individuals and social organizations over time.

Caregiver burden: the term used to describe the stress that caregivers experience in the daily management of their afflicted relative.

Caregivers: individuals, usually family, who provide support to people with chronic diseases.

Case report: research method that provides in-depth data from a relatively small number of individuals.

Caspase: enzymes that are lethal to neurons.

Cataract: a clouding or opacity in the lens of the eye.

Cattell–Horn–Carroll (CHC) model of intelligence: proposal that there is a three-tier structure to intelligence.

Centenarians: people who are 100 years old and older.

Center for Epidemiological Studies Scale for Depression (CES-D): a 20-item questionnaire that screens for depressive symptoms.

Centers for Medicare and Medicaid Services (CMS): the federal agency that oversees, administers, and analyzes the nation's major health care programs.

Cerebrovascular accident: also known as a "stroke" or "brain attack," an acute condition in which an artery leading to the brain bursts or is clogged by a blood clot or other particle.

Choice reaction time tasks: tasks used to measure processing speed in which respondents must make one response for one stimulus and another response for a different stimulus.

Chromosomes: distinct, physically separate units of coiled threads of DNA and associated protein molecules.

Chronic obstructive pulmonary disease (COPD): a group of diseases that involve obstruction of the airflow into the respiratory system.

Chronosystem: from the ecological perspective, changes that take place over time.

Circadian rhythm: the daily variations in various bodily functions.

Classic aging pattern: an inverted U-shaped pattern, with a peak of intelligence in early adulthood followed by steady decline.

Climacteric: the gradual winding down of reproductive ability in men and women.

Clinical interview: a series of questions that clinicians administer in face-to-face interaction with clients.

Cognition: the way the mind works; specifically, the processes of attention, memory, intelligence, problem-solving, and the use of language.

Cognitive-behavioral therapy (CBT): an approach in which the clinician encourages clients to develop more adaptive behaviors and ways of thinking about their experiences.

Cohabitation effect: the greater likelihood of divorce among couples who cohabitate before becoming engaged.

Cohabitation: living in a stable relationship prior to or instead of marrying.

Cohort effects: the social, historical, and culture influences that affect people during a particular period of time.

Cohort: a term used to describe the year (or period) of a person's birth.

Cohort-sequential design: method in which cohorts are compared at different ages.

Collagen: the fibrous protein that makes up about one-quarter of all bodily proteins.

Communicative ecology model of successful aging (CEMSA): approach to successful aging proposing that the way older adults communicate about aging influences the way they feel about aging and, ultimately, their actual ability to age successfully.

Communication predicament model: model proposing that when older adults are thought of as mentally incapacitated, leading younger people to speak to them in a simplified manner (using elderspeak). Over time, this can have the effect of reducing the older adult's actual ability to use language.

Compensation-Related Utilization of Neural Circuits Hypothesis (CRUNCH) model: approach to aging of the brain proposing that the demands of cognitively challenging tasks cause an overall excitation of neural activity in older adults.

Competence–press model: predicts an optimal level of adjustment that institutionalized persons will experience when their levels of competence match the demands, or "press," of the institutional environment.

Comprehension knowledge (Gc): originally called crystallized intelligence, represents the acquisition of specific skills and information that people gain as the result of their exposure to the language, knowledge, and conventions of their culture.

Compression of morbidity: the concept that the illness burden to a society can be reduced if people become disabled closer to the time of their death.

Computed axial tomography (CAT or CT scan): an imaging method that clinicians and researchers use to provide an image of a cross-sectional slice of the brain from any angle or level.

Congestive heart failure (or heart failure): a condition in which the heart is unable to pump enough blood to meet the needs of the body's other organs.

Congruence: situation in which one's vocational type matches one's occupational environment.

Conjunction visual search: search in which the target differs from the distractors in more than one way.

Contextual influences on development: the effects of sex, race, ethnicity, social class, income, religion, and culture on development.

Contingency theory: proposal that parents may provide help to their children because they perceive that the children need this support.

Continuing care retirement community (CCRC): a housing community that provides different levels of care based on the needs of the residents.

Continuity principle: the changes that people experience in later adulthood build on what they lived through in their earlier years.

Continuity theory of retirement: proposal that retired individuals maintain the ties they had to society when they were working.

Continuity theory: proposal that whether disengagement or activity is beneficial to the older adult depends on the individual's personality.

Coping: the actions people take to reduce stress.

Core self-evaluations: a person's appraisal of people, events, and things in relation to oneself.

Coronary (ischemic) heart disease: a condition caused by atherosclerosis, which blocks the blood supply to the heart muscle.

Correlation: statistic that expresses the strength and direction of a relationship between two variables.

Correlational design: a research design in which researchers investigate relationships among two or more variables.

Correspondence principle: proposal that people's life events that reflect their personality traits; once these events occur, they further affect people's personalities.

Cortisol: the hormone produced by the adrenal gland.

Creative potential: the total number of works that a person could hypothetically produce in a life span with no upper limits.

Creativity: the ability to generate products or ideas that are original, appropriate, and have an impact on others.

Crisp retirement pattern: a pattern of retirement in which workers leave the workplace in a single, unreversed, low tomoderate exit.

Cross-linking theory: proposal that aging causes deleterious changes in cells of the body that make up much of the body's connective tissue.

Cross-sectional design: a research design where groups of people are compared with different ages at one point in time.

Cross-sequential design: method in which cohorts are examined at different times of measurement.

Crude death rate: the number of deaths divided by population alive during a certain time period.

Crystallized intelligence: represents the acquisition of specific skills and information that people gain as the result of their exposure to the language, knowledge, and conventions of their culture.

Culture Change Movement: philosophy that services for older adults should promote person-centered care, allowing individuals to feel "at home" despite living in institutional settings.

Daily diary method: a research method in which participants enter data on a daily basis.

Death: the irreversible cessation of circulatory and respiratory functions, or when all the structures of the brain have irreversibly ceased to function.

Death ethos: the prevailing philosophy of death of a culture.

Death with dignity: the idea that death should not involve extreme physical dependency or the loss of control of bodily functions.

Debriefing: a procedure that reveals a study's purpose and answers to the participant after testing has completed.

Default network: a circuit in the brain that is active while the brain is at rest.

Dehydroepiandrosterone (DHEA): a weak male steroid (androgen) produced by the adrenal glands.

Delirium: an acute cognitive disorder that is characterized by temporary confusion.

Dementia: term no longer in clinical use that referred to a loss of cognitive abilities.

Deoxyribonucleic acid (DNA): a molecule capable of replicating itself that encodes information needed to produce proteins.

Dependent variable: the outcome of a manipulation that researchers observe.

Dermis: the middle layer of the skin containing protein molecules of elastin and collagen, among which various nerve cells, glands, and the hair follicles reside.

Descriptive (single-factor) research design: method that catalogs information about how people perform based on their age but does not attempt to rule out social or historical factors.

Developmental schism: situation when there is a gap between the two generations in how much they value the relationship and whether they wish to be independent.

Developmental science: a term replacing "developmental psychology" that expands the focus of life span development to include a broader variety of domains.

Diabetes: a disease where individuals are unable to metabolize glucose, a simple sugar that is a major source of energy for the body's cells.

Diagnostic and Statistical Manual (DSM): the major reference used by mental health professionals in the United States and Canada to diagnose people with psychological disorders.

Dialectical thinking: related to the postformal stage of cognitive development involving an interest in and appreciation for debate, arguments, and counterarguments.

Diffuse tensor imaging: brain scanning method that reveals the structure and integrity of white matter.

Disengagement theory: the view that the normal and natural evolution of life causes older adults to wish to loosen their social ties.

Disillusionment pathway: relationship type where a couple starts out happy but gradually falls out of love.

Divorce proneness: tendency for people to be likely to contemplate divorce when their marriage is in trouble.

Dizziness: an uncomfortable sensation of feeling light-headed and even floating.

Do not resuscitate (DNR) order: directs health care workers not to use resuscitation if the patient experiences cardiac or pulmonary arrest.

Doing gender: a term that refers to the tendency of women and men to behave in stereotypically gendered ways.

Donepezil hydrochloride: a generic version of the drug Aricept.

Donut hole: the coverage gap in Medicare Part D within each calendar year when patients pay a higher percentage of certain drugs until they reach a certain threshold.

Dual-process model of coping with bereavement: proposal that the practical adaptations to loss are as important to the bereaved person's adjustment as the emotional.

Durable power of attorney for health care (DPAHC): also known as a health care proxy, is appointed to make decisions to act on a person's behalf should that person become incapacitated.

Dyadic withdrawal: the process of reducing the individual friendships of the couple and increasing the joint friendships.

Dying: the period during which the organism loses its vitality.

Dying trajectory: the temporal pattern of the disease process leading to a patient's death

Dysphoria: sad mood.

Dysthermia: a condition in which the individual shows an excessive raising of body temperature (hyperthermia) or excessive lowering of body temperature (hypothermia).

Early-onset Alzheimer's disease: a form of Alzheimer's that strikes at the relatively young age of 40 to 50 years.

Ecological perspective: identifies multiple levels of the environment as they affect the individual's development.

Ego integrity versus despair: stage in Erikson's theory in which individuals face psychosocial issues related to aging and facing their mortality.

Ego psychology: the belief that the ego plays a central role in actively directing behavior.

Ego: the part of the mind that controls rational thought.

Elastase: an enzyme that breaks down the elastin found in lung tissue.

Elder abuse: a large category of actions taken directly against older adults that inflict physical or psychological harm.

Elderspeak: a speech pattern directed at older adults similar to the way people talk to babies.

Electroconvulsive therapy (ECT): a method of treatment for depression in which an electric current is applied through electrodes attached across the head.

Electroencephalogram (EEG): a brain scanning method that measures electrical activity in the brain.

Emergent distress pathway: couple whose relationship problems develop over time.

Emerging adulthood: the transition prior to assuming the full responsibilities associated with adulthood normally associated with the years 18 to 29.

Emotional labor: the requirement of service-oriented jobs in which workers must smile and maintain a friendly attitude regardless of their own personal feelings or emotions.

Emotion-focused coping: coping in which people attempt to reduce their stress by changing the ways they think about the situation.

Empty nest: describes the period in a couple's life that occurs when their children permanently depart from the home.

Endocrine system: a large and diverse set of glands that regulate the actions of the body's other organ systems.

Enduring dynamics pathway: proposal that how a couple interacts early in their relationship will characterize the course of the relationship over time.

Epidemiology: the study of the distribution and determinants of health-related states or events (including disease).

Epidermis: the outermost layer of the skin that protects the underlying tissue.

Epigenetic principle: in Erikson's theory, the proposal that asserts that each stage unfolds from the previous stage according to a predestined order.

Episodic memory: memory for events that took place in the past.

Equal odds rule: the principle that creative individuals who produce more works are more likely to produce one or more of high quality than are those who produce fewer works.

Equilibrium: process occuring when assimilation and accommodation are perfectly balanced.

Equity theory: proposal that partners are satisfied in a relationship if they feel they are getting what they deserve.

Erectile dysfunction: a condition in which a man is unable to achieve an erection sustainable for intercourse.

Error catastrophe theory: proposal that the errors that accumulate with aging are ones that are vital to life itself.

Error theories: proposal that mutations acquired over the organism's lifetime lead to the malfunctioning of the body's cells.

Ethnicity: captures the cultural background of an individual, reflecting the predominant values, attitudes, and expectations in which the individual has been raised.

Euthanasia: a process where physicians take actions that cause the patient to die, with the intention of preventing the suffering associated with a prolonged ending of life.

Event-related potentials (ERPs): brain scan that records brain's pattern of electricity in response to stimuli.

Everyday problem-solving: involves problems that typically occur in people's daily lives, that can be solved in more than one way, and that require the problem solver to decide which strategy will lead to the desired result.

Evidence-based practice: proposal that clinicians should integrate the best available research evidence and clinical expertise in the context of the cultural background, preferences, and characteristics of clients.

Executive functioning: higher-order cognitive skills, including judgment, knowledge, and decision-making.

Exosystem: from the ecological perspective, includes the environments that people do not closely experience on a regular basis but that impact them nevertheless.

Experimental design: research method in which an independent variable is manipulated and scores are then measured on the dependent variable. Involves random assignment of respondents to treatment and control groups.

Extrinsic factors in vocational satisfaction: features that accompany the job but are not central to its performance.

Fat-free mass (FFM): lean tissue in the body.

Fear of falling: the anxiety about the fear of falling; this anxiety can create a vicious cycle in which older individuals increasingly restrict their movement.

Filial anxiety: the fear of having to take care of an aging, infirmed parent.

Filial maturity: occurs when children reach the age of relating to their parents as equals.

Filial obligation or **filial piety:** the cultural values that adult children are expected to care for their parents, meaning that they feel committed to taking care of their parents should this become necessary.

Five-Factor model (FFM): a theory intended to capture all the essential characteristics of personality in a set of five broad dispositions.

Flashbulb memory: the recall of important and distinctive events that stand out from other memories of past events.

Fluid reasoning (Gf): the individual's innate abilities to carry out higher-level cognitive operations involving the integration, analysis, and synthesis of new information.

Fluid-crystallized theory (Gf-Gc): the view that intelligence should be divided into two distinct factors.

Focus group: research method in which respondents meet and discuss a particular topic that the researcher assigns to them.

Formal operations: the ability of adolescents and adults to use logic and abstract symbols to arrive at solutions to complex problems.

FOXO genes: a group of genes that are involved in crucial cellular processes regulating stress resistance, metabolism, the cell cycle, and the death of cells.

Free radical theory: proposal that the cause of aging is the increased activity of unstable compounds that compromise the cell's functioning.

Free radicals: unstable compounds produced when certain molecules in cells react with oxygen.

Friendship styles: individual differences in approaches toward friendships.

Frontotemporal neurocognitive disorder (FTD): a neurocognitive disorder that involves specifically the frontal lobes of the brain.

Functional age: approach defining age based on performance rather than chronological age.

Functional magnetic resonance imaging (fMRI): a type of scan that can be used to show changes in the brain over the course of a mental activity.

g or **general factor:** the ability to infer and apply relationships on the basis of experience.

Galantamine: a drug (brand name Razadyne) used to treat dementia caused by Alzheimer's disease.

Gender gap: expressed as a proportion of women's to men's salaries.

Gender: an individual's identification as male, female, or nonbinary.

Gene: the functional unit of a DNA molecule carrying a particular set of instructions for producing a specific protein.

General slowing hypothesis: proposal that the increase in reaction time reflects a general decline of information processing speed within the nervous system of the aging individual.

Generalized anxiety disorder: disorder in which the individual experiences an overall sense of uneasiness and concern without specific focus.

Generativity versus stagnation: stage in Erikson's theory when middle-aged adults focus on the psychosocial issues of procreation, productivity, and creativity.

Genome: the complete set of instructions for "building" all the cells that make up an organism.

Genome-wide association study: a method used in behavior genetics in which researchers search for genetic variations related to complex diseases by scanning the entire genome.

Genome-wide linkage study: a method used in behavior genetics in which researchers study the families of people with specific psychological traits or disorders.

Geriatric Depression Scale (GDS): a depression screening instrument that asks individuals to answer a true–false set of questions about symptoms of depression.

Geriatric partial hospital: provides older adults living in the community who need psychiatric care with a range of mental health services.

Geriatrics: the medical specialty in aging.

Gerontology: the scientific study of the aging process.

Gini coefficent: an index of income inequality in a given economy.

Glaucoma: a group of conditions causing blindness related to changes in pressure within the eyeball.

Glucocorticoid cascade hypothesis: the view that increased cortisol levels accelerate neuronal loss in the hippocampus and that repeated (cascading) increases in cortisol over the lifetime lead to further degeneration.

Gompertz function: a plot showing the relationship between age and death rates for a given species.

Good death: the opportunity for patients to have autonomy in making decisions about the type, site, and duration of the care that they receive at the end of life.

Government-assisted housing: housing provided for individuals with low-to-moderate incomes who need affordable housing or rental assistance.

Green House model: an alternative to the traditional nursing homes; offers older adults individual homes within a small community of 6 to 10 residents and skilled nursing staff.

Health: a state of complete physical, mental, and social well-being; not merely the absence of disease or infirmity.

Health expectancy: the number of years a person could expect to live in good health if current mortality and morbidity rates persist.

Helicopter parents: parents who are seen as smothering and overprotecting their overly dependent children.

Hemispheric Asymmetry Reduction in Older Adults (HAROLD) model: model of plasticity in which the brains of older adults become activated in the opposite hemisphere when the original area suffers deficits.

Hierarchical linear modeling (HLM): a statistical methodology where researchers study the patterns of change within individuals over time.

High-density lipoproteins (HDLs): known as "good" cholesterol, which transport lipids out of the body.

Hippocampus: the structure in the brain responsible for consolidating memories.

Hispanic mortality paradox: the longer life expectancy of people of Hispanic (or Latino) ethnicity despite living in harsher conditions within the United States.

Hoarding: disorder in which people collect and store seemingly useless items that they cannot discard.

Holland's vocational development theory: proposal that people express their personalities in their vocational aspirations and interests.

Home health services: provide assistance to older adults within their own private residences.

Hormone replacement therapy (HRT): a therapeutic administration of lower doses of estrogen than in estrogen-replacement therapy (ERT) along with progestin to reduce the cancer risk associated with ERT.

Hormones: the chemical messengers produced by the endocrine systems.

Hospice: a site or program that provides medical and supportive services for dying patients.

Hypertension: a disease in which an individual chronically suffers from abnormally elevated blood pressure.

Hypothalamus-releasing factors (HRFs): hormones produced by the hypothalamus that regulate the secretion of hormones in turn produced by the anterior pituitary gland.

Identity: a composite of how people view themselves in the biological, psychological, and social domains of life.

Identity accommodation: the process of making changes in identity in response to experiences that challenge people's current view of themselves.

Identity achievement versus identity diffusion: stage in Erikson's theory when individuals must decide "who" they are and what they wish to get out of life.

Identity assimilation: process involving the interpretation of new experiences in terms of a person's existing identity.

Identity balance: process involving the dynamic equilibrium that occurs when people tend to view themselves consistently but can make changes when called for by their experiences.

Identity process theory: proposal that identity continues to change in adulthood in a dynamic manner.

Identity status interview: examines the degree of commitment held by the individual to identity issues and the degree of exploration the individual used to arrive at this commitment.

Immune senescence: the belief that there are widespread age-related declines in immune system functioning.

Implicit memory: long-term memory for information that people acquire without intending to do so.

Incidence statistics: data that provide estimates of the percent of people who *first* develop symptoms in a given period.

Independent variable: the factor that the researcher manipulates.

Individuality: a principle of adult development and aging that asserts that as people age, they become more different from each other.

Industry versus inferiority: stage in Erikson's theory that involves the individual's identifying with the world of work and developing a work ethic.

Informed consent: written agreement to participate in research based on knowing what participation will involve.

Inhibitory control: the process of turning off one response while performing another.

Inhibitory deficit hypothesis: proposal that aging reduces the individual's ability to inhibit or tune out irrelevant information.

Initiative versus guilt: stage in Erikson's theory when the child becomes able to engage in creative self-expression without fear of making a mistake.

Inoculation hypothesis: the belief that older minorities and women have actually become immune to the effects of ageism through years of exposure to discrimination and stereotyping.

Institutional facility: a group residential setting that provides individuals with medical or psychiatric care.

Instrumental activities of daily living (IADL): the ability to use the telephone, go shopping, prepare meals, complete housekeeping tasks, do laundry, use private or public transportation, take medications, and handle finances.

Intelligence: an individual's mental ability.

Intelligence test: assessment of an individual's overall cognitive status along a set of standardized dimensions.

Interactionist model: the view that not only do genetics and environment interact in complex ways to produce their effects on the individual but also that individuals actively shape their own development.

Intergenerational solidarity model (ISM): summarizes the six relevant dimensions of families that span at least two generations.

Intergenerational stake hypothesis: proposal that parents are higher in affectual solidarity toward their children than children are toward their parents.

Interindividual differences: differences between people.

Intermediate care facility: facility in which health-related services are provided to individuals who do not require hospital or skilled nursing facility care but do require some type of institutional care.

International Statistical Classification of Diseases and Related Health Problems (ICD): the reference guide to all medical illnesses, including psychological disorders.

Interpersonal therapy (IPT): an approach that helps clients learn to understand and change their relationships with others.

Intersectionality: the notion that multiple "isms" such as ageism, sexism, and racism do not just add up, but interact with one another to influence the discriminatory ways in which people reflecting more than one group are treated.

Intimacy versus isolation: stage in Erikson's theory when individuals are faced with making commitments to close relationships.

Intraindividual differences: variations within the same individual.

Intrinsic factors in vocational satisfaction: the tasks required to perform the work itself.

Invisible death: the current Western attitude of a desire for death to retreat from the family and to be confined to hospitals.

Job tenure: the length of time a person has spent in the job.

Korsakoff syndrome: a form of neurocognitive disorder progressing from Wernicke's disease to a chronic form of alcohol-induced neurocognitive disorder.

Labor force: includes all civilians in the over-16 population who live outside of institutions and have sought or are actively seeking employment.

Laboratory studies: the testing of participants in a systematic fashion using standardized procedures.

Lastingness: the quality of an older artist's work that allows it to persist over time.

Latent variable: a statistical composite of several variables.

Late-onset Alzheimer's disease: a form of Alzheimer's disease that starts after the age of 60 or 65 years.

Late-onset schizophrenia: a form of schizophrenia originating in adults over the age of 45 years.

Late-onset stress symptomatology (LOSS): a phenomenon observed in aging veterans who were exposed to stressful combat situations in young adulthood.

Legitimization of biography: steps to leave a legacy that will continue to define oneself after one is gone.

Life course perspective: the norms, roles, and attitudes about age that have an impact on the shape of each person's life.

Life course perspective on retirement: proposal that changes in the work role in later life are best seen as logical outgrowths of earlier life events.

Life expectancy: the average number of years of life remaining to people born within a similar period of time.

Life satisfaction: the overall assessment of an individual's feelings and attitudes about one's life at a particular point in time.

Life span: the maximum length of life for a given species.

Life-span perspective: the view of development as continuous from childhood through old age.

Life story: the individual's narrative view of his or her own past.

Living will: part of an advance directive that stipulates the conditions under which a patient will accept or refuse treatment.

Life structure: the way that the individual's life is patterned at a given point in time.

Living apart together (LAT): living arrangement increasingly adopted by unmarried older adults in an intimate relationship who do not wish to share a residence.

Logistic regression: a method in which researchers test the likelihood of an individual receiving a score on a discrete yes–no variable.

Longitudinal design: a research design in which people are followed repeatedly from one test occasion to another.

Long-term memory: the repository of information that is held for a period of time ranging from several minutes to a lifetime.

Low-density lipoproteins (LDLs): known as "bad" cholesterol, the transport mechanisms that send cholesterol to the arteries.

Lung age: a mathematical function showing how old your lung is based on a combination of your age and a measure obtained from a spirometer called forced expiratory volume.

Macrosystem: from the ecological perspective, includes the larger social institutions ranging from a country's economy to its laws and social norms.

Magnetic resonance imaging (MRI): a brain imaging method that uses radio waves to construct a picture of the living brain based on the water content of various tissues.

Major depressive disorder: disorder in which the major symptom of which is an extremely sad mood that lasts most of the time for at least 2 weeks and is atypical of the individual's usual mood.

Marriage: a legally sanctioned union between two adults.

Maturation hypothesis: the belief that people who have personality disorders that involve "immature" symptoms, such as acting out, being entitled, and having an unstable sense of self, improve or at least become more treatable later in life.

Mechanics of intelligence: involves cognitive operations such as speed, working memory, and fluid intelligence.

Mechanistic model: proposal that people's behavior changes gradually over time, shaped by the outside forces that cause them to adapt to their environments.

Mediation: a method used to compare the correlation between two variables with and without their joint correlation to a third variable.

Medicaid: a federal and state matching entitlement program that provides medical assistance for certain individuals and families with low incomes and resources.

Medical model: a perspective that focuses primarily on the physiological causes of a psychological disorder.

Medical Order for Life-Sustaining Treatment (MOLST): component of an advance directive that contains orders for a physician's assistant or nurse practitioner.

Medicare: the federal health care funding agency passed and signed into law in 1965, designated as "Health Insurance for the Aged and Disabled."

Medicare Modernization Act (MMA): U.S. legislation passed in 2003 that created the prescription drug benefit in Medicare.

Medicare Part A (Hospital Insurance or HI): provides coverage that includes all medically necessary services and supplies provided during a patient's stay in the hospital and subsequent rehabilitation in an approved facility.

Medicare Part B: provides benefits for a range of medical services available to people 65 and older who pay a monthly insurance premium.

Melatonin: the hormone manufactured by the pineal gland responsible in part for the sleep–wake cycles.

Memantine: a type of medication for Alzheimer's disease that targets the excitatory neurotransmitter glutamate.

Memory controllability: beliefs about the effects of the aging process on memory, such as the extent to which the individual believes that memory decline is inevitable with age.

Memory self-efficacy: the degree to which an individual believes he/she can successfully complete a memory task.

Menopause: the point in a woman's life when menstruation stops permanently.

Mental status examination: assessment of qualities of the client including appearance, attitudes, behavior, mood and affect, speech, thought processes, content of thought, perception, cognition, insight, and judgment.

Mesosystem: from the ecological perspective, the system in which interactions take place among two or more microsystems.

Meta-analysis: a statistical procedure that allows for a combination of findings from independently conducted studies.

Metabolic syndrome: a cluster of symptoms associated with high-risk factors for cardiovascular (and other) diseases, including high levels of abdominal obesity, high blood fats, abnormal levels of blood cholesterol, hypertension, and high glucose.

Microsystem: from the ecological perspective, the setting in which people have their daily interactions and that therefore have the most direct impact on their lives.

Midlife crisis: a period of self-scrutiny and reevaluation of goals triggered by the individual's entry into middle age.

Mild cognitive impairment (MCI): a form of neurocognitive disorder that signifies that the individual may be at risk for developing Alzheimer's disease.

Millennials: the generation reaching young adulthood in the early 21st century.

Mini-Mental State Examination (MMSE): a brief, structured tool that clinicians use as a screening device to assess dementia.

Moderation: condition in which two variables are believed to have a joint influence on a third.

Modernization hypothesis: proposal that the increasing urbanization and industrialization of Western society is what causes older adults to be devalued.

Most Efficient Design: a set of three designs manipulating the variables of age, cohort, and time of measurement.

Motivation crowding out: describes workers who feel that they cannot fulfill their intrinsic needs because their motivation is controlled entirely by extrinsic factors.

Multidirectionality: the idea that development can proceed in multiple directions within the same person.

Multi-infarct dementia or MID: the most common form of vascular neurocognitive disorder; caused by transient ischemic attacks.

Multiple jeopardy hypothesis: proposal that older individuals who fit more than one discriminated-against category are affected by biases against each of these categorizations.

Multiple regression analysis: form of correlational study in which one set of variables are designated as predictors of performance on another variable designated as the outcome.

Multiple threshold model: proposal that individuals realize that they are getting older through a stepwise process as aging-related changes occur.

Multivariate correlational design: a research design where researchers simultaneously evaluate the effects of more than two variables.

Mutations: alterations in genes that lead to changes in their functions.

Myocardial infarction: an acute condition in which the blood supply to part of the heart muscle (the myocardium) is severely reduced or blocked.

Need complementarity hypothesis: proposal that people seek and are more satisfied with marital partners who are the opposite of themselves.

NEO-PI-R: a questionnaire containing 240 items measuring the 30 facets of the Five-Factor model.

Nephrons: cells in the kidneys that serve as millions of tiny filters that cleanse the blood of metabolic waste.

Neurocognitive disorder with Lewy bodies: condition first identified in 1961; similar to Alzheimer's disease in that it causes progressive loss of memory, language, calculation, and reasoning as well as other higher mental functions.

Neurocognitive disorder: a condition in which an individual experiences a loss of cognitive function severe enough to interfere with normal daily activities and social relationships.

Neurofibrillary tangles: abnormally twisted fibers within the neurons that occurs in Alzheimer's disease.

Neuronal fallout model: proposal that individuals progressively lose brain tissue over the life span because neurons do not have the ability to replace themselves when they die.

Neuropsychological assessment: method of gathering information about a client's brain functioning from a series of standardized cognitive tests.

New modes of retirement: the view that the characteristics of the person's spouse and lifelong family responsibilities play a role in retirement decisions and adjustment.

Niche-picking: the proposal that genetic and environmental factors work together to influence the direction of a child's life.

Nonnormative influences: the random idiosyncratic events that occur throughout life.

Normal aging is different from disease: the principle that growing older does not necessarily mean growing sicker.

Normal-pressure hydrocephalus: a reversible form of neurocognitive disorder that can cause cognitive impairment, dementia, urinary incontinence, and difficulty in walking.

Normative age-graded influences: influences that lead people to choose experiences that their culture and historical period attach to certain ages or points in the life span.

Normative history-graded influences: events that occur to everyone within a certain culture or geopolitical unit (regardless of age).

Nursing Home Reform Act (NHRA): a U.S. federal law mandating that facilities meet physical standards, provide adequate professional staffing and services, and maintain policies governing their administrative and medical procedures.

Nursing home: a type of medical institution that provides a room, meals, skilled nursing and rehabilitative care, medical services, and protective supervision.

O*NET, the Occupational Information Network: an interactive national database of occupations.

Observational method: a way for researchers to conduct a systematic examination of what people do in particular settings.

Obsessive-compulsive disorder: disorder characterized by unrelenting, irrational, and distracting obsessions, or repetitive thoughts and compulsions, or repetitive behaviors.

Obsessive-compulsive personality disorder: personality disorder with symptoms that include excessive rigidity, preoccupation with details and rules, excessive perfectionism, and over-conscientiousness.

Occupational reinforcement patterns (ORPs): the work values and needs likely to be reinforced or satisfied by a particular occupation.

Old Age and Survivors Disability Insurance (OASDI): combines Old-Age Survivors Insurance and Disability Insurance.

Old age style: a special quality common to the work of older artists and writers.

Oldest-old: a subgroup of older adults between the ages of 85 and older.

Old-old: a subgroup of older adults between the ages of 75 and 84.

Optimal aging: growing older in a way that slows or alters the process.

Organismic model: proposal that heredity drives the course of development throughout life.

Orientation: reflects whether examinees know where they are (orientation to place), what time it is (orientation to time), and who they are (orientation to person).

Osteoarthritis: a painful, degenerative joint disease that often involves the hips, knees, neck, lower back, or the small joints of the hands.

Osteoporosis: a disease that occurs when the bone mineral density reaches the point that is more than 2.5 standard deviations below the mean of young, White, non-Hispanic women.

Overactive bladder: a condition whose symptoms include incontinence and the need to urinate more frequently than normal.

Overtreatment: occurs when patients do not have their DNRs respected but instead receive active life support that includes resuscitation.

Palliative care: a request by dying patients that will provide them with relief from symptoms such as nausea, pain, and dyspnea as well as with some services such as physical and occupational therapy.

Panic disorder: disorder that involves the experience of panic attacks in which people have the physical sensation that they are about to die.

Paradox of well-being: findings from research on successful aging that so many older adults maintain high subjective well-being despite facing challenges from their objective circumstances.

Parkinson's disease: a disease that shows a variety of motor disturbances, including tremors, speech impediments, slowing of movement, muscular rigidity, shuffling gait, and postural instability or the inability to maintain balance.

Part C of Medicare: also called Medicare Advantage; provides coverage in conjunction with private health plans.

Part D of Medicare: a prescription-drug benefit plan that provides coverage for a portion of the enrollee's costs.

Path analysis: a method in which researchers test all possible correlations among a set of variables to see if they can be explained by a single model.

Patient Self-Determination Act (PSDA): passed in 1990, guarantees the right of all competent adults to have an active role in decisions about their care.

Perimenopause: a 3- to 5-year span in which a woman gradually loses her reproductive ability; it ends in menopause when a woman has not had her menstrual period for 1 year.

Peripheral ties: friendships that are not characterized by a high degree of closeness.

Personal aging: changes that occur within the individual and reflect the influence of time's passage on the body's structures and functions.

Personality disorder: a long-standing pattern of inner experience and behavior that has maladaptive qualities.

Person–environment correspondence theory: proposal that people are most satisfied when their workplaces respond to their needs.

Photoaging: age-related changes in the skin due to radiation from the sun.

Physician's Order for Life-Sustaining Treatment (POLST): component of an advance directive that contains orders for the physician.

Physician-assisted suicide (PAS): a process through which terminally ill individuals make the conscious decision, while they are still able to do so, that they want their lives to end before dying becomes a protracted process.

Pick's disease: a form of neurocognitive disorder that involves severe atrophy of the frontal and temporal lobes.

Pikes Peak Model of Geropsychology: a set of competencies that professional geropsychologists are expected to have when working with older adults.

Planck hypothesis: the tendency of peak scientific productivity to occur in early adulthood.

Plasticity in development: the course of development may be altered (is "plastic") depending on the nature of the individual's specific interactions in the environment.

Plasticity model: a view of the aging nervous system that proposal that although some neurons die, the remaining ones continue to develop.

Plaque: hard deposits inside the arterial walls consisting of cholesterol, cellular waste products, calcium, and fibrin.

Polypharmacy: a condition in which an individual takes multiple drugs.

Positive psychology: view intended to provide a greater understanding of the strengths and virtues that enable individuals and communities to thrive.

Positron emission tomography (PET) scan: a brain scan method that shows radioactive compounds in the blood as they pass through the brain.

Possible selves: model proposing that the individual's view of the self, or self-schema, guides the choice and pursuit of future endeavors.

Posterior-Anterior Shift with Aging (PASA) model: proposal that the front (anterior) of the brain in older adults becomes more responsive to make up for the lower responsiveness found in the rear (posterior) of the brain.

Postformal operations: a stage proposed by adult development researchers that refers to the way that adults structure their thinking over and beyond that of adolescents.

Post-traumatic stress disorder (PTSD): the diagnosis given to people whose symptoms persist for more than a month after a trauma and include the intrusion of distressing reminders of an event; dissociative symptoms, such as feeling numb or detached from others; avoidance of situations that might serve as reminders of the event; and hyperarousal, including sleep disturbances or irritability.

Pragmatics of intelligence: an individual's aptitude to apply his or her abilities to the solution of real-life problems.

Presbycusis: an age-related hearing loss due to degenerative changes in the cochlea or auditory nerve leading from the cochlea to the brain.

Presbyopia: the loss of the ability to focus vision on near objects.

Presenilin genes (PS1 and PS2): genes that may lead APP to increase its production of beta-amyloid, which in turn causes neurofibrillary tangles and amyloid plaques.

Prevalence statistics: data that provide estimates of the percentage of people who have ever had symptoms in a particular period.

Primary aging or normal aging: a set of changes built into the hard wiring of an organism that progress at different rates among individuals but are universal, intrinsic, and progressive.

Primary Mental Abilities Test (PMAT): assesses the seven abilities of Verbal Meaning, Word Fluency, Number, Spatial Relations, Memory, Perceptual Speed, and General Reasoning.

Problem-focused coping: coping in which people attempt to reduce their stress by changing something about the situation.

Problem-solving therapy (PST): form of therapy for major depressive disorder in which clients are taught ways to identify and solve their actual life problems.

Procedural memory: the recall of the actions involved in particular tasks, such as sewing on a button, playing the piano, and riding a bike.

Processing speed: the brain's efficiency in processing information.

Professional geropsychology: the application of gerontology to the psychological treatment of older adults.

Programmed aging theories: proposal that aging and death are built into the hardwiring of all organisms and are therefore part of the genetic code.

Prospective memory: the recall of events to be performed in the future.

Prospective study: a variant of longitudinal design in which researchers sample from a population of interest before they develop a particular type of illness or experience a particular type of life event.

Protean career: a career in which individuals are both self-directed and driven internally by their own values.

Pseudodementia: a condition where cognitive symptoms appear, causing impairment similar to neurocognitive disorder.

Psychodynamic perspective: emphasizes the ways in which unconscious motives and impulses express themselves in people's personalities and behavior.

Psychodynamic therapy: focuses on the client's underlying conflicts; however, these traditional models are changing, and therapists working from this framework may emphasize other issues, such as the client's attachment style.

Psychological age: the performance that an individual achieves on measures of such qualities as reaction time, memory, learning ability, and intelligence.

Psychological assessment: a procedure in which a clinician provides a formal evaluation of an individual's cognitive, personality, and psychosocial functioning.

Psychological disorders: include the range of behaviors and experiences that fall outside of social norms, create adaptational difficulty for the individual on a daily basis, and put the individual or others at risk of harm.

Psychopathy: a set of traits that include a lack of remorse and an impulsive lifestyle.

Psychosocial theory of development: the view proposed by Erikson that at certain points in life, a person's biological, psychological, and social changes come together to influence his or her personality.

Psychotherapeutic medications: medications intended to reduce an individual's psychological symptoms.

Qualitative method: method in which researchers use a flexible approach to understand the main themes in their data.

Quasi-experimental design: a research design where groups are compared on predetermined characteristics.

Race: defined in biological terms as the classification within the species based on physical and structural characteristics.

Random error theories: proposal that aging reflects unplanned changes in an organism over time.

Reaction time: the basic measure of processing speed.

Reciprocity in development: principle that people both influence and are influenced by the events in their lives.

Recycling: the process through which workers change their main field of career activity part way into occupational life.

Reliability: a measure's consistency and whether it produces the same results each time it is used.

Religion: an individual's identification with an organized belief system.

Reminiscence bump: period of clear memories from the age of about 10 to 30 years.

Remote memory: the recall of information from the distant past in general.

Replicative senescence: the loss of the ability of cells to reproduce.

Reserve capacity: abilities that are there to be used but are currently untapped.

Residential care facility: facility that provides 24-hour supportive care services and supervision to individuals who do not require skilled nursing care.

Resilience: the ability to recover from stress.

Resource model: theory that an individual's adjustment to retirement reflects his or her physical, cognitive, motivational, financial, social, and emotional resources; the more resources, the more favorable will be the individual's adjustment at any one point through the retirement transition.

Respite care: service that provides family caregivers with a break while allowing the older adult to receive needed support.

Retirement: the withdrawal of an individual in later life from the labor force.

Retrieval-induced forgetting: being unable to remember information that a person knew at one time in the past.

Reversible neurocognitive disorders: disorders due to the presence of a medical condition that affects but does not destroy brain tissue.

RIASEC model: the six basic types that characterize an individual's vocational interests.

Rivastigmine: a generic version of the drug Exelon.

Role reversal: the family situation in which adult children take over in the role as parent because the parents are unable to care for themselves.

Role theory of retirement: proposal that retirement has deleterious effects because the loss of the work role loosens the ties between the individual and society.

Rowe and Kahn definition of successful aging: the absence of disease, high cognitive and physical function, and engagement with life.

Sandwich generation: proposal that midlife caregivers are sandwiched between their aging parents and their teenaged children.

Sarcopenia: a progressive age-related loss of muscle mass with a consequent loss of strength.

Scaffolding theory: proposal that older adults are able to recruit alternate neural circuits as needed by task demands to make up for losses suffered elsewhere.

Schemas: the mental structures people use to understand the world.

Schizophrenia: a disorder in which individuals experience a distorted perception of reality and impairment in thinking, behavior, affect, and motivation.

Secondary aging or impaired aging: changes due to disease.

Secretases: in healthy aging, the part of APP remaining outside the neuron is trimmed by enzymes.

Secure attachment style: attachment style in which individuals feel able to rely on other people.

Selective attrition: the observation that the people who drop out of a longitudinal study are not necessarily representative of the sample that was originally tested.

Selective optimization with compensation model (SOC): proposal that adults attempt to preserve and maximize the abilities that are of central importance and put less effort into maintaining those that are not.

Self-determination theory: theory that focuses on the amount of control that workers have over their jobs as influences on vocational satisfaction.

Self-Directed Search (SDS): a self-administered questionnaire that allows one to assess where one fits on the RIASEC dimensions.

Self-efficacy: a term used in the social psychological literature to refer to a person's feelings of competence at a particular task.

Semantic memory: the ability to recall word meanings and factual information.

Sequential design: data collection strategies consisting of different combinations of the variables of age, cohort, and time of measurement.

Set point perspective: the view that people's personalities influence their level of well-being throughout life.

Sex: an individual's inherited predisposition to develop the physiological characteristics typically associated with maleness or femaleness.

Similarity hypothesis: proposal that the similarity of personality and values predicts both initial interpersonal attraction and satisfaction within long-term relationships.

Simple reaction time tasks: tasks used to measure processing speed in which participants are instructed to make a response, such as pushing a key as soon as a target appears.

Simple visual search: search in which the target differs from the other stimuli by only one feature, such as shape, color, or size.

Single-nucleotide polymorphisms (SNPs): small genetic variations that can occur in a person's DNA sequence.

Single-photon emission computed tomography (SPECT): a brain scan method that detects radioactive compounds as they pass through the brain.

Skilled nursing facility: a type of nursing home that provides the most intensive nursing care available outside of a hospital.

Skip generation family: a family living situation in which children live with their grandparents and not their parents.

Sleep apnea: a disorder in which the individual becomes temporarily unable to breathe while asleep.

Social age: calculated by evaluating where people are compared to the "typical" ages expected for people to be when they occupy certain positions in life.

Social aging: the effects of a person's exposure to a changing environment.

Social anxiety disorder: disorder in which the individual experiences extreme anxiety about being watched by other people.

Social clock: the expectations for the ages at which a society associates with major life events.

Social comparison: the process that occurs when people rate themselves relative to their primary reference group.

Social death: the process through which the dying become treated as nonpersons by family or health care workers as they are left to spend their final months or years in a hospital or nursing home.

Social exchange theory: theory that predicts why some relationships succeed and others fail in terms of whether the relationship's rewards exceed its costs.

Social indicators: objective measures of social and economic welfare and an individual's level of psychological well-being.

Social indicator model of well-being: the view that demographic and social structural variables account for individual differences in levels of well-being.

Social Security Act: federal legislation that guarantees income for retirees and others who are unable to work as well as a lump sum in death benefits for survivors.

Socioeconomic status (SES): or "social class," reflects people's position in the educational and occupational ranks of a society.

Socioemotional selectivity theory: proposal that throughout adulthood, people structure the nature and range of their relationships to maximize gains and minimize risks.

Somatopause of aging: a decline in the somatotrophic axis (GH and IGF-1).

Source memory: the recall of where or how an individual acquires information.

Specific phobia: disorder in which the individual has having an irrational fear of a particular object or situation.

Stages of dying: the process considered to occur universally among terminally ill patients including denial, anger, bargaining, depression, and acceptance.

Stereotype threat: proposal that people perform in ways consistent with negative stereotypes of the group to which they see themselves as belonging.

Stress incontinence: a condition in which the individual is unable to retain urine while engaging in some form of physical exertion.

Stress: the perception that a situation overwhelms the individual's ability to manage effectively in that situation.

Strong Vocational Interest Inventory (SVII): consists of items in which respondents indicate their preferences for occupations, topics of study, activities, and types of people.

Structural ambivalence: the idea that society's structures do not make clear how family members should behave.

Structural equation modeling (SEM): a process where researchers test models involving relationships that include latent variables.

Subcutaneous: the bottommost layer of skin, giving the skin its opacity and smoothing the curves of the arms, legs, and face.

Subdural hematoma: a blood clot that creates pressure on brain tissue.

Subjective well-being: an individual's overall sense of happiness.

Successful cognitive aging: defined as cognitive performance that is above the average for an individual's age group as objectively measured.

Suffocation model of marriage: contemporary adults place more emphasis on marriage as a source of self-expression and fulfillment, but have less time to devote to maintaining their marriages than ever before.

Superagers: individuals 80 years and older with episodic memory that is comparable to, or superior than, that of middle-aged adults.

Super's life-span life-stage theory: focuses on the role of the self and proposal that people attempt to realize their inner potential through their career choices.

Supercentenarians: people who are 110 years old and older.

Survey method: a method to gain information about a sample that can then be generalized to a larger population.

Survivor principle: idea that people who live to old age outlive the many threats that could have caused their deaths at earlier ages.

Sustained attention: type of attention in which participants completing a task must respond when they see a particular target appear out of a continuous stream of stimuli.

Swan song: the last burst of creativity of an older musician.

Tamed death: the prevailing view until the Middle Ages in which death was viewed as familiar and simple, a transition to eternal life.

Tau: the protein that makes up neurofibrillary tangles.

Telomeres: repetitive DNA sequences at the ends of chromosomes.

Terminal decline: the gradual loss of cognitive abilities as an individual draws closer to death.

Terror management theory: proposal that people regard with panic and dread the thought of the finitude of their lives.

Tertiary aging: the rapid loss of functions experienced at the very end of life.

Testing the limits: the process of continuing to train people until they show no further improvements.

Tetrahydroaminoacridine (THA): medication also called tacrine and given the brand name Cognex.

Theory of multiple intelligences: theory that intelligence includes several traditional abilities as well as others not usually tapped in intelligence tests.

Time of measurement: the year or period in which a person is tested.

Time-sequential design: method in which data are organized by age and time of measurement.

Tinnitus: a symptom in which the individual perceives sounds in the head or ear (such as a ringing noise) when there is no external source.

Trait: a stable, enduring disposition that persists over time.

Trait perspective: a theory based on the assumption that the organization of the personal dispositions known as traits guide the individual's behavior.

Transient ischemic attack (TIA): a condition caused by the development of clots in the cerebral arteries; also called a ministroke.

Transition to parenthood (TtP): the period of adjustment to the new family status represented by the presence of a child in the home.

Triglycerides: fats that are stored in the body's cells.

Two-factor motivational theory: proposal that intrinsic and extrinsic factors play different roles in contributing to vocational satisfaction.

Type A behavior pattern: a collection of traits that include being highly competitive, being impatient, feeling a strong sense of time urgency, and being highly achievement-oriented.

Urge incontinence: a form of urinary incontinence in which the individual experiences a sudden need to urinate and may even leak urine.

Useful field of view (UFOV): test of people's ability to respond to stimuli appearing in the periphery of their vision.

Validity: a test's ability to measure what it is supposed to measure.

Variable: a characteristic that "varies" from individual to individual.

Vascular neurocognitive disorder: a progressive loss of cognitive functioning due to damage to the arteries supplying the brain.

Vertigo: the sensation of spinning when the body is at rest.

Visual search tasks: tasks that require that the observer locate a specific target among a set of distractors.

Vocation: a person's choice of an occupation.

Vocational satisfaction: the extent to which people find their work to be enjoyable.

Wear and tear theory: proposal that as people age, they believe they are "falling apart."

Wechsler Adult Intelligence Scale (WAIS): the most well-known individual test of adult intelligence.

Wernicke's disease: an acute condition caused by chronic alcohol abuse involving delirium, eye movement disturbances, difficulties maintaining balance and movement, and deterioration of the nerves to the hands and feet.

White matter hyperintensities (WMH): abnormalities in the brain thought to be made up of parts of deteriorating neurons.

Whitehall II: a survey of a large sample of British adults focusing on the relationships among health, social class, and occupation.

Widowhood effect: the greater probability of death in those who have become widowed compared to those who are married.

Work–family conflict model: proposal that people have a fixed amount of time and energy to spend on their life roles.

Work–family enrichment model: proposal that experiences in one role improve the quality of life in the other.

Working memory: memory process that keeps information temporarily available and active in consciousness.

World Health Organization definition of active aging: the process of optimizing opportunities for health, participation, and security in order to enhance quality of life as people age.

Young-old: a subgroup of older adults between the ages of 65 and 74.

REFERENCES

Aartsen, M. J., Van Tilburg, T., Smits, C. H., Comijs, H. C., & Knipscheer, K. C. (2005). Does widowhood affect memory performance of older persons? *Psychological Medicine, 35*(2), 217–226.

Abbasi, J. (2019). For mortality, busting the myth of 10000 steps per day. *Journal of the American Medical Association.* doi: 10.1001/jama.2019.10042

Abdouni, A., Djaghloul, M., Thieulin, C., Vargiolu, R., Pailler-Mattei, C., & Zahouani, H. (2017). Biophysical properties of the human finger for touch comprehension: Influences of ageing and gender. *Royal Society Open Science, 4*(8), 170321. doi: 10.1098/rsos.170321

Abrahin, O., Rodrigues, R. P., Nascimento, V. C., Da Silva-Grigoletto, M. E., Sousa, E. C., & Marcal, A. C. (2014). Single- and multiple-set resistance training improves skeletal and respiratory muscle strength in elderly women. *Clinical Interventions in Aging, 9,* 1775–1782. doi: 10.2147/CIA.S68529 cia-9-1775 [pii]

Acierno, R., Hernandez, M. A., Amstadter, A. B., Resnick, H. S., Steve, K., Muzzy, W., & Kilpatrick, D. G. (2010). Prevalence and correlates of emotional, physical, sexual, and financial abuse and potential neglect in the United States: The National Elder Mistreatment Study. *American Journal of Public Health, 100*(2), 292–297. doi: AJPH.2009.163089 [pii] 10.2105/AJPH.2009.163089

Adachi, D., Yamada, M., Nishiguchi, S., Fukutani, N., Hotta, T., Tashiro, Y., ... Aoyama, T. (2015). Age-related decline in chest wall mobility: A cross-sectional study among community-dwelling elderly women. *Journal of the American Osteopathic Association, 115*(6), 384–389. doi: 10.7556/jaoa.2015.079 2300622 [pii]

Adams, R. G., & Blieszner, R. (1994). An integrative conceptual framework for friendship research. *Journal of Social and Personal Relationships, 11,* 163–184.

Ades, P. A., & Toth, M. J. (2005). Accelerated decline of aerobic fitness with healthy aging: What is the good news? *Circulation, 112*(5), 624–626. doi: 10.1161/circulationaha.105.553321

Administration for Community Living. (2019). Advancing independence, integration, and inclusion throughout life. From https://acl.gov/

Administration on Aging. (2018). A profile of older Americans: 2017. From https://www.acl.gov/sites/default/files/Aging%20and%20Disability%20in%20America/2017OlderAmericansProfile.pdf

Adnan, A., Beaty, R., Silvia, P., Spreng, R. N., & Turner, G. R. (2019). Creative aging: Functional brain networks associated with divergent thinking in older and younger adults. *Neurobiology of Aging, 75,* 150–158. doi: 10.1016/j.neurobiolaging.2018.11.004

Adrian, J., Moessinger, M., Charles, A., & Postal, V. (2019). Exploring the contribution of executive functions to on-road driving performance during aging: A latent variable analysis. *Accident Analysis and Prevention, 127,* 96–109. doi: 10.1016/j.aap.2019.02.010

Agostinho, D., & Paço, A. (2012). Analysis of the motivations, generativity and demographics of the food bank volunteer. *International Journal of Nonprofit and Voluntary Sector Marketing, 17*(3), 249–261. doi: 10.1002/nvsm.1427

Aizpurua, A., & Koutstaal, W. (2015). A matter of focus: Detailed memory in the intentional autobiographical recall of older and younger adults. *Consciousness and Cognition, 33,* 145–155. doi: 10.1016/j.concog.2014.12.006

Ajdzanovic, V. Z., Trifunovic, S., Miljic, D., Sosic-Jurjevic, B., Filipovic, B., Miler, M., ... Milosevic, V. (2018). Somatopause, weaknesses of the therapeutic approaches and the cautious optimism based on experimental ageing studies with soy isoflavones. *EXCLI Journal: Experimental and Clinical Sciences, 17,* 279–301. doi: 10.17179/excli2017-956

Akbaraly, T. N., Kivimaki, M., Shipley, M. J., Tabak, A. G., Jokela, M., Virtanen, M., ... Singh-Manoux, A. (2009). Metabolic syndrome over 10 years and cognitive functioning in late mid life: The Whitehall II study. *Diabetes Care.* doi: dc09-1218 [pii] 10.2337/dc09-1218

Al-Turk, W., & Al-Dujaili, E. A. (2016). Effect of age, gender and exercise on salivary dehydroepiandrosterone circadian rhythm profile in human volunteers. *Steroids, 106,* 19–25. doi: 10.1016/j.steroids.2015.12.001

Alameel, T., Andrew, M. K., & Macknight, C. (2010). The association of fecal incontinence with institutionalization and mortality in older adults. *American Journal of Gastroenterology.* doi: ajg201077 [pii] 10.1038/ajg.2010.77

Aldwin, C. M., & Gilmer, D. F. (1999). Health and optimal aging. In J. C. Cavanaugh & S. K. Whitbourne (Eds.), *Gerontology: Interdisciplinary perspectives* (pp. 123–154). New York: Oxford University Press.

Alkatan, M., Baker, J. R., Machin, D. R., Park, W., Akkari, A. S., Pasha, E. P., & Tanaka, H. (2016). Improved function and reduced pain after swimming and cycling training in patients with osteoarthritis. *The Journal of Rheumatology, 43*(3), 666–672. doi: 10.3899/jrheum.151110

Allen, E. S., & Atkins, D. C. (2012). The association of divorce and extramarital sex in a representative U.S. sample. *Journal of Family Issues, 33*(11), 1477–1493. doi: 10.1177/0192513x12439692

Allen, H. K., Beck, K. H., & Zanjani, F. (2019). Driving concerns among older adults: Associations with driving skill, behaviors, and experiences. *Traffic Injury Prevention, 20*(1), 45–51. doi: 10.1080/15389588.2018.1528358

Allen, K. R., & Walker, A. J. (2000). Qualitative research. In C. Hendrick & S. S. Hendrick (Eds.), *Close relationships* (pp. 19–30). Thousand Oaks, CA: Sage Publications.

Allen, M. T. (2016). *Young adult offenders in Canada, 2014.* Juristat Article. Canada: Canadian Centre for Justice Statistics.

Allen, M. T., Handy, J. D., Blankenship, M. R., & Servatius, R. J. (2018). The distressed (Type D) personality factor of social inhibition, but not negative affectivity, enhances eyeblink conditioning. *Behavioural Brain Research, 345*, 93–103. doi: 10.1016/j.bbr.2018.02.035

Almeida, O. P., Hankey, G. J., Yeap, B. B., & Flicker, L. (2018). Impact of a prudent lifestyle on the clinical outcomes of older men with bipolar disorder. *Aging and Mental Health*, 1–7. doi: 10.1080/13607863.2018.1553233

Alonso-Fernandez, P., Puerto, M., Mate, I., Ribera, J. M., & de la Fuente, M. (2008). Neutrophils of centenarians show function levels similar to those of young adults. *Journal of the American Geriatrics Society.* doi: 10.1111/j.1532-5415.2008.02018.x

Alzheimer's Association. (2019). 2019 Alzheimer's disease facts and figures. From https://www.alz.org/media/Documents/alzheimers-facts-and-figures-2019-r.pdf

Amato, P. R., & Afifi, T. D. (2006). Feeling caught between parents: Adult children's relations with parents and subjective well-being. *Journal of Marriage and the Family, 68*(1), 222–235.

American Psychiatric Association. (2013). *DSM-5 diagnostic and statistical manual of mental disorders 5.* Washington, DC: American Psychiatric Association.

American Psychological Association. (2014). Guidelines for psychological practice with older adults. *American Psychologist, 69*, 34–65.

American Psychological Association. (2018). Ethical principles of psychologists and code of conduct. From https://www.apa.org/ethics/code/

American Psychological Association Presidential Task Force on Evidence-Based Practice. (2006). Evidence-based practice in psychology. *American Psychologist, 61*(4), 271–285. doi: 10.1037/0003-066x.61.4.271

An, J. S., & Cooney, T. M. (2006). Psychological well-being in mid to late life: The role of generativity development and parent-child relationships across the lifespan. *International Journal of Behavioral Development, 30*(5), 410–421.

Ancoli-Israel, S. (2009). Sleep and its disorders in aging populations. *Sleep Medicine, 10*(Suppl 1), S7–S11. doi: 10.1016/j.sleep.2009.07.004

Anderson, L. (2019). The opioid prescribing rate and grandparents raising grandchildren: State and county analysis. *Working Paper #SEHSD-WP2019-04.*

Andreoletti, C., Veratti, B. W., & Lachman, M. E. (2006). Age differences in the relationship between anxiety and recall. *Aging and Mental Health, 10*(3), 265–271.

Angelucci, L. (2000). The glucocorticoid hormone: From pedestal to dust and back. *European Journal of Pharmacology, 405*(1–3), 139–147. doi: S0014299900005471 [pii]

Anger, J. T., Saigal, C. S., & Litwin, M. S. (2006). The prevalence of urinary incontinence among community dwelling adult women: Results from the National Health and Nutrition Examination Survey. *Journal of Urology, 175*(2), 601–604. doi: S0022-5347(05)00242-9 [pii] 10.1016/S0022-5347(05)00242-9

Ansado, J., Monchi, O., Ennabil, N., Faure, S., & Joanette, Y. (2012). Load-dependent posterior-anterior shift in aging in complex visual selective attention situations. *Brain Research, 1454*, 14–22. doi: 10.1016/j.brainres.2012.02.061

Antonini, F. M., Magnolfi, S. U., Petruzzi, E., Pinzani, P., Malentacchi, F., Petruzzi, I., & Masotti, G. (2008). Physical performance and creative activities of centenarians. *Archives of Gerontology and Geriatrics, 46*(2), 253–261.

Aoi, W. (2009). Exercise and food factors. *Forum in Nutrition, 61*, 147–155. doi: 000212747 [pii] 10.1159/000212747

Arbesman, M., & Pellerito, J. M., Jr. (2008). Evidence-based perspective on the effect of automobile-related modifications on the driving ability, performance, and safety of older adults. *American Journal of Occupational Therapy, 62*(2), 173–186. doi: 10.5014/ajot.62.2.173

Ariès, P. (1974). *Western attitudes toward death: From the middle ages to the present.* Baltimore, MD: Johns Hopkins University Press.

Ariès, P. (1981). *The hour of our death.* New York: Alfred A. Knopf.

Armstrong, P. I., & Anthoney, S. F. (2009). Personality facets and RIASEC interests: An integrated model. *Journal of Vocational Behavior, 75*(3), 346–359.

Arnett, J. J. (2000). Emerging adulthood: A theory of development from the late teens through the twenties. *American Psychologist, 55*(5), 469–480.

Arnold, J. T., Liu, X., Allen, J. D., Le, H., McFann, K. K., & Blackman, M. R. (2007). Androgen receptor or estrogen receptor-beta blockade alters DHEA-, DHT-, and E(2)-induced proliferation and PSA production in human prostate cancer cells. *Prostate, 67*(11), 1152–1162. doi: 10.1002/pros.20585

Arnoldussen, I. A. C., Sundh, V., Backman, K., Kern, S., Ostling, S., Blennow, K., … Gustafson, D. R. (2018). A 10-year follow-up of adiposity and dementia in Swedish adults aged 70 years and older. *Journal of Alzheimer's Disease, 63*(4), 1325–1335. doi: 10.3233/jad-180099

Arsenis, N. C., You, T., Ogawa, E. F., Tinsley, G. M., & Zuo, L. (2017). Physical activity and telomere length: Impact of aging and potential mechanisms of action. *Oncotarget, 8*(27), 45008–45019. doi: 10.18632/oncotarget.16726

Artistico, D., Cervone, D., & Pezzuti, L. (2003). Perceived self-efficacy and everyday problem solving among young and older adults. *Psychology and Aging, 18*, 68–79.

Artistico, D., Orom, H., Cervone, D., Krauss, S., & Houston, E. (2010). Everyday challenges in context: The influence of contextual factors on everyday problem solving among young, middle-aged, and older adults. *Experimental Aging Research, 36*(2), 230–247. doi: 10.1080/03610731003613938

Atchley, R. C. (1989). A continuity theory of normal aging. *Gerontologist, 29*, 183–190.

Ausburn, L. J. (2004). Course design elements most valued by adult learners in blended online education environments: An American perspective. *Educational Media International, 41*(4), 327–337. doi: 10.1080/0952398042000314820

Baan, R., Grosse, Y., Straif, K., Secretan, B., El Ghissassi, F., Bouvard, V., ... Cogliano, V. (2009). A review of human carcinogens—Part F: Chemical agents and related occupations. *Lancet Oncology, 10*(12), 1143–1144.

Baird, B. M., Lucas, R. E., & Donnellan, M. B. (2010). Life satisfaction across the lifespan: Findings from two nationally representative panel studies. *Social Indicators Research, 99*(2), 183–203. doi: 10.1007/s11205-010-9584-9

Baker, P. R., Francis, D. P., Hairi, N. N., Othman, S., & Choo, W. Y. (2016). Interventions for preventing abuse in the elderly. *Cochrane Database Systematic Reviews, 8*, Cd010321. doi: 10.1002/14651858.CD010321.pub2

Ball, F. C., & Miller, M. L. (2019). Life tables for the United States Social Security Area 1900-2100: Actuarial study No. 120. Retrieved 04/30/2019, from https://www.ssa.gov/oact/NOTES/as120/LifeTables_Tbl_7_2020.html

Ball, K., Berch, D. B., Helmers, K. F., Jobe, J. B., Leveck, M. D., Marsiske, M., ... Willis, S. L. (2002). Effects of cognitive training interventions with older adults: A randomized controlled trial. *Journal of the American Medical Association, 288*(18), 2271–2281.

Balsam, K. F., Rothblum, E. D., & Wickham, R. E. (2017). Longitudinal predictors of relationship dissolution among same-sex and heterosexual couples. *Couple and Family Psychology: Research and Practice, 6*(4), 247–257. doi: 10.1037/cfp0000091

Baltes, P. B. (1979). Life-span developmental psychology: Some converging observations on history and theory. In P. B. Baltes & J. O. G. Brim (Eds.), *Life-span development and behavior* (Vol. 2, pp. 255–279). New York: Academic Press.

Baltes, P. B., & Baltes, M. M. (1990). Psychological perspectives on successful aging: A model of selective optimization with compensation. In P. B. Baltes & M. M. Baltes (Eds.), *Successful aging: Perspectives from the behavioral sciences* (pp. 1–34). New York: Cambridge University Press.

Baltes, P. B., & Kliegl, R. (1992). Further testing of limits of cognitive plasticity: Negative age differences in a mnemonic skill are robust. *Developmental Psychology, 28*, 121–125.

Baltes, P. B., & Schaie, K. W. (1976). On the plasticity of intelligence in adulthood and old age: Where Horn and Donaldson fail. *American Psychologist, 31*, 720–725.

Baltes, P. B., & Smith, J. (2008). The fascination of wisdom: Its nature, ontogeny, and function. *Perspectives on Psychological Science, 3*, 56–64.

Baltes, P. B., Staudinger, U. M., Maercker, A., & Smith, J. (1995). People nominated as wise: A comparative study of wisdom-related knowledge. *Psychology and Aging, 10*, 155–166.

Bandura, A. (1977). Self-efficacy: Toward a unifying theory of behavioral change. *Psychological Review, 84*, 191–215.

Barber, S. J., Opitz, P. C., Martins, B., Sakaki, M., & Mather, M. (2016). Thinking about a limited future enhances the positivity of younger and older adults' recall: Support for socioemotional selectivity theory. *Memory and Cognition, 44*(6), 869–882. doi: 10.3758/s13421-016-0612-0

Barber, S. J., & Tan, S. C. (2018). Ageism affects the future time perspective of older adults. *GeroPsych: The Journal of Gerontopsychology and Geriatric Psychiatry, 31*(3), 115–126. doi: 10.1024/1662-9647/a000189

Barcelos, N., Shah, N., Cohen, K., Hogan, M. J., Mulkerrin, E., Arciero, P. J., ... Anderson-Hanley, C. (2015). Aerobic and cognitive exercise (ACE) pilot study for older adults: Executive function improves with cognitive challenge while exergaming. *Journal of the International Neuropsychological Society: JINS, 21*(10), 768–779. doi: 10.1017/s1355617715001083

Barelds, D. P. H., & Dijkstra, P. (2011). Positive illusions about a partner's personality and relationship quality. *Journal of Research in Personality, 45*(1), 37–43. doi: 10.1016/j.jrp.2010.11.009

Bartels, S. J., Moak, G. S., & Dums, A. R. (2002). Mental health services in nursing homes: Models of mental health services in nursing homes: A review of the literature. *Psychiatric Services, 53*, 1390–1396.

Basseches, M. (1984). *Dialectical thinking and adult development.* Norwood, NJ: Ablex.

Bauer, J. J. (2008). How the ego quiets as it grows: Ego development, growth stories, and eudaimonic personality development. In H. A. Wayment & J. J. Bauer (Eds.), *Transcending self-interest: Psychological explorations of the quiet ego* (pp. 199–210). Washington, DC: American Psychological Association.

Bavelier, D., Green, C. S., Pouget, A., & Schrater, P. (2012). Brain plasticity through the life span: Learning to learn and action video games. *Annual Review of Neuroscience, 35*, 391–416. doi: 10.1146/annurev-neuro-060909-152832

Bayl-Smith, P. H., & Griffin, B. (2014). Age discrimination in the workplace: Identifying as a late-career worker and its relationship with engagement and intended retirement age. *Journal of Applied Social Psychology, 44*(9), 588–599. doi: 10.1111/jasp.12251

Bayl-Smith, P. H., & Griffin, B. (2018). Maintenance of D-A fit through work adjustment behaviors: The moderating effect of work style fit. *Journal of Vocational Behavior, 106*, 209–219. doi: 10.1016/j.jvb.2018.02.006

Beach, S. R. H., Whitaker, D. J., Jones, D. J., & Tesser, A. (2001). When does performance feedback prompt complementarity in romantic relationships? *Personal Relationships*, 8(3), 231–248. doi: 10.1111/j.1475-6811.2001.tb00038.x

Becker, E. (1973). *The denial of death*. New York: Free Press.

Bedford, V. H., Volling, B. L., & Avioli, P. S. (2000). Positive consequences of sibling conflict in childhood and adulthood. *International Journal of Aging and Human Development*, 51, 53–69.

Beehr, T. A., Glazer, S., Nielson, N. L., & Farmer, S. J. (2000). Work and nonwork predictors of employees' retirement ages. *Journal of Vocational Behavior*, 57(2), 206–225.

Beghetto, R. A., & Kaufman, J. C. (2007). Toward a broader conception of creativity: A case for 'mini-c' creativity. *Psychology of Aesthetics, Creativity, and the Arts*, 1(2), 73–79. doi: 10.1037/1931-3896.1.2.73

Benichov, J., Cox, L. C., Tun, P. A., & Wingfield, A. (2012). Word recognition within a linguistic context: Effects of age, hearing acuity, verbal ability, and cognitive function. *Ear and Hearing*, 33(2), 250–256. doi: 10.1097/AUD.0b013e31822f680f

Benjamin, E. J., Muntner, P., Alonso, A., Bittencourt, M. S., Callaway, C. W., Carson, A. P., … Virani, S. S. (2019). Heart disease and stroke statistics-2019 update: A report from the American Heart Association. *Circulation*, 139(10), e56–e528. doi: 10.1161/cir.0000000000000659

Bennett, K. M. (2010). How to achieve resilience as an older widower: Turning points or gradual change? *Ageing & Society*, 30(3), 369–382. doi: 10.1017/S0144686X09990572

Benson, J. J., & Coleman, M. (2016). Older adult descriptions of living apart together. *Family Relations*, 65(3), 439–449. doi: 10.1111/fare.12203

Benson, L. A., McGinn, M. M., & Christensen, A. (2012). Common principles of couple therapy. *Behavior Therapy*, 43(1), 25–35. doi: 10.1016/j.beth.2010.12.009

Benson, N., Hulac, D. M., & Kranzler, J. H. (2010). Independent examination of the Wechsler Adult Intelligence Scale—Fourth Edition (WAIS-IV): What does the WAIS-IV measure? *Psychological Assessment*, 22(1), 121–130. doi: 10.1037/a0017767

Berg, J. M., Grant, A. M., & Johnson, V. (2010). When callings are calling: Crafting work and leisure in pursuit of unanswered occupational callings. *Organization Science*, 21(5), 973–994. doi: 10.1287/orsc.1090.0497

Berko, J., Ingram, D. D., Saha, S., & Parker, J. D. (2014). Deaths attributed to heat, cold, and other weather events in the United States, 2006–2010. *National Health Statistics Reports, No. 76*.

Berlingeri, M., Danelli, L., Bottini, G., Sberna, M., & Paulesu, E. (2013). Reassessing the HAROLD model: Is the hemispheric asymmetry reduction in older adults a special case of compensatory-related utilisation of neural circuits? *Experimental Brain Research*, 224(3), 393–410. doi: 10.1007/s00221-012-3319-x

Bersamin, M. M., Zamboanga, B. L., Schwartz, S. J., Donnellan, M. B., Hudson, M., Weisskirch, R. S., … Caraway, S. J. (2014). Risky business: Is there an association between casual sex and mental health among emerging adults? *Journal of Sex Research*, 51(1), 43–51. doi: 10.1080/00224499.2013.772088

Bhakuni, R., & Mutha, P. K. (2015). Learning of bimanual motor sequences in normal aging. *Frontiers in Aging Neuroscience*, 7, 76. doi: 10.3389/fnagi.2015.00076

Bhar, S. S., & Brown, G. K. (2012). Treatment of depression and suicide in older adults. *Cognitive and Behavioral Practice*, 19(1), 116–125. doi: 10.1016/j.cbpra.2010.12.005

Bhave, D. P., & Glomb, T. M. (2016). The role of occupational emotional labor requirements on the surface acting–job satisfaction relationship. *Journal of Management*, 42(3), 722–741. doi: 10.1177/0149206313498900

Bherer, L. (2015). Cognitive plasticity in older adults: Effects of cognitive training and physical exercise. *Annals of the New York Academy of Sciences*, 1337, 1–6. doi: 10.1111/nyas.12682

Bialystok, E. (2011). Reshaping the mind: The benefits of bilingualism. *Canadian Journal of Experimental Psychology/Revue canadienne de psychologie expérimentale*, 65(4), 229–235. doi: 10.1037/a0025406

Bialystok, E., Craik, F. I. M., Green, D. W., & Gollan, T. H. (2009). Bilingual minds. *Psychological Science in the Public Interest*, 10(3), 89–129. doi: 10.1177/1529100610387084

Bieman-Copland, S., & Ryan, E. B. (2001). Social perceptions of failures in memory monitoring. *Psychology and Aging*, 16(2), 357–361.

Birditt, K. S., Fingerman, K. L., Lefkowitz, E. S., & Dush, C. M. K. (2008). Parents perceived as peers: Filial maturity in adulthood. *Journal of Adult Development*, 15(1), 1–12. doi: 10.1007/s10804-007-9019-2

Birditt, K. S., Miller, L. M., Fingerman, K. L., & Lefkowitz, E. S. (2009a). Tensions in the parent and adult child relationship: Links to solidarity and ambivalence. *Psychology and Aging*, 24(2), 287–295. doi: 10.1037/a0015196

Birditt, K. S., Rott, L. M., & Fingerman, K. L. (2009b). "If you can't say anything nice don't say anything at all": Coping with interpersonal tensions in the parent-child relationship during adulthood. *Journal of Family Psychology*, 23(6), 769–778.

Birditt, K. S., Tighe, L. A., Fingerman, K. L., & Zarit, S. H. (2012). Intergenerational relationship quality across three generations. *The Journals of Gerontology: Series B: Psychological Sciences and Social Sciences*, 67B(5), 627–638. doi: 10.1093/geronb/gbs050

Bitzer, M., & Wiggins, J. (2016). Aging biology in the kidney. *Advances in Chronic Kidney Disease*, 23(1), 12–18. doi: 10.1053/j.ackd.2015.11.005 S1548-5595(15)00145-7 [pii]

Blagosklonny, M. V. (2013). Aging is not programmed: Genetic pseudo-program is a shadow of developmental growth. *Cell Cycle*, 12(24), 3736–3742. doi: 10.4161/cc.27188

Blanchflower, D. G., & Oswald, A. J. (2016). Antidepressants and age: A new form of evidence for U-shaped well-being through life. *Journal of Economic Behavior & Organization*, 127, 46–58. doi: 10.1016/j.jebo.2016.04.010

Blieszner, R. (2006). A lifetime of caring: Dimensions and dynamics in late-life close relationships. *Personal Relationships*, *13*(1), 1–18.

Boards of Trustees of the Federal Hospital Insurance and Federal Supplementary Medical Insurance Trust Funds. (2019). 2019 Annual Report of the Boards of Trustees of the Federal Hospital Insurance Trust Fund and the Federal Supplementary Medical Insurance Trust Fund. From https://www.cms.gov/Research-Statistics-Data-and-Systems/Statistics-Trends-and-Reports/ReportsTrustFunds/Downloads/TR2019.pdf

Böckerman, P., Johansson, E., & Saarni, S. (2012). Institutionalisation and subjective wellbeing for old-age individuals: Is life really miserable in care homes? *Ageing & Society*, *32*(7), 1176–1192. doi: 10.1017/s0144686x1100081x

Bodill, K., & Roberts, L. D. (2013). Implicit theories of intelligence and academic locus of control as predictors of studying behaviour. *Learning and Individual Differences*, *27*, 163–166. doi: https://doi.org/10.1016/j.lindif.2013.08.001

Bolzetta, F., Veronese, N., Stubbs, B., Noale, M., Vaona, A., Demurtas, J., … Solmi, M. (2019). The relationship between dietary Vitamin K and depressive symptoms in late adulthood: A cross-sectional analysis from a large cohort study. *Nutrients*, *11*(4), E787. doi: 10.3390/nu11040787

Bonnefond, A., Härmä, M., Hakola, T., Sallinen, M., Kandolin, I., & Virkkala, J. (2006). Interaction of age with shift-related sleep-wakefulness, sleepiness, performance, and social life. *Experimental Aging Research*, *32*(2), 185–208.

Boot, W. R., Kramer, A. F., Simons, D. J., Fabiani, M., & Gratton, G. (2008). The effects of video game playing on attention, memory, and executive control. *Acta Psychologica*, *129*(3), 387–398. doi: 10.1016/j.actpsy.2008.09.005

Bortz, W. (2010). Disuse and aging, 2009. *The Journals of Gerontology: Series A: Biological Sciences and Medical Sciences*, *65*(4), 382–385. doi: 10.1093/gerona/glp164

Bosch-Farré, C., Garre-Olmo, J., Bonmati-Tomas, A., Malagon-Aguilera, M. C., Gelabert-Vilella, S., Fuentes-Pumarola, C., & Juvinya-Canal, D. (2018). Prevalence and related factors of Active and Healthy Ageing in Europe according to two models: Results from the Survey of Health, Ageing and Retirement in Europe (SHARE). *PLoS ONE*, *13*(10), e0206353. doi: 10.1371/journal.pone.0206353

Botwinick, J. (1977). Intellectual abilities. In J. E. Birren & K. W. Schaie (Eds.), *Handbook of the psychology of aging* (pp. 580–605). New York: Van Nostrand Reinhold.

Boudreaux, M. J., South, S. C., & Oltmanns, T. F. (2019). Symptom-level analysis of DSM–IV/DSM–5 personality pathology in later life: Hierarchical structure and predictive validity across self- and informant ratings. *Journal of Abnormal Psychology*, *128*(5), 365–384. doi: 10.1037/abn0000444 10.1037/abn0000444.supp (Supplemental)

Boustani, M., Baker, M. S., Campbell, N., Munger, S., Hui, S. L., Castelluccio, P., … Callahan, C. (2010). Impact and recognition of cognitive impairment among hospitalized elders. *Journal of Hospital Medicine*, *5*(2), 69–75. doi: 10.1002/jhm.589

Bowers, B., Nolet, K., & Jacobson, N. (2016). Sustaining culture change: Experiences in the green house model. *Health Services Research*, *51*(Suppl 1), 398–417. doi: 10.1111/1475-6773.12428

Bowling, N. A., Eschleman, K. J., & Wang, Q. (2010). A meta-analytic examination of the relationship between job satisfaction and subjective well-being. *Journal of Occupational and Organizational Psychology*, *83*(4), 915–934. doi: 10.1348/096317909x478557

Boylan, S., Welch, A., Pikhart, H., Malyutina, S., Pajak, A., Kubinova, R., … Bobak, M. (2009). Dietary habits in three Central and Eastern European countries: The HAPIEE study. *BMC Public Health*, *9*(1), 439. doi: 1471-2458-9-439 [pii] 10.1186/1471-2458-9-439

Boyle, P. A., Yu, L., Leurgans, S. E., Wilson, R. S., Brookmeyer, R., Schneider, J. A., & Bennett, D. A. (2018). Attributable risk of Alzheimer's dementia attributed to age-related neuropathologies. *Annals of Neurology*. doi: 10.1002/ana.25380

Boyle, S. H., Jackson, W. G., & Suarez, E. C. (2007). Hostility, anger, and depression predict increases in C3 over a 10-year period. *Brain Behavior and Immunology*. doi: 10.1016/j.bbi.2007.01.008

Bradbury, K. E., Murphy, N., & Key, T. J. (2019). Diet and colorectal cancer in UK Biobank: A prospective study. *International Journal of Epidemiology*. doi: 10.1093/ije/dyz064

Brady, C. B., Pless Kaiser, A., Spiro, A., 3rd, Davison, E., King, D., & King, L. (2019). Late-onset stress symptomatology (LOSS) scale – short form: Development and validation. *Aging and Mental Health*, *23*(8), 952–960. doi: 10.1080/13607863.2018.1450831

Braitman, K. A., Kirley, B. B., Chaudhary, N. K., & Ferguson, S. A. (2006). Factors leading to older drivers' intersection crashes. From http://www.iihs.org/research/topics/pdf/older_drivers.pdf

Brenes, G. A., Kritchevsky, S. B., Mehta, K. M., Yaffe, K., Simonsick, E. M., Ayonayon, H. N., … Penninx, B. W. (2007). Scared to death: Results from the health, aging, and body composition study. *American Journal of Geriatric Psychiatry*, *15*(3), 262–265.

Bresee, C., Dubina, E. D., Khan, A. A., Sevilla, C., Grant, D., Eilber, K. S., & Anger, J. T. (2014). Prevalence and correlates of urinary incontinence among older community-dwelling women. *Female Pelvic Medicine and Reconstructive Surgery*, *20*(6), 328–333. doi: 10.1097/spv.0000000000000093

Breslin, C. W., & Safer, M. A. (2013). Aging and long-term memory for emotionally valenced events. *Psychology and Aging*, *28*(2), 346–351. doi: 10.1037/a0029554

Brill, F. (1967). *Matisse*. London: Paul Hamlyn.

Brim, O. G., Jr. (1976). Theories of the male mid-life crisis. *The Counseling Psychologist*, *6*, 2–9.

Briody, E. K., & Briller, S. H. (2017). Pursuing a desired future: Continuity and change in a long-term-care community. *Journal of Applied Gerontology*, *36*(10), 1197–1227. doi: 10.1177/0733464815608496

Briscoe, J. P., Hall, D. T., & Frautschy DeMuth, R. L. (2006). Protean and boundaryless careers: An empirical exploration. *Journal of Vocational Behavior, 69*(1), 30–47.

Bronfenbrenner, U. (1994). Ecological models of human development. In T. Husen & T. N. Postlethwaite (Eds.), *International encyclopedia of education* (2nd ed., Vol. 3, pp. 1643–1647). Oxford: Pergamon Press and Elsevier Science.

Bronfenbrenner, U., & Ceci, S. J. (1994). Nature-nurture reconceptualized in developmental perspective: A bioecological model. *Psychological Review, 101*, 568–586.

Brookmeyer, R., Abdalla, N., Kawas, C. H., & Corrada, M. M. (2018). Forecasting the prevalence of preclinical and clinical Alzheimer's disease in the United States. *Alzheimer's & Dementia, 14*(2), 121–129. doi: 10.1016/j.jalz.2017.10.009

Brown, S. L., Bulanda, J. R., & Lee, G. R. (2012). Transitions into and out of cohabitation in later life. *Journal of Marriage and the Family, 74*(4), 774–793.

Bruckenthal, P., Marino, M. A., & Snelling, L. (2016). Complementary and integrative therapies for persistent pain management in older adults: A review. *Journal of Gerontological Nursing, 42*(12), 40–48. doi: 10.3928/00989134-20161110-08

Bugg, J. M., DeLosh, E. L., & Clegg, B. A. (2006). Physical activity moderates time-of-day differences in older adults' working memory performance. *Experimental Aging Research, 32*(4), 431–446. doi: R15X03172KNU7782 [pii] 10.1080/03610730600875833

Buitenweg, J. I. V., van de Ven, R. M., Prinssen, S., Murre, J. M. J., & Ridderinkhof, K. R. (2017). Cognitive flexibility training: A large-scale multimodal adaptive active-control intervention study in healthy older adults. *Frontiers in Human Neuroscience, 11*, 529. doi: 10.3389/fnhum.2017.00529

Bureau of Labor Statistics. (2015). Educational attainment, employment, and unemployment among African Americans. *News Releases*. From https://www.bls.gov/opub/ted/2015/educational-attainment-employment-and-unemployment-among-african-americans.htm

Bureau of Labor Statistics. (2018). Women in the labor force: A databook. From https://www.bls.gov/opub/reports/womens-databook/2018/home.htm

Bureau of Labor Statistics. (2019a). Economic news release. From https://www.bls.gov/news.release/wkyeng.t04.htm

Bureau of Labor Statistics. (2019b). Employment situation. *News Releases*. From https://www.bls.gov/news.release/empsit.toc.htm

Bureau of Labor Statistics. (2019c). Employment situation of veterans. *News Release*. From http://www.bls.gov/news.release/pdf/vet.pdf

Bureau of Labor Statistics. (2019d). Labor force participation rate for workers age 75 and older projected to be over 10 percent by 2026. *News Releases*. From https://www.bls.gov/opub/ted/2019/labor-force-participation-rate-for-workers-age-75-and-older-projected-to-be-over-10-percent-by-2026.htm

Bureau of Labor Statistics. (2019e). Labor force statistics from the Current Population Survey. From https://www.bls.gov/cps/cpsaat03.htm

Bureau of Labor Statistics. (2019f). Unemployment rates and earnings by educational attainment. From https://www.bls.gov/emp/chart-unemployment-earnings-education.htm

Burn, K., & Szoeke, C. (2015). Grandparenting predicts late-life cognition: Results from the Women's Healthy Ageing Project. *Maturitas, 81*(2), 317–322. doi: 10.1016/j.maturitas.2015.03.013

Burnes, D., Henderson, C. R., Jr., Sheppard, C., Zhao, R., Pillemer, K., & Lachs, M. S. (2017). Prevalence of financial fraud and scams among older adults in the United States: A systematic review and meta-analysis. *American Journal of Public Health, 107*(8), e13–e21. doi: 10.2105/ajph.2017.303821

Burnes, D., Pillemer, K., Caccamise, P. L., Mason, A., Henderson, C. R., Jr., Berman, J., … Lachs, M. S. (2015). Prevalence of and risk factors for elder abuse and neglect in the community: A population-based study. *Journal of the American Geriatrics Society, 63*(9), 1906–1912. doi: 10.1111/jgs.13601

Burton, C. L., Strauss, E., Hultsch, D. F., & Hunter, M. A. (2006). Cognitive functioning and everyday problem solving in older adults. *Clinical Neuropsychology, 20*(3), 432–452. doi: 10.1080/13854040590967063

Burton, C. L., Strauss, E., Hultsch, D. F., & Hunter, M. A. (2009). The relationship between everyday problem solving and inconsistency in reaction time in older adults. *Neuropsychology and Developmental Cognition B: Aging Neuropsychology and Cognition, 16*(5), 607–632. doi: 914159307 [pii] 10.1080/13825580903167283

Burzynska, A. Z., Nagel, I. E., Preuschhof, C., Gluth, S., Bäckman, L., Li, S. C., … Heekeren, H. R. (2012). Cortical thickness is linked to executive functioning in adulthood and aging. *Human Brain Mapping, 33*(7), 1607–1620. doi: 10.1002/hbm.21311

Butler, K. M., & Zacks, R. T. (2006). Age deficits in the control of prepotent responses: Evidence for an inhibitory decline. *Psychology and Aging, 21*(3), 638–643. doi: 2006-11398-019 [pii] 10.1037/0882-7974.21.3.638

Byberg, L., Melhus, H. K., Gedeborg, R., Sundstrom, J., Ahlbom, A., Zethelius, B., … Michaelsson, K. (2009). Total mortality after changes in leisure time physical activity in 50 year old men: 35 year follow-up of population based cohort. *British Medical Journal, 338*(7700).

Byrne, C. M., Solomon, M. J., Young, J. M., Rex, J., & Merlino, C. L. (2007). Biofeedback for fecal incontinence: Short-term outcomes of 513 consecutive patients and predictors of successful treatment. *Diseases of the Colon and Rectum, 50*(4), 417–427. doi: 10.1007/s10350-006-0846-1

Cabello, M., Miret, M., Ayuso-Mateos, J. L., Caballero, F. F., Chatterji, S., Tobiasz-Adamczyk, B., … Borges, G. (2019). Cross-national prevalence and factors associated with suicide ideation and attempts in older and young-and-middle age people. *Aging and Mental Health*, 1–10. doi: 10.1080/13607863.2019.1603284

Cabeza, R., Albert, M., Belleville, S., Craik, F. I. M., Duarte, A., Grady, C. L., … Rajah, M. N. (2018). Maintenance, reserve and compensation: The cognitive neuroscience of healthy ageing. *Nature Reviews Neuroscience, 19*(11), 701–710. doi: 10.1038/s41583-018-0068-2

Cahana-Amitay, D., Spiro, A., 3rd, Cohen, J. A., Oveis, A. C., Ojo, E. A., Sayers, J. T., … Albert, M. L. (2015). Effects of metabolic syndrome on language functions in aging. *Journal of the International Neuropsychological Society, 21*(2), 116–125. doi: 10.1017/s1355617715000028

Calle, E. E., Rodriguez, C., Walker-Thurmond, K., & Thun, M. J. (2003). Overweight, obesity, and mortality from cancer in a prospectively studied cohort of U.S. adults. *New England Journal of Medicine, 348*(17), 1625–1638. doi: 10.1056/NEJMoa021423 348/17/1625 [pii]

Campbell, A., Grace, F., Ritchie, L., Beaumont, A., & Sculthorpe, N. (2019). Long-term aerobic exercise improves vascular function into old age: A systematic review, meta-analysis and meta regression of observational and interventional studies. *Frontiers in Physiology, 10*, 31. doi: 10.3389/fphys.2019.00031

Campos, M. W., Serebrisky, D., & Castaldelli-Maia, J. M. (2016). Smoking and cognition. *Current Drug Abuse Reviews, 9*(2), 76–79. doi: 10.2174/1874473709666160803101633

Canuto, A., Weber, K., Baertschi, M., Andreas, S., Volkert, J., Dehoust, M. C., … Harter, M. (2018). Anxiety disorders in old age: Psychiatric comorbidities, quality of life, and prevalence according to age, gender, and country. *American Journal of Geriatric Psychiatry, 26*(2), 174–185. doi: 10.1016/j.jagp.2017.08.015

Cao, J. J., Wronski, T. J., Iwaniec, U., Phleger, L., Kurimoto, P., Boudignon, B., & Halloran, B. P. (2005). Aging increases stromal/osteoblastic cell-induced osteoclastogenesis and alters the osteoclast precursor pool in the mouse. *Journal of Bone and Mineral Research, 20*(9), 1659–1668.

Carlson, D. S., Thompson, M. J., Crawford, W. S., & Kacmar, K. M. (2019). Spillover and crossover of work resources: A test of the positive flow of resources through work–family enrichment. *Journal of Organizational Behavior.* doi: 10.1002/job.2363

Carr, E., Hagger-Johnson, G., Head, J., Shelton, N., Stafford, M., Stansfeld, S., & Zaninotto, P. (2016). Working conditions as predictors of retirement intentions and exit from paid employment: A 10-year follow-up of the English Longitudinal Study of Ageing. *European Journal of Ageing, 13*(1), 39–48. doi: 10.1007/s10433-015-0357-9

Carroll, C. C., Dickinson, J. M., Haus, J. M., Lee, G. A., Hollon, C. J., Aagaard, P., … Trappe, T. A. (2008). Influence of aging on the in vivo properties of human patellar tendon. *Journal of Applied Physiology, 105*(6), 1907–1915. doi: 10.1152/japplphysiol.00059.2008

Carroll, J. B. (1993). *Human cognitive abilities: A survey of factor-analytic studies.* New York: Cambridge University Press.

Caruso, C., Candore, G., Colonna Romano, G., Lio, D., Bonafe, M., Valensin, S., & Franceschi, C. (2000). HLA, aging, and longevity: A critical reappraisal. *Human Immunology, 61*(9), 942–949.

Casares, D. R., & White, C. C. (2018). The phenomenological experience of parents who live with a boomerang child. *American Journal of Family Therapy.* doi: 10.1080/01926187.2018.1495133

Castellano, C. A., Hudon, C., Croteau, E., Fortier, M., St-Pierre, V., Vandenberghe, C., … Cunnane, S. C. (2019). Links between metabolic and structural changes in the brain of cognitively normal older adults: A 4-year longitudinal follow-up. *Frontiers in Aging Neuroscience, 11*, 15. doi: 10.3389/fnagi.2019.00015

Castro-Costa, E., Diniz, B. S., Firmo, J. O. A., Peixoto, S. V., de Loyola Filho, A. I., Lima-Costa, M. F., & Blay, S. L. (2019). Diabetes, depressive symptoms, and mortality risk in old age: The role of inflammation. *Depression and Anxiety.* doi: 10.1002/da.22908

Cattell, R. B. (1963). Theory of fluid and crystallized intelligence: A critical experiment. *Journal of Educational Psychology, 54*, 1–22.

Cattell, R. B. (1971). *Abilities: Their structure, growth, and action.* Boston, MA: Houghton Mifflin.

Cavan, R. S., Burgess, E. W., Havighurst, R. J., & Goldhamer, H. (1949). *Personal adjustment in old age.* Chicago, IL: Science Research Associates.

Centers for Disease Control and Prevention. (2012). *Principles of epidemiology in public health practice. An introduction to applied epidemiology and biostatistics* (3rd ed.). From https://www.cdc.gov/csels/dsepd/ss1978/lesson3/section3.html

Centers for Disease Control and Prevention. (2017). National Diabetes Statistics Report, 2017. Retrieved 5/23/2019, from http://www.cdc.gov/nchs/data/nhhcs/2007hospicecaresurvey.pdf

Centers for Disease Control and Prevention. (2019a). Current cigarette smoking among adults in the United States. From https://www.cdc.gov/tobacco/data_statistics/fact_sheets/adult_data/cig_smoking/index.htm#anchor_1549902047693

Centers for Disease Control and Prevention. (2019b). Home and recreational safety. From https://www.cdc.gov/homeandrecreationalsafety/falls/adultfalls.html

Centers for Disease Control and Prevention. (2019c). Marriage and divorce. From https://www.cdc.gov/nchs/fastats/marriage-divorce.htm

Centers for Disease Control and Prevention. (2019d). Quick-Stats: Death rates attributed to excessive cold or hypothermia among persons aged ≥15 years, by urbanization level and age group—National Vital Statistics System, 2015–2017. *MMWR Morbidity and Mortality Weekly Report, 68*, 187. doi: http://dx.doi.org/10.15585/mmwr.mm6807a8External

Centers for Disease Control and Prevention National Center for Injury Prevention and Control. (2017). Healthy weight. From https://www.cdc.gov/healthyweight/assessing/bmi/adult_bmi/index.html#InterpretedAdults

Centers for Medicare & Medicaid Services. (2015). Nursing home data compendium 2015 edition. From https://www.cms.gov/Medicare/Provider-Enrollment-and-Certification/Certificationand Complianc/downloads/nursinghomedatacompendium_508-2015.pdf

Centers for Medicare & Medicaid Services. (2019a). CMS drug spending. From https://www.cms.gov/Research-Statistics-Data-and-Systems/Statistics-Trends-and-Reports/Information-on-Prescription-Drugs/index.html

Centers for Medicare & Medicaid Services. (2019b). Design for nursing home compare Five-Star Quality Rating System.

From https://www.cms.gov/Medicare/Provider-Enrollment-and-Certification/CertificationandComplianc/Downloads/usersguide.pdf

Centers for Medicare & Medicaid Services. (2019c). Design for nursing home compare Five-Star Quality Rating System: Technical users guide April 2019. From https://www.cms.gov/Medicare/Provider-Enrollment-and-Certification/CertificationandComplianc/downloads/usersguide.pdf

Centers for Medicare & Medicaid Services. (2019d). National health expenditures 2017 highlights. From http://www.cms.hhs.gov/NationalHealthExpendData/downloads/highlights.pdf

Cerasoli, C. P., Nicklin, J. M., & Ford, M. T. (2014). Intrinsic motivation and extrinsic incentives jointly predict performance: A 40-year meta-analysis. *Psychological Bulletin, 140*(4), 980–1008. doi: 10.1037/a0035661

Cerella, J., Poon, L. W., & Williams, D. M. (1980). Age and the complexity hypothesis. In L. W. Poon (Ed.), *Aging in the 1980s* (pp. 332–340). Washington, DC: American Psychological Association.

Chaabna, K., Cheema, S., Abraham, A., Alrouh, H., & Mamtani, R. (2018). Adult mortality trends in Qatar, 1989-2015: National population versus migrants. *PLoS ONE, 13*(9), e0203996. doi: 10.1371/journal.pone.0203996

Chandola, T., Rouxel, P., Marmot, M. G., & Kumari, M. (2018). Retirement and socioeconomic differences in diurnal cortisol: Longitudinal evidence from a cohort of British Civil Servants. *Journal of Gerontology Series B: Psychological Science and Social Science, 73*(3), 447–456. doi: 10.1093/geronb/gbx058

Chang, Y. K., & Etnier, J. L. (2009). Exploring the dose-response relationship between resistance exercise intensity and cognitive function. *Journal of Sports Exercise Psychology, 31*(5), 640–656.

Charlson, F. J., Ferrari, A. J., Santomauro, D. F., Diminic, S., Stockings, E., Scott, J. G., ... Whiteford, H. A. (2018). Global epidemiology and burden of schizophrenia: Findings from the Global Burden of Disease Study 2016. *Schizophrenia Bulletin, 44*(6), 1195–1203. doi: 10.1093/schbul/sby058

Chau, R., Kissane, D. W., & Davison, T. E. (2019). Risk factors for depression in long-term care: A prospective observational cohort study. *Clinical Gerontology*, 1–14. doi: 10.1080/07317115.2019.1635548

Chedraui, P., Perez-Lopez, F. R., Mendoza, M., Leimberg, M. L., Martinez, M. A., Vallarino, V., & Hidalgo, L. (2010). Factors related to increased daytime sleepiness during the menopausal transition as evaluated by the Epworth sleepiness scale. *Maturitas, 65*(1), 75–80. doi: S0378-5122(09)00402-2 [pii] 10.1016/j.maturitas.2009.11.003

Chen, L., Selvendra, A., Stewart, A., & Castle, D. (2018). Risk factors in early and late onset schizophrenia. *Comprehensive Psychiatry, 80*, 155–162. doi: 10.1016/j.comppsych.2017.09.009

Cherkas, L. F., Aviv, A., Valdes, A. M., Hunkin, J. L., Gardner, J. P., Surdulescu, G. L., ... Spector, T. D. (2006). The effects of social status on biological aging as measured by white-blood-cell telomere length. *Aging Cell, 5*(5), 361–365.

Cherkas, L. F., Hunkin, J. L., Kato, B. S., Richards, J. B., Gardner, J. P., Surdulescu, G. L., ... Aviv, A. (2008). The association between physical activity in leisure time and leukocyte telomere length. *Archives of Internal Medicine, 168*(2), 154–158. doi: 168/2/154 [pii] 10.1001/archinternmed.2007.39

Cherry, K. E., Lyon, B. A., Boudreaux, E. O., Blanchard, A. B., Hicks, J. L., Elliott, E. M., ... Jazwinski, S. M. (2019). Memory self-efficacy and beliefs about memory and aging in oldest-old adults in the Louisiana Healthy Aging Study (LHAS). *Experimental Aging Research, 45*(1), 28–40. doi: 10.1080/0361073x.2018.1560107

Cherry, K. E., Silva, J. L., & Galea, S. (2009). Natural disasters and the oldest-old: A psychological perspective on coping and health in late life. In K. E. Cherry (Ed.), *Lifespan perspectives on natural disasters: Coping with Katrina, Rita, and other storms* (pp. 171–193). New York: Springer Science + Business Media.

Cheshire, J. (2012). Lives on the line: Mapping life expectancy along the London Tube Network. *Environment and Planning A, 44*(7). doi: 10.1068/a45341

Chetan, P., Tandon, P., Singh, G. K., Nagar, A., Prasad, V., & Chugh, V. K. (2013). Dynamics of a smile in different age groups. *Angle Orthodontics, 83*(1), 90–96. doi: 10.2319/040112-268.1

Cheung, E. N. M., Benjamin, S., Heckman, G., Ho, J. M., Lee, L., Sinha, S. K., & Costa, A. P. (2018). Clinical characteristics associated with the onset of delirium among long-term nursing home residents. *BMC Geriatrics, 18*(1), 39. doi: 10.1186/s12877-018-0733-3

Chinoy, E. D., Duffy, J. F., & Czeisler, C. A. (2018). Unrestricted evening use of light-emitting tablet computers delays self-selected bedtime and disrupts circadian timing and alertness. *Physiological Reports, 6*(10), e13692. doi: 10.14814/phy2.13692

Chiriaco, G., Cauci, S., Mazzon, G., & Trombetta, C. (2016). An observational retrospective evaluation of 79 young men with long-term adverse effects after use of finasteride against androgenetic alopecia. *Andrology, 4*(2), 245–250. doi: 10.1111/andr.12147

Chitaley, K., Kupelian, V., Subak, L., & Wessells, H. (2009). Diabetes, obesity and erectile dysfunction: Field overview and research priorities. *Journal of Urology, 182* (Suppl 6), S45–S50. doi: S0022-5347(09)01946-6 [pii] 10.1016/j.juro.2009.07.089

Choi, J., Tantisira, K. G., & Duan, Q. L. (2018). Whole genome sequencing identifies high-impact variants in well-known pharmacogenomic genes. *Pharmacogenomics Journal*. doi: 10.1038/s41397-018-0048-y

Choi, J. W., Kim, T. H., Shin, J., & Han, E. (2019). Poverty and suicide risk in older adults: A retrospective longitudinal cohort study. *International Journal of Geriatric Psychiatry*. doi: 10.1002/gps.5166

Christensen, D. S., Flensborg-Madsen, T., Garde, E., Hansen, A. M., & Mortensen, E. L. (2019). Big Five personality traits and allostatic load in midlife. *Psychological Health, 34*(8), 1011–1028. doi: 10.1080/08870446.2019.1585851

Christiansen, S. L., & Palkovitz, R. (2001). Why the 'good provider' role still matters: Providing as a form of paternal involvement. *Journal of Family Issues, 22*(1), 84–106.

Christoffersen, M., & Tybjaerg-Hansen, A. (2016). Visible aging signs as risk markers for ischemic heart disease: Epidemiology, pathogenesis and clinical implications. *Ageing Research Review, 25,* 24–41. doi: 10.1016/j.arr.2015.11.002

Chu, K. H., Baker, M. A., & Murrmann, S. K. (2012). When we are onstage, we smile: The effects of emotional labor on employee work outcomes. *International Journal of Hospitality Management, 31*(3), 906–915. doi: 10.1016/j.ijhm.2011.10.009

Chua, C. H. M., Jiang, Y., Lim, S., Wu, V. X., & Wang, W. (2019). Effectiveness of cognitive behavior therapy-based multicomponent interventions on fear of falling among community-dwelling older adults: A systematic review and meta-analysis. *Journal of Advanced Nursing.* doi: 10.1111/jan.14150

Chung, C. S., Lee, Y. C., & Wu, M. S. (2015). Prevention strategies for esophageal cancer: Perspectives of the East vs. West. *Best Practice and Research. Clinical Gastroenterology, 29*(6), 869–883. doi: 10.1016/j.bpg.2015.09.010

Cicirelli, V. G. (1988). A measure of filial anxiety regarding anticipated care of elderly parents. *Gerontologist, 28,* 478–482.

Cicirelli, V. G. (2010). Attachment relationships in old age. *Journal of Social and Personal Relationships, 27*(2), 191–199. doi: 10.1177/0265407509360984

Clark, K. (2006). The artist grows old. *Daedalus, 135*(1), 77–90.

Clark, D. J., & Fielding, R. A. (2012). Neuromuscular contributions to age-related weakness. *Journal of Gerontology Series A: Biological Sciences and Medical Sciences, 67*(1), 41–47. doi: 10.1093/gerona/glr041

Clark, M. A., Robertson, M. M., & Carter, N. T. (2018). You spin me right round: A within-person examination of affect spin and voluntary work behavior. *Journal of Management, 44*(8), 3176–3199. doi: 10.1177/0149206316662315

Clarke, P., Marshall, V. W., & Weir, D. (2012). Unexpected retirement from full time work after age 62: Consequences for life satisfaction in older Americans. *European Journal of Ageing, 9*(3), 207–219. doi: 10.1007/s10433-012-0229-5

Clouston, S. A. P., Deri, Y., Diminich, E., Kew, R., Kotov, R., Stewart, C., … Luft, B. J. (2019). Posttraumatic stress disorder and total amyloid burden and amyloid-beta 42/40 ratios in plasma: Results from a pilot study of World Trade Center responders. *Alzheimer's & Dementia, 11,* 216–220. doi: 10.1016/j.dadm.2019.01.003

Cobaugh, D. J., Miller, M. J., Pham, T. T., & Krenzelok, E. P. (2015). Risk of major morbidity and death in older adults with suicidal intent: A cross-sectional analysis from the National Poison Data System, 2000-2009. *Journal of the American Geriatrics Society, 63*(3), 501–507. doi: 10.1111/jgs.13323

Cock, C., & Omari, T. (2018). Systematic review of pharyngeal and esophageal manometry in healthy or dysphagic older persons (>60 years). *Geriatrics, 3*(4). doi: 10.3390/geriatrics3040067

Cohan, C. L., & Kleinbaum, S. (2002). Toward a greater understanding of the cohabitation effect: Premarital cohabitation and marital communication. *Journal of Marriage and the Family, 64*(1), 180–192.

Cohen-Mansfield, J., Shmotkin, D., Malkinson, R., Bartur, L., & Hazan, H. (2013). Parental bereavement increases mortality in older persons. *Psychological Trauma: Theory, Research, Practice, and Policy, 5*(1), 84–92. doi: 10.1037/a0029011

Cohen-Mansfield, J., Thein, K., & Marx, M. S. (2014). Predictors of the impact of nonpharmacologic interventions for agitation in nursing home residents with advanced dementia. *The Journal of Clinical Psychiatry, 75*(7), e666–671. doi: 10.4088/JCP.13m08649

Cohen, C. I. (2018). Very late-onset schizophrenia-like psychosis: Positive findings but questions remain unanswered. *Lancet Psychiatry, 5*(7), 528–529. doi: 10.1016/s2215-0366(18)30174-3

Cohen, P. (2018). The coming divorce decline. *SocArXiv.* doi: 10.1177/2378023119873497

Coles, R. L. (2015). Single-father families: A review of the literature. *Journal of Family Theory & Review, 7*(2), 144–166. doi: 10.1111/jftr.12069

Collet, J., de Vugt, M. E., Verhey, F. R., & Schols, J. M. (2010). Efficacy of integrated interventions combining psychiatric care and nursing home care for nursing home residents: A review of the literature. *International Journal of Geriatric Psychiatry, 25*(1), 3–13. doi: 10.1002/gps.2307

Colman, R. J., Beasley, T. M., Kemnitz, J. W., Johnson, S. C., Weindruch, R., & Anderson, R. M. (2014). Caloric restriction reduces age-related and all-cause mortality in rhesus monkeys. *Nature Communication, 5,* 3557. doi: 10.1038/ncomms4557

Colpo, G. D., Leffa, D. D., Köhler, C. A., Kapczinski, F., Quevedo, J., & Carvalho, A. F. (2015). Is bipolar disorder associated with accelerating aging? A meta-analysis of telomere length studies. *Journal of Affective Disorders, 186,* 241–248. doi: 10.1016/j.jad.2015.06.034

Coltrane, S. (2000). Research on household labor: Modeling and measuring the social embeddedness of routine family work. *Journal of Marriage and the Family, 62*(4), 1208–1233.

Comijs, H. C., Gerritsen, L., Penninx, B. W., Bremmer, M. A., Deeg, D. J., & Geerlings, M. I. (2010). The association between serum cortisol and cognitive decline in older persons. *American Journal of Geriatric Psychiatry, 18*(1), 42–50. doi: 10.1097/JGP.0b013e3181b970ae

Commons, M., Richards, F., & Armon, C. (Eds.). (1984). *Beyond formal operations: Late adolescent and adult cognitive development.* New York: Praeger.

Congdon, N., Vingerling, J. R., Klein, B. E., West, S., Friedman, D. S., Kempen, J., … Taylor, H. R. (2004). Prevalence of cataract and pseudophakia/aphakia among adults in the United States. *Archives of Ophthalmology, 122*(4), 487–494. doi: 10.1001/archopht.122.4.487 122/4/487 [pii]

Connidis, I. A., & McMullin, J. A. (2002). Sociological ambivalence and family ties: A critical perspective. *Journal of Marriage and the Family, 64*(3), 558–567. doi: 10.1111/j.1741-3737.2002.00558.x

Connors, M. H., Quinto, L., & Brodaty, H. (2018). Longitudinal outcomes of patients with pseudodementia: A systematic review. *Psychological Medicine,* 1–11. doi: 10.1017/s0033291718002829

Conradie, M., Conradie, M. M., Scher, A. T., Kidd, M., & Hough, S. (2015). Vertebral fracture prevalence in black and white South African women. *Archives of Osteoporosis, 10*, 203. doi: 10.1007/s11657-015-0203-x

Consedine, N. S., & Magai, C. (2003). Attachment and emotion experience in later life: The view from emotions theory. *Attachment in Human Development, 5*(2), 165–187. doi: 10.1080/1461673031000108496 98U1YMG3H66RMMCY [pii]

Constantinople, A. (1969). An Eriksonian measure of personality development in college students. *Developmental Psychology, 1*(4), 357–372.

Conti, E. C., Kraus-Schuman, C., & Stanley, M. A. (2017). Cognitive-behavioral therapy in older adults. In S. G. Hofmann & G. J. G. Asmundson (Eds.), *The science of cognitive behavioral therapy* (pp. 223–255). San Diego, CA: Elsevier Academic Press.

Cook Maher, A., Kielb, S., Loyer, E., Connelley, M., Rademaker, A., Mesulam, M. M., ... Rogalski, E. (2017). Psychological well-being in elderly adults with extraordinary episodic memory. *PLoS ONE, 12*(10), e0186413. doi: 10.1371/journal.pone.0186413

Cooper, L. D., Balsis, S., & Oltmanns, T. F. (2014). Aging: Empirical contribution: A longitudinal analysis of personality disorder dimensions and personality traits in a community sample of older adults: Perspectives from selves and informants. *Journal of Personality Disorders, 28*(1), 151–165. doi: 10.1521/pedi.2014.28.1.151

Copen, C. E., Daniels, K., Vespa, J., & Mosher, W. D. (2012). First marriages in the United States: Data from the 2006–2010 National Survey of Family Growth. *National Health Statistics Reports*, Number 49 (March 22, 2012). From http://www.cdc.gov/nchs/data/nhsr/nhsr049.pdf

Cornelius, S., Gordon, C., & Ackland, A. (2011). Towards flexible learning for adult learners in professional contexts: An activity-focused course design. *Interactive Learning Environments, 19*(4), 381–393. doi: 10.1080/10494820903298258

Cornwell, B. (2012). Spousal network overlap as a basis for spousal support. *Journal of Marriage and the Family, 74*(2), 229–238. doi: 10.1111/j.1741-3737.2012.00959.x

Corona, G., & Maggi, M. (2010). The role of testosterone in erectile dysfunction. *Nature Review Urology, 7*(1), 46–56. doi: nrurol.2009.235 [pii] 10.1038/nrurol.2009.235

Costa, P. T., Jr., & McCrae, R. R. (1992). *NEO-PI-R manual.* Odessa, FL: Psychological Assessment Resources.

Costa, P. T. J., & McCrae, R. R. (1978). Objective personality assessment. In M. Storandt, I. C. Siegler & M. F. Elias (Eds.), *The clinical psychology of aging* (pp. 119–143). New York: Plenum.

Côté, J. E. (2014). The dangerous myth of emerging adulthood: An evidence-based critique of a flawed developmental theory. *Applied Developmental Science, 18*(4), 177–188. doi: 10.1080/10888691.2014.954451

Coutanche, M. N., & Paulus, J. P. (2018). An empirical analysis of popular press claims regarding Linguistic change in President Donald J. Trump. *Frontiers in Psychology, 9*, 2311. doi: 10.3389/fpsyg.2018.02311

Cowgill, D. O., & Holmes, L. D. (1972). *Aging and modernization.* New York: Appleton-Century-Crofts.

Coyne, K. S., Sexton, C. C., Vats, V., Thompson, C., Kopp, Z. S., & Milsom, I. (2011). National community prevalence of overactive bladder in the United States stratified by sex and age. *Urology, 77*(5), 1081–1087. doi: 10.1016/j.urology.2010.08.039

Craik, F. I. M., & Rose, N. S. (2012). Memory encoding and aging: A neurocognitive perspective. *Neuroscience and Biobehavioral Reviews, 36*(7), 1729–1739. doi: 10.1016/j.neubiorev.2011.11.007

Cramer, P. (2003). Personality change in later adulthood is predicted by defense mechanism use in early adulthood. *Journal of Research in Personality, 37*, 76–104.

Cramer, P., & Jones, C. J. (2007). Defense mechanisms predict differential lifespan change in self-control and self-acceptance. *Journal of Research in Personality, 41*(4), 841–855.

Cramer, P., & Jones, C. J. (2008). Narcissism, identification, and longitudinal change in psychological health: Dynamic predictions. *Journal of Research in Personality, 42*(5), 1148–1159.

Crawford, S., & Channon, S. (2002). Dissociation between performance on abstract tests of executive function and problem solving in real-life-type situations in normal aging. *Aging and Mental Health, 6*(1), 12–21.

Crosnoe, R., & Elder, G. H., Jr. (2002). Life course transitions, the generational stake, and grandparent-grandchild relationships. *Journal of Marriage and the Family, 64*, 1089–1096.

Cross, N. E., Carrier, J., Postuma, R. B., Gosselin, N., Kakinami, L., Thompson, C., ... Dang-Vu, T. T. (2019). Association between insomnia disorder and cognitive function in middle-aged and older adults: A cross-sectional analysis of the Canadian Longitudinal Study on Aging. *Sleep.* doi: 10.1093/sleep/zsz114

Crowe, F., Roddam, A., Key, T., Appleby, P., Overvad, K., Jakobsen, M., ... Riboli, E. (2011). Fruit and vegetable intake and mortality from ischaemic heart disease: Results from the European Prospective Investigation into Cancer and Nutrition (EPIC)-Heart study. *European Heart Journal, 32*(10), 1235–1243.

Cruitt, P. J., & Oltmanns, T. F. (2018). Age-related outcomes associated with personality pathology in later life. *Current Opinion in Psychology, 21*, 89–93. doi: https://doi.org/10.1016/j.copsyc.2017.09.013

Cruz-Jimenez, M. (2017). Normal changes in gait and mobility problems in the elderly. *Physical Medicine Rehabilitation Clinics of North America, 28*(4), 713–725. doi: 10.1016/j.pmr.2017.06.005

Cumming, E., & Henry, W. E. (1961). *Growing old: The process of disengagement.* New York: Basic Books.

Cushman, M., Cantrell, R. A., McClure, L. A., Howard, G., Prineas, R. J., Moy, C. S., ... Howard, V. J. (2008). Estimated 10-year stroke risk by region and race in the United States: Geographic and racial differences in stroke risk. *Annals of Neurology, 64*(5), 507–513. doi: 10.1002/ana.21493

Deary, I. J. (2012). Intelligence. *Annual Review of Psychology, 63*, 453–482. doi: 10.1146/annurev-psych-120710-100353 da Silva Lara, L. A., Useche, B., Rosa, E. S. J. C., Ferriani, R. A., Reis, R. M., de Sa, M. F., … de Sa Rosa, E. S. A. C. (2009). Sexuality during the climacteric period. *Maturitas*, 62(2), 127–133. doi: S0378-5122(08)00399-X [pii] 10.1016/j.maturitas.2008.12.014

Dangour, A. D., Allen, E., Elbourne, D., Fletcher, A., Richards, M., & Uauy, R. (2009). Fish consumption and cognitive function among older people in the UK: Baseline data from the OPAL study. *Journal of Nutrition, Health, and Aging*, 13(3), 198–202.

Damian, R. I., Spengler, M., Sutu, A., & Roberts, B. W. (2018). Sixteen going on sixty-six: A longitudinal study of personality stability and change across 50 years. *Journal of Personality and Social Psychology*. doi: 10.1037/pspp0000210

Darrell, A., & Pyszczynski, T. (2016). Terror management theory: Exploring the role of death in life. In L. A. Harvell & G. S. Nisbett (Eds.), *Denying death: An interdisciplinary approach to terror management theory* (pp. 1–15). New York: Routledge/Taylor & Francis Group.

Davis, M. A. (2003). Factors related to bridge employment participation among private sector early retirees. *Journal of Vocational Behavior*, 63(1), 55–71.

Davis, S. D., Lebow, J. L., & Sprenkle, D. H. (2012). Common factors of change in couple therapy. *Behavior Therapy*, 43(1), 36–48. doi: 10.1016/j.beth.2011.01.009

Davison, E. H., Pless, A. P., Gugliucci, M. R., King, L. A., King, D. W., Salgado, D. M., … Bachrach, P. (2006). Late-life emergence of early-life trauma: The phenomenon of late-onset stress symptomatology among aging combat veterans. *Research on Aging*, 28(1), 84–114. doi: 10.1177/0164027505281560

Davison, T. E., McCabe, M. P., & Mellor, D. (2009). An examination of the "gold standard" diagnosis of major depression in aged-care settings. *American Journal of Geriatric Psychiatry*, 17(5), 359–367. doi: 10.1097/JGP.0b013e318190b901

Dawis, R. (2002). Person–Environment–Correspondence theory. In S. D. Brown (Ed.), *Career choice and development* (4th ed., pp. 427–464). San Francisco, CA: Jossey Bass.

Dawson-Hughes, B., & Bischoff-Ferrari, H. A. (2007). Therapy of osteoporosis with calcium and vitamin D. *Journal of Bone and Mineral Research*, 22 (Suppl 2), V59–63. doi: 10.1359/jbmr.07s209

De Raedt, R., & Ponjaert-Kristoffersen, I. (2006). Self-serving appraisal as a cognitive coping strategy to deal with age-related limitations: An empirical study with elderly adults in a real-life stressful situation. *Aging and Mental Health*, 10(2), 195–203.

De Vries, B., & Megathlin, D. (2009). The meaning of friendships for gay men and lesbians in the second half of life. *Journal of GLBT Family Studies*, 5(1-2), 82–98.

Deary, I. J., & Brett, C. E. (2015). Predicting and retrodicting intelligence between childhood and old age in the 6-Day Sample of the Scottish Mental Survey 1947. *Intelligence*, 50, 1–9. doi: 10.1016/j.intell.2015.02.002

Deary, I. J., & Ritchie, S. J. (2016). Processing speed differences between 70- and 83-year-olds matched on childhood IQ. *Intelligence*, 55, 28–33. doi: 10.1016/j.intell.2016.01.002

Deci, E. L., & Ryan, R. M. (2008). Self-determination theory: A macrotheory of human motivation, development, and health. *Canadian Psychology/Psychologie Canadienne*, 49(3), 182–185.

Delbanco, N. (2011). *Lastingness: The art of old age*. New York: Grand Central Publishing.

Delbeke, J., Hoffman, L., Mols, K., Braeken, D., & Prodanov, D. (2017). And then there was light: Perspectives of optogenetics for deep brain stimulation and neuromodulation. *Frontiers in Neuroscience*, 11, 663. doi: 10.3389/fnins.2017.00663

Delgoulet, C., & Marquie, J. C. (2002). Age differences in learning maintenance skills: A field study. *Experimental Aging Research*, 28(1), 25–37.

Dellenbach, M., & Zimprich, D. (2008). Typical intellectual engagement and cognition in old age. *Neuropsychology and Developmental Cognition B: Aging Neuropsychology and Cognition*, 15(2), 208–231. doi: 781708432 [pii] 10.1080/13825580701338094

DeMaris, A. (2010). The 20-year trajectory of marital quality in enduring marriages: Does equity matter? *Journal of Social and Personal Relationships*, 27(4), 449–471. doi: 10.1177/0265407510363428

Deng, C.-P., Armstrong, P. I., & Rounds, J. (2007). The fit of Holland's RIASEC model to US occupations. *Journal of Vocational Behavior*, 71(1), 1–22. doi: 10.1016/j.jvb.2007.04.002

Desapriya, E., Harjee, R., Brubacher, J., Chan, H., Hewapathirane, D. S., Subzwari, S., & Pike, I. (2014). Vision screening of older drivers for preventing road traffic injuries and fatalities. *The Cochrane Database of Systematic Reviews*, (2), Cd006252. doi: 10.1002/14651858.CD006252.pub4

Devine, A., Dick, I. M., Islam, A. F., Dhaliwal, S. S., & Prince, R. L. (2005). Protein consumption is an important predictor of lower limb bone mass in elderly women. *American Journal of Clinical Nutrition*, 81(6), 1423–1428.

Dhamoon, M. S., Cheung, Y. K., DeRosa, J. T., Gutierrez, J., Moon, Y. P., Sacco, R. L., … Wright, C. B. (2018). Association between subclinical brain infarcts and functional decline trajectories. *Journal of the American Geriatrics Society*, 66(11), 2144–2150. doi: 10.1111/jgs.15557

Di Bonito, P., Di Fraia, L., Di Gennaro, L., Vitale, A., Lapenta, M., Scala, A., … Capaldo, B. (2007). Impact of impaired fasting glucose and other metabolic factors on cognitive function in elderly people. *Nutrition, Metabolism, and Cardiovascular Diseases*, 17(3), 203–208.

Diab, T., Condon, K. W., Burr, D. B., & Vashishth, D. (2006). Age-related change in the damage morphology of human cortical bone and its role in bone fragility. *Bone*, 38(3), 427–431.

Dich, N., Hansen, A. M., Avlund, K., Lund, R., Mortensen, E. L., Bruunsgaard, H., & Rod, N. H. (2015). Early life adversity potentiates the effects of later life stress on cumulative physiological dysregulation. *Anxiety, Stress, and Coping*, 28(4), 372–390. doi: 10.1080/10615806.2014.969720

Dickin, D. C., Brown, L. A., & Doan, J. B. (2006). Age-dependent differences in the time course of postural control during sensory perturbations. *Aging: Clinical and Experimental Research*, 18(2), 94–99.

Dickinson, G. E. (2012). Diversity in death: Body disposition and memorialization. *Illness, Crisis, & Loss*, 20(2), 141–158. doi: 10.2190/IL.20.2.d

Didikoglu, A., Maharani, A., Payton, A., Pendleton, N., & Canal, M. M. (2019). Longitudinal change of sleep timing: Association between chronotype and longevity in older adults. *Chronobiology International*, 1–16. doi: 10.1080/07420528.2019.1641111

Diekelmann, S., Biggel, S., Rasch, B., & Born, J. (2012). Offline consolidation of memory varies with time in slow wave sleep and can be accelerated by cuing memory reactivations. *Neurobiology of Agingogy of Learning and Memory*, 98(2), 103–111. doi: 10.1016/j.nlm.2012.07.002

Dietrich, A. (2004). The cognitive neuroscience of creativity. *Psychonomic Bulletin & Review*, 11(6), 1011–1026.

Diez, J. J., & Iglesias, P. (2004). Spontaneous subclinical hypothyroidism in patients older than 55 years: An analysis of natural course and risk factors for the development of overt thyroid failure. *Journal of Clinical Endocrinology and Metabolism*, 89(10), 4890–4897.

Diez, J. J., & Iglesias, P. (2009). An analysis of the natural course of subclinical hyperthyroidism. *American Journal of Medical Science*, 337(4), 225–232.

Ding, C., Cicuttini, F., Blizzard, L., Scott, F., & Jones, G. (2007). A longitudinal study of the effect of sex and age on rate of change in knee cartilage volume in adults. *Rheumatology*, 46(2), 273–290. doi: kel243 [pii] 10.1093/rheumatology/kel243

Diokno, A. C., Newman, D. K., Low, L. K., Griebling, T. L., Maddens, M. E., Goode, P. S., … Burgio, K. L. (2018). Effect of group-administered behavioral treatment on urinary incontinence in older women: A randomized clinical trial. *JAMA Internal Medicine*, 178(10), 1333–1341. doi: 10.1001/jamainternmed.2018.3766

Dixon, R. A., & Hultsch, D. F. (1999). Intelligence and cognitive potential in late life. In J. C. Cavanaugh & S. K. Whitbourne (Eds.), *Gerontology: Interdisciplinary perspectives* (pp. 213–237). New York: Oxford University Press.

do Amaral, M. A., Neto, M. G., de Queiroz, J. G., Martins-Filho, P. R., Saquetto, M. B., & Oliveira Carvalho, V. (2016). Effect of music therapy on blood pressure of individuals with hypertension: A systematic review and meta-analysis. *International Journal of Cardiology*, 214, 461–464. doi: 10.1016/j.ijcard.2016.03.197

Dobbs, B. M. (2008). Aging baby boomers--a blessing or challenge for driver licensing authorities. *Traffic and Injury Prevention*, 9(4), 379–386. doi: 901525511 [pii] 10.1080/15389580802045823

Dobrow Riza, S., Ganzach, Y., & Liu, Y. (2018). Time and job satisfaction: A longitudinal study of the differential roles of age and tenure. *Journal of Management*, 44(7), 2558–2579. doi: 10.1177/0149206315624962

Dobrow, S. R., & Tosti-Kharas, J. (2011). Calling: The development of a scale measure. *Personnel Psychology*, 64(4), 1001–1049. doi: 10.1111/j.1744-6570.2011.01234.x

Dockree, P. M., Brennan, S., O'Sullivan, M., Robertson, I. H., & O'Connell, R. G. (2015). Characterising neural signatures of successful aging: Electrophysiological correlates of preserved episodic memory in older age. *Brain and Cognition*, 97, 40–50. doi: 10.1016/j.bandc.2015.04.002

Dolcos, S. M., & Daley, D. (2009). Work pressure, workplace social resources, and work-family conflict: The tale of two sectors. *International Journal of Stress Management*, 16(4), 291–311.

Dols, A., Kessing, L. V., Strejilevich, S. A., Rej, S., Tsai, S. Y., Gildengers, A. G., … Sajatovic, M. (2016). Do current national and international guidelines have specific recommendations for older adults with bipolar disorder? A brief report. *International Journal of Geriatric Psychiatry*, 31(12), 1295–1300. doi: 10.1002/gps.4534

Dommes, A., Cavallo, V., Vienne, F., & Aillerie, I. (2012). Age-related differences in street-crossing safety before and after training of older pedestrians. *Accident Analysis and Prevention*, 44(1), 42–47. doi: 10.1016/j.aap.2010.12.012

Doniec, K., Stefler, D., Murphy, M., Gugushvili, A., McKee, M., Marmot, M., … King, L. (2019). Education and mortality in three Eastern European populations: Findings from the PrivMort retrospective cohort study. *European Journal of Public Health*, 29(3), 549–554. doi: 10.1093/eurpub/cky254

D'Onofrio, B., & Emery, R. (2019). Parental divorce or separation and children's mental health. *World Psychiatry: Official Journal of the World Psychiatric Association (WPA)*, 18(1), 100–101. doi:10.1002/wps.20590

Donohue, R. (2006). Person-environment congruence in relation to career change and career persistence. *Journal of Vocational Behavior*, 68(3), 504–515.

Dorshkind, K., & Swain, S. (2009). Age-associated declines in immune system development and function: Causes, consequences, and reversal. *Current Opinion in Immunology*, 21(4), 404–407. doi: S0952-7915(09)00138-1 [pii] 10.1016/j.coi.2009.07.001

Downes, S. M. (2016). Ultraviolet or blue-filtering intraocular lenses: What is the evidence? *Eye*, 30(2), 215–221. doi: 10.1038/eye.2015.267

Dozier, M. E., Porter, B., & Ayers, C. R. (2016). Age of onset and progression of hoarding symptoms in older adults with hoarding disorder. *Aging and Mental Health*, 20(7), 736–742. doi: 10.1080/13607863.2015.1033684

Drew, L. M., & Smith, P. K. (2002). Implications for grandparents when they lose contact with their grandchildren: Divorce, family feud, and geographical separation. *Journal of Mental Health & Aging*, 8, 95–119.

Duffy, J. F., Scheuermaier, K., & Loughlin, K. R. (2016). Age-related sleep disruption and reduction in the circadian rhythm of urine output: Contribution to nocturia? *Currents in Aging Science*, 9(1), 34–43.

Duffy, J. F., Zitting, K. M., & Chinoy, E. D. (2015). Aging and circadian rhythms. *Sleep Medicine Clinics*, 10(4), 423–434. doi: 10.1016/j.jsmc.2015.08.002 S1556-407X(15)00099-5 [pii]

Duffy, R. D., Douglass, R. P., Gensmer, N. P., England, J. W., & Kim, H. J. (2019). An initial examination of the work as calling theory. *Journal of Counseling Psychology, 66*(3), 328–340. doi: 10.1037/cou0000318

Dufour, A., & Candas, V. (2007). Ageing and thermal responses during passive heat exposure: Sweating and sensory aspects. *European Journal of Applied Physiology, 100*(1), 19–26. doi: 10.1007/s00421-007-0396-9

Dufour, A. B., Broe, K. E., Nguyen, U.-S. D. T., Gagnon, D. R., Hillstrom, H. J., Walker, A. H., … Hannan, M. T. (2009). Foot pain: Is current or past shoewear a factor? *Arthritis and Rheumatism, 61*(10), 1352–1358. doi: 10.1002/art.24733

Dunifon, R., & Bajracharya, A. (2012). The role of grandparents in the lives of youth. *Journal of Family Issues, 33*(9), 1168–1194. doi: 10.1177/0192513x12444271

Dustman, R. E., Emmerson, R. Y., Steinhaus, L. A., & Shearer, D. E. (1992). The effects of videogame playing on neuropsychological performance of elderly individuals. *Journals of Gerontology, 47*(3), P168–P171.

Duys, D. K., Ward, J. E., Maxwell, J. A., & Eaton-Comerford, L. (2008). Career counseling in a volatile job market: Tiedeman's perspective revisited. *The Career Development Quarterly, 56*(3), 232–241. doi: 10.1002/j.2161-0045.2008.tb00037.x

Dwyer-Lindgren, L., Bertozzi-Villa, A., Stubbs, R. W., Morozoff, C., Kutz, M. J., Huynh, C., … Murray, C. J. (2016). US county-level trends in mortality rates for major causes of death, 1980-2014. *Journal of the American Medical Association, 316*(22), 2385–2401. doi: 10.1001/jama.2016.13645

Dy, S., & Lynn, J. (2007). Getting services right for those sick enough to die. *British Medical Journal, 334*(7592), 511–513.

Dye, B. A., Thornton-Evans, G., Li, X., & Iafolla, T. J. (2015). Dental caries and tooth loss in adults in the United States, 2011-2012. *NCHS data brief (197)*.

Dye, M. W. G., Green, C. S., & Bavelier, D. (2009). Increasing speed of processing with action video games. *Current Directions in Psychological Science, 18*(6), 321–326. doi: 10.1111/j.1467-8721.2009.01660.x

Earl, J. K., Gerrans, P., & Halim, V. A. (2015). Active and adjusted: Investigating the contribution of leisure, health and psychosocial factors to retirement adjustment. *Leisure Sciences, 37*(4), 354–372. doi: 10.1080/01490400.2015.1021881

Edelstein, B. A., Martin, R. R., & Gerolimatos, L. A. (2013). Assessment in geriatric settings. In J. R. Graham, J. A. Naglieri & I. B. Weiner (Eds.), *Handbook of psychology. Assessment psychology* (2nd ed., Vol. 10, pp. 425–447). Hoboken, NJ: John Wiley & Sons Inc.

Edwards, J. R., & Rothbard, N. P. (2000). Mechanisms linking work and family: Clarifying the relationship between work and family constructs. *The Academy of Management Review, 25*(1), 178–199. doi: 10.2307/259269

Eissa, G., & Lester, S. W. (2017). Supervisor role overload and frustration as antecedents of abusive supervision: The moderating role of supervisor personality. *Journal of Organizational Behavior, 38*(3), 307–326. doi: 10.1002/job.2123

Eliasson, L., Birkhed, D., Osterberg, T., & Carlen, A. (2006). Minor salivary gland secretion rates and immunoglobulin A in adults and the elderly. *European Journal of Oral Sciences, 114*(6), 494–499.

Eliot, L. (2011). The trouble with sex differences. *Neuron, 72*(6), 895–898. doi: https://doi.org/10.1016/j.neuron.2011.12.001

Ellis, R. R., & Simmons, T. (2014). Coresident grandparents and their grandchildren: 2012 *Current population reports, P20-576*. Washington, DC.: U.S. Census Bureau.

Emaus, N., Berntsen, G. K., Joakimsen, R., & Fonnebo, V. (2006). Longitudinal changes in forearm bone mineral density in women and men aged 45-84 years: The Tromso Study, a population-based study. *American Journal of Epidemiology, 163*(5), 441–449.

Engvig, A., Fjell, A. M., Westlye, L. T., Moberget, T., Sundseth, Ø., Larsen, V. A., & Walhovd, K. B. (2012). Memory training impacts short-term changes in aging white matter: A longitudinal diffusion tensor imaging study. *Human Brain Mapping, 33*(10), 2390–2406. doi: 10.1002/hbm.21370

Erickson, K. I., Hillman, C., Stillman, C. M., Ballard, R. M., Bloodgood, B., Conroy, D. E., … Powell, K. E. (2019). Physical activity, cognition, and brain outcomes: A review of the 2018 physical activity guidelines. *Medicine and Science in Sports and Exercise, 51*(6), 1242–1251. doi: 10.1249/mss.0000000000001936

Erickson, K. I., & Kramer, A. F. (2009). Aerobic exercise effects on cognitive and neural plasticity in older adults. *British Journal of Sports Medicine, 43*(1), 22–24. doi: bjsm.2008.052498 [pii] 10.1136/bjsm.2008.052498

Erikson, E. H. (1963). *Childhood and society* (2nd ed.). New York: W.W. Norton.

Erikson, E. H., Erikson, J. M., & Kivnick, H. Q. (1986). *Vital involvement in old age*. New York: W.W. Norton.

Erlangsen, A., Stenager, E., & Conwell, Y. (2015). Physical diseases as predictors of suicide in older adults: A nationwide, register-based cohort study. *Social Psychiatry and Psychiatric Epidemiology, 50*(9), 1427–1439. doi: 10.1007/s00127-015-1051-0

Eshelman, A. J., & Rottinghaus, P. J. (2015). Viewing adolescents' career futures through the lenses of socioeconomic status and social class. *The Career Development Quarterly, 63*(4), 320–332. doi: 10.1002/cdq.12031

Espiritu, J. R. (2008). Aging-related sleep changes. *Clinics in Geriatric Medicine, 24*(1), 1–14, v. doi: S0749-0690(07)00072-9 [pii] 10.1016/j.cger.2007.08.007

Esposito, C., Plati, A., Mazzullo, T., Fasoli, G., De Mauri, A., Grosjean, F., … Dal Canton, A. (2007). Renal function and functional reserve in healthy elderly individuals. *Journal of Nephrology, 20*(5), 617–625.

Esposito, K., Giugliano, F., Maiorino, M. I., & Giugliano, D. (2010). Dietary factors, Mediterranean diet and erectile dysfunction. *Journal of Sexual Medicine, 7*(7), 2338–2345. doi: 10.1111/j.1743-6109.2010.01842.x

European Union. (2019). European Innovation Partnership on Active and Healthy Ageing. https://ec.europa.eu/eip/ageing/home_en

Falck, R. S., Davis, J. C., Best, J. R., Crockett, R. A., & Liu-Ambrose, T. (2019). Impact of exercise training on physical and cognitive function among older adults: A systematic review and meta-analysis. *Neurobiology of Aging, 79,* 119–130. doi: 10.1016/j.neurobiolaging.2019.03.007

Falkowski, J., Atchison, T., Debutte-Smith, M., Weiner, M. F., & O'Bryant, S. (2014). Executive functioning and the metabolic syndrome: A project FRONTIER study. *Archives of Clinical Neuropsychology, 29*(1), 47–53. doi: 10.1093/arclin/act078

Farley, C., Alimi, Y., Espinosa, L. R., Perez, S., Knechtle, W., Hestley, A., … Rizzo, M. (2015). Tanning beds: A call to action for further educational and legislative efforts. *Journal of Surgical Oncology, 112*(2), 183–187. doi: 10.1002/jso.23969

Farrell, M. P., & Rosenberg, S. D. (1981). *Men at midlife.* Boston, MA: Auburn House.

Favero, G., Franceschetti, L., Buffoli, B., Moghadasian, M. H., Reiter, R. J., Rodella, L. F., & Rezzani, R. (2017). Melatonin: Protection against age-related cardiac pathology. *Ageing Research Reviews, 35,* 336–349. doi: 10.1016/j.arr.2016.11.007

Federal Interagency Forum on Aging-Related Statistics. (2016). *Older Americans 2016: Key indicators of well-being.* Washington, DC: U.S. Government Printing Office.

Feist, G. J., & Barron, F. X. (2003). Predicting creativity from early to late adulthood: Intellect, potential, and personality. *Journal of Research in Personality, 37*(2), 62–88.

Feldman, H. A., Longcope, C., Derby, C. A., Johannes, C. B., Araujo, A. B., Coviello, A. D., … McKinlay, J. B. (2002). Age trends in the level of serum testosterone and other hormones in middle-aged men: Longitudinal results from the Massachusetts male aging study. *Journal of Clinical Endocrinology and Metabolism, 87*(2), 589–598.

Felicissimo, M. F., Carneiro, M. M., Saleme, C. S., Pinto, R. Z., da Fonseca, A. M., & da Silva-Filho, A. L. (2010). Intensive supervised versus unsupervised pelvic floor muscle training for the treatment of stress urinary incontinence: A randomized comparative trial. *International Urogynecology: Journal of Pelvic Floor Dysfunction.* doi: 10.1007/s00192-010-1125-1

Ferguson, R., & Brohaugh, B. (2010). The aging of aquarius. *Journal of Consumer Marketing, 27*(1), 76–81.

Fernandez-Ballesteros, R., Bustillos, A., & Huici, C. (2015). Positive perception of aging and performance in a memory task: Compensating for stereotype threat? *Experimental Aging Research, 41*(4), 410–425. doi: 10.1080/0361073x.2015.1053757

Ferraro, K. F., & Farmer, M. M. (1996). Double jeopardy, aging as leveler, or persistent health inequality? A longitudinal analysis of white and black Americans. *Journal of Gerontology: Social Sciences, 51*(6), S319–328.

Ferri, R., Gschliesser, V., Frauscher, B., Poewe, W., & Hogl, B. (2009). Periodic leg movements during sleep and periodic limb movement disorder in patients presenting with unexplained insomnia. *Clinics in Neurophysiology, 120*(2), 257–263. doi: S1388-2457(08)01257-1 [pii] 10.1016/j.clinph.2008.11.006

Ferrucci, L., Cooper, R., Shardell, M., Simonsick, E. M., Schrack, J. A., & Kuh, D. (2016). Age-related change in mobility: Perspectives from life course epidemiology and geroscience. *Journal of Gerontology Series A: Biological Sciences, 71*(9), 1184–1194. doi: 10.1093/gerona/glw043

Fetto, J. (2002). Friends forever. Retrieved 2/20/13, from http://adage.com/article/american-demographics/friends-forever/44657/

Field, N. P., Gal-Oz, E., & Bonanno, G. A. (2003). Continuing bonds and adjustment at 5 years after the death of a spouse. *Journal of Consulting and Clinical Psychology, 71,* 110–117.

Fien, S., Climstein, M., Quilter, C., Buckley, G., Henwood, T., Grigg, J., & Keogh, J. W. L. (2017). Anthropometric, physical function and general health markers of Masters athletes: A cross-sectional study. *PeerJ, 5,* e3768. doi: 10.7717/peerj.3768

Fiksenbaum, L. M., Greenglass, E. R., & Eaton, J. (2006). Perceived social support, hassles, and coping among the elderly. *Journal of Applied Gerontology, 25*(1), 17–30.

Fingerman, K. L. (2001). *Aging mothers and their adult daughters: A study in mixed emotions.* New York: Springer.

Fingerman, K. L., Cheng, Y. P., Wesselmann, E. D., Zarit, S., Furstenberg, F., & Birditt, K. S. (2012). Helicopter parents and landing pad kids: Intense parental support of grown children. *Journal of Marriage and the Family, 74*(4), 880–896.

Fingerman, K. L., & Griffiths, P. C. (1999). Seasons greetings: Adults' social contacts at the holiday season. *Psychology and Aging, 14,* 192–205.

Fingerman, K. L., Hay, E. L., & Birditt, K. S. (2004). The best of ties, the worst of ties: Close, problematic, and ambivalent social relationships. *Journal of Marriage and the Family, 66*(3), 792–808.

Fingerman, K. L., Pitzer, L. M., Chan, W., Birditt, K. S., Franks, M., & Zarit, S. H. (2010). Who gets what and why? Help middle-aged adults provide to parents and grown children. *Journal of Gerontology: Social Sciences.* doi: 10.1093/geronb/gbq009

Finkel, E. J., Cheung, E. O., Emery, L. F., Carswell, K. L., & Larson, G. M. (2015). The suffocation model: Why marriage in America is becoming an all-or-nothing institution. *Current Directions in Psychological Science, 24*(3), 238–244. doi: 10.1177/0963721415569274

Finkel, E. J., Hui, C. M., Carswell, K. L., & Larson, G. M. (2014). The suffocation of marriage: Climbing Mount Maslow without enough oxygen. *Psychological Inquiry, 25*(1), 1–41. doi: 10.1080/1047840X.2014.863723

Fiocco, A. J., & Yaffe, K. (2010). Defining successful aging: The importance of including cognitive function over time. *Archives of Neurology, 67*(7), 876–880. doi: 10.1001/archneurol.2010.130

Fiorito, G., McCrory, C., Robinson, O., Carmeli, C., Rosales, C. O., Zhang, Y., … Polidoro, S. (2019). Socioeconomic position, lifestyle habits and biomarkers of epigenetic aging: A multi-cohort analysis. *Aging, 11*(7), 2045–2070. doi: 10.18632/aging.101900

Fishleder, S., Schonfeld, L., Corvin, J., Tyler, S., & VandeWeerd, C. (2016). Drinking behavior among older adults in a planned retirement community: Results from The Villages survey. *International Journal of Geriatric Psychiatry, 31*(5), 536–543. doi: 10.1002/gps.4359

Fjell, A. M., Walhovd, K. B., Fennema-Notestine, C., McEvoy, L. K., Hagler, D. J., Holland, D., ... Dale, A. M. (2009). One-year brain atrophy evident in healthy aging. *Journal of Neuroscience, 29*(48), 15223–15231. doi: 29/48/15223 [pii] 10.1523/JNEUROSCI.3252-09.2009

Flatt, J. D., Williams, B. A., Barnes, D., Goldenson, J., & Ahalt, C. (2017). Post-traumatic stress disorder symptoms and associated health and social vulnerabilities in older jail inmates. *Aging and Mental Health, 21*(10), 1106–1112. doi: 10.1080/13607863.2016.1201042

Flaxman, S. R., Bourne, R. R. A., Resnikoff, S., Ackland, P., Braithwaite, T., Cicinelli, M. V., ... Taylor, H. R. (2017). Global causes of blindness and distance vision impairment 1990-2020: A systematic review and meta-analysis. *Lancet Global Health, 5*(12), e1221–e1234. doi: 10.1016/s2214-109x(17)30393-5

Fleming, R., & Bennett, K. (2015). Assessing the quality of environmental design of nursing homes for people with dementia: Development of a new tool. *Australasian Journal on Ageing, 34*(3), 191–194. doi: 10.1111/ajag.12233

Flora, C. (2013). *Friendfluence: The surprising ways friends make us who we are.* New York: Random House.

Foley, P. F., & Lytle, M. C. (2015). Social cognitive career theory, the theory of work adjustment, and work satisfaction of retirement-age adults. *Journal of Career Development, 42*(3), 199–214. doi: 10.1177/0894845314553270

Folstein, M. F., Folstein, S. E., & McHugh, P. R. (1975). Mini-mental state: A practical method for grading the cognitive state of patients for the clinician. *Journal of Psychiatric Research, 12,* 189–198.

Ford, D. H., & Lerner, R. M. (Eds.). (1992). *Developmental systems theory: An integrative approach.* Newbury Park, CA: Sage Publications.

Forsmo, S., Langhammer, A., Forsen, L., & Schei, B. (2005). Forearm bone mineral density in an unselected population of 2,779 men and women--The HUNT Study, Norway. *Osteoporosis International, 16*(5), 562–567.

Fotso Soh, J., Klil-Drori, S., & Rej, S. (2019). Using lithium in older age bipolar disorder: Special considerations. *Drugs and Aging, 36*(2), 147–154. doi: 10.1007/s40266-018-0628-1

Fowler, C., Gasiorek, J., & Giles, H. (2015). The role of communication in aging well: Introducing the communicative ecology model of successful aging. *Communication Monographs, 82*(4), 431–457. doi: 10.1080/03637751.2015.1024701

Fraade-Blanar, L. A., Sears, J. M., Chan, K. C. G., Thompson, H. J., Crane, P. K., & Ebel, B. E. (2017). Relating older workers' injuries to the mismatch between physical ability and job demands. *Journal of Occupational and Environmental Medicine, 59*(2), 212–221. doi: 10.1097/JOM.0000000000000941

França, L. H. F., & Hershey, D. A. (2018). Financial preparation for retirement in Brazil: A cross-cultural test of the interdisciplinary financial planning model. *Journal of Cross-Cultural Gerontology, 33*(1), 43–64. doi: 10.1007/s10823-018-9343-y

Fraser, J., Maticka-Tyndale, E., & Smylie, L. (2004). Sexuality of Canadian women at midlife. *Canadian Journal of Human Sexuality, 13*(3), 171–188.

Fraser, M. A., Shaw, M. E., & Cherbuin, N. (2015). A systematic review and meta-analysis of longitudinal hippocampal atrophy in healthy human ageing. *Neuroimage, 112,* 364–374. doi: 10.1016/j.neuroimage.2015.03.035

Frazer, K. A., Ballinger, D. G., Cox, D. R., Hinds, D. A., Stuve, L. L., Gibbs, R. A., ... Stewart, J. (2007). A second generation human haplotype map of over 3.1 million SNPs. *Nature, 449*(7164), 851–861. doi: nature06258 [pii] 10.1038/nature06258

Frazier, L., Barreto, M., & Newman, F. (2012). Self-regulation and eudaimonic well-being across adulthood. *Experimental Aging Research, 38*(4), 394–410. doi: 10.1080/0361073x.2012.699367

Frazier, L. D., Johnson, P. M., Gonzalez, G. K., & Kafka, C. L. (2002). Psychosocial influences on possible selves: A comparison of three cohorts of older adults. *International Journal of Behavioral Development, 26,* 308–317.

Fredriksen, E., von Soest, T., Smith, L., & Moe, V. (2019). Depressive symptom contagion in the transition to parenthood: Interparental processes and the role of partner-related attachment. *Journal of Abnormal Psychology.* doi: 10.1037/abn0000429

Freitas, H. R., Ferreira, Gustavo da Costa, Trevenzoli, I. H., Oliveira, Karen de Jesus, & de Melo Reis, R. A. (2017). Fatty acids, antioxidants and physical activity in brain aging. *Nutrients, 9*(11), 1263. doi: 10.3390/nu9111263

Friedman, M., & Rosenman, R. H. (1974). *Type A behavior and your heart.* New York: Alfred A. Knopf.

Frisby, B. N., Booth-Butterfield, M., Dillow, M. R., Martin, M. M., & Weber, K. D. (2012). Face and resilience in divorce: The impact on emotions, stress, and post-divorce relationships. *Journal of Social and Personal Relationships, 29*(6), 715–735. doi: 10.1177/0265407512443452

Froidevaux, A., Hirschi, A., & Wang, M. (2016). The role of mattering as an overlooked key challenge in retirement planning and adjustment. *Journal of Vocational Behavior, 94,* 57–69. doi: 10.1016/j.jvb.2016.02.016

Froudist-Walsh, S., Lopez-Barroso, D., Jose Torres-Prioris, M., Croxson, P. L., & Berthier, M. L. (2018). Plasticity in the working memory system: Life span changes and response to injury. *Neuroscientist, 24*(3), 261–276. doi: 10.1177/1073858417717210

Fung, H. H., Lu, A. Y., Goren, D., Isaacowitz, D. M., Wadlinger, H. A., & Wilson, H. R. (2008). Age-related positivity enhancement is not universal: Older Chinese look away from positive stimuli. *Psychology and Aging, 23*(2), 440–446.

Funk, L. M. (2004). Who wants to be involved? Decision-making preferences among residents of long-term care facilities. *Canadian Journal of Aging, 23,* 47–58.

Garber, C. E., Blissmer, B., Deschenes, M. R., Franklin, B. A., Lamonte, M. J., Lee, I. M., ... Swain, D. P. (2011). American College of Sports Medicine position stand. Quantity and quality of exercise for developing and maintaining cardiorespiratory, musculoskeletal, and neuromotor fitness in apparently healthy adults: Guidance for prescribing exercise. *Medicine & Science in Sports & Exercise, 43*(7), 1334–1359. doi: 10.1249/MSS.0b013e318213fefb

Garcia-Piqueras, J., Garcia-Mesa, Y., Carcaba, L., Feito, J., Torres-Parejo, I., Martin-Biedma, B., … Vega, J. A. (2019). Ageing of the somatosensory system at the periphery: Age-related changes in cutaneous mechanoreceptors. *Journal of Anatomy.* doi: 10.1111/joa.12983

Garcia, M. A., & Umberson, D. (2019). Marital strain and psychological distress in same-sex and different-sex couples. *Journal of Marriage and the Family.* doi: 10.1111/jomf.12582

Garden, S. E., Phillips, L. H., & MacPherson, S. E. (2001). Midlife aging, open-ended planning, and laboratory measures of executive function. *Neuropsychology, 15*(4), 472–482.

Gardner, H. (1993). *Multiple intelligences: The theory in practice.* New York: Basic Books.

Garg, S. K., Delaney, C., Toubai, T., Ghosh, A., Reddy, P., Banerjee, R., & Yung, R. (2014). Aging is associated with increased regulatory T-cell function. *Aging Cell, 13*(3), 441–448. doi: 10.1111/acel.12191

Gaunt, R. (2006). Couple similarity and marital satisfaction: Are similar spouses happier? *Journal of Personality, 74*(5), 1401–1420.

Gavrin, J., & Chapman, C. R. (1995). Clinical management of dying patients. *Western Journal of Medicine, 163,* 268–277.

Geard, D., Reaburn, P. R. J., Rebar, A. L., & Dionigi, R. A. (2017). Masters athletes: Exemplars of successful aging? *Journal of Aging and Physical Activity, 25*(3), 490–500. doi: 10.1123/japa.2016-0050

Gefen, T., Kim, G., Bolbolan, K., Geoly, A., Ohm, D., Oboudiyat, C., … Geula, C. (2019). Activated microglia in cortical white matter across cognitive aging trajectories. *Frontiers in Aging Neuroscience, 11,* 94. doi: 10.3389/fnagi.2019.00094

Geirsdottir, O. G., Chang, M., Jonsson, P. V., Thorsdottir, I., & Ramel, A. (2019). Obesity, physical function, and training success in community-dwelling nonsarcopenic old adults. *Journal of Aging Research, 5340328.* doi: 10.1155/2019/5340328

Gerstorf, D., Ram, N., Hoppmann, C., Willis, S. L., & Schaie, K. W. (2011). Cohort differences in cognitive aging and terminal decline in the Seattle Longitudinal Study. *Developmental Psychology, 47*(4), 1026–1041. doi: 10.1037/a0023426

Gerstorf, D., Ram, N., Lindenberger, U., & Smith, J. (2013). Age and time-to-death trajectories of change in indicators of cognitive, sensory, physical, health, social, and self-related functions. *Developmental Psychology, 8*(4), 562–574. doi: 10.1037/a0031340

Geurts, T., Poortman, A.-R., van Tilburg, T., & Dykstra, P. A. (2009). Contact between grandchildren and their grandparents in early adulthood. *Journal of Family Issues, 30*(12), 1698–1713.

Geurts, T., van Tilburg, T. G., & Poortman, A.-R. (2012). The grandparent–grandchild relationship in childhood and adulthood: A matter of continuation? *Personal Relationships, 19*(2), 267–278.

Ghate, V. M., Lewis, S. A., Prabhu, P., Dubey, A., & Patel, N. (2016). Nanostructured lipid carriers for the topical delivery of tretinoin. *European Journal of Pharmaceutics and Biopharmaceutics, 108,* 253–261. doi: 10.1016/j.ejpb.2016.07.026

Ghisletta, P., Rabbitt, P., Lunn, M., & Lindenberger, U. (2012). Two thirds of the age-based changes in fluid and crystallized intelligence, perceptual speed, and memory in adulthood are shared. *Intelligence, 40*(3), 260–268. doi: 10.1016/j.intell.2012.02.008

Gillsjö, C., Schwartz-Barcott, D., & von Post, I. (2011). Home: The place the older adult cannot imagine living without. *BMC Geriatrics, 11*(1), 10. doi: 10.1186/1471-2318-11-10

Gimeno, D., Tabak, A. G., Ferrie, J. E., Shipley, M. J., De Vogli, R., Elovainio, M., … Kivimaki, M. (2010). Justice at work and metabolic syndrome: The Whitehall II study. *Occupational and Environmental Medicine, 67*(4), 256–262. doi: oem.2009.047324 [pii] 10.1136/oem.2009.047324

Gladyshev, V. N. (2014). The free radical theory of aging is dead. Long live the damage theory! *Antioxidants & Redox Signaling, 20*(4), 727–731. doi: 10.1089/ars.2013.5228

Glaser, B. G., & Strauss, A. L. (1968). *Time for dying.* Chicago, IL: Aldine.

Global BMI Mortality Collaboration, Di Angelantonio, E., Bhupathiraju, Sh. N., Wormser, D., Gao, P., Kaptoge, S., … Hu, F. B. (2016). Body-mass index and all-cause mortality: Individual-participant-data meta-analysis of 239 prospective studies in four continents. *Lancet, 388*(10046), 776–786. doi: 10.1016/s0140-6736(16)30175-1

Gluck, J., & Bluck, S. (2007). Looking back across the life span: A life story account of the reminiscence bump. *Memory and Cognition, 35*(8), 1928–1939.

Goh, J. O., & Park, D. C. (2009). Neuroplasticity and cognitive aging: The scaffolding theory of aging and cognition. *Restorative Neurology and Neuroscience, 27*(5), 391–403. doi: 2170W040X0229571 [pii] 10.3233/RNN-2009-0493

Goldberg, A. E., Frost, R. L., Manley, M. H., & Black, K. A. (2018). Meeting other moms: Lesbian adoptive mothers' relationships with other parents at school and beyond. *Journal of Lesbian Studies, 22*(1), 67–84. doi: 10.1080/10894160.2016.1278349

Goldberg, A. E., & Smith, J. Z. (2011). Stigma, social context, and mental health: Lesbian and gay couples across the transition to adoptive parenthood. *Journal of Counseling Psychology, 58*(1), 139–150. doi: 10.1037/a0021684

Goldberg, J., Magruder, K. M., Forsberg, C. W., Friedman, M. J., Litz, B. T., Vaccarino, V., … Smith, N. L. (2016). Prevalence of post-traumatic stress disorder in aging Vietnam-era veterans: Veterans administration cooperative study 569: Course and consequences of post-traumatic stress disorder in Vietnam-era veteran twins. *The American Journal of Geriatric Psychiatry, 24*(3), 181–191. doi: 10.1016/j.jagp.2015.05.004

Goldstein, J. H., Cajko, L., Oosterbroek, M., Michielsen, M., van Houten, O., & Salverda, F. (1997). Video games and the elderly. *Social Behavior and Personality, 25*(4), 345–352. doi: 10.2224/sbp.1997.25.4.345

Golob, E. J., & Mock, J. R. (2019). Auditory spatial attention capture, disengagement, and response selection in normal aging. *Attention, Perception, & Psychophysics, 81*(1), 270–280.

Gompertz, B. (1825). On the nature of the function expressive of the law of human mortality, and on the mode of determining the value of life contingencies. *Philosophical Transactions of the Royal Society, 115*, 513–585.

Gottman, J. M., & Driver, J. L. (2005). Dysfunctional marital conflict and everyday marital interaction. *Journal of Divorce & Remarriage, 43*(3), 63–78.

Gouin, J. P., Hantsoo, L., & Kiecolt-Glaser, J. K. (2008). Immune dysregulation and chronic stress among older adults: A review. *Neuroimmunomodulation, 15*(4-6), 251–259. doi: 000156468 [pii] 10.1159/000156468

Government Accountability Office. (2008). Nursing homes: Federal monitoring surveys demonstrate continued understatement of serious care problems and CMS oversight weaknesses. Government Accountability Office.

Government Accountability Office. (2019). *Elder justice: Goals and outcome measures would provide DOJ with clear direction and a means to assess its efforts.* Highlights of GAO-19-365: Government Accountability Office.

Graham-Bailey, M., Richardson Cheeks, B. L., Blankenship, B. T., Stewart, A. J., & Chavous, T. M. (2018). Examining college students' multiple social identities of gender, race, and socioeconomic status: Implications for intergroup and social justice attitudes. *Journal of Diversity in Higher Education.* doi: 10.1037/dhe0000098

Grand, J. H., Stawski, R. S., & MacDonald, S. W. (2016). Comparing individual differences in inconsistency and plasticity as predictors of cognitive function in older adults. *Journal of Clinical Experimental Neuropsychology, 38*(5), 534–550. doi: 10.1080/13803395.2015.1136598

Greaney, J. L., Stanhewicz, A. E., Kenney, W. L., & Alexander, L. M. (2015). Impaired increases in skin sympathetic nerve activity contribute to age-related decrements in reflex cutaneous vasoconstriction. *Journal of Physiology, 593*(9), 2199–2211. doi: 10.1113/jp270062

Green, A. (2012). The Central African Republic's silent health crisis. *Lancet, 380*(9846), 964–965. doi: 10.1016/s0140-6736(12)61523-2

Green, C. S., & Bavelier, D. (2003). Action video game modifies visual selective attention. *Nature, 423*(6939), 534–537.

Green, C. S., & Bavelier, D. (2006). Effect of action video games on the spatial distribution of visuospatial attention. *Journal of Experimental Psychology: Human Perception and Performance, 32*(6), 1465–1478. doi: 10.1037/0096-1523.32.6.1465

Green, E. D., Watson, J. D., & Collins, F. S. (2015). Human Genome Project: Twenty-five years of big biology. *Nature, 526*(7571), 29–31. doi: 10.1038/526029a

Green, T. L., & Darity, W. A., Jr. (2010). Under the skin: Using theories from biology and the social sciences to explore the mechanisms behind the black-white health gap. *American Journal of Public Health, 100*(Suppl 1), S36–40. doi: AJPH.2009.171140 [pii] 10.2105/AJPH.2009.171140

Greenberg, J., Helm, P., Maxfield, M., & Schimel, J. (2017). How our mortal fate contributes to ageism: A terror management perspective. In T. D. Nelson (Ed.), *Ageism: Stereotyping and prejudice against older persons* (pp. 105–132). Cambridge, MA: MIT Press.

Greenwood, P. M. (2007). Functional plasticity in cognitive aging: Review and hypothesis. *Neuropsychology, 21*(6), 657–673. doi: 10.1037/0894-4105.21.6.657

Gregory, T., Nettelbeck, T., & Wilson, C. (2010). Openness to experience, intelligence, and successful ageing. *Personality and Individual Differences, 48*(8), 895–899. doi: 10.1016/j.paid.2010.02.017

Greif, G. L., & Deal, K. H. (2012). Platonic couple love: How couples view their close couple friends. In M. A. Paludi (Ed.), *The psychology of love* (Vols. 1–4, pp. 19–33). Santa Barbara, CA: Praeger/ABC-CLIO.

Gross, A. L., Brandt, J., Bandeen-Roche, K., Carlson, M. C., Stuart, E. A., Marsiske, M., & Rebok, G. W. (2014). Do older adults use the method of loci? Results from the ACTIVE study. *Experimental Aging Research, 40*(2), 140–163. doi: 10.1080/0361073x.2014.882204

Grossmann, I., Karasawa, M., Izumi, S., Na, J., Varnum, M. E. W., Kitayama, S., & Nisbett, R. E. (2012). Aging and wisdom: Culture matters. *Psychological Science, 23*(10), 1059–1066. doi: 10.1177/0956797612446025

Grossmann, I., Na, J., Varnum, M. E. W., Park, D. C., Kitayama, S., & Nisbett, R. E. (2010). Reasoning about social conflicts improves into old age. *Proceedings of the National Academy of Sciences, 107*(16), 7246–7250. doi: 10.1073/pnas.1001715107

Grossmann, I., Oakes, H., & Santos, H. C. (2019). Wise reasoning benefits from emodiversity, irrespective of emotional intensity. *Journal of Experimental Psychology General, 148*(5), 805–823. doi: 10.1037/xge0000543

Grosul, M., & Feist, G. J. (2014). The creative person in science. *Psychology of Aesthetics, Creativity, and the Arts, 8*(1), 30–43. doi: 10.1037/a0034828

Grosz, M. P., Göllner, R., Rose, N., Spengler, M., Trautwein, U., Rauthmann, J. F., … Roberts, B. W. (2019). The development of narcissistic admiration and machiavellianism in early adulthood. *Journal of Personality and Social Psychology, 116*(3), 467–482. doi: 10.1037/pspp0000174

Grote, N. K., Clark, M. S., & Moore, A. (2004). Perceptions of injustice in family work: The role of psychological distress. *Journal of Family Psychology, 18*(3), 480–492.

Grubeck-Loebenstein, B. (2010). Fading immune protection in old age: Vaccination in the elderly. *Journal of Comparative Physiology, 142*(Suppl 1), S116–S119. doi: S0021-9975(09)00326-0 [pii] 10.1016/j.jcpa.2009.10.002

Grundy, E., & Henretta, J. C. (2006). Between elderly parents and adult children: A new look at the intergenerational care provided by the 'sandwich generation'. *Ageing & Society, 26*(5), 707–722. doi: 10.1017/s0144686x06004934

Grundy, S. M. (2016). Metabolic syndrome update. *Trends in Cardiovascular Medicine, 26*(4), 364–373. doi: 10.1016/j.tcm.2015.10.004

Grundy, S. M., Cleeman, J. I., Daniels, S. R., Donato, K. A., Eckel, R. H., Franklin, B. A., ... Costa, F. (2006). Diagnosis and management of the metabolic syndrome: An American Heart Association/National Heart, Lung, and Blood Institute scientific statement. *Current Opinions in Cardiology, 21*(1), 1–6.

Grydeland, H., Vertes, P. E., Vasa, F., Romero-Garcia, R., Whitaker, K., Alexander-Bloch, A. F., ... Bullmore, E. T. (2019). Waves of maturation and senescence in micro-structural MRI markers of human cortical myelination over the lifespan. *Cerebral Cortex, 29*(3), 1369–1381. doi: 10.1093/cercor/bhy330

Guerreiro, M. J., Eck, J., Moerel, M., Evers, E. A., & Van Gerven, P. W. (2015). Top-down modulation of visual and auditory cortical processing in aging. *Brain and Behavior Research, 278,* 226–234. doi: 10.1016/j.bbr.2014.09.049

Guerville, F., Roubaud-Baudron, C., Duc, S., Salles, N., Rainfray, M., & Bourdel-Marchasson, I. (2019). Discrepancy between equations estimating kidney function in geriatric care: A study of implications for drug prescription. *Drugs and Aging, 36*(2), 155–163. doi: 10.1007/s40266-018-0618-3

Guillén, L., & Kunze, F. (2019). When age does not harm innovative behavior and perceptions of competence: Testing interdepartmental collaboration as a social buffer. *Human Resource Management.* doi: 10.1002/hrm.21953

Guntern, S., Korpershoek, H., & van der Werf, G. (2016). Prestige added to Holland's vocational interest scales for the prediction of medical students' aspired work environments. *Journal of Career Assessment, 24*(2), 333–346. doi: 10.1177/1069072715580418

Gurrentz, B. (2018a). Living with an unmarried partner now common for young adults. Retrieved 6/14/2019, from https://www.census.gov/library/stories/2018/11/cohabitaiton-is-up-marriage-is-down-for-young-adults.html

Gurrentz, B. (2018b). Millennial marriage: How much does economic security matter to marriage rates for young adults? Working paper number SEHSD-WP2018-09. Retrieved 6/14/2019, from https://www.census.gov/library/stories/2018/06/millennial-marriages.html

Habes, M., Erus, G., Toledo, J. B., Zhang, T., Bryan, N., Launer, L. J., ... Davatzikos, C. (2016). White matter hyperintensities and imaging patterns of brain ageing in the general population. *Brain, 139*(Pt 4), 1164–1179. doi: 10.1093/brain/aww008

Hafkemeijer, A., van der Grond, J., & Rombouts, S. A. (2012). Imaging the default mode network in aging and dementia. *Biochimica et Biophysica Acta, 1822*(3), 431–441. doi: 10.1016/j.bbadis.2011.07.008

Hafstrom, A. (2018). Perceived and functional balance control is negatively affected by diminished touch and vibration sensitivity in relatively healthy older adults and elderly. *Gerontology and Geriatric Medicine, 4,* 2333721418775551. doi: 10.1177/2333721418775551

Hagestad, G. O., & Neugarten, B. L. (1985). Age and the life course. In R. H. Binstock & E. Shanas (Eds.), *Handbook of aging and the social sciences* (pp. 35–61). New York: Van Nostrand Reinhold.

Hakulinen, C., Hintsanen, M., Munafo, M. R., Virtanen, M., Kivimaki, M., Batty, G. D., & Jokela, M. (2015). Personality and smoking: Individual-participant meta-analysis of nine cohort studies. *Addiction, 110*(11), 1844–1852. doi: 10.1111/add.13079

Hales, C. M., Carroll, M. D., Fryar, C. D., & Ogden, C. L. (2017). Prevalence of obesity among adults and youth: United States 2015–2016. *NCHS Data Brief* (288).

Hall, K. S., Morey, M. C., Bosworth, H. B., Beckham, J. C., Pebole, M. M., Sloane, R., & Pieper, C. F. (2019). Pilot randomized controlled trial of exercise training for older veterans with PTSD. *Journal of Behavioral Medicine.* doi: 10.1007/s10865-019-00073-w

Hall, P. A., Dubin, J. A., Crossley, M., Holmqvist, M. E., & D'Arcy, C. (2009). Does executive function explain the IQ-mortality association? Evidence from the Canadian Study on Health and Aging. *Psychosomatic Medicine, 71*(2), 196–204.

Hamilton, B. E., Martin, J. A., Osterman, M. J. K., & Rosen, L. M. (2019). Births: Provisional data for 2018. *Vital Statistics Rapid Release, No. 7.* Hyattsville, MD: National Center for Health Statistics.

Hare, R. D., & Neumann, C. S. (2006). The PCL-R assessment of psychopathy: Development, structural properties, and new directions. In C. J. Patrick (Ed.), *Handbook of psychopathy* (pp. 58–88). New York: Guilford Press.

Harley, T. A., Jessiman, L. J., & MacAndrew, S. B. G. (2011). Decline and fall: A biological, developmental, and psycholinguistic account of deliberative language processes and ageing. *Aphasiology, 25*(2), 123–153. doi: 10.1080/02687031003798262

Harms, C. A., & Rosenkranz, S. (2008). Sex differences in pulmonary function during exercise. *Medicine and Science in Sports and Exercise, 40*(4), 664–668. doi: 10.1249/MSS.0b013e3181621325

Harold, D., Abraham, R., Hollingworth, P., Sims, R., Gerrish, A., Hamshere, M. L., ... Williams, J. (2009). Genome-wide association study identifies variants at CLU and PICALM associated with Alzheimer's disease. *Nature Genetics, 41*(10), 1088–1093. doi: ng.440 [pii] 10.1038/ng.440

Harrington, C., Carrillo, H., Garfield, R., Musumeci, M., Squires, E., & Kaiser Family Foundation. (2018). Nursing facilities, staffing, residents, and facility deficiencies, 2009 through 2016. From http://files.kff.org/attachment/REPORT-Nursing-Facilities-Staffing-Residents-and-Facility-Deficiencies-2009-2016

Harris-Kojetin, L., Sengupta, M., Lendon, J. P., Rome, V., Valverde, R., & Caffrey, C. (2019). Long-term care providers and service users in the United States, 2015–2016. National Center for Health Statistics. *Vital and Health Statistics, 34*(3).

Harrison, T. M., Weintraub, S., Mesulam, M. M., & Rogalski, E. (2012). Superior memory and higher cortical volumes in unusually successful cognitive aging. *Journal of the International Neuropsychological Society, 18*(6), 1081–1085. doi: 10.1017/s1355617712000847

Hart, C. L., Gruer, L., & Watt, G. C. M. (2011). Cause specific mortality, social position, and obesity among women who had never smoked: 28 year cohort study. *British Medical Journal*, *343*(7813), 1–14.

Hart, H. M., McAdams, D. P., Hirsch, B. J., & Bauer, J. J. (2001). Generativity and social involvement among African Americans and White adults. *Journal of Research in Personality*, *35*(2), 208–230. doi: 10.1006/jrpe.2001.2318

Hartup, W. W., & Stevens, N. (1997). Friendships and adaptation in the life course. *Psychological Bulletin*, *121*, 355–370.

Harvey, P. D., & Bowie, C. R. (2013). Schizophrenia spectrum conditions. In G. Stricker, T. A. Widiger & I. B. Weiner (Eds.), *Handbook of psychology. Clinical psychology* (2nd ed., Vol. 8, pp. 240–261). Hoboken, NJ: John Wiley & Sons Inc.

Hasher, L., Goldstein, F., & May, C. (2005). It's about time: Circadian rhythms, memory and aging. In C. Izawa & N. Ohta (Eds.), *Human learning and memory: Advances in theory and application* (Vol. 18, pp. 179–186). Mahwah, NJ: Lawrence Erlbaum Associates.

Hastings, E. C., & West, R. L. (2009). The relative success of a self-help and a group-based memory training program for older adults. *Psychology and Aging*, *24*(3), 586–594.

Hatfield, E., & Rapson, R. L. (2012). Equity theory in close relationships. In P. A. M. Van Lange, A. W. Kruglanski & E. T. Higgins (Eds.), *Handbook of theories of social psychology* (Vol. 2, pp. 200–217). Thousand Oaks, CA: Sage Publications.

Hatfield, E., Rapson, R. L., & Aumer-Ryan, K. (2008). Social justice in love relationships: Recent developments. *Social Justice Research*, *21*(4), 413–431. doi: 10.1007/s11211-008-0080-1

Hauger, A. V., Bergland, A., Holvik, K., Stahle, A., Emaus, N., & Strand, B. H. (2018). Osteoporosis and osteopenia in the distal forearm predict all-cause mortality independent of grip strength: 22-Year follow-up in the population-based Tromso Study. *Osteoporosis International*, *29*(11), 2447–2456. doi: 10.1007/s00198-018-4653-z

Hausler, N., Lisan, Q., van Sloten, T., Haba-Rubio, J., Perier, M. C., Thomas, F., … Empana, J. P. (2019). Cardiovascular health and sleep disturbances in two population-based cohort studies. *Heart*. doi: 10.1136/heartjnl-2018-314485

Hayflick, L. (1994). *How and why we age*. New York: Ballantine Books.

Hazlett-Stevens, H., Singer, J., & Chong, A. (2019). Mindfulness-based stress reduction and mindfulness-based cognitive therapy with older adults: A qualitative review of randomized controlled outcome research. *Clinical Gerontology*, *42*(4), 347–358. doi: 10.1080/07317115.2018.1518282

He, W., Goodkind, D., & Kowal, P. (2016). *An aging world: 2015* (Vol. P95/16-1). U.S. Bureau of the Census.

Head, D., Kennedy, K. M., Rodrigue, K. M., & Raz, N. (2009). Age differences in perseveration: Cognitive and neuroanatomical mediators of performance on the Wisconsin Card Sorting Test. *Neuropsychologia*, *47*(4), 1200–1203. doi: S0028-3932(09)00006-2 [pii] 10.1016/j.neuropsychologia.2009.01.003

Headey, B., & Yong, J. (2019). Happiness and longevity: Unhappy people die young, otherwise happiness probably makes

no difference. *Social Indicators Research*, *142*(2), 713–732. doi: 10.1007/s11205-018-1923-2

Hebblethwaite, S., & Norris, J. (2011). Expressions of generativity through family leisure: Experiences of grandparents and adult grandchildren. *Family Relations: An Interdisciplinary Journal of Applied Family Studies*, *60*(1), 121–133. doi: 10.1111/j.1741-3729.2010.00637.x

Heckhausen, J. (1997). Developmental regulation across adulthood: Primary and secondary control of age-related challenges. *Developmental Psychology*, *33*(1), 176–187. doi: 10.1037/0012-1649.33.1.176

Heid, A. R., Pruchno, R., Cartwright, F. P., & Wilson-Genderson, M. (2017). Exposure to Hurricane Sandy, neighborhood collective efficacy, and post-traumatic stress symptoms in older adults. *Aging and Mental Health*, *21*(7), 742–750. doi: 10.1080/13607863.2016.1154016

Heidari, M., Ghodusi, M., Rezaei, P., Kabirian Abyaneh, S., Sureshjani, E. H., & Sheikhi, R. A. (2019). Sexual function and factors affecting menopause: A systematic review. *Journal of Menopausal Medicine*, *25*(1), 15–27. doi: 10.6118/jmm.2019.25.1.15

Heilmann, S. G., Holt, D. T., & Rilovick, C. Y. (2008). Effects of career plateauing on turnover: A test of a model. *Journal of Leadership & Organizational Studies*, *15*(1), 59–68.

Helfand, B. T., Evans, R. M., & McVary, K. T. (2009). A comparison of the frequencies of medical therapies for overactive bladder in men and women: Analysis of more than 7.2 million aging patients. *European Urologist*. doi: S0302-2838(09)01272-X [pii] 10.1016/j.eururo.2009.12.025

Henz, U. (2010). Parent care as unpaid family labor: How do spouses share? *Journal of Marriage and the Family*, *72*(1), 148–164.

Heraclides, A., Chandola, T., Witte, D. R., & Brunner, E. J. (2009). Psychosocial stress at work doubles the risk of type 2 diabetes in middle-aged women: Evidence from the Whitehall II study. *Diabetes Care*, *32*(12), 2230–2235. doi: dc09-0132 [pii] 10.2337/dc09-0132

Hermansen, K., Bengtsen, M., Kjaer, M., Vestergaard, P., & Jorgensen, J. O. L. (2017). Impact of GH administration on athletic performance in healthy young adults: A systematic review and meta-analysis of placebo-controlled trials. *Growth Hormone & IGF Research*, *34*, 38–44. doi: 10.1016/j.ghir.2017.05.005

Hertzog, C., Kramer, A. F., Wilson, R. S., & Lindenberger, U. (2008). Enrichment effects on adult cognitive development: Can the functional capacity of older adults be preserved and enhanced? *Psychological Science in the Public Interest*, *9*(1), 1–65. doi: 10.1111/j.1539-6053.2009.01034.x

Herzberg, F., Mausner, B., & Bloch Snyderman, B. (2005). *The motivation to work*. New Brunswick, NJ: Transaction Publishers.

Hess, T. M., Auman, C., Colcombe, S. J., & Rahhal, T. A. (2003). The impact of stereotype threat on age differences in memory performance. *Journals of Gerontology Series B: Psychological Sciences and Social Sciences*, *58*(1), P3–11.

Hess, T. M., & Hinson, J. T. (2006). Age-related variation in the influences of aging stereotypes on memory in adulthood. *Psychology and Aging*, *21*(3), 621–625.

Hicks, G. E., Sions, J. M., & Velasco, T. O. (2018). Hip symptoms, physical performance, and health status in older adults with chronic low back pain: A preliminary investigation. *Archives of Physical Medicine and Rehabilitation, 99*(7), 1273–1278. doi: 10.1016/j.apmr.2017.10.006

Hobfoll, S. E. (2002). Social and psychological resources and adaptation. *Review of General Psychology, 6*(4), 307–324. doi: 10.1037/1089-2680.6.4.307

Hodges, A. L., & Walker, D. K. (2017). Skin care for women. *Nursing for Womens Health, 20*(6), 609–613. doi: 10.1016/j.nwh.2016.10.001

Hofäcker, D., & Naumann, E. (2015). The emerging trend of work beyond retirement age in Germany: Increasing social inequality? *Zeitschrift für Gerontologie und Geriatrie, 48*(5), 473–479. doi: 10.1007/s00391-014-0669-y

Hofer, S. M., & Sliwinski, M. J. (2006). Design and analysis of longitudinal studies on aging. In J. E. Birren & K. W. Schaire (Eds.), *Handbook of the psychology of aging* (6th ed., pp. 15–37). Amsterdam, Netherlands: Elsevier.

Hoffman, B. J., & Woehr, D. J. (2006). A quantitative review of the relationship between person-organization fit and behavioral outcomes. *Journal of Vocational Behavior, 68*(3), 389–399.

Hoffman, H. J., Rawal, S., Li, C. M., & Duffy, V. B. (2016). New chemosensory component in the U.S. National Health and Nutrition Examination Survey (NHANES): First-year results for measured olfactory dysfunction. *Reviews in Endocrine and Metabolic Disorders, 17*(2), 221–240. doi: 10.1007/s11154-016-9364-1

Hoffman, L., Hofer, S. M., & Sliwinski, M. J. (2011). On the confounds among retest gains and age-cohort differences in the estimation of within-person change in longitudinal studies: A simulation study. *Psychology and Aging, 26*(4), 778–791. doi: 10.1037/a0023910

Hofland, B. F., Willis, S. L., & Baltes, P. B. (1980). Fluid performance in the elderly: Intraindividual variability and conditions of assessment. *Journal of Educational Psychology, 73*, 573–586.

Hogan, M. J., Staff, R. T., Bunting, B. P., Deary, I. J., & Whalley, L. J. (2012). Openness to experience and activity engagement facilitate the maintenance of verbal ability in older adults. *Psychology and Aging, 27*(4), 849–854. doi: 10.1037/a0029066

Hogerbrugge, M. J. A., & Silverstein, M. D. (2015). Transitions in relationships with older parents: From middle to later years. *The Journals of Gerontology: Series B: Psychological Sciences and Social Sciences, 70*(3), 481–495. doi: 10.1093/geronb/gbu069

Hogh, A., Hansen, Å. M., Mikkelsen, E. G., & Persson, R. (2012). Exposure to negative acts at work, psychological stress reactions and physiological stress response. *Journal of Psychosomatic Research, 73*(1), 47–52. doi: 10.1016/j.jpsychores.2012.04.004

Holland, J. L. (1997). *Making vocational choices: A theory of vocational personalities and work environments* (3rd ed.). Odessa, FL: Psychological Assessment Resources.

Hook, J. L., & Chalasani, S. (2008). Gendered expectations? Reconsidering single fathers' child-care time. *Journal of Marriage and the Family, 70*(4), 978–990.

Horn, J. L., & Cattell, R. B. (1966). Refinement and test of the theory of fluid and crystallized intelligence. *Journal of Educational Psychology, 57*, 253–270.

Hornsby, P. J. (2009). Senescence and life span. *Pflügers Archives.* doi: 10.1007/s00424-009-0723-6

Horslen, B. C., Dakin, C. J., Inglis, J. T., Blouin, J. S., & Carpenter, M. G. (2015). CrossTalk proposal: Fear of falling does influence vestibular-evoked balance responses. *Journal of Physiology, 593*(14), 2979–2981. doi: 10.1113/jp270269

Houlfort, N., Fernet, C., Vallerand, R. J., Laframboise, A., Guay, F., & Koestner, R. (2015). The role of passion for work and need satisfaction in psychological adjustment to retirement. *Journal of Vocational Behavior, 88*, 84–94. doi: 10.1016/j.jvb.2015.02.005

Howard, D., & Adams, E. (2012). Mammography rates after the 2009 US Preventive Services Task Force breast cancer screening recommendation. *Preventive Medicine, 55*(5), 485–487.

Huang, H.-W., Meyer, A. M., & Federmeier, K. D. (2012). A "concrete view" of aging: Event related potentials reveal age-related changes in basic integrative processes in language. *Neuropsychologia, 50*(1), 26–35. doi: 10.1016/j.neuropsychologia.2011.10.018

Huentelman, M. J., Piras, I. S., Siniard, A. L., De Both, M. D., Richholt, R. F., Balak, C. D., … Rogalski, E. J. (2018). Associations of MAP2K3 gene variants with superior memory in Super-Agers. *Frontiers in Aging Neuroscience, 10*, 155. doi: 10.3389/fnagi.2018.00155

Huisingh, C., Levitan, E. B., Irvin, M. R., Owsley, C., & McGwin, G., Jr. (2016). Driving with pets and motor vehicle collision involvement among older drivers: A prospective population-based study. *Accident Analysis and Prevention, 88*, 169–174. doi: 10.1016/j.aap.2015.12.015

Hülür, G., Ram, N., Willis, S. L., Schaie, K. W., & Gerstorf, D. (2015). Cognitive dedifferentiation with increasing age and proximity of death: Within-person evidence from the Seattle Longitudinal Study. *Psychology and Aging, 30*(2), 311–323. doi: 10.1037/a0039260

Humphrey, D. (1991). *Final exit: The practicalities of self-deliverance and assisted suicide for the dying.* Eugene, OR: Hemlock Society.

Hurd Clarke, L. (2006). Older women and sexuality: Experiences in marital relationships across the life course. *Canadian Journal of Aging, 25*(2), 129–140.

Huston, T. L. (2009). What's love got to do with it? Why some marriages succeed and others fail. *Personal Relationships, 16*(3), 301–327. doi: 10.1111/j.1475-6811.2009.01225.x

Huxhold, O., Miche, M., & Schüz, B. (2014). Benefits of having friends in older ages: Differential effects of informal social activities on well-being in middle-aged and older adults. *The Journals of Gerontology: Series B: Psychological Sciences and Social Sciences, 69*(3), 366–375. doi: 10.1093/geronb/gbt029

Iacono, D., Zandi, P., Gross, M., Markesbery, W. R., Pletnikova, O., Rudow, G., & Troncoso, J. C. (2015). APOε2 and education in cognitively normal older subjects with high levels of AD pathology at autopsy: Findings from the Nun Study. *Oncotarget, 6*(16), 14082–14091. doi: 10.18632/oncotarget.4118

Ilies, R., Johnson, M. D., Judge, T. A., & Keeney, J. (2011). A within-individual study of interpersonal conflict as a work stressor: Dispositional and situational moderators. *Journal of Organizational Behavior, 32*(1), 44–64. doi: 10.1002/job.677

Imoscopi, A., Inelmen, E. M., Sergi, G., Miotto, F., & Manzato, E. (2012). Taste loss in the elderly: Epidemiology, causes and consequences. *Aging Clinical and Experimental Research, 24*(6), 570–579. doi: 10.3275/8520

Institute of Medicine. (2014). Dying in America: Improving quality and honoring individual preferences near the end of life. From http://www.nationalacademies.org/hmd/Reports/2014/Dying-In-America-Improving-Quality-and-Honoring-Individual-Preferences-Near-the-End-of-Life.aspx

Institute of Medicine Board on Health Sciences Policy Committee on the Public Health Dimensions of Cognitive Aging. (2015). *Cognitive aging: Progress in understanding and opportunities for action.* Washington, DC: National Academies Press.

Isaacowitz, D. M. (2012). Mood regulation in real time: Age differences in the role of looking. *Current Directions in Psychological Science, 21*(4), 237–242. doi: 10.1177/0963721412448651

Isaacowitz, D. M. (2014). Aging: Commentary. Change in perceptions of personality disorder in late life: The view from socioemotional aging. *Journal of Personality Disorders, 28*(1), 166–171. doi: 10.1521/pedi.2014.28.1.166

Isaacowitz, D. M., Livingstone, K. M., Richard, M., & Seif El-Nasr, M. (2018). Aging and attention to self-selected emotional content: A novel application of mobile eye tracking to the study of emotion regulation in adulthood and old age. *Psychology and Aging, 33*(2), 361–372. doi: 10.1037/pag0000231

Isaacowitz, D. M., Toner, K., & Neupert, S. D. (2009). Use of gaze for real-time mood regulation: Effects of age and attentional functioning. *Psychology and Aging, 24*(4), 989–994.

Isaacowitz, D. M., Wadlinger, H. A., Goren, D., & Wilson, H. R. (2006). Selective preference in visual fixation away from negative images in old age? An eye-tracking study. *Psychology and Aging, 21*(1), 40–48.

Islam, S., Muthumala, M., Matsuoka, H., Uehara, O., Kuramitsu, Y., Chiba, I., & Abiko, Y. (2019). How each component of betel quid is involved in oral carcinogenesis: Mutual interactions and synergistic effects with other carcinogens-a review article. *Current Oncology Reports, 21*(6), 53. doi: 10.1007/s11912-019-0800-8

Janse, E. (2009). Processing of fast speech by elderly listeners. *Journal of the Acoustical Society of America, 125*(4), 2361–2373. doi: 10.1121/1.3082117

Jansen, I. E., Savage, J. E., Watanabe, K., Bryois, J., Williams, D. M., Steinberg, S., … Posthuma, D. (2019). Genome-wide meta-analysis identifies new loci and functional pathways influencing Alzheimer's disease risk. *Nature Genetics, 51*(3), 404–413. doi: 10.1038/s41588-018-0311-9

Janson, C., Lindberg, E., Gislason, T., Elmasry, A., & Boman, G. (2001). Insomnia in men-A10-year prospective population based study. *Sleep, 24*(4), 425–430.

Jaques, E. (1965). Death and the mid-life crisis. *International Journal of Psychoanalysis, 46*, 502–514.

Jayarajan, J., & Radomski, S. B. (2013). Pharmacotherapy of overactive bladder in adults: A review of efficacy, tolerability, and quality of life. *Research and Reports in Urology, 6*, 1–16. doi: 10.2147/rru.s40034

Jimenez, D. E., Alegria, M., Chen, C. N., Chan, D., & Laderman, M. (2010). Prevalence of psychiatric illnesses in older ethnic minority adults. *Journal of the American Geriatrics Society, 58*(2), 256–264. doi: JGS2685 [pii] 10.1111/j.1532-5415.2009.02685.x

Jimenez, M. C., Manson, J. E., Cook, N. R., Kawachi, I., Wassertheil-Smoller, S., Haring, B., … Rexrode, K. M. (2019). Racial variation in stroke risk among women by stroke risk factors. *Stroke, 50*(4), 797–804. doi: 10.1161/strokeaha.117.017759

Jobe, T. H., & Harrow, M. (2010). Schizophrenia course, long-term outcome, recovery, and prognosis. *Current Directions in Psychological Science, 19*(4), 220–225. doi: 10.1177/0963721410378034

Johansson, H., Bertero, C., Berg, K., & Jonasson, L. L. (2019). To live a life with COPD—The consequences of symptom burden. *International Journal of Chronic and Obstructive Pulmonary Diseases, 14*, 905–909. doi: 10.2147/copd.s192280

Johnson, A. A., Akman, K., Calimport, S. R. G., Wuttke, D., Stolzing, A., & de Magalhães, J. P. (2012). The role of DNA methylation in aging, rejuvenation, and age-related disease. *Rejuvenation Research, 15*(5), 483–494. doi: 10.1089/rej.2012.1324

Jonas, J. B., Cheung, C. M. G., & Panda-Jonas, S. (2017). Updates on the epidemiology of age-related macular degeneration. *Asia-Pacific Journal of Ophthalmology, 6*(6), 493–497. doi: 10.22608/apo.2017251

Jones, K. M., Whitbourne, S., Whitbourne, S. B., & Skultety, K. M. (2009). Identity processes and memory controllability in middle and later adulthood. *Journal of Applied Gerontology, 28*(5), 582–599. doi: 10.1177/0733464808330823

Juhl, J., & Routledge, C. (2016). Putting the terror in terror management theory: Evidence that the awareness of death does cause anxiety and undermine psychological well-being. *Current Directions in Psychological Science, 25*(2), 99–103. doi: 10.1177/0963721415625218

Junco, R. (2012). Too much face and not enough books: The relationship between multiple indices of Facebook use and academic performance. *Computers in Human Behavior, 28*(1), 187–198. doi: 10.1016/j.chb.2011.08.026

Jung, S. H., Kwon, O. Y., Yi, C. H., Cho, S. H., Jeon, H. S., Weon, J. H., & Hwang, U. J. (2018). Predictors of dysfunction and health-related quality of life in the flexion pattern subgroup of patients with chronic lower back pain: The STROBE study. *Medicine, 97*(29), e11363. doi: 10.1097/md.0000000000011363

Kaiser, J., Allaire, B., Fein, P. M., Lu, D., Jarraya, M., Guermazi, A., … Morgan, E. F. (2018). Correspondence between bone mineral density and intervertebral disc degeneration across age and sex. *Archives of Osteoporosis, 13*(1), 123. doi: 10.1007/s11657-018-0538-1

Kalapatapu, R. K., Ventura, M. I., & Barnes, D. E. (2017). Lifetime alcohol use and cognitive performance in older adults.

Journal of Addictive Diseases, 36(1), 38–47. doi: 10.1080/10550887.2016.1245029

Kalmijn, M. (2003). Shared friendship networks and the life course: An analysis of survey data on married and cohabiting couples. *Social Networks, 25*(3), 231–249.

Kalmijn, M., & De Graaf, P. M. (2012). Life course changes of children and well-being of parents. *Journal of Marriage and the Family, 74*(2), 269–280. doi: 10.1111/j.1741-3737.2012.00961.x

Kamel, N. S., & Gammack, J. K. (2006). Insomnia in the elderly: Cause, approach, and treatment. *American Journal of Medicine, 119*(6), 463–469.

Kanagaratnam, L., Drame, M., Novella, J. L., Trenque, T., Joachim, C., Nazeyrollas, P., … Mahmoudi, R. (2017). Risk factors for adverse drug reactions in older subjects hospitalized in a dedicated dementia Unit. *American Journal of Geriatric Psychiatry, 25*(3), 290–296. doi: 10.1016/j.jagp.2016.07.002

Kang, S., Aldwin, C. M., Choun, S., & Spiro, A., 3rd. (2016). A life-span perspective on combat exposure and PTSD symptoms in later life: Findings from the VA Normative Aging Study. *Gerontologist, 56*(1), 22–32. doi: 10.1093/geront/gnv120

Karam, Z., & Tuazon, J. (2013). Anatomic and physiologic changes of the aging kidney. *Clinics in Geriatric Medicine, 29*(3), 555–564. doi: 10.1016/j.cger.2013.05.006

Karel, M. J., Knight, B. G., Duffy, M., Hinrichsen, G. A., & Zeiss, A. M. (2010). Attitude, knowledge, and skill competencies for practice in professional geropsychology: Implications for training and building a geropsychology workforce. *Training and Education in Professional Psychology, 4*(2), 75–84. doi: 10.1037/a0018372

Karney, B., & Bradbury, T. (1997). Neuroticism, marital interaction, and the trajectory of marital satisfaction. *Journal of Personality and Social Psychology, 72,* 1075–1092.

Kelley, N. J., & Schmeichel, B. J. (2015). Mortality salience increases personal optimism among individuals higher in trait self-control. *Motivation and Emotion, 39*(6), 926–931. doi: 10.1007/s11031-015-9504-z

Kelly, B., Handley, T., Kissane, D., Vamos, M., & Attia, J. (2019). "An indelible mark" The response to participation in euthanasia and physician-assisted suicide among doctors: A review of research findings. *Palliative and Supportive Care,* 1–7. doi: 10.1017/s1478951519000518

Kempen, R., Roewekaemper, J., Hattrup, K., & Mueller, K. (2019). Daily affective events and mood as antecedents of life domain conflict and enrichment: A weekly diary study. *International Journal of Stress Management, 26*(2), 107–119. doi: 10.1037/str0000104

Kemper, S., Greiner, L. H., Marquis, J. G., Prenovost, K., & Mitzner, T. L. (2001). Language decline across the life span: Findings from the Nun Study. *Psychology and Aging, 16*(2), 227–239.

Kemper, S., Marquis, J., & Thompson, M. (2001). Longitudinal change in language production: Effects of aging and dementia on grammatical complexity and propositional content. *Psychology and Aging, 16*(4), 600–614.

Kennedy, C., Brooks-Young, P., Brunton Gray, C., Larkin, P., Connolly, M., Wilde-Larsson, B., … Chater, S. (2014).

Diagnosing dying: An integrative literature review. *BMJ Supportive and Palliative Care, 4*(3), 263–270. doi: 10.1136/bmjspcare-2013-000621

Kessel, L., Jorgensen, T., Glumer, C., & Larsen, M. (2006). Early lens aging is accelerated in subjects with a high risk of ischemic heart disease: An epidemiologic study. *BMC Ophthalmology, 6,* 16.

Kessler, R. C., Chiu, W. T., Jin, R., Ruscio, A. M., Shear, K., & Walters, E. E. (2006). The epidemiology of panic attacks, panic disorder, and agoraphobia in the National Comorbidity Survey Replication. *Archives of General Psychiatry, 63*(4), 415–424. doi: 63/4/415 [pii] 10.1001/archpsyc.63.4.415

Khaddouma, A., Norona, J. C., & Whitton, S. W. (2015). Individual, couple, and contextual factors associated with same-sex relationship instability. *Couple and Family Psychology: Research and Practice, 4*(2), 106–125. doi: 10.1037/cfp0000043

Kidd, T., Hamer, M., & Steptoe, A. (2013). Adult attachment style and cortisol responses across the day in older adults. *Psychophysiology, 50*(9), 841–847. doi: 10.1111/psyp.12075

Kieffer, K. M., Schinka, J. A., & Curtiss, G. (2004). Person-environment congruence and personality domains in the prediction of job performance and work quality. *Journal of Counseling Psychology, 51*(2), 168–177.

Kilb, A., & Naveh-Benjamin, M. (2015). The effects of divided attention on long-term memory and working memory in younger and older adults: Assessment of the reduced attentional resources hypothesis. In R. H. Logie & R. G. Morris (Eds.), *Working memory and ageing* (pp. 48–78). New York: Psychology Press.

Kim, H. (2012). A dual-subsystem model of the brain's default network: Self-referential processing, memory retrieval processes, and autobiographical memory retrieval. *Neuroimage, 61*(4), 966–977. doi: 10.1016/j.neuroimage.2012.03.025

Kim, J. M., Stewart, R., Kim, S. W., Yang, S. J., Shin, I. S., & Yoon, J. S. (2009). Insomnia, depression, and physical disorders in late life: A 2-year longitudinal community study in Koreans. *Sleep, 32*(9), 1221–1228.

Kim, S., & Hasher, L. (2005). The attraction effect in decision making: Superior performance by older adults. *The Quarterly Journal of Experimental Psychology A: Human Experimental Psychology, 58A*(1), 120–133. doi: 10.1080/02724980443000160

Kimmel, D. C., Hinrichs, K. L. M., & Fisher, L. D. (2015). Understanding lesbian, gay, bisexual, and transgender older adults. In P. A. Lichtenberg, B. T. Mast, B. D. Carpenter, J. Loebach Wetherell, P. A. Lichtenberg, B. T. Mast, B. D. Carpenter & J. Loebach Wetherell (Eds.), *APA handbook of clinical geropsychology. History and status of the field and perspectives on aging* (Vol. 1, pp. 459–472). Washington, DC: American Psychological Association.

Kinsey, D., Pretorius, S., Glover, L., & Alexander, T. (2016). The psychological impact of overactive bladder: A systematic review. *Journal of Health Psychology, 21*(1), 69–81. doi: 10.1177/1359105314522084

Kirchner, C., Bock, O. L., & Völker, I. (2017). The effects of priming with age stereotypes on a PC-based mail-sorting task. *Ergonomics*, *60*(4), 512–517. doi: 10.1080/00140139.2016.1182219

Kirkham, J. G., Choi, N., & Seitz, D. P. (2016). Meta-analysis of problem solving therapy for the treatment of major depressive disorder in older adults. *International Journal of Geriatric Psychiatry*, *31*(5), 526–535. doi: 10.1002/gps.4358

Kirkwood, T. B. L. (2015). Deciphering death: A commentary on Gompertz (1825) 'On the nature of the function expressive of the law of human mortality, and on a new mode of determining the value of life contingencies'. *Philosophical Transactions of the Royal Society B: Biological Sciences*, *370*, 20140379. doi: 10.1098/rstb.2014.0379

Kishimoto, H., Ohara, T., Hata, J., Ninomiya, T., Yoshida, D., Mukai, N., … Kiyohara, Y. (2016). The long-term association between physical activity and risk of dementia in the community: The Hisayama Study. *European Journal of Epidemiology*, *31*(3), 267–274. doi: 10.1007/s10654-016-0125-y

Kite, M. E., & Wagner, L. S. (2002). Attitudes toward older adults. In T. D. Nelson (Ed.), *Ageism: Stereotyping and prejudice against older persons* (pp. 129–161). Cambridge, MA: The MIT Press.

Kiviniemi, M., & Hay, J. (2012). Awareness of the 2009 US Preventive Services Task Force recommended changes in mammography screening guidelines, accuracy of awareness, sources of knowledge about recommendations, and attitudes about updated screening guidelines in women ages 40–49 and 50+. *BMC Public Health*, *12*, 899.

Kliegel, M., Ballhausen, N., Hering, A., Ihle, A., Schnitzspahn, K. M., & Zuber, S. (2016). Prospective memory in older adults: Where we are now and what is next. *Gerontology*, *62*(4), 459–466. doi: 10.1159/000443698

Kjorholt, K. E., Kristensen, N. R., Prieto-Alhambra, D., Johnsen, S. P., & Pedersen, A. B. (2019). Increased risk of mortality after postoperative infection in hip fracture patients. *Bone*. doi: 10.1016/j.bone.2019.07.023

Klainin-Yobas, P., Oo, W. N., Suzanne Yew, P. Y., & Lau, Y. (2015). Effects of relaxation interventions on depression and anxiety among older adults: A systematic review. *Aging and Mental Health*, *19*(12), 1043–1055. doi: 10.1080/13607863.2014.997191

Klauer, S. G., Ehsani, J. P., McGehee, D. V., & Manser, M. (2015). The effect of secondary task engagement on adolescents' driving performance and crash risk. *Journal of Adolescent Health*, *57*(Suppl 1), S36–43. doi: 10.1016/j.jadohealth.2015.03.014

Klemmack, D. L., Roff, L. L., Parker, M. W., Koenig, H. G., Sawyer, P., & Allman, R. M. (2007). A cluster analysis typology of religiousness/spirituality among older adults. *Research on Aging*, *29*(2), 163–183.

Klenfeldt, I. F., Karlsson, B., Sigstrom, R., Backman, K., Waern, M., Ostling, S., … Skoog, I. (2014). Prevalence of obsessive–compulsive disorder in relation to depression and cognition in an elderly population. *American Journal of Geriatric Psychiatry*, *22*(3), 301–308. doi: 10.1016/j.jagp.2012.09.004

Klerman, E. B., Duffy, J. F., Dijk, D. J., & Czeisler, C. A. (2001). Circadian phase resetting in older people by ocular bright light exposure. *Journal of Investigative Medicine*, *49*(1), 30–40.

Knight, B. G., & Kellough, J. (2013). Psychotherapy with older adults within a family context. In G. Stricker, T. A. Widiger & I. B. Weiner (Eds.), *Handbook of psychology.: Clinical psychology* (2nd ed., Vol. 8, pp. 474–488). Hoboken, NJ: John Wiley & Sons Inc.

Knoester, C., & Eggebeen, D. J. (2006). The effects of the transition to parenthood and subsequent children on men's well-being and social participation. *Journal of Family Issues*, *27*(11), 1532–1560.

Kochanek, K. D., Murphy, S. L., Xu, Z., & Arias, E. (2019). Deaths: Final data for 2017 *National Vital Statistics Reports* (Vol. 68, No. 9). Hyattsville, MD: National Center for Health Statistics.

Kohen, S. A., & Nair, R. (2019). Improving hospital-based communication and decision-making about scope of treatment using a standard documentation tool. *BMJ Open Quality*, *8*(2), e000396. doi: 10.1136/bmjoq-2018-000396

Kok, R. M., & Reynolds, C. F., 3rd. (2017). Management of depression in older adults: A review. *Journal of the American Medical Association*, *317*(20), 2114–2122. doi: 10.1001/jama.2017.5706

Kokkeler, K. J. E., van den Berg, K. S., Comijs, H. C., Oude Voshaar, R. C., & Marijnissen, R. M. (2019). Sarcopenic obesity predicts nonremission of late-life depression. *International Journal of Geriatric Psychiatry*. doi: 10.1002/gps.5121

König, K., Raue, M., D'Ambrosio, L. A., & Coughlin, J. F. (2019). Physical and emotional support of the neighborhood for older adults: A comparison of the United States and Germany. *Journal of Environmental Psychology*, *62*, 84–94. doi: 10.1016/j.jenvp.2019.01.008

Kononova, A., Li, L., Kamp, K., Bowen, M., Rikard, R. V., Cotten, S., & Peng, W. (2019). The use of wearable activity trackers among older adults: Focus group study of tracker perceptions, motivators, and barriers in the maintenance stage of behavior change. *JMIR Mhealth Uhealth*, *7*(4), e9832. doi: 10.2196/mhealth.9832

Koppel, S., Kuo, J., Berecki-Gisolf, J., Boag, R., Hue, Y. X., & Charlton, J. L. (2015). Examining physiological responses across different driving maneuvers during an on-road driving task: A pilot study comparing older and younger drivers. *Traffic and Injury Prevention*, *16*, 225–233. doi: 10.1080/15389588.2014.933478

Koropeckyj-Cox, T. (2002). Beyond parental status: Psychological well-being in middle and old age. *Journal of Marriage and the Family*, *64*, 957–971.

Kousaie, S., & Phillips, N. A. (2012). Ageing and bilingualism: Absence of a "bilingual advantage" in Stroop interference in a nonimmigrant sample. *The Quarterly Journal of Experimental Psychology*, *65*(2), 356–369. doi: 10.1080/17470218.2011.604788

Kouvonen, A., Stafford, M., De Vogli, R., Shipley, M. J., Marmot, M. G., Cox, T., … Kivimäki, M. (2011). Negative aspects of close relationships as a predictor of increased body mass index and waist circumference: The Whitehall II Study. *American Journal of Public Health*, *101*(8), 1474–1480. doi: 10.2105/AJPH.2010.300115

Kramer, A. F., Boot, W. R., McCarley, J. S., Peterson, M. S., Colcombe, A., & Scialfa, C. T. (2006). Aging, memory and visual search. *Acta Psychologica, 122*(3), 288–304.

Krasnova, A., Eaton, W. W., & Samuels, J. F. (2019). Antisocial personality and risks of cause-specific mortality: Results from the Epidemiologic Catchment Area study with 27 years of follow-up. *Social Psychiatry and Psychiatric Epidemiology, 54*(5), 617–625. doi: 10.1007/s00127-018-1628-5

Kraus, V. B., Sprow, K., Powell, K. E., Buchner, D., Bloodgood, B., Piercy, K., … Kraus, W. E. (2019). Effects of physical activity in knee and hip osteoarthritis: A systematic umbrella review. *Medicine & Science in Sports & Exercise, 51*(6), 1324–1339. doi: 10.1249/mss.0000000000001944

Kreider, R. M., & Gurrentz, B. T. (2019). *Changes to the household relationship data in the Current Population Survey: SESHD Working Paper #2019-13 CBDRB-FY19-ROSS-B0066.* Washington, DC: U.S. Bureau of the Census.

Krendl, A. C., Ambady, N., & Kensinger, E. A. (2015). The dissociable effects of stereotype threat on older adults' memory encoding and retrieval. *Journal of Applied Research in Memory and Cognition, 4*(2), 103–109. doi: 10.1016/j.jarmac.2015.02.001

Kristiansen, C. B., Kjær, J. N., Hjorth, P., Andersen, K., & Prina, A. M. (2019a). The association of time since spousal loss and depression in widowhood: A systematic review and meta-analysis. *Social Psychiatry and Psychiatric Epidemiology: The International Journal for Research in Social and Genetic Epidemiology and Mental Health Services.* doi: 10.1007/s00127-019-01680-3

Kristiansen, C. B., Kjær, J. N., Hjorth, P., Andersen, K., & Prina, A. M. (2019b). Prevalence of common mental disorders in widowhood: A systematic review and meta-analysis. *Journal of Affective Disorders, 245*, 1016–1023. doi: 10.1016/j.jad.2018.11.088

Kroger, J., & Marcia, J. E. (2011). The identity statuses: Origins, meanings, and interpretations. In S. J. Schwartz, K. Luyckx & V. L. Vignoles (Eds.), *Handbook of identity theory and research* (Vols. 1 and 2, pp. 31–53). New York: Springer Science + Business Media.

Kryger, A. I., & Andersen, J. L. (2007). Resistance training in the oldest old: Consequences for muscle strength, fiber types, fiber size, and MHC isoforms. *Scandinavian Journal of Medicine and Science in Sports, 17*(4), 422–430. doi: SMS575 [pii] 10.1111/j.1600-0838.2006.00575.x

Kübler-Ross, E. (1969). *On death and dying.* New York: MacMillan.

Kubo, N., Kato, A., & Nakamura, K. (2006). Deterioration of planning ability with age in Japanese monkeys (Macaca fuscata). *Journal of Comparative Psychology, 120*(4), 449–455.

Kubzansky, L. D., Cole, S. R., Kawachi, I., Vokonas, P., & Sparrow, D. (2006). Shared and unique contributions of anger, anxiety, and depression to coronary heart disease: A prospective study in the Normative Aging Study. *Annals of Behavioral Medicine, 31*(1), 21–29.

Kuerbis, A., & Sacco, P. (2012). The impact of retirement on the drinking patterns of older adults: A review. *Addictive Behaviors, 37*(5), 587–595. doi: 10.1016/j.addbeh.2012.01.022

Kuhlmann, B. G., & Boywitt, C. D. (2016). Aging, source memory, and the experience of "remembering". *Neuropsychology and Developmental Cognition B: Aging Neuropsychology and Cognition, 23*(4), 477–498. doi: 10.1080/13825585.2015.1120270

Kukat, A., & Trifunovic, A. (2009). Somatic mtDNA mutations and aging – facts and fancies. *Experimental Gerontology, 44*(1–2), 101–105. doi: S0531-5565(08)00154-X [pii] 10.1016/j.exger.2008.05.006

Kunar, M. A., Cole, L., Cox, A., & Ocampo, J. (2018). It is not good to talk: Conversation has a fixed interference cost on attention regardless of difficulty. *Cognitive Research: Principles and Applications, 3*, 33. doi: 10.1186/s41235-018-0124-5

Kundrat, A. L., & Nussbaum, J. F. (2003). The impact of invisible illness on identity and contextual age across the life span. *Health Communication, 15*(3), 331–347. doi: 10.1207/s15327027hc1503_5

Kunze, F., & Menges, J. I. (2017). Younger supervisors, older subordinates: An organizational-level study of age differences, emotions, and performance. *Journal of Organizational Behavior, 38*(4), 461–486. doi: 10.1002/job.2129

Kunzmann, U., Nowak, J., Thomas, S., & Nestler, S. (2018). Value relativism and perspective taking are two distinct facets of wisdom-related knowledge. *Journal of Gerontology Series B: Psychological Science and Social Science, 73*(8), 1384–1392. doi: 10.1093/geronb/gbx136

Laaksonen, S. (2018). A research note: Happiness by age is more complex than U-shaped. *Journal of Happiness Studies: An Interdisciplinary Forum on Subjective Well-Being, 19*(2), 471–482. doi: 10.1007/s10902-016-9830-1

Lachman, M. E. (2004). Development in midlife. *Annual Review of Psychology, 55*, 305–331.

Lachman, M. E. (2006). Perceived control over aging-related declines. *Current Directions in Psychological Science, 15*, 282–286.

Lachman, M. E., & Andreoletti, C. (2006). Strategy use mediates the relationship between control beliefs and memory performance for middle-aged and older adults. *Journals of Gerontology Series B: Psychological Sciences and Social Sciences, 61*(2), P88–94.

Lachman, M. E., Rosnick, C. B., Rocke, C., Bosworth, H. B., & Hertzog, C. (2009). The rise and fall of control beliefs and life satisfaction in adulthood: Trajectories of stability and change over ten years. *Aging and cognition: Research methodologies and empirical advances* (pp. 143–160). Washington, DC: American Psychological Association.

Lachman, M. E., Teshale, S., & Agrigoroaei, S. (2015). Midlife as a pivotal period in the life course: Balancing growth and decline at the crossroads of youth and old age. *International Journal of Behavioral Development, 39*(1), 20–31. doi: 10.1177/0165025414533223

Lamina, S., Okoye, C. G., & Dagogo, T. T. (2009). Therapeutic effect of an interval exercise training program in the management of erectile dysfunction in hypertensive patients. *Journal of Clinical Hypertension, 11*(3), 125–129. doi: JCH086 [pii] 10.1111/j.1751-7176.2009.00086.x

Lampi, K. J., Wilmarth, P. A., Murray, M. R., & David, L. L. (2014). Lens beta-crystallins: The role of deamidation and related modifications in aging and cataract. *Progress in Biophysics and Molecular Biology, 115*(1), 21–31. doi: 10.1016/j.pbiomolbio.2014.02.004

Lang, F. R., & Carstensen, L. L. (2002). Time counts: Future time perspective, goals, and social relationships. *Psychology and Aging, 17*, 125–139.

Lang, T., Streeper, T., Cawthon, P., Baldwin, K., Taaffe, D. R., & Harris, T. B. (2009). Sarcopenia: Etiology, clinical consequences, intervention, and assessment. *Osteoporosis International.* doi: 10.1007/s00198-009-1059-y

Lapalme, M.-È., Tremblay, M., & Simard, G. (2009). The relationship between career plateauing, employee commitment and psychological distress: The role of organizational and supervisor support. *The International Journal of Human Resource Management, 20*(5), 1132–1145. doi: 10.1080/09585190902850323

Larson, E. B., Shadlen, M. F., Wang, L., McCormick, W. C., Bowen, J. D., Teri, L., & Kukull, W. A. (2004). Survival after initial diagnosis of Alzheimer disease. *Annals of Internal Medicine, 140*(7), 501–509.

Lavender, A. P., & Nosaka, K. (2007). Fluctuations of isometric force after eccentric exercise of the elbow flexors of young, middle-aged, and old men. *European Journal of Applied Physiology, 100*(2), 161–167. doi: 10.1007/s00421-007-0418-7

Lawton, M. P., & Brody, E. M. (1969). Assessment of older people: Self-maintaining and instrumental activities of daily living. *The Gerontologist, 9*(3, Pt 1), 179–186. doi: 10.1093/geront/9.3_Part_1.179

Lawton, M. P., & Nahemow, L. (1973). Ecology and the aging process. In C. Eisdorfer & M. P. Lawton (Eds.), *The psychology of adult development and aging*. Washington, DC: American Psychological Association.

Leboeuf-Yde, C., Nielsen, J., Kyvik, K. O., Fejer, R., & Hartvigsen, J. (2009). Pain in the lumbar, thoracic or cervical regions: Do age and gender matter? A population-based study of 34,902 Danish twins 20-71 years of age. *BMC Musculoskeletal Disorders, 10*, 39. doi: 1471–2474-10-39 [pii] 10.1186/1471-2474-10-39

Lee, R. K., Chughtai, B., Te, A. E., & Kaplan, S. A. (2012). Sexual function in men with metabolic syndrome. *Urologic Clinics of North America, 39*(1), 53–62. doi: 10.1016/j.ucl.2011.09.008

Lehman, H. C. (1953). *Age and achievement*. Princeton, NJ: Princeton University Press.

Lentz, E., & Allen, T. D. (2009). The role of mentoring others in the career plateauing phenomenon. *Group and Organization Management, 34*(3), 358–384.

Leonardelli, G. J., Hermann, A. D., Lynch, M. E., & Arkin, R. M. (2003). The shape of self-evaluation: Implicit theories of intelligence and judgments of intellectual ability. *Journal of Research in Personality, 37*(3), 141–168. doi: https://doi.org/10.1016/S0092-6566(02)00565-2

Leopold, T., & Skopek, J. (2015). Convergence or continuity? The gender gap in household labor after retirement. *Journal of Marriage and the Family, 77*(4), 819–832. doi: 10.1111/jomf.12199

Lerner, R. M. (1995). Developing individuals within changing contexts: Implications of developmental contextualism for human development, research, policy, and programs. In T. J. Kindermann & J. Valsiner (Eds.), *Development of person-context relations* (pp. 13–37). Hillsdale, NJ: Lawrence Erlbaum Associates.

Lerner, R. M. (1996). Relative plasticity, integration, temporality, and diversity in human development: A developmental contextual perspective about theory, process, and method. *Developmental Psychology, 32*, 781–786.

Levinson, D. J., Darrow, C. N., Klein, E. B., Levinson, M. H., & McKee, B. (1978). *The seasons of a man's life*. New York: Alfred A. Knopf.

Levinson, D. J., & Levinson, J. D. (1996). *The seasons of a woman's life*. New York: Alfred A. Knopf.

Levy, B. R., Slade, M. D., Kunkel, S. R., & Kasl, S. V. (2002). Longevity increased by positive self-perceptions of aging. *Journal of Personality and Social Psychology, 83*(2), 261–270.

Lewis, J. M., & Kreider, R. M. (2015). *Remarriage in the United States*. Washington, DC: U.S. Bureau of the Census.

Li, J., Zhang, C.-X., Liu, Y.-M., Chen, K.-L., & Chen, G. (2017). A comparative study of anti-aging properties and mechanism: Resveratrol and caloric restriction. *Oncotarget, 8*(39), 65717–65729. doi: 10.18632/oncotarget.20084

Li, S., Stampfer, M. J., Williams, D. R., & VanderWeele, T. J. (2016). Association of religious service attendance with mortality among women. *Journal of the American Medical Association Internal Medicine, 176*(6), 777–785. doi: 10.1001/jamainternmed.2016.1615

Lichters, M., Bengart, P., Sarstedt, M., & Vogt, B. (2017). What really matters in attraction effect research: When choices have economic consequences. *Marketing Letters, 28*(1), 127–138. doi: 10.1007/s11002-015-9394-6

Lindau, S. T., & Gavrilova, N. (2010). Sex, health, and years of sexually active life gained due to good health: Evidence from two US population based cross sectional surveys of ageing. *British Medical Journal, 340*(7746).

Lindauer, M. S. (1993). The old-age style and its artists. *Empirical Studies of the Arts, 11*(2), 135–146. doi: 10.2190/KMH5-UFVJ-8QRC-KLTQ

Lindemann, D. J. (2017). Doing and undoing gender in commuter marriages. *Sex Roles: A Journal of Research.* doi: 10.1007/s11199-017-0852-x

Lipton, S. A. (2006). Paradigm shift in neuroprotection by NMDA receptor blockade: Memantine and beyond. *Nature Reviews: Drug Discovery, 5*(2), 160–170.

Liu-Ambrose, T., Nagamatsu, L. S., Graf, P., Beattie, B. L., Ashe, M. C., & Handy, T. C. (2010). Resistance training and executive functions: A 12-month randomized controlled trial. *Archives of Internal Medicine, 170*(2), 170–178. doi: 170/2/170 [pii] 10.1001/archinternmed.2009.494

Liu, B., Luo, Z., Pinto, J. M., Shiroma, E. J., Tranah, G. J., Wirdefeldt, K., … Chen, H. (2019). Relationship between poor olfaction and mortality among community-dwelling older adults: A Cohort study. *Annals of Internal Medicine*. doi: 10.7326/m18-0775

Liu, C. Y., Zhou, H. D., Xu, Z. Q., Zhang, W. W., Li, X. Y., & Zhao, J. (2009). Metabolic syndrome and cognitive impairment amongst elderly people in Chinese population: A cross-sectional study. *European Journal of Neurology*, 16(9), 1022–1027. doi: ENE2640 [pii] 10.1111/j.1468-1331.2009.02640.x

Liu, H. Y., Yang, C. T., Tseng, M. Y., Chen, C. Y., Wu, C. C., Cheng, H. S., … Shyu, Y. L. (2018). Trajectories in postoperative recovery of elderly hip-fracture patients at risk for depression: A follow-up study. *Rehabilitation Psychology*, 63(3), 438–446. doi: 10.1037/rep0000130

Liu, P. Y., Beilin, J., Meier, C., Nguyen, T. V., Center, J. R., Leedman, P. J., … Handelsman, D. J. (2007). Age-related changes in serum testosterone and sex hormone binding globulin in Australian men: Longitudinal analyses of two geographically separate regional cohorts. *Journal of Clinical and Endocrinological Metabolism*, 92(9), 3599–3603. doi: 10.1210/jc.2007-0862

Livingstone, K. M., & Isaacowitz, D. M. (2019). Age similarities and differences in spontaneous use of emotion regulation tactics across five laboratory tasks. *Journal of Experimental Psychology General*. doi: 10.1037/xge0000556

Lockhart, S. N., Mayda, A. B. V., Roach, A. E., Fletcher, E., Carmichael, O., Maillard, P., … DeCarli, C. (2012). Episodic memory function is associated with multiple measures of white matter integrity in cognitive aging. *Frontiers in Human Neuroscience*, 6. doi: 10.3389/fnhum.2012.00056

Lodi-Smith, J., Jackson, J., Bogg, T., Walton, K., Wood, D., Harms, P., & Roberts, B. W. (2010). Mechanisms of health: Education and health-related behaviours partially mediate the relationship between conscientiousness and self-reported physical health. *Psychology and Health*, 25(3), 305–319. doi: 10.1080/08870440902736964

Lodi-Smith, J., Ponterio, E. J., Poulin, M. J., Newton, N. J., Baranski, E., & Whitbourne, S. K. (In preparation). Development of generativity and well-being into later life.

Lohr, J. B., Palmer, B. W., Eidt, C. A., Aailaboyina, S., Mausbach, B. T., Wolkowitz, O. M., … Jeste, D. V. (2015). Is post-traumatic stress disorder associated with premature senescence? A review of the literature. *American Journal of Geriatric Psychiatry*, 23(7), 709–725. doi: 10.1016/j.jagp.2015.04.001

Lombardi, G., Tauchmanova, L., Di Somma, C., Musella, T., Rota, F., Savanelli, M. C., & Colao, A. (2005). Somatopause: Dismetabolic and bone effects. *Journal of Endocrinological Investigation*, 28(Suppl 10), 36–42.

Looker, A. C., Sarafrazi Isfahani, N., Fan, B., & Shepherd, J. A. (2017). Trends in osteoporosis and low bone mass in older US adults, 2005–2006 through 2013–2014. *Osteoporosis International*, 28(6), 1979–1988. doi: 10.1007/s00198-017-3996-1

Lu, B., Qian, Z., Cunningham, A., & Li, C.-L. (2012). Estimating the effect of premarital cohabitation on timing of marital disruption: Using propensity score matching in event history analysis. *Sociological Methods & Research*, 41(3), 440–466. doi: 10.1177/0049124112452395

Lunney, J. R., Lynn, J., Foley, D. J., Lipson, S., & Guralnik, J. M. (2003). Patterns of functional decline at the end of life. *Journal of the American Medical Association*, 289(18), 2387–2392. doi: 10.1001/jama.289.18.2387

Luo, L., Craik, F. I. M., Moreno, S., & Bialystok, E. (2012). Bilingualism interacts with domain in a working memory task: Evidence from aging. *Psychology and Aging*. doi: 10.1037/a0030875

Lupien, S. J., McEwen, B. S., Gunnar, M. R., & Heim, C. (2009). Effects of stress throughout the lifespan on the brain, behaviour and cognition. *Nature Reviews Neuroscience*, 10(6), 434–445. doi: nrn2639 [pii] 10.1038/nrn2639

Luszcz, M. A., Anstey, K. J., & Ghisletta, P. (2015). Subjective beliefs, memory and functional health: Change and associations over 12 years in the Australian Longitudinal Study of Ageing. *Gerontology*, 61(3), 241–250. doi: 10.1159/000369800

Lynn, J., Teno, J. M., Phillips, R. S., Wu, A. W., Desbiens, N., Harrold, J., … Connors, A. F., Jr. (1997). Perceptions by family members of the dying experience of older and seriously ill patients. SUPPORT Investigators. Study to Understand Prognoses and Preferences for Outcomes and Risks of Treatments. *Annals of Internal Medicine*, 126(2), 97–106.

Lyons, H. Z., & O'Brien, K. M. (2006). The role of person-environment fit in the job satisfaction and tenure intentions of African American employees. *Journal of Counseling Psychology*, 53(4), 387–396.

Lyssens-Danneboom, V., & Mortelmans, D. (2015). Living apart together: Longing for the couple, enjoying being single. *Family Science*, 6(1), 11–22. doi: 10.1080/19424620.2015.1009932

Ma, H., Lee, Y., Hayama, T., Van Dyken, C., Marti-Gutierrez, N., Li, Y., … Mitalipov, S. (2018). Germline and somatic mtDNA mutations in mouse aging. *PLoS ONE*, 13(7), e0201304. doi: 10.1371/journal.pone.0201304

Maccallum, F., Galatzer-Levy, I. R., & Bonanno, G. A. (2015). Trajectories of depression following spousal and child bereavement: A comparison of the heterogeneity in outcomes. *Journal of Psychiatric Research*, 69, 72–79. doi: 10.1016/j.jpsychires.2015.07.017

Maddodi, N., Jayanthy, A., & Setaluri, V. (2012). Shining light on skin pigmentation: The darker and the brighter side of effects of UV radiation. *Photochemistry and Photobiology*, 88(5), 1075–1082. doi: 10.1111/j.1751-1097.2012.01138.x

Magnusson, D. (Ed.). (1996). *The lifespan development of individuals: Behavioral, neurobiological, and psychosocial perspectives: A synthesis*. New York: Cambridge University Press.

Majer, I. M., Nusselder, W. J., Mackenbach, J. P., & Kunst, A. E. (2011). Socioeconomic inequalities in life and health expectancies around official retirement age in 10 Western-European countries. *Journal of Epidemiological and Community Health*, 65(11), 972–979. doi: 10.1136/jech.2010.111492

Malakou, E., Linardakis, M., Armstrong, M. E. G., Zannidi, D., Foster, C., Johnson, L., & Papadaki, A. (2018). The combined effect of promoting the Mediterranean Diet and physical activity on metabolic risk factors in adults: A systematic review and meta-analysis of randomised controlled trials. *Nutrients, 10*(11). doi: 10.3390/nu10111577

Malyutina, S., Laurinavichyute, A., Terekhina, M., & Lapin, Y. (2018). No evidence for strategic nature of age-related slowing in sentence processing. *Psychology and Aging, 33*(7), 1045–1059. doi: 10.1037/pag0000302

Manenti, R., Cotelli, M., & Miniussi, C. (2011). Successful physiological aging and episodic memory: A brain stimulation study. *Brain and Behavior Research, 216*(1), 153–158. doi: 10.1016/j.bbr.2010.07.027

Marcia, J. E. (1966). Development and validation of ego-identity status. *Journal of Personality and Social Psychology, 3*, 551–558.

Markland, A. D., Richter, H. E., Burgio, K. L., Bragg, C., Hernandez, A. L., & Subak, L. L. (2009). Fecal incontinence in obese women with urinary incontinence: Prevalence and role of dietary fiber intake. *American Journal of Obstetrics and Gynecology, 200*(5), 566 e561–566. doi: S0002-9378(08)02238-2 [pii] 10.1016/j.ajog.2008.11.019

Markus, H., & Nurius, P. (1986). Possible selves. *American Psychologist, 41*, 954–969.

Marmot, M. G., Shipley, M. J., Hemingway, H., Head, J., & Brunner, E. J. (2008). Biological and behavioural explanations of social inequalities in coronary heart disease: The Whitehall II study. *Diabetologia, 51*(11), 1980–1988. doi: 10.1007/s00125-008-1144-3

Marshall, V. W. (1980). *Last chapters: A sociology of aging and dying.* Monterey, CA: Brooks-Cole.

Marsiglio, W., Amato, P., Day, R. D., & Lamb, M. E. (2002). Scholarship on fatherhood in the 1990s and beyond. *Journal of Marriage and the Family, 62*, 1173–1191.

Marsiske, M., & Margrett, J. A. (2006). Everyday problem solving and decision making. In J. E. Birren & K. W. Schaire (Eds.), *Handbook of the psychology of aging* (pp. 315–342). London: Elsevier.

Marson, S. M., & Powell, R. M. (2014). Goffman and the infantilization of elderly persons: A theory in development. *Journal of Sociology and Social Welfare, 41*(4), 143–158.

Martin-Joy, J. S., Malone, J. C., Cui, X. J., Johansen, P. O., Hill, K. P., Rahman, M. O., ... Vaillant, G. E. (2017). Development of adaptive coping from mid to late life: A 70-year longitudinal study of defense maturity and its psychosocial correlates. *Journal of Nervous and Mental Disease, 205*(9), 685–691. doi: 10.1097/nmd.0000000000000711

Martin, C. O., Pontbriand-Drolet, S., Daoust, V., Yamga, E., Amiri, M., Hubner, L. C., & Ska, B. (2018). Narrative discourse in young and older adults: Behavioral and NIRS analyses. *Frontiers in Aging Neuroscience, 10*, 69. doi: 10.3389/fnagi.2018.00069

Martinson, M., & Berridge, C. (2015). Successful aging and its discontents: A systematic review of the social gerontology literature. *The Gerontologist, 55*(1), 58–69. doi: 10.1093/geront/gnu037

Masayesva, B. G., Mambo, E., Taylor, R. J., Goloubeva, O. G., Zhou, S., Cohen, Y., ... Califano, J. (2006). Mitochondrial DNA content increase in response to cigarette smoking. *Cancer Epidemiology Biomarkers and Prevention, 15*(1), 19–24.

Masuda, A. D., McNall, L. A., Allen, T. D., & Nicklin, J. M. (2012). Examining the constructs of work-to-family enrichment and positive spillover. *Journal of Vocational Behavior, 80*(1), 197–210. doi: 10.1016/j.jvb.2011.06.002

Matsuba, M. K., Pratt, M. W., Norris, J. E., Mohle, E., Alisat, S., & McAdams, D. P. (2012). Environmentalism as a context for expressing identity and generativity: Patterns among activists and uninvolved youth and midlife adults. *Journal of Personality, 80*(4), 1091–1115. doi: 10.1111/j.1467-6494.2012.00765.x

Matta Mello Portugal, E., Cevada, T., Sobral Monteiro-Junior, R., Teixeira Guimaraes, T., da Cruz Rubini, E., Lattari, E., ... Camaz Deslandes, A. (2013). Neuroscience of exercise: From neurobiology mechanisms to mental health. *Neuropsychobiology, 68*(1), 1–14. doi: 10.1159/000350946

Matthews, B., & Minton, J. (2018). Rethinking one of criminology's 'brute facts': The age-crime curve and the crime drop in Scotland. *European Journal of Criminology, 15*(3), 296–320. doi: 10.1177/1477370817731706

Mayer, P., Guldenpfennig, F., & Panek, P. (2019). Towards smart adaptive care toilets. *Studies in Health Technology and Informatics, 260*, 9–16.

Mayhew, P. M., Thomas, C. D., Clement, J. G., Loveridge, N., Beck, T. J., Bonfield, W., ... Reeve, J. (2005). Relation between age, femoral neck cortical stability, and hip fracture risk. *Lancet, 366*(9480), 129–135.

Maywald, M., & Rink, L. (2015). Zinc homeostasis and immunosenescence. *Journal of Trace Elements in Medicine and Biology, 29*, 24–30. doi: 10.1016/j.jtemb.2014.06.003

McAdams, D. P. (2008). Generativity, the redemptive self, and the problem of a noisy ego in American life. In H. A. Wayment & J. J. Bauer (Eds.), *Transcending self-interest: Psychological explorations of the quiet ego* (pp. 235–242). Washington, DC: American Psychological Association.

McAuley, E., Marquez, D. X., Jerome, G. J., Blissmer, B., & Katula, J. (2002). Physical activity and physique anxiety in older adults: Fitness, and efficacy influences. *Aging and Mental Health, 6*(3), 222–230.

McCartney, G., Hearty, W., Arnot, J., Popham, F., Cumbers, A., & McMaster, R. (2019). Impact of political economy on population health: A systematic review of reviews. *American Journal of Public Health, 109*(6), e1–e12. doi: 10.2105/ajph.2019.305001

McCrae, R. R., & Costa, P. T. J. (2003). *Personality in adulthood, personality in adulthood: A five-factor theory perspective* (2nd ed.), New York: Guilford.

McFadden, J. R., & Rawson Swan, K. T. (2012). Women during midlife: Is it transition or crisis? *Family and Consumer Sciences Research Journal, 40*(3), 313–325. doi: 10.1111/j.1552-3934.2011.02113.x

McGinnis, D. (2012). Susceptibility to distraction during reading in young, young–old, and old–old adults. *Experimental Aging Research, 38*(4), 370–393.

McGue, M., & Christensen, K. (2002). The heritability of level and rate-of-change in cognitive functioning in Danish twins aged 70 years and older. *Experimental Aging Research, 28*, 435–451.

McKay, S. M., & Maki, B. E. (2010). Attitudes of older adults toward shooter video games: An initial study to select an acceptable game for training visual processing. *Gerontechnology*, 9(1), 5–17. doi: 10.4017/gt.2010.09.01.001.00

McKeith, I. G., Boeve, B. F., Dickson, D. W., Halliday, G., Taylor, J. P., Weintraub, D., … Kosaka, K. (2017). Diagnosis and management of dementia with Lewy bodies: Fourth consensus report of the DLB Consortium. *Neurology*, 89(1), 88–100. doi: 10.1212/wnl.0000000000004058

McKhann, G., Drachman, D., Folstein, M., Katzman, R., Price, D., & Stadlan, E. M. (1984). Clinical diagnosis of Alzheimer's disease: Report of the NINCDS-ADRDA Work Group under the auspices of Department of Health and Human Services Task Force on Alzheimer's disease. *Neurology*, 34, 939–944.

McLean, K. C. (2008). Stories of the young and the old: Personal continuity and narrative identity. *Developmental Psychology*, 44(1), 254–264. doi: 2007-19851-026 [pii]10.1037/0012-1649.44.1.254

Medicare. (2019a). Nursing home compare. From https://www.medicare.gov/nursinghomecompare/search.html?

Medicare. (2019b). Your medicare costs. From https://www.medicare.gov/your-medicare-costs

Medicare. (2019c). Your rights and protections as a nursing home resident. From https://downloads.cms.gov/medicare/Your_Resident_Rights_and_Protections_section.pdf

Medina-Garrido, J. A., Biedma-Ferrer, J. M., & Ramos-Rodríguez, A. R. (2019). Moderating effects of gender and family responsibilities on the relations between work–family policies and job performance. *The International Journal of Human Resource Management*. doi: 10.1080/09585192.2018.1505762

Mehra, A., Grover, S., Agarwal, A., Bashar, M., & Avasthi, A. (2019). Prevalence of elder abuse and its association with psychiatric morbidity in a rural setting. *Journal of Neurosciences in Rural Practice*, 10(2), 218–224. doi: 10.4103/jnrp.jnrp_338_18

Meijer, W. A., van Boxtel, M. P. J., Van Gerven, P. W. M., van Hooren, S. A. H., & Jolles, J. (2009). Interaction effects of education and health status on cognitive change: A 6-year follow-up of the Maastricht Aging Study. *Aging and Mental Health*, 13(4), 521–529. doi: 10.1080/13607860902860821

Meredith, D., & Kozbelt, A. (2014). A swan song for the swan-song phenomenon: Multi-level evidence against robust end-of-life effects for classical composers. *Empirical Studies of the Arts*, 32(1), 5–25. doi: 10.2190/EM.EOV

Messe, P.-J., & Wolff, F.-C. (2019). The short-term effects of retirement on health within couples: Evidence from France. *Social Science & Medicine*, 221, 27–39. doi: 10.1016/j.socscimed.2018.12.008

Messier, V., Rabasa-Lhoret, R., Barbat-Artigas, S., Elisha, B., Karelis, A. D., & Aubertin-Leheudre, M. (2011). Menopause and sarcopenia: A potential role for sex hormones. *Maturitas*, 68(4), 331–336. doi: 10.1016/j.maturitas.2011.01.014

Methqal, I., Marsolais, Y., Wilson, M. A., Monchi, O., & Joanette, Y. (2019). More expertise for a better perspective: Task and strategy-driven adaptive neurofunctional reorganization for word production in high-performing older adults. *Neuropsychology and Developmental Cognition B: Aging Neuropsychology and Cognition*, 26(2), 190–221. doi: 10.1080/13825585.2017.1423021

Meunier, N., Beattie, J. H., Ciarapica, D., O'Connor, J. M., Andriollo-Sanchez, M., Taras, A., … Polito, A. (2005). Basal metabolic rate and thyroid hormones of late-middle-aged and older human subjects: The ZENITH study. *European Journal of Clinical Nutrition*, 59(Suppl 2), S53–57. doi: 1602299 [pii] 10.1038/sj.ejcn.1602299

Miceli, S., Maniscalco, L., & Matranga, D. (2019). Social networks and social activities promote cognitive functioning in both concurrent and prospective time: Evidence from the SHARE survey. *European Journal of Aging*, 16(2), 145–154. doi: 10.1007/s10433-018-0486-z

Michaelson, C., & Tosti-Kharas, J. (2019). Serving self or serving others? Close relations' perspectives on ethics and calling. *Journal of Vocational Behavior*. doi: 10.1016/j.jvb.2019.02.005

Miche, M., Huxhold, O., & Stevens, N. L. (2013). A latent class analysis of friendship network types and their predictors in the second half of life. *The Journals of Gerontology: Series B: Psychological Sciences and Social Sciences*, 68(4), 644–652. doi: 10.1093/geronb/gbt041

Mike, A., King, H., Oltmanns, T. F., & Jackson, J. J. (2018). Obsessive, compulsive, and conscientious? The relationship between OCPD and personality traits. *Journal of Personality*, 86(6), 952–972. doi: 10.1111/jopy.12368

Milligan-Saville, J. S., Paterson, H. M., Harkness, E. L., Marsh, A. M., Dobson, M., Kemp, R. I., … Harvey, S. B. (2017). The amplification of common somatic symptoms by posttraumatic stress disorder in firefighters. *Journal of Traumatic Stress*, 30(2), 142–148. doi: 10.1002/jts.22166

Miner-Rubino, K., Winter, D. G., & Stewart, A. J. (2004). Gender, social class, and the subjective experience of aging: Self-perceived personality change from early adulthood to late midlife. *Personality and Social Psychology Bulletin*, 30(12), 1599–1610.

Minority Staff Special Investigations Division Committee on Government Reform U.S. House of Representatives. (2001, July 30, 2001). Abuse of residents is a major problem in U.S. nursing homes prepared for Rep. Henry A. Waxman. From http://www.cbsnews.com/htdocs/pdf/waxman_nursing.pdf

Mireles, D. E., & Charness, N. (2002). Computational explorations of the influence of structured knowledge on age-related cognitive decline. *Psychology and Aging*, 17(2), 245–259.

Mitchell, B. A., & Lovegreen, L. D. (2009). The empty nest syndrome in midlife families: A multimethod exploration of parental gender differences and cultural dynamics. *Journal of Family Issues*, 30(12), 1651–1670. doi: 10.1177/0192513x09339020

Mitchell, S. L., Teno, J. M., Kiely, D. K., Shaffer, M. L., Jones, R. N., Prigerson, H. G., … Hamel, M. B. (2009). The clinical course of advanced dementia. *New England Journal of Medicine*, 361(16), 1529–1538. doi: 361/16/1529 [pii] 10.1056/NEJMoa0902234

Mitchell, V., & Helson, R. M. (2016). The place of purpose in life in women's positive aging. *Women & Therapy, 39*(1–2), 213–234. doi: 10.1080/02703149.2016.1116856

Mitnick, D. M., Heyman, R. E., & Smith Slep, A. M. (2009). Changes in relationship satisfaction across the transition to parenthood: A meta-analysis. *Journal of Family Psychology, 23*(6), 848–852. doi: 10.1037/a0017004 10.1037/a0017004.supp (Supplemental)

Mitty, E. (2009). Nursing care of the aging foot. *Geriatric Nursing, 30*(5), 350–354. doi: S0197–4572(09)00307-3 [pii] 10.1016/j.gerinurse.2009.08.004

Miyake, A., Friedman, N. P., Emerson, M. J., Witzki, A. H., Howerter, A., & Wager, T. D. (2000). The unity and diversity of executive functions and their contributions to complex "frontal lobe" tasks: A latent variable analysis. *Cognitive Psychology, 41*(1), 49–100. doi: http://dx.doi.org/10.1006/cogp.1999.0734

Moffitt, T. E. (2018). Male antisocial behaviour in adolescence and beyond. *Nature and Human Behaviour, 2*, 177–186.

Montpetit, M. A., Bergeman, C. S., Deboeck, P. R., Tiberio, S. S., & Boker, S. M. (2010). Resilience-as-process: Negative affect, stress, and coupled dynamical systems. *Psychology and Aging, 25*(3), 631–640. doi: 10.1037/a0019268

Moore, T. S. (2018). Why don't employees use family-friendly work practices? *Asia Pacific Journal of Human Resources*. doi: 10.1111/1744-7941.12212

Morgan, W. B., Perry, S. J., & Wang, Y. (2018). The angry implications of work-to-family conflict: Examining effects of leadership on an emotion-based model of deviance. *Journal of Vocational Behavior, 108*, 13–27. doi: 10.1016/j.jvb.2018.05.009

Mori, M. (2014). Conflicting ideologies and language policy in Adult ESL: Complexities of language socialization in a majority-L1 classroom. *Journal of Language, Identity & Education, 13*(3), 153–170. doi: 10.1080/15348458.2014.919810

Morrill, G. A., Kostellow, A. B., & Gupta, R. K. (2017). Computational comparison of a calcium-dependent jellyfish protein (apoaequorin) and calmodulin-cholesterol in short-term memory maintenance. *Neuroscience Letters, 642*, 113–118. doi: 10.1016/j.neulet.2017.01.069

Morris, M. C., Evans, D. A., Tangney, C. C., Bienias, J. L., & Wilson, R. S. (2005). Fish consumption and cognitive decline with age in a large community study. *Archives of Neurology, 62*(12), 1849–1853.

Motter, J. N., Devanand, D. P., Doraiswamy, P. M., & Sneed, J. R. (2016). Clinical trials to gain FDA approval for computerized cognitive training: What is the ideal control condition? *Frontiers in Aging Neuroscience, 8*, 249. doi: 10.3389/fnagi.2016.00249

Mroczek, D. K., & Kolarz, C. M. (1998). The effect of age on positive and negative affect: A developmental perspective on happiness. *Journal of Personality and Social Psychology, 75*, 1333–1349.

Mueller, M. M., Wilhelm, B., & Elder, G. H., Jr. (2002). Variations in grandparenting. *Research on Aging, 24*, 360–388.

Muratore, A. M., & Earl, J. K. (2015). Improving retirement outcomes: The role of resources, pre-retirement planning and transition characteristics. *Ageing & Society, 35*(10), 2100–2140. doi: 10.1017/S0144686X14000841

Murphy, D. R., Daneman, M., & Schneider, B. A. (2006). Why do older adults have difficulty following conversations? *Psychology and Aging, 21*(1), 49–61.

Murphy, E., Kapur, N., Webb, R., Purandare, N., Hawton, K., Bergen, H., … Cooper, J. (2012). Risk factors for repetition and suicide following self-harm in older adults: Multicentre cohort study. *The British Journal of Psychiatry, 200*(5), 399–404. doi: 10.1192/bjp.bp.111.094177

Murphy, T., Dias, G. P., & Thuret, S. (2014). Effects of diet on brain plasticity in animal and human studies: Mind the gap. *Neural Plasticity, 563160*. doi: 10.1155/2014/563160

Murphy, S. L., Xu, J., Kochanek, K. D., Curtin, S. C., & Arias, E. (2017). *Deaths: Final data for 2015*. Washington, DC: U.S. Department of Health and Human Services.

Musich, S., Wang, S. S., Slindee, L., Kraemer, S., & Yeh, C. S. (2019). Association of resilience and social networks with pain outcomes among older adults. *Population Health Management*. doi: 10.1089/pop.2018.0199

Nascimento, C. M., Ingles, M., Salvador-Pascual, A., Cominetti, M. R., Gomez-Cabrera, M. C., & Vina, J. (2019). Sarcopenia, frailty and their prevention by exercise. *Free Radicals in Biological Medicine, 132*, 42–49. doi: 10.1016/j.freeradbiomed.2018.08.035

National Cancer Institute. (2019). Cancer statistics. From https://www.cancer.gov/about-cancer/understanding/statistics?redirect=true

National Center for Education Statistics. (2013). Digest of education statistics: 2011. Retrieved 6/5/2019, from http://nces.ed.gov/programs/digest/d11/tables/dt11_439.asp?referrer=list

National Center for Education Statistics. (2019). Digest of education statistics. Retrieved 6/5/2019, from https://nces.ed.gov/programs/digest/d16/tables/dt16_303.40.asp?current=yes

National Center for Health Statistics. (2019). *Key statistics from the National Survey of Family Growth-C listing*. Washington, DC: U.S. Department of Health and Human Services.

National Center for Statistics and Analysis. (2017). *Alcohol impaired driving: 2016 data* (Traffic Safety Facts. Report No. DOT HS 812 450). Washington, DC: National Highway Traffic Safety Administration.

National Collaborating Centre for Women's and Children's Health. (2015). *National Institute for Health and Care Excellence: Clinical guidelines*. London: National Institute for Health and Care Excellence Copyright (c) 2015 National Collaborating Centre for Women's and Children's Health.

National Institute of Aging. (2019). Spotting the signs of elder abuse. From https://www.nia.nih.gov/health/infographics/spotting-signs-elder-abuse

National Institute of Mental Health. (2019). Suicide. Retrieved 3/8/19, from https://www.nimh.nih.gov/health/statistics/suicide.shtml

National Institute on Alcohol Abuse and Alcoholism. (2013). Older adults. Retrieved 10/21/2018, from http://www.niaaa.nih.gov/alcohol-health/special-populations-co-occurring-disorders/older-adults

Negaresh, R., Ranjbar, R., Baker, J. S., Habibi, A., Mokhtarzade, M., Gharibvand, M. M., & Fokin, A. (2019). Skeletal muscle hypertrophy, Insulin-like Growth Factor 1, myostatin and follistatin in healthy and sarcopenic elderly men: The effect of whole-body resistance training. *International Journal of Preventive Medicine*, *10*, 29. doi: 10.4103/ijpvm.IJPVM_310_17

Neider, M. B., Boot, W. R., & Kramer, A. F. (2010). Visual search for real world targets under conditions of high target-background similarity: Exploring training and transfer in younger and older adults. *Acta Psychologica*, *134*(1), 29–39. doi: 10.1016/j.actpsy.2009.12.001

Neider, M. B., & Kramer, A. F. (2011). Older adults capitalize on contextual information to guide search. *Experimental Aging Research*, *37*(5), 539–571. doi: 10.1080/0361073x.2011.619864

Nelson, E. A., & Dannefer, D. (1992). Aged heterogeneity: Fact or fiction? The fate of diversity in gerontological research. *Gerontologist*, *32*, 17–23.

Neugarten, B. L. (1974). Age groups in American Society and the rise of the young-old. *The ANNALS of the American Academy of Political and Social Science*, *415*(1), 187–198. doi: 10.1177/000271627441500114

Neugarten, B. L., & Weinstein, K. K. (1964). The changing American grandparent. *Journal of Marriage and the Family*, *26*, 199–204.

Neupert, S. D., Almeida, D. M., Mroczek, D. K., & Spiro, A. I. (2006). Daily stressors and memory failures in a naturalistic setting: Findings from the VA Normative Aging Study. *Psychology and Aging*, *21*(2), 424–429.

Neupert, S. D., Lachman, M. E., & Whitbourne, S. B. (2009). Exercise self-efficacy and control beliefs: Effects on exercise behavior after an exercise intervention for older adults. *Journal of Aging and Physical Activity*, *17*(1), 1–16.

Newton, N. J., Chauhan, P. K., & Pates, J. L. (2019). Facing the future: Generativity, stagnation, intended legacies, and well-being in later life. *Journal of Adult Development*. doi: 10.1007/s10804-019-09330-3

Ng, T. P., Feng, L., Nyunt, M. S., Feng, L., Gao, Q., Lim, M. L., … Yap, K. B. (2016). Metabolic syndrome and the risk of mild cognitive impairment and progression to dementia: Follow-up of the Singapore Longitudinal Ageing Study Cohort. *JAMA Neurology*, *73*(4), 456–463. doi: 10.1001/jamaneurol.2015.4899

Ng, T. W. H., & Feldman, D. C. (2013). Does longer job tenure help or hinder job performance? *Journal of Vocational Behavior*, *83*(3), 305–314. doi: 10.1016/j.jvb.2013.06.012

Nielsen, M. K., Neergaard, M. A., Jensen, A. B., Bro, F., & Guldin, M. B. (2016). Do we need to change our understanding of anticipatory grief in caregivers? A systematic review of caregiver studies during end-of-life caregiving and bereavement. *Clinical Psychology Reviews*, *44*, 75–93. doi: 10.1016/j.cpr.2016.01.002

Nielsen, T. T., Moller, T. K., & Andersen, L. L. (2019). Feasibility and health effects of a 15-Week combined exercise programme for sedentary elderly: A randomised controlled trial. *Biomedical Research International*, 3081029. doi: 10.1155/2019/3081029

Nikitin, N. P., Loh, P. H., de Silva, R., Witte, K. K., Lukaschuk, E. I., Parker, A., … Cleland, J. G. (2006). Left ventricular morphology, global and longitudinal function in normal older individuals: A cardiac magnetic resonance study. *International Journal of Cardiology*, *108*(1), 76–83.

Nilsson, L.-G., Sternäng, O., Rönnlund, M., & Nyberg, L. (2009). Challenging the notion of an early-onset of cognitive decline. *Neurobiology of Aging*, *30*(4), 521–524. doi: 10.1016/j.Neurobiology of Agingaging.2008.11.013

Nimrod, G., & Rotem, A. (2012). An exploration of the innovation theory of successful ageing among older tourists. *Ageing & Society*, *32*(3), 379–404. doi: 10.1017/s0144686x1100033x

Nordin, S., McKee, K., Wallinder, M., von Koch, L., Wijk, H., & Elf, M. (2017a). The physical environment, activity and interaction in residential care facilities for older people: A comparative case study. *Scandinavian Journal of Caring Sciences*, *31*(4), 727–738. doi: 10.1111/scs.12391

Nordin, S., McKee, K., Wijk, H., & Elf, M. (2017b). The association between the physical environment and the well-being of older people in residential care facilities: A multilevel analysis. *Journal of Advanced Nursing*, *73*(12), 2942–2952. doi: 10.1111/jan.13358

Nova Scotia Legislature. (2019). Human Organ and Tissue Donation Act. From https://novascotia.ca/organdonation/ Human Organ and Tissue Donation Act (2019).

Nugent, C. N., & Daugherty, J. (2018). A demographic, attitudinal, and behavioral profile of cohabiting adults in the United States, 2011–2015. *National Health Statistics Reports*; No. 111. (May 31, 2018 ed.). Hyattsville, MD: National Center for Health Statistics.

Nunes, A., & Kramer, A. F. (2009). Experience-based mitigation of age-related performance declines: Evidence from air traffic control. *Journal of Experimental Psychology: Applied*, *15*(1), 12–24. doi: 2009-03685-002 [pii] 10.1037/a0014947

O'Donovan, D., Hausken, T., Lei, Y., Russo, A., Keogh, J., Horowitz, M., & Jones, K. L. (2005). Effect of aging on transpyloric flow, gastric emptying, and intragastric distribution in healthy humans—impact on glycemia. *Digestive Diseases and Sciences*, *50*(4), 671–676.

O'Loughlin, K., Kendig, H., Hussain, R., & Cannon, L. (2017). Age discrimination in the workplace: The more things change …. *Australasian Journal on Ageing*, *36*(2), 98–101. doi: 10.1111/ajag.12429

O'Suilleabhain, P. S., Gallagher, S., & Steptoe, A. (2019). Loneliness, living alone, and all-cause mortality: The role of emotional and social loneliness in the elderly during 19 years of follow-up. *Psychosomatic Medicine*, *81*(6), 521–526. doi: 10.1097/psy.0000000000000710

Ohtani, N., Mann, D. J., & Hara, E. (2009). Cellular senescence: Its role in tumor suppression and aging. *Cancer Science*,

100(5), 792–797. doi: CAS1123 [pii] 10.1111/j.1349-7006.2009.01123.x

Okolie, C., Dennis, M., Simon Thomas, E., & John, A. (2017). A systematic review of interventions to prevent suicidal behaviors and reduce suicidal ideation in older people. *International Psychogeriatrics*, *29*(11), 1801–1824. doi: 10.1017/s1041610217001430

Okuro, M., & Morimoto, S. (2014). Sleep apnea in the elderly. *Current Opinion in Psychiatry*, *27*(6), 472–477. doi: 10.1097/yco.0000000000000105

Olafsen, A. H., Niemiec, C. P., Halvari, H., Deci, E. L., & Williams, G. C. (2017). On the dark side of work: A longitudinal analysis using self-determination theory. *European Journal of Work and Organizational Psychology*, *26*(2), 275–285. doi: 10.1080/1359432X.2016.1257611

Olaya, B., Moneta, M. V., Miret, M., Ayuso-Mateos, J. L., & Haro, J. M. (2019). Course of depression and cognitive decline at 3-year follow-up: The role of age of onset. *Psychology and Aging*, *34*(4), 475–485. doi: 10.1037/pag0000354

Olfson, M., Gerhard, T., Huang, C., Crystal, S., & Stroup, T. S. (2015). Premature mortality among adults with schizophrenia in the United States. *JAMA Psychiatry*, *72*(12), 1172–1181. doi: 10.1001/jamapsychiatry.2015.1737

Olij, B. F., Barmentloo, L. M., Smilde, D., van der Velde, N., Polinder, S., Schoon, Y., & Erasmus, V. (2019). Factors associated with participation of community-dwelling older adults in a home-based falls prevention program. *International Journal of Environmental Research and Public Health*, *16*(6). doi: 10.3390/ijerph16061087

Olsson, G., Hemstrom, O., & Fritzell, J. (2009). Identifying factors associated with good health and ill health: Not just opposite sides of the same coin. *International Journal of Behavioral Medicine*, *16*(4), 323–330. doi: 10.1007/s12529-009-9033-9

Ong, A. D., Bergeman, C. S., Bisconti, T. L., & Wallace, K. A. (2006). Psychological resilience, positive emotions, and successful adaptation to stress in later life. *Journal of Personality and Social Psychology*, *91*(4), 730–749.

Ostenson, J. A., & Zhang, M. (2014). Reconceptualizing marital conflict: A relational perspective. *Journal of Theoretical and Philosophical Psychology*, *34*(4), 229–242. doi: 10.1037/a0034517

Otsuki, T., Maeda, S., Kesen, Y., Yokoyama, N., Tanabe, T., Sugawara, J., … Matsuda, M. (2006). Age-related reduction of systemic arterial compliance induces excessive myocardial oxygen consumption during sub-maximal exercise. *Hypertension Research*, *29*(2), 65–73.

Overdorp, E. J., Kessels, R. P., Claassen, J. A., & Oosterman, J. M. (2016). The combined effect of neuropsychological and neuropathological deficits on instrumental activities of daily living in older adults: A systematic review. *Neuropsychology Reviews*, *26*(1), 92–106. doi: 10.1007/s11065-015-9312-y

Packer, D. J., & Chasteen, A. L. (2006). Looking to the future: How possible aged selves influence prejudice toward older adults. *Social Cognition*, *24*(3), 218–247.

Pailhé, A., & Solaz, A. (2018). Is there a wage cost for employees in family-friendly workplaces? The effect of different employer policies. *Gender, Work and Organization*. doi: 10.1111/gwao.12295

Palmeira, M. (2014). Frontline employees' self-perception of ageism, sexism, and lookism: Comparative analyses of prejudice and discrimination in fashion and food retailing. In F. Musso & E. Druica (Eds.), *Handbook of research on retailer-consumer relationship development* (pp. 275–296). Hershey, PA: Business Science Reference/IGI Global.

Palmiero, M., Di Giacomo, D., & Passafiume, D. (2016a). Can creativity predict cognitive reserve? *The Journal of Creative Behavior*, *50*(1), 7–23. doi: 10.1002/jocb.62

Palmiero, M., Nori, R., & Piccardi, L. (2016b). The relationship between visual creativity and visual mental imagery in ageing. In G. B. Moneta & J. Rogaten (Eds.), *Psychology of creativity: Cognitive, emotional, and social processes* (pp. 69–81). Hauppauge, NY: Nova Science Publishers.

Panegyres, P. K., Berry, R., & Burchell, J. (2016). Early dementia screening. *Diagnostics*, *6*(1). doi: 10.3390/diagnostics6010006

Paolieri, D., Marful, A., Morales, L., & Bajo, M. T. (2018). The modulating effect of education on semantic interference during healthy aging. *PLoS ONE*, *13*(1), e0191656. doi: 10.1371/journal.pone.0191656

Papa, R., & Papa, J. (2011). Leading adult learners: Preparing future leaders and professional development of those they lead. In R. Papa (Ed.), *Technology leadership for school improvement* (pp. 91–107). Thousand Oaks, CA: Sage Publications.

Parmenter, B. J., Mavros, Y., Ritti Dias, R., King, S., & Fiatarone Singh, M. (2019). Resistance training as a treatment for older persons with peripheral artery disease: A systematic review and meta-analysis. *British Journal of Sports Medicine*. doi: 10.1136/bjsports-2018-100205

Patten, S. B., Williams, J. V. A., Lavorato, D. H., Wang, J. L., Bulloch, A. G. M., & Sajobi, T. (2016). The association between major depression prevalence and sex becomes weaker with age. *Social Psychiatry and Psychiatric Epidemiology*, *51*(2), 203–210. doi: 10.1007/s00127-015-1166-3

Paulson, D., Bassett, R., Kitsmiller, E., Luther, K., & Conner, N. (2017). When employment and caregiving collide: Predictors of labor force participation in prospective and current caregivers. *Clinical Gerontologist: The Journal of Aging and Mental Health*, *40*(5), 401–412. doi: 10.1080/07317115.2016.1198856

Payne, B. A. I., & Chinnery, P. F. (2015). Mitochondrial dysfunction in aging: Much progress but many unresolved questions. *Biochimica et Biophysica Acta*, *1847*(11), 1347–1353. doi: 10.1016/j.bbabio.2015.05.022

Payne, B. R., Gao, X., Noh, S. R., Anderson, C. J., & Stine-Morrow, E. A. (2012). The effects of print exposure on sentence processing and memory in older adults: Evidence for efficiency and reserve. *Neuropsychology and Developmental Cognition B: Aging Neuropsychology and Cognition*, *19*(1–2), 122–149. doi: 10.1080/13825585.2011.628376

Payne, B. R., Gross, A. L., Hill, P. L., Parisi, J. M., Rebok, G. W., & Stine-Morrow, E. A. L. (2017). Decomposing the relationship between cognitive functioning and self-referent memory beliefs in older adulthood: What's memory got to do with it? *Neuropsychology and Developmental Cognition B: Aging Neuropsychology and Cognition*, 24(4), 345–362. doi: 10.1080/13825585.2016.1218425

Pearson, E. S., Hall, C. R., & Gammage, K. L. (2013). Self-presentation in exercise: Changes over a 12-week cardiovascular programme for overweight and obese sedentary females. *European Journal of Sport Science*, 13(4), 407–413. doi: 10.1080/17461391.2012.660504

Pearson, K. J., Baur, J. A., Lewis, K. N., Peshkin, L., Price, N. L., Labinskyy, N., … de Cabo, R. (2008). Resveratrol delays age-related deterioration and mimics transcriptional aspects of dietary restriction without extending life span. *Cell Metabolism*, 8(2), 157–168. doi: S1550-4131(08)00182-4 [pii] 10.1016/j.cmet.2008.06.011

Peelle, J. E., & Wingfield, A. (2016). The neural consequences of age-related hearing loss. *Trends in Neuroscience*, 39(7), 486–497. doi: 10.1016/j.tins.2016.05.001

Pelegrini, L. N. C., Mota, G. M. P., Ramos, C. F., Jesus, E., & Vale, F. A. C. (2019). Diagnosing dementia and cognitive dysfunction in the elderly in primary health care: A systematic review. *Dementia and Neuropsychologica*, 13(2), 144–153. doi: 10.1590/1980-57642018dn13-020002

Pelletier, A., Periot, O., Dilharreguy, B., Hiba, B., Bordessoules, M., Chanraud, S., … Catheline, G. (2015). Age-related modifications of diffusion tensor imaging parameters and White Matter Hyperintensities as inter-dependent processes. *Frontiers in Aging Neuroscience*, 7, 255. doi: 10.3389/fnagi.2015.00255

Pelletier, A. L., Thomas, J., & Shaw, F. R. (2009). Vision loss in older persons. *American Family Physician*, 79(11), 963–970.

Peretz, C., Korczyn, A. D., Shatil, E., Aharonson, V., Birnboim, S., & Giladi, N. (2011). Computer-based, personalized cognitive training versus classical computer games: A randomized double-blind prospective trial of cognitive stimulation. *Neuroepidemiology*, 36(2), 91–99. doi: 10.1159/000323950

Perrig-Chiello, P., & Hopflinger, F. (2005). Aging parents and their middle-aged children: Demographic and psychosocial challenges. *European Journal of Ageing*, 2(3), 183–191.

Persson, G. R. (2018). Periodontal complications with age. *Periodontology 2000*, 78(1), 185–194. doi: 10.1111/prd.12227

Perry, T. E., Andersen, T. C., & Kaplan, D. B. (2014). Relocation remembered: Perspectives on senior transitions in the living environment. *The Gerontologist*, 54(1), 75–81. doi: 10.1093/geront/gnt070

Peterson, B. E. (2006). Generativity and successful parenting: An analysis of young adult outcomes. *Journal of Personality*, 74(3), 847–869. doi: 10.1111/j.1467-6494.2006.00394.x

Petrofsky, J. S., McLellan, K., Bains, G. S., Prowse, M., Ethiraju, G., Lee, S., … Schwab, E. (2009). The influence of ageing on the ability of the skin to dissipate heat. *Medical Science Monitor*, 15(6), CR261–268. doi: 869673 [pii]

Pew Research Center. (2009). Growing old in America: Expectations vs. reality. From http://pewresearch.org/pubs/1269/aging-survey-expectations-versus-reality

Pfisterer, M. H., Griffiths, D. J., Schaefer, W., & Resnick, N. M. (2006). The effect of age on lower urinary tract function: A study in women. *Journal of the American Geriatrics Society*, 54(3), 405–412.

Pfoh, E., Mojtabai, R., Bailey, J., Weiner, J. P., & Dy, S. M. (2015). Impact of medicare annual wellness visits on uptake of depression screening. *Psychiatric Services*, 66(11), 1207–1212. doi: 10.1176/appi.ps.201400524

Phan, W. M. J., & Rounds, J. (2018). Examining the duality of Holland's RIASEC types: Implications for measurement and congruence. *Journal of Vocational Behavior*, 106, 22–36. doi: 10.1016/j.jvb.2017.11.011

Pienta, A. M. (2003). Partners in marriage: An analysis of husbands' and wives' retirement behavior. *Journal of Applied Gerontology*, 22(3), 340–358. doi: 10.1177/0733464803253587

Piersol, C. V., Canton, K., Connor, S. E., Giller, I., Lipman, S., & Sager, S. (2017). Effectiveness of interventions for caregivers of people with Alzheimer's disease and related major neurocognitive disorders: A systematic review. *American Journal of Occupational Therapy*, 71(5), 7105180020p1-7105180020p10. doi: 10.5014/ajot.2017.027581

Pilarska, A. (2017). Contributions of cognitive-motivational factors to the sense of identity. *Current Psychology*, 36(3), 468–482. doi: 10.1007/s12144-016-9435-1

Piot, A., Chapurlat, R. D., Claustrat, B., & Szulc, P. (2019). Relationship between sex steroids and deterioration of bone microarchitecture in older men: The prospective STRAMBO Study. *Journal of Bone and Mineral Research*. doi: 10.1002/jbmr.3746

Pistono, A., Busigny, T., Jucla, M., Cabirol, A., Dinnat, A. L., Pariente, J., & Barbeau, E. J. (2019). An analysis of famous person semantic memory in aging. *Experimental Aging Research*, 45(1), 74–93. doi: 10.1080/0361073x.2018.1560118

Platts-Mills, T. F., Nebolisa, B. C., Flannigan, S. A., Richmond, N. L., Domeier, R. M., Swor, R. A., … McLean, S. A. (2017). Post-traumatic stress disorder among older adults experiencing motor vehicle collision: A multicenter prospective cohort study. *American Journal of Geriatric Psychiatry*, 25(9), 953–963. doi: 10.1016/j.jagp.2017.03.011

Plaut, V. C., Markus, H. R., & Lachman, M. E. (2003). Place matters: Consensual features and regional variation in American well-being and self. *Journal of Personality and Social Psychology*, 83, 160–184.

Plemons, J. K., Willis, S. L., & Baltes, P. B. (1978). Modifiability of fluid intelligence in aging: A short-term longitudinal training approach. *Journal of Gerontology*, 33, 224–231.

Poh, S., Mohamed Abdul, R. B., Lamoureux, E. L., Wong, T. Y., & Sabanayagam, C. (2016). Metabolic syndrome and eye diseases. *Diabetes Research and Clinical Practice*, 113, 86–100. doi: 10.1016/j.diabres.2016.01.016

Pollock, D., Ziaian, T., Pearson, E., Cooper, M., & Warland, J. (2019). Understanding stillbirth stigma: A scoping literature review. *Women Birth*. doi: 10.1016/j.wombi.2019.05.004

Ponce-Bravo, H., Ponce, C., Feriche, B., & Padial, P. (2015). Influence of two different exercise programs on physical fitness and cognitive performance in active older adults: Functional resistance-band exercises vs. recreational oriented exercises. *Journal of Sports Science & Medicine*, 14(4), 716–722.

Pope, C. A., 3rd, Lefler, J. S., Ezzati, M., Higbee, J. D., Marshall, J. D., Kim, S. Y., … Burnett, R. T. (2019). Mortality risk and fine particulate air pollution in a large, representative cohort of U.S. adults. *Environmental Health Perspectives*, 127(7), 77007. doi: 10.1289/ehp4438

Porell, F. W., & Carter, M. W. (2012). Risk of mortality and nursing home institutionalization after injury. *Journal of the American Geriatrics Society*, 60(8), 1498–1503. doi: 10.1111/j.1532-5415.2012.04053.x

Porter, G., Tales, A., Troscianko, T., Wilcock, G., Haworth, J., & Leonards, U. (2010). New insights into feature and conjunction search: I Evidence from pupil size, eye movements and ageing. *Cortex: A Journal Devoted to the Study of the Nervous System and Behavior*, 46(5), 621–636. doi: 10.1016/j.cortex.2009.04.013

Potter, C. M., Kaiser, A. P., King, L. A., King, D. W., Davison, E. H., Seligowski, A. V., … Spiro, A., 3rd. (2013). Distinguishing late-onset stress symptomatology from posttraumatic stress disorder in older combat veterans. *Aging and Mental Health*, 17(2), 173–179. doi: 10.1080/13607863.2012.717259

Powers, A. D., & Oltmanns, T. F. (2012). Personality disorders and physical health: A longitudinal examination of physical functioning, healthcare utilization, and health-related behaviors in middle-aged adults. *Journal of Personality Disorders*, 26(4), 524–538. doi: 10.1521/pedi.2012.26.4.524

Prediger, D. J., & Vansickle, T. R. (1992). Who claims Holland's hexagon is perfect? *Journal of Vocational Behavior*, 40(2), 210–219. doi: 10.1016/0001-8791(92)90070-G

President's Commission for the Study of Ethical Problems in Medicine and Biomedical and Behavioral Research. (1981). *Defining death*. Washington, DC: U.S. Government Printing Office.

Pyun, J. M., Kang, M. J., Kim, D., Baek, M. J., Wang, M. J., & Kim, S. (2018). Driving cessation and cognitive dysfunction in patients with mild cognitive impairment. *Journal of Clinical Medicine*, 7(12). doi: 10.3390/jcm7120545

Radloff, L. S. (1977). The CES-D Scale: A self-report depression scale for research in the general population. *Applied Psychological Measurement*, 1(3), 385–401. doi: 10.1177/014662167700100306

Rahhal, T. A., Colcombe, S. J., & Hasher, L. (2001). Instructional manipulations and age differences in memory: Now you see them, now you don't. *Psychology and Aging*, 16(4), 697–706.

Ralston, S. H. (2007). Genetics of osteoporosis. *Proceedings of the Nutrition Society*, 66(2), 158–165. doi: 10.1017/s002966510700540x

Ram, N., Rabbitt, P., Stollery, B., & Nesselroade, J. R. (2005). Cognitive performance inconsistency: Intraindividual change and variability. *Psychology and Aging*, 20(4), 623–633.

Ramírez-Esparza, N., Harris, K., Hellermann, J., Richard, C., Kuhl, P. K., & Reder, S. (2012). Socio-interactive practices and personality in adult learners of English with little formal education.

Language Learning, 62(2), 541–570. doi: 10.1111/j.1467-9922.2011.00631.x

Ramscar, M., Hendrix, P., Shaoul, C., Milin, P., & Baayen, H. (2014). The myth of cognitive decline: Non-linear dynamics of lifelong learning. *Topics in Cognitive Science*, 6(1), 5–42. doi: 10.1111/tops.12078

Randall, A. K., Tao, C., Totenhagen, C. J., Walsh, K. J., & Cooper, A. N. (2017). Associations between sexual orientation discrimination and depression among same-sex couples: Moderating effects of dyadic coping. *Journal of Couple & Relationship Therapy*, 16(4), 325–345. doi: 10.1080/15332691.2016.1253520

Rathbun, A. M., Schuler, M. S., Stuart, E. A., Shardell, M. D., Yau, M. S., Gallo, J. J., … Hochberg, M. C. (2019). Depression subtypes in persons with or at risk for symptomatic knee osteoarthritis. *Arthritis Care & Research*. doi: 10.1002/acr.23898

Raudenbush, S. W., & Bryk, A. S. (2002). *Hierarchical linear models: Applications and data analysis methods* (2nd ed.). Newbury Park, CA: Sage Publications.

Raue, P. J., Ghesquiere, A. R., & Bruce, M. L. (2014). Suicide risk in primary care: Identification and management in older adults. *Current Psychiatry Reports*, 16(9), 466. doi: 10.1007/s11920-014-0466-8

Raue, P. J., McGovern, A. R., Kiosses, D. N., & Sirey, J. A. (2017). Advances in psychotherapy for depressed older adults. *Current Psychiatry Reports*, 19(9), 57–57. doi: 10.1007/s11920-017-0812-8

Rawson, N. E. (2006). Olfactory loss in aging. *Science of Aging Knowledge Environment*, 2006(5), pe6.

Ray, L., Lipton, R. B., Zimmerman, M. E., Katz, M. J., & Derby, C. A. (2011). Mechanisms of association between obesity and chronic pain in the elderly. *Pain*, 152(1), 53–59. doi: 10.1016/j.pain.2010.08.043

Reas, E. T., Laughlin, G. A., Bergstrom, J., Kritz-Silverstein, D., Richard, E. L., Barrett-Connor, E., & McEvoy, L. K. (2019). Lifetime physical activity and late-life cognitive function: The Rancho Bernardo study. *Age and Ageing*. doi: 10.1093/ageing/afy188

Rebok, G. W., Ball, K., Guey, L. T., Jones, R. N., Kim, H. Y., King, J. W., … Willis, S. L. (2014). Ten-year effects of the advanced cognitive training for independent and vital elderly cognitive training trial on cognition and everyday functioning in older adults. *Journal of the American Geriatrics Society*, 62(1), 16–24. doi: 10.1111/jgs.12607

Reeves, N. D., Narici, M. V., & Maganaris, C. N. (2006). Myotendinous plasticity to ageing and resistance exercise in humans. *Experimental Physiology*, 91(3), 483–498.

Regnier, V., & Denton, A. (2009). Ten new and emerging trends in residential group living environments. *NeuroRehabilitation*, 25(3), 169–188. doi: A47W1V1R0705P026 [pii] 10.3233/NRE-2009-0514

Reilly, D., Neumann, D. L., & Andrews, G. (2016). Sex and sex-role differences in specific cognitive abilities. *Intelligence*, 54, 147–158. doi: https://doi.org/10.1016/j.intell.2015.12.004

Reinders, I., Murphy, R. A., Martin, K. R., Brouwer, I. A., Visser, M., White, D. K., … Harris, T. B. (2015). Body mass index trajectories in relation to change in lean mass and physical function:

The health, aging and body composition study. *Journal of the American Geriatrics Society*, *63*(8), 1615–1621. doi: 10.1111/jgs.13524

Remond, D., Shahar, D. R., Gille, D., Pinto, P., Kachal, J., Peyron, M. A., … Vergeres, G. (2015). Understanding the gastrointestinal tract of the elderly to develop dietary solutions that prevent malnutrition. *Oncotarget*, *6*(16), 13858–13898. doi: 10.18632/oncotarget.4030

Resnick, B., Shaughnessy, M., Galik, E., Scheve, A., Fitten, R., Morrison, T., … Agness, C. (2009). Pilot testing of the PRAISEDD intervention among African American and low-income older adults. *Journal of Cardiovascular Nursing*, *24*(5), 352–361. doi: 10.1097/JCN.0b013e3181ac0301

Reuter-Lorenz, P. A., & Park, D. C. (2014). How does it STAC up? Revisiting the scaffolding theory of aging and cognition. *Neuropsychology Reviews*, *24*(3), 355–370. doi: 10.1007/s11065-014-9270-9

Reynolds, C. A., Finkel, D., Gatz, M., & Pedersen, N. L. (2002). Sources of influence on rate of cognitive change over time in Swedish twins: An application of latent growth models. *Experimental Aging Research*, *28*, 407–433.

Rhee, T. G., Barry, L. C., Kuchel, G. A., Steffens, D. C., & Wilkinson, S. T. (2019). Associations of adverse childhood experiences with past-year DSM-5 psychiatric and substance use disorders in older adults. *Journal of the American Geriatrics Society*. doi: 10.1111/jgs.16032

Richards, J. B., Kavvoura, F. K., Rivadeneira, F., Styrkarsdottir, U., Estrada, K., Halldorsson, B. V., … Spector, T. D. (2009). Collaborative meta-analysis: Associations of 150 candidate genes with osteoporosis and osteoporotic fracture. *Annals of Internal Medicine*, *151*(8), 528–537. doi: 151/8/528 [pii]

Riesenhuber, M. (2004). An action video game modifies visual processing. *Trends in Neurosciences*, *27*(2), 72–74. doi: 10.1016/j.tins.2003.11.004

Rijs, K. J., Cozijnsen, R., & Deeg, D. J. H. (2012). The effect of retirement and age at retirement on self-perceived health after three years of follow-up in Dutch 55–64-year-olds. *Ageing & Society*, *32*(2), 281–306. doi: 10.1017/s0144686x11000237

Rioux, L., & Werner, C. (2011). Residential satisfaction among aging people living in place. *Journal of Environmental Psychology*, *31*(2), 158–169. doi: 10.1016/j.jenvp.2010.12.001

Ritchie, R. A., Meca, A., Madrazo, V. L., Schwarz, S. J., Hardy, S. A., Zamboanga, B. L., … Lee, R. M. (2013). Identity dimensions and related processes in emerging adulthood: Helpful or harmful? *Journal of Clinical Psychology*. doi: 10.1002/jclp.21960

Rizzoli, R., Stevenson, J. C., Bauer, J. M., van Loon, L. J., Walrand, S., Kanis, J. A., … Reginster, J. Y. (2014). The role of dietary protein and vitamin D in maintaining musculoskeletal health in postmenopausal women: A consensus statement from the European Society for Clinical and Economic Aspects of Osteoporosis and Osteoarthritis (ESCEO). *Maturitas*, *79*(1), 122–132. doi: 10.1016/j.maturitas.2014.07.005

Rizzuto, D., Orsini, N., Qiu, C., Wang, H.-X., & Fratiglioni, L. (2012). Lifestyle, social factors, and survival after age 75:

Population based study. *British Medical Journal*, *345*(7876), 1–10.

Roberto, K. A. (1990). Grandparent and grandchild relationships. In T. H. Brubaker (Ed.), *Family relationships in later life* (2nd ed., pp. 100–112). Newbury Park, CA: Sage Publications.

Roberts, B. W., & DelVecchio, W. F. (2000). The rank-order consistency of personality traits from childhood to old age: A quantitative review of longitudinal studies. *Psychological Bulletin*, *126*(1), 3–25.

Roberts, B. W., Donnellan, M. B., & Hill, P. L. (2013). Personality trait development in adulthood. In H. Tennen, J. Suls & I. B. Weiner (Eds.), *Handbook of psychology. Personality and social psychology* (2nd ed., Vol. 5, pp. 183–196). Hoboken, NJ: John Wiley & Sons Inc.

Roberts, B. W., Walton, K. E., & Viechtbauer, W. (2006). Patterns of mean-level change in personality traits across the life course: A meta-analysis of longitudinal studies. *Psychological Bulletin*, *132*(1), 1–25. doi: 10.1037/0033-2909.132.1.1

Roberts, B. W., Wood, D., & Caspi, A. (2008). The development of personality traits in adulthood. In O. P. John, R. W. Robins & L. A. Pervin (Eds.), *Handbook of personality: Theory and research* (pp. 375–398). New York: Guilford Press.

Robertson, T., Batty, G. D., Der, G., Fenton, C., Shiels, P. G., & Benzeval, M. (2013). Is socioeconomic status associated with biological aging as measured by telomere length? *Epidemiologic Reviews*, *35*(1), 98–111. doi: 10.1093/epirev/mxs001

Robinson, O. C., & Wright, G. R. T. (2013). The prevalence, types and perceived outcomes of crisis episodes in early adulthood and midlife: A structured retrospective-autobiographical study. *International Journal of Behavioral Development*, *37*(5), 407–416. doi: 10.1177/0165025413492464

Rodella, L. F., Bonazza, V., Labanca, M., Lonati, C., & Rezzani, R. (2014). A review of the effects of dietary silicon intake on bone homeostasis and regeneration. *The Journal of Nutrition, Health, and Aging*, *18*(9), 820–826. doi: 10.1007/s12603-014-0484-6

Rodrigues, R., Butler, C. L., & Guest, D. (2019). Antecedents of protean and boundaryless career orientations: The role of core self-evaluations, perceived employability and social capital. *Journal of Vocational Behavior*, *110*(Part A), 1–11. doi: 10.1016/j.jvb.2018.11.003

Rodriguez-Prat, A., Balaguer, A., Booth, A., & Monforte-Royo, C. (2017). Understanding patients' experiences of the wish to hasten death: An updated and expanded systematic review and meta-ethnography. *BMJ Open*, *7*(9), e016659. doi: 10.1136/bmjopen-2017-016659

Rodriguez-Sanz, D., Tovaruela-Carrion, N., Lopez-Lopez, D., Palomo-Lopez, P., Romero-Morales, C., Navarro-Flores, E., & Calvo-Lobo, C. (2018). Foot disorders in the elderly: A mini-review. *Disease a Month*, *64*(3), 64–91. doi: 10.1016/j.disamonth.2017.08.001

Rodriguez, L., Schwartz, S. J., & Whitbourne, S. K. (2010). American identity revisited: The relation between national, ethnic, and personal identity in a multiethnic sample of emerging adults. *Journal of Adolescent Research, 25*(2), 324–349. doi: 10.1177/0743558409359055

Rogers, C. H., Floyd, F. J., Seltzer, M. M., Greenberg, J., & Hong, J. (2008). Long-term effects of the death of a child on parents' adjustment in midlife. *Journal of Family Psychology, 22*(2), 203–211. doi: 2008-03770-003 [pii] 10.1037/0893-3200.22.2.203

Roig, M., Macintyre, D. L., Eng, J. J., Narici, M. V., Maganaris, C. N., & Reid, W. D. (2010). Preservation of eccentric strength in older adults: Evidence, mechanisms and implications for training and rehabilitation. *Experimental Gerontology*. doi: S0531-5565(10)00122-1 [pii] 10.1016/j.exger.2010.03.008

Roman, M. A., & Rossiter, H. B. (2016). Exercise, ageing and the lung. *European Respiratory Journal, 48*(5), 1471–1486. doi: 10.1183/13993003.00347-2016

Ronald, L. A., McGregor, M. J., Harrington, C., Pollock, A., & Lexchin, J. (2016). Observational evidence of for-profit delivery and inferior nursing home care: When is there enough evidence for policy change? *PLoS Medicine, 13*(4), e1001995. doi: 10.1371/journal.pmed.1001995

Rosenberg, S. D., Rosenberg, H. J., & Farrell, M. P. (1999). The midlife crisis revisited. In J. D. Reid & S. L. Willis (Eds.), *Life in the middle: Psychological and social development in middle age* (pp. 25–45). San Diego, CA: Academic Press.

Rosenbloom, C., & Bahns, M. (2006). What can we learn about diet and physical activity from master athletes? *Holistic Nursing Practice, 20*(4), 161–166; quiz 167-168.

Rostila, M., Saarela, J., & Kawachi, I. (2012). Mortality in parents following the death of a child: A nationwide follow-up study from Sweden. *Journal of Epidemiological and Community Health, 66*(10), 927–933. doi: 10.1136/jech-2011-200339

Roth, G. A., Johnson, C., Abajobir, A., Abd-Allah, F., Abera, S. F., Abyu, G., ... Murray, C. (2017). Global, regional, and national burden of cardiovascular diseases for 10 Causes, 1990 to 2015. *Journal of the American College of Cardiology, 70*(1), 1–25. doi: 10.1016/j.jacc.2017.04.052

Rothbard, N. P., & Wilk, S. L. (2011). Waking up on the right or wrong side of the bed: Start-of-workday mood, work events, employee affect, and performance. *Academy of Management Journal, 54*(5), 959–980. doi: 10.5465/amj.2007.0056

Rouxel, P., Heilmann, A., Demakakos, P., Aida, J., Tsakos, G., & Watt, R. G. (2017). Oral health-related quality of life and loneliness among older adults. *European Journal of Ageing, 14*(2), 101–109. doi: 10.1007/s10433-016-0392-1

Rowe, G., Hasher, L., & Turcotte, J. (2009). Age and synchrony effects in visuospatial working memory. *Quarterly Journal of Experimental Psychology, 62*(10), 1873–1880. doi: 911473077 [pii] 10.1080/17470210902834852

Rowe, J. W., & Kahn, R. L. (1998). *Successful aging*. New York: Pantheon Books.

Ruangthai, R., & Phoemsapthawee, J. (2019). Combined exercise training improves blood pressure and antioxidant capacity in elderly individuals with hypertension. *Journal of Exercise Science and Fitness, 17*(2), 67–76. doi: 10.1016/j.jesf.2019.03.001

Rubin, D. C., Rahhal, T. A., & Poon, L. W. (1998). Things learned in early adulthood are remembered best. *Memory and Cognition, 26*(1), 3–19.

Rubio, C., Osca, A., Recio, P., Urien, B., & Peiró, J. M. (2015). Work-family conflict, self-efficacy, and emotional exhaustion: A test of longitudinal effects. *Journal of Work and Organizational Psychology, 31*(3), 147–154. doi: 10.1016/j.rpto.2015.06.004

Ruigrok, A. N. V., Salimi-Khorshidi, G., Lai, M.-C., Baron-Cohen, S., Lombardo, M. V., Tait, R. J., & Suckling, J. (2014). A meta-analysis of sex differences in human brain structure. *Neuroscience & Biobehavioral Reviews, 39*, 34–50. doi: https://doi.org/10.1016/j.neubiorev.2013.12.004

Runco, M. A., & Beghetto, R. A. (2019). Primary and secondary creativity. *Current Opinion in Behavioral Sciences, 27*, 7–10. doi: 10.1016/j.cobeha.2018.08.011

Rupp, D. E., Vodanovich, S. J., & Crede, M. (2006). Age bias in the workplace: The impact of ageism and causal attributions. *Journal of Applied Social Psychology, 36*, 1337–1364.

Rutjes, A. W., Denton, D. A., Di Nisio, M., Chong, L. Y., Abraham, R. P., Al-Assaf, A. S., ... McCleery, J. (2018). Vitamin and mineral supplementation for maintaining cognitive function in cognitively healthy people in mid and late life. *Cochrane Database of Systematic Reviews, 12*, Cd011906. doi: 10.1002/14651858.CD011906.pub2

Rutkowska, A. Z., Szybiak, A., Serkies, K., & Rachon, D. (2016). Endocrine disrupting chemicals as potential risk factor for estrogen-dependent cancers. *Polish Archives of Medicine, 126*(7–8), 562–570. doi: 10.20452/pamw.3481

Ryan, C. L., & Bauman, K. (2016). Educational attainment in the United States: 2015 *Current Population Reports P20-578*. Washington, DC: U.S. Bureau of the Census.

Ryan, E. B., Hummert, M. L., & Boich, L. H. (1995). Communication predicaments of aging: Patronizing behavior toward older adults. *Journal of Language and Social Psychology, 14*(1–2), 144–166.

Ryazanov, A. A., Knutzen, J., Rickless, S. C., Christenfeld, N. J. S., & Nelkin, D. K. (2018). Intuitive probabilities and the limitation of moral Imagination. *Cognitive Science, 42*(Suppl 1), 38–68. doi: 10.1111/cogs.12598

Ryder, K. M., Shorr, R. I., Bush, A. J., Kritchevsky, S. B., Harris, T., Stone, K., ... Tylavsky, F. A. (2005). Magnesium intake from food and supplements is associated with bone mineral density in healthy older white subjects. *Journal of the American Geriatrics Society, 53*(11), 1875–1180.

Sabia, S., Kivimaki, M., Shipley, M. J., Marmot, M. G., & Singh-Manoux, A. (2009). Body mass index over the adult life course and cognition in late midlife: The Whitehall II Cohort Study. *American Journal of Clinical Nutrition, 89*(2), 601–607. doi: ajcn.2008.26482 [pii] 10.3945/ajcn.2008.26482

Sacher, G. A. (1977). Life table modification and life prolongation. In C. E. Finch & L. Hayflick (Eds.), *Handbook of the biology of aging* (pp. 582–638). New York: Van Nostrand Reinhold.

Sachs-Ericsson, N., Joiner, T. E., Cougle, J. R., Stanley, I. H., & Sheffler, J. L. (2016). Combat exposure in early adulthood interacts with recent stressors to predict PTSD in aging male veterans. *Gerontologist*, 56(1), 82–91. doi: 10.1093/geront/gnv036

Saeed Mirza, S., Ikram, M. A., Freak-Poli, R., Hofman, A., Rizopoulos, D., & Tiemeier, H. (2018). 12 year trajectories of depressive symptoms in community-dwelling older adults and the subsequent risk of death over 13 years. *Journal of Gerontology Series A: Biological Sciences*, 73(6), 820–827. doi: 10.1093/gerona/glx215

Sahni, S., Hannan, M. T., Blumberg, J., Cupples, L. A., Kiel, D. P., & Tucker, K. L. (2009). Inverse association of carotenoid intakes with 4-y change in bone mineral density in elderly men and women: The Framingham Osteoporosis Study. *American Journal of Clinical Nutrition*, 89(1), 416–424. doi: ajcn.2008.26388 [pii] 10.3945/ajcn.2008.26388

Saito, M., & Marumo, K. (2009). Collagen cross-links as a determinant of bone quality: A possible explanation for bone fragility in aging, osteoporosis, and diabetes mellitus. *Osteoporosis International*. doi: 10.1007/s00198-009-1066-z

Sajatovic, M., Jenkins, J. H., Safavi, R., West, J. A., Cassidy, K. A., Meyer, W. J., & Calabrese, J. R. (2008). Personal and societal construction of illness among individuals with rapid-cycling bipolar disorder: A life-trajectory perspective. *American Journal of Geriatric Psychiatry*, 16(9), 718–726. doi: JGP.0b013e3180488346 [pii] 10.1097/JGP.0b013e3180488346

Sajatovic, M., Strejilevich, S. A., Gildengers, A. G., Dols, A., Al Jurdi, R. K., Forester, B. P., … Shulman, K. I. (2015). A report on older-age bipolar disorder from the International Society for Bipolar Disorders Task Force. *Bipolar Disorders*, 17(7), 689–704. doi: 10.1111/bdi.12331

Salari, S. M., & Rich, M. (2001). Social and environmental infantilization of aged persons: Observations in two adult day care centers. *International Journal of Aging and Human Development*, 52(2), 115–134.

Salthouse, T. A. (1996). The processing-speed theory of adult age differences in cognition. *Psychological Review*, 103(3), 403–428.

Salthouse, T. A. (2009). When does age-related cognitive decline begin? *Neurobiology of Aging*, 30(4), 507–514. doi: 10.1016/j.Neurobiology of Aging.2008.09.023

Samaras, N., Papadopoulou, M.-A., Samaras, D., & Ongaro, F. (2014). Off-label use of hormones as an antiaging strategy: A review. *Clinical Interventions in Aging*, 9, 1175–1186. doi: 10.2147/CIA.S48918

Sargent-Cox, K. A., Windsor, T., Walker, J., & Anstey, K. J. (2011). Health literacy of older drivers and the importance of health experience for self-regulation of driving behaviour. *Accident Analysis and Prevention*, 43(3), 898–905. doi: 10.1016/j.aap.2010.11.012

Satizabal, C. L., Beiser, A. S., Chouraki, V., Chene, G., Dufouil, C., & Seshadri, S. (2016). Incidence of dementia over three decades in the Framingham Heart Study. *New England Journal of Medicine*, 374(6), 523–532. doi: 10.1056/NEJMoa1504327

Sattler, F. R. (2013). Growth hormone in the aging male. *Best Practices in Research in Clinical Endocrinology and Metabolism*, 27(4), 541–555. doi: 10.1016/j.beem.2013.05.003

Scarr, S., & McCartney, K. (1983). How people make their own environments: A theory of genotype → environment effects. *Child Development*, 54, 424–435.

Schaie, K. W. (1965). A general model for the study of developmental change. *Psychological Bulletin*, 64, 92–107.

Schaie, K. W. (1996). Intellectual development in adulthood. In J. E. Birren, K. W. Schaie, R. P. Abeles, M. Gatz & T. A. Salthouse (Eds.), *Handbook of the psychology of aging* (4th ed., pp. 266–286). San Diego, CA: Academic Press.

Schaie, K. W. (2009). 'When does age-related cognitive decline begin?' Salthouse again reifies the 'cross-sectional fallacy.' *Neurobiology of Aging*, 30(4), 528–529. doi: 10.1016/j.Neurobiology of Agingaging.2008.12.012

Schaie, K. W., Willis, S. L., & Caskie, G. I. (2004). The Seattle Longitudinal Study: Relationship between personality and cognition. *Aging, Neuropsychology and Cognition*, 11(2–3), 304–324.

Schaie, K. W., & Zanjani, F. A. K. (2006). Intellectual development across adulthood. In C. Hoare (Ed.), *Handbook of adult development and learning* (pp. 99–122). New York: Oxford University Press.

Schattner, E. (2019). Correcting a decade of negative news about mammography. *Clinical Imaging*. doi: 10.1016/j.clinimag.2019.03.011

Schenk, S., Lech, R. K., & Suchan, B. (2017). Games people play: How video games improve probabilistic learning. *Behavioural Brain Research*, 335, 208–214. doi: 10.1016/j.bbr.2017.08.027

Schneider-Garces, N. J., Gordon, B. A., Brumback-Peltz, C. R., Shin, E., Lee, Y., Sutton, B. P., … Fabiani, M. (2010). Span, CRUNCH, and beyond: Working memory capacity and the aging brain. *Journal of Cognitive Neuroscience*, 22(4), 655–669. doi: 10.1162/jocn.2009.21230

Schneider, T., Gleissner, J., Merfort, F., Hermanns, M., Beneke, M., & Ulbrich, E. (2011). Efficacy and safety of vardenafil for the treatment of erectile dysfunction in men with metabolic syndrome: Results of a randomized, placebo-controlled trial. *Journal of Sexual Medicine*, 8(10), 2904–2911. doi: 10.1111/j.1743-6109.2011.02383.x

Scholtens, R. M., van Munster, B. C., van Kempen, M. F., & de Rooij, S. E. (2016). Physiological melatonin levels in healthy older people: A systematic review. *Journal of Psychosomatic Research*, 86, 20–27. doi: 10.1016/j.jpsychores.2016.05.005

Schott, J. M., Aisen, P. S., Cummings, J. L., Howard, R. J., & Fox, N. C. (2019). Unsuccessful trials of therapies for Alzheimer's disease. *Lancet*, 393(10166), 29. doi: 10.1016/s0140-6736(18)31896-8

Schrodt, P. (2016). Coparental communication with nonresidential parents as a predictor of children's feelings of being caught in stepfamilies. *Communication Reports*, 29(2), 63–74. doi: 10.1080/08934215.2015.1020562

Schroeck, J. L., Ford, J., Conway, E. L., Kurtzhalts, K. E., Gee, M. E., Vollmer, K. A., & Mergenhagen, K. A. (2016). Review of safety and efficacy of sleep medicines in older adults. *Clinical Therapeutics*, 38(11), 2340–2372. doi: 10.1016/j.clinthera.2016.09.010

Schuch, F. B., Vancampfort, D., Rosenbaum, S., Richards, J., Ward, P. B., Veronese, N., ... Stubbs, B. (2016). Exercise for depression in older adults: A meta-analysis of randomized controlled trials adjusting for publication bias. *Brazilian Journal of Psychiatry*, 38(3), 247–254. doi: 10.1590/1516-4446-2016-1915

Schulte, T., Müller-Oehring, E. M., Chanraud, S., Rosenbloom, M. J., Pfefferbaum, A., & Sullivan, E. V. (2009). Age-related reorganization of functional networks for successful conflict resolution: A combined functional and structural MRI study. *Neurobiology of Aging*, 32(11), 2075–2090.

Schuster, J. P., Hoertel, N., Le Strat, Y., Manetti, A., & Limosin, F. (2013). Personality disorders in older adults: Findings from the National Epidemiologic Survey on Alcohol and Related Conditions. *American Journal of Geriatric Psychiatry*, 21(8), 757–768. doi: 10.1016/j.jagp.2013.01.055

Schwartz, S. J., Beyers, W., Luyckx, K., Soenens, B., Zamboanga, B. L., Forthun, L. F., ... Waterman, A. S. (2011). Examining the light and dark sides of emerging adults' identity: A study of identity status differences in positive and negative psychosocial functioning. *Journal of Youth and Adolescence*, 40(7), 839–859. doi: 10.1007/s10964-010-9606-6

Schwartz, S. J., Kim, S. Y., Whitbourne, S. K., Zamboanga, B. L., Weisskirch, R. S., Forthun, L. F., ... Luyckx, K. (2012). Converging identities: Dimensions of acculturation and personal identity status among immigrant college students. *Cultural Diversity and Ethnic Minority Psychology*. doi: 10.1037/a0030753

Schwartz, S. J., Kim, S. Y., Whitbourne, S. K., Zamboanga, B. L., Weisskirch, R. S., Forthun, L. F., ... Luyckx, K. (2013). Converging identities: Dimensions of acculturation and personal identity status among immigrant college students. *Cultural Diversity and Ethnic Minority Psychology*, 19(2), 155–165. doi: 10.1037/a0030753

Scollon, C. N., & Diener, E. (2006). Love, work, and changes in extraversion and neuroticism over time. *Journal of Personality and Social Psychology*, 91(6), 1152–1165.

Sebastiani, P., & Perls, T. T. (2012). The genetics of extreme longevity: Lessons from the New England Centenarian Study. *Frontiers in Genetics*, 3, 277. doi: 10.3389/fgene.2012.00277

Semba, R. D., Bandinelli, S., Sun, K., Guralnik, J. M., & Ferrucci, L. (2010). Relationship of an advanced glycation end product, plasma carboxymethyl-lysine, with slow walking speed in older adults: The InCHIANTI study. *European Journal of Applied Physiology*, 108(1), 191–195. doi: 10.1007/s00421-009-1192-5

Sergi, G., Bano, G., Pizzato, S., Veronese, N., & Manzato, E. (2017). Taste loss in the elderly: Possible implications for dietary habits. *Critical Reviews in Food Science and Nutrition*, 57(17), 3684–3689. doi: 10.1080/10408398.2016.1160208

Settersten, R. A., Jr. (2006). Aging and the life course. In R. H. Binstock & L. K. George (Eds.), *Handbook of aging and the social sciences* (6th ed., pp. 3–19). Amsterdam, Netherlands: Elsevier.

Shafto, M. A. (2015). Proofreading in young and older adults: The effect of error category and comprehension difficulty. *International Journal of Environmental Research and Public Health*, 12(11), 14445–14460. doi: 10.3390/ijerph121114445

Shafto, M. A., & Tyler, L. K. (2014). Language in the aging brain: The network dynamics of cognitive decline and preservation. *Science*, 346(6209), 583–587. doi: 10.1126/science.1254404

Shafto, M. A., Burke, D. M., Stamatakis, E. A., Tam, P. P., & Tyler, L. K. (2007). On the tip-of-the-tongue: Neural correlates of increased word-finding failures in normal aging. *Journal of Cognitive Neuroscience*, 19(12), 2060–2070. doi: 10.1162/jocn.2007.19.12.2060

Shafto, M. A., Stamatakis, E. A., Tam, P. P., & Tyler, L. K. (2009). Word retrieval failures in old age: The relationship between structure and function. *Journal of Cognitive Neuroscience*. doi: 10.1162/jocn.2009.21321

Shah, A., Morthland, M., Scogin, F., Presnell, A., DiNapoli, E. A., DeCoster, J., & Yang, X. (2018). Audio and computer cognitive behavioral therapy for depressive symptoms in older adults: A pilot randomized controlled trial. *Behavior Therapy*, 49(6), 904–916. doi: 10.1016/j.beth.2018.06.002

Shao, J., Zhang, Q., Ren, Y., Li, X., & Lin, T. (2019). Why are older adults victims of fraud? Current knowledge and prospects regarding older adults' vulnerability to fraud. *Journal of Elder Abuse and Neglect*, 31(3), 225–243. doi: 10.1080/08946566.2019.1625842

Shapiro, D. (2014). Stepparents and parenting stress: The roles of gender, marital quality, and views about gender roles. *Family Process*, 53(1), 97–108. doi: 10.1111/famp.12062

Shapses, S. A., & Sukumar, D. (2012). Bone metabolism in obesity and weight loss. *Annual Reviews of Nutrition*, 32, 287–309. doi: 10.1146/annurev.nutr.012809.104655

Sharma, M., Naik, V., & Deogaonkar, M. (2016). Emerging applications of deep brain stimulation. *Journal of Neurosurgical Science*, 60(2), 242–255.

Shay, J. W. (2018). Telomeres and aging. *Current Opinion in Cell Biology*, 52, 1–7. doi: https://doi.org/10.1016/j.ceb.2017.12.001

Sheehy, G. (1974). *Passages: Predictable passages of adult life.* New York: Dutton.

Sheppard, P., & Monden, C. (2019). Becoming a first-time grandparent and subjective well-being: A fixed effects approach. *Journal of Marriage and the Family*. doi: 10.1111/jomf.12584

Sherrington, C., Fairhall, N. J., Wallbank, G. K., Tiedemann, A., Michaleff, Z. A., Howard, K., ... Lamb, S. E. (2019). Exercise for preventing falls in older people living in the community. *Cochrane Database Systematic Reviews*, 1, Cd012424. doi: 10.1002/14651858.CD012424.pub2

Sherzai, D., Sherzai, A., Lui, K., Pan, D., Chiou, D., Bazargan, M., & Shaheen, M. (2016). The association between diabetes and dementia among elderly individuals: A nationwide inpatient sample analysis. *Journal of Geriatric Psychiatry and Neurology*, 29(3), 120–125. doi: 10.1177/0891988715627016

Sheu, Y., Cauley, J. A., Wheeler, V. W., Patrick, A. L., Bunker, C. H., Kammerer, C. M., & Zmuda, J. M. (2009). Natural history and correlates of hip BMD loss with aging in men of African ancestry: The Tobago Bone Health Study. *Journal of Bone Mineral Research, 24*(7), 1290–1298. doi: 10.1359/jbmr.090221

Shier, V., Khodyakov, D., Cohen, L. W., Zimmerman, S., & Saliba, D. (2014). What does the evidence really say about culture change in nursing homes? *Gerontologist, 54*(Suppl 1), S6–S16. doi: 10.1093/geront/gnt147

Shim, Y. S., Roe, C. M., Buckles, V. D., & Morris, J. C. (2013). Clinicopathologic study of Alzheimer's disease: Alzheimer mimics. *Journal of Alzheimer's Disease, 35*(4), 799–811. doi: 10.3233/jad-121594

Shing, Y. L., Werkle-Bergner, M., Brehmer, Y., Muller, V., Li, S. C., & Lindenberger, U. (2010). Episodic memory across the lifespan: The contributions of associative and strategic components. *Neuroscience and Biobehavioural Reviews, 34*(7), 1080–1091. doi: 10.1016/j.neubiorev.2009.11.002

Shor, E., Roelfs, D., & Vang, Z. M. (2017). The "Hispanic mortality paradox" revisited: Meta-analysis and meta-regression of life-course differentials in Latin American and Caribbean immigrants' mortality. *Social Science and Medicine, 186*, 20–33. doi: 10.1016/j.socscimed.2017.05.049

Shrestha, S., Stanley, M. A., Wilson, N. L., Cully, J. A., Kunik, M. E., Novy, D. M., ... Amspoker, A. B. (2015). Predictors of change in quality of life in older adults with generalized anxiety disorder. *International Psychogeriatrics, 27*(7), 1207–1215. doi: 10.1017/S1041610214002567

Sideri, O., Tsaousis, K. T., Li, H. J., Viskadouraki, M., & Tsinopoulos, I. T. (2019). The potential role of nutrition on lens pathology: A systematic review and meta-analysis. *Surveys of Ophthalmology, 64*(5), 668–678. doi: 10.1016/j.survophthal.2019.03.003

Siflinger, B. (2017). The effect of widowhood on mental health—An analysis of anticipation patterns surrounding the death of a spouse. *Health Economics, 26*(12), 1505–1523. doi: 10.1002/hec.3443

Sigurdsson, G., Aspelund, T., Chang, M., Jonsdottir, B., Sigurdsson, S., Eiriksdottir, G., ... Lang, T. F. (2006). Increasing sex difference in bone strength in old age: The Age, Gene/Environment Susceptibility-Reykjavik study (AGES-REYKJAVIK). *Bone, 39*(3), 644–651.

Silverstein, M., & Parker, M. G. (2002). Leisure activities and quality of life among the oldest old in Sweden. *Research on Aging, 24*, 528–547.

Silverstein, N. M., Hendricksen, M., Bowen, L. M., Fonte Weaver, A. J., & Whitbourne, S. K. (2019). Developing an Age-Friendly University (AFU) audit: A pilot study. *Gerontology & Geriatrics Education, 40*(2), 203–220. doi: 10.1080/02701960.2019.1572006

Simonton, D. K. (1989). The swan-song phenomenon: Last-works effects for 172 classical composers. *Psychology and Aging, 4*, 42–47.

Simonton, D. K. (1998). Achieved eminence in minority and majority cultures: Convergence versus divergence in the assessments of 294 African Americans. *Journal of Personality and Social Psychology, 74*, 804–817.

Simonton, D. K. (2012). Creative productivity and aging: An age decrement- or not? In S. K. Whitbourne & M. J. Sliwinski (Eds.), *Handbook of adult development and aging* (pp. 477–496). Oxford: Wiley-Blackwell.

Simonton, D. K. (2015). On praising convergent thinking: Creativity as blind variation and selective retention. *Creativity Research Journal, 27*(3), 262–270. doi: 10.1080/10400419.2015.1063877

Simpson, J. A., & Rholes, W. S. (2019). Adult attachment orientations and well-being during the transition to parenthood. *Current Opinion in Psychology, 25*, 47–52. doi: 10.1016/j.copsyc.2018.02.019

Sindi, S., Fiocco, A. J., Juster, R. P., Lord, C., Pruessner, J., & Lupien, S. J. (2014). Now you see it, now you don't: Testing environments modulate the association between hippocampal volume and cortisol levels in young and older adults. *Hippocampus, 24*(12), 1623–1632. doi: 10.1002/hipo.22341

Sinnott, J. D. (1989). A model for solution of ill-structured problems: Implications for everyday and abstract problem-solving. In J. D. Sinnott (Ed.), *Everyday problem solving: Theory and applications* (pp. 72–99). New York: Praeger.

Sizzano, F., Collino, S., Cominetti, O., Monti, D., Garagnani, P., Ostan, R., ... Palini, A. (2018). Evaluation of lymphocyte response to the induced oxidative stress in a cohort of ageing subjects, including semisupercentenarians and their offspring. *Mediators of Inflammation, 2018*, 7109312. doi: 10.1155/2018/7109312

Skultety, K. M., & Whitbourne, S. K. (2004). Gender differences in identity processes and self-esteem in middle and later adulthood. *Journal of Women and Aging, 16*(1), 175–188.

Smith-Ruig, T. (2009). Exploring career plateau as a multi-faceted phenomenon: Understanding the types of career plateaux experienced by accounting professionals. *British Journal of Management, 20*(4), 610–622. doi: 10.1111/j.1467-8551.2008.00608.x

Smith, C. D., Walton, A., Loveland, A. D., Umberger, G. H., Kryscio, R. J., & Gash, D. M. (2005). Memories that last in old age: Motor skill learning and memory preservation. *Neurobiology of Aging, 26*(6), 883–890.

Snedeker, J. G., & Gautieri, A. (2014). The role of collagen crosslinks in ageing and diabetes—The good, the bad, and the ugly. *Muscles, Ligaments and Tendons Journal, 4*(3), 303–308.

Sneed, J. R., & Whitbourne, S. K. (2003). Identity processing and self-consciousness in middle and later adulthood. *Journals of Gerontology Series B: Psychological Sciences and Social Sciences, 58*(6), P313–P319.

Sneed, J. R., Whitbourne, S. K., Schwartz, S. J., & Huang, S. (2012). The relationship between identity, intimacy, and midlife well-being: Findings from the Rochester Adult Longitudinal Study. *Psychology and Aging, 27*(2), 318–323. doi: 10.1037/a0026378

Snitz, B. E., O'Meara, E. S., Carlson, M. C., Arnold, A. M., Ives, D. G., Rapp, S. R., ... DeKosky, S. T. (2009). Ginkgo biloba for preventing cognitive decline in older adults: A randomized trial. *Journal of the American Medical Association, 302*(24), 2663–2670. doi: 302/24/2663 [pii] 10.1001/jama.2009.1913

Social Security Administration. (2019a). Fact Sheet. From https://www.ssa.gov/news/press/factsheets/basicfact-alt.pdf

Social Security Administration. (2019b). Monthly statistical snapshot, May 2019. From http://www.ssa.gov/policy/docs/quickfacts/stat_snapshot/

Sohal, R. S., & Orr, W. C. (2012). The redox stress hypothesis of aging. *Free Radical Biology Medicine*, *52*(3), 539–555. doi: 10.1016/j.freeradbiomed.2011.10.445

Soldz, S., & Vaillant, G. E. (1998). A 50-year longitudinal study of defense use among inner city men: A validation of the DSM-IV defense axis. *Journal of Nervous and Mental Disease*, *186*(2), 104–111.

Solem, P. E., Syse, A., Furunes, T., Mykletun, R. J., De Lange, A., Schaufeli, W., & Ilmarinen, J. (2016). To leave or not to leave: Retirement intentions and retirement behaviour. *Ageing & Society*, *36*(2), 259–281. doi: 10.1017/S0144686X14001135

Spearman, C. (1904). "General intelligence:" Objectively determined and measured. *American Journal of Psychology*, *15*, 201–292.

Spence, R., Jacobs, C., & Bifulco, A. (2018). Attachment style, loneliness and depression in older age women. *Aging and Mental Health*, 1–3. doi: 10.1080/13607863.2018.1553141

Spreng, R. N., DuPre, E., Selarka, D., Garcia, J., Gojkovic, S., Mildner, J., … Turner, G. R. (2014). Goal-congruent default network activity facilitates cognitive control. *Journal of Neuroscience*, *34*(42), 14108–14114. doi: 10.1523/jneurosci.2815-14.2014

Spengler, M., Brunner, M., Damian, R. I., Ludtke, O., Martin, R., & Roberts, B. W. (2015). Student characteristics and behaviors at age 12 predict occupational success 40 years later over and above childhood IQ and parental socioeconomic status. *Developmental Psychology*, *51*(9), 1329–1340. doi: 10.1037/dev0000025

St Jacques, P. L., Montgomery, D., & Schacter, D. L. (2015). Modifying memory for a museum tour in older adults: Reactivation-related updating that enhances and distorts memory is reduced in ageing. *Memory*, *23*(6), 876–887. doi: 10.1080/09658211.2014.933241

Starr, J. M., Deary, I. J., Fox, H. C., & Whalley, L. J. (2007). Smoking and cognitive change from age 11 to 66 years: A confirmatory investigation. *Addictive Behaviors*, *32*(1), 63–68.

Statistics Canada. (2019). Leading causes of death, total population, by age group. From https://www150.statcan.gc.ca/t1/tbl1/en/tv.action?pid=1310039401

Staudinger, U. M., & Gluck, J. (2011). Psychological wisdom research: Commonalities and differences in a growing field. *Annual Review of Psychology*, *62*, 215–241. doi: 10.1146/annurev.psych.121208.131659

Staudinger, U. M., Marsiske, M., & Baltes, P. B. (1995). Resilience and reserve capacity in later adulthood: Potentials and limits of development across the life span. In D. Cicchetti & D. J. Cohen (Eds.), *Developmental psychopathology. Risk, disorder, and adaptation* (Vol. 2, pp. 801–847). New York: Wiley.

Stawski, R. S., Sliwinski, M. J., & Smyth, J. M. (2006). Stress-related cognitive interference predicts cognitive function in old age. *Psychology and Aging*, *21*(3), 535–544. doi: 10.1037/0882-7974.21.3.535

Steele, C. M., Spencer, S. J., Aronson, J., & Zanna, M. P. (2002). Contending with group image: The psychology of stereotype and social identity threat. In P. Devine (Ed.), *Advances in experimental social psychology* (Vol. 34, pp. 379–440). San Diego, CA: Academic Press.

Stefanetti, R. J., Voisin, S., Russell, A., & Lamon, S. (2018). Recent advances in understanding the role of FOXO3. *F1000Research*, *7*, F1000 Faculty Rev-1372. doi: 10.12688/f1000research.15258.1

Stella, F., Radanovic, M., Canineu, P. R., de Paula, V. J., & Forlenza, O. V. (2015). Anti-dementia medications: Current prescriptions in clinical practice and new agents in progress. *Therapeutic Advances in Drug Safety*, *6*(4), 151–165. doi: 10.1177/2042098615592116

Steptoe, A., Deaton, A., & Stone, A. A. (2015). Subjective well-being, health, and ageing. *Lancet*, *385*(9968), 640–648. doi: 10.1016/s0140-6736(13)61489-0

Steptoe, A., Easterlin, E., & Kirschbaum, C. (2017). Conscientiousness, hair cortisol concentration, and health behaviour in older men and women. *Psychoneuroendocrinology*, *86*, 122–127. doi: 10.1016/j.psyneuen.2017.09.016

Sterns, H. L., & Gray, J. H. (1999). Work, leisure, and retirement. In J. C. Cavanaugh & S. K. Whitbourne (Eds.), *Gerontology: Interdisciplinary perspectives* (pp. 355–390). New York: Oxford University Press.

Stojan, R., & Voelcker-Rehage, C. (2019). A systematic review on the cognitive benefits and neurophysiological correlates of exergaming in healthy older adults. *Journal of Clinical Medicine*, *8*(5). doi: 10.3390/jcm8050734

Story, T. N., Berg, C. A., Smith, T. W., Beveridge, R., Henry, N. J., & Pearce, G. (2007). Age, marital satisfaction, and optimism as predictors of positive sentiment override in middle-aged and older married couples. *Psychology and Aging*, *22*(4), 719–727. doi: 2007-18670-007 [pii] 10.1037/0882-7974.22.4.719

Straif, K., Benbrahim-Tallaa, L., Baan, R., Grosse, Y., Secretan, B., El Ghissassi, F., … Cogliano, V. (2009). A review of human carcinogens—Part C: Metals, arsenic, dusts, and fibres. *Lancet Oncology*, *10*(5), 453–454.

Strenger, C. (2009). Paring down life to the essentials: An epicurean psychodynamics of midlife changes. *Psychoanalytic Psychology*, *26*(3), 246–258.

Stringhini, S., Berkman, L., Dugravot, A., Ferrie, J. E., Marmot, M., Kivimaki, M., & Singh-Manoux, A. (2012). Socioeconomic status, structural and functional measures of social support, and mortality: The British Whitehall II Cohort Study, 1985–2009. *American Journal of Epidemiology*, *175*(12), 1275–1283. doi: 10.1093/aje/kwr461

Stroebe, M., Schut, H., & Boerner, K. (2010). Continuing bonds in adaptation to bereavement: Toward theoretical integration. *Clinical Psychology Reviews*, *30*(2), 259–268. doi: 10.1016/j.cpr.2009.11.007

Stuenkel, C. A. (2015). Menopausal hormone therapy: Current considerations. *Endocrinological and Metabolic Clinics of North*

America, 44(3), 565–585. doi: 10.1016/j.ecl.2015.05.006 S0889-8529(15)00047-X [pii]

Stypinska, J., & Turek, K. (2017). Hard and soft age discrimination: The dual nature of workplace discrimination. *European Journal of Ageing, 14*(1), 49–61. doi: 10.1007/s10433-016-0407-y

Suarez, E. C., Williams, R. B., Kuhn, C. M., & Zimmerman, E. A. (1991). Biobehavioral basis of coronary-prone behavior in middle-aged men: II. Serum cholesterol, the Type A behavior pattern, and hostility as interactive modulators of physiological reactivity. *Psychosomatic Medicine, 53*(5), 528–537.

Substance Abuse and Mental Health Services Administration. (2018). National Survey from the 2017 National Survey on Drug Use and Health: Detailed Tables. *National Survey of Drug Use and Health*. Rockville, MD: Center for Behavioral Health Statistics and Quality.

Suitor, J. J., Sechrist, J., Plikuhn, M., Pardo, S. T., Gilligan, M., & Pillemer, K. (2009). The role of perceived maternal favoritism in sibling relations in midlife. *Journal of Marriage and the Family, 71*(4), 1026–1038.

Sun, N., Youle, R. J., & Finkel, T. (2016). The mitochondrial basis of aging. *Molecular Cell, 61*(5), 654–666. doi: 10.1016/j.molcel.2016.01.028

Sung, J., Song, Y. M., & Hong, K. P. (2019). Relationship between the shift of socioeconomic status and cardiovascular mortality. *European Journal of Preventive Cardiology*, 2047487319856125. doi: 10.1177/2047487319856125

Super, D. E. (1990). A life span, life-space approach to career development. In D. Brown & L. Brooks (Eds.), *Career choice and development* (2nd ed.). San Francisco, CA: Jossey-Bass.

Sutin, A. R., Beason-Held, L. L., Resnick, S. M., & Costa, P. T. (2009). Sex differences in resting-state neural correlates of openness to experience among older adults. *Cerebral Cortex, 19*(12), 2797–2802.

Sutin, A. R., Stephan, Y., Damian, R. I., Luchetti, M., Strickhouser, J. E., & Terracciano, A. (2019). Five-factor model personality traits and verbal fluency in 10 cohorts. *Psychology and Aging, 34*(3), 362–373. doi: 10.1037/pag0000351

Sutin, A. R., Stephan, Y., & Terracciano, A. (2018). Facets of conscientiousness and objective markers of health status. *Psychological Health, 33*(9), 1100–1115. doi: 10.1080/08870446.2018.1464165

Sutphin, S. T. (2010). Social exchange theory and the division of household labor in same-sex couples. *Marriage & Family Review, 46*(3), 191–206. doi: 10.1080/01494929.2010.490102

Sweeney, M. M., & Cancian, M. (2004). The changing importance of White women's economic prospects for assortative mating. *Journal of Marriage and Family, 66*(4), 1015–1028.

Swick, K. J., & Williams, R. D. (2006). An analysis of Bronfenbrenner's bio-ecological perspective for early childhood educators: Implications for working with families experiencing stress. *Early Childhood Education Journal, 33*(5), 371–378. doi: 10.1007/s10643-006-0078-y

Szanton, S. L., Xue, Q. L., Leff, B., Guralnik, J., Wolff, J. L., Tanner, E. K., … Gitlin, L. N. (2019). Effect of a biobehavioral environmental approach on disability among low-income older adults: A randomized clinical trial. *JAMA Internal Medicine*. doi: 10.1001/jamainternmed.2018.6026

Tanaka, H., Nusselder, W. J., Bopp, M., Nussbaum, J. F., Kalediene, R., Lee, J. S., … Mackenbach, J. P. (2019a). Mortality inequalities by occupational class among men in Japan, South Korea and eight European countries: A national register-based study, 1990–2015. *Journal of Epidemiological and Community Health, 73*(8), 750–758. doi: 10.1136/jech-2018-211715

Tanaka, H., & Seals, D. R. (2003). Invited review: Dynamic exercise performance in Masters athletes: Insight into the effects of primary human aging on physiological functional capacity. *Journal of Applied Physiology, 95*(5), 2152–2162.

Tanaka, M., Kusaga, M., Nyamathi, A. M., & Tanaka, K. (2019b). Effects of brief cognitive behavioral therapy for insomnia on improving depression among community-dwelling older adults: A randomized controlled comparative study. *Worldviews on Evidence-Based Nursing, 16*(1), 78–86. doi: 10.1111/wvn.12342

Tang, H. Y., Harms, V., Speck, S. M., Vezeau, T., & Jesurum, J. T. (2009). Effects of audio relaxation programs for blood pressure reduction in older adults. *European Journal of Cardiovascular Nursing, 8*(5), 329–336. doi: S1474-5151(09)00061-9 [pii] 10.1016/j.ejcnurse.2009.06.001

Tang, J., Liu, M.-S., & Liu, W.-B. (2017). How workplace fun influences employees' performance: The role of person–organization value congruence. *Social Behavior and Personality: An International Journal, 45*(11), 1787–1802. doi: 10.2224/sbp.6240

Tanuseputro, P., Hsu, A., Chalifoux, M., Talarico, R., Kobewka, D., Scott, M., … Perri, G. (2019). Do-not-resuscitate and do-not-hospitalize orders in nursing homes: Who gets them and do they make a difference? *Journal of the American Medical Directors Association*. doi: 10.1016/j.jamda.2019.02.017

Taylor, J. (2017). Over-the-counter medicines and diabetes care. *Canadian Journal of Diabetes, 41*(6), 551–557. doi: 10.1016/j.jcjd.2017.06.015

Teichtahl, A. J., Wluka, A. E., Wang, Y., Hanna, F., English, D. R., Giles, G. G., & Cicuttini, F. M. (2009). Obesity and adiposity are associated with the rate of patella cartilage volume loss over 2 years in adults without knee osteoarthritis. *Annals of the Rheumatic Diseases, 68*(6), 909–913. doi: ard.2008.093310 [pii] 10.1136/ard.2008.093310

Teixeira, C. V. L., Gobbi, L. T. B., Corazza, D. I., Stella, F., Costa, J. L. R., & Gobbi, S. (2012). Non-pharmacological interventions on cognitive functions in older people with mild cognitive impairment (MCI). *Archives of Gerontology and Geriatrics, 54*(1), 175–180.

Teno, J. M., Weitzen, S., Fennell, M. L., & Mor, V. (2001). Dying trajectory in the last year of life: Does cancer trajectory fit other diseases? *Journal of Palliative Medicine, 4*(4), 457–464. doi: 10.1089/109662101753381593

Tentori, K., Osherson, D., Hasher, L., & May, C. (2001). Wisdom and aging: Irrational preferences in college students but not older adults. *Cognition, 81*(3), B87–96.

Teruya, S. A., & Bazargan-Hejazi, S. (2013). The immigrant and Hispanic paradoxes: A systematic review of their predictions and effects. *Hispanic Journal of Behavioral Sciences*, 35(4), 486–509. doi: 10.1177/0739986313499004

Tham, Y.-C., Li, X., Wong, T. Y., Quigley, H. A., Aung, T., & Cheng, C.-Y. (2014). Global prevalence of glaucoma and projections of glaucoma burden through 2040: A systematic review and meta-analysis. *Ophthalmology*, 121(11), 2081–2090. doi: 10.1016/j.ophtha.2014.05.013

The President's Council on Bioethics. (2005). *Taking care: Ethical caregiving in our aging society*. Washington, DC.

The US Burden of Disease Collaborators. (2018). The State of US Health, 1990–2016: Burden of diseases, injuries, and risk factors Among US states. *Journal of the American Medical Association*, 319(14), 1444–1472. doi: 10.1001/jama.2018.0158

Theodoraki, A., & Bouloux, P. M. (2009). Testosterone therapy in men. *Menopause International*, 15(2), 87–92. doi: 15/2/87 [pii] 10.1258/mi.2009.009025

Thomas, M. L., Kaufmann, C. N., Palmer, B. W., Depp, C. A., Martin, A. S., Glorioso, D. K., ... Jeste, D. V. (2016). Paradoxical trend for improvement in mental health with aging: A community-based study of 1,546 adults aged 21–100 years. *Journal of Clinical Psychiatry*, 77(8), e1019–1025. doi: 10.4088/JCP.16m10671

Thomas, P. A., Lodge, A. C., & Reczek, C. (2019). Do support and strain with adult children affect mothers' and fathers' physical activity? *Research on Aging*, 41(2), 164–185. doi: 10.1177/0164027518792904

Thornton, W. J. L., & Dumke, H. A. (2005). Age differences in everyday problem-solving and decision-making effectiveness: A meta-analytic review. *Psychology and Aging*, 20(1), 85–99.

Thornton, W. L., Paterson, T. S. E., & Yeung, S. E. (2013). Age differences in everyday problem solving: The role of problem context. *International Journal of Behavioral Development*, 37(1), 13–20. doi: 10.1177/0165025412454028

Thorp, S. R., Glassman, L. H., Wells, S. Y., Walter, K. H., Gebhardt, H., Twamley, E., ... Wetherell, J. (2019). A randomized controlled trial of prolonged exposure therapy versus relaxation training for older veterans with military-related PTSD. *Journal of Anxiety Disorders*, 64, 45–54. doi: 10.1016/j.janxdis.2019.02.003

Tillmann, T., Pikhart, H., Peasey, A., Kubinova, R., Pajak, A., Tamosiunas, A., ... Bobak, M. (2017). Psychosocial and socioeconomic determinants of cardiovascular mortality in Eastern Europe: A multicentre prospective cohort study. *PLoS Medicine*, 14(12), e1002459. doi: 10.1371/journal.pmed.1002459

Tinetti, M. E., & Kumar, C. (2010). The patient who falls: "It's always a trade-off". *Journal of the American Medical Association*, 303(3), 258–266. doi: 303/3/258 [pii] 10.1001/jama.2009.2024

Tolppanen, A.-M., Solomon, A., Kulmala, J., Kåreholt, I., Ngandu, T., Rusanen, M., ... Kivipelto, M. (2015). Leisure-time physical activity from mid- to late life, body mass index, and risk of dementia. *Alzheimer's & Dementia: The Journal of the Alzheimer's Association*, 11(4), 434–443. doi: 10.1016/j.jalz.2014.01.008

Tomás, J. M., Sancho, P., Galiana, L., & Oliver, A. (2016). A double test on the importance of spirituality, the 'forgotten factor', in successful aging. *Social Indicators Research*, 127(3), 1377–1389. doi: 10.1007/s11205-015-1014-6

Tomlinson, J., Baird, M., Berg, P., & Cooper, R. (2018). Flexible careers across the life course: Advancing theory, research and practice. *Human Relations*, 71(1), 4–22. doi: 10.1177/0018726717733313

Tostain, J. L., & Blanc, F. (2008). Testosterone deficiency: A common, unrecognized syndrome. *National Clinical Practice Urology*, 5(7), 388–396. doi: ncpuro1167 [pii] 10.1038/ncpuro1167

Travison, T. G., Araujo, A. B., Beck, T. J., Williams, R. E., Clark, R. V., Leder, B. Z., & McKinlay, J. B. (2009). Relation between serum testosterone, serum estradiol, sex hormone-binding globulin, and geometrical measures of adult male proximal femur strength. *Journal of Clinical Endocrinology and Metabolism*, 94(3), 853–860. doi: jc.2008-0668 [pii] 10.1210/jc.2008-0668

Tremblay, S., & Pierce, T. (2011). Perceptions of fatherhood: Longitudinal reciprocal associations within the couple. *Canadian Journal of Behavioural Science/Revue canadienne des sciences du comportement*, 43(2), 99–110. doi: 10.1037/a0022635

Troll, L. E. (1985). The contingencies of grandparenting. In V. L. Bengston & J. F. Robertson (Eds.), *Grandparenthood* (pp. 135–149). Beverly Hills, CA: Sage Publications.

Trouillet, R. l., Gana, K., Lourel, M., & Fort, I. (2009). Predictive value of age for coping: The role of self-efficacy, social support satisfaction and perceived stress. *Aging and Mental Health*, 13(3), 357–366.

Trunk, D. L., & Abrams, L. (2009). Do younger and older adults' communicative goals influence off-topic speech in autobiographical narratives? *Psychology and Aging*, 24(2), 324–337.

Tucker-Drob, E. M. (2011). Neurocognitive functions and everyday functions change together in old age. *Neuropsychology*, 25(3), 368–377. doi: 10.1037/a0022348

Turcotte, M. (2006). Parents with adult children living at home. *Canadian Social Trends*, 11–14.

Turiano, N. A., Spiro, A., 3rd, & Mroczek, D. K. (2012). Openness to experience and mortality in men: Analysis of trait and facets. *Journal of Aging and Health*, 24(4), 654–672. doi: 10.1177/0898264311431303

Turner-Zwinkels, F. M., & Spini, D. (2019). (Mis-)coordinating identities in the transition to parenthood: Investigating the co-development of partners' parenting, domestic and provider identities before and after the birth of the first child. *European Journal of Social Psychology*. doi: 10.1002/ejsp.2591

Turner, J. E., & Brum, P. C. (2017). Does regular exercise Counter T Cell immunosenescence reducing the risk of developing cancer and promoting successful treatment of malignancies? *Oxidative Medicine and Cell Longevity*, 4234765. doi: 10.1155/2017/4234765

Tyagi, T., Alarab, M., Leong, Y., Lye, S., & Shynlova, O. (2019). Local oestrogen therapy modulates extracellular matrix and immune response in the vaginal tissue of post-menopausal women with severe pelvic organ prolapse. *Journal of Cellular and Molecular Medicine*, 23(4), 2907–2919. doi: 10.1111/jcmm.14199

Tyrovolas, S., Koyanagi, A., Olaya, B., Ayuso-Mateos, J. L., Miret, M., Chatterji, S., ... Haro, J. M. (2016). Factors associated with skeletal muscle mass, sarcopenia, and sarcopenic obesity in older adults: A multi-continent study. *Journal of Cachexia Sarcopenia Muscle*, 7(3), 312–321. doi: 10.1002/jcsm.12076

U.S. Bureau of the Census. (2012). America's families and living arrangements: 2011. Table FG6.

U.S. Bureau of the Census. (2016). Living arrangements of children under 18. Retrieved 6/19/2019, from https://www.census.gov/library/visualizations/2016/comm/cb16-192_living_arrangements.html

U.S. Bureau of the Census. (2017a). 2014 National Population Projections Tables. From https://www.census.gov/data/tables/2014/demo/popproj/2014-summary-tables.html

U.S. Bureau of the Census. (2017b). LGBTQ family fact sheet in support of August 2017 presentation to NAC undercount of young children working group.

U.S. Bureau of the Census. (2017c). Grandparents still work to support grandchildren.

U.S. Bureau of the Census. (2018a). America's families and living arrangements: 2018.

U.S. Bureau of the Census. (2018b). American fact finder. Retrieved 8/20/2018. From https://factfinder.census.gov/faces/tableservices/jsf/pages/productview.xhtml?pid=PEP_2017_PEPAGESEX&prodType=table

U.S. Bureau of the Census. (2018c). Fatherly figures: A snapshot of dads today. From https://www.census.gov/library/visualizations/2018/comm/fathers-day.html

U.S. Bureau of the Census. (2018d). From pyramid to pillar: A century of change, population of the U.S. From https://www.census.gov/library/visualizations/2018/comm/century-of-change.html

U.S. Bureau of the Census. (2018e). Women's earnings by occupation. Retrieved 6/21/2019, from https://www.census.gov/content/dam/Census/library/visualizations/2018/comm/womens-occupations.pdf

U.S. Bureau of the Census. (2019a). Characteristics of same-sex couple households: 2005 to present. Retrieved 6/18/2019, from https://www.census.gov/data/tables/time-series/demo/same-sex-couples/ssc-house-characteristics.html

U.S. Bureau of the Census. (2019b). Median age at first marriage: 1890 to present. Figure MS-2.

U.S. Department of Health and Human Services. (2017). Costs of care. From https://longtermcare.acl.gov/costs-how-to-pay/costs-of-care.html

U.S. Department of Labor. (2015). Equal pay infographic. From https://digitalcommons.ilr.cornell.edu/key_workplace/1583

United Nations. (2015). Sustainable development goals. From https://www.un.org/sustainabledevelopment/health/

United Nations. (2019). World mortality, 2017. From https://www.un.org/en/development/desa/population/publications/pdf/mortality/World-Mortality-2017-Data-Booklet.pdf

United Nations Population Fund. (2016). Stunning plunge in maternal deaths recorded in Maldives. From https://www.unfpa.org/news/stunning-plunge-maternal-deaths-recorded-maldives

Urien, B., & Kilbourne, W. (2011). Generativity and self-enhancement values in eco-friendly behavioral intentions and environmentally responsible consumption behavior. *Psychology & Marketing*, 28(1), 69–90. doi: 10.1002/mar.20381

Vaden, K. I., Jr., Matthews, L. J., Eckert, M. A., & Dubno, J. R. (2017). Longitudinal changes in audiometric phenotypes of age-related hearing loss. *Journal of the Association for Research in Otolaryngology*, 18(2), 371–385. doi: 10.1007/s10162-016-0596-2

Vaillant, G. E. (1993). *The wisdom of the ego*. Cambridge, MA: Harvard University Press.

Vaillant, G. E. (2000). Adaptive mental mechanisms: Their role in a positive psychology. *American Psychologist*, 55, 89–98.

Valentijn, S. A. M., Hill, R. D., Van Hooren, S. A. H., Bosma, H., Van Boxtel, M. P. J., Jolles, J., & Ponds, R. W. H. M. (2006). Memory self-efficacy predicts memory performance: Results from a 6-year follow-up study. *Psychology and Aging*, 21(1), 165–172.

Valian, V. (2014). Bilingualism and cognition. *Bilingualism: Language and Cognition*, 18(1), 3–24. doi: 10.1017/S1366728914000522

Valiathan, R., & Asthana, D. (2016). Increase in frequencies of circulating Th-17 cells correlates with microbial translocation, immune activation and exhaustion in HIV-1 infected patients with poor CD4 T-cell reconstitution. *Immunobiology*, 221(5), 670–678. doi: 10.1016/j.imbio.2016.01.002 S0171-2985(16)30004-3 [pii]

Van Benthem, K., & Herdman, C. M. (2016). Cognitive factors mediate the relation between age and flight path maintenance in general aviation. *Aviation Psychology and Applied Human Factors*, 6(2), 81–90. doi: 10.1027/2192-0923/a000102

van der Wiel, R., Mulder, C. H., & Bailey, A. (2018). Pathways to commitment in living-apart-together relationships in the Netherlands: A study on satisfaction, alternatives, investments and social support. *Advances in Life Course Research*, 36, 13–22. doi: https://doi.org/10.1016/j.alcr.2018.03.001

van Drongelen, A., Boot, C. R., Hlobil, H., Smid, T., & van der Beek, A. J. (2017). Risk factors for fatigue among airline pilots. *International Archives of Occupational and Environmental Health*, 90(1), 39–47. doi: 10.1007/s00420-016-1170-2

van Hooff, M. L., Geurts, S. A., Taris, T. W., Kompier, M. A., Dikkers, J. S., Houtman, I. L., & van den Heuvel, F. M. (2005). Disentangling the causal relationships between work-home interference and employee health. *Scandinavian Journal of Work and Environmental Health*, 31(1), 15–29.

Van Ness, P. H., & Larson, D. B. (2002). Religion, senescence, and mental health: The end of life is not the end of hope. *American Journal of Geriatric Psychiatry*, 10(4), 386–397.

Van Volkom, M. (2006). Sibling relationships in middle and older adulthood: A review of the literature. *Marriage and Family Review*, 40(2), 151–170.

Vauclair, C.-M., Marques, S., Lima, M. L., Bratt, C., Swift, H. J., & Abrams, D. (2015). Subjective social status of older people across countries: The role of modernization and employment. *The Journals of Gerontology: Series B: Psychological Sciences and Social Sciences*, 70(4), 650–660. doi: 10.1093/geronb/gbu074

Velagaleti, R. S., & O'Donnell, C. J. (2010). Genomics of heart failure. *Heart Failure Clinics*, 6, 115–124.

Velez, B. L., & Moradi, B. (2012). Workplace support, discrimination, and person–organization fit: Tests of the theory of work adjustment with LGB individuals. *Journal of Counseling Psychology*, 59(3), 399–407. doi: 10.1037/a0028326

Ventura, J., Subotnik, K. L., Gitlin, M. J., Gretchen-Doorly, D., Ered, A., Villa, K. F., … Nuechterlein, K. H. (2015). Negative symptoms and functioning during the first year after a recent onset of schizophrenia and 8 years later. *Schizophrenia Research*, 161(2–3), 407–413. doi: 10.1016/j.schres.2014.10.043

Verloo, H., Goulet, C., Morin, D., & von Gunten, A. (2016). Nursing intervention versus usual care to improve delirium among home-dwelling older adults receiving homecare after hospitalization: Feasibility and acceptability of a randomized controlled trail. *BMC Nursing*, 15, 19. doi: 10.1186/s12912-016-0140-z

Verweij, L. M., van Schoor, N. M., Deeg, D. J., Dekker, J., & Visser, M. (2009). Physical activity and incident clinical knee osteoarthritis in older adults. *Arthritis Rheumatology*, 61(2), 152–157. doi: 10.1002/art.24233

Vespa, J. (2009). Gender ideology construction: A life course and intersectional approach. *Gender & Society*, 23(3), 363–387. doi: 10.1177/0891243209337507

Vespa, J. (2014). Historical trends in the marital intentions of one-time and serial cohabitors. *Journal of Marriage and the Family*, 76(1), 207–217. doi: 10.1111/jomf.12083

Vespa, J. (2017). The changing economics and demographics of young adulthood: 1975–2016. Report #P20-579.

Vespa, J., Armstrong, D. M., & Medina, L. (2018). Demographic turning points for the United States: Population projections for 2020 to 2060: Current population reports P25-1144: U.S. Bureau of the Census.

Videler, A. C., Hutsebaut, J., Schulkens, J. E. M., Sobczak, S., & van Alphen, S. P. J. (2019). A life span perspective on borderline personality disorder. *Current Psychiatry Reports*, 21(7), 51. doi: 10.1007/s11920-019-1040-1

Videman, T., Battie, M. C., Gibbons, L. E., & Gill, K. (2014). Aging changes in lumbar discs and vertebrae and their interaction: A 15-year follow-up study. *The Spine Journal*, 14(3), 469–478. doi: 10.1016/j.spinee.2013.11.018

Villa, J. C., Gianakos, A., & Lane, J. M. (2016). Bisphosphonate treatment in osteoporosis: Optimal duration of therapy and the incorporation of a drug holiday. *HSS Journal: The Musculoskeletal Journal of Hospital for Special Surgery*, 12(1), 66–73. doi: 10.1007/s11420-015-9469-1

Vita, A., & Barlati, S. (2018). Recovery from schizophrenia: Is it possible? *Current Opinion in Psychiatry*, 31(3), 246–255. doi: 10.1097/yco.0000000000000407

Vitale, S., Cotch, M. F., & Sperduto, R. D. (2006). Prevalence of visual impairment in the United States. *Journal of the American Medical Association*, 295(18), 2158–2163.

Vogelzangs, N., Comijs, H. C., Oude Voshaar, R. C., Stek, M. L., & Penninx, B. W. (2014). Late-life depression symptom profiles are differentially associated with immunometabolic functioning. *Brain Behavior and Immunology*, 41, 109–115. doi: 10.1016/j.bbi.2014.05.004 S0889-1591(14)00126-3 [pii]

Volling, B. L. (2003). Sibling relationships. In M. H. Bornstein, L. Davidson, C. L. M. Keyes & K. A. Moore (Eds.), *Well-being: Positive development across the life course* (pp. 205–220). Mahwah, NJ: Lawrence Erlbaum Associates.

Voorpostel, M., & Blieszner, R. (2008). Intergenerational solidarity and support between adult siblings. *Journal of Marriage and Family*, 70(1), 157–167.

Vural, E. M., van Munster, B. C., & de Rooij, S. E. (2014). Optimal dosages for melatonin supplementation therapy in older adults: A systematic review of current literature. *Drugs & Aging*, 31(6), 441–451. doi: 10.1007/s40266-014-0178-0

Wada, M., Hanamoto, A., & Kawashima, A. (2019). Elderly patients with lower-jaw mobility require careful food texture modification: A cohort study. *Journal of General Family Medicine*, 20(3), 93–100. doi: 10.1002/jgf2.240

Waite, L. J., Laumann, E. O., Das, A., & Schumm, L. P. (2009). Sexuality: Measures of partnerships, practices, attitudes, and problems in National Social Life, Health, and Aging Study. *The Journals of Gerontology: Series B: Psychological Sciences and Social Sciences*, 64B(Suppl 1), 156–166.

Waiter, G. D., Deary, I. J., Staff, R. T., Murray, A. D., Fox, H. C., Starr, J. M., & Whalley, L. J. (2010). Exploring possible neural mechanisms of intelligence differences using processing speed and working memory tasks: An fMRI study. *Intelligence*, 37(2), 199–206.

Walford, R. L., Mock, D., Verdery, R., & MacCallum, T. (2002). Calorie restriction in biosphere 2: Alterations in physiologic, hematologic, hormonal, and biochemical parameters in humans restricted for a 2-year period. *Journal of Gerontology Series A: Biological Sciences and Medical Sciences*, 57(6), B211–224.

Walker, A. E., Eskurza, I., Pierce, G. L., Gates, P. E., & Seals, D. R. (2009). Modulation of vascular endothelial function by low-density lipoprotein cholesterol with aging: Influence of habitual exercise. *American Journal of Hypertension*, 22(3), 250–256. doi: ajh2008353 [pii] 10.1038/ajh.2008.353

Walster, E., Walster, G. W., & Berscheid, E. (1978). *Equity: Theory and research*. Boston, MA: Allyn & Bacon.

Walston, J. D. (2012). Sarcopenia in older adults. *Current Opinion in Rheumatology*, 24(6), 623–627. doi: 10.1097/BOR.0b013e328358d59b

Wang, M., & Shi, J. (2014). Psychological research on retirement. *Annual Review of Psychology*, 65, 209–233. doi: 10.1146/annurev-psych-010213-115131

Ward, E. V. (2018). Reduced recognition and priming in older relative to young adults for incidental and intentional information. *Consciousness and Cognition*, 57, 62–73. doi: 10.1016/j.concog.2017.11.006

Waring, J. D., Seiger, A. N., Solomon, P. R., Budson, A. E., & Kensinger, E. A. (2014). Memory for the 2008 presidential election in healthy ageing and mild cognitive impairment. *Cognition and Emotion*, 28(8), 1407–1421. doi: 10.1080/02699931.2014.886558

Wassertheil-Smoller, S., Kaplan, R. C., & Salazar, C. R. (2014). Stroke findings in the Women's Health Initiative. *Seminars in Reproductive Medicine*, 32(6), 438–446. doi: 10.1055/s-0034-1384627

Watad, A., Bragazzi, N. L., Adawi, M., Amital, H., Toubi, E., Porat, B. S., & Shoenfeld, Y. (2017). Autoimmunity in the elderly: Insights from basic science and clinics—A mini-review. *Gerontology*, 63(6), 515–523.

Watson, K. B., Carlson, S. A., Gunn, J. P., Galuska, D. A., O'Connor, A., Greenlund, K. J., & Fulton, J. E. (2016). Physical inactivity among adults aged 50 Years and older United States, 2014. *Morbidity and Mortality Weekly Report*, 65, 954–958. doi: doi:10.15585/mmwr.mm6536a3external

Webb, C. E., Turney, I. C., & Dennis, N. A. (2016). What's the gist? The influence of schemas on the neural correlates underlying true and false memories. *Neuropsychologia*, 93(Pt A), 61–75. doi: 10.1016/j.neuropsychologia.2016.09.023

Wechsler, D. (2008). Wechsler Adult Intelligence Scales- IV. From http://www.pearsonassessments.com/HAIWEB/Cultures/en-us/Productdetail.htm?Pid=015-8980-808

Weinberger, M. I., Hofstein, Y., & Whitbourne, S. K. (2008). Intimacy in young adulthood as a predictor of divorce in midlife. *Personal Relationships*, 15(4), 551–557. doi: 10.1111/j.1475-6811.2008.00215.x

Weinberger, M. I., & Whitbourne, S. K. (2010). Depressive symptoms, self-reported physical functioning, and identity in community-dwelling older adults. *Ageing International*. doi: 10.1007/s12126-010-9053-4

Weiss, D. (2018). On the inevitability of aging: Essentialist beliefs moderate the impact of negative age stereotypes on older adults' memory performance and physiological reactivity. *Journals of Gerontology Series B: Psychological Sciences and Social Sciences*, 73(6), 925–933. doi: 10.1093/geronb/gbw087

Weiss, A., & Costa, P. T., Jr. (2005). Domain and facet personality predictors of all-cause mortality among medicare patients aged 65 to 100. *Psychosomatic Medicine*, 67(5), 724–733. doi: 67/5/724 [pii] 10.1097/01.psy.0000181272.58103.18

Weiss, H. M., & Cropanzano, R. (1996). Affective events theory: A theoretical discussion of the structure, causes and consequences of affective experiences at work. In B. M. Staw & L. L. Cummings (Eds.), *Research in organizational behavior: An annual series of analytical essays and critical reviews* (Vol. 18, pp. 1–74). Middlesex: Elsevier Science/JAI Press.

Weltman, A., Weltman, J. Y., Roy, C. P., Wideman, L., Patrie, J., Evans, W. S., & Veldhuis, J. D. (2006). Growth hormone response to graded exercise intensities is attenuated and the gender difference abolished in older adults. *Journal of Applied Physiology*, 100(5), 1623–1629.

Wen, W., Schlundt, D., Andersen, S. W., Blot, W. J., & Zheng, W. (2019). Does religious involvement affect mortality in low-income Americans? A prospective cohort study. *BMJ Open*, 9(7), e028200. doi: 10.1136/bmjopen-2018-028200

Wennberg, A. M. V., Hagen, C. E., Machulda, M. M., Hollman, J. H., Roberts, R. O., Knopman, D. S., … Mielke, M. M. (2018). The association between peripheral total IGF-1, IGFBP-3, and IGF-1/IGFBP-3 and functional and cognitive outcomes in the Mayo Clinic Study of Aging. *Neurobiology of Aging*, 66, 68–74. doi: 10.1016/j.Neurobiology of Agingaging.2017.11.017

Werner, P., Buchbinder, E., Lowenstein, A., & Livni, T. (2005). Mediation across generations: A tri-generational perspective. *Journal of Aging Studies*, 19(4), 489–502.

West, A., Lewis, J., Roberts, J., & Noden, P. (2017). Young adult graduates living in the parental home: Expectations, negotiations, and parental financial support. *Journal of Family Issues*, 38(17), 2449–2473. doi: 10.1177/0192513X16643745

West, G. L., Al-Aidroos, N., & Pratt, J. (2013). Action video game experience affects oculomotor performance. *Acta Psychologica*, 142(1), 38–42. doi: http://dx.doi.org/10.1016/j.actpsy.2011.08.005t

West, R., & Schwarb, H. (2006). The influence of aging and frontal function on the neural correlates of regulative and evaluative aspects of cognitive control. *Neuropsychology*, 20(4), 468–481.

West, R. L., Bagwell, D. K., & Dark-Freudeman, A. (2008). Self-efficacy and memory aging: The impact of a memory intervention based on self-efficacy. *Neuropsychology and Developmental Cognition B: Aging Neuropsychology and Cognition*, 15(3), 302–329.

Westerhof, G. J., Whitbourne, S. K., & Freeman, G. P. (2012). The aging self in a cultural context: The relation of conceptions of aging to identity processes and self-esteem in the United States and the Netherlands. *The Journals of Gerontology: Series B: Psychological Sciences and Social Sciences*, 67B(1), 52–60. doi: 10.1093/geronb/gbr075

Wetherell, J. L., Reynolds, C. A., Gatz, M. P., & Nancy, L. (2002). Anxiety, cognitive performance, and cognitive decline in normal aging. *Journals of Gerontology Series B: Psychological Sciences and Social Sciences*, 57B, P246–P255.

Wethington, E., Kessler, R. C., Pixley, J. E., Brim, O. G., & Ryff, C. D. (2004). Turning points in adulthood. In O. G. Brim, C. D. Ryff & R. C. Kessler (Eds.), *How healthy are we? A national study of well-being at midlife* (pp. 586–613). Chicago, IL: University of Chicago Press.

Wettstein, M., Tauber, B., Kuzma, E., & Wahl, H. W. (2017). The interplay between personality and cognitive ability across 12 years in middle and late adulthood: Evidence for reciprocal associations. *Psychology and Aging*, 32(3), 259–277. doi: 10.1037/pag0000166

Wetzel, M., Bowen, C. E., & Huxhold, O. (2019). Level and change in economic, social, and personal resources for people retiring from paid work and other labour market statuses. *European Journal of Ageing*. doi: 10.1007/s10433-019-00516-y

Whalley, L. J., Staff, R. T., Fox, H. C., & Murray, A. D. (2016). Cerebral correlates of cognitive reserve. *Psychiatry Research Neuroimaging*, 247, 65–70. doi: 10.1016/j.pscychresns.2015.10.012

Whisman, M. A., Uebelacker, L. A., Tolejko, N., Chatav, Y., & McKelvie, M. (2006). Marital discord and well-being in older adults: Is the association confounded by personality? *Psychology and Aging, 21*(3), 626–631.

Whitbourne, S. K. (1985). The life-span construct as a model of adaptation in adulthood. In J. E. Birren & K.W. Schaie (Eds.), *Handbook of the psychology of aging* (2nd ed., pp. 594–618). NewYork: Van Nostrand Reinhold.

Whitbourne, S. K. (1986). *The me I know: A study of adult identity.* New York: Springer.

Whitbourne, S. K. (2010). *The search for fulfillment.* New York: Ballantine.

Whitbourne, S. K. (2019). *Abnormal psychology: Clinical perspectives on psychological disorders* (9th ed.). New York: McGraw-Hill.

Whitbourne, S. K., & Collins, K. C. (1998). Identity and physical changes in later adulthood: Theoretical and clinical implications. *Psychotherapy, 35,* 519–530.

Whitbourne, S. K., & Connolly, L. A. (1999). The developing self in midlife. In J. D. Reid & S. L. Willis (Eds.), *Life in the middle: Psychological and social development in middle age* (pp. 25–45). San Diego, CA: Academic Press.

Whitbourne, S. K., Culgin, S., & Cassidy, E. (1995). Evaluation of infantilizing intonation and content of speech directed at the aged. *International Journal of Aging and Human Development, 41,* 107–114.

Whitbourne, S. K., Ellenberg, S., & Akimoto, K. (2013). Reasons for playing casual video games and perceived benefits among adults 18 to 80 years old. *Cyberpsychology, Behavior and Sociology Networking, 16*(12), 892–897. doi: 10.1089/cyber.2012.0705

Whitbourne, S. K., & Martins, B. S. (2020). Psychotherapy with the underserved older adult population In J. Zimmerman, J. Barnett & L. Campbell (Eds.), *Bringing psychotherpay to the underserved.* New York: Oxford University Press.

Whitbourne, S. K., & Meeks, S. (2011). Psychopathology, bereavement, and aging. In K. W. Schaie & S. L. Willis (Eds.), *Handbook of the psychology of aging* (pp. 311–323). New York: Cambridge University Press.

Whitbourne, S. K., & Montepare, J. M. (2017). What's holding us back? Ageism in higher education *Ageism: Stereotyping and prejudice against older persons* (pp. 263–289). Cambridge, MA: MIT Press.

Whitbourne, S. K., & Sneed, J. R. (2002). The paradox of well-being, identity processes, and stereotype threat: Ageism and its potential relationships to the self in later life. In T. D. Nelson (Ed.), *Ageism: Stereotyping and prejudice against older persons* (pp. 247–273). Cambridge, MA: The MIT Press.

Whitbourne, S. K., Sneed, J. R., & Sayer, A. (2009). Psychosocial development from college through midlife: A 34-year sequential study. *Developmental Psychology, 45*(5), 1328–1340. doi: 2009-12605-011 [pii] 10.1037/a0016550

Whitbourne, S. K., Sneed, J. R., & Skultety, K. M. (2002). Identity processes in adulthood: Theoretical and methodological challenges. *Identity, 2,* 29–45.

Whitbourne, S. K., & Waterman, A. S. (1979). Psychosocial development during the adult years: Age and cohort comparisons. *Developmental Psychology, 15*(4), 373–378.

Whitbourne, S. K., & Willis, S. L. (Eds.). (2006). *The baby boomers grow up: Contemporary perspectives on midlife.* Mahwah, NJ: Lawrence Erlbaum Associates.

Whitbourne, S. K., Zuschlag, M. K., Elliot, L. B., & Waterman, A. S. (1992). Psychosocial development in adulthood: A 22-year sequential study. *Journal of Personality and Social Psychology, 63*(2), 260–271.

Whiteside, D. M., Kealey, T., Semla, M., Luu, H., Rice, L., Basso, M. R., & Roper, B. (2016). Verbal fluency: Language or executive function measure? *Applied Neuropsychology: Adult, 23*(1), 29–34. doi: 10.1080/23279095.2015.1004574

Whitfield, K. E., Allaire, J. C., & Wiggins, S. A. (2004). Relationships among health factors and everyday problem solving in African Americans. *Health Psychology, 23*(6), 641–644.

Whiting, W. L., Madden, D. J., Pierce, T. W., & Allen, P. A. (2005). Searching from the top down: Ageing and attentional guidance during singleton detection. *Quarterly Journal of Experimental Psychology: Section A, 58*(1), 72–97. doi: 10.1080/02724980443000205

Whitton, S. W., Kuryluk, A. D., & Khaddouma, A. M. (2015). Legal and social ceremonies to formalize same-sex relationships: Associations with commitment, social support, and relationship outcomes. *Couple and Family Psychology: Research and Practice, 4*(3), 161–176. doi: 10.1037/cfp0000045

Whitton, S. W., Stanley, S. M., Markman, H. J., & Johnson, C. A. (2013). Attitudes toward divorce, commitment, and divorce proneness in first marriages and remarriages. *Journal of Marriage and the Family, 75*(2), 276–287. doi: 10.1111/jomf.12008

Wiernik, B. M., & Kostal, J. W. (2019). Protean and boundaryless career orientations: A critical review and meta-analysis. *Journal of Counseling Psychology, 66*(3), 280–307. doi: 10.1037/cou0000324 10.1037/cou0000324.supp (Supplemental)

Wille, B., Hofmans, J., Feys, M., & De Fruyt, F. (2014). Maturation of work attitudes: Correlated change with big five personality traits and reciprocal effects over 15 years. *Journal of Organizational Behavior, 35*(4), 507–529. doi: 10.1002/job.1905

Williams, B. R., Zhang, Y., Sawyer, P., Mujib, M., Jones, L. G., Feller, M. A., … Ahmed, A. (2011). Intrinsic association of widowhood with mortality in community-dwelling older women and men: Findings from a prospective propensity-matched population study. *The Journals of Gerontology: Series A: Biological Sciences and Medical Sciences, 66A*(12), 1360–1368. doi: 10.1093/gerona/glr144

Williams, K. N., & Warren, C. A. (2009). Communication in assisted living. *Journal of Aging Studies, 23*(1), 24–36. doi: 10.1016/j.jaging.2007.09.003

Willis, S. L., Blieszner, R., & Baltes, P. B. (1981). Intellectual training research in aging: Modification of performance on the fluid ability of figural relations. *Journal of Educational Psychology, 73,* 41–50.

Willis, S. L., & Schaie, K. W. (2009). Cognitive training and plasticity: Theoretical perspective and methodological consequences. *Restorative Neurology and Neuroscience, 27*(5), 375–389.

Willis, S. L., Schaie, K. W., Martin, M., Bengston, V. L., Gans, D., Pulney, N. M., & Silverstein, M. (2009). Cognitive plasticity. *Handbook of theories of aging* (2nd ed., pp. 295–322). New York: Springer.

Wilson, R. S., Arnold, S. E., Tang, Y., & Bennett, D. A. (2006). Odor identification and decline in different cognitive domains in old age. *Neuroepidemiology, 26*(2), 61–67.

Winch, R. F. (1958). *Mate selection: A study of complementary needs.* New York: Harper & Row.

Wittchen, H. U., Gloster, A. T., Beesdo-Baum, K., Fava, G. A., & Craske, M. G. (2010). Agoraphobia: A review of the diagnostic classificatory position and criteria. *Depression and Anxiety, 27*(2), 113–133. doi: 10.1002/da.20646

Wlodarczyk, O. M., & Barinow-Wojewodzki, A. (2015). The impact of resistance respiratory muscle training with a SpiroTiger((R)) device on lung function, exercise performance, and health-related quality of life in respiratory diseases. *Kardiochir Torakochirurgia Pol, 12*(4), 386–390. doi: 10.5114/kitp.2015.56796

Wolf, E. J., & Schnurr, P. P. (2016). Posttraumatic stress disorder-related cardiovascular disease and accelerated cellular aging. *Psychiatric Annals, 46*(9), 527–532. doi: 10.3928/00485713-20160729-01

Wolfe, C. J., Rennie, K. E., & Truffer, C. J. (2017). 2017 Actuarial report on the financial outlook for Medicaid. From https://www.cms.gov/Research-Statistics-Data-and-Systems/Research/ActuarialStudies/Downloads/MedicaidReport2017.pdf

Wolffsohn, J. S., & Davies, L. N. (2019). Presbyopia: Effectiveness of correction strategies. *Progress in Retinal Eye Research, 68*, 124–143. doi: 10.1016/j.preteyeres.2018.09.004

Wong, I. Y., Smith, S. S., Sullivan, K. A., & Allan, A. C. (2016). Toward the multilevel older person's transportation and road safety model: A new perspective on the role of demographic, functional, and psychosocial factors. *The Journals of Gerontology. Series B, Psychological Sciences and Social Sciences, 71*(1), 71–86. doi: 10.1093/geronb/gbu099

Woods, S. P., Weinborn, M., Li, Y. R., Hodgson, E., Ng, A. R., & Bucks, R. S. (2015). Does prospective memory influence quality of life in community-dwelling older adults? *Neuropsychology and Developmental Cognition B: Aging Neuropsychology and Cognition, 22*(6), 679–692. doi: 10.1080/13825585.2015.1027651

Woolf, S. H. (2010). The 2009 breast cancer screening recommendations of the US Preventive Services Task Force. *Journal of the American Medical Association, 303*(2), 162–163. doi: 303/2/162 [pii] 10.1001/jama.2009.1989

World Health Organization. (1948). Preamble to the Constitution of the World Health Organization as adopted by the International Health Conference, New York, 19–22 June, 1946; signed on 22 July 1946 by the representatives of 61 States (Official Records of the World Health Organization, no. 2, p. 100) and entered into force on 7 April 1948.

World Health Organization. (2002a). *Active ageing: A policy framework.* Geneva, Switzerland: World Health Organization.

World Health Organization. (2002b). *National cancer control programmes: Policies and managerial guidelines.* Geneva, Switzerland: World Health Organization.

World Health Organization. (2016). Global report on diabetes. Retrieved 5/23/2019, from https://apps.who.int/iris/bitstream/handle/10665/204871/9789241565257_eng.pdf;jsessionid=D677FDF5C0C8737F19AF4BAABE1D8921?sequence=1

World Health Organization. (2017). Cardiovascular diseases (CVDs). Retrieved 5/17/19, from https://www.who.int/en/news-room/fact-sheets/detail/cardiovascular-diseases-(cvds)

World Health Organization. (2018a). Cancer. Retrieved 5/21/2019, from https://www.who.int/en/news-room/fact-sheets/detail/cancer

World Health Organization. (2018b). Diabetes. Retrieved 5/22/19, from https://www.who.int/news-room/fact-sheets/detail/diabetes

World Health Organization. (2018c). Fact file: Misconceptions on ageing and health. Retrieved 8/31/2018, from http://www.who.int/ageing/features/misconceptions/en/

World Health Organization. (2018d). The global network for age-friendly cities and communities: Looking back over the last decade, looking forward to the next. Retrieved 7/31/21019, from https://www.who.int/ageing/publications/gnafcc-report-2018/en/

World Health Organization. (2018e). Noncommunicable diseases. Retrieved 5/17/2019, from https://www.who.int/en/news-room/fact-sheets/detail/noncommunicable-diseases

World Health Organization. (2018f). Obesity and overweight. Retrieved 5/21/2019, from https://www.who.int/en/news-room/fact-sheets/detail/obesity-and-overweight

World Health Organization. (2018g). The Global Network for Age-friendly Cities and Communities: Looking back over the last decade, looking forward to the next. Retrieved 7/31/21019, from https://www.who.int/ageing/publications/gnafcc-report-2018/en/

World Health Organization. (2019a). Dementia. Retrieved 5/22/19, from https://www.who.int/news-room/fact-sheets/detail/dementia

World Health Organization. (2019b). Global health observatory: Overweight and obesity. Retrieved 5/7/2019, from https://www.who.int/gho/ncd/risk_factors/overweight_obesity/bmi_trends_adults/en/

World Health Organization. (2019c). Skin cancers. Retrieved 5/21/2019, from https://www.who.int/uv/faq/skincancer/en/index1.html

Worthy, D. A., Gorlick, M. A., Pacheco, J. L., Schnyer, D. M., & Maddox, W. T. (2011). With age comes wisdom: Decision making in younger and older adults. *Psychological Science, 22*(11), 1375–1380. doi: 10.1177/0956797611420301

Worthy, D. A., & Maddox, W. T. (2012). Age-based differences in strategy use in choice tasks. *Frontiers in Neuroscience, 5*, 145. doi: 10.3389/fnins.2011.00145

Wright, N. C., Looker, A. C., Saag, K. G., Curtis, J. R., Delzell, E. S., Randall, S., & Dawson-Hughes, B. (2014). The recent prevalence of osteoporosis and low bone mass in the United States based on bone mineral density at the femoral neck or lumbar spine. *Journal of Bone and Mineral Research, 29*(11), 2520–2526. doi: 10.1002/jbmr.2269

Wunderlich, G. S., Kohler, P. O., & Committee on Improving Quality in Long-Term Care Division of Health Care Services Institute of Medicine (Eds.). (2001). *Improving the quality of long-term care*. Washington, DC: National Academies Press.

Wuthrich, V. M., & Frei, J. (2015). Barriers to treatment for older adults seeking psychological therapy. *International Psychogeriatrics, 27*(7), 1227–1236. doi: 10.1017/S1041610215000241

Xekardaki, A., Santos, M., Hof, P., Kovari, E., Bouras, C., & Giannakopoulos, P. (2012). Neuropathological substrates and structural changes in late-life depression: The impact of vascular burden. *Acta Neuropathologica, 124*(4), 453–464. doi: 10.1007/s00401-012-1021-5

Xu, Z., Murphy, S. L., Kochanek, K. D., Bastian, B., & Arias, E. (2018). Deaths: Final data for 2016 *National Vital Statistics Reports* (Vol. 67, No. 5). Hyattsville, MD: National Center for Health Statistics.

Yabiku, S. T., & Gager, C. T. (2009). Sexual frequency and the stability of marital and cohabiting unions. *Journal of Marriage and the Family, 71*(4), 983–1000.

Yadav, K. N., Gabler, N. B., Cooney, E., Kent, S., Kim, J., Herbst, N., … Courtright, K. R. (2017). Approximately one in three US adults completes any type of advance directive for end-of-life care. *Health Affairs, 36*(7), 1244–1251. doi: 10.1377/hlthaff.2017.0175

Yang, W.-N., Niven, K., & Johnson, S. (2019). Career plateau: A review of 40 years of research. *Journal of Vocational Behavior, 110*(Part B), 286–302. doi: 10.1016/j.jvb.2018.11.005

Yeung, S. E., Fischer, A. L., & Dixon, R. A. (2009). Exploring effects of type 2 diabetes on cognitive functioning in older adults. *Neuropsychology, 23*(1), 1–9. doi: 2008-19137-001 [pii] 10.1037/a0013849

Yilmaz, M., & Kayancicek, H. (2018). A new inflammatory marker: Elevated monocyte to HDL cholesterol ratio associated with smoking. *Journal of Clinical Medicine, 7*(4). doi: 10.3390/jcm7040076

Yohannes, A. M., & Tampubolon, G. (2014). Changes in lung function in older people from the English Longitudinal Study of Ageing. *Expert Reviews in Respiratory Medicine, 8*(4), 515–521. doi: 10.1586/17476348.2014.919226

Yoon, J. Y., Brown, R. L., Bowers, B. J., Sharkey, S. S., & Horn, S. D. (2015). Longitudinal psychological outcomes of the small-scale nursing home model: A latent growth curve zero-inflated Poisson model. *International Psychogeriatrics, 27*(6), 1009–1016. doi: 10.1017/s1041610214002865

Yuen, J. K., Reid, M. C., & Fetters, M. D. (2011). Hospital do-not-resuscitate orders: Why they have failed and how to fix them. *Journal of General Internal Medicine, 26*(7), 791–797. doi: 10.1007/s11606-011-1632-x

Zahodne, L. B., Ajrouch, K. J., Sharifian, N., & Antonucci, T. C. (2019). Social relations and age-related change in memory. *Psychology and Aging*. doi: 10.1037/pag0000369

Zamboanga, B. L., Pesigan, I. J. A., Tomaso, C. C., Schwartz, S. J., Ham, L. S., Bersamin, M., … Hurley, E. A. (2015). Frequency of drinking games participation and alcohol-related problems in a multiethnic sample of college students: Do gender and ethnicity matter? *Addictive Behaviors, 41*, 112–116. doi: 10.1016/j.addbeh.2014.10.002

Zaval, L., Markowitz, E. M., & Weber, E. U. (2015). How will I be remembered? Conserving the environment for the sake of one's legacy. *Psychological Science, 26*(2), 231–236. doi: 10.1177/0956797614561266

Zekveld, A. A., Kramer, S. E., & Festen, J. M. (2011). Cognitive load during speech perception in noise: The influence of age, hearing loss, and cognition on the pupil response. *Ear and Hearing, 32*(4), 498–510. doi: 10.1097/AUD.0b013e31820512bb

Zhang, J., Andreano, J. M., Dickerson, B. C., Touroutoglou, A., & Barrett, L. F. (2019). Stronger functional connectivity in the default mode and salience networks is associated with youthful memory in superaging. *Cerebral Cortex*. doi: 10.1093/cercor/bhz071

Ziegler, M., Cengia, A., Mussel, P., & Gerstorf, D. (2015). Openness as a buffer against cognitive decline: The openness-fluid-crystallized-intelligence (OFCI) model applied to late adulthood. *Psychology and Aging, 30*(3), 573–588. doi: 10.1037/a0039493

Ziegler, M., Schroeter, T. A., Ludtke, O., & Roemer, L. (2018). The enriching interplay between openness and interest: A theoretical elaboration of the OFCI model and a first empirical test. *Journal of Intelligence, 6*(3). doi: 10.3390/jintelligence6030035

AUTHOR INDEX

SUBJECT INDEX